NAPOLEONIC ARTILLERY

Statue of Napoleon at the Musée de L'Armée, Paris. (Paul Dawson)

NAPOLEONIC ARTILLERY

ANTHONY L. DAWSON, PAUL L. DAWSON
AND STEPHEN SUMMERFIELD

THE CROWOOD PRESS

First published in 2007 by
The Crowood Press Ltd
Ramsbury, Marlborough
Wiltshire SN8 2HR

www.crowood.com

British Library Cataloguing-in-Publication Data
A catalogue record for this book is available from the British Library.

ISBN 978 1 86126 9232

Disclaimer
The author and the publisher do not accept any responsibility in any manner whatsoever for any error or omission, nor any loss, damage, injury or liability of any kind incurred as a result of the use of any of the information contained in this book, or reliance upon it.

Dedicated to Jane Dawson

Edited by Martin Windrow

Index by Stephen Summerfield

Typeset in Times by Bookcraft Ltd, Stroud, Gloucestershire

Printed and bound in Great Britain by The Cromwell Press, Trowbridge

Contents

Foreword

The authors of this very impressive work have invested years of thorough and painstaking research into the entire, extensive spectrum of the development of European artillery, from the 18th century through to the end of the Napoleonic era at Waterloo. Rarely have I seen such a truly astounding compilation of facts and figures on the various facets of the weapons, their design and development, the panoply of projectiles, the gun carriages, limbers and other artillery vehicles, the battlefield tactics and even the intimate details of the composition of the different gunpowders and of the paints used on the vehicles. Field artillery, horse artillery, siege artillery and even mountain artillery are all included.

I was able to see the Association Britannique de la Garde Impériale (est. 1972) exercising their practical artillery drills at the re-enactment of the Battle of Jena on 14 October 2006. The experience of these experimental historians in constructing, limbering, moving, siting, and loading the cannon of Napoleon's armies has imparted indelible lessons as to what men and horses could achieve on the march and in battle.

Those who know more about artillery than I will be pleasantly reassured to encounter all their old friends from the tales of the history of this arm, as well as some new ones. The popular names of Gribeauval, Liechtenstein, Smola, the du Teil brothers, Congreve Snr, Shrapnel and – of course – Napoleon are all there, together with details of their contributions. Several popular myths and misconceptions associated with some of these names are revealed and explored.

To them are added those of the perhaps lesser well known, such as Rumford of Bavaria; Blomefield and Desaguliers of Britain; Manson, Maritz and Vallière of France; Dieskau, Euler, Linger, Holtzmann and Scharnhorst of Prussia; Arakcheev of Russia and many others who contributed sometimes critically important thoughts, theories and practical advances into the developments of artillery, but whose work has since slipped into the background.

The introductory chapter includes a potted history of the martial and political events of the Revolutionary and Napoleonic era, setting the scene for even the most novice reader. All European states that contributed to this development are covered in depth. It quickly becomes apparent that – as in all scientific fields – there have always been designers and teams of craftsmen in different countries, working on parallel lines of exploration into any problem in the field of ballistics, casting of gun barrels, carriage design, battlefield mobility, gun drill or the associated aspects of getting the best performance out of the artillery. The cross-fertilisation of ideas and designs is an interesting story.

The work is lavishly illustrated and there are many tables to support the theories of ballistics. It is a milestone publication on the development of artillery and richly deserves to succeed. Every serious student of military history should have a copy on his bookshelf; I wish it well.

Digby Smith
Thetford 2007

Preface

The French Revolutionary and Napoleonic wars (1792–1815) saw the transition from the small professional armies of the 18th century to large national conscript armies, and the transformation of the artillery from a professional guild into a major branch of the army that could dominate the battlefield. In 1796 the French Army of Italy had only sixty artillery pieces; just sixteen years later, the combined artillery of both sides at Borodino totalled about 1,200 guns. These fired an average of 15,000 rounds per hour during the course of that battle, on a frontage of only about two miles. Napoleon Bonaparte himself was a born gunner, who used his artillery with a calm, sure skill, improving his techniques from campaign to campaign.

The weapons used in Europe during the wars of 1792–1815 were superficially similar to each other, but each country's system for using their guns varied. The guns themselves had been transformed by the 18th-century arms race from the slow, lumbering and immobile artillery of the 17th century into a mobile arm that would ultimately become a battle-winning weapon rather than merely providing static infantry support. These new guns developed during the 18th century were the cornerstone of the artillery tactics of the Napoleonic Wars.

As the guns evolved, so did the doctrine for their employment, championed by the Austrian artilleryman Smola and the Emperor Napoleon. It was under Napoleon that artillery tactics came of age, and artillerymen could finally claim to be the great deciders of battles. The tasks of the artillery were to clear gaps in the enemy lines that could be exploited by the foot and horse, to halt the enemy's attacks, and to support those launched against him. The key to achieving this was the concentration of a large number of guns at a single point. The Coalition Allies learnt this tactic from the French, but ultimately failed to employ it with as much success as Napoleon. However, massed batteries returned battles to something resembling a 'siege mentality', last experienced in the 1750s, with both sides slugging it out in pursuit of an eventual victory of attrition, rather than pursuing the nimble and flowing tactics of the Revolutionary and early Napoleonic campaigns. After 1809, there was increasing use of massed batteries to pave the way for the infantry assault, and the artillerymen engaged enemy assault columns head-on during both offensive and defensive operations. The decline in quality of the French infantry required an increase in the number of guns.[1] Napoleon saw artillery as crucial to stiffening poor-quality infantry, but also to supporting good infantry,[2] thus minimising tactical casualties and winning battles at the lowest possible cost in lives.[3] Napoleon believed that a revolution in tactics, with artillery at its core, should include massed batteries and near-continuous fire.

The artillery of the Napoleonic Wars, in both equipment and doctrine, was built upon the accumulated experience of previous generations.

In 1731, Prussia restricted the number of calibres in use to reduce the logistical problems of supplying ammunition, and France followed suit in 1732. This was not as successful as might have been expected, since there was no standard system of measurement that applied throughout Europe.

The aftermath of the War of the Austrian Succession (1740–48) saw radical changes in Austrian artillery after it was found to be inferior to that of Prussia. In 1753, Austria's Liechtenstein system set such a high standard in terms of design and technical excellence that it was used as the point of inspiration for the artillery of the majority of the major European powers. In Russia, a new system of artillery was created to compete with that of Prussia. However, Prussia herself would have to turn to her neighbours for inspiration by the latter decades of the century.

The Seven Years War (1756–63) marked the end of artillery tactics based almost exclusively on static defence and siege warfare. Frederick the

Great introduced artillery into the heart of the battlefield, equipping his infantry regiments with two Light 6-pdr pieces and one Light 7-pdr howitzer. In April 1759 he created a horse artillery battery. The M1732 Vallière system of the French was too heavy and cumbersome to operate effectively in the more mobile battlefield environment of the second half of the 18th century. Their next step was the Gribeauval system, which like all successful technologies borrowed heavily from the best existing models, mainly from Austria and to a lesser extent from Prussia. Many other countries were influenced by elements of this system, principally the metal axle, the reduction of windage of the gun tube, and the preference for the elevating screw over the *Rechtsmaschine*.

Jacques (Jakob) Manson, a colleague of Gribeauval, took the standardisation of wheel size and gun carriages still further by producing two types when he was working for Bavaria. He also realised that Gribeauval's gun tubes were capable of taking a larger weight of shot, so modified the Gribeauval 4-pdr design by boring it out to take a 6-pdr shot.

The experience gained from the American and the French Revolutionary Wars led many European countries to overhaul their artillery. Their systems were found to be inadequate to cope with the changes to tactics that occurred at this time, the catalyst being the way in which Napoleon used his artillery. It was these artillery systems, modified through combat experience, that were used in the Napoleonic Wars. During those wars the main difference between the Coalition and French artilleries lay not in the quality of guns or gunners, but in the fact that Napoleon used artillery offensively while Coalition commanders saw its main purpose as to defend cavalry and infantry; this can be said of the Russian, Prussian and British artilleries. Their reserve artillery batteries joined the battle in a piecemeal manner at the request of local divisional commanders, or were despatched by commanders-in-chief to support a line that was too weak or hard-pressed. In contrast, Napoleon's artillery prepared the way for the final blow that would decide the battle, employing anything between 50 and 150 pieces at once.

This work aims to trace the evolution of European land-based, muzzle-loading artillery from the lumbering and relatively immobile artillery of the 17th century to the mobile lightweight artillery of the late 18th century that became the battle-winning weapon of the Napoleonic Wars. The artillery of any one country was influenced by its neighbours. For example, Jean-Baptiste de Vaquette Gribeauval (1715–89), who has been credited as the father of Napoleonic artillery, was influenced by existing French, Austrian and Prussian designs. It is commonly accepted that, in every area of science, great advances have always been built upon the shoulders of giants; this study cannot be restricted to the actual years of the Napoleonic Wars, because most artillery systems were conceived and put into operation about fifty years before those conflicts began.

Chapter 1 explores the terminology, and how the guns were loaded, aimed and fired. Chapter 2 follows the story of the intertwined development of Austrian, Prussian and Russian ordnance, one or other of which enjoyed ascendancy during the 18th-century arms race. Chapter 3 examines French field ordnance and its influence upon the closely related systems of Bavaria, Piedmont (Italy), Saxony and Württemberg. Chapter 4 addresses the complex and sometimes confusing story of British and Hanoverian field ordnance. During the Revolutionary and Napoleonic wars a large amount of foreign equipment was employed by all countries, especially France; the first part of Chapter 5 looks at the field guns of the Confederation of the Rhine and of other French allies, the latter part at those of Britain's allies. Chapter 6 examines light and mountain ordnance – often neglected, but essential in many of the less well-known actions in the Alps, Italy, Portugal and Spain. Chapter 7 goes to the other extreme: the use of heavy guns, howitzers and mortars in the attack and defence of coastal and field fortifications and garrisons.

Chapter 8 begins a series of thematic chapters on the details of actual use, with consideration of how guns were moved to and around the battlefield: by draft animals and limbers, by manhandling, and by draft without limbers. In Chapter 9 the appearance of the field pieces and attendant items is discussed, including the source and manufacture of the pigments used to paint them – an often neglected subject.

Chapter 10 addresses the absolutely central subject of artillery ammunition – the types used in this period, and their effectiveness. The range limitations of guns firing particular types of round contributed directly to the way in which guns were used (the sagest advice was perhaps that of the French artillery officer General Foy: 'Get up close, and shoot fast'.) The ready supply of munitions depended upon various types of caissons and wagons, which are examined in the last part of this chapter.

The fundamental changes in artillery usage and deployment were born of the decades of technical improvements, the refinement of tactical doctrine and the rise in status of artillery officers. Chapter 11 attempts to set these developments in context, showing the radical tactical advances that were achieved at the beginning of the 19th century by artillery whose equipment was little removed technologically from the mid-18th century. The artillery came of age through the improvements in its organisation, employment, command and control; Chapter 12 discusses the different types of regimental, field and horse artillery as an introduction to the organisational diagrams.

The maps have been included in this book as an aid to identifying those various states that existed in the period under discussion but which have since disappeared from the face of Europe. Obviously, a number of states outside Europe – in North and South America, in Asia and the Indian sub-continent – were involved in various contemporaneous wars, but to attempt to cover them here would have vastly increased the size of the present work.

In this text, for ease of understanding, the word *battery* refers to a tactical unit upon the battlefield, although this term was not in common use until later in the 19th century. *Gun tube length* refers to the barrel of the cannon, and is given in metric measurement. *Bore length* is given conventionally in calibres (i.e. the number of diameters of the bore that would fit in the length of the tube).

In order to produce consistency in weights and measures, the native units have been converted into metric to ease comparison between the artillery of various nations (*see* the Appendix). To add to the confusion, foreign ordnance has often been referred to in the writer's own units of weight and measurement; this was particularly so for the French, who used large quantities of captured ordnance. This has often produced errors that have been compounded down the years. For example:

> a French 6 *pouce* (often written as 6in) howitzer is a 6.9in (160mm) howitzer and the 24-pdr howitzer with 5 *pouce* 6 *ligne* calibre (often written as 5.5.in, 5.6in or 5.72in) is a 5.9in (150mm) howitzer. The *pouce de Paris* was slightly larger than the Imperial inch, hence the discrepancy. France, unlike most other countries, referred to the weight of shot for howitzers in metal weight rather than the stone weight. A French 24-pdr howitzer had the same calibre as an Austrian 7-pdr howitzer. The use of both a calibre measure and weight of shot measure has led some authors to assume that the M1808 24-pdr howitzer was different from the M1808 5.9in howitzer, when they are in fact the same weapon.

The great challenge in completing this work has been to synthesise data collected from over a decade of searching libraries and archives throughout Europe, Canada and the USA. We would encourage readers to contact us via our publishers if they have any relevant information or corrections to contribute to further works on the subject. Many of the questions that we set ourselves have been answered, but many more have inevitably come to light. We hope that this book in some way opens up this fascinating subject for the general reader.

Paul L. Dawson, FINS, and Anthony L. Dawson
Wakefield, England
Dr Stephen Summerfield, CSci, CChem
Loughborough University, England
July 2007

Acknowledgements

We would like to thank members of the Association Britannique de la Garde Impériale from Britain, France and Poland, who have explored the practical aspects of gunnery science that cannot be learned from books, particularly Mark Hanson (the ever-reliable sergeant) and Paul R. Laverick (logistics officer). This book would not have been written without the learning, wisdom and infectious enthusiasm for the Emperor Napoleon's artillery of Mr M.S. Pendlebury and Mr D.R. Mellard. The experience of commanding, operating and manoeuvring a full battery in the field, such as at the bicentenary of Jena (2006), has given us some insight into the devastating effect of mobile artillery during the period, and into how artillery operated at higher levels than a single gun or a two-gun section.

We are indebted for the assistance of the members of the Napoleonic Artillery Research Group, namely Dave Hollins (Austria), Pawel Nowaczek and Mrs Waldemar Zubek (Poland and Duchy of Warsaw), and Geert van Uythoven (Kingdom of Holland and the Netherlands), who have each made invaluable contributions. Norman Swales has provided a number of fine CAD drawings taken from the original plans.

Mark Conrad, Don Graves, John Henderson, Dr M. Kloeffler, Oliver Schmidt, Joerg Schreibe, Markus Stein, Joerg Titzer and Hans-Karl Weiss have supplied us with advice guidance, and a number of interesting documents and illustrations. Access to Steven H. Smith's library, and his ability to find rare books and illustrations, has made this work a pleasure to write. The provision by Patrick Ehresmann of copies of many of the French artillery manuals has greatly enhanced our understanding both of that country's systems and, through their comments, of those of other countries. We wish to acknowledge the assistance of Chris Hunt, Philip A. Magrath (Curator of Artillery, Royal Armouries at Fort Nelson), Howie Muir and Digby Smith, for their time and comments upon the manuscript.

We would also like to thank Mr J. Tremelling, Miss D. Tremelling and Horses Through History for the images of the reconstructed Napoleonic horse team and input on the use of horses in the period. Mr Tremelling's reconstruction of period horse harness, which are the only known examples in Europe, has allowed us to understand much more about the role of horses and their needs in a battery than could be gleaned from books. The internationally renowned wheelwright Mr R. Hurford has also been of great assistance in discussing the design of wheels, and wood types used in the construction of the gun carriages and vehicles.

The contributors to The Napoleon Series website, such as Bob Burnham, Kevin Kiley, and Alexander Zhmodikov, have underlined a necessity to bring together in one place an introduction to this fascinating subject.

We thank the staff of the Musée de l'Armée (Paris), the Royal Armouries Library Service (Leeds, and Fort Nelson, Portsmouth), the British Library, Woolwich Arsenal, and the Royal Engineers Museum (Chatham), Dr S. Efimov of the Engineers and Artillery Museum (St Petersburg) and the National Archives (former Public Record Office) in the United Kingdom have been invaluable in allowing access to their collections of books, journals and drawings. The Bavarian Army Museum (Ingolstadt), Copenhagen Army Museum (Denmark), HMG (Vienna), Krakow Museum (Poland), the Kremlin (Moscow), Leipzig Museum (Saxony), and Warsaw Museum (Poland) have been invaluable in supplying obscure papers, books and images. Chris Jones of Sheffield University has been of great assistance by finding information on the casting of British guns at Walkers of Sheffield. We also acknowledge the assistance of the University Libraries of Greenwich, Hull, Leeds, Loughborough, Sheffield and Wolverhampton, and of the Royal Society of Chemistry.

It is sad to record the deaths of Jerry Groombridge, RA (retired), and Keith Sherman (engineer and former armourer at Bisley) over the time of writing; both were much valued for their contributions to the understanding of the subject over the last two decades.

Not least, we should acknowledge our long-suffering mothers, girlfriends and friends, without whom this would have been such a lonely road.

1 Napoleonic Ordnance

A CONDENSED CHRONOLOGY

A constant theme throughout the 18th and the early 19th century was the mutual hostility of Britain and France. The Seven Years War that ended in 1763 exhausted Europe and many of the participants went through a long period of military rationalisation during which there was an interplay of influences between armies that had fought side by side. Europe was at relative peace for almost 30 years, although this was punctuated by hostilities between Britain on the one hand and France and Spain on the other during the American Revolutionary War (1775–83); and by the limited War of the Bavarian Succession (1778–79) between Austria and Prussia. Re-armament began in many states in response to the spread of revolutionary ideals to Holland, Belgium and France in 1787–89.

Following the decline of Prussia and of the Holy Roman Empire in the last decades of the 18th century, France was once more the pre-eminent power in Europe, with the second largest population after Russia – some 27.4 million.[4] The political turmoil in France following the Revolution of 1789 was the root cause of the Revolutionary Wars (1792–1801) and Napoleonic Wars (1803–15). The German states retained the old confused organisation of the Holy Roman Empire, with an outward appearance of a federal state that elected an emperor through an assembly (the Diet), but the Empire had no real power. A number of its sovereigns had possessions outside the Holy Roman Empire, including Austria, Hanover and Prussia.[5] The smaller German states were for centuries caught between the rivalries of France, Prussia and Austria. Enlightened reform had started in many of these polities in the late 18th century, but was hampered by the thousand-year-old grip on their privileges defended by the nobles, clerics and free cities.[6] The majority of educated Germans initially greeted the French Revolution of 1789 as evidence that France was catching up with their own reforms, but the ruling elites were afraid of revolutionary contagion.

In October 1790, Britain and Spain were at war over the Nootka Sound incident. The Declaration of Pilnitz (27 August 1791) signed by the King of Prussia and the Holy Roman Emperor threatened intervention in France; and on 7 February 1792 they signed the Treaty of Berlin, guaranteeing each other's territory and agreeing mutual support in the event of a declaration of war by France. Many German states, as part of their obligation to the Empire, would send contingents to fight against the French on the side of the Coalition armies, their troops normally following the customs and styles of Austria and Prussia. Nevertheless, since the Revolutionary Wars coincided with the final disappearance of an independent Poland – partitioned between Austria, Prussia and Russia in 1793 and 1795 – some German states were concerned that they too might be absorbed by Austria and Prussia.

On 20 April 1792 the French National Assembly declared war on the Holy Roman Emperor. Austria and Prussia formed the First Coalition in response on 24 July 1792. After the execution of King Louis XVI of France on 21 January 1793, France declared war on Britain and Holland (1 February 1793) and then Spain (7 March 1793). On 23 January 1793, Prussia and Russia co-operated in the Second Partition of Poland. Prussia withdrew from the Coalition in March 1795, signing the First Treaty of Basel (5 April 1795), in order to concentrate upon the final dismemberment of Poland with Austria and Russia. By mid-1796 only Britain, Austria and Naples remained in the alliance against France. Holland had been transformed into the Batavian Republic (16 May 1795) and had made peace; Spain had withdrawn by the Second Treaty of Basel (22 July 1795), and Sardinia had followed suit (May 1796); and on 8 October 1796, Spain declared war on Britain. This in effect left Austria to fight alone on land in

Europe. Her armies were defeated in Italy by General Napoleon Bonaparte in 1796–97, and she concluded the Treaty of Campo Formio (17 October 1797), by which Austria recognised France's absorption of the Austrian Netherlands – roughly, Belgium – and the Cisalpine Republic in northern Italy, and France's frontier on the Rhine, in return for the Republic of Venice.

The Second Coalition was completed by the signing of an Austro-British alliance (29 December 1798), through a series of treaties between Britain, Russia, Portugal, Naples, the Ottoman Empire and the Vatican. War broke out with France on 1 March 1799, while Bonaparte was absent leading an expeditionary army in Egypt; in August he abandoned this command – which would surrender to British forces in September 1801 – and sailed for France. A Russian army defeated the French in Italy and advanced into Switzerland; but in October 1799, following the French defeat of Anglo-Russian forces in Holland, Russia withdrew from the coalition. On 9–10 November 1799, General Bonaparte carried out the '*coup* of Brumaire', overthrowing the Directory and assuming dictatorial powers as First Consul. After he and General Jean-Victor Moreau defeated Austrian armies at Marengo and Hohenlinden respectively (14

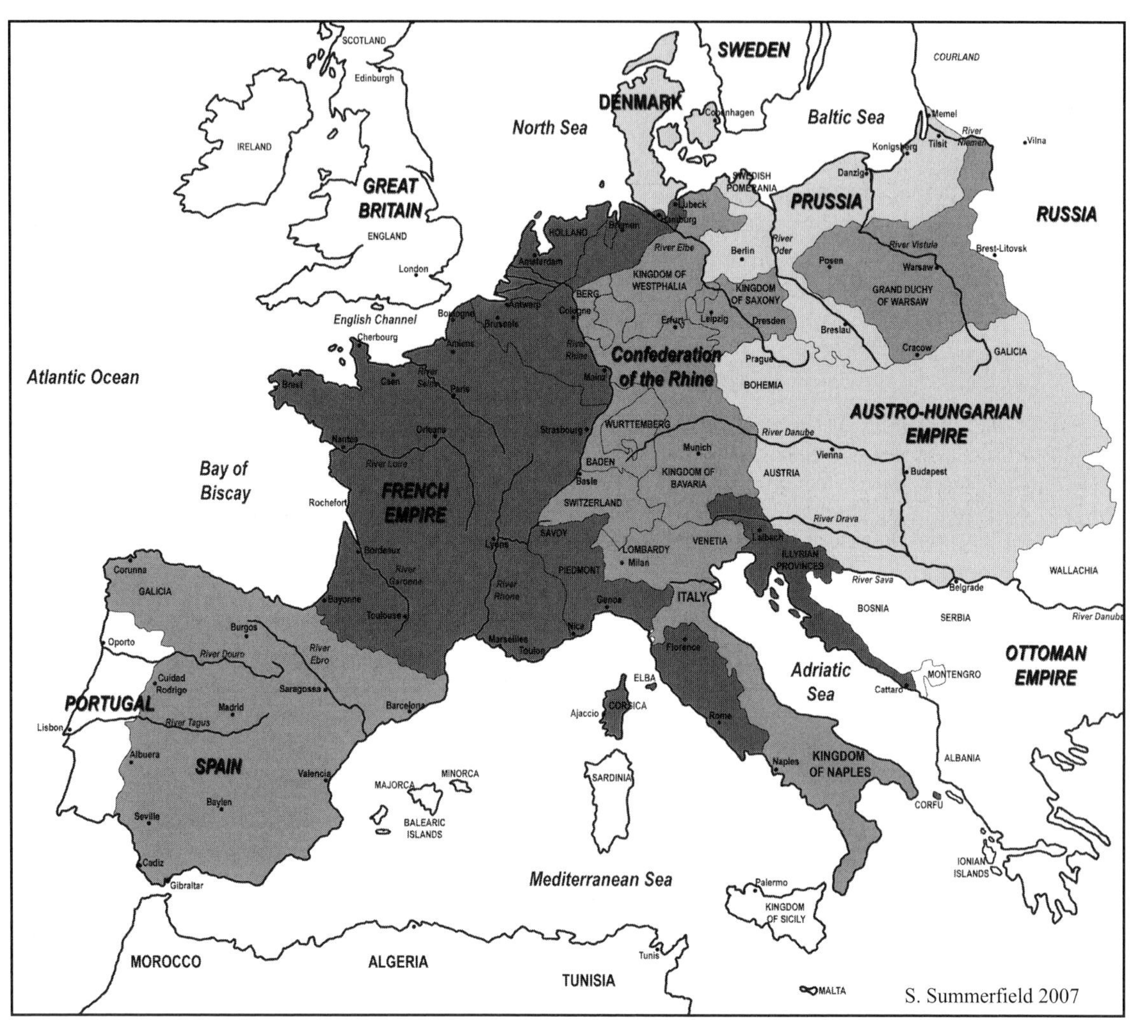

Europe in 1811. Napoleon's Imperial France included Belgium, Holland, northern Westphalia, Piedmont, eastern Italy and the Illyrian Provinces.

June and 3 December 1800), Austria sued for peace. This was concluded at Luneville (15 January 1801); Austria ceded to France all territory west of the Rhine including Belgium and Luxembourg, and recognised the Cisalpine, Ligurian, Batavian and Helvetic Republics.

Austria's exit left Britain alone; she was also challenged by the League of Armed Neutrality signed by Denmark, Russia, Sweden and later Prussia on 18 December 1800, to protect Baltic shipping against British attempts to strangle French commerce. Prussia invaded Hanover, and the Royal Navy destroyed the Danish fleet in Copenhagen. On 23 February 1801, Tsar Paul I was assassinated and was succeeded by his son Alexander I, who chose to leave the League. The Peace of Amiens was signed between Britain and France on 27 March 1802.

War broke out again on 18 May 1803 when Britain resumed the naval blockade of France and began operations in the Mediterranean and against French overseas possessions. By the end of that year a 150,000-strong French 'Army of England' was concentrated on the northern French coast around Boulogne for an invasion of Britain, which could never be launched in the face of British naval superiority.

On 2 December 1804, Napoleon crowned himself Emperor of the French in Notre Dame Cathedral, while the helpless Pope Pius VII looked on. In Germany – as in the Netherlands, Switzerland and Italy – the series of French victories had swept away ancient institutions; France acquired land up to the Rhine, giving her a dominant role in reshaping central Europe. In compensation, the rulers of Prussia and Bavaria had sought to absorb territories east of the Rhine. On 27 April 1803 all the ecclesiastical states were secularised, and 45 of the 51 independent free cities were annexed to the neighbouring states. The largest loser was the German Catholic Church, which had ruled 15% of the territory and 11.4% of its population; a seventh part of the Holy Roman Empire's population (about 3.2 million) and 10,000km^2 of territory were now transferred. On 1 June 1803, the French occupied Hanover. France's annexation of her neighbours in the Low Countries, on the left bank of the Rhine and in Italy brought a cosmopolitan nature to some of her forces, and many units were able to keep their identity after being absorbed into the French Army.

In 1805 the Third Coalition was organised between Austria (9 August), Britain, Russia, Sweden and some minor German states, against France and Spain. Austrian forces invaded Bavaria (2 September 1805), unaware that two days earlier Napoleon's Grande Armée encamped around Boulogne had begun a rapid march eastwards. The Austrian invasion took place without a declaration of war, and consequently Bavaria, Baden, Hesse-Darmstadt and Württemberg allied themselves with Napoleon. Napoleon encircled an Austrian army in Ulm and forced it to surrender (17 October 1805), and by mid-November he had occupied Vienna. He decisively defeated the combined Austro-Russian armies at Austerlitz (2 December 1805), and two days later Austria surrendered unconditionally. By the Treaty of Pressburg (26 December 1805), Austria surrendered Venice to the Kingdom of Italy, the Tyrol to Bavaria and the Swabian territories to Baden and Württemberg; Napoleon elevated Bavaria and Württemberg to sovereign kingdoms.

In May 1806, Napoleon approved the draft drawn up by Talleyrand for the creation of a military alliance of the sixteen southern and central German states within a confederation under French protection. The Confederation of the Rhine was formed on 16 July 1806, with Napoleon as 'Protector'. Each state pledged a military contingent in case of war, these initially totalled 63,000 men; a few of the tiniest states substituted cash contributions. In return, France pledged 200,000 men to the common defence. The smaller of the German states saw this Confederation of the Rhine as their best defence against further consolidation by the larger; in just a few years the number of sovereign states had decreased from 300 to 38, with most of the territory divided between Baden, Bavaria, Württemberg and Würzburg. In the north, the territories of the Princes of Anhalt, Lippe, Reuss and the Saxon duchies were not disturbed.

Francis II abdicated as Holy Roman Emperor in August 1806, and became Emperor Francis I of Austria. On 15 September 1806 the Fourth Coalition was formed by Britain, Prussia, Russia and Saxony against France. On 26 September, Prussia

Firing procedure performed by the gunners of L'Association Britannique de la Garde Impériale, taking post with a full-size M1765 Gribeauval 12-pdr gun.

demanded the dissolution of the Confederation of the Rhine and the withdrawal of all French troops from the east bank of the Rhine. Predictably, Napoleon refused, and marched his 200,000-strong Grande Armée northwards. The Prussian army was destroyed in the battles of Jena and Auerstädt (14 October 1806) and the subsequent pursuit into Poland. Napoleon's battle against a Russian army at Eylau (8 February 1807) was costly but indecisive; that at Friedland (14 June 1807) was a crushing victory, and Russia requested terms. By the Peace of Tilsit (7–9 July 1807) between France, Russia and Prussia, the latter paid a huge indemnity and lost half of her territory – all that between the Elbe and the Rhine, and her Polish acquisitions, which became the Duchy of Warsaw.

Napoleon was now the master of virtually the whole of western and central Europe. By 1808 there were thirty-five states in the Confederation of the Rhine, and Neufchatel and Switzerland were also his vassals. His stepson Eugène de Beauharnais ruled the Kingdom of Italy as his viceroy, and the Duchy of Warsaw – administered from Saxony – provided some of the best troops in the Grande Armée.

Meanwhile, Napoleon's Berlin Decrees (21 November 1806) had forbidden any of his subject or client states to carry on trade with Britain – the so-called Continental System. Only Portuguese ports remained open to British shipping and in response the French invaded Portugal through their ally Spain, occupying Lisbon on 1 December 1807. Napoleon took this opportunity to site French garrisons at strategic points along his rear lines; and in March 1808 this army, reinforced and commanded by Marshal Murat, forced King Charles IV (19 March 1808) and his son Ferdinand (6 May 1808) to abdicate the throne. On 6 June, Napoleon proclaimed his brother Joseph Bonaparte as the new King of Spain so provoking bloody insurrections in May–July 1808, and the landing of the first British expeditionary forces in Portugal. With British funding and direct assistance, Portugal and the Spanish patriots rebuilt their armies and waged the Peninsular War, which tied down large French and French-allied forces until winter 1813–14. In February 1814 the French were finally driven back over the Pyrenees and into south-western France, pursued by a British army commanded by the Duke of Wellington.

On 9 April 1809, encouraged by the French distraction in the Peninsula, Austria invaded Bavaria, revealing her partnership with Britain in a Fifth Coalition; another army invaded northern Italy, and rebels rose against Bavaria in the Tyrol. Napoleon won a number of actions during April, and captured Vienna once again, but was defeated at Aspern-Essling (21–22 May 1809). Regrouping, he re-crossed the Danube and defeated the Austrians decisively at Wagram (5–6 July 1809). For this war the Confederation of the Rhine contributed 120,680 men to Napoleon's armies.[7] By the Treaty of Schönbrunn (14 October 1809), Austria ceded the Illyrian Provinces to France, Salzburg and much of upper Austria to Bavaria, and most of western Galicia to the Duchy of Warsaw.

France's satellite states, and her forced 'allies' Austria, Prussia and Russia, chafed under the ruinous Continental System, and Russia formally abandoned the embargo on 31 December 1810. Napoleon bided his time, concluding treaties with Prussia and Austria (24 February and 10 March 1811), from whom he would demand auxiliary corps for his eventual campaign against Russia. By the Treaty of Abo (9 April 1812) Sweden agreed to cede Finland to Russia, and to supply 30,000 men to support Russia in the event of war with Napoleon, in return for assurance of Russian support for Sweden to secure Norway. On 28 May 1812, Russia made peace with the Ottoman Empire by the Treaty of Bucharest. By these two treaties Russia had secured her northern and southern flanks, releasing 100,000 men to fight against the expected French invasion.

On 24 June 1812, Napoleon launched the invasion of Russia when the advance elements of his nearly half-million strong Grande Armée crossed to the east bank of the River Niemen, and began the long march towards Moscow. Throughout the summer the Russians conducted a series of retreats and rearguard actions, trading territory for time. They finally stood to fight at Borodino (7 September 1812), some 60 miles west of their capital; the Grande Armée fought a very costly battle of attrition, and the Russians withdrew in reasonable order. Napoleon occupied Moscow from 14 September; the Russians refused to conclude a peace, and on 19 October his precarious lines of supply and communication obliged him to order a retreat upon Smolensk. The Russian forces harried the winter retreat all the way back to Polish territory, and the Grande Armée virtually ceased to exist. On 8 December 1812, Napoleon abandoned the remnants at Smorgoni and returned to France to begin raising a new army, reaching Paris on 18 December.

The Prussian and Austrian auxiliary corps had avoided serious combat in Russia, and on 17 March 1813 Prussia's declaration of war against France heralded the formation of the Sixth Coalition. At the Treaty of Reichenbach (27 July 1813), Austria, Prussia and Russia agreed to abolish the Duchy of Warsaw and the Confederation of the Rhine, and in August, Austria finally joined the Coalition. The Austrian statesman Metternich recognised that fear of loss of sovereignty was delaying the defection of German princes from France, and concluded separate treaties with the individual German states, starting with Bavaria (8 October 1813); the only principalities which failed to take advantage of Austrian guarantees were Saxony, Frankfurt and Isenburg-Birstein. After the 'Battle of the Nations' at Leipzig (16–19 October), when Austrian, Prussian, Russian and Swedish armies defeated Napoleon and forced him to fall back to the Rhine, most of his former Rheinbund allies joined the Coalition with varying levels of enthusiasm.

By 1814, France was alone and assailed on all fronts; Napoleon conducted a brilliant campaign of mobile defence, but was hopelessly outnumbered. On 6 April 1814, he attempted to abdicate in favour of his son, but was finally forced to surrender unconditionally on 11 April. Louis XVIII was installed as King of France, and Napoleon went into exile on the small Mediterranean island of Elba. The Treaty of Paris (30 May 1814) restored France to her 1792 boundaries.

On 1 March 1815, Napoleon and a handful of troops landed unopposed at Cannes on the southern French coast and marched for Paris; by the time he reached his capital (20 March) he had been acclaimed by many of his former soldiers. The allied powers assembled at the Congress of Vienna declared him an international outlaw on 13 March 1815, and organised the Seventh Coalition. Some

German states provided at least small contingents to the Coalition armies during the subsequent Hundred Days campaign, although the Saxons mutinied against Prussian command.[8] Napoleon made a surprise advance into Belgium (15 June); he drove a Prussian army under Blücher back from Ligny (16 June), but failed to prevent it coming to the support of Wellington's Anglo-Netherlands-German army at Waterloo (18 June), where his Army of the North was routed. He was subsequently banished to the remote Atlantic island of St Helena, where he died on 5 May 1821.

On 20 November 1815 Austria, Britain, Prussia and Russia signed the Quadruple Alliance. The next stage of the unification of Germany was confirmed by the final Act of Vienna (15 May 1820).[9] Each state was to be independent, but war between the individual states was forbidden, and a war could only be declared with the consent of the confederacy. The Napoleonic territorial order in Germany essentially survived through Bismarck's re-ordering in 1866 following the Prussian defeat of Austria, and the foundation of the Second Empire in 1871 following the defeat of France by the Prussian-led German confederation.[10]

BASIC TERMS USED IN THE TEXT

During the Napoleonic Wars four principal types of ordnance were used: guns (cannon), carronades, howitzers and mortars.

Guns were used to fire roundshot, more or less horizontally and were normally between 12 and 24 calibres long. They were distinguished one from another by their weight of shot in pounds (e.g. '12-pounder/pdr'), and were often subdivided into light, medium and heavy categories, or short and long.

Carronades were shorter, lighter guns employed almost exclusively by navies (initially the Royal Navy, from 1779) and by garrisons. The British also employed them occasionally in sieges, to limited effect.

Howitzers had a greater ratio of bore diameter to weight than guns. Invented by the Dutch in the 1690s, they had a short barrel with a large powder chamber, and fired shells by lower propellant charges at higher elevations than guns. Their trunnions *(see below)* were placed at the reinforce rather than at the breech, as in many mortars. They were distinguished by bore size (Britain and France) expressed in inches or national equivalent, or by

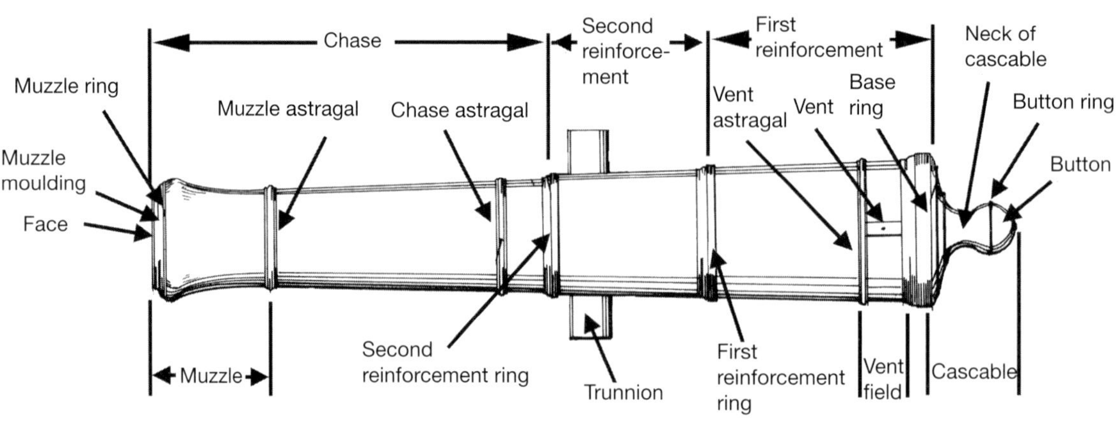

The parts of a British M1732 Armstrong 12-pdr gun.

British 32-pdr carronade on an iron Land Service carriage.

weight of shot in pounds of iron (France) or pounds of stone (Austria and Prussia).

Mortars were very short weapons that fired shells (bombs) at high angles, and were used exclusively for siege work. Some fired at a fixed elevation of 45 degrees, their range being adjusted by altering the powder charge. Other mortars had trunnions at either the base or the point of balance, clamped by metal caps to sturdy wooden beds; in such cases elevation was changed using a wooden quoin. Coehorn mortars were small, with calibres of between 60mm and 120mm; they could be carried by two men using the handles fixed to the bed, and fired small shells or hand grenades to ranges of about 140m.

Field artillery ammunition was generally of three types: roundshot (the most common), exploding shell, and anti-personnel – such as grape, canister, and spherical case (or 'shrapnel', after Henry Shrapnel). There were also specialised types of ammunition, such as the incendiary 'carcass' used against built-up areas and fortifications, and illuminating shells.[11]

Solid iron *roundshot* (or hereafter, simply 'shot') fired by field guns were used against massed troop formations. Generally, regardless of calibre, artillery started to engage targets at a maximum of 1km. This range could be doubled at the expense of accuracy by ricochet fire, accomplished with a low trajectory over hard ground; the roundshot would graze the ground and bounce forwards into the enemy formation. (The Austrian artillery expert Smola observed that for bouncing shot, elevation should not exceed 4 degrees.) This was very destructive, even when the shot was rolling slowly; Coignet gives a convincing description of ricochets hitting the Guard infantry at Aspern-Essling in 1809.[12]

Mortars and howitzers fired *common shell* – hollow spheres of relatively thin cast iron filled with gunpowder, pierced with a hole to receive the fuse. Even an unexploded shell, hissing and smoking as it rolled around at the feet of enemy troops, could have a powerfully unnerving effect and might lead to men breaking ranks. Some countries, including Britain and Russia, fired common shell by ricochet.

Anti-personnel ammunition came in two main types, grapeshot and canister. *Grapeshot* consisted of a number of cast iron or lead balls arranged around a central wooden spigot and secured with a cloth wrapping and cord. *Canister* consisted of a thin metal or wooden cylindrical case containing iron balls varying from 50g to 450g (2oz–16oz) weight; the case ruptured on impact with the ground, scattering its contents with the effect of a

British Coehorn mortar, cast in 1814, on a wooden bed.

giant shotgun. At close range gunners might load two rounds of canister for greater effect; the results could be ruinous to formations of men and horses.

Howitzers and larger artillery guns also fired *spherical case* (shrapnel), consisting of a shell filled with musket balls around a bursting charge.

Siege, garrison and coastal defence guns, in addition to roundshot, canister, grape and in some cases spherical case, might use *hot shot*. This was undersized roundshot heated to red-hot, in order to set fire to ships, buildings, or emplacements constructed from fascines and gabions, and to ignite powder stores.

A gun tube was generally cast from either iron or bronze (the latter often referred to in contemporary literature as brass or gunmetal). Despite bronze being 20.7% heavier than cast iron due to its higher density, bronze guns were preferred for field service because they could be produced with thinner walls, making them lighter and less liable to burst when fired quickly.[13] However, they could suffer from 'muzzle droop' when fired continuously.[14] The British, as most other countries, considered good cast iron guns to be superior in all other respects, especially for siege, naval and garrison service.[15]

Bronze is an alloy of copper and tin. The French recipe of 90% copper to 10% tin could be made more brittle if the absorption of oxygen occurred during manufacture resulting in the presence of tin dioxide in the alloy.[16] According to Landmann (1801), British cannon were made of 92.6% copper and 7.4% tin. Mortars were made of 89.3% copper and 11.7% tin, as greater hardness was required.[17] Zinc was frequently added to act as an oxygen-inhibiter, resulting in a gunmetal alloy that had good tensile strength and resistance to corrosion.[18] Up to 3% lead could be added to produce cleaner castings and improve machining properties.[19] This could be a liability if the gun was heated above 300ºC, as the lead would exude; this was observed by Dickson, when ancient 18- and 24-pdr Portuguese siege guns overheated due to prolonged firing during the siege operations of the Peninsular War.[20] A modern analysis of a French bronze gun-tube gives 93% copper, 5% tin, 0.5% zinc and 1% lead.

Cast iron is an iron-carbon alloy with between 1.8 and 4.5% carbon; it is a hard, brittle and impure iron obtained by re-melting pig iron with limestone.[21] This strong, inflexible alloy was considered to be most suitable for guns and mortars, and cost a tenth as much as those made from bronze.[22]

Wrought iron was produced at temperatures too low to render it fluid, and then hammered to elongate the metal granules.[23] This was used in the production of projectiles, and many of the fittings on gun carriages and vehicles.

The smoothbore muzzle-loading gun was essentially a tube of cast metal closed at one end; this *breech* was pierced with a *vent* through which the gunpowder charge was ignited. *Trunnions* projected from each side of the tube, by which the gun was held on its carriage. The longer the tube length (the internal *bore*, including the *chamber* for the gunpowder charge), generally the more accurate the piece would be, but accuracy also depended on keeping the *windage* (the difference between the diameters of bore and projectile) as small as possible.[24] The bore diameter is the cannon diameter at its muzzle, measured from inside wall to inside wall in a smoothbore. The *calibre* is this inside diameter expressed in inches or millimetres.

The gun is divided into five parts: the *cascable* between the rear extremity and the base ring; the *first reinforce* (two-sevenths of the gun length); the *second reinforce* (one-seventh of the gun length plus one bore diameter); the *chase* (four-sevenths of the gun length minus one bore diameter); and the *muzzle*. The external diameter of the gun tapered gradually within each of these sections and rather more at the junction between them, so that a neck just behind the muzzle had a diameter probably 60% of that of the base, before flaring out again around the muzzle. The muzzle opening was bevelled to prevent abrasion and to facilitate loading. The breech around the chamber was the thickest part of the gun, since it needed to withstand over 1,000 atmospheres of pressure upon detonation of the gunpowder.

The *cascable* (or back-weight) and *dolphins* (two bracket-shaped handles which might be placed over the centre of gravity of a bronze gun) facilitated the handling of the gun when mounting and dismounting, and when moving it when it was off the carriage. The tubes of 16th- to 18th-century pieces had decorated dolphins, a coat of arms or escutcheon on the first reinforce and another on the chase. In the search for lighter pieces the dolphins and adornment were omitted in the designs of Blomefield of England, Rumford of Bavaria, and the French Year XI system.

Howitzers, mortars and 'unicorns' (Russian gun-howitzers fired at lower trajectories than conventional howitzers) had chambers smaller than the diameter of the rest of the bore. In the mid-18th century, Prussia produced a number of chambered cannon that influenced the later Russian unicorns. Most howitzers had cylindrical chambers smaller than the main bore, with either a rounded or a squared end. Early mortars used the spherical chamber, where the sphere was joined to the bore by a small cylinder. Gomer mortars and some howitzers had conical chambers.

Proving

Before they were 'proved', to ensure that they would not fail in service, guns were measured by their internal and external dimensions. In Britain, iron guns up to 12-pdr were proved with powder equivalent to the weight of the shot.[25] Bronze guns were proved with increasing charges up to three times the normal charge. At each stage they were inspected for any pits or irregularities.

In Austria, gun tubes were proved with ten shots and howitzers with three. The tubes were laid on a horizontal bed and aimed at an earth bank 300m away. They were loaded with a larger than normal charge, and packed with a sod of turf twice the depth of the ball; the ball was then placed on top, firmly packed with straw. The turf contained the powder charge longer than would be the case in service, so exposing any pitting or weaknesses in the tube walls to the explosive force for longer.

Artillery Carriages

The various types of ordnance in use were fixed on an iron or wooden mounting called a carriage; these were classified as field, siege, garrison, coastal defence and naval carriages.

The field artillery used either a wooden bracket carriage or a block- trail carriage. The *bracket carriage* was formed from two full-length longitudinal 'cheeks', separated by lateral 'transoms'. The *block-trail carriage* (or *stock trail*) had short cheeks supporting the tube attached to each side of a single central stock, cut from a single piece of timber or laminated from three pieces. British block-trail carriages, like French gun carriages, had iron axles. The trail was the part of the stock of the gun carriage behind the cheeks that rested on the ground when the gun was unlimbered. Either the trail hooked up

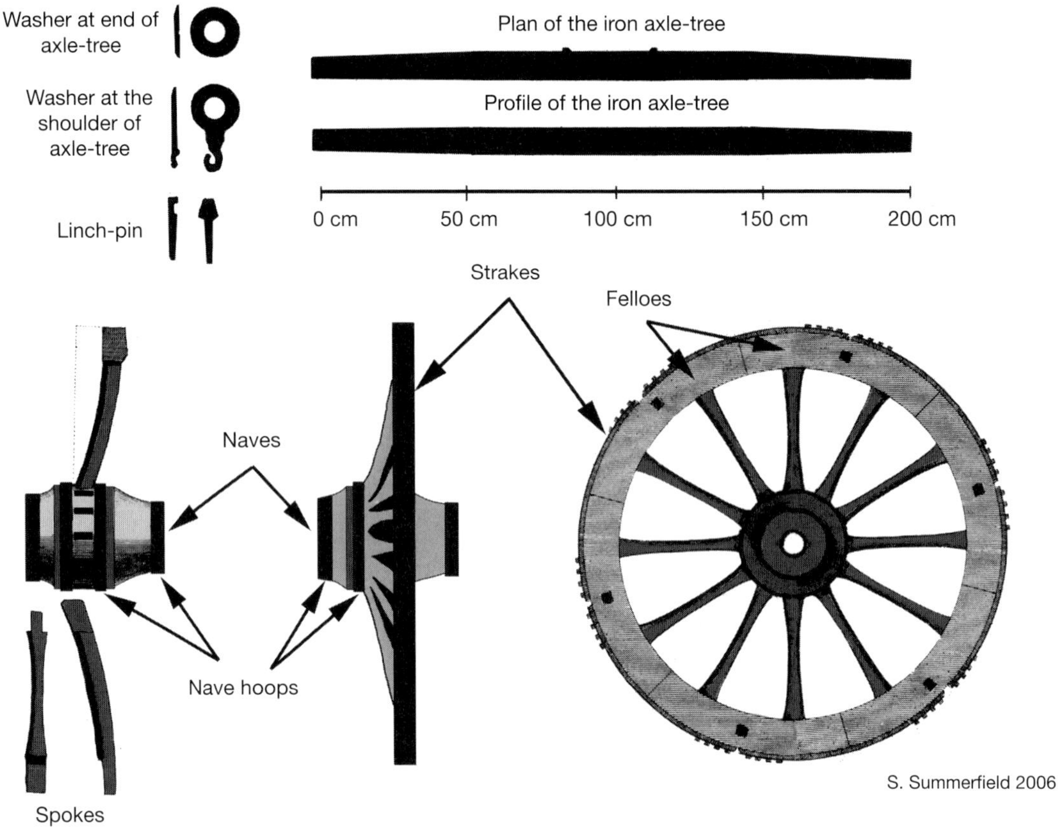

Wooden wheels with iron tyres, and iron axle-tree, of a French M1765 Gribeauval 8-pdr gun.

to a crooked pintail (as in British service) or a hole through the transom plate to a straight pintail on the limber, so that gun and limber together formed a four-wheeled vehicle (*see* Chapter 8).

Carriages had two large wheels ranging from 120cm to 160cm in diameter. Gun wheels had two light elm *naves* (hubs), oak radial spokes and ash *felloes* (the circumference); they were designated as heavy or light depending on the thickness of the spokes and felloes. Where wooden axles were used, these tended to be made from ash.[26] Two types of wheel were used. The *carriage wheel* had dished spokes flared away from the gun carriage, which made the body of the carriage wider, and increased the axle strength by reducing its length; these were used for field artillery carriages.[27] The *artillery wheel*, with spokes in the vertical plane, was used for heavy siege guns and lighter calibres of coastal defence and garrison carriages, since it was inherently stronger than the dished wheel.[28]

Oak, ash and elm were normally used in carriage construction. For example, a British M1776 Congreve bracket field carriage for 3-pdr to 12-pdr pieces had elm cheeks and transoms, an ash axle-tree and pine ammunition boxes.

The gun tube was held in place on the carriage by means of trunnion positions; semi-circular recesses were cut out of the top edge of the cheeks, and plated with iron for reinforcement, to receive the trunnions on the gun tube. In order to stop the tube bouncing out of the trunnion positions when the piece was moved or fired, the trunnions were held in place by *cap squares* – semi-cylindrical iron plates which closed over the trunnions to secure them.

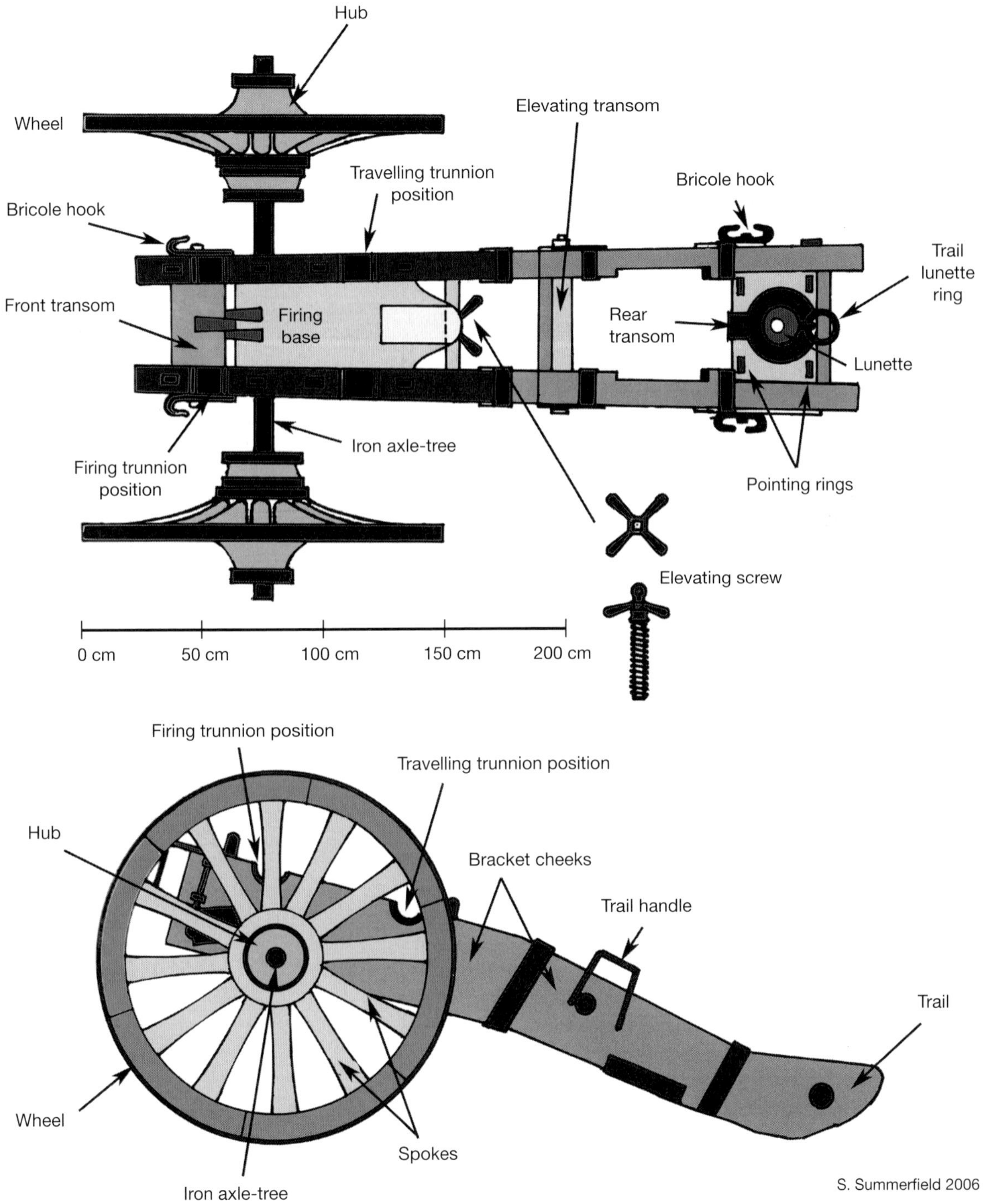

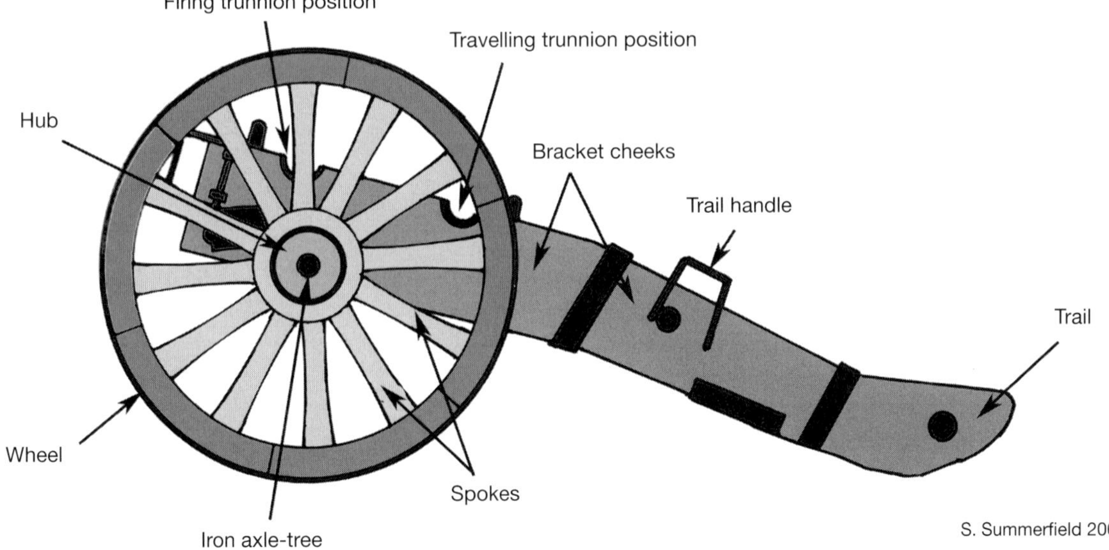

The parts of the bracket carriage for a French M1765 Gribeauval 8-pdr gun.

Rechtsmaschinen *of a Russian M1805 ¼-pud unicorn (left); an Austrian M1753 3-pdr field gun (centre); and a Russian M1805 6-pdr gun. (Paul Dawson and Dr S. Efimov)*

Elevating screws, of a French M1765 12-pdr, cast in 1821 (left); a French M1808 12-pdr (centre); and a Prussian M1809 6-pdr. (Paul Dawson)

There were four main types of elevating mechanism. The most primitive was a large wooden *quoin* or wedge, adjusted by blows of a wooden mallet. In the 1740s Prussia introduced a screw-driven quoin, known as the *Rechtsmaschine,* which gave greater precision. Meanwhile in France, Marshal Saxe developed the *elevating screw* of wrought bronze – a threaded metal cylinder with a four-pronged handle attached to one end. The vertical elevating screw either fitted into a socket on the gun tube or acted upon the bottom of the breech via a semi-circular cup. The gunner would turn this screw to elevate or depress the breech, thus depressing or elevating the muzzle.

Siege carriages were formed with two oak brackets connected by three transoms, and varied according to the nature of the gun; the British also used block-trail carriages. The guns were conveyed either on the carriage or on a separate wagon.[29] Mortars were mounted on wooden or iron beds and transported on specially constructed wagons called 'sling carts'. Garrison carriages were normally made of oak, since they were exposed to the weather for long periods. Iron carriages were also employed,

Vertical elevating screws, of a M1760 Armstrong-Frederick 5½in howitzer, cast by the Verbruggens in 1782 (left); a Sikh 9-pdr on a Congreve-style carriage (centre); and a Blomefield M1788 6-pdr, cast in 1796 by Francis Kinman. (Courtesy the Trustees of the RAHT; photographs S. Summerfield)

although, being cast iron, these tended to be rather brittle. Garrison carriages could be raised above a parapet by means of a traversing-platform.[30] Naval carriages were made of elm, lighter and cheaper than oak. They could take the forms of a rear chock carriage, sliding carriage or jamming carriage.[31]

MANNING AND FIRING

Artillerymen considered themselves elite troops. Ideally they were selected from among bigger and stronger men than their infantry and cavalry comrades, since serving the guns was heavy, gruelling work, and not only in combat. Before and after battle the guns needed cleaning, having been fouled by hours of firing. The tubes, carriages, and vehicles needed to be maintained; vehicles and carriages might appear strong and sturdy, but prolonged firing and travel over execrable roads could quite literally shake them apart – in today's parlance, the artillery arm was 'maintenance intensive'.

The way in which the various artillery systems were used in Europe during this period was virtually identical, in that all guns were muzzle-loaders. Serving the guns efficiently required the gunners to undergo long hours at 'crew-drill' (*see* accompanying drawing for crew positions):

When the gun was first cleared for action, the loader would remove the *tompion* (a wooden stopper that fitted into the muzzle to protect the bore from the weather) and the ventsman would remove the *apron* (a piece of sheet lead or leather used to protect the vent). These were suspended from the carriage when guns were in action or moving only short distances.

The rammer, standing on the right-hand side, would take his tools – some combination of *ramrod, brush and sponge,* and a separate *worm* or wad-hook – from the rack and, on command, check that the gun tube was clear by using the sponge.

The firer, standing behind the rammer, would unhook the water bucket and place it outside the right hand wheel, and then check his own equipment. He then turned about face, and planted his *boute-feu* or *linstock* in the ground. He lit the *porte-feu* (port-fire) from the slowmatch of the linstock, and held its short shaft *(porte-lance)* in his right hand with the smouldering end pointing at the ground.

Once the rammer had declared the tube empty, the gun commander (usually a corporal) would order the gun to be loaded, specifying the type of ammunition and the speed of loading. During the ramming procedure the ventsman would stop the vent using a *thumb-stall* (buckskin pad stuffed with horsehair, actually worn on the third or fourth finger rather than the thumb), to prevent the rush of air through the bore from igniting any unseen sparks from the last round and thus setting off the powder charge prematurely.

The ammunition would be carried from the *caisson* or *limber box* by the ammunition number and presented to the loader, who stood to the left of the muzzle. The ammunition could be inserted into the muzzle either separately (a fabric cartridge bag, followed by the roundshot attached to a sabot), or as *fixed ammunition* (the roundshot attached to the powder cartridge). Once inserted, the ammunition would be rammed down the bore of the piece by the rammer and loader, and seated at the breech with three firm thrusts of the ramrod. Each man cupped the ramrod shaft across the palm of one hand so that, should the piece discharge prematurely, he was unlikely to lose a whole hand. Once the ammunition had been seated at the breech the rammer and loader would retire to their positions.

The gun commander, assisted by two gunners levering with *handspikes*, would point the piece and alter the elevation as necessary to bring it to bear on the allocated target. To do so he would place his right leg between the cheeks of the gun carriage, so he could sight down the length of the tube using the back sight, his hand within easy reach of the elevating mechanism. He indicated the need to train the piece left or right by tapping with his right hand the inner or outer face of the gun cheek, as a signal for the men on the trail spikes to turn the trail right or left respectively.

In 1786, the *Hausse sight* was introduced to French service by Professor Lombard; this enabled the gun commander not to lose sight of the target,

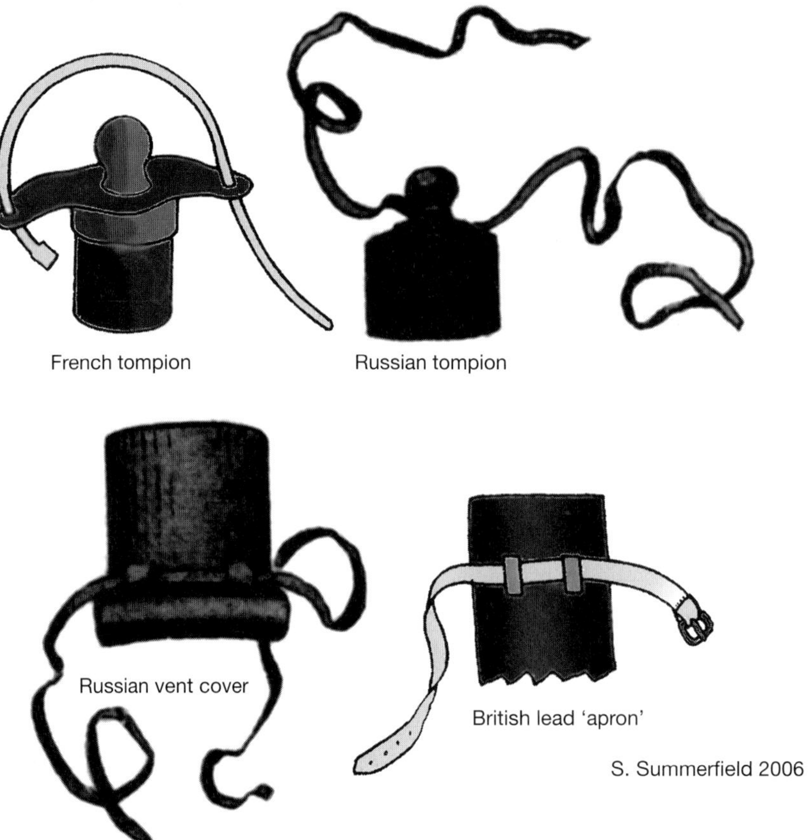

Tompions and aprons, used to protect the muzzle and vent of a gun from the elements.

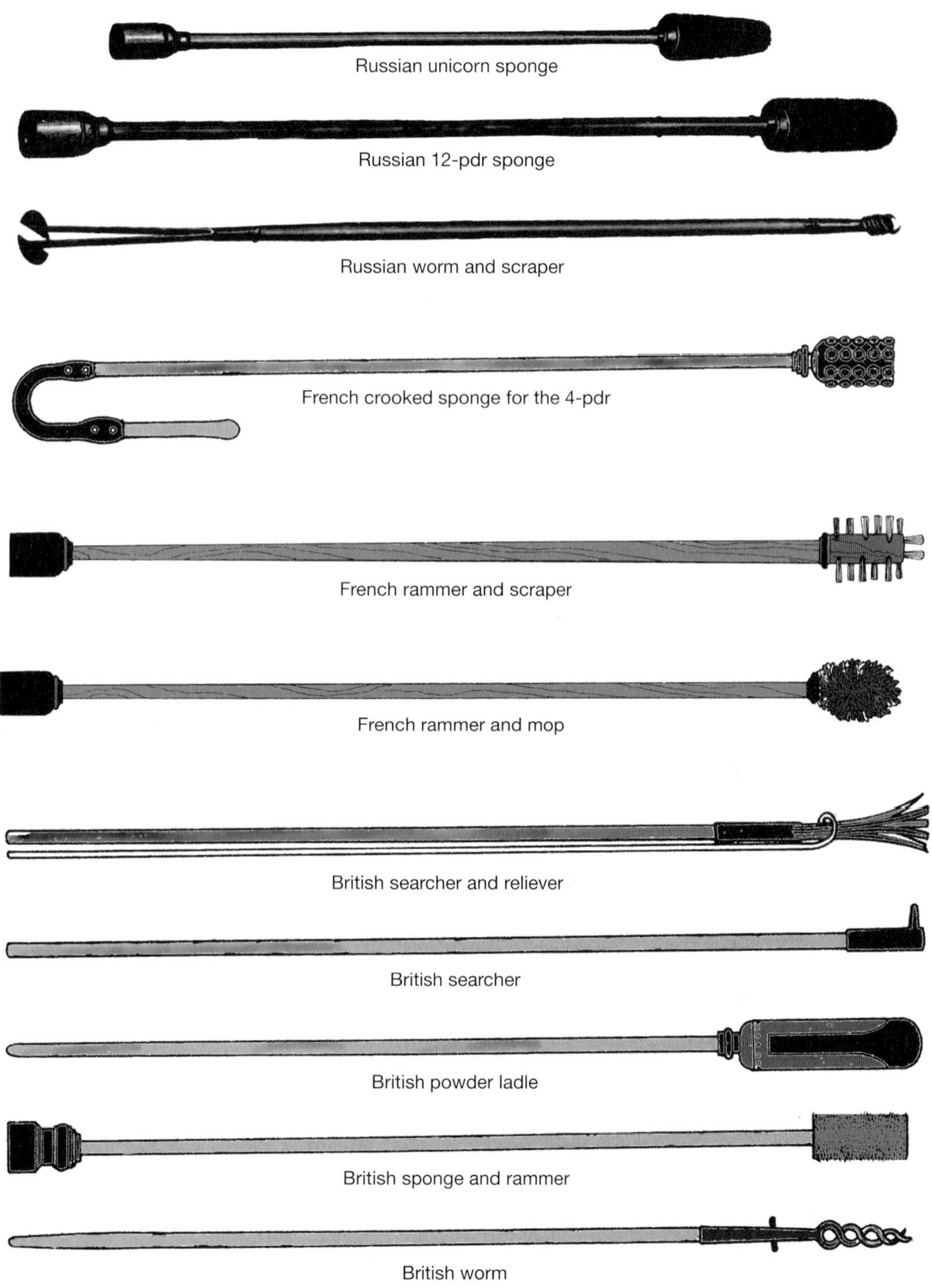

British, French and Russian tools used by the rammer and loader of a gun crew.

M1765 Gribeauval 12-pdr

The ammunition has been rammed home in this 12-pdr by the rammer, assisted by the loader. The ventsman is preparing to place the fuse into the vent, after piercing the cartridge bag with the ventspike. The two ammunition numbers, with their munition satchels each holding three rounds of fixed ammunition, stand to attention in front of the *coffret* or ammunition box. (L'Association Britannique de la Garde Impériale)

and to know exactly how to elevate his piece. It made training a gun crew quicker and easier, so that any man in the crew could take over the commander's job. It permitted French artillery to shoot more accurately, and thus saved ammunition.

Once the gun was on target, the ventsman would thrust his pricker or *ventspike* (a bronze or iron spike, also known as a *priming wire*) down the vent to pierce the cartridge. He would then prime the gun by placing a *fuse* (a powder-filled tube, originally of quill, reed or later paper, but by the Napoleonic period often of thin metal) in the vent and thence into the cartridge through the hole pierced in the bag. The pricker and fuses were carried on the ventsman's waist belt, respectively looped to and inside a small leather pouch.

Once the gun was armed, the gun commander reported to the section commander (a sergeant in the French army, a lieutenant in others) that the piece was ready to fire. Upon command, the gunner allocated to fire the piece would ignite the fuse, either by a slowmatch attached to a linstock or by a portfire. Since the discharge up the vent might blow the end off the portfire match, this would be trimmed anew with special cutters after each shot.

Upon ignition, the exploding charge would propel the projectile out of the gun tube and cause gun and carriage to recoil – the distance depended upon the nature and inclination of the ground, the trunnion position, angle of elevation, weight of the piece and strength of the charge. After the discharge the gun tube was scoured with a scraper (usually made from hog bristles, and dipped in water from the sponge bucket) in order to pull out any remaining small parts of the charge bag and extinguish any burning embers. A worm or wad-hook, shaped like a double corkscrew, was used to pull any misfires, or larger bits of debris that had remained in the bore when the gun was fired. The gun was swabbed (with a wet mop or sponge, usually made from sheepskin) after every round, both to extinguish any last sparks and to cool the tube; if it became excessively heated a bronze tube could droop, or prematurely ignite the next powder charge.

The gun had to be run forward again after each discharge, and re-laid before another round was fired. Veteran crews could get off four rounds per minute in emergencies, while the 'sustained rate of fire' for most guns was two rounds per minute, even for the Heavy 12-pdr.

The drill for firing shells from a howitzer was more demanding, since the time fuse of the shell had to be cut to length, and the shell placed into the bore carefully, to ensure that the firing of the charge

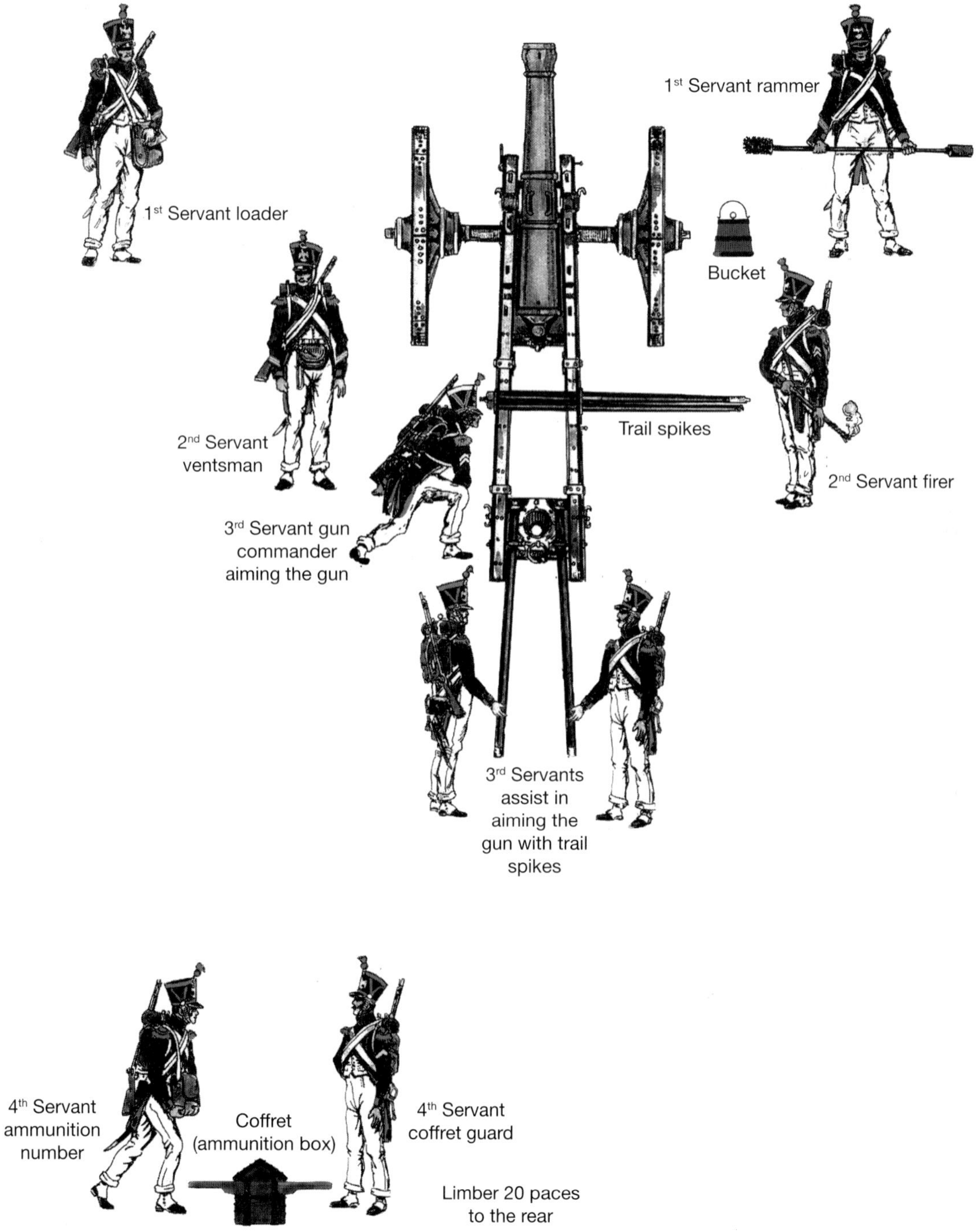

1st Servant loader
1st Servant rammer
Bucket
2nd Servant ventsman
Trail spikes
2nd Servant firer
3rd Servant gun commander aiming the gun
3rd Servants assist in aiming the gun with trail spikes
4th Servant ammunition number
Coffret (ammunition box)
4th Servant coffret guard
Limber 20 paces to the rear
NARG 2007

The regulation crew for a French 8-pdr field gun.

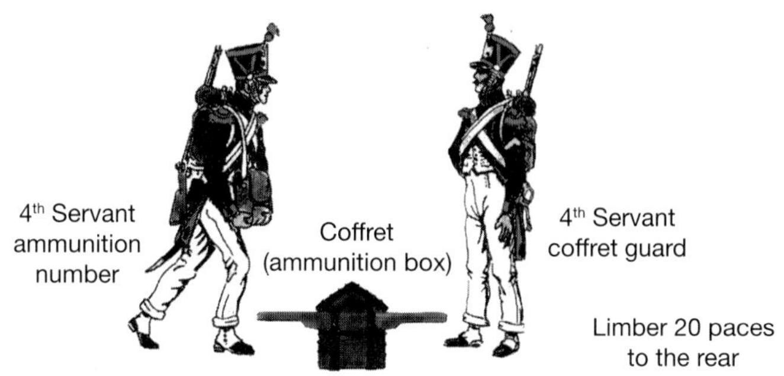

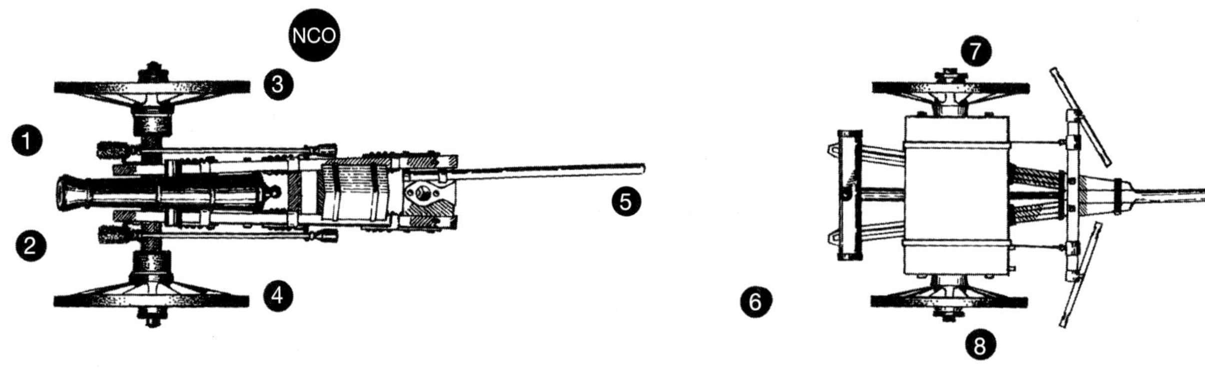

Crew positions for a Prussian M1768 6-pdr gun. (1) Rammer, (2) loader, (3) firer, (4) ventsman, (5) assistant gun-layer, (6) and (8) ammunition numbers, (7) limber ammunition guard, (NCO) gun commander.

would also ignite the fuse; the sustained rate of fire for shell may have been as low as one every two minutes.

National Variations

Prior to 1757, when Liechtenstein of Austria assigned the duties of the members of gun crews, the service of the guns was haphazard. On campaign, gunners and infantry 'servants' were assigned a particular gun from the artillery park for the duration of the campaign, at the end of which it was returned to the park. In the next campaign the crew would serve on a different gun, which might be either a field or a siege piece; they might even be serving a 24-pdr siege gun one day, and an 8-pdr field gun the next, and were thus liable to be unfamiliar with the characteristics of any particular gun. This practice persisted in Britain, where each piece had a specialist crew of five to six gunners who were only assigned to their pieces when on active service.

In France, a decree of 1759 regularised the number and position of the gunners and infantry servants for each gun and the organisation of the artillery as a whole. (This predated Gribeauval's decree of 16 March 1769 concerning the manufacture and testing of new field artillery.)[32] Based on the Swedish system, this decree established permanent gun crews, and organised the artillery into two battalions that became the 47e Régiment de Ligne. In 1791 this title was changed to the 62e and 63e de Ligne.[33] During time of peace the officers and gunners were instructed in artillery theory, learning the difference in capabilities between weapons from 24-pdrs to 4-pdrs, their range, when to use certain types of ammunition, and their effectiveness.

It was not until the 1780s that a French manual was produced for artillery officers to use in the field.[34] A similar manual had been published in Austria in 1757, covering organisation, administration, drill, artillery skills, mathematics, construction of fortifications and mines, and this heavily influenced Gribeauval in his reforms of the French artillery arm. He separated the artillery into the three distinct branches of siege, garrison and field artillery, as had been done in Austria in 1772.[35]

According to the 1809 manual by General Gassendi, the duties of the gunners differed little throughout Europe, as a gun could be fired safely with a minimum number of men:[36]

Rammer (First servant to the right): ensured the *cartouche* presented to the muzzle by the loader was inserted correctly, and that the ventsman closed off the vent when it was inserted. When the gun was cleared for action, he removed the tompion from the muzzle, and hung it on a hook on the side of the carriage.

Loader (first servant to the left): was of comparable build to the rammer, and responsible for inserting the correct cartridge and assisting in ramming when the order *'Refoulez'* was given. He carried three rounds of ammunition in his ready-bag.

Firer (second servant to the right): fired the piece on the orders of the ventsman, and was responsible for ensuring that the slowmatch *(corde à feu)* was burning properly at all times. He carried a container with two packs of ten port-fires, and a pair of pincers to trim the port-fire after each shot. When clearing the gun for action, he unhooked the water bucket and placed it by the wheel.

Ventsman (second servant to the left): pushed the pricker *(étoupille)* into the vent to prepare the piece for firing; wore a thumb-stall on the third finger of the right hand; and carried at his waist a pouch with 20 fuses. On being ordered to clear the gun for action, he removed the apron from the vent and hung it from the cascable.

Gun commander (third servant to the left – typically, a corporal): aimed the gun, commanded the gun, was responsible for the welfare of the crew, and was directly responsible to the sergeant section commander.

Ammunition numbers (fourth servants): two gunners responsible for the contents of the *coffret* (ammunition chest), and for supplying ammunition to the loader when needed.

The manning of Prussian guns was specified in the Prussian artillery manual of 1812.[37] Each gun was commanded by a non-commissioned officer, and each howitzer was commanded by a *Feuerwerker*. Prussian 6-pdr and 12-pdr cannon and 7-pdr and 10-pdr howitzers had crews of nine, thirteen, twelve and fifteen men respectively. The manual specified the following (*see* accompanying drawing for crew positions):[38]

Prussian 6-pdr gun with roundshot: When No.2 has emptied his bag of cartridges, he is replaced by No.6, who carries the reserve bag. No.2 will go back to the limber to have his bag refilled there by No.5, and takes the position of No.6. The Nos.2 and 6 are constantly exchanging their positions.

6-pdr gun with canister: No.2 takes the round from the box on the carriage. No.6 immediately fetches a new round from No.5, who gives it to him from the limber box; he then replaces No.2, who will go back to the limber to fetch more ammunition. The round in the gun carriage box is only there in order to have a shot immediately to hand whenever necessary.

12-pdr gun: When No.2 has emptied his bag, he is replaced by No.6, and the latter is replaced by No.10 (who was standing at the side of the ammunition wagon, 20 or 40 paces behind the guns). Then No.2 will have his bag refilled at the limber or at the ammunition wagon. If grapeshot is fired, Nos.11 and 12 will also help to fetch the rounds.

2 Austrian, Prussian and Russian Ordnance

ADVANCES IN BALLISTICS

The development of artillery in Austria, Prussia and Russia was particularly intertwined with the flow of ideas, and officers, between these countries and others. The science of ballistics was transformed by the gradual adoption of modern calculus. The founders of modern calculus were Sir Isaac Newton (1642–1727) and Gottfried Wilhelm von Leibnitz (1646–1716).[39] The Swiss brothers Jakob (Jacques) Bernoulli (1654–1705) and Johann (Jean) Bernoulli (1667–1748) made further developments, and gave the first public lectures on calculus.[40]

After the debacle of Narva (20 November 1700), where King Charles XII of Sweden routed a much larger Russian army leaving 145 cannon and 32 mortars on the field, Tsar Peter the Great (r.1686–1725) set out to reorganise and re-equip his forces. The lightening of Russian gun tubes and the development of uniform designs for carriages and supply vehicles, which began under the talented James Bruce (1669–1735), anticipated later Western developments.[41] Bruce was the son of a Scottish émigré, and became a colonel for the capture of Azov (July 1696). In 1704 he was appointed commander of the Russian artillery, a major-general, and governor of Novgorod. From 1714 an imperial decree concentrated the management of the artillery in St Petersburg. Daniel Bernoulli (1700–82), assisted by Leonhard Euler (1707–83), who was in his first year at St Petersburg Academy of Sciences, undertook ballistic experiments under General Gunther, Master-General of Ordnance at St Petersburg in 1727.

The Prussian M1731 system of General Christian von Linger (1669–1755) adopted Swiss carriage designs and standardised calibres at 3-, 6-, 12- and 24-pdr guns. These calibres were later adopted in Austria and subsequently by the rest of Europe, except for France and some of the lesser German states.

Traditionally the accepted weight of powder charge for any calibre of piece was two-thirds the weight of the ball. In 1731, Bernard Forest de Belidor (1673–1761) discovered that powder charges could be reduced without affecting range.[42] This research took cannon development in Prussia and Russia down a different path from the rest of Europe. By reducing the powder charge the thickness of metal at the breech could also be reduced, making the tube lighter. The reduced powder charge occupied less space than previously, so it was thought best to contain it in a small chamber; this increased the thrust that the projectile received, thus both saving powder and reducing further the thickness of metal required around the breech.

After joining the Berlin Academy of Sciences in 1741 from Russia, Leonhard Euler acted as a consultant to King Frederick the Great (1713–86), and was instrumental in developing Belidor's work on reducing powder charges; a range of chambered guns was subsequently introduced.

Daniel Bernoulli published experiments in his *Hydrodynamica* (1738), where he employed Newton's Law of Air Resistance to determine the initial pressure of gunpowder detonation in the breech as being 10,000 atmospheres. A few years later the English scientist Benjamin Robins (1707–51), in his *New Principles of Gunnery* (1742), transformed gunnery into a Newtonian calculus-based science. The most important breakthrough was the ballistics pendulum, which consisted of a flat plate connected to a bar suspended from a tripod; this measured muzzle velocity and consequently the influence of air resistance by moving the pendulum progressively farther from the gun. The velocity of the projectile was derived from the deflection of the pendulum after the impact of a ball upon the plate. Robins calculated that the initial pressure was in fact 1,000 atmospheres, a tenth of that calculated by Bernoulli.

In Euler's translation of *New Principles of Gunnery* into German for the Prussian artillery corps in 1745, he pointed out that Robins had failed to take a number of factors into account: gunpowder does not explode instantly; not all the gunpowder becomes a gas (a solid residue remains); there is air resistance in the barrel; and pressure is lost due to windage and through the touchhole. When these were taken into account, Euler calculated the initial gas pressure as being 5,000 atmospheres.[43]

These calculations were the basis for the designs of the Linger, Holtzmann and Dieskau chambered pieces of Prussia, hence contradicting Robins' assertion that changing the chamber size had little effect. Euler concluded that increasing the rate of explosion would be beneficial; in the 1770s and 1780s Lavoisier and Congreve Snr, directors of the French and British gunpowder administrations respectively, also came to the same conclusions.

Oberst-Leutnant Ernst von Holtzmann of Prussia invented the screw-driven elevating wedge or *Rechtsmaschine* in 1747 (*see* previous chapter), and this great improvement over the previous method was adopted by Austria in the M1753 system. Another Prussian officer, Lieutenant Paul Jacobi, constructed an exhaustive set of ballistic tables based upon exterior ballistic analysis in 1753 (five years later he would be killed at the siege of Olmütz in the Seven Years War).

During the War of the Austrian Succession (1740–48), Austrian artillery performed poorly compared to their Prussian opponents. In response Prince Joseph Wenzel von Liechtenstein, instigated the standardisation of equipment by completely redesigning Austrian artillery, with the emphasis on mobility and commonality. In 1748 he became the head of his family – which owned a quarter of Moravia, as well as the poor Principality of Liechtenstein on the Swiss border – upon the unexpected death of Prince Johann Carl. His considerable fortune was used to fund costly experiments and improve the professionalism of the artillery corps, projects that were beyond the capacity of state finances. Changes were made to ammunition, gun tubes, gun carriages, caissons, limbers, pontoons and all the other vehicles and stores necessary for a mobile army.

Prince Joseph Wenzel von Liechtenstein (1696–1772), who presided over – and to a large extent paid for – the Austrian artillery reforms of the 1750s. (Dave Hollins)

The major innovation of the M1753 Liechtenstein system was the reduction in windage, making guns more accurate and longer-ranged. Austrian tubes were now cast from a sand mould that took six men five hours to prepare. Liechtenstein's new furnaces took just one hour to melt the bronze, compared to 30–36 hours previously. The newly cast gun tube took 24 hours to cool, compared to five or six days in the old lime moulds. The tubes were bored out to half their desired internal diameter using a 6–8 horsepower water-powered machine that turned at 16 rpm; the vent was then drilled, the trunnions were finished, and the bore was then drilled out to its full width. A 3-pdr required 20 hours of boring, a 6-pdr 24 hours, a 7-pdr howitzer 22 hours, and a 12-pdr

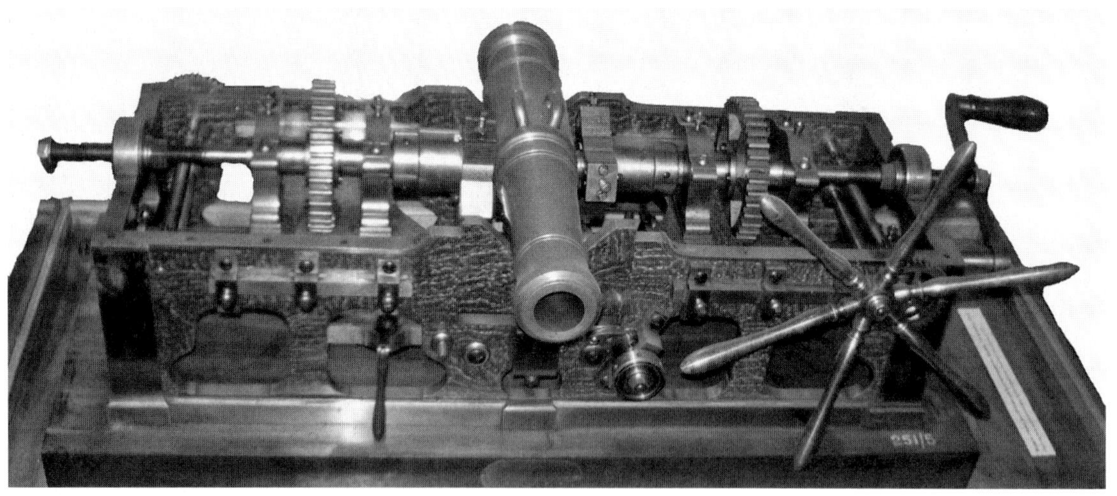

Model of a trunnion-turning machine, made in 1823 by students from the Artillery Technical School in St Petersburg, Russia. (Dr S. Efimov)

28 hours to complete the process. Production took place at either the Imperial Bohrwerke in Mechelen (Belgium) or at Ebergassing near Vienna.[44]

The Liechtenstein M1753 gun system introduced the following features:

- The brass Hausse sight
- Standardised ordnance and gunners' equipment
- A standard ammunition wagon, pulled by two horses
- A second, travelling trunnion positions for 12-pdr and 18-pdr guns, thus improving the weight distribution when the gun was limbered up for long movements
- The principle of standardised parts made to a common specification
- Reducing the bore-length by a third and most of the decoration from the tubes, thus halving their weight
- The *bricole* (men's harness or drag rope) and handspikes, which allowed guns to be manhandled more easily, without hitching up the team for many battlefield movements
- The rounding of the rearmost bottom corners of the bracket carriage, allowing guns to be moved by horse team with the *Schleppseil* rope or manhandled with *bricoles* without having to limber up.

The Seven Years War (1756–63) was caused by fear of Prussia's growing territorial expansion under Frederick the Great. Ranged against Frederick was a coalition of the Holy Roman Empire (Austria), France, Russia, Saxony and Sweden. The only major Prussian ally was Britain, already engaged in a colonial and maritime war against France. This war had a great influence upon ordnance. Frederick attempted to improve the mobility of his field guns by using the reduced-charge, chambered pieces of the Holtzmann M1741 and Dieskau M1758 systems. However, these were outclassed in range and hitting-power by the superior Austrian Liechtenstein M1753 designs. Indeed, Prussia introduced Austrian 12-pdrs in lieu of their own pieces, as they were far lighter than either of the two types then in use.[45]

In Russia, the chambered gun was used as the basis for a shell-firing cannon termed a 'unicorn', designed by Field Marshal Count Peter Ivanovich Shuvalov (1710–62), who became the head of the Artillery and Weapons Chancelleries in 1757, and Mikhail Vasilevich Danilov (1722–90). Unicorns were introduced into Russian service in the late 1750s, and copied by Saxony in 1766. It was Shuvalov who introduced the Russian M1757 system.

In the same year, Liechtenstein introduced new uniforms for the Austrian artillery; the first regulation to standardise crew positions; annual tests

General Alexei Adreevich Arakcheev

General Alexei Adreevich Arakcheev (1769–1834) was appointed in September 1792 as Senior Adjutant to the Inspector of Artillery, and Governor of Tsarevich Paul's Gatchina Model Army. After Paul I's coronation, on 7 November 1796, Arakcheev was appointed as the Commandant of the St Petersburg Garrison. In 1799 he became Inspector of Artillery, and started the reorganisation of that branch and its equipment. In May 1803, Tsar Alexander I reappointed him as Inspector of Artillery, a position he held until 1808; he reformed the units, improved the training of officers, amended the new regulations, and developed the M1805 system, which restricted the field artillery to five calibres. During the campaign of 1805 against France, Arakcheev worked on supplying the army with enough artillery ammunition. Promoted in January 1808 to Defence Minister to the Tsar and Inspector-General of the entire infantry and artillery, he continued his army reforms, and played an important part in directing the Swedish War of 1809. In 1810, Barclay de Tolly succeeded him as Defence Minister; during the Patriotic War of 1812, Arakcheev oversaw the management of supplies. In 1825, upon the accession of Tsar Nicolas I, he was exiled to Novgorod.[47] (Authors' collection)

and firing exercises for all gunners; a new, larger four-horse ammunition wagon used for all calibres except the 3-pdr, and new gun tools. Most of these were soon adopted by other countries. Ten years later, Austria published a handbook for the field artillery dealing for the first time with the technical aspects of ballistics and howitzer use.[46]

With the end of the Seven Years War, Frederick began an overhaul of his artillery. General C.W. Dieskau removed the 'dolphins' from the tubes of his new M1768 guns to reduce weight, and these replaced the chambered pieces of the Prussian M1744/58 system, which had proved unsatisfactory. In 1768, Georg Friedrich von Templehoff of Prussia published his translation of D'Antoni's *Treatise on Gunpowder*. He then conducted extensive exterior ballistics analysis, which he published as *La Bombardier Prussien* (1781). He clearly explained the distance a projectile travelled in relationship to the weight of propellant charge, elevation and length of tube and projectile weight, as well as air resistance and numerous minor perturbations acting on the projectile. These confirmed the relationship between bore length, propellant charge and range, as had already been established in France in 1768–69 in practical tests carried out by General Manson. The charge of one-third of the weight of shot and a length of 18 calibres gave the shortest length of bore for a maximum range of 1,100m. Thus, the length of gun tubes could be reduced without diminishing the range, so long as the ratio between powder and shot weights was maintained.

Tsarina Catherine the Great (1729–96) sent Russian technicians to Britain, to study more modern methods of producing gun tubes during their visits to the Carron Foundry near Falkirk and Mathew Boulton's works near Birmingham. Nikolai Ivanovich Korsakov visited the Carron Foundry (April 1775–July 1777); he was provided with a written description of the works, but was not allowed to view the secret cannon-boring machinery. Korsakov drew plans from memory of what he had seen.

General Gerhard Johann David von Scharnhorst

General Gerhard Johann David von Scharnhorst (1755–1813) was born in Bordenau, Hanover. In 1782 he received an appointment to the new Artillery School in Hanover, where he taught until 1793. In 1801, King Frederick William III of Prussia gave him a patent of nobility, the rank of lieutenant-colonel, and twice the salary. He was employed at the Berlin War Academy (where Clausewitz was one of his pupils), and founded the Berlin Military Society. Promoted to major-general a few days after the Peace of Tilsit (July 1807), he became the head of a reform commission that included Gneisenau, Grolmann and Boyen. In 1811, when France forced Prussia into an alliance against Russia, Scharnhorst left Berlin on unlimited leave of absence.[48] (Authors' collection)

Grand Admiral Greig of the Russian Navy, Governmental Registrar to the Olonets Armoury, was unhappy with this second-hand information, so offered an engagement to Charles Gascoigne, the director of the Carron Foundry (1769–86) and reputedly the inventor of the carronade (which was known for a short time as the 'gasconade' in his honour). The Carron Foundry exported large quantities of iron ordnance for the Russian Navy; for example, in August 1784 the foundry shipped £3,400-worth of gun tubes.

On 28 April 1786 the Lord Advocate of Scotland ruled that Gascoigne was allowed to take plans and cannon-boring machinery to Russia. He arrived at Kronstadt in May 1786, and by an edict of 2 September he reorganised the Alexandrovski Foundry at Petrozavodsk (founded in 1765 by Frenchmen Pierre Barral and Denis Charmony), and the nearby Konchezerski Foundry, along the same lines as the Carron Foundry. Gascoigne later set up a foundry on Kotlin Island near Kronstadt to supply guns for the navy, followed by others at Mariupol in the Crimea (annexed from the Turks in 1783) and in the Sea of Azov area. Gascoigne prospered in Russia, receiving the Order of St Vladimir and being appointed a business consultant to Catherine II. With the succession of Tsar Paul I (1777–1801) Gascoigne became advisor to the state, and was awarded the Order of St Ann on 8 October 1798 – as well as a gift of 2,000 serfs.

The War of the First Coalition (1792–98) against Revolutionary France revealed many deficiencies of the Coalition artillery, mainly those of Russia and Prussia. As a result, new Russian ordnance was introduced by Tsar Paul I. The introduction of cannon-boring machines was fundamental to Arakcheev's reforms of 1805; no longer were guns made with cast-in bores, and reduced their reliance on imported tubes. Russia was perhaps the last European country to introduce the cannon-boring machine, but she was finally self-sufficient in ordnance.

Because of financial problems Prussia still clung to her increasingly ineffective and outdated ordnance. During the Peace of Amiens (1802–03) David von Scharnhorst, who had transferred from Hanoverian to Prussian service, was tasked with researching a new artillery system. In 1806 he published a three-volume treatise on artillery that covered all contemporary systems in great detail. Out of this study came the Prussian M1809 and M1816 systems, which were developed after the massive loss of Prussian artillery following the defeats at Jena and Auerstädt in October 1806.

AUSTRIA

Maria Theresa had inherited a range of ordnance dating from as far back as 1718; there was no formal system of artillery, and the outdated guns were too cumbersome to move on the battlefield. Many guns were lost at Mollwitz (10 April 1741), Chotusitz (17 May 1742) and Hohenfriedberg (4 June 1745) during the War of the Austrian Succession (1740–48). Thereafter the Austrian artillery arm clearly needed a radical overhaul, and Prince Joseph Wenzel von Liechtenstein who had been Feld- und Haus-Artillerie General-Director since 1744, introduced a completely new system in 1753. This provided Austria with the best artillery in Europe during the Seven Years War (1756–63).

Liechtenstein had decided on the need for reform after being impressed by the Prussian guns at Chotusitz; he did not wish to see the dismal failure of the Austrian artillery during the War of the Austrian Succession repeated in future conflicts. Between 1744 and 1750 he and his staff, led by his chief designer Andreas Franz Feuerstein von Feuersteinberg (1697–1774), tested a number of new types. The key objective was to produce light and manoeuvrable pieces for field warfare. Feuerstein's M1744 3-pdr (13.5 calibres long) was shown to be unsuccessful during the Rhine campaign of 1744, when a number of them quickly overheated. There followed ten years of experimentation to develop a comprehensive new system.

In 1748, after unexpectedly inheriting an enormous fortune, Liechtenstein poured his personal resources

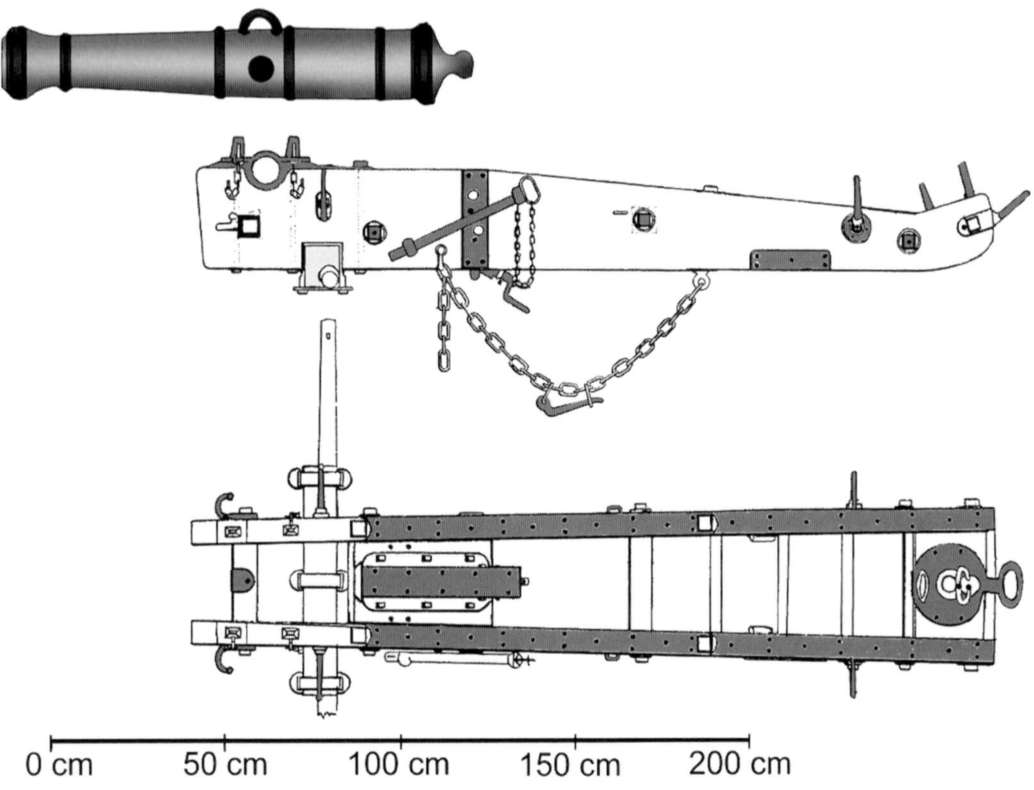

Austrian M1753 3-pdr gun carriage. This is the post-1780 design, with the ammunition box removed to the limber and the iron fittings for the advancing poles removed.

Table 2.1: Austrian Ordnance (Smola, 1839)

	Calibre	Bore length	Tube length	Tube weight	Windage	Projectile weight	Charge weight
M1753							
18-pdr Long	136mm	20.5 calibres	299cm	2190kg	5.5mm	8250g	ND
18-pdr Short	136mm	18.5 calibres	272cm	2020kg	5.5mm	8250g	ND
12-pdr	119.5mm	14.6 calibres	191cm	812kg	6mm	5500g	1600g
12-pdr Long	119.5mm	23.5 calibres	299cm	1517kg	6mm	5500g	1600g
12-pdr Short	119.5mm	21.5 calibres	275cm	1486kg	6mm	5500g	1600g
6-pdr	95.7mm	14.6 calibres	152cm	414kg	5.2mm	2750g	800g
3-pdr	75.5mm	14.6 calibres	121cm	240kg	3.8mm	1370g	409g
7-pdr Howitzer	153mm	4.1 calibres	94cm	280kg	8.5mm	7500g	572g
10-pdr Howitzer	171mm	4 calibres	94cm	280kg	7.5mm	10.6kg	ND
M1757							
1-pdr	53mm	14.6 calibres	85cm	98kg	3.8mm	450g	ND
M1764							
18-pdr Medium	136mm	20.5 calibres	299cm	2200kg	5.5mm	8250g	ND
12-pdr Medium	119.5mm	23.5 calibres	287cm	1500kg	6mm	5500g	1600g
M1780							
3-pdr	75.5mm	10 calibres	108cm	169kg	3.8mm	1370g	409g
1-pdr	52.6mm	14.6 calibres	84cm	96kg	3.4mm	450g	ND
M1811							
7-pdr Short	149.2mm	4 calibres	149cm	272kg	4.7mm	7500g	572g

into his work, bringing together some of the best designers in Europe at his own expense. Jaquet (a Swiss carpenter) and Schroder (from Berlin) worked at the Ebergassing foundry near Vienna on the new carriage and gun tube designs. Schroder used a horizontal boring machine; some say that he invented the technique, although it is normally attributed to Jean Maritz I (1680–1743) from Switzerland.[49] Other members of the team included Major Adolph Nicolai Alfson from Norway, in 1754; the Austrian Ignaz Walther von Waldenau (1713–60), killed at Torgau; and Johann Theodor Rouvroy (1727–1789), who came from Saxon service in 1753. In 1759, Rouvroy introduced Prussian-style horse artillery into the Austrian service, although it was disbanded in 1763 after the Seven Years War.

M1753 Liechtenstein System

The Liechtenstein M1753 system was so successful that it remained in service until 1859 with minor modifications, and can be considered the first unified systems of field artillery in the world. The barrels were lightened by reducing their thickness and length as well as removing any unnecessary adornments. The new bronze 3-pdr, 6-pdr and 12-pdr field guns were all 16 calibres long. There was now a systematic approach to boring the barrels, and the windage was halved on field guns. Casting techniques were improved; a key change was the exact casting of the roundshot (Müller (1811) notes that Austrian rounds were cast in graphite moulds). The *Traube* (cascable) was more pointed initially, but was rounded in Polish style from 1774. The original design had the vent drilled at an angle through the back of the gun, and supported by a vent support, so that the fuse would be thrown clear when firing. In 1780 this design was changed to a vertical vent in the main part of the tube, that was easier to bore and, being shorter, was less prone to blockages.

Liechtenstein brought a fresh and rational approach to the design of the gun carriages, which

Austrian M1770 3-pdr gun carriage found in Graz, with a Gribeauval 4-pdr gun tube fitted. (Dave Hollins)

were straight and no longer in the 'broken' style adopted by the French. (For carriage dimensions *see* Table 2.2.) Built from the best quality oak or elm, they retained the overall shape of the earlier Austrian system while being significantly lighter. The cheeks were reduced to one calibre in thickness and bound with a complete iron strap around the edges; in addition there were three iron cross ties towards the lower part of the carriage. The trunnion positions were moved in front of the axle to make the carriage easier to lift from the trail end. To facilitate road transport, an additional rear pair of trunnion positions were provided on the 12-pdr, to spread the weight of the tube more evenly between the limber and carriage.[50] This innovation was copied in the French Gribeauval system in 1765. Liechtenstein introduced metal trunnion plates which reduced the shaking of the carriage when the piece was fired. These carriages had a distinct advantage over previous designs, allowing a howitzer to have up to 30.5-degree elevation and 6-degree declination.

So thorough was Liechtenstein's evaluation of designs that the form of wheels was tested to identify the best ratio of felloes and spokes; the wheels for the field limber and 2-horse wagon had, and all others had, six felloes.

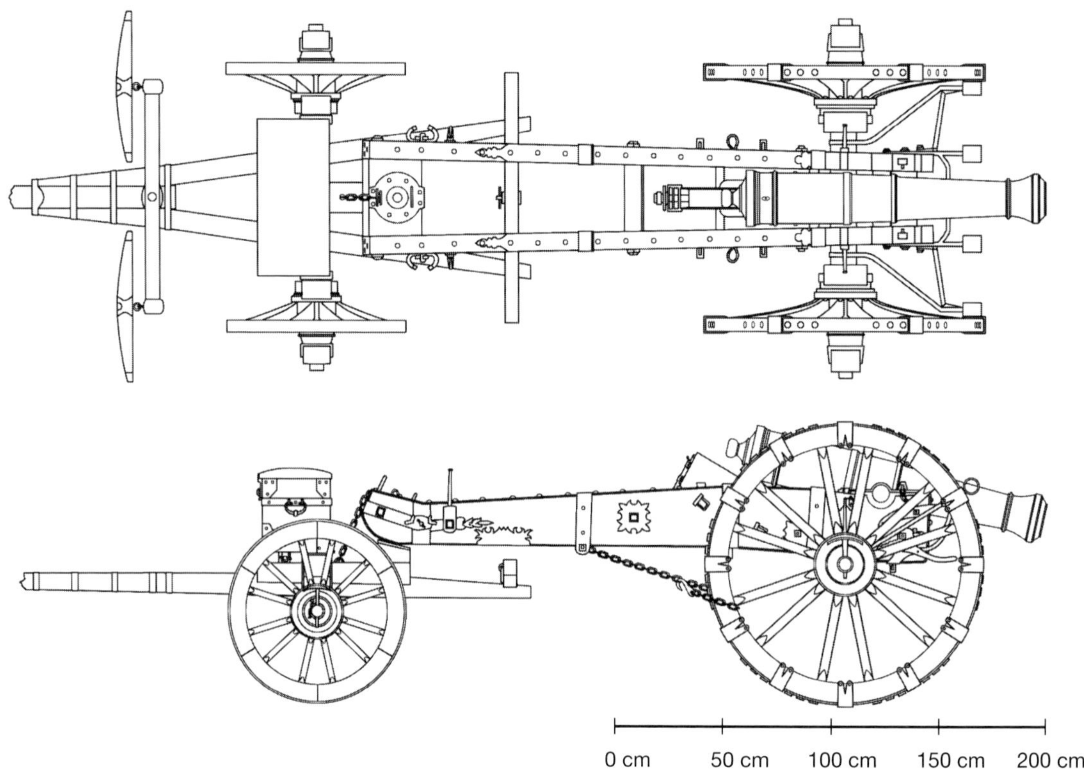

Austrian M1753 6-pdr gun, retaining the 'advancing handles', hooked to a M1774 limber.

M1776 'Wurst' Guns

The Saxon officer Rouvroy designed the Austrian M1776 cavalry guns that saw service in the War of the Bavarian Succession (1778). The most distinctive part of the carriage was the padded leather *Wurst* ('sausage') seat over the long ready-use ammunition chest; the 6-pdr seat was designed to carry four men astride the chest, one behind the other, and that for the 7-pdr howitzer, four men. The sponge and traversing handspikes were stowed under the carriage (which would inspire tool stowage on some designs of British gun carriages later in the century). The transmission *Rechtsmaschine* was worked by a handle on the left-hand side of the gun carriage, because the Wurst seat prevented the use of the normal layout, and also prevented the gun tubes from having a cascable. The operating handle turned a screw that raised or lowered a V-shaped platform with the open ends to the front. Howitzers could be elevated to 18.5 degrees and the 6-pdr to 15.4 degrees. In order to mount the Wurst seat, the gun carriage was longer than normal (*see* Table 2.3). In 1778, Rouvroy introduced the *prolonge* to Austrian service but it saw little use, the *Schleppseil* being deemed superior. While the *prolonge* attaching the gun to the limber could only be used to retreat a gun, the Schleppseil allowed both retreating and advancing without having to limber the piece using the lead horses (*see* Chapter 8).

The equipment allocation for Austrian units was as follows:

- *6-pdr brigade battery, 1808–12:* 8× 6-pdr guns, 8× four-wheeled ammunition wagons
- *6-pdr brigade battery, 1813:* 6× 6-pdr guns, 2× 7-pdr howitzers, 8× four-wheeled ammunition wagons

Table 2.2: Austrian gun carriages (Hollins, 2005)

	Length	Weight	Diameter of wheels
16-pdr	323cm	655kg	130cm
12-pdr	323cm	491kg	130cm
6-pdr	262cm	483kg	128cm
3-pdr	231cm	319kg	128cm
7-pdr Howitzer	270cm	475kg	128cm

Table 2.3: Comparison of Austrian field guns to cavalry (Wurst) guns

	6-pdr	7-pdr Howitzer	6-pdr Wurst	7-pdr Wurst Howitzer
Gun tube	388kg	274kg	386kg	274kg
Carriage	398kg	411kg	435kg	482kg
Wurst seat	none	none	69kg	72kg
Limber	259kg	248kg	183kg	183kg
Ammunition	88kg	57kg	60kg	88kg
Men riding	none	none	364kg (4 gunners)	291kg (3 gunners)
Total	1133kg	990kg	1497kg	1390kg

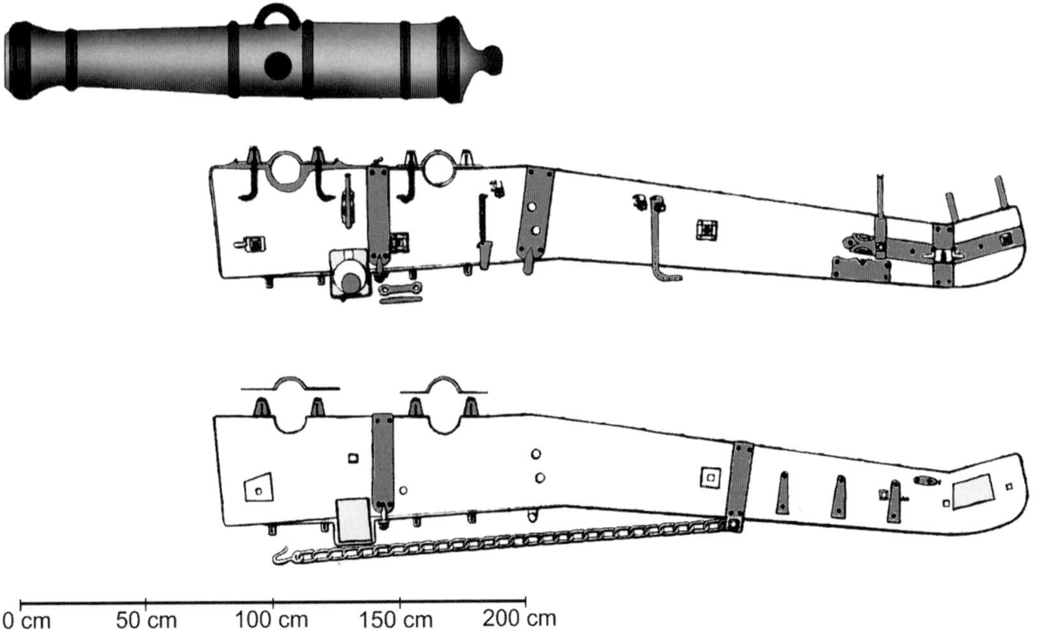

Austrian M1753 12-pdr gun carriage; this design, with two trunnion positions, influenced Gribeauval's design for his 8-pdr and 12-pdr carriage.

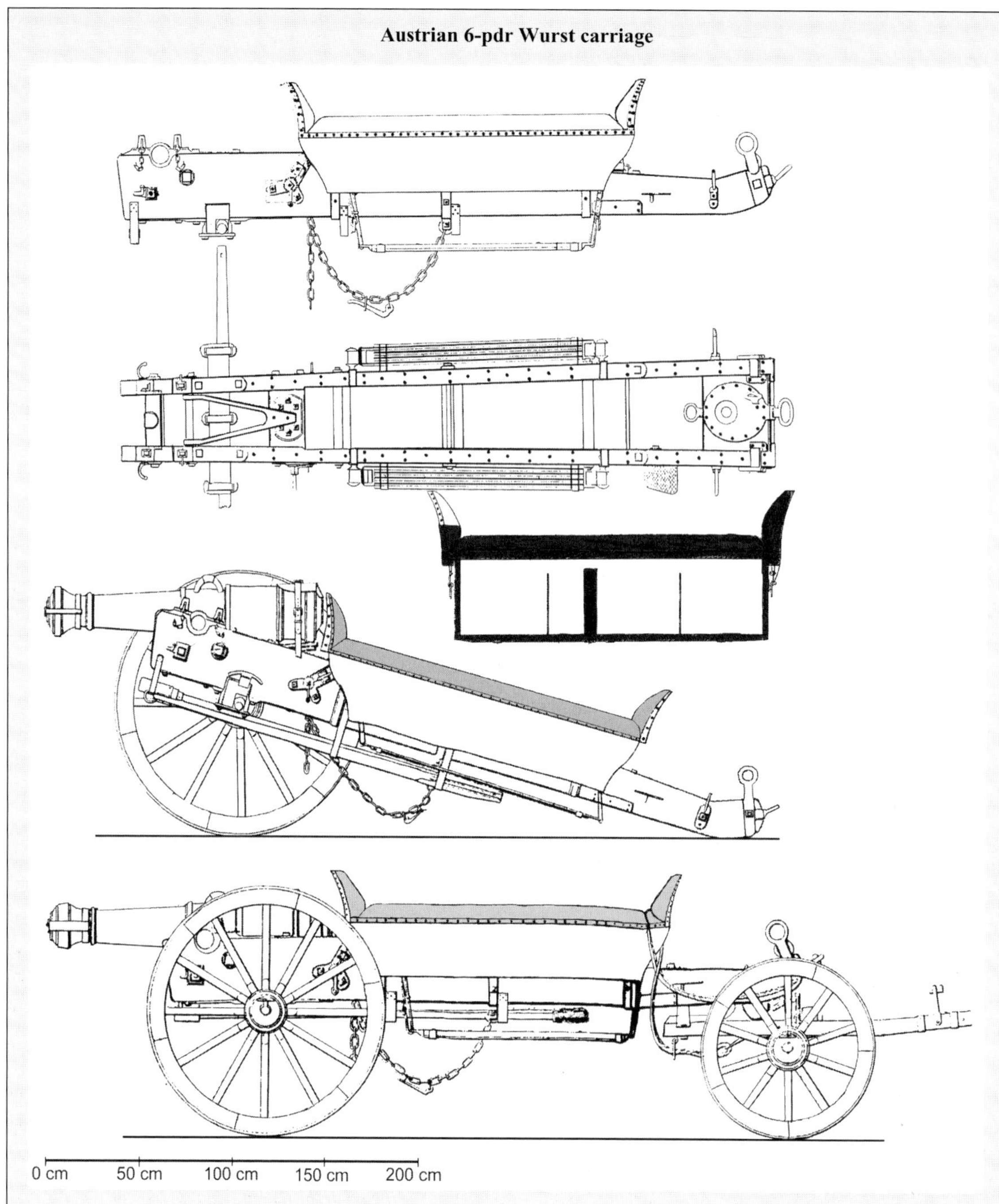

Austrian 6-pdr Wurst carriage. Note the transmission Rechtsmaschine elevating mechanism acting through the carriage, and the absence of the backweight. Handspikes were placed in the iron eyes protruding above the trail end to elevate it for limbering or unlimbering; this positioning of the handspikes made Austrian guns far easier to handle, since the lifting-point was as far away from the fulcrum as possible. On the French Gribeauval equipment the lifting-point was half the distance from the fulcrum to the trail end.

- *12-pdr position battery:* 4× 12-pdr guns, 2× 7-pdr howitzers, 3× four-wheeled ammunition wagons
- *Horse battery:* 4× 6-pdr Wurst guns, 2× 7-pdr Wurst howitzers, 3× four-wheeled ammunition wagons and 6× packhorses

PRUSSIA

To understand the artillery used by Prussia in the Napoleonic Wars we must consider the developments of the previous century, when Frederick the Great entered an arms race with Austria that almost bankrupted his country.[51] The complexity of Prussian artillery is shown by the summary of major tube types (*see* Table 2.4).

In 1731, the M1731 system of General von Linger standardised Prussian calibres at 3-pdr, 6-pdr, 12-pdr and 24-pdr, and introduced a Swiss carriage design. The Linger 3-pdr and 6-pdr were restricted to infantry support, and pulled by six-horse teams. The 12-pdr and 24-pdr were used as position artillery emplaced in temporary field fortifications, due to their weight and lack of manoeuvrability.[52]

In 1741–42, Prussia put Belidor's theories into practice under the leadership of Oberst-Leutnant

Prussian M1731 12-pdr or 'Brummer', *held in the collections of the French Musée de l'Armée. These 12-pdr guns were used in fixed positions and weighed over 3.5 tonnes. (Paul Dawson)*

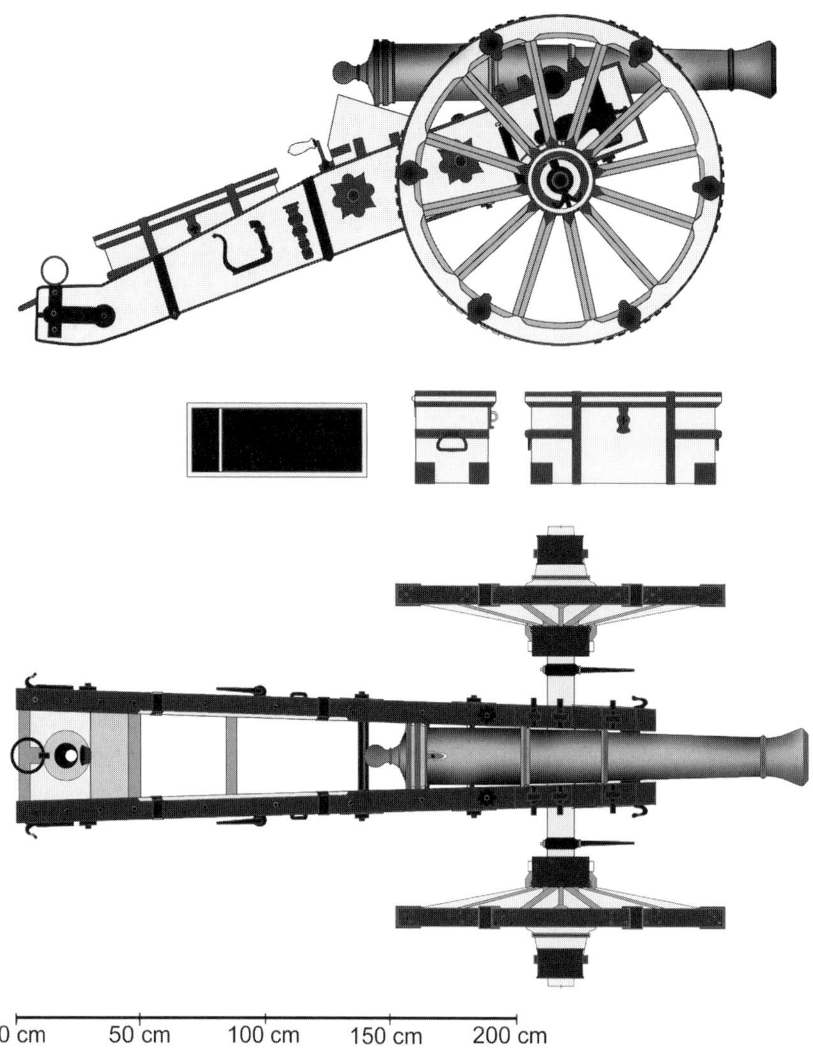

The Prussian M1768 6-pdr gun.

Ernst von Holtzmann, ably advised by Leonhard Euler. The guns were cast at Prussia's new armaments factory founded by Linger. In 1741, Frederick the Great wrote to Leopold of Anhalt-Dessau suggesting that the 3-pdr should be recast as the new M1741 6-pdr gun. The piece was pulled by three horses, and had a chambered bore like a howitzer in order to reduce the powder charge. However, these guns were found to be insufficiently mobile, so Frederick introduced the 3-pdr to replace the 6-pdr piece. In 1747, Holtzmann invented the screw-driven elevating wedge called the *Rechtsmaschine* (*see* Chapter 1).

Samuel von Schmettau, recruited from Austrian service, was appointed 'Grand Master' of Artillery, and succeeded Major-General Linger in April 1755 as Chief of the Field Artillery Regiment. The M1741 3-pdr had less hitting-power than Linger's M1731 6-pdr, so, as a compromise, Inspector-General of Artillery Karl Wilhelm von Dieskau (1701–77) instigated a longer-barrelled 3-pdr and a new 6-pdr design that was pulled by four horses. A total of 84 of the new light Dieskau M1755 6-pdrs were cast in Berlin.

Apparently Holtzmann carried out tests there to find the best way of making the ordnance lighter,

The Prussian M1809 6-pdr carriage in the Musée de l'Armée has a French M1808 6-pdr gun tube. (Paul Dawson)

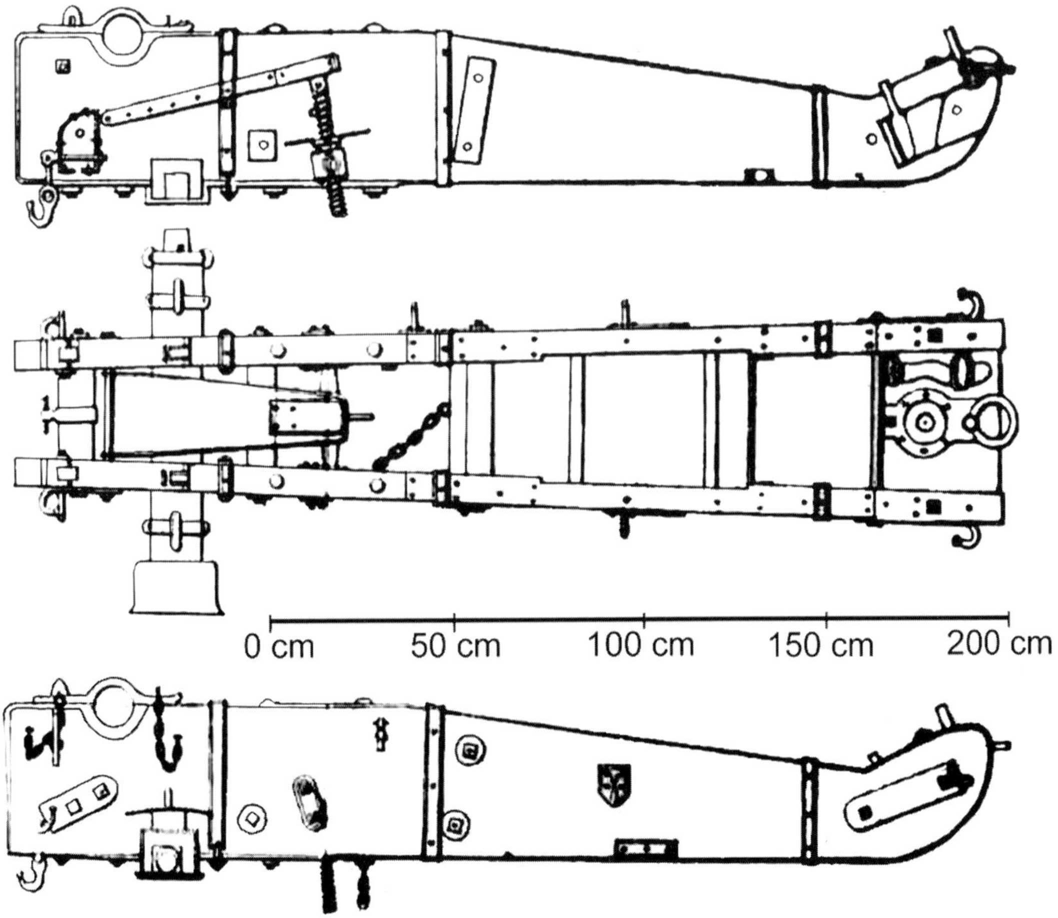

0 cm 50 cm 100 cm 150 cm 200 cm

The Prussian M1809 6-pdr carriage.

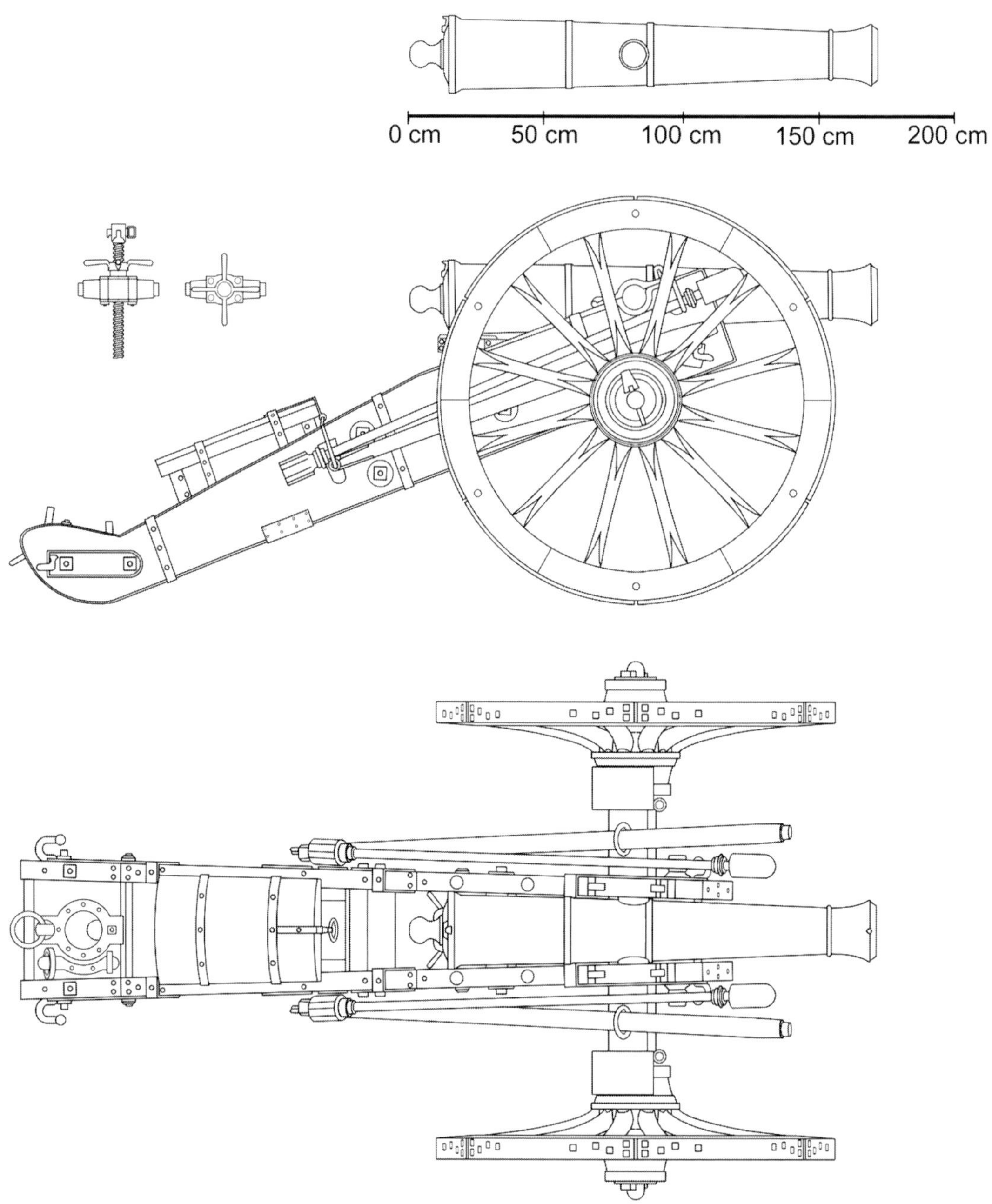

The Prussian M1816 6-pdr gun.

Table 2.4: Eighteenth-century Prussian ordnance (M1731 to M1790)

	Calibre	Bore length	Tube length	Tube weight	Projectile weight	Charge weight
Linger 1731						
12-pdr M1731 Brummer	122mm	16 calibres	182cm	487kg	5600g	1630g
6-pdr Linger M1731	95mm	ND	ND	ND	ND	ND
3-pdr Linger M1731	73mm	20 calibres	144cm	207kg	1400g	580g
Holtzmann M1740 (chambered pieces)						
24-pdr M1741	150mm	16 calibres	230cm	1150kg	11.2kg	2800g
12-pdr M1741	122mm	16 calibres	182cm	570kg	5600g	1400g
6-pdr M1742 (conical)	95mm	16 calibres	145cm	440kg	2800g	900g
6-pdr M1741 (cylindrical)	95mm	16 calibres	145cm	220kg	2800g	700g
3-pdr M1742 (conical)	73mm	16 calibres	115cm	220kg	1400g	470g
3-pdr M1741 (cylindrical)	73mm	16 calibres	115cm	144kg	1400g	340g
10-pdr M1743 Long Howitzer	173mm	5 calibres	135cm	ND	12.6kg	2100g
Linger M1744-1746						
12-pdr M1744 (conical)	122mm	16 calibres	182cm	487kg	5600g	1630g
3-pdr M1746 (conical)	73mm	20 calibres	144cm	207kg	1400g	580g
Dieskau M1754 (chambered pieces)						
24-pdr M1754	150mm	16 calibres	230cm	1764kg	11.2kg	4700g
12-pdr M1754 (conical)	122mm	14 calibres	160cm	358kg	5600g	1600g
6-pdr M1754 (conical)	95mm	16 calibres	145cm	268kg	3000g	1400g
Dieskau M1758						
Light 12-pdr M1758	122mm	14 calibres	196cm	397kg	5600g	1600g
12-pdr M1758	122mm	18 calibres	250cm	1385kg	5600g	2300g
6-pdr M1758	95mm	25 calibres	256cm	660kg	3000g	1400g
3-pdr M 1758	73mm	17.5 calibres	148cm	327kg	1400g	580g
2-pdr M1758	68mm	14 calibres	119cm	ND	1000g	470g
M1759-1762						
12-pdr M1759 Austrian	119.5mm	16.4 calibres	214cm	952kg	5930g	1800g
12-pdr M1761 Brummer	122mm	22 calibres	262cm	1492kg	5930g	2300g
6-pdr M1762 Heavy Dieskau	95mm	22 calibres	199cm	ND	5930g	1400g
Dieskau M1762-1766 Howitzers						
10-pdr M1763 Howitzer	173mm	4.4 calibres	94cm	590kg	12.6kg	1400g
10-pdr M1766 Howitzer	173mm	ND	121cm	1732kg	12.6kg	2300g
7-pdr M1762 Howitzer	148mm	4.5 calibres	95cm	792kg	6540g	900g
Dieskau M1768						
12-pdr M1768	119mm	16 calibres	210cm	838kg	5930g	1600g
Heavy 6-pdr M1768	94mm	24 calibres	244cm	925kg	3000g	1400g
Light 6pdr M1768	94mm	16.5 calibres	164cm	500kg	3000g	1400g
3-pdr M1768	73mm	16.5 calibres	132cm	280kg	1400g	580g
Dieskau M1771						
3-pdr 1771	73mm	18.5 calibres	146cm	530kg	1400g	470g
Holtzmann M1774						
3-pdr 1774	73mm	18.5 calibres	146cm	526kg	1400g	470g
M1787-1790						
6-pdr M 1787	94mm	16.5 calibres	164cm	902kg	3000g	890g
7-pdr M1790 HA	148mm	4.5 calibres	94.7cm	343kg	6080g	690g

Table 2.5: Prussian Field Artillery 1809–1816

	Calibre	Bore length	Tube length	Tube weight	Projectile weight	Charge weight
M1809						
12-pdr M1809	119mm	16.4 calibres	214cm	900kg	5930g	1600g
6-pdr M1809 FA	94mm	16.5 calibres	169cm	880kg	3000g	890g
6-pdr M1809 HA	94mm	16.5 calibres	164cm	491kg	3000g	890g
3-pdr M1809	76mm	18.5 calibres	146cm	230kg	1400g	600g
7-pdr M1809 Howitzer	148mm	4.5 calibres	94. cm	410kg	6950g	690g
M1816						
12-pdr M1816	119mm	ND	214cm	ND	5930g	1600g
6-pdr M1816	94mm	ND	164cm	ND	3000g	890g
7-pdr M1816 Howitzer	148mm	ND	ND	ND	6950g	690g

and concluded that a ratio of 112:1 metal in the gun tube to shot was sufficiently strong for service in the field artillery, the length of the tube being 16 calibres. Frederick insisted that the 3-pdr, 6-pdr and 12-pdr had chambered breeches akin to that of a gun-howitzer (unicorn). Holtzmann's work was a development of Linger's: the former had introduced a tapered bore to the field artillery, replaced by Holtzmann with a chamber proper. Frederick the Great was a great supporter of howitzers, and his influence is evident in the adoption of gun-howitzers for the field army. These new guns were introduced in 1755, and it was Frederick's intention to arm the front-line infantry regiments with the 6-pdr and second-line units with the 3-pdr; a new chambered 12-pdr was also introduced.

M1758 System

By the end of the 1750s, practical wartime experience clearly demonstrated that the chambered field guns were inferior to the new Austrian artillery in terms of range and hitting-power. The Dieskau modified M1741 system was deemed a failure, and was only in service for three years; despite this, Dieskau's carriage designs formed the basis of a new M1758 system designed by Linger assisted by General Dieskau.

From 1758, fully bored 3-pdr and 6-pdr guns were introduced, and the M1731 Linger 12-pdr was reintroduced. Some of the chambered guns may also have been bored out as a matter of economy. Dieskau also introduced a Light 7-pdr howitzer, which proved such an effective weapon that one was attached to each infantry battalion by the end of the Seven Years War; this piece supplemented the excellent 18-pdr and 10-pdr howitzers introduced in 1744. A Light 12-pdr based on Austrian designs was introduced to act as a support for the battalion guns, keeping the old 12-pdr as a reserve. Dieskau also founded the artillery train and horse artillery. The latter was clearly inspired by the Austrian M1753 Liechtenstein system, since it had medium wheels (130cm) for 6-pdr guns, limbers, and the front of four-wheel ammunition wagons, and large wheels (147cm) for 12-pdr guns, limbers, and the rear wheels of ammunition carts. The original screw-driven elevating plate was replaced with the *Rechtsmaschine*. The M1758 carriages were virtually identical to those of Liechtenstein – indeed, the limber-mounted ammunition box had identical dimensions.

By 1761 the number of guns in Prussian service had almost doubled, from 360 in 1756 to some 626 pieces. However, the Austrians still outgunned them. In 1762, King Frederick's brother Ferdinand proposed that every infantry regiment have two 3-pdr guns and one 7-pdr howitzer, and every infantry brigade two Austrian 12-pdrs, two Heavy 6-pdrs, two Light 6-pdrs and two 10-pdr howitzers. Frederick also realised that heavier shot was more effective because of its greater hitting-power. In 1763 he ordered the production of a Medium 10-pdr howitzer, and assembled an artillery reserve of 70 pieces. However, his kingdom could not afford the expense of introducing an entire new system, and continued to employ a wide variety of types and calibres.

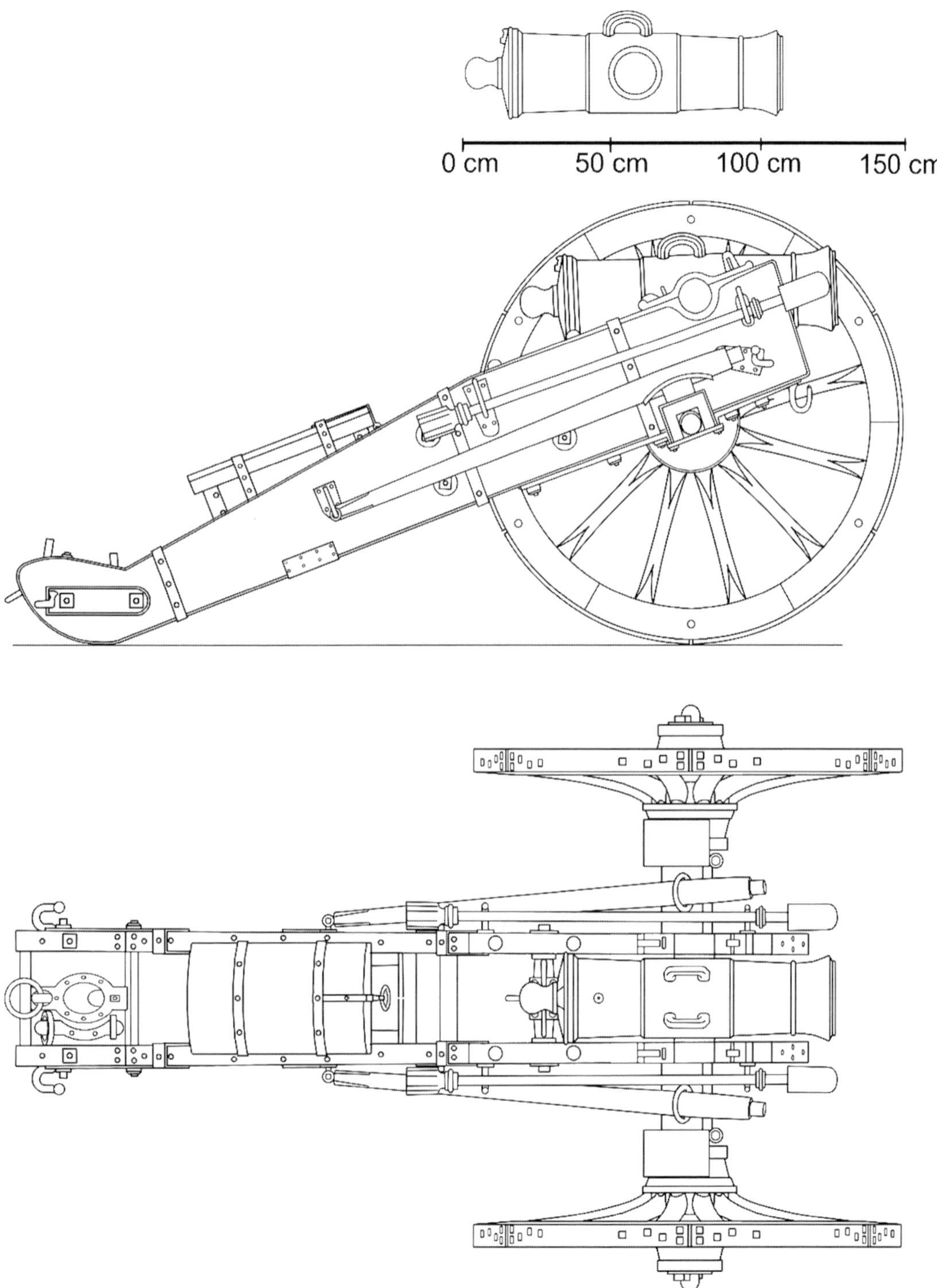

The Prussian M1816 7-pdr howitzer.

M1768 Dieskau System

Dieskau, who had been General-Inspector of Artillery since 1763, overhauled Prussian artillery yet again, with a new longer-barrelled 3-pdr of 20 calibres, a Light 6-pdr for the horse artillery, and a Heavy 6-pdr for the foot artillery, in accordance with the desires of Prince Ferdinand. In order to reduce the weight of the tube the dolphins were removed (except from the 12-pdr and howitzers). Between 1768 and 1773 over 50,000 *thalers* was spent on improving the artillery.

According to William Congreve Snr, during the War of the Bavarian Succession the battalion artillery was organised so that every grenadier and musketeer battalion was issued with four 6-pdrs, and each fusilier battalion with four 3-pdrs, which were to be 16 calibres in length and weigh some 438kg. The park artillery was to consist of 6-pdr and 12-pdr guns of both light and heavy varieties, the 6-pdr being the same model as for the battalion artillery. The Light 12-pdr was described as weighing 730kg, and rather than having the tube walls one calibre thick at the breech, they were to be 0.75, and 0.5 calibre at the muzzle. The Heavy 6-pdr was 24 calibres in length and weighed 600kg. The Heavy 12-pdr was described as being 24 calibres in length, weighing 1000kg or more, and was 'doubly fortified'. The 24-pdr or battery guns were noted to be 27 calibres in length, and weighed from 1500kg upwards. Howitzers were noted as being of 7-, 10-, 18- and 25-pdr varieties.

In 1787 the Light 12-pdr were recast as a Heavy 6-pdr, and the howitzers were no longer to be used as battalion guns. In 1790, the Light 7-pdr howitzer was introduced to service for use with the horse artillery.[53] For the Jena campaign of 1806, Prussia had 24× 'bombardment pieces', 84× normal 12-pdrs, 120× Heavy 6-pdrs, 320× Light 6-pdrs, 16× 10-pdr mortars, 76× 10-pdr howitzers and 34× 7-pdr howitzers.

Reconstruction, 1808–15

By the time of the French Revolution (1789) the artillery was perhaps the worst arm of the Prussian army, and after suffering heavy losses in the 1806 campaign it had to be rebuilt over a number of years. Battalion guns were abolished under the new regulations of 1812.[54] The lack of field artillery pieces was to some extent made up by gifts of artillery and powder captured by the Russians; Britain supplied gun tubes in 1807 and again in 1813, fitted on British or Prussian double-bracket carriages. For example, the 24th 6-pdr Foot Battery (Captain Vahrenkampff) was formed with 6× Light British 6-pdrs with block carriages and 2 × Prussian 7-pdr howitzers with wooden axles – one of the great drawbacks of Prussian artillery – and British ammunition wagons; all eight NCOs of the battery were mounted.

Between 1808 and 1812 the total number of artillery pieces, including fortress pieces, increased from 1,318 (of which 149 field pieces) to 1,659 – still a mere fraction of the 7,095 guns that had been available in 1806. In 1811, Friedrich Krupp started the small Prussian forge that blossomed into a great steel and ordnance empire of the 19th–20th centuries.

New guns introduced into the Prussian army in 1816–17 were based on the French Gribeauval system.[55] The *Rechtsmaschine* had been replaced with the hinged wooden plate and elevating screw of the Gribeauval system. Iron axles were used, and the trail ends of existing carriages were made more rounded. The wheels were of two sizes. Another novel aspect of the system was the standardisation to three carriages for the field artillery (12-pdr, 6-pdr and howitzer).

RUSSIA

The artillery arm enjoyed a pre-eminent position in Tsar Peter the Great's new model army of 1704. Its creator James Bruce produced a battle-winning system of artillery from scratch by standardising carriage design, reducing barrel weights (e.g. the 12-pdr from 1835kg to just 495kg) so increasing mobility and created the artillery regiment. In just five years, Russia had manufactured 1006 cannon. This resulted in the 102 Russian guns shredding the attacking Swedish infantry at the battle of Poltava (28 June 1709) with little response from the four 4-pdrs.

Russian artillery during the French Revolutionary Wars: two M1757 light 12-pdr cannon, with vent covers and tompions in place. The carriages were painted green with black metalwork. (By kind permission Landes u. Universitätsbibliothek Darmstadt; photograph Marcus Stein)

Baron Count Burkhard Christoph von Munnich (1683–1767), born in Oldenburg, reformed the system, with a greater emphasis on the use of the four 3-pdr guns per infantry regiment, and developed the professionalism of the service by founding the cadet corps. This officer – often referred to in Russian sources as 'Burkhard Kristof Munikh' – became a field-marshal and President of the Council of War in 1732, but was sent into exile for 20 years in 1742.[56] The Imperial Arms Factory became the centre of the Russian armaments industry established by Tsar Peter the Great in 1712.

M1757 Shuvalov System

The Russian army was strong in artillery when it took the field against Prussia at the start of the Seven Years War (1756–63). This conflict was the catalyst for the artillery reforms of Peter Shuvalov in 1757, but they fell far short of the scale of change seen in other European countries. The field artillery consisted of 3-pdr regimental guns, and 6-, 8- and 12-pdrs of a mixture of designs by Wilhelm de Hennin, Mikhail Danilov and Shuvalov himself. The guns were more heavily reinforced

Gun tube of a Russian M1757 ¼-pud (10-pdr) unicorn, cast in 1787, on a horse artillery carriage. (Steven H. Smith)

and more cumbersome than those of other countries. The Master-General of Artillery stipulated the basic dimensions, and then permitted the individual contractors or regimental commanders to produce carriages to their own designs.

The Russians also produced a variety of unusual or experimental guns. The 'secret' M1759 unicorn of 18 calibres, designed by Mikhail Danilov, had an oval rather than a round bore; this scattered small canister-shot in a wide, flat swathe parallel with the ground.[57] To preserve the secrecy surrounding this piece, on campaign the muzzle was shielded with a copper tompion fastened with a lock until it was brought into action. In 1759 there were 181 of these pieces in service, in place of the more reliable 3-pdr.

The unicorn, designed by Danilov assisted by S.A. Martynov, was intended to replace both the field gun and the howitzer with a 10 calibre tube

An M1805 light 12-pdr field gun, cast at the St Petersburg Arsenal by Master Pashkov; it has a calibre of 121mm, a gun tube length of 172cm, and weight of 479kg. (Dr S. Efimov)

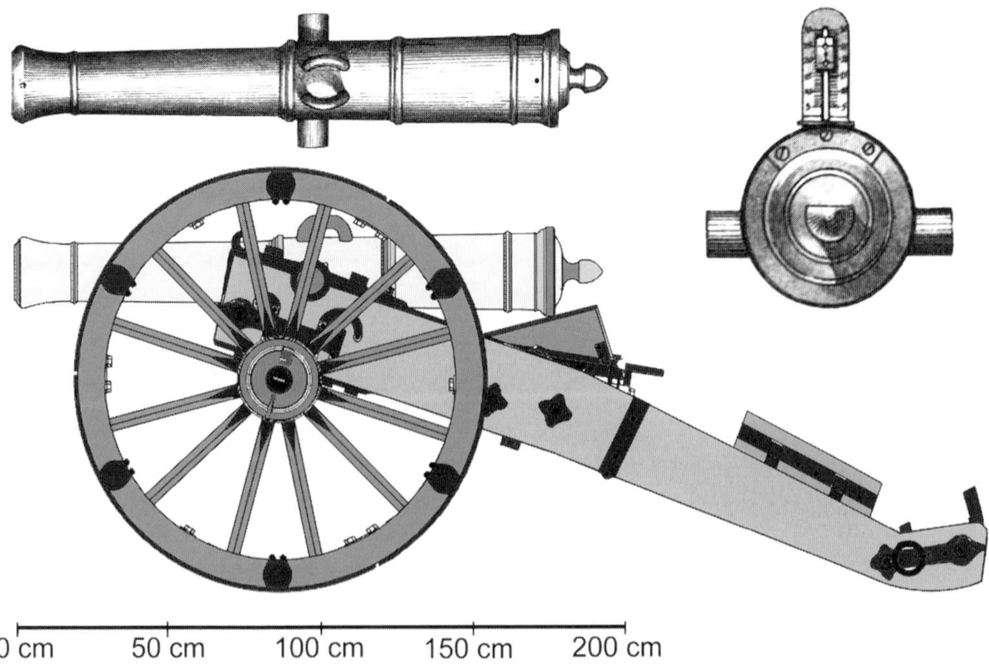

The Russian M1805 medium 12-pdr field gun; at top right, the Markevich sight.

and conical breech. The first example of this cross between a field gun, a howitzer and a mortar to see service was an 8-pdr in 1758, followed by 10-, 20-, 40- and 80-pdr variants.[58] Although it fired canister out to the same range as the 'secret' howitzer, it was capable of firing ball, and was quicker to load. The piece was relatively light and therefore more mobile, but the conical chamber caused problems: it limited the powder charge that could be used, and therefore reduced the range to less than guns of conventional tube design. The M1759 1-pud (20-pdr) version was issued to the regimental artillery, with the remainder attached to the 'secret' howitzer corps until it was disbanded.

From 1758 the Light 8-pdr unicorns were issued to the four-gun horse artillery batteries allocated to each cavalry brigade. In 1759 the larger unicorns entered service, and began to replace the 6-pdr guns of the

Table 2.6: Russian M1805 gun carriages (Smirnov A.A., 1998)

	Length	Weight	Wheel diameter
Cannon			
12-pdr medium	283cm	672kg	137cm
12-pdr light	262cm	500kg	137cm
6-pdr	228cm	393kg	122cm
Unicorns			
20-pdr (½ pud) unicorn	310cm	688kg	137cm
10-pdr (¼ pud) unicorn	237cm	410kg	122cm
10-pdr (¼ pud) horse unicorn	237cm	360kg	122cm
3-pdr unicorn	170cm	278kg	122cm

A Russian M1805 6-pdr field gun, cast by Master Zhdanov in 1806 at St Petersburg Arsenal. The calibre is 95mm, gun tube length 175cm and weight 369kg. (Dr S. Efimov)

field artillery; the 6-pdrs were re-assigned to the regimental artillery alongside the light unicorns.[59]

M1805 Arakcheev System

During the French Revolutionary Wars the limitations of the Russian artillery became apparent, and Tsar Paul I implemented changes that brought some order out of the prevailing chaos. The new artillery was much lighter than the M1757 system. It consisted of a Light and a Medium 12-pdr, a 6-pdr, ½-pud (20-pdr) and ¼-pud (10-pdr) unicorns that had been designed for his Gatchina Model Army – which mimicked the Prussian army that Frederick the Great set up in 1783. Special attention was paid to improving the construction quality of tubes and carriages.

In 1801, Tsar Paul was murdered; the following year Tsar Alexander I created a special commission for modernising the artillery under the chairmanship of General Arakcheev, who had participated in the reforms of the new Tsar's predecessor. The commission of 1802 included A.O. Bazin, I.G. Gogel, A.I. Kutaisov (who commanded the artillery of the 1st Western Army in 1812), A.I. Markevich (who designed the M1802 sights), G.A. Plotto, D.P. Rezvy and General K.L. Euler (who improved the design of gun carriages).[60] In 1803, Arakcheev was appointed as the Inspector of Artillery.

In 1804 the Provisional Artillery Committee was established to consider changes in garrison artillery, and their remit was widened in February 1805 to embrace all scientific work, projects and tests related to artillery. Many improvements had already

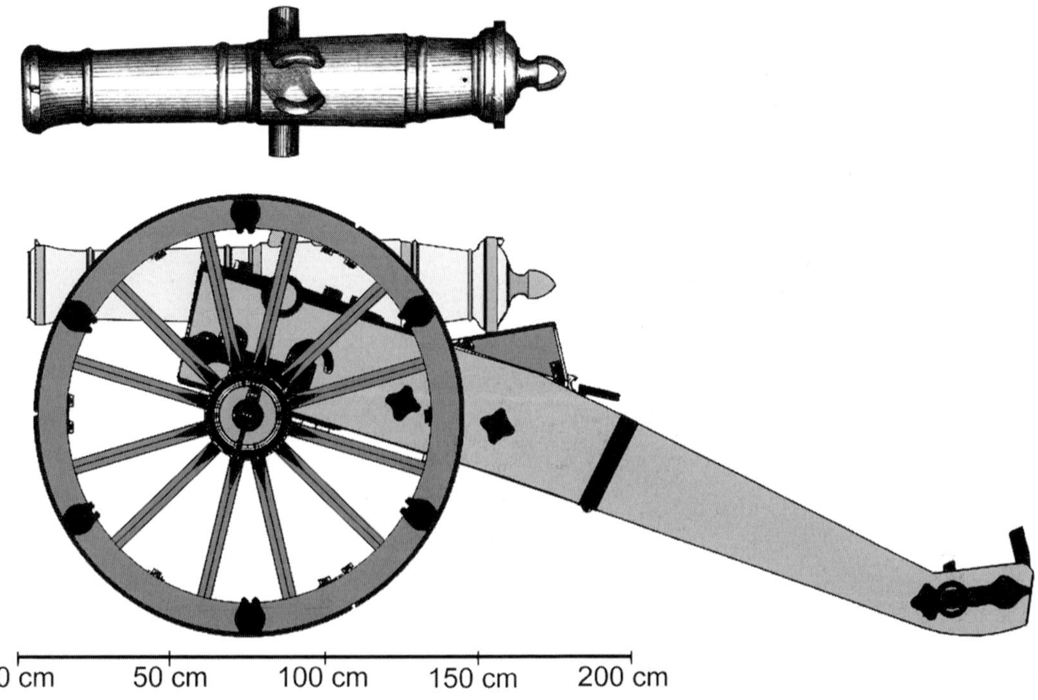

The Russian M1805 ½-pud (20-pdr) unicorn.

been made by that date, including the M1802 aiming sight (dioptre) designed by A.I. Markevich, to allow the 12-pdr to be fired with accuracy up to 1,200m. However, during the 1805–07 campaigns it was found that the Markevich device produced significant errors when the piece was placed upon uneven ground, as it was unable to take into account the axis of the trunnions to the horizon. In 1811 it was gradually replaced by the M1811 Kabanov device that was weighted at the lower end; when hung from a pin inserted in a bracket screwed on top of the breech so it was always kept vertical irrespective of the angle that the trunnions made to the horizon. However, it was difficult to use in strong winds, and had to be removed after each shot. Not all artillery companies were supplied with this device before 1815.

Table 2.7: Russian M1805 gun tubes

	Calibre	Bore length	Tube length	Tube weight	Windage	Projectile weight	Charge weight
Cannon							
12-pdr medium	120mm	15.8 calibres	198cm	819kg	4.6mm	5720g	1630g
12-pdr light	120mm	12.3 calibres	156cm	475kg	4.6mm	5720g	1630g
6-pdr	95.5mm	16.3 calibres	162cm	369kg	3.8mm	2860g	810g
Unicorns							
20-pdr (½ pud) unicorn	152mm	8.5 calibres	129cm	688kg	5.0mm	8100g	1630g
10-pdr (¼ pud) unicorn	122mm	8.5 calibres	135cm	360kg	5.0mm	3880g	810g
10-pdr (¼ pud) horse unicorn	122mm	7.5 calibres	123cm	316kg	5.0mm	3880g	810g
3-pdr unicorn	83mm	8.5 calibres	70.6cm	106kg	3.8mm	1020g	600g

This M1805 ¼-pud (10-pdr) field artillery unicorn was cast in 1805 at the St Petersburg Arsenal. The calibre is 125mm, gun tube length 153cm and weight 354kg. (Dr S. Efimov)

In 1805 the Artillery Committee issued a set of drawings of all artillery equipment, and distributed copies to all artillery works. This new M1805 Arakcheev system was based upon that of Tsar Paul I. It replaced the 3-, 6-, 8- and 12-pdr and the unicorns of the previous systems, which were withdrawn to the arsenals. The new system restricted the field artillery to 6- and 12-pdr field guns and 3-, 10- and 20-pdr unicorns. The 3-pdr unicorn was allocated to Jäger regiments, but was withdrawn in 1810. The minimum number of gunners to serve a light piece was specified as three, and for a heavy piece, five gunners.[61]

The construction of the guns was simplified by the removal of all excess adornments from both the tubes and carriages. So successful were these reforms that the gun carriages of Arakcheev's system were in service until 1845. Each calibre of gun had its own unique carriage design (*see* Table 2.6). The number of axles was reduced to two, with three types of wheel: Light and Heavy 54in (137cm), and 48in (122cm). One important innovation was the adoption of the metal axle, and the use of the *Rechtsmaschine* elevating system to replace the quoin. The M1805 reforms abolished the 3-pdr field guns and the 6-pdr Coehorn mortars used as regimental guns.[62]

In M1805 gun tubes now had flat rather than spherical base to the bore, and the vent was moved from the rear of the piece to the top in front of the base ring.[63] At the end of the breech the tube wall thickness was 0.75 calibre for field guns and one calibre for siege guns. At the start of the muzzle swelling the thickness of the metal was 0.5 calibre for bronze guns and 0.75 calibre for iron (i.e. fortress

A later M1805 ¼-pud horse artillery unicorn cast at St Petersburg Arsenal in 1816 by Master Rusinov. The calibre is 123mm, gun tube length 141cm and weight 320kg. (Dr S. Efimov)

and coastal defence guns). The trunnions of field guns were placed in line with the bore and exactly halfway along the length of the tube (excluding the back-weight).

The trunnions for M1805 unicorns were placed 44 to 46% of the distance from muzzle to base ring, in order to make the tube balance. The chamber of the unicorn was two calibres deep, the tube walls 0.5 calibre thick reducing to 0.25 calibre at the muzzle.[64] For specifications of the gun tubes see Table 2.7.

Equipment allocation for Russian units in 1812 was as follows:

- *Light artillery company:* 8× 6-pdr guns, 4× ¼-pud (10-pdr) unicorns, 12× four-horse limbers, 24× three-horse ammunition caissons, 4× reserve gun carriages, 8× artillery carriages, 1× field forge and 11× provision wagons; 124× draft horses
- *Position battery:* 4× Medium 12-pdr guns, 4× Light 12-pdr guns, 4× ½-pud (20-pdr) unicorns, 12× six-horse limbers, 34× three-horse ammunition caissons, 6× reserve gun carriages, 1× field forge and 15× provision wagons; 179× draft horses
- *Horse artillery company:* 6× 6-pdr guns, 6× ¼-pud (10-pdr) unicorns, 12× four-horse limbers, 24× three-horse ammunition wagons, 4× reserve gun carriages, 8× artillery carriages, 1× field forge and 15× provision wagons; 124 draft horses.

3 French and French-allied Ordnance

INTRODUCTION

During the 16th and 17th centuries French artillery was considered the best in Europe. In 1680, St Remy reduced the French calibres to 4-, 8-, 12-, 16- and 24-pdr, with a barrel length of about 3m. He did not distinguish between guns used for field work, sieges or in fixed fortifications. This was the first time that the calibres of guns had been standardised, thus simplifying the ammunition supply; previously artillery came in a multitude of calibres, often with a variance within the same calibre according to where it was produced. Henceforth, a 4-pdr used a fixed diameter of shot regardless of where it was manufactured. The early 18th-century French artillery of St Remy and Vallière – respectively, the M1685 and M1732 – was the point of inspiration for many other artillery systems.

Traditionally, the gun tube was cast with the bore already in place. Both Vallière and later Gribeauval noted that the mould tended to bend due to the length of the bore, thus causing the finished tube to fire imperfectly or even to be useless. In 1704, Jean Maritz I (1680–1743) built a horizontal boring machine at the gun foundry in Geneva; this was one of the most important inventions for the development of artillery. The mould for the gun tube, made from the casting compound of fine sand mixed with clay, was taken off a pewter master, and the gun tube was cast solid. After removing the casting compound from the cooled tube, it was placed on a Maritz water-powered horizontal boring machine, where the tube was rotated around a static cutting head to cut the bore of the tube. The tube exterior was then finished on a lathe to remove imperfections. Finally, the vent was drilled from the outside of the tube to the bore at an angle of 7 degrees. Only mortars and howitzers continued to have cast bores – their shortness meant that imperfections were of little consequence.[65]

General Jean-Florent de Vallière was so impressed by the horizontal boring machine during a visit to the Geneva foundry that he sought to obtain Jean Maritz I for the French service in 1727. Five years later, the first machine was erected in Lyon to bore the new M1732 ordnance designed by Vallière, who had restricted French ordnance to 4-, 8-, 12-, 16- and 24-pdr calibres.[66]

In 1731 B.F. Belidor, working at Le Fere, carried out experiments to ascertain the best charge for a gun, and these were later repeated at Metz in 1739–40. He determined that a charge of about one-third of the weight of the ball did not reduce the range or penetration compared to the accepted two-thirds charge, and this permitted the construction of gun tubes with thinner walls and of chambered pieces. Prussia was the first country to put Belidor's research into practice, as discussed in Chapter 2. It would be these light guns that caused a radical redesign of the artillery of Austria and subsequently of France.[67]

In 1738, Jean Maritz I built a second horizontal boring machine in the foundry at Strasbourg, with a third machine being supplied in 1746 to the foundry at Douai. The latter differed from the others in that it enabled the simultaneous drilling of the bore of the gun and lathing smooth of its exterior. In 1744, Jean Maritz II (1717–90), the son of Jean Maritz I, insisted on more thorough testing of guns. Guns were proved with two discharges of two-thirds the weight of the ball and then three of half the weight of the ball.[68] The 'searcher' or 'cat' (later modified by Gribeauval in 1769) was used to check for casting imperfections under water pressure.[69] In 1746, Maritz II also introduced a wrought-bronze vent that was screwed into place; wrought bronze was far stronger than cast bronze and so less likely to melt at the high temperatures achieved when the gun was discharged.

In 1752, Jean Maritz II further developed the cannon-boring machine at the Rocheford Foundry for the iron guns used by the French navy.[70] His son-in-law Berenger, also a gun-founder, developed iron casting and founding technology at the Douai foundry. The next year Jean Maritz II equipped the coastal defence fortresses and the navy with new designs of iron guns, and boring machines were set up at Rochefort and Toulon. In 1760 Jean Maritz II standardised the bronze for guns as 90% copper, 9% tin and 1% lead. By this time he had installed twenty-six horizontal boring machines in the eleven forging mills throughout Metropolitan France.[71]

By the middle of the 18th century French artillery had become outmoded by those of Austria, Prussia and Russia. The Seven Years War (1756–63) was disastrous for French artillery, and much of their ordnance was lost due to its lack of mobility. In 1761, Jean Maritz II lightened gun tubes by removing all the ornamentation from the outside, but despite this the guns still remained too heavy.

The lack of mobility was overcome by the work of Generals Müy and Gribeauval amongst others. For a new artillery system for France, they drew heavily upon Gribeauval's experience of Austrian and Prussian ordnance from his foreign service during the Seven Years War, as shown in the accompanying diagram.

On 17 August 1765, Secretary of State for War, Duc de Choiseul issued a decree introducing a new system of artillery as championed by Müy, Gribeauval and du Coudray. However, it appears that the system was far from finalised as a subsequent decree by the Secretary State for War concerning siege, garrison and coast artillery was issued on 16 March 1769. No all-embracing decree was published until 1771 concerning field, siege, garrison and coast artillery to the designs of Müy, Gribeauval and others due to the lengthy progenesis of the new artillery system and its incomplete adoption.[72] There then followed an extended dispute between the followers of the old Vallière system *('les rouges')* and the supporters of the new designs *('les bleus')*. On 23 August 1772, Secretary of State for War Monteynard reintroduced the system of M1732 by political influence, and appointed Vallière the Younger (1717–76) as Director-General of Artillery. The controversy lasted until 1774, when a committee of four marshals proposed that the Gribeauval system be reintroduced and ratified by a new ordinance of 3 October 1774. However, it was only after the death of Vallière the Younger in 1776, and Gribeauval's subsequent appointment as Inspector-General of Artillery with the backing of Secretary of State for War Claude Louis de Saint Germain, that the sweeping changes to French ordnance were consolidated. The decree of 3

Jean-Florent de Vallière

Jean-Florent de Vallière (1667–1759) was a lieutenant of Miners in 1690; he became Colonel-Inspector of Artillery in 1720 and was promoted lieutenant-general in 1732. As Director-General of Artillery, he restricted the French artillery to five types of cannon and two types of mortar by the Royal Ordinance of 7 October 1732. He was Director-General of the Manufacture of Arms between 1726 and 1747.

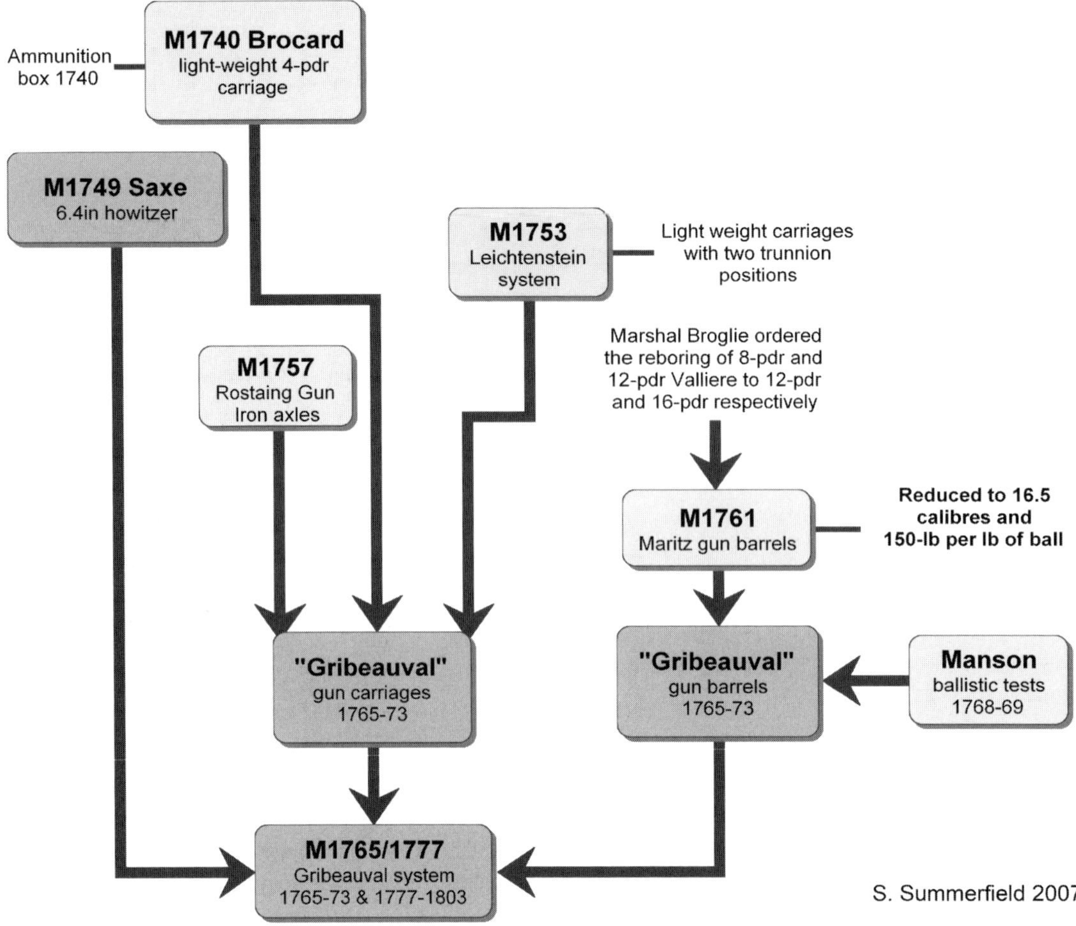

Origins of the Gribeauval system guns and carriages.

November 1776 formally introduced the Gribeauval system only for the field artillery, the old Vallière siege artillery being retained in modified form.[73]

The uniformity of components was the most important concept that Gribeauval copied from the Liechtenstein system. Previously, each component was unique to the vehicle or gun, and this lack of interchangeability hampered their repair or replacement. Gribeauval and his collaborators made all parts for field guns and rolling stock interchangeable, by means of detailed specifications distributed to all the workshops manufacturing components so that they could be fabricated consistently. Each battery carried sufficient spares to be able to replace entire gun carriages and other items of rolling stock in the field. Further spares could be obtained from the regimental depot, or from regimental artifisers using the same detailed specifications and plans as the workshops back in France. This permitted the artillery battery to be essentially self-sufficient for spares and maintenance.[74]

With the implementation in 1776 of Gribeauval's system, a tolerance of 5mm was set for the internal and external diameters of the gun tube, and 4mm in the location of the trunnions. In order to achieve this, standard reference measures made from bronze were distributed to the foundries; this was the first time that a common measure had been adopted in France, so a measurement in Paris would be the same as in Lyon or Marseille. This was one of the most important pre-Napoleonic reforms to take place in France.

General Jean Baptiste Vacquette de Gribeauval

General Jean Baptiste Vacquette de Gribeauval (1715–89) was an engineer – a specialist in the attack and defence of fortified places – and in 1752 he was a captain in the Miners. In 1757, at the height of the Seven Years War, he exchanged into Austrian service, where he was able briefly to study the best artillery in Europe at that time, although he was primarily involved with setting up a corps of sappers. On 1 November 1758 he was promoted to the rank of *Generalfeldwachtmeister* in Austrian service, and served with the miners at the siege of Schweidnitz (1763) under Major Johann Theodor Rouvroy (1727–1789) and Lieutenant-Field-Marshal Graf Guasco von Clavières (1714–80). In 1764 Gribeauval returned to France on the recommendation of the War Minister, Choiseul. Gribeauval's M1765–89 artillery designs drew very heavily upon the M1753 Liechtenstein system.

Gribeauval also imparted a greater robustness to his carriage designs than Liechtenstein's by introducing cast-iron axles instead of wood, and increasing the wheel diameter to give better cross-country performance. He also replaced the delicate *Rechtsmaschine* with a screw-driven elevating plate.

In 1772 Assistant Professor M.N. Dupuy at the Artillery School of Grenoble translated Robins' (1742) *New Principles of Gunnery*, despite its being shown to be in error by Euler in 1771. The following year, Euler's theories of interior ballistics were used to defend the M1732 Vallière system against Gribeauval's new designs, as the Vallière guns fired larger powder charges. However, the supporters of Vallière failed to appreciate that muzzle velocity was only one aspect of ballistics.

In 1775, Lavoisier of the Royal Gunpowder Administration introduced improvements in the production of gunpowder and the refining of saltpetre. These improvements made it possible to reduce the size of charges, but stronger gun tubes were needed to cope with their increased potency.

In 1780, Professor Jean Louis Lombard (better known as the tutor to Napoleon) began work in Auxonne on ballistics based on the work of Benjamin Robins of England, D'Antoni of Piedmont, Lavoisier of France and Euler of Prussia. Lombard published his *Treatise on the Movements of Projectiles when Fired from Cannon*, and translated Euler's interior ballistics into French with a commentary that supported Euler's rather than Robins' conclusions; this book was highly prized by Gassendi.[75] Lombard carried out further tests to identify the relationship between angle and range that were published as the *Tables de Tire Experimentals* in 1787, and a paper on point-blank shooting two years later. These built upon the 1768 work of Jakob Manson, who produced calibration tables of charge-to-range and angle-to-range that were of immense importance in improving the accuracy of artillery.

Lombard designed a Hausse sight that was mounted on the back of the gun tube behind the vent; the M1789 design that was put into service fitted into a recess in the back of the gun tube.[76] This new sight enabled the gun commander never to lose sight of the target, to determine suitable elevation, and to correct the fall of shot easily,

Joseph-Florent de Vallière the Younger

Joseph-Florent de Vallière the Younger (1717–1776) blocked the adoption of the Gribeauval system, in favour of his father's designs, until his death.

allowing him to hit his target with his second or third shot.

Piedmont introduced their M1786 system based on the researches of Papacino D'Antoni, who had published his *Treatise on Gunpowder* (1765) and *Treatise on Firearms* (1780). D'Antoni demonstrated that the powder burned almost instantaneously, with the gases produced upon detonation exerting maximum force to move the projectile from its moment of inertia. The huge increase in gas pressure was contained by the breech and was quickly dissipated as the projectile moved down the tube, so that the gun tube wall could safely be tapered towards the muzzle. In 1793, Lieutenant Joseph Hohnal produced an updated version of D'Antoni's treatise that emphasised interior ballistics. He stated that the charge burned before the projectile was displaced, exerting the maximum force at this point, but that it was not instantaneous as D'Antoni had assumed.

In 1780, France provided Gribeauval guns to the rebel colonists in North America, where they were operationally tested and shown to be successful at the siege of Yorktown in 1783. The practical experience of the American Revolutionary War (1776–83) and French Revolutionary Wars (1793–99) exposed a number of defects in the Gribeauval system. Compared to the artillery of Austria and Piedmont the gun tubes were too heavy, and attending rolling stock was inferior to the British carriages encountered in America and Flanders. Modifications to the coastal, garrison and siege artillery took place (*see* Chapter 7); changes to the field artillery were proposed in 1789, but the French Revolution threw all these plans into disarray.

The Revolution also resulted in a mass exodus of influential artillery officers. Importantly, one of Gribeauval's colleagues, Jakob Manson, left France for Bavaria, where he rationalised the Gribeauval system and corrected many of the defects, including removing the ammunition box from the gun carriage; this had to be lifted on and off before the gun could be limbered or unlimbered.

Jean-Pierre du Teil succeeded Gribeauval as First Inspector of Artillery, but was executed for Royalist sympathies six years later. The uncertainty of the Revolutionary Wars and the Directory period ended when Napoleon came to power as the First Consul in 1801. The Peace of Amiens (1802–03) permitted changes to be made to the French armed forces, the artillery being no exception. General (later Marshal) Auguste Marmont combined Jakob Manson's version of the Gribeauval system carriages and equipment used in Bavaria with Austrian carriage designs and Piedmont M1786 gun tubes, to create what became known as the system of M1803 (AnXI). The guns were principally cast in Turin, later at Strasbourg and Douai, in batches of six tubes. These smooth gun tubes became the standard throughout the French Empire and the satellite states, and provided the basic design for muzzle-loading artillery developments throughout the 19th century.

French artillery systems were also exported to their allies, including Baden, Hesse-Darmstadt, Kleve-Berg and Westphalia. The Gribeauval system existed in Spain and Naples before the French Revolutionary Wars began, as it was the standard artillery equipment for all Bourbon kingdoms. It was 1827 before France replaced it with the Valée system.

Jacque Charles (Jakob) Manson

Jacque Charles (Jakob) Manson (1724–1809) was born in Provence and joined the French artillery in 1742. He worked alongside Gribeauval and others to introduce reforms after the Seven Years War, and wrote several influential papers on ballistics. He was director of the Strasbourg Arsenal from 1774 to 1791, and Inspector-General of Colonial Artillery, a post which also included responsibility for coastal artillery. He served in America under Rochambeau in 1780–82. In 1784 he introduced the Wurst wagon into French service; and on 9 March 1788 he was made a marshal of France. In 1792 he published Gribeauval's treatise before leaving France to serve in the Army of Condé. In 1797 he joined the Russian army and was given general rank.

In 1799, Manson was invited into the Bavarian service by the new Elector Maximilian Joseph; this monarch had been colonel-in-chief of the Royal Alsace Infantry Regiment since 1780, and was a French general and commandant of Strasbourg before transferring to Austrian service in 1795.[77] On 6 February 1800, Manson was made Lieutenant-General of Artillery and on 1 October 1801 he founded the Bavarian Artillery School. From 1800 until his death he was the Zeughaus Director, designing artillery rolling stock as well as holding responsibility for the metals used in the cannon foundry and for saltpetre production. He died in Munich in 1809.

FRANCE

As noted above, the Seven Years War (1756–63) was a disastrous experience for the French artillery designed by Vallière. This was due in the main to poor mobility; the gun tubes of Vallière were almost double the weight of the Austrian M1753 and later French Gribeauval guns.

M1732 Vallière System

By the Royal Ordinance of 7 October 1732, Lieutenant-General Jean-Florent de Vallière (1669–1759), Inspector-General of Artillery, restricted French artillery pieces to five calibres: 4-, 8-, 12-, 16- and 24-pdr; there were also two types of mortar (8 and 12 pouce).[80] He abolished the short, medium and long forms of each gun of the M1685 St Remy system, replacing them with a single piece of each type. The reforms only applied to the guns and did not change the construction of the carriages or the rolling stock. Vallière simplified the chaotic system of artillery then prevalent in France, but it was not a great technological advance. A veteran of the wars of Louis XIV, he was greatly influenced by the renowned French military engineer Sebastien Le Prestre de Vauban (1633–1707), and the Dutch military engineer Menno van Coehorn (1641–1704), both of whom considered siege-craft more important than open-field battles. Consequently, Vallière's guns reflected the need for range and hitting-power rather than mobility. Nor did he advocate specialisation in gun tube and carriage designs: the same gun and carriage would be used for garrison, siege

Table 3.1: French artillery pieces [Gassendi (1809, 1819) and Musee de l'Armee]

	Calibre	Shot diameter	Bore length	Tube length	Weight	Windage	Projectile weight	Charge weight
M1685 St Remy								
12-pdr	121mm	117.4mm	23 calibres	291cm	1640kg	3.6mm	6.0kg	4kg
8-pdr	106mm	102.9mm	23 calibres	257cm	1080kg	3.1mm	4.0kg	2.7kg
4-pdr (long)	84mm	81.5mm	30 calibres	258cm	720kg	2.5mm	1.8kg	1.1kg
4-pdr (short)	84mm	81.5mm	22 calibres	195cm	540kg	2.5mm	1.8kg	1.1kg
M1732 Vallière								
12-pdr	121.3mm	117.4mm	23.2 calibres	293cm	1565kg	3.6mm	6.0kg	2kg
8-pdr	106mm	102.9mm	24 calibres	265cm	1030kg	3.1mm	4.0kg	1.3kg
M1740 "Swedish gun" (used 1740–3 and 1757–98)								
Brocard M1750 4-pdr	84mm	82mm	16.5 calibres	146cm	325kg	2mm	1.8kg	0.6kg
M1749 Saxe								
6.4 inch M1749 Howitzer	160mm	156.1mm	3 calibres	77cm	320kg	3.9mm	12.4kg	2.2kg
Rostaing M1757								
1-pdr	53mm	ND	20.6 calibres	114cm	115kg	ND	ND	ND
M1765/M1777 Gribeauval								
12-pdr	121.2mm	118.7mm	16.5 calibres	211cm	985kg	2.1mm	6.1kg	2.0kg
8-pdr	106mm	104mm	16.5 calibres	2184cm	580kg	2.1mm	4.0kg	1.3kg
4-pdr	84mm	82mm	16.5 calibres	146cm	290kg	2mm	2.0kg	0.8kg
M1792 6-pdr (Brocard M1740 "Swedish gun")								
M1792 Brocard 6-pdr	95mm	90.4mm	16.5 calibres	146cm	325kg	3.6mm	2.7kg	1.0kg
M1795 "Prussian"								
6.8in (10-pdr) Howitzer	165.8mm	163.7mm	4.3 calibres	108cm	680kg	2.1mm	14.6kg	2.2kg
M1803 (AnIX)								
12-pdr	121.3mm	120mm	16.8 calibres	210cm	760kg	1.3mm	6.1kg	2.0kg
6-pdr	95.9mm	94mm	16.6 calibres	166cm	390kg	1.9mm	3.0kg	1.1kg
7-pdr Howitzer	151.5mm	149mm	5 calibres	101cm	300kg	2.1mm	6.6kg	1.1kg
M1808 System								
6-pdr	95.9mm	94mm	17.2 calibres	180cm	392kg	1.9mm	3kg	1.0kg
24-pdr (5.9in) Howitzer	148mm	146.1mm	7 calibres	120cm	327kg	2.9mm	6.1kg	1.0kg

and battlefield work. In practice, the guns would be placed in position and not moved.

The mobility and hitting-power of Prussian and Austrian artillery at the beginning of the Seven Years War came as a shock to the French, and it was clear that a redesign of the ordnance was required. Fortunately, France had a number of capable artillery officers who could contribute to these reforms, including Marshal Broglie, Generals Manson, Müy and Gribeauval (the latter two being the co-designers of the gun carriages and elevation system), General Berthelot (designer of the coastal defence guns and traversing carriages introduced in 1769–86). Also France had the services of a number of innovative gun-founders including Jean Maritz II (1711–90), his son-in-law Jean Francois Berenger (1720–1801) of the Douai Foundry and Poitevin brothers of the Strasbourg Foundry.

Marshal Maurice de Saxe (1696–1759), the illegitimate son of Augustus II of Saxony and victor of Fontenoy (10 May 1745), introduced a Light M1740 4-pdr (known as a 'Swedish gun'), one of which was attached to each infantry battalion. This gun weighed 150 times its own weight of shot,

M1732 Vallière 12-pdr

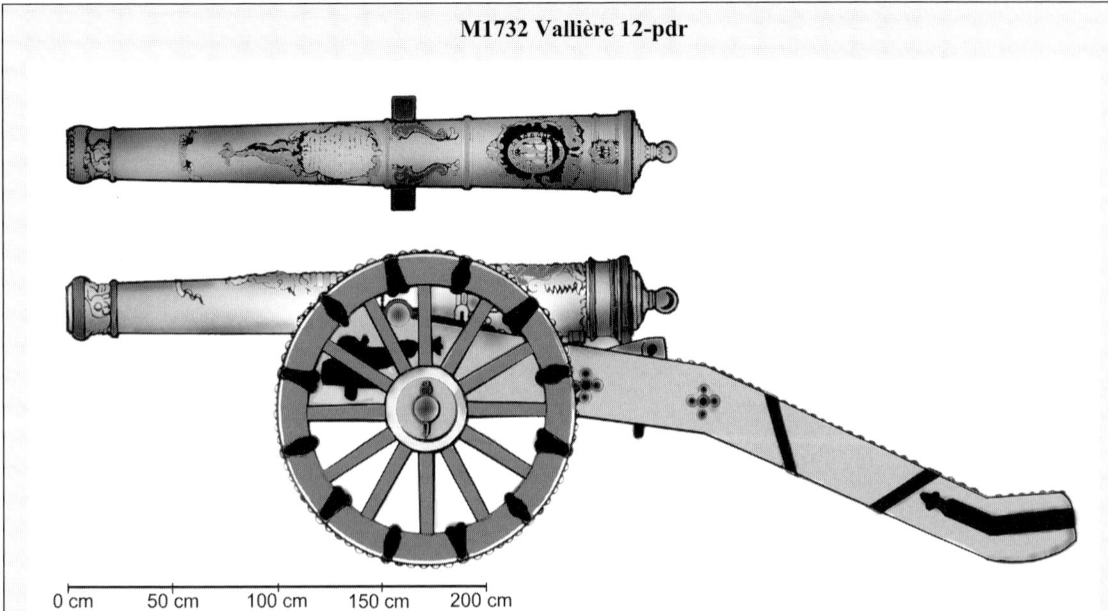

The M1732 Vallière 12-pdr, and a gun tube cast in 1733. It bears the royal arms – a sun in splendour with the motto 'Nec Pluribus Impar'; the arms of the Grand Maitre de l'Artillerie with the motto 'Ultima Ratio Regum'; and the name of the gun. The tube was 23.2 calibres long (293cm) and weighed 1570kg; the carriage was 374cm long. Interestingly, the different calibres were distinguished by the decoration of the cascable. The 4-pdr had a sun in splendour with a club issuing from its mouth; the 8-pdr, the head of a monkey; the 12-pdr, the head of a cockerel; the 16-pdr, a Medusa head, and the 24-pdr the head of Bacchus.

The Maritz M1761 12-pdr of 121mm bore was 18 calibres long (234cm) and mounted on a 292cm-long carriage. These guns were lighter than the M1732 Vallière 12-pdrs, because the carriage was shorter and the gun tube undecorated. (Musee de L'Armee)

compared to 280:1 for the Vallière 4-pdr. In 1759 Marshal Broglie (1718–1804) ordered the re-boring of Vallière's 4-, 8- and 12-pdr tubes to 6-, 12- and 16-pdr respectively, thus demonstrating that Vallière gun tubes could be lightened and still retain their effectiveness. The following year he ordered that new gun tubes of the Vallière system were to be cast without the ornamentation, and mounted on shorter, lighter carriages.

In 1761, King Louis XV charged Jean Maritz II to redesign the field artillery barrels to make them as light as possible.[81] Maritz II continued the work of Marshal Broglie in lightening Vallière gun tubes, and settled on producing 4-, 8-, 12- and 16-pdr guns. Under the Royal Ordinance of December 1761, guns were shortened to 18 calibres, compared to the previous Vallière system of 20 to 24 calibres. This choice of bore length was based on observation of the Austrian and Prussian systems. Maritz II also reduced the tube weight from 300:1 to 150:1 of metal to weight of ball; this was, however, still heavier than Austria at 120:1, and Prussia at 100:1.

Maritz II also made subtle alterations to the Vallière tube designs. He placed the trunnions more centrally, at 6.3mm rather than 0.5 calibres below the axis of the tube; this prevented the breech from kicking up after firing and damaging both tube and carriage. This was not a problem when the breech sat on a solid transom plate as in the M1732 system, but a kicking breech would easily damage the elevating screw and plate designed by Müy and Gribeauval. Maritz II introduced *rimbases* (thickening of the metal of the trunnions next to the tube body) so that the barrel was centred on the carriage, thus allowing the shock of the recoil to be absorbed equally by each cheek.[82] He also placed reinforcing rings at regular intervals along the tube to make it easier to machine.

In 1764, Gribeauval tests of Maritz II's new gun barrels at Strasbourg demonstrated – as Liechtenstein had already done – that shorter barrels were just as effective as longer barrels. Unfortunately, Vallière the Younger, and those who considered this reduction in weight to be excessive, opposed Maritz II's changes.

M1765 Gribeauval System

Maritz II's shorter gun tubes, and the lightweight gun carriage of General Brocard – introduced by the Royal Ordinance of 20 January 1750 – were a promising start in reforming French artillery equipment, but far bolder steps were required. The 4-pdr M1750 Brocard gun carriage for the 'Swedish' light gun was lighter than the Vallière version by reducing the thickness of the cheeks and reinforcing them with iron strapping. An elevating screw, instead of quoins, was introduced to make laying the gun quicker. An ammunition chest (*coffret*) was mounted between the cheeks of the carriage to improve immediate ammunition supply. Firing was made more reliable by using a fuse rather than loose powder. The size of the

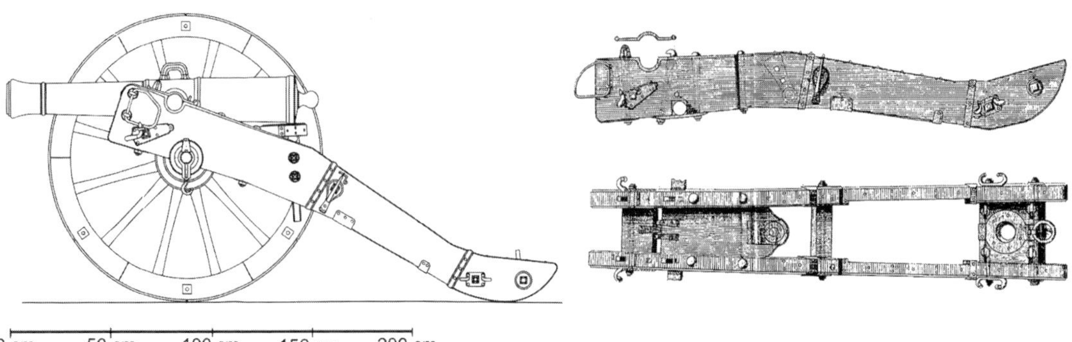

The Gribeauval 4-pdr carriage dated back to Brocard's M1740 design. The carriage was 236cm long and the cheeks 81mm thick; the wheels were 135cm in diameter, and mounted on a 197cm-long iron axle, replacing the original wooden axle. (Drawing by Andrew Menkov)

A M1765 Gribeauval 6.4in bronze howitzer, cast in Strasbourg under the guidance of Darshen, Commissioner-in-Chief for the Artillery Foundries, on 7 August 1793. The barrel length is 95cm and the weight 352kg. (Dr S. Efimov)

limber wheels was increased to make the limbered field piece more stable and improve its mobility.

In the meantime, as described in Chapter 2, Austrian artillery had undergone a comprehensive overhaul by Liechtenstein to standardise and lighten the carriages and barrels, creating a mobile field ordnance augmented by a separate series of heavier siege and fortress guns. In 1758, Empress Maria Theresa of Austria requested technical personnel from France, and King Louis XV transferred some able artillery and mining officers. (At this time the Austrian military miners were a section of the artillery branch, and this may be the origin of confusion over applying the term 'engineer' to Gribeauval - his fundamental profession was the building and attacking of fortresses.)

As mentioned above in the Introduction, the 1765 Decree led to an extended dispute between supporters of the new system and those of the old Vallière system. It was only by the decree of 3 November 1776 that the Gribeauval system was introduced, for the field artillery only and the M1732 Vallière guns were retained for the siege guns.

Gribeauval's initial reforms did not encompass any of the rolling stock except a universal limber and a smaller version for the 4-pdr, based heavily upon the Liechtenstein design. The Marshal de Saxe 6.4in howitzer with its wooden axle remained unaltered from the decree of 1760.

Experience of the American Revolutionary Wars (1775–83) coupled with observations of the Austrian Artillery in Bavarian War of Succession (1778–79),

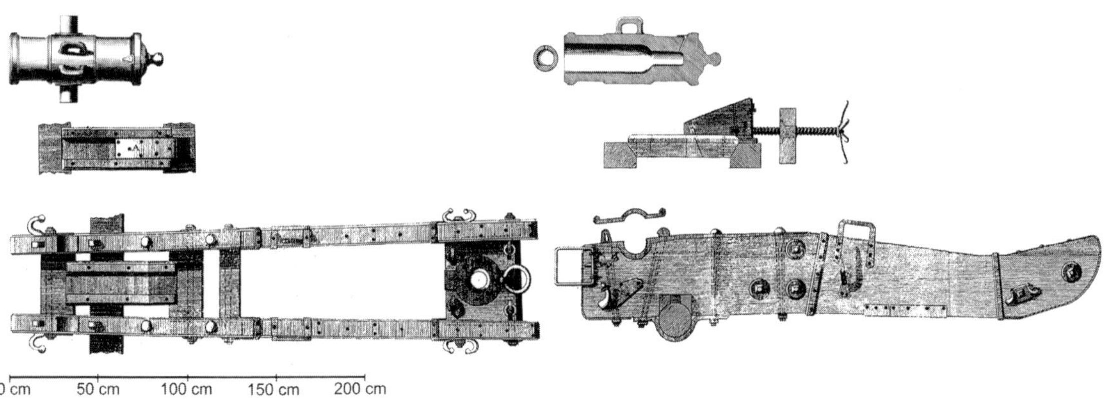

The Gribeauval 6.4in howitzer carriage (after De Scheel, 1800). This was a copy of the M1743 Prussian 10-pdr howitzer carriage, even down to the Rechtsmaschine elevating system; this was discontinued from 1792 in favour of a vertically-mounted screw acting on the breech of the gun tube.

M1765 Gribeauval 12-pdr gun

A M1765 Gribeauval 12-pdr gun cast in 1780 on a carriage built in 1821, now at the Musée de l'Armée. This design was used from 1765 to 1827, although there were minor modifications when it was reintroduced to the field army in 1808. From 1814, the smaller 8-pdr carriage was used for the 6-pdr cannon and 24-pdr howitzer, with the second trunnion positions eliminated. (Paul Dawson)

showed many flaws in the artillery equipment. Marshal Manson and Comt de Rostaing modified the ordnance by introducing a new elevating system for siege, garrison and coast artillery, rationalised the number of wheels used, replaced the Gribeauval two-wheeled field forge and many other modifications. At the same time the tactical ideas of the du Teil were enshrined in the Guibert Committee 1788 report as artillery doctrine. King Louis XVI appointed Gribeauval Inspector-General of the Grand Arsenal, shortly before the latter's death in Paris on 9 May 1789. This modified artillery system was enshrined in the Manson Artillery Treatise of 1792 which replaced that of Müy and Gribeauval.[83]

The lighter and shorter tubes of Jean Maritz II subsequently permitted Müy and Gribeauval to design lighter carriages, by modifying Brocard's 4-pdr carriage and using the Liechtenstein 12-pdr carriage as model for their own 8- and 12-pdr carriages. Both the 8- and 12-pdr had two trunnion positions four calibres apart; for moving over one mile by limber, the barrel was moved to the rear trunnion position so the weight of the tube was evenly distributed between the carriage axle and that of the limber. This made the limbered gun more stable, and reduced the likelihood of damage to the tube by increasing the clearance from the ground. The gun crew could move the tube without the need for a crane or gin, unlike the heavy Vallière tubes. The carriages had iron axles with brass bushes greased with suet and oil, to permit the wheels to move more freely than the wooden axles of the Liechtenstein system. In addition, this facilitated the mass production of the iron axles to a single specification. The elevation system was changed from wedges to a screw-driven wooden plate. The screw bolts connecting the cheeks and transoms allowed these to be replaced when they became worn or damaged; this useful feature is often overlooked, and was probably common throughout Europe at the time.

A recess was made in the cheeks of the carriage to accept an ammunition chest *(coffret)*, which ensured that some ammunition was instantly at hand in emergencies. The box for the 12-pdr contained 9 rounds, 20 fuses, 2 portfires and a linstock; that for the 8-pdr, 15 rounds, 20 fuses, 3 portfires and a linstock; the chest for the 4-pdr contained 18 rounds, 24 fuses, 3 portfires and a linstock; and that for the howitzer, 4 rounds, 6 fuses, 1 portfire and a linstock. On the march this box was suspended by transverse carrying bars; it was dismounted in action, and placed 5m away from the gun, the limber and the horse teams in

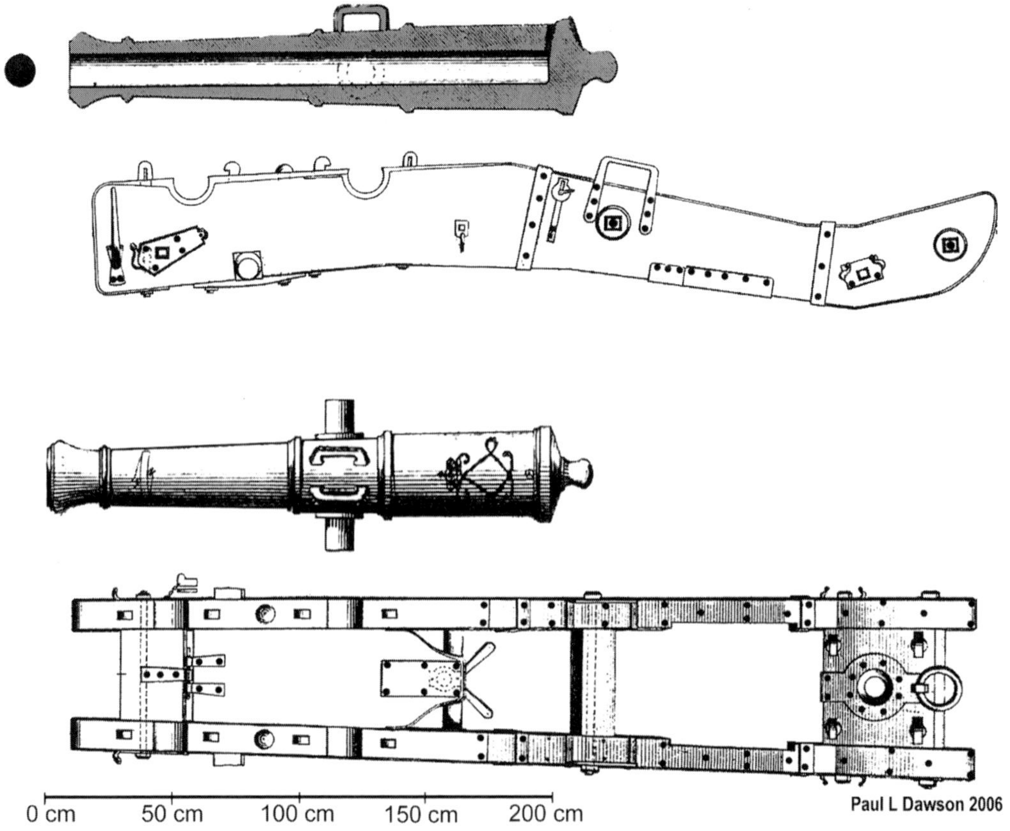

The Gribeauval 12-pdr gun carriage. The 8-pdr carriage was marginally shorter (285cm rather than 293cm), with thinner cheeks (9.5cm rather than 10.8cm). Wheels of the same 146cm diameter, running on the same 209cm iron axle, were used for both carriages. (After Manson, 1792)

order to reduce the risk of damage by explosion of the ammunition. The limber and team were never supposed to be exposed to enemy fire. A leather satchel protected the charges from rain and sparks when the ammunition was carried from the caisson to the box and from the box to the gun. A water bucket copied from Brocard's 4-pdr carriage was placed at the side of the carriage, and was designed to be difficult to overturn.

Instead of the single handspike used by the Swedish guns and in the Liechtenstein system, two handspikes were used with the Gribeauval carriages; this reduced the strain upon the crew, as two men could lift the trail together. Iron rings held the handspikes; two manoeuvre rings were placed opposite the supporting transom, and two small handspikes could be placed in them, which served to push the piece backward and forward and to lift the trail on limbering or unlimbering.

Though lighter than before, the 12- and 16-pdr field guns were designed as position pieces and so seldom moved during a battle. This clearly shows that Gribeauval and his collaborators were designing an artillery system to suit the tactics of the Seven Years War, and its defects became evident during the more fluid warfare of the French Revolutionary and Napoleonic Wars. It is undeniable that the Gribeauval system transformed French artillery and was the precursor of the mass production of standardised parts.

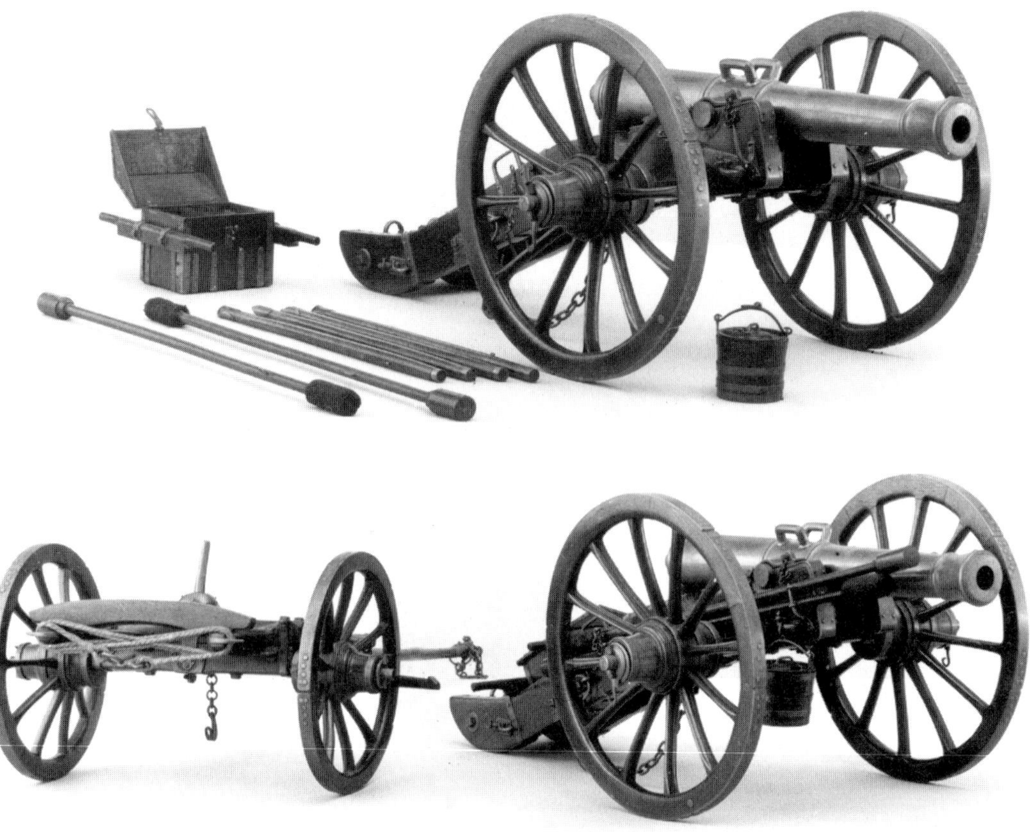

The Gribeauval 8-pdr is shown here deployed ready for action (top), and with crew equipment attached, next to its limber (bottom). (Paul Dawson)

Reforming the Gribeauval System, 1790–1803

In 1790, the French National Assembly established a committee of artillery 'to treat with the minister on all the businesses relating to the services and work of artillery'. However, the committee was only convened in 1795 under the law of 18 Floréal, Year III (7 May 1795) and the three subsequent decrees. The committee was charged to deliver opinions on the artillery service as well of the personnel and material, as directed by the government; to present the work of the inspections; and to give advice to government on the improvement of the artillery service in general. Moreover, it was in charge of quality control for the workshops engaged in production, and the uniformity of the instruments used by the inspectors of weapons and ammunition. Lastly, the committee was authorised by the Minister of War to undertake experiments on new designs.

During the Revolutionary Wars, France captured large quantities of Austrian and Prussian 6-pdr ammunition that could not be used by the existing French ordnance, so in 1792 the National Assembly decreed that the M1740 Brocard 4-pdrs were to be re-bored to 6-pdr with a calibre of 95mm. The re-boring of existing guns proved an unsatisfactory solution to the lack of ordnance and ammunition, but France had neither the money nor the time to design and cast new guns.[84] These converted guns were withdrawn from service in 1798.

The decree of 1792 also sanctioned the use of captured ordnance for which sufficient ammunition was available. In 1793–95 the amount of captured ammunition was so great that Prussian 10-pdr (6.8in)

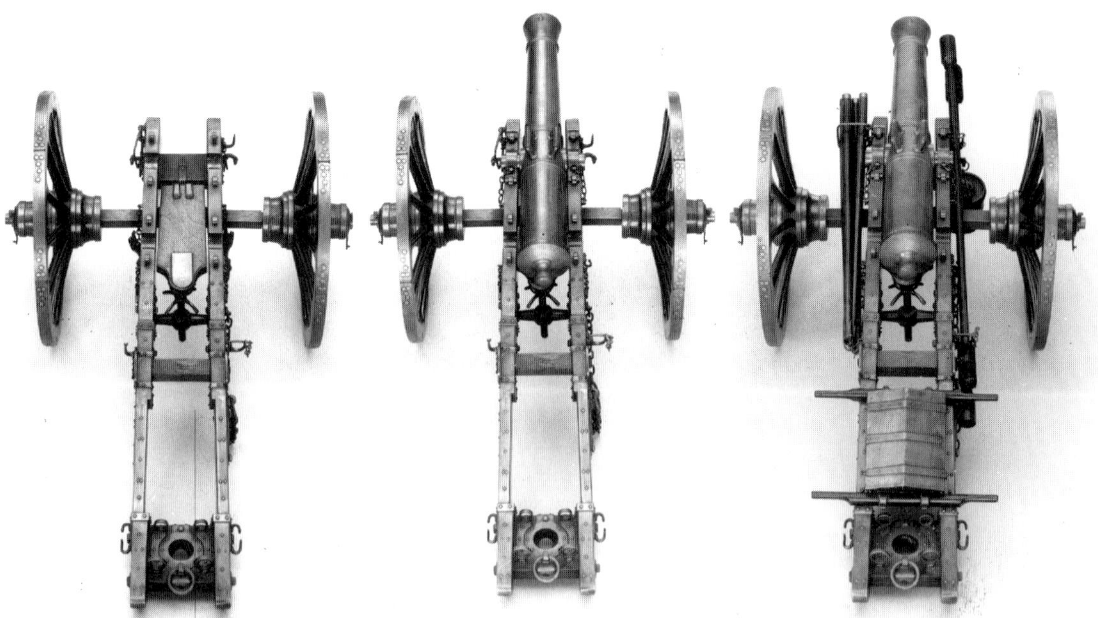

Gribeauval 8-pdr field gun models in the Musée de l'Armée: the carriage without gun tube (left), the carriage with gun tube (centre), and the complete gun with equipment. (Paul Dawson)

howitzers were officially introduced to replace the unsatisfactory M1749 6.4in howitzer; the Prussian piece had greater range and accuracy due to the length of its barrel. The original Prussian carriage was retained, and used with the Gribeauval limber and carriage-mounted ammunition box. It could fire both Austrian and Prussian 10-pdr howitzer ammunition.[85]

During the 1800 campaign General Marmont noted problems with the artillery system then in use. Whilst in Turin, Napoleon ordered General Allix to form a new artillery train of 250 guns to make up the deficit in artillery. He was unable to cast sufficient new 6-pdrs at the arsenal in Turin to supplement captured Austrian 6-pdr guns and 7-pdr howitzers. These guns were formally introduced into the army by an order of 2 March 1803, although they were actually in service in 1801.

Whatever the merits of General Gribeauval's reforms of the 1760s, the experience of the Revolutionary Wars led a group of influential French artillery officers to be critical of the equipment. The

An example of a M1803 12-pdr now in the Musée de l'Armée. (Paul Dawson)

main complaints were that the 4-pdr was too small to be effective and the 8-pdr too heavy for close infantry support. The First Consul re-created the title of Inspector-General of Artillery for the head of the committee. On 16 November 1799, just eight days after the creation of the Consulate, Bonaparte ordered the committee to present an assessment of their activities since their creation.

On 24 February 1800 the committee reported to Napoleon a wish to adopt new models of howitzer and shells. The report stressed the necessity to preserve the heavy base of shells and reduce the shell wall thickness to make them break easier and contain more powder. The committee also wished to carry out tests on hardening of wrought iron, cast iron and steel.

Introducing serving senior artillery generals to debate a new artillery system was Napoleon's rational response to this less than impressive fruit of ten years' deliberations. However, their attendance was poor as many of these officers were serving with the field army; only five out of twelve were able to attend the first meeting on 4 November 1800. On 29 December 1801, Napoleon replaced the committee with a council that included all the Inspector-Generals of Artillery, charged with improving the equipment of the artillery arm.[86] The council ceased meeting in January 1803. Henceforward the First Inspector of Artillery decided the technical direction of the arm, while also being the commander-in-chief of Grande Armée artillery in the field until 1811.[87]

AnXI System, 1803–05

The Artillery Committee created by Napoleon was presided over by the 70-year-old General d'Aboville (the First Inspector of Artillery). The other members were Generals La Martillerie, Marmont, Andreossy, Eble, Songis, Faultrier

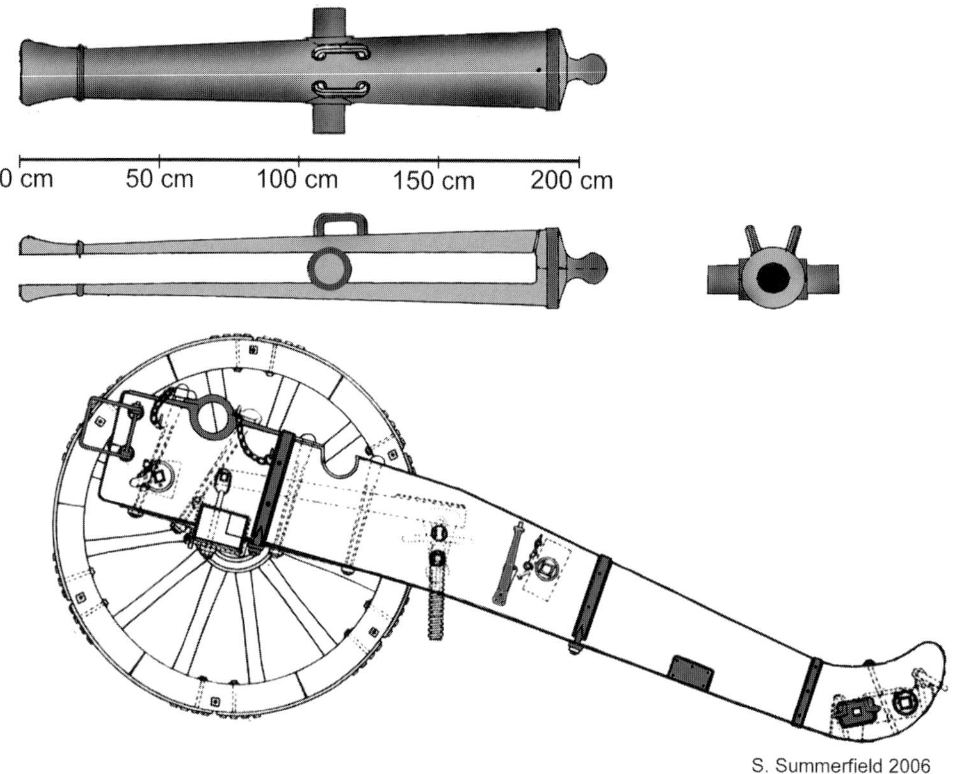

A M1803 (AnXI) system 12-pdr field gun. The reinforcing band was introduced between the two trunnion positions to overcome the tendency of the Gribeauval carriage to split behind the iron axle on firing.

M1803 (AnXI) 6-pdr field gun

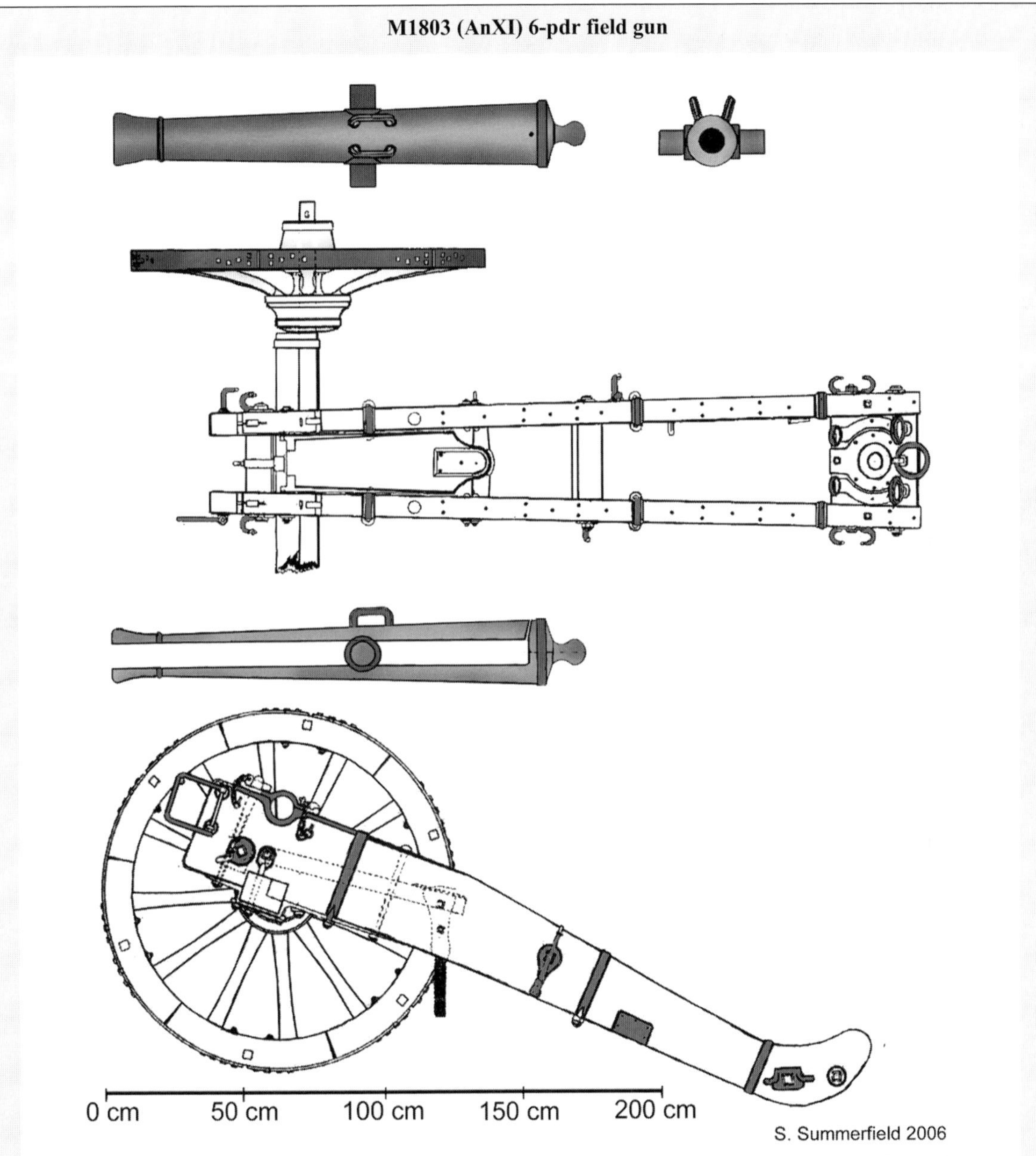

The M1803 (AnXI) 6-pdr field gun had a gun tube based upon the Piedmontese M1786, with the reinforcing rings along the tube removed as Jean Maritz II had proposed back in the 1760s. The two handles on top of the carriage, where two handspikes were placed for limbering, were removed and the handspikes were positioned under the carriage so the trail could be lifted higher. The recess in the carriage for the ammunition box was eliminated. The axle was of iron construction encased in wood rather than all iron, thus reducing recoil.

M1803 24-pdr bronze howitzer, cast by Master Berenger in 1805. Length, 101cm; weight, 278kg. (Dr S. Efimov)

An example of an M1803 howitzer carriage with a M1765 Gribeauval howitzer tube, now in the Musée de l'Armée. The carriage was modified in 1808 to have an iron rather than wooden axle, and the recess for the ammunition box was discontinued. (Paul Dawson)

and Gassendi (Head of Artillery at the Ministry of War). The task they faced was immense: to redesign the artillery by critically examining the reformed Gribeauval's system and then evaluating any changes made to the designs. The theoretical research began on 11 January 1802 and ended on 21 July 1802. Colonel (later Général de Division) François de Faultrier (1760–1805) identified the principal faults as follows:[88]

1 Moving the barrel between trunnion positions quickly fatigued the gun crews.
2 Moving the ammunition box quickly fatigued the crews, and made limbering the carriage even more cumbersome.
3 The carriage-mounted ammunition box held less ammunition than the limber-mounted boxes of Austria, Prussia and Bavaria.
4 The 4-pdr was mobile but lacked the 'hitting-power' of the 8-pdr.
5 The caisson was not waterproof and lacked suspension, causing damage to ammunition; it was top-heavy, difficult to manoeuvre over rough ground due to the small front wheels, and could not turn sharply. The spare wheel and axle was difficult to use, so were often discarded.

The proposals of the report included:[89]

1 The requirement for a method of moving by *prolonge* without shifting the barrel between trunnion positions.
2 Moving the ammunition box to the limber to allow more ammunition to be carried and make deploying quicker.
3 Auguste de Lespinasse, writing in 1800, stressed the value of pack mules to carry ammunition, as used by the Austrians for over 20 years, and this suggestion was supported by Napoleon.

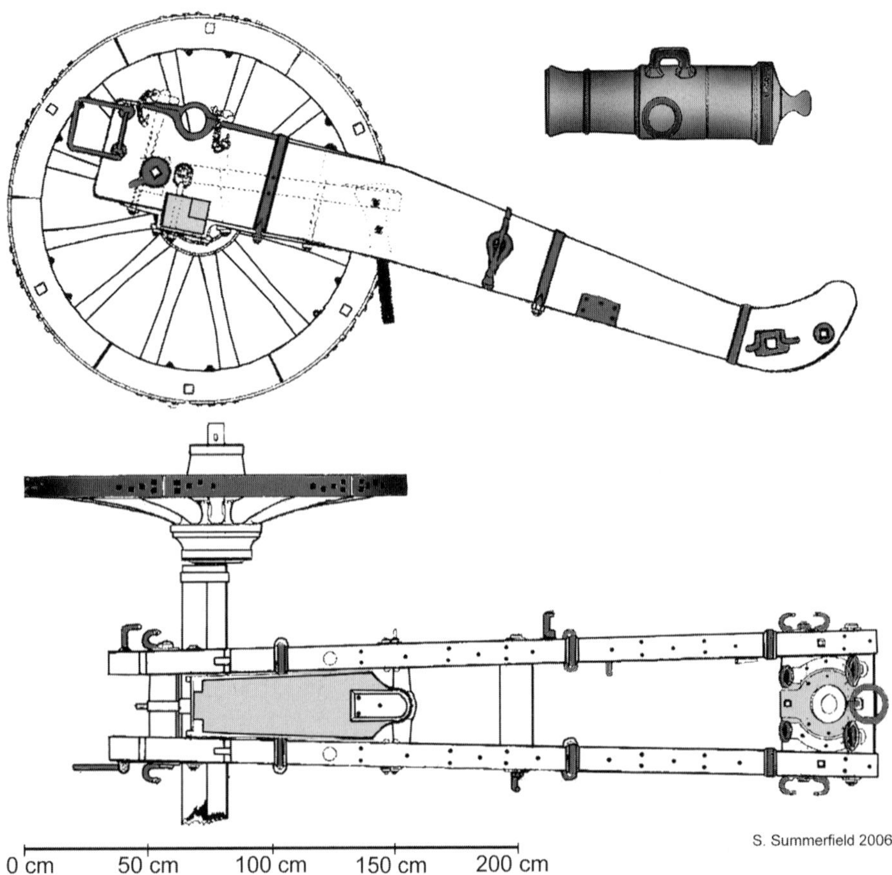

The M1803 (AnXI) system 24-pdr howitzer. Note that the Rechtsmaschine of the Gribeauval system has been replaced with the screw-driven elevating plate as used on the field guns.

4 If the gun crews could ride on the carriage, the foot artillery could move at the same speed as the horse artillery and light infantry.

5 The 4-pdr should be replaced with a new 6-pdr gun, and the 8- and 12-pdrs should be retained.

6 General Eble was commissioned to design a new caisson.

Generals Gassendi and Songis were critical of this report, and were opposed to any changes to the Gribeauval system.[90] General Marmont appealed to Napoleon to become involved in the discussions, and the latter's view concisely guided the way that the committee should think:

> The artillery should have but four calibres, the 6-, 12- and 24-pdr and the 5.9in [24-pdr] howitzer. In this way, we abolish four calibres. We should add a 3-pdr for mountain equipment. In abolishing the Rostaing guns, we get rid of stubborn beasts not worth the trouble they give. The 3-pdr should be of a minimum calibre.

Chef de Bataillon Parisot made a number of suggestions that foreshadowed the work of Valée in the 1820s. He recommended that a single calibre cannon (8-pdr) and howitzer (24-pdr) be used for the field army, both with 152cm carriage wheels, and that the caissons and field forge wagons be reduced to a single type. He proposed an elevating system using the Gribeauval elevating screw acting directly on the neck of the cascable, as used in the British and Bavarian M1791 Rumford; and a single handspike should be used for traversing the piece instead of two. The limber should have large 145.8cm wheels copied directly from the British Desaguliers limber; and the bracket trail should be limbered to the hook on the back of the axle block by a large iron ring protruding from the transom plate, as in the British Butler gun carriages noted by Scharnhorst in 1806. Parisot's progressive suggestions - clearly inspired by the work of Graf von Rumford, Thomas Desaguliers and Butler - were disregarded, apparently on political grounds.[91]

On 2 May 1803 the council reported back to Napoleon, based on the experience of the Army of Germany with the re-bored Brocard guns and the Army of Italy's use of captured Piedmont M1786 6-pdrs. They recommended that a new 6-pdr gun tube based on the Piedmont design, and mounted on a carriage of French design, be brought into service. Article 1 of the decree abolished the 4- and 8-pdr, and reduced the number of different axles and wheels used. Three axles were to replace the four of the Gribeauval system. Three wheel sizes were to replace the 25 different types in the Gribeauval system, namely 152.5cm (12-pdr, 6-pdr and 5.9in howitzer); 145.8cm (caissons' and other vehicles' rear wheels); and 132cm (limbers, and front wheels of vehicles). Originally it was proposed to use only 152.5cm and 145.8cm diameter wheels, but the size of wheels increased the turning circle of the vehicles when compared to the smaller 132cm wheel of the Gribeauval system.[92]

The Year XI Report concluded that the new 6-pdr gun had 75% of the effective range of a 12-pdr, with the hitting-power of an 8-pdr. It was lighter and shorter than the 8-pdr, with a calibre of 95.8mm, intermediate between the 4- and 8-pdrs; however, the enormous quantities of captured Austrian 6-pdr ammunition could not be used by the M1803 (AnXI) 6-pdr. Since the carriage was based loosely on the Austrian 6-pdr, there was also no need to move the gun tube from the firing trunnion to the moving trunnion position or vice versa, thus solving one of the main problems of the old Gribeauval 8-pdr. The ammunition box was moved from the carriage to the limber and was enlarged to contain 15× roundshot, 3× canister rounds, 24× fuses, 3× portfires and a linstock. The bore for this gun was only 16 calibres long (the same as used in the Austrian service), and had 100:1 of metal to weight of ball, as in the Prussian system.

The 24-pdr howitzer of 5 calibres tube length required only two powder charges, compared to the three required by the 6.4in howitzer. Construction of the Gribeauval carriage for the 6.4in howitzer was ordered to cease in 1803, and the 8-pouce (8.5in) howitzer was abandoned in 1805.

In 1803 the committee proposed that the field army should be equipped with 6-pdr (increased to 16.6 calibres) and 12-pdr cannon, cast with a ratio of 130:1 of metal to weight of ball, plus a 24-pdr howitzer. This lightness of the 6-pdr would be criticised in later years for reducing the range, durability and hitting-power of the gun. The new carriages had new wheels with iron axles mounted in wood to improve shock absorption. The travelling trunnions of the 12-pdr were moved closer together to resemble the Austrian 12-pdr carriage design, and the curve of the trail was reduced.

In 1795 the French had undertaken tests firing explosive shells from 18-, 24- and 36-pdr coastal artillery cannon against a wooden target; further tests were carried out in 1797 with 24-pdrs at Toulon and Cherbourg. This resulted in a special commission being formed a year later. As part of the French AnXI Committee tests, General Lariboissière made further trials at Strasbourg using a 24-pdr siege gun.[93] Gassendi was present at both tests, and wrote enthusiastically about the potential of this new method of shooting shells. Consequently the AnXI Committee instructed the production of a new 24-pdr cannon, 24-pdr howitzer and 24-pdr mortar with the same calibre of 5.9in (148mm), and able to fire the same shells.[94] No tests appear to have been carried out to ascertain if shells could be fired from field artillery guns.

M1808 System

On 9 November 1805, Napoleon ordered the construction of guns to be halted as many of the designs were incomplete and the French were already on campaign.[95] On 14 April 1806, Napoleon ordered Gassendi to sort out the chaos of artillery equipment, noting that he would raise the matter with the

Gribeauval M1765 gun tube

The Gribeauval M1765 gun tube named 'Voltaire', cast in 1794, is seen here mounted on the M1808 carriage. This was virtually identical to that of the M1765 design, except that the trail end had became more rounded, copying the shape of the carriage for the 6-pdr and the 24-pdr howitzer. (Courtesy the Board of Trustees of the Royal Armouries; photograph Stephen Summerfield)

First Inspector in person when they met in the field. He instructed Gassendi to construct at Mayence, Landau, Strasbourg, Neuf-Brisach and Alessandrie 1,750 new field guns and carriages, as well as 1,700 new caissons, to replace all of the current equipment then in use.

In 1807 the Grande Armée had only 104 Gribeauval guns (85× 8-pdr and 19× 4-pdr), compared to 166 captured Austrian and Hanoverian 6-pdrs that served as a universal gun for both foot and horse batteries. The army as a whole had only 40× 12-pdrs, most of which were not French.

In order to discuss any changes a second committee was formed. On 10 January 1808 it reported that the innovations of the M1803 (AnXI) system were disappointing and the artillery had the logistical nightmare of two systems (French and captured) in use at the same time, in some cases within the same battery. They concluded that it was impossible to harmonise the artillery equipment because the French army was spread all over Europe.[96] They voted to return to the Gribeauval system, by converting existing carriages and rolling stock where possible, or constructing replacements. The Gribeauval caisson was reintroduced with modifications. The carriages for the 6.4in howitzer, 24-pdr howitzer, and Heavy 10-pdr (6.8in) howitzer were redesigned on the Gribeauval principal; the howitzer tubes were also redesigned, with Gomer chambers. Production of the M1803 (AnXI) 12-pdr carriage was halted, and by 1812 all M1803 (AnXI) carriages had been replaced with Gribeauval-based designs. The copy of the Austrian 7-pdr howitzer – with a calibre of 151.5mm and tube length of

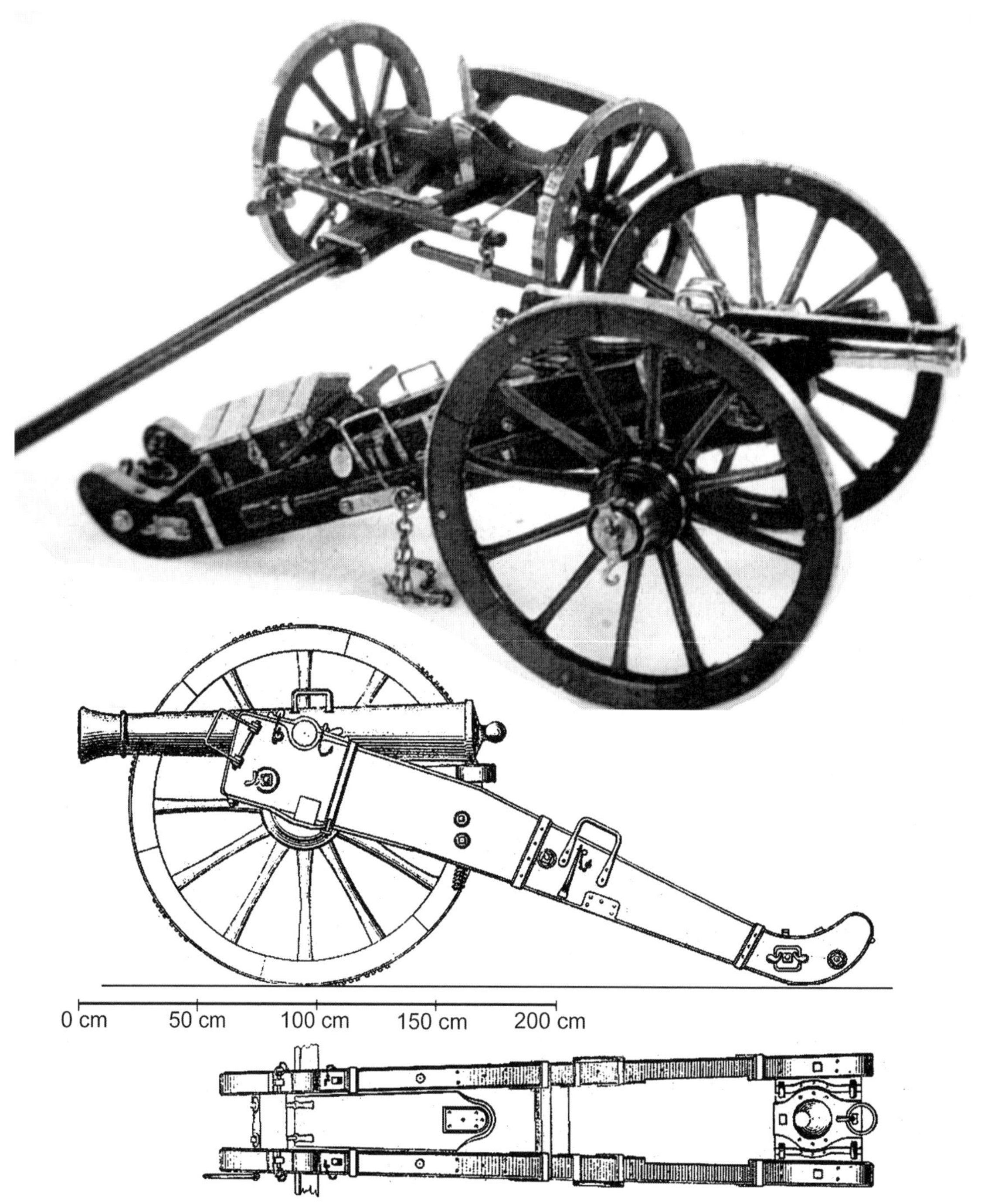

The M1808 6-pdr gun; (top) a model of this piece in the Musée de l'Armée.

M1808 24-pdr howitzer limbered to an M1814 limber of the horse artillery, c.*1822. (Auguste de Moltzheim,* L'Armée Française sous la Restauration, 1814–1830, *Editions du Cannonier, Nantes, France)*

101cm, mounted on a carriage that enabled vertical shooting – was abandoned.

Napoleon was fundamentally in favour of the new carriage and 24-pdr (5.9in) howitzer. Gassendi and others had complained that the 6-pdr tube was too light and insufficiently strong at 130:1 of metal to ball weight; so the gun tube metal was increased to 150:1, and the bore lengthened to 17 calibres – so creating, in effect, a lightweight version of the Gribeauval 8-pdr. A new carriage based on the Gribeauval principles was introduced. The ammunition box on the limber *'à la Bavaroise'* was discontinued and the Gribeauval limber reintroduced; new carriages also reintroduced the recess for the *coffret*, and any M1803 (AnXI) rolling stock were either converted or replaced.

In Russia in 1812, Napoleon lost more than 1,000 guns and howitzers. Under the edict of Tsar Alexander I of 14 November 1813, 875 captured gun tubes were collected in Moscow.[97] Out of 353 pieces of French ordnance captured, 58 (16.4%) were 12-pdrs (made between 1767 and 1811); 184 (52%) were 6-pdr barrels (1804–11); 26 (7.4%) were 4-pdrs (1766–93); and 85 (24%) were 24-pdr howitzers

(1804–07). This clearly shows that the new howitzer had replaced the old Gribeauval pieces entirely by 1812; the 4-pdr was regimental artillery, meaning that the 6-pdr was already in universal use by 1812, and the 12-pdr was used by the Guard and reserve batteries. The 6-pdr became the standard field gun for all European armies during the latter stages of the Napoleonic wars. Indeed, General von Scharnhorst favoured the Prussian 6-pdr, as he demonstrated that the cost of equipping and manning a 12-pdr cannon was double that of a 6-pdr. Also taking into account the mobility of the two calibres, and the efficient arrangement for battle of the 6-pdr, the latter was to be preferred. This matter of economy was also important to Napoleon from 1812 onwards, as he was in desperate need of men, horses, artillery and money. Again, the absence of 8-pdrs from this list of captures suggests that none were taken on the Russian campaign.[98]

M1814 System

In 1811 the Artillery Committee was disbanded. On 1 January 1814, Napoleon issued a decree that sought to standardise French artillery in a first step towards rationalising the guns and carriages then in service. The decree stipulated that the a new limber design would be introduced that was in essence the M1765 Gribeauval 12-pdr limber with the pintail moved to the rear bolster and replaced with a smaller ammunition box than the M1803 (AnXI) version. This was to be achieved by altering existing limbers or making new where necessary. The M1765 8-pdr carriage was to become the standard gun carriage for all field ordnance; 6-pdr and 12-pdr, 24-pdr (5.9in) and 7-pdr howitzers.[99] These carriages were retained until 1827.

The Restoration, 1814–27

Shortly after the restoration of the Bourbon monarchy, the Artillery Committee was reformed by an ordinance of 12 May 1814, and was charged to examine and discuss all the projects made by the Minister for War. Two further decrees augmented this original order. That of 3 November 1814 added that the committee should, in addition to the usual tasks, subject the artillery system to a simple, economic and uniform construction, by drawing as many parts as may be possible from the existing system. General Ruty, president of the committee, carried out tests on the 6-pdr, whose construction was stopped until the committee published its report. General Allix, on his own initiative, prepared a report for a new system of artillery.

Ruty wrote in his report of December 1814 that 'the 8-pdr gun has, in all respects, an undeniable advantage over the 6-pdr gun. The use of the former in preference to the latter could not be put in doubt if we disregarded all economic considerations in the use of resources.' As well as looking at the economics behind the use of the 4- and 8-pdr, Ruty also noted that the new gun (6-pdr) was disliked by the artillery; that the superiority of the horse artillery was reduced by having only 6-pdrs; and that twenty years of success had sanctified the 8-pdr.

A royal ordinance of 30 January 1815 in theory restored Gribeauval's system until a new system could be introduced, but was not acted upon until 31 October 1824.[100] Rather than being abandoned in 1814, the system of AnXI/M1808 lasted into the 1820s: the AnXI/M1808 6-pdr went out of service in 1825, the Prussian M1795 10-pdr (6.8in) howitzer in 1818, the M1808 24-pdr (5.9in) howitzer in 1828, and the M1808 field forge in 1827.

In 1815–16, the artillery consisted of the 6- and 12-pdr for the foot artillery, supported by the 24-pdr (5.9in) and 6.4in howitzers. The horse artillery used 8-pdrs and 24-pdr (5.9in) howitzers. The siege artillery remained unchanged. The regulation of March 1819 reduced the variations in vent diameter to three and confirmed the use of 4-, 6-, 8-, and 12-pdr field guns, 12- and 16-pdr garrison guns, and 16- and 24-pdr siege guns.

In 1823, new axles and 156cm wheels were supplied for all field guns and 138cm wheels for all limbers. The Light 156cm wheels were used on the infantry munition caissons and other rolling stock. New howitzers were developed between 1820 and 1822 at La Fere, Toulouse and Vincennes, using the block-trail carriage. By 1824, some 1.5 million francs had been spent to improve the Gribeauval system, yet it still had a number of major failings, the main ones being the lack of limber ammunition boxes and the caissons. Many artillery officers argued for a new system based upon that used in Britain.

Rather than going to the expense of designing and building an entirely new system, General Valée convinced the Minister for War to follow the policy of the committee, which insisted that improving and supplementing the Gribeauval material was the best solution. He set about designing new rolling stock to utilise the Gribeauval and Vallière gun tubes.

In 1827, the Gribeauval system was theoretically replaced with a new Valée system that retained the Gribeauval 8- and 12-pdrs and the Vallière 16- and 24-pdrs, and introduced two new howitzers with a common block-trail carriage.

BAVARIA

Throughout most of the period, Bavarian ordnance designers were under the leadership of Graf von Rumford (Sir Benjamin Thompson) and Jakob Manson. These men produced a series of innovative guns that were the basis for the artillery systems of other nations. From 1785, Liechtenstein M1753 3-, 6- and 12-pdr guns and 7-pdr howitzers were cast in Bavaria, replacing the Vallière-style guns. In 1800–01 Bavaria cast small numbers of M1785 'Austrian-style' guns tubes for Hesse-Darmstadt.

M1791 Rumford System

The Graf von Rumford introduced his M1791 3- and 6-pdr field guns and a 7-pdr howitzer serving as battalion guns. His new carriage designs were based on his observation of British artillery in England and during his military service in America in 1781–83. Rumford took the concept of the Desaguliers block trail and modified this for his 3-pdr gun.

Rumford also devised a new howitzer that could be elevated to 86 degrees and could be fired while still attached to the limber; he designed heavy siege guns, mortars, a 12-pdr field gun, and a 7-pdr howitzer. Both the 7-pdr howitzer and 6-pdr field gun shared a common bracket carriage design, while the Light 3-pdr was mounted on a block trail.

Table 3.2: Bavarian field gun specifications

Model	Calibre	Diameter of shot	Bore length	Tube length	Weight	Windage	Shot weight	Powder charge
M1785 "Austrian style"								
12-pdr	117mm	115mm	15 calibres	191cm	812kg	6mm	5500g	1600g
6-pdr	94.5mm	90mm	15 calibres	152cm	414kg	5.2mm	2750g	800g
3-pdr	75mm	72mm	15 calibres	121cm	240kg	3.8mm	1370g	409g
7-pdr Howitzer	148mm	146mm	4.3 calibres	94cm	280kg	8.5mm	7500g	572g
M1791 Rumford								
6-pdr Heavy	94.5mm	90mm	14.4 calibres	144cm	430kg	4.5mm	3000g	1100g
6-pdr Light	94.5mm	90mm	14.4 calibres	145cm	400kg	4.5mm	3000g	1100g
3-pdr Block Trail	75mm	72mm	14.4 calibres	120cm	ND	3mm	ND	ND
7-pdr Howitzer	148mm	146mm	3.5 calibres	79cm	ND	2mm	6600g	ND
30-pdr Howitzer	240mm	236mm	3 calibres	65cm	508kg	4mm	ND	ND
M1800 Manson								
12-pdr	117mm	115mm	16.8 calibres	222cm	801kg	1.3mm	6100g	1958g
6-pdr	94.5mm	90mm	16.6 calibres	176cm	409kg	4mm	3000g	1100g
3-pdr	75mm	72mm	14 calibres	125cm	238kg	3mm	ND	ND
7-pdr Howitzer	148mm	146mm	7 calibres	101cm	300kg	2 mm	6600g	1000g
M1806 (modified Austrian Wurstguns)								
6-pdr	94.5mm	90mm	14.6 calibres	151cm	385kg	4mm	2740g	800g
7-pdr Howitzer	150mm	146mm	4.1 calibres	91.5cm	275kg	4mm	7150g	572g

A Bavarian M1785 6-pdr gun tube, as based on the Austrian M1753 Liechtenstein system. (Bavarian Artillery Museum)

Bavaria – consisting of the Electorates of Bavaria and the Rhineland Palatinate, plus the Duchies of Berg, Jülich and Zweibrücken – mobilised a contingent against Revolutionary France in accordance with her commitment to the Holy Roman Empire, but by October 1792 declared herself neutral. Diplomats from all the warring states met at the Congress of Ratstatt in 1796 to redraw the map of Europe, but before the treaty could be finalised war broke out again. The new Elector Maximilian Joseph IV, who succeeded his brother in 1799, was sympathetic to French ideas, having served in the French army for many years. He inherited a bankrupt economy and ruined army after the débâcle of Hohenlinden in 1800, and thereafter he worked to modernise, organise and train the Bavarian army on the French model. The British Graf Rumford lost his patronage, and so left Bavarian service.

Palatinate Artillery

The Palatinate artillery consisted of a company of gunners armed with French Vallière guns. In 1778, Bavaria and the neighbouring Rhineland Palatinate were unified; the Palatinate retained its separate artillery establishment and outdated ordnance despite this unification.

Georg Alexander Schweinichen (1752–1832) had served in the Prussian army, 1768–79, before retiring due to ill health; he went on to serve in the United Belgian and Dutch artillery, 1790–93, before joining the Palatinate service on 8 August 1799. With the rank of captain, he was directed to improve that state's artillery by Elector Maximillian Joseph IV of Bavaria. He was promoted major on 25 April 1801, before once more retiring on 14 March 1804. On 28 March 1809 he returned to the colours, becoming Oberst-Leutnant and commandant of the Palatinate artillery.

Manson M1800 System

At the time when the Bavarian elector signed a separate peace with France, most of the 80 guns were those designed by Graf von Rumford. Maximilian Joseph was ably assisted in his project to modernise his army along French lines by Jakob Manson, the French émigré who had served with him in Strasbourg. Manson was made a lieutenant-general and Director of Artillery in 1800.

The new M1800 system of artillery that Manson created for the unified Bavaria was designed by a group that Manson brought together from the French Royalist Army of Condé. These included Karl Julien Zoller (1773–1849), a gentleman cadet of artillery from Anhalt, who had entered French service by 1792 and the Army of Condé in 1795. Transferring to Bavarian service in 1799 with the rank of Oberst, Zoller was made a military commissioner (1818) and major-general (1824). He introduced a new artillery system in 1836, and retired as a lieutenant-general and Bavaria's Commander of Artillery. Also prominent in Manson's team were Sebastian-Joseph de Comeau de Cherry; one Lintz, a master-carpenter from Alsace who designed the new carriages; and the Baron Colonge brothers. The younger brother (1754–1837) became General-Director of Bavarian Artillery in 1822; their father had worked with Gribeauval in the 1760s and had been a general in the French army in the 1770s.

Graf von Rumford

Graf von Rumford (Sir Benjamin Thompson, 1753–1814) was born in Massachusetts. Between 1777 and 1781 he served as Under-Secretary of State in Lord North's British government. In 1779 he carried out tests on gunpowder that led to 'red LG' (large grain) gunpowder, and wrote an important treatise; the same year he was elected a Fellow of the Royal Society in recognition of his scientific work. Two years later he returned to North America at the fall of North's ministry, as colonel of the King's American Dragoons regiment, and saw the Desaguliers block-trail gun carriage in action. In 1783 he returned to England and retired on half-pay; he was knighted on 23 February 1784.

Thompson joined the service of Elector Theodor I of Bavaria after being given leave to enter foreign service by King George III in 1785. Over the following decade he reformed the Bavarian army, altering their uniforms and gunpowder production, and introducing the Rumford system of artillery. As Inspector-General of Artillery he oversaw experiments in cannon-boring. He also served as Minister of War and Police, and Grand Chamberlain. In 1792 he was elevated to Graf (Count) von Rumford of the Holy Roman Empire, taking his title from his birthplace near Concord, New Hampshire.

In 1798 the Elector sent him to London as the Bavarian ambassador to England, but his credentials were refused as he was a British citizen. His artillery designs were so highly regarded that in 1799 US President John Adams considered making him superintendent of the new military academy being set up at West Point. He lost patronage in Bavaria when Maximilian Joseph became Elector of Bavaria and the Palatinate on 16 February 1799.

Rumford co-founded the Royal Institution in London in 1800. He moved to Paris in May that year, and married the widow of the chemist Lavoisier on 24 October 1805. Returning to Bavaria, he chaired the Artillery Committee. On 21 August 1814 he died of 'nervous fever' in Auteuil, France. He had furthered the careers of General Wrede, and of Humphrey Davy, whom he appointed as lecturer in chemistry to the Royal Institution.[101]

The M1791 Rumford 3-pdr and 6-pdr cannon and 7-pdr howitzer were retained. Manson introduced new 6- and 12-pdrs, 18 calibres long, based on an amalgam of Gribeauval and M1803 (AnXI) gun tube and carriage designs, in the same calibres used by Rumford's system. They had the same metal-to-weight ratio, of 150:1 to weight of shot, as the Gribeauval system. The carriages used the Gribeauval elevating screw and plate rather than the vertical screw acting on the cascable, as used by Rumford. The 7-pdr howitzer was 6 calibres long.

A new Wurst wagon was introduced to replace the M1785 wagon, and new limbers were based on the Austrian M1780. Ammunition supply to the guns was from the limber box, copied in 1803 by France; this could carry 10 roundshot and 10 canister rounds for the 6-pdr; 8 shot and 9 canister for the 12-pdr; and 5 shells and 5 canister for the howitzer. Manson used a 144cm wheel for the 12-pdr and 6-pdr and the rear wheels of wagons and caissons, and a 116cm wheel for limbers and the front wheels of wagons.

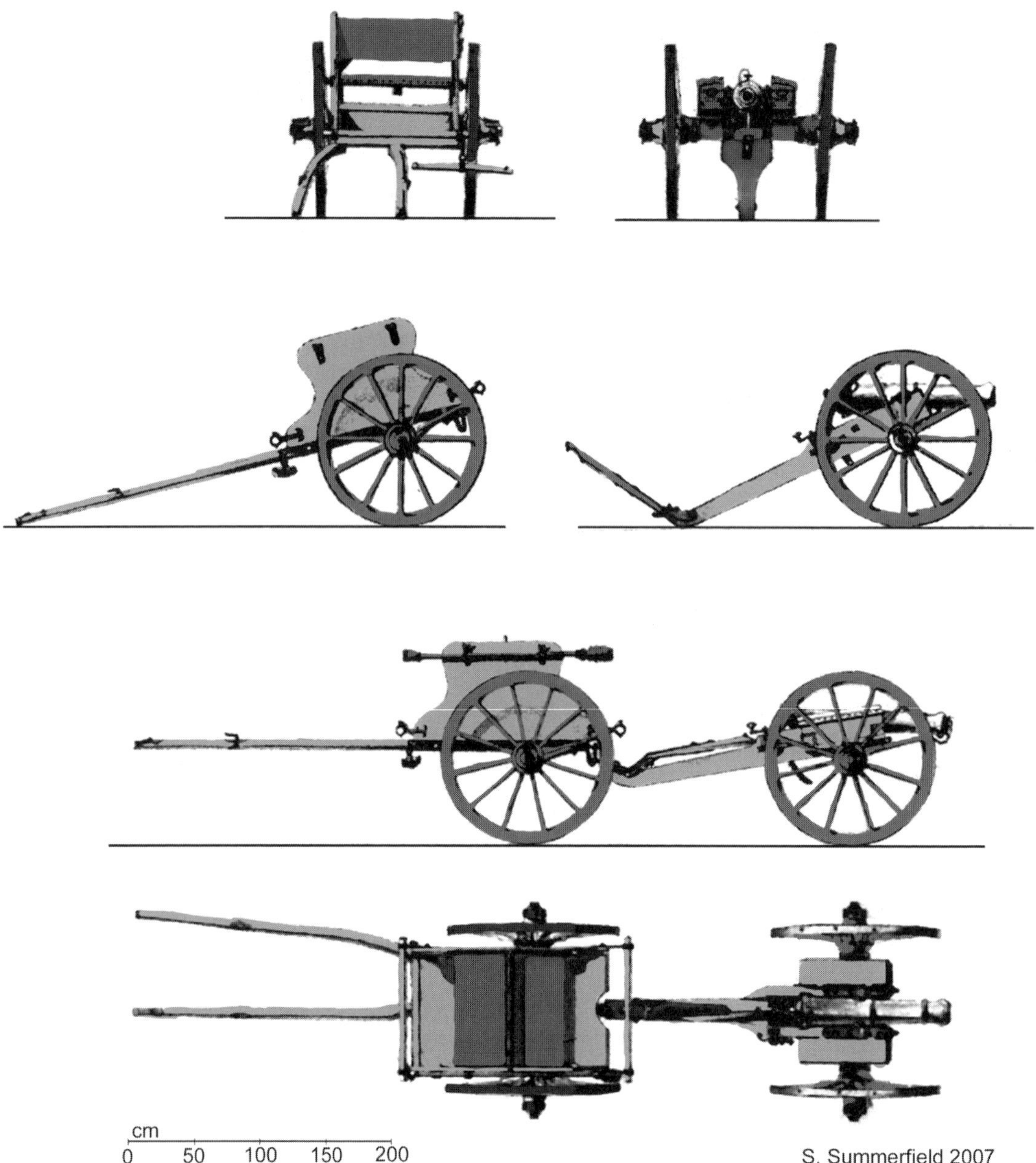

Bavarian M1791 Rumford 3-pdr field gun for use as battalion and light artillery, taken from drawings by Graf von Rumford. The limber and gun carriage were based on the British M1778 Desaguliers system.

In 1805, Rumford returned to Bavaria as Director of Artillery. The artillery commission at that time consisted of Rumford, Jakob Manson (Director-General), Baron Zoller (Adjutant-General), Oberst Comeau (Under-Director) and his assistant, Oberst-Leutnant Colonge. These were assisted by Heinrich Othon von Schell (1745–1807) from Denmark. Better known as Otto de Scheel, he published a commentary on Müy and Gribeauval's *Treatise of 1771* (by the appearance of the second edition in 1795 there had been many changes to the Gribeauval system, making this work out of date). Another

Bavarian M1791 6-pdr gun and carriage

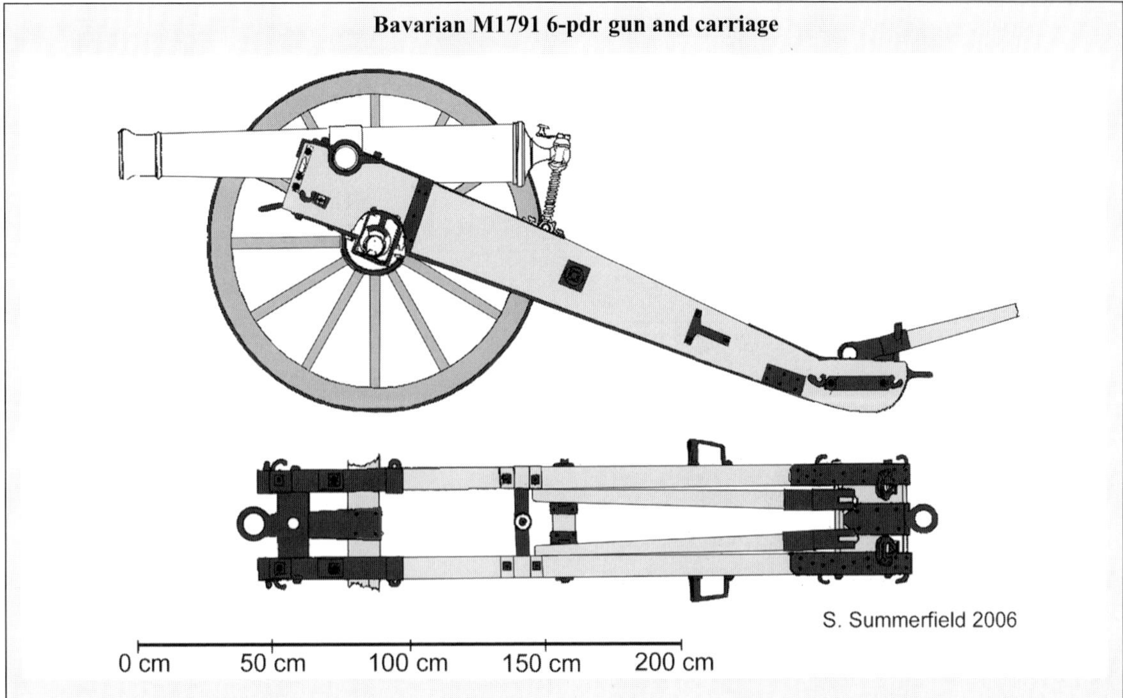

Bavarian M1791 6-pdr gun and carriage designed by Graf von Rumford. Notice that the dolphins have been removed to slightly lighten the gun tube. The elevation system was a version of that used in Britain in both the Congreve and Desaguliers systems. The folding hand-spikes and parallel carriage cheeks were innovations of Rumford, copied later in the century in Prussia, Russia and Württemberg. The basic concept of this carriage was applied to the French artillery under the 1803 committee recommendations, but was never put into practice.

contributor to the commission's work was one de Pirah from Switzerland.

In May 1805, Bavaria cast a series of M1800 guns for Baden and also equipped Kleve-Berg. A total of 76 guns of M1800 type had been cast by 1806. As a reward for Bavarian support during the 1805 campaign, Napoleon presented the Elector Maximilian Joseph with two batteries of Austrian 6-pdr cavalry guns (12× Austrian M1774 6-pdrs and 4× M1774 7-pdr howitzers) and support vehicles, which were used to mobilise two more batteries during the occupation of Vienna. In 1806, Manson removed the Wurst seats from the guns themselves, the gunners thereafter riding on the M180 Wurst wagon.

Napoleon also presented Bavaria with cannon-boring machines and other manufacturing equipment from the Vienna Arsenal. These were set up in Munich and Amberg, where cannon production was increased with Austrian calibres. For the first time, a paid gun-founder was appointed. Gun production was handled by the *Ouvriers* company, split into a Zug (platoon) each of wheelwrights, cannon-borers, smiths and carpenters, and commanded by Oberst Lintz. From 21 June 1807 they came under the direct control of the Director of Arsenals.

Napoleon elevated Bavaria to a kingdom in 1806; she was the most powerful state of the Confederation of the Rhine, with a contingent of 30,000 men – she actually raised 47,000 in 1809 when the Austrians invaded. With Manson's death on 5 January 1809 the directorship of the arsenal was taken over by Oberst Comeau and Captain von Reichenbach. The 1809 Bavarian 6-pdr batteries had 4× 6-pdr guns and 2× 7-pdr howitzers.

Table 3.3: Losses of Bavarian artillery equipment 1806–15

	3-pdr	6-pdr	12-pdr	Howitzer	Munition wagons
1807	none	2	none	none	none
1809	4	3	1	3	5
1812	none	20	6	12	365
1813	none	7	none	2	39
1814	none	none	none	none	1
1815	none	none	none	none	none
Total	4	32	17	410	

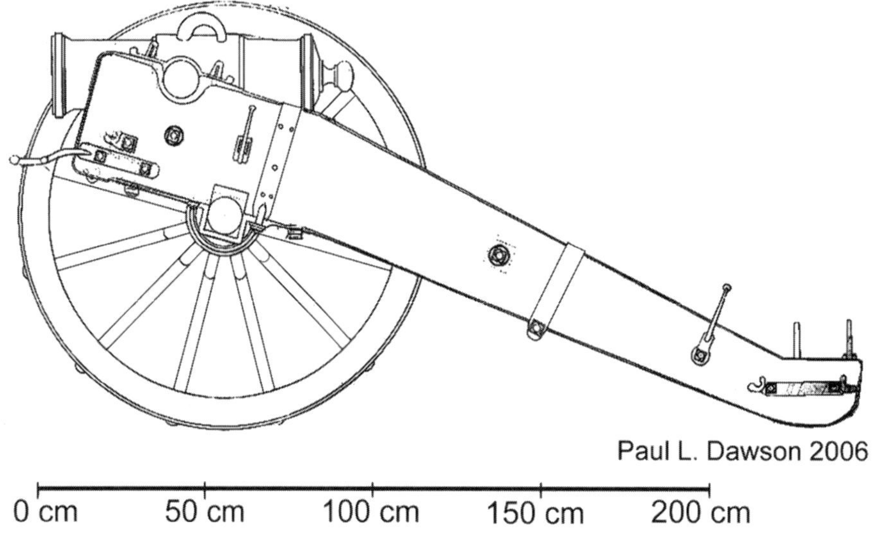

Bavarian M1791 Rumford 7-pdr howitzer. (After Scharnhorst, 1806)

An 18th-century Palatinate 3-pdr gun based upon the French Vallière system. Notice the gryphon mouldings on the dolphins and cascable. (HMG, Vienna)

Bavarian foot artillery crew loading a M1800 Manson 6-pdr in 1809. (By kind permission Landes u. Universitätsbibliothek Darmstadt; photograph Marcus Stein)

By 1812 the Director of Artillery was Dreierlei. In that year the allocation of equipment to Bavarian units was as follows:

6-pdr battery: 6× 6-pdr guns, 2× 7-pdr howitzers, 14× 6-pdr caissons, 4× howitzer caissons, 1× infantry munition wagon, 1× field forge, 1× coal wagon, 1× supply wagon; 112× men and 68× horses

12-pdr battery: 4× 12-pdrs, 2× 7-pdr howitzers, 10× 12-pdr caissons, 4× howitzer caissons, 1× field forge, 1× coal wagon, 1× supply wagon; 124× men and 64× horses

Horse artillery company: 4× 6-pdrs, 2× 7-pdr howitzers, 4× 6-pdr Wurst wagons, 2× howitzer Wurst wagons, 5× munition wagons, 1× cavalry munition wagon, 1× field forge, 1× coal wagon, 1× supply wagon.

The bulk of the artillery that was fielded in the 1812 campaign was lost during the retreat from Russia, and the field artillery had to be rebuilt around surviving guns. By March 1813, 120 field guns and 436 caissons of the French pattern were in service.[102] A report of 1 August 1813 lists the Bavarian artillery as ten foot batteries (each with 6× 6-pdrs and 2× 24-pdr howitzers); four Light (Wurst) batteries (each 4× 6-pdr guns and 2× 24-pdr howitzers); and two reserve batteries (each 6× 12-pdr and 2× 6.4in howitzers). In theory, the Light Wurst batteries should have had 6x 6-pdrs according to a decision of March 1813, but shortages seem to have prevented this being put into effect. French M1808 guns had replaced those of the Bavarian Manson M1800 system.

The ammunition allocation was as follows:

Light battery (1813): 210× 6-pdr roundshot, 185× howitzer shells
Foot battery (1813): 155× 6-pdr roundshot, 185× howitzer shells
12-pdr battery (1813): 180× 6-pdr roundshot, 185× howitzer shells.

It appears that the light artillery companies used either Manson M1800 Wurst caissons or converted French caissons, as they were still listed as being vehicle-mounted.

A siege train was re-established in October 1813. In that month the Bavarian army is noted as having received French-manufactured ordnance to replace the 1812 losses: 2× 12-pdrs, 10× 6-pdrs and 4× 24-pdr howitzers. Also in October 1813, General von Wrede was hampered by the lack of ammunition for his Bavarian artillery, as the French guns had a larger calibre than those of Austria; Austrian ammunition could be fired, but the greater windage dramatically reduced the effectiveness of the guns. French guns were still used in 1814, when sufficient Bavarian equipment could be produced.

In 1836, the M1836 Zoller system replaced the Manson equipment. The M1800 equipment was still used by garrison and reserve units until at least 1854.

PIEDMONT

Since the 16th century the northern Italian Kingdom of Piedmont had been ruled by the House of Savoy which, from 1720, also held the Kingdom of Sardinia. By 1750, Piedmont-Sardinia had become the principal military state in Italy. The kingdom's defeat by Napoleon at Montenotte (11–12 April 1796) followed by the Armistice of Cherasco (28 April 1796) gave France control of all the Piedmontese fortresses. In October 1798, King Charles Emmanuel IV, faced with liberal unrest in Turin, fled to the island of Sardinia and the protection of the British Royal Navy. From 1799 until 1814, Piedmont formed four departments within Metropolitan France.[103]

M1770 System

The M1770 system of Piedmont-Sardinia, with ordnance cast in Turin, included a light mountain 4-pdr, a Heavy field 4-pdr, a Light 8-pdr and a Heavy 8-pdr. Light and Heavy 16-pdrs had a similar calibre to French 12-pdrs; and Light and Heavy 32-pdrs, equivalent to French 24-pdrs, were used in fortresses and the siege train. Howitzers appear to have been of 7-pdr and 10-pdr calibres. These guns were made to the designs of Vincenti.

Table 3.4: Piedmont M1770 and M1786 Ordnance

Model	Calibre	Shot diameter	Bore length	Tube length	Weight	Windage	Shot weight	Charge weight
Piedmontese M1770								
Heavy 16-pdr	122mm	120mm	18 calibres	244cm	ND	2mm	ND	ND
Heavy 8-pdr	97mm	94.5mm	18 calibres	194cm	ND	2mm	ND	ND
Heavy 4-pdr	77mm	74mm	18 calibres	157cm	ND	2mm	ND	ND
Piedmontese M1786								
32-pdr	155mm	153mm	19 calibres	323cm	2630kg	2mm	ND	ND
16-pdr (12-pdr)	122mm	120mm	16 calibres	224cm	982.8kg	2mm	6000g	1900g
8-pdr (6-pdr)	96.5mm	94.5mm	17 calibres	174cm	409.5kg	2mm	3000g	1100g
4-pdr (3-pdr)	76mm	74mm	16 calibres	155cm	311.2kg	2.2mm	1000g	800g
1-pdr	53mm	50mm	ND	ND	ND	2mm	ND	ND
7-pdr Howitzer	140mm	138mm	7 calibres	115cm	294.8kg	2mm	ND	ND

Piedmont M1770 4-pdr field gun designed by Vincenti, now in Vienna. Note the absence of dolphins, and the single reinforcing band in front of the trunnions. These reinforcing bands were removed from the M1786 ordnance.

Piedmont M1786 4-pdr gun, a precursor of the French M1803 (AnXI) guns cast in Turin for the Kingdom of Italy. (HMG, Vienna).

M1786 System

The M1786 guns were based upon the ballistics research of D'Antoni published in 1780. The Piedmont M1786 gun tubes designed by Vincenti were revolutionary in that they took the ideas of Jean Maritz II one stage further to ease mass and standardised production, by removing all the reinforcing bands from the exterior of the tube except for one in front of the muzzle swell, giving a smooth, tapering section. The ornamentation was also removed to lighten the tubes further. The cascable and tulip-shaped muzzle were retained. These weapons were precursors to the French M1803 (AnXI) guns. They were produced as Medium and Heavy 4-, 8-, 16- and 32-pdrs according to Piedmont weights – equivalent to 3-, 6-, 12- and 24-pdrs in French weights.

SAXONY

The history of the Saxon army is complex, and can be touched upon only briefly here. The relationship

Table 3.5: Saxon ordnance, M1772 Hoyer and M1810 Raabe

	Calibre	Tube length	Tube weight	Carriage weight	Limber weight	Shot weight	Charge weight
Hoyer M1772							
Heavy 12-pdr	115mm	184cm	1121kg	740kg	313kg	5610g	2340g
Light 12-pdr	115mm	184cm	794kg	640kg	297kg	5610g	1870g
Heavy 8-pdr	100.6mm	161cm	748kg	533kg	239kg	3740g	1520g
Light 8-pdr	100.6mm	161cm	523kg	462kg	220kg	3740g	1400g
Heavy 4-pdr	78.7mm	165cm	420kg	426kg	200kg	1870g	930g
Light 4-pdr	78.7mm	126cm	313kg	426kg	200kg	1870g	580g
8-pdr Howitzer	154.8mm	93cm	398kg	878kg	193kg	8410g	700g
4-pdr Granatstück	154.8mm	124cm	325kg	491kg	312kg	1870g	640g
Raabe M1810							
12-pdr	115mm	207cm	585kg	640kg	300kg	5610g	1816g
6-pdr	92.6mm	167cm	392kg	530kg	200kg	2800g	908g
8-pdr Howitzer	154.8mm	80cm	320kg	790kg	300kg	8410g	700g

Saxon M1766 Light 4-pdr quick-firing gun. (Bottom left) Cipher of Elector Frederick Augustus III (1750–1824), elector 1763–1806 and king 1806–24, and a casting date of 1769, on the gun shown above, now in the Borodino Museum (photograph: Steven H. Smith). The drawing (top right) shows clearly the flat cascable to which the elevating system was attached. (Below right) This Saxon Artillery model was purchased from Colonel Hoyer in 1812 by the Board of Ordnance.

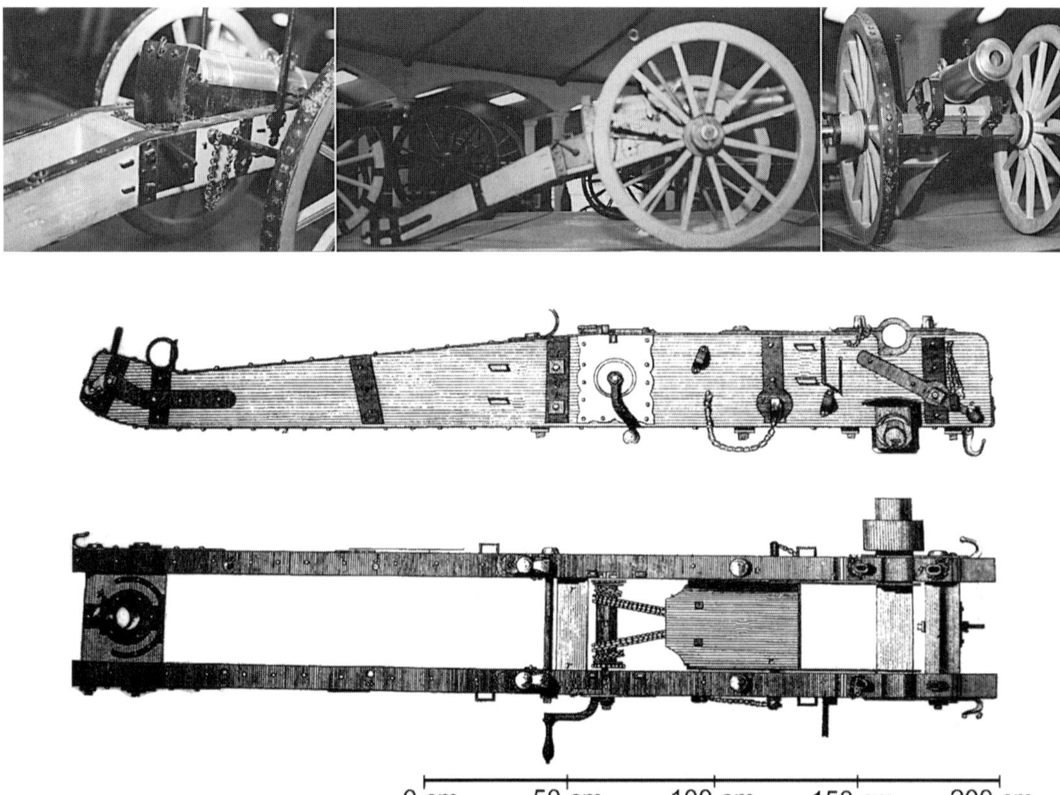

(Top) Model of a Saxon M1772 heavy 8-pdr, with the flat cascable to which the elevating system was attached. (Courtesy the Trustees of the RAHT; photograph Norman Swales) (Below) Drawing of the carriage, showing the unique elevating system. (After Scharnhorst, 1806)

between Prussia and Saxony was somewhat cool during the Revolutionary Wars. In 1806, Saxony was forced into alliance by Prussia and supplied her with 20,000 men. In contrast to the flight of the Prussians from Jena-Auerstädt, contemporary accounts describe the Saxon units retreating from the battlefield in perfect order with bands playing. The Electorate of Saxony was raised to a kingdom by Napoleon, and the new King Friedrich August entered into an alliance with France, being obliged to contribute 20,000 men if called upon to do so. This alliance came to an end at the battle of Leipzig in October 1813.

M1772 Hoyer System

In 1772, Saxony adopted Gribeauval style caisson. The ordnance designed by Oberst Johann Frederich Hoyer (1726–1802) as Director of the Artillery School, assisted by Major Raabe, was not a completely new system. The 8- and 12-pdr gun tubes (both light and heavy models) were retained, but mounted on new carriages that had a unique elevating system permitting 10-degree elevation and 5-degree depression. This was apparently an improvement on the designs of the Hanoverian system. The ordnance was 16 calibres long except for the Heavy 4-pdr, which was 21 calibres long, and the 8-pdr howitzer with a tube length of 6 calibres.

Hoyer and Raabe also designed a light quick-firing 4-pdr introduced in 1766, a 24-pdr for siege and position work, and a 4-pdr Granatstück (grenade-thrower). This Granatstück, 9 calibres long, fired only 4-pdr case-shot grenades, and was able to carry 50–60 rounds in its ammunition chest. Its canister round, containing 28 balls of eight *Loth* (116.8g)

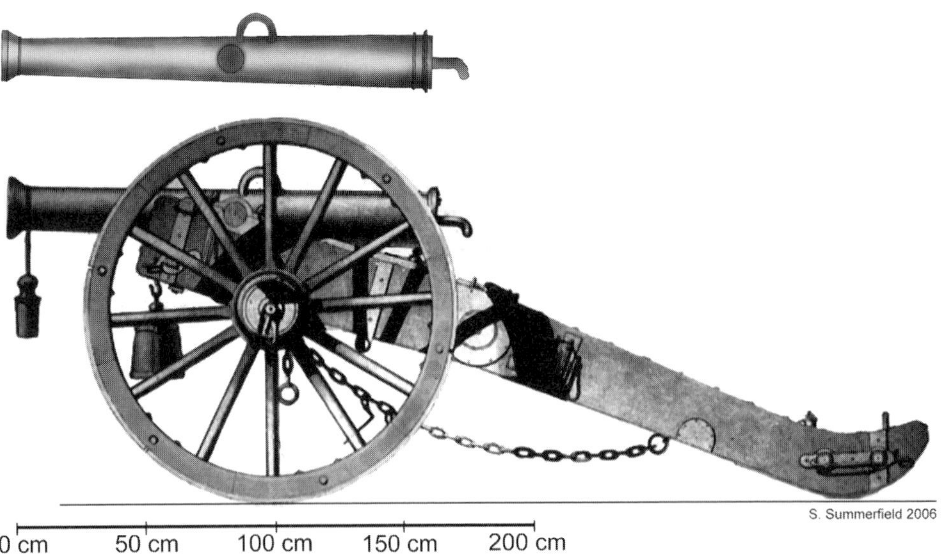

Saxon M1810 12-pdr field gun.

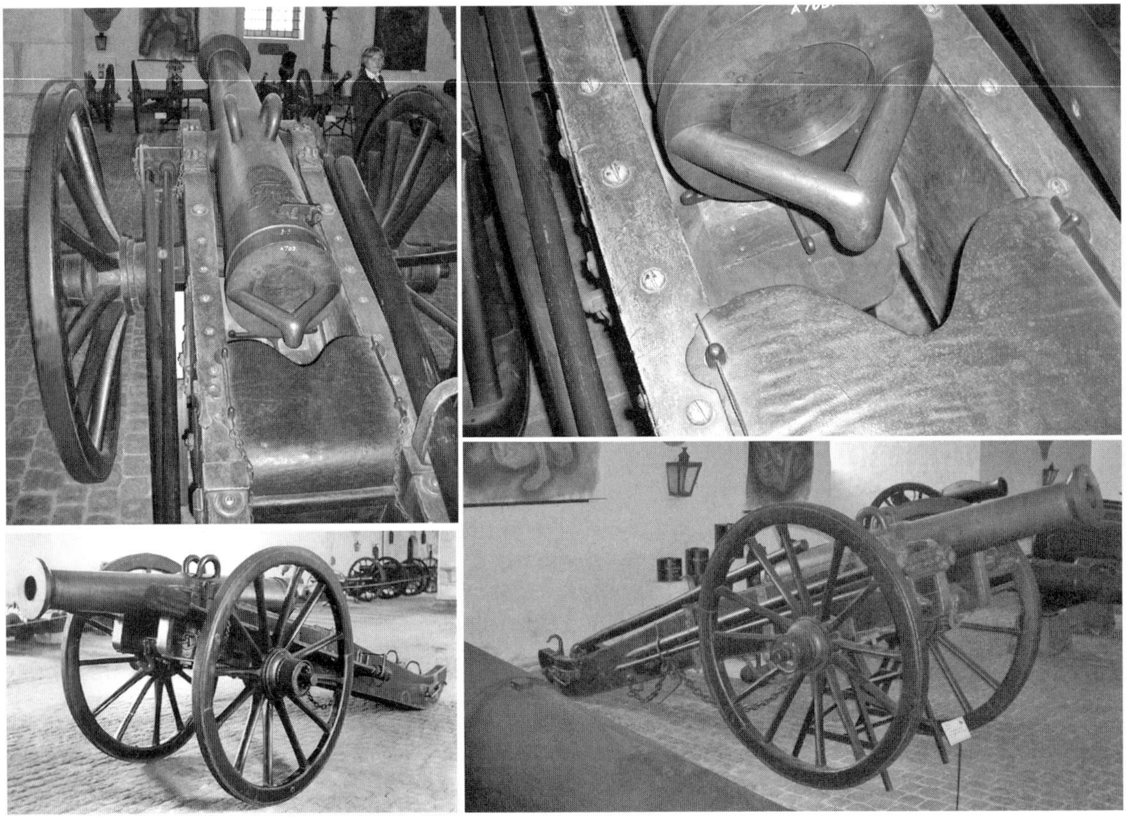

Saxon M1810 12-pdr field gun, now in Copenhagen. (Jeorg Titze)

weight each, had an effective range of 756 paces (475 m).[104] When horse artillery was assigned to outpost duty it was suggested that the Granatstück be used, since it combined the advantages of a howitzer and the accuracy of a cannon. It was essentially a light gun-howitzer similar to the Russian unicorn. The chance of grenades failing to explode was very small, so long as care was taken in the preparation of the fuse. The rounds mentioned appear to have been spherical.

M1810 Raabe System

This system was designed by the artillery staff led by Major Raabe and Frederick Gustav Rouvroy (1777–1839), the nephew of Johann Theodor Rouvroy. It introduced new 6-pdr and 12-pdr field guns as well as a new 8-in howitzer, and the gun carriages were lightened. The gun tubes had a bore length of 18 calibres, and the howitzers of 7 calibres. The 4-pdr grenade-thrower was retained, but the tube was modified to make it lighter. The 24-pdr field gun was assigned to the siege train.

Unique features of these guns were the replacement of the cascable with a handle; suppression of the reinforcements; and the fact that gun carriages were made with all-bronze fittings rather than iron. New caissons were introduced, as well as a new training manual. One aspect of the M1810 reforms was the use of only two wheel sizes: small 113cm wheels for limbers, and large 119cm wheels (either heavy or light) for guns and the rear wheels of vehicles. All guns had a loading gauge of 113cm.

The 56 guns of the Saxon artillery commanded by Oberst-Leutnant Johann Friedrich Hoyer formed part of Reynier's Corps during the 1812 Russian campaign; some of these had been cast as long ago as 1766. Only 12 guns, one officer, 146 men and 167 horses returned to Saxony.

WÜRTTEMBERG

Before 1808, Austria supplied 3-, 6- and 12-pdr guns and 7- and 10-pdr howitzers. In December 1783 the arsenal at Ludwigsburg had 20× howitzers, 6× pierriers, 12× 12-pdrs, 12× 6-pdrs, 50× bronze 3-pdrs, 4× iron 3-pdrs, 12× falconets and 6× Jäger (light) pieces. In 1783, a horse artillery company was raised and armed with 3-pdrs.

During the 1790s some Austrian officers were also seconded to the Württemberg service. In May 1792, Württemberg sent 5× Heavy 12-pdrs, 2× Light 12-pdrs, 1× Heavy and 4× Light 6-pdrs to participate in the First Coalition.

By 1799, the horse artillery had replaced its 3-pdrs with 6-pdrs (18 calibres long, and weighing 504kg) devised by General-Intendant von Camrer, and the 7-pdr howitzer. The ammunition box of the Light 6-pdr contained 15 roundshot and weighed 148kg loaded. The *Rechtsmaschine*, *prolonge* and locking chains together weighed 33.6kg. Both the Light 6-pdr and the 7-pdr howitzer were drawn by six horses. At 13mm (½ *Zoll*) elevation, the 6-pdr had a range of 630–760m, which was longer than the light artillery of other nations. Some countries had begun to use 8- and 12-pdr guns in horse artillery by this time, principally France and Britain.

Until 1799 the horse artillery battery had 8 pieces, 4× 6-pdr guns and 4× 7-pdr howitzers; this was then reduced to 4× 6-pdrs and 2× 7-pdr howitzers.[105] At this time the horse artillery became vehicle-mounted along French Artillerie Légère principals, with the introduction of the Wurst wagon. The four 6-pdr guns had two Wurst wagons carrying 100 roundshot and 9 canister rounds, and the pair of howitzers had a single Wurst wagon carrying 60 shells and 10 canister rounds. The 6-pdrs had a reserve caisson containing 200 roundshot, and the howitzers a reserve caisson with 100 shells; both were drawn by eight horses. Thus, a battery needed 129 horses, plus two for the trumpeters, in total 131 horses. The Wurst wagons were abandoned in 1803.

In 1800, each foot company had eight pieces (6× 6-pdrs, 2× 7-pdr howitzers) drawn by four-horse teams; 10× two-horse caissons, 6× two-horse infantry ammunition wagons, a two-horse Jäger ammunition wagon, a two-horse field forge, a four-horse requisition wagon, a two-horse staff ambulance wagon, a four-horse light horse staff wagon, 2× packhorses, 3× four-horse infantry battalion staff wagons, plus 4× packhorses and a three-horse cart for the Jägers, 15× packhorses for the infantry, 17× four-horse tent wagons, and 67 riding horses.

In 1808 a foundry was set up at Ludwigsburg. In addition, powder mills were established at Rottweil,

Tübingen, Neuthgen, Korchen and Menzingen to reduce reliance on imported Austrian powder, since this commerce was no longer politically expedient. Captured guns were also used: there are references to French 8-pdrs, as well as ordnance from Prussia including Heavy and Light 12-pdrs, Heavy and Light 6-pdrs being used to fill gaps left by lost ordnance.

In 1809 the Austrian guns were augmented by French guns, principally the 6- and 12-pdr and the 24-pdr howitzer. The 3-pdr was placed in the regimental artillery. Now that Württemberg was self-sufficient in ordnance, an artillery commission was formed, headed by Captain Theilen; this designed the M1809 artillery system based on Gribeauval. The new Württemberg guns owed much to the French M1803 (AnXI) equipment; the calibres chosen were 6- and 12-pdr guns and a 7-pdr howitzer (a direct copy of the French 24-pdr). The munitions wagon was based on Gribeauval's designs but had a limber designed to be interchangeable with other vehicles. Three types of limber were used for the field gun, howitzer and vehicle. The field forge was the French M1808 four-wheeled version.

The concept of interchangeable parts was taken a step further, so that the 12-pdr gun and 7-pdr howitzer shared a carriage. (This concept was followed by France in 1814, when the Gribeauval 8-pdr carriage was used for both the 6-pdr field gun and the 24-pdr howitzer.) The 12-pdr gun tube was 17 calibres long, and the 6-pdr for light and horse artillery was apparently based on British design principles. All rolling stock was made to this new Württemberg system, as were all gun carriages, for ease of repair. A small Wurst seat was introduced to the trail of the 6-pdr gun used by the horse artillery, enabling two to four gunners to ride back-to-back on the gun rather than astride the seat, so making dismounting quicker and safer. The smaller Wurst seat had lower ends than those of Austrian designs, permitting the standard *Rechtsmaschine* elevating system and gun tubes with a cascable to be used.

In both foot and horse artillery, two gunners rode on the carriage with two more on top of the padded toolbox. The horse artillery had the rest of the gun crew mounted on the new ammunition wagon, which was padded on the front half to seat them.

In 1810 the organisation and equipment allocation of Württemberg artillery was as follows:

1st, 2nd and 3rd Foot Companies: each 6× 6-pdr guns, 2× 7-pdr howitzers, 8× caissons
4th (Heavy) Foot Company: 4× 12-pdr guns, 2× Heavy howitzers, 6× caissons
1st and 2nd Horse Artillery Companies: each 4× 6-pdr guns, 2× 7-pdr howitzers, 6× caissons, 1× tool wagon
3rd Horse Artillery (half-) Company: 3× 6-pdr guns, 1× 7-pdr howitzer, 4× caissons, 1× tool wagon.

In June 1812 the issue of ordnance to III (Ney) Corps (continued on pages 94–5). Württemberg provided two foot batteries and a 12-pdr battery to

Table 3.6: Württemberg ordnance

	Calibre	Bore length	Tube length	Tube weight	Windage	Projectile weight	Charge weight
Pre-1808 (Austrian gun tubes)							
18-pdr	130mm	22 calibres	295cm	1310kg	5mm	6000g	1600g
12-pdr	118mm	14.6 calibres	191cm	812kg	6mm	5500g	1600g
M1796 Light 6-pdr	93mm	18 calibres	ND	504kg	ND	2740g	1000g
6-pdr	93mm	14.6 calibres	157cm	385kg	4mm	2740g	1000g
3-pdr	76mm	14.6 calibres	121cm	240kg	3mm	1300g	409g
7-pdr Howitzer	150mm	4.1 calibres	92cm	275kg	4mm	7150g	572g
M1809 (French inspired)							
M1809 12-pdr	121mm	16.8 calibres	210cm	760kg	1.3mm	6100g	1958g
M1809 6-pdr	95mm	16.6 calibres	170cm	390kg	1.9mm	3000g	1100g
M1809 7-pdr Howitzer	148mm	7 calibres	120cm	327kg	2.9mm	6100g	1000g

Pre-1808 Württemberg 12-pdr

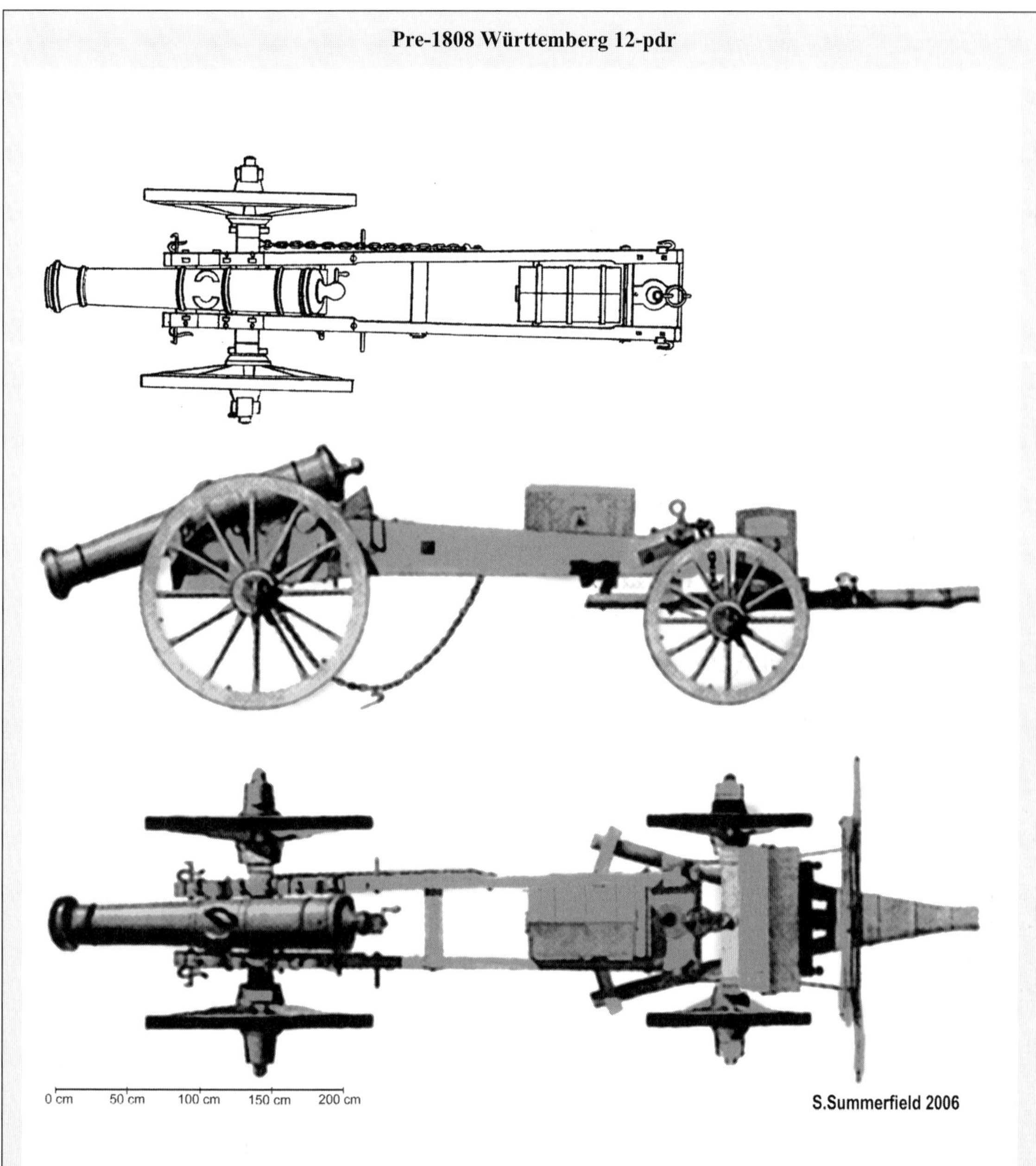

The pre-1808 Württemberg 12-pdr cannon was a version of an Austrian Liechtenstein gun tube and carriage. The carriage-mounted ammunition box was retained in Württemberg despite being discontinued in Austria in 1774. The M1774 Austrian ammunition limber was adopted in the 1780s, enabling the gun to fight more independently of the caissons.

Table 3.7: Technical data for M1809 Württemberg carriages

	12-pdr	6-pdr	7-pdr Howitzer
Length of axle	180.4cm	180.4cm	180.4cm
Length of limber axle	177cm	177cm	177cm
Length of wooden saddle over the axle	130.7cm	130.7cm	130.7cm
Weight of gun with loaded ammunition chest	1729kg	1528kg	1680kg
Weight of loaded caisson with spare wheel	1729kg	563kg	1697kg
Length of gun and limber	851cm	802cm	766cm

the 25th Division and a half horse artillery battery each to the 9th and 14th Light Cavalry Brigades.

10th (French) Division, III Corps (60 vehicles):
Field Artillery: 10× French 6-pdrs, 4× French 24-pdr howitzers, 1× spare 6-pdr carriage, 15× 6-pdr caissons, 8× 24-pdr howitzer caissons, 16× infantry caissons, 4× ammunition wagons, 2× field forges
Regimental Artillery: 8× 3-pdrs, 8× 3-pdr caissons, 11× infantry caissons, 4× field forges

11th (French) Division, III Corps (60 vehicles):
Field Artillery: 10× French 6-pdrs, 4× French 24-pdr howitzers, 1× spare 6-pdr carriage, 15× 6-pdr caissons, 8× 24-pdr howitzer caissons, 16× infantry caissons, 4× ammunition wagons, 2× field forges
Regimental Artillery: 6× 3-pdrs, 8× 3-pdr caissons, 11× infantry caissons, 3× field forges

25th Württemberg Division (119 vehicles):
6× M1809 Wurst 6-pdrs, 8× M1809 6-pdrs, 6× Austrian 12-pdrs, 8× M1809 7-pdr howitzers, 1× spare 7-pdr carriage, 18× 12-pdr caissons, 26× 6-pdr caissons, 16× 7-pdr howitzer caissons, 16× infantry caissons, 7× park caissons, 5× ammunition wagons, 2× field forges

Model of a Württemberg M1809 6-pdr with Wurst seat, as used by the horse artillery; these units were fully vehicle-mounted by this period. (Rastatt Military Museum; photograph Uwe Ehmek)

Model of a Württemberg M1809 12-pdr with a Gribeauval-pattern carriage, and an M1809 Wurst limber; this was a modified Austrian M1774 limber. (Rastatt Military Museum)

French Reserve Artillery (73 vehicles):
12× French 12-pdrs, 4× Austrian 10-pdr howitzers, 2× spare 12-pdr carriages, 1× spare 10-pdr howitzer carriage, 36× 12-pdr caissons, 12× 10-pdr howitzer caissons, 4× ammunition wagons, 2× field forges

French Light Cavalry Corps (31 vehicles):
8× 6-pdrs (197x fixed 6-pdr rounds), 4× 24-pdr howitzers (20× 24-pdr howitzer rounds), 10× 6-pdr caissons (958 6-pdr rounds), 6× 24-pdr howitzer caissons, 1× field forge, 2× ammunition wagons (298× 24-pdr howitzer powder charges, drawn from caissons)

Park (88 vehicles):
1× spare 12-pdr carriage, 4× spare 6-pdr carriages, 3× spare 7-pdr howitzer carriages, 8× 12-pdr caissons, 20× 6-pdr caissons, 6× 10-pdr howitzer caissons, 10× 7-pdr howitzer caissons, 21× infantry caissons, 1× park caisson, 7× ammunition wagons, 1× tool wagon, 1× pontoon wagon, 5× field forges

Oddly, it appears that Württemberg gunners managed to drag a spare gun carriage for a 6-pdr all the way back to France from Russia, along with 5× caissons, 3× empty ammunition wagons and a field forge. These vehicles must have been used to transport the gunners and other personnel.

In 1813 the army was re-equipped with newly cast guns to the previous designs.

4 British and Hanoverian Ordnance

INTRODUCTION

Unlike other countries, in Britain the artillery arm was separate from the regular army and was run by the Board of Ordnance. The origins of this institution went back to the 14th century, when the English Wardrobe of Arms developed into the Privy Wardrobe of the Tower, specialising in the provision of arms. Enlarged by King Henry VIII, in 1597 it was formally constituted as a Board by Queen Elizabeth I, with responsibilities for armaments, munitions and the upkeep and repair of forts and castles. The Board of Ordnance remained administratively separate from the army and navy, and had both civil and military wings. Many of the surveyors and draughtsmen who designed fortifications and barracks were civilians. By the 19th century the Board was increasingly dominated by army officers, and it was merged with the War Office in 1855.

The artillery did not receive the royal warrant until the 18th century. The artillery and engineering arms were run by the 'Ordnance Board' under the Master-General of Ordnance; it was based at Woolwich, which served as both the artillery school and depot and was controlled by the Adjutant-General of Artillery. British artillery personnel were not paid by the Crown but were instead employees of the Board of Ordnance. The Master-General of the Ordnance was usually a serving general officer; he was responsible for all British artillery, engineers, fortifications and military supplies. The appointment was often combined with a seat in the cabinet, especially in the late 18th and early 19th centuries. (The post of Master-General of the Ordnance has survived the abolition of the Board of Ordnance in 1855 to this day, as the title of the fourth member of the Army Board, who oversees procurement, research and development.)

Unlike the absolutist monarchies of the Continental powers, that of Great Britain was constitutionally limited, and ministers exercised the king's ostensible powers in practice. The Tory party in Parliament tended to uphold the powers of the monarchy, while the Whigs sought to extend parliamentary prerogatives. The Hanoverian dynasty had something of a tradition of the king and his eldest son being estranged; during the late 18th century this effectively created two factions supporting King George III and the Prince of Wales, which became involved in wrangling over practical decisions.

King George III suffered his first attack of mental instability (as a result of porphyria) in 1788, and subsequent bouts occurred in March 1801, in 1804, and finally in November 1810 following the death of his youngest daughter, Princess Amelia. On 5 February 1811 the Regency Act 1811 established the Prince of Wales as regent, with limited powers for twelve months. The Royal Artillery used two distinct types of gun carriage during the Napoleonic Wars: the traditional bracket carriage was employed by the foot and park artillery, and the more radical Desaguliers block-trail by the new horse artillery. The Whig friends of the prince regent supported and were closely involved in the creation of the Royal Horse Artillery and the introduction of the block-trail.

On 18 February 1812 the restrictions on the Prince Regent's powers came to an end, and it is interesting that the changes to British uniforms and the order initiating the conversion of the old bracket carriages occurred in the same year. William Congreve Snr, Desaguliers and Townshend were all part of George III's circle, whereas William Congreve Jnr (1772–1828), was prominent among the friends of the Prince of Wales, and became his senior equerry in 1817 – a friendship that probably advanced the development of the Rocket Troops

The cipher of the monarch was usually placed on the first reinforcement of British gun tubes, often with the numerals incorporated: George I (1714–27), George II (1727–60), and George III (1760–1820). On some pieces the entire coat of arms was displayed.

and Royal Horse Artillery in place of the older more conservative ideas favoured by those officers who were friends with George III. Richard Bogue who commanded the Rocket Troop was also part of the Prince Regent's circle.

Scientific Influence on British Ordnance

The design of ordnance and practice of gunnery before the application of mathematics was based upon empirical reasoning; these skills were difficult to master except through a great deal of trial and error. In Britain, Benjamin Robins (1707–51) in his *New Principles of Gunnery* (1742) transformed gunnery into a Newtonian, calculus-based science rather than an art or craft. This started the trend towards the use of lower charges, and consequently lighter and more mobile guns. In 1747, Robins argued for exactly this when he proposed the production of guns to replace Royal Navy weapons up to 18-pdrs with larger-calibre pieces but of the same weight, so increasing the potential broadside.

Muller's *A Treatise on Artillery*, first published in 1757, was a comprehensive introduction to ordnance, including ballistics, the construction of guns, mortars and howitzers, the manufacture of ammunition and fuses, and an account of the service of artillery in the field. Although subsequent editions were not fully revised it was still considered by contemporaries a useful text as there were few other textbooks available in English.

In 1777, Hugh Brown translated Euler's 1745 commentaries upon Robins' work into English as *The True Principle of Gunnery*; this had a great influence on British gunnery, correcting a number of Robins' assumptions (as discussed above in Chapter 2). Benjamin Thompson (later Graf von Rumford) relied upon it for his own investigations and experiments into gunpowder and ballistics. In 1791, Charles Hutton, mathematics professor at the Royal Military Academy at Woolwich (1773–1807), proved Euler over Robins.

Captain Ralph Willet Adye (1764–1804) first published his *Bombardier and Pocket Gunner* in 1798. This was perhaps one of the most influential books for the Royal Artillery until the 1830s, and after Adye's death revised and expanded volumes were published.

The Royal Brass Foundry

The construction of the Royal Brass Foundry at Woolwich was started on 19 June 1716 and was completed the following year; it became part of a complex of buildings and proving-grounds known as the Warren, located on Crown land next to the Royal Dockyard that had been established by King Henry VIII. In August 1716 the Swiss Andreas Schalch (1692–1776), who had received training at the Douai foundry in France, was appointed as Master Founder.[106] On 22 March 1722, Schalch installed his vertical boring machine, thus doing away with the old method of casting around a core; this was a fundamental advance in British gun-founding.

In general, bronze gun tubes were cast by the Woolwich foundry, with commercial founders being contracted to cast iron guns for the Board of Ordnance. Private contractors sold their guns to the Board on a purely commercial basis, but were obliged to produce such weapons to government designs. The Board bought the guns by weight, so it was not surprising that foundries preferred to make larger, heavier guns than smaller ones; this resulted in iron gun tubes being generally larger than the regulation drawings. By 1716 full-sized drawings were sent to the gun-founders so that they were made to a common pattern rather than one determined by individual founders.

Iron guns were cast from a wooden model, in sand-boxes that could be opened along the sides, since the model did not admit the casting being drawn from the box like a smooth cylinder.[107] The cast tube was then 'fettled' and bored out using a combination lathe and boring machine.[108] From the 1730s, brass 'rammers' were sent from the Ordnance Office to form the cores, to ensure that the bore was even more accurate. After delivery to the Ordnance, the gun tube was proved before the gun-founder was paid; it was tested with twice the normal powder charge, and if the tube survived it was then carefully examined for cracks by pressure-testing with water.

In 1755, Jan Verbruggen (1712–81), Master Founder at the Hague Arsenal in Holland, started designing a boring machine with the aid of the ambitious Johan Jacob Siegler, who professed to have worked for 15 years at the Douai foundry and to have practical experience of the Maritz horizontal boring machine. Between 1755 and 1758, Verbruggen and Siegler constructed their first combination boring machine and finishing lathe.[109] It was at this time that Pieter Verbruggen, newly graduated in law, joined his father at the Hague foundry.

While the new equipment solved the machining problems, controversy soon erupted over the suitability of the furnace designed by Verbruggen's superior, General de Creuznach. While de Creuznach was absent in 1759, Verbruggen rashly demolished the furnace and constructed another to his own design. There is evidence that Siegler – described by his French employer, Master Berenger, as an over-ambitious troublemaker – tried to profit by the situation, and was sacked for his disloyalty by Verbruggen in November 1760. In retaliation, on 24 January 1761 Siegler wrote a letter to the State Council of the Netherlands accusing the Verbruggens of corruption by using substandard brass. This caused the government to reject ordnance from the Hague factory between 1761 and 1770.[110]

During the Seven Years War (1756–63), Woolwich produced only 136 guns while private contractors produced at least 527 pieces. In 1763, Sir Joseph Yorke, British Ambassador to the Netherlands, urged the Board of Ordnance to hire Jan Verbruggen as a replacement for Schalch at the Royal Brass Foundry, but he failed to convince them. Two years later, Jan travelled to Paris and visited Jean-Francois Berenger at the Douai foundry, where he was probably inspired by what he saw.[111] Father and son Verbruggen fled to Britain in 1769; and on 12 January the following year Andrew Schalch was dismissed as Master Founder at Woolwich by the Board of Ordnance, and Jan Verbruggen was appointed in his place. Gun tubes cast by the Verbruggens all bore their 'signature' – I & P Verbruggens Fecerunt on the base ring, with weight (hundredweights, quarters and pounds) and calibre marked on the gun tube. The Woolwich foundry was in a poor state after more than fifty years of production with little or no maintenance. The only inventory available was that made in 1753; even this could not be found, and Schalch claimed that all the tools were his, since he had made them.[112]

The Verbruggens installed a new horizontal boring/finishing machine in May 1771, and a second one that July. On 13 July 1773, King George III visited the Royal Brass Foundry and issued the first warrants for six Heavy 12-pdr guns. The first was

Monogram initial of the Master-General of Ordnance

Charles Lennox, 3rd Duke of Richmond
1782–1783 1784–1795

Charles, 1st Marquess Cornwallis
1795–1797 1798–1801

John Pitt, 2nd Earl of Chatham
1801–1806 and 1807–1810

Henry Phipps, 1st Earl of Mulgrave
1810–1818

S. Summerfield 2007

The monogram initial of the Master-General of Ordnance, with the appropriate coronet, was placed on the chase until 1855. These examples are (left to right, top and bottom):

George Townshend, 4th Viscount Townshend (1714–1807), Master-General 1772–82 and 1783–84 (not shown).

Charles Lennox, 3rd Duke of Richmond (1735–1806), Master-General 1782–83 and 1784–95.

Charles, 1st Marquess Cornwallis (1738–1805), Master-General 1795–1801.

John Pitt, 2nd Earl of Chatham (1756–1835), Master-General 1801–06 and 1807–10.

Francis Rawdon Hastings, 2nd Earl of Moira (1754–1826), Master-General 1806–07 (not shown).

Henry Phipps, 1st Earl of Mulgrave (1755–1831), Master-General 1810–18.

The name of the founder and the date in Roman numerals were placed on the base ring, as were the quarter-sight scales. The weight in hundredweight, quarters and pounds, separated by dots, was marked on the top of the breech. Other marks, such as numbers on the trunnions, were normally manufacturers' serial numbers.

completed in December that year; and in April 1774 the first proofs of the Verbruggen cannon were all successful. The Board of Ordnance stopped contracting for brass ordnance to private companies.[113] Within four years the Verbruggens had completely renovated the Arsenal, and were producing guns of unsurpassed quality.

During the summer of 1770 the Royal Navy suffered from a large number of iron cannon produced by Carron of Falkirk bursting under training conditions. In response, Anthony Bacon devised a method of casting a solid iron barrel and then boring it out at his Merthyr Tydfil foundry in South Wales in 1773. On 27 January 1774, John Wilkinson patented an iron-boring mill that was certainly based upon those of Maritz in France or Holland. After a successful series of extraordinary proofs upon Bacon's solid-cast bored-out 18-pdr, he received an order on 10 May 1774 for 56× 32-pdr, 9× 24-pdr and 102× 9-pdr iron cannon, at £18 per ton. From 15 August 1776 all iron guns were bored from solid, because the metal produced was more durable and less likely to fail in proof.[114]

Woolwich produced the bulk of the army's requirements during the American Revolutionary War (1775–83), when the Verbruggens manufactured well over 500 pieces, including innovative new light guns. On 8 February 1775 the Verbruggens received the order to cast six of Colonel Pattison's M1775 Light 3-pdrs (*see* Chapter 6); and the next year Armstrong-Frederick designed the M1760 Light Common 6-pdr gun.[115] The production of the Congreve M1776 Light 3-pdr designed by Captain (later General Sir) William Congreve Snr (died 1814) was started on 24 January 1776. (He should not be confused with his eldest son, Sir William Congreve Jnr, Second Baronet, 1772–1828, who became Comptroller of the Royal Laboratory, and invented the Congreve rocket based upon the work of Desaguliers in 1770.) Later that year, Congreve experimented with two Light 6-pdrs cast by the Verbruggens, and a third boring machine was authorised. In November 1776 a number of French Gribeauval M1765 4-pdrs were bored out to 6-pdr under the instruction of General Desaguliers. In October 1781, Pieter Verbruggen (1735–86) succeeded his father as Master Founder at the Royal Brass Foundry. In 1782 the output of the Royal Brass Foundry was cut by 42%, and Pieter Verbruggen reported an urgent need for repairs to the brass foundry.[116]

Major (later Sir) Thomas Blomefield was appointed Inspector-General of Ordnance in 1780, and attempted to standardise all the guns in use by the army and navy into a unified system. However, the conservatism of the Board of Ordnance, coupled with the fact that the pieces of Desaguliers (and others) were no more than a decade old, frustrated this ambition, so Blomefield's weapons merely increased the number of types in use. Blomefield stipulated that guns that passed proof should be rejected if the weight did not match the specification or if they were not bored accurately enough. He recommended the use of bronze for the casting of gun tubes for mobile artillery, and iron for naval ordnance and fortress guns. Blomefield's gun tubes are characterised by their shallow muzzle flare and pronounced vent field. The iron Blomefield tubes had a breeching loop above the cascable.[117]

The Verbruggens had been producing sub-standard gun tubes and were accused of swindling the Ordnance Board. Blomefield failed more than 490 tubes in proof in his first year of office, and in 1783 he succeeded in having a royal warrant issued which totally reorganised the Royal Brass Foundry; this made him not only Inspector of the Royal Brass Foundry but also Inspector of Artillery for both the army and the Royal Navy. The following year Blomefield dismissed the Verbruggens, and John and Henry King were appointed Founders at Woolwich, being promoted to Master Founder and Assistant Founder respectively in 1797.

From March 1803 the examination, reproofing and withdrawal of older guns was undertaken with 'the utmost dispatch', although the Board of Ordnance did not order the return of all 'old pattern' guns until February 1810 and by 1811 these had been scrapped. At the same time private contractors were permitted to tender for the production of brass gun tubes while the Royal Brass Foundry was reorganised. Francis Kinman, who had premises at New Street Square and later Shoe Lane in London, was the main supplier from 1799 until 1825.

Samuel Walker (1742–92) – son of the founder – worked with Thomas Blomefield on designs for moulds and the technology of casting new gun tubes of the 'Blomefield System of Ordnance'. He introduced a new method of casting iron guns in 1786. The Walker company (est 1742) had foundries across Great Britain and even in Holland. From 1773 they were the most prolific suppliers to the Board of Ordnance, of 22,000 iron gun tubes, howitzers, mortars and mortar beds. They introduced their own pattern of 'gun boring and finishing mill' in May 1776, and six years later introduced steam-powered gun-boring machinery that enabled an increase in production.[118] It was estimated that the 32-pdr took 48 hours to drill, allowing for stoppages to re-sharpen the drill bit, and guns were produced in batches.[119] Walkers also had their own in-house proofing arsenal; and from 1787 they started patented casting of both iron artillery shot and lead shot.[120]

Henry Shrapnel – who designed the British version of spherical case shot that later bore his name – became Senior Assistant Inspector of Artillery in 1804. Upon the death of John King his son Cornelius succeeded him as Assistant Founder at Woolwich in 1813, and Henry became the Master Founder.

The American Revolutionary War (1775–83) had demonstrated the need for highly mobile, lightweight artillery. Such pieces were developed in the 1770s and 1780s to replace the heavy guns of the first half of the 18th century. Conversely, the poor performance of British artillery during the French Revolutionary Wars of the 1790s led the artillery reformers, such as Blomefield, to develop heavier artillery to match their continental counterparts. Although British artillery never benefited from a unified system like those introduced in Austria, France or Russia, Blomefield was heavily influenced by the Austrian system, and it was his guns that were the most common in service during the Napoleonic Wars.

BRITAIN

Guns

During the Napoleonic period the Royal Artillery used three generations of gun tubes mounted on as many different generations of carriage. Guns designed by Armstrong-Frederick in 1760, Desaguliers in 1776–8, and Belford and Blomefield from 1784 were in use simultaneously. In 1760, the M1732 Armstrong guns were re-designed by Sir Charles Frederick based upon that of St Remy, Belidor, Bernoulli and Vallière.

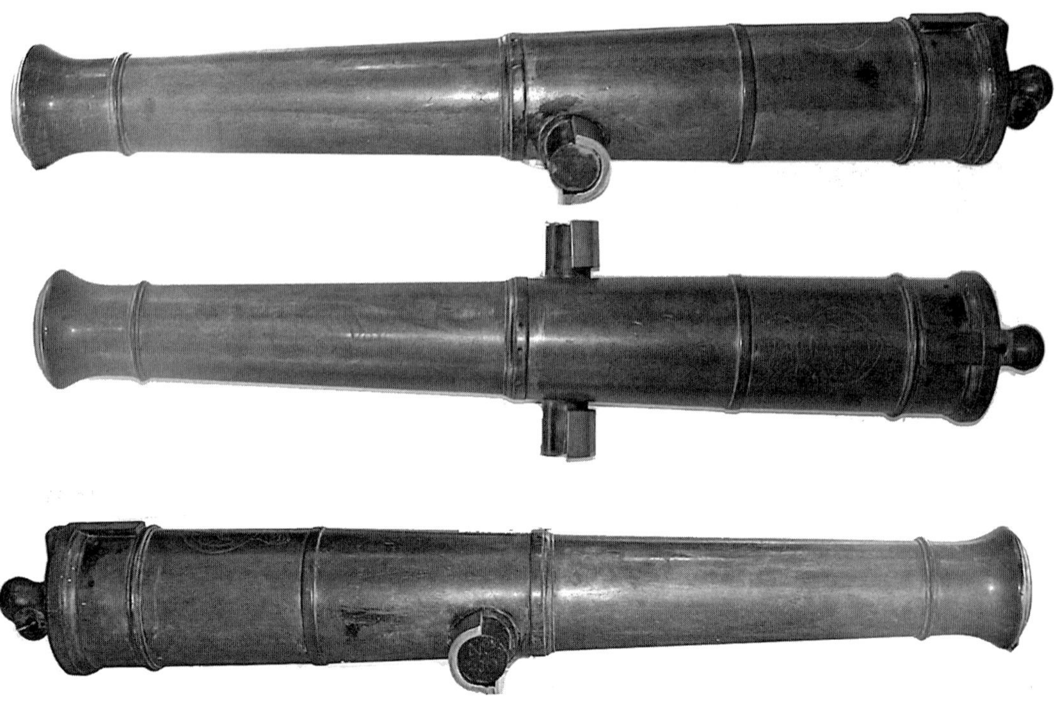

Blomefield M1788 Light 6-pdr gun tube now at the Royal Armouries in Leeds. (Courtesy the Board of Trustees of the Royal Armouries; photograph Stephen Summerfield)

From the surviving gun tubes it would appear that the Royal Artillery was re-equipped during the period 1792–1800. This was not surprising, given the major reduction and stagnation of the Royal Artillery following defeat in the American Revolutionary War, and the energetic reforms of Sir Thomas Blomefield.

One of the major figures of this period was General William Belford (1709–80), the son-in-law of Colonel Albert Borgard, who re-established The Warren, Woolwich. In 1747 he designed the elevating screw to replace the wooden wedge or quoin based on the French M1746 system. In *c.*1778 he designed his Light 6-pdr gun that was used by the Horse Artillery in 1780s.

General Thomas Desaguliers (1721–80) was the son of the French Huguenot émigré scientist Jean-Théophile Desaguliers (1683–1744). On 1 April 1748, Thomas was appointed Chief Firemaster (superintendent) of The Warren, Woolwich, and was responsible for the design of gun tubes and carriages. In 1765 he published *The Actual State of Artillery*.

From 1770 he experimented with rockets; in 1773 he designed wheels, and in 1776 the block-trail carriage that was introduced into the system of

Table 4.1: British ordnance used during the Napoleonic period

	Calibre	Tube length	Tube length	Tube length	Tube weight	Tube weight
Armstrong-Frederick M1760						
Light Common 6-pdr	93.2mm	4'6"	137cm	14 calibres	5cwt	255kg
Light Common 3-pdr	74.4mm	3'6"	107cm	14 calibres	2.6cwt	133kg
8 inch Howitzer	203mm	3'1"	94cm	5 calibres	12.75cwt	649kg
5½ inch Howitzer	142mm	2'7"	79cm	4.5 calibres	4.4cwt	208kg
4 2/5 inch Howitzer	110mm	1'10"	56cm	4 calibres	2.5cwt	127kg
Desaguliers M1778						
Desaguliers 12-pdr	117.4mm	7'6"	229cm	19 calibres	22.4cwt	1142kg
Long (Desaguliers) 6-pdr	93.2mm	7'	213cm	22 calibres	12cwt	611kg
Long (Desaguliers) 3-pdr	74.4mm	6'	183cm	24 calibres	6cwt	305kg
Belford M1780						
Belford 6-pdr	93.2mm	5'	152cm	16 calibres	5.5cwt	280kg
Blomefield M1788 (Designs and trials started in 1784)						
Light 24-pdr	131mm	6'3"	191cm	13 calibres	24cwt	1221kg
M1788 Medium 12-pdr	117.4mm	7'2"	218cm	17 calibres	18cwt	916kg
M1794 Light 12 pdr	117.4mm	5'6"	168cm	13 calibres	12cwt	611kg
Heavy 6-pdr	93.2mm	5'2.4"	158cm	17 calibres	9cwt	458kg
Light 6-pdr	93.2mm	5'	152cm	16 calibres	6cwt	305kg
Heavy 5½ inch Howitzer	143mm	3'2"	96cm	5 calibres	10cwt	509kg
Light 5½ inch Howitzer	143mm	2'2¾"	68cm	4 calibres	4cwt	204kg
Blomefield M1805						
M1805 Blomefield 9-pdr	106.7mm	6'	183cm	17 calibres	13.5cwt	687kg
Blomefield M1810 (Adye, 1813)						
M1810 Light 6-pdr	93.2mm	5'	152cm	13 calibres	10cwt	509kg
M1810 New Medium 6-pdr	93.2mm	5'6"	168cm	15 calibres	9cwt	458kg
M1810 Reduced 6-pdr	93.2mm	5'6"	168cm	15 calibres	8.1cwt	412kg

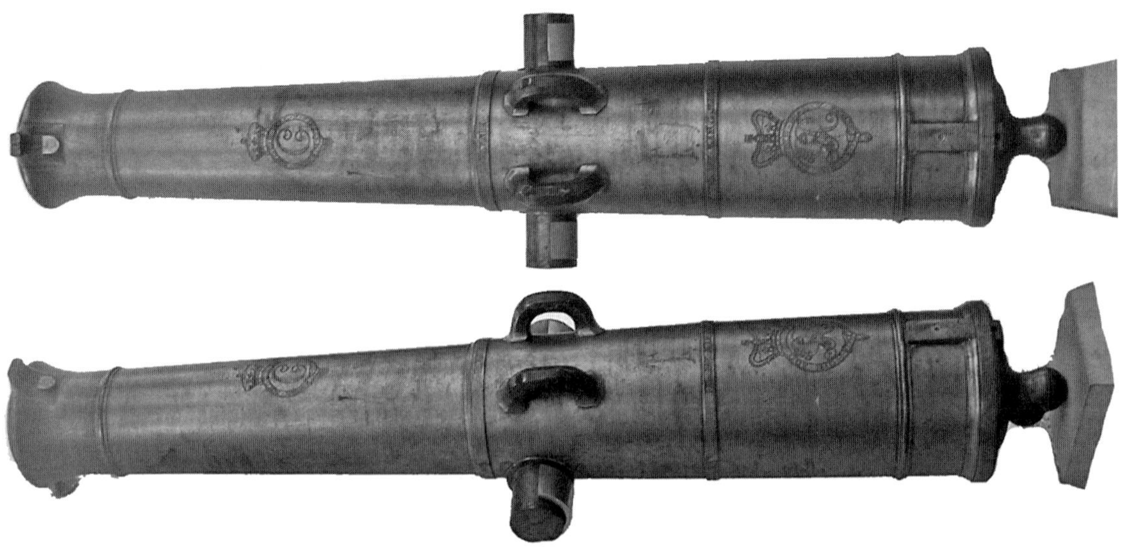

M1788 Blomefield Medium 12-pdr gun tube, cast in 1795 by John and Henry King. It is 218cm (7ft 2in) long and weighs 918kg (18cwt 9lb). (Courtesy the Board of Trustees of the Royal Armouries; photograph Stephen Summerfield)

ordnance in 1778. He was probably the first English artilleryman to apply science to the design of gun tubes, and was appointed a member of the Royal Society shortly before his death in March 1780.[121] His weapons, based on the work of Vallière, were tested at Woolwich in 1776, and the 'Desaguliers System' was published in 1778. Desaguliers' guns were about 20 calibres in length, so were accurate, but heavy.[122] To reduce weight and simplify construction most extraneous decoration was removed, only the 12-pdr having dolphins. The Long 3-pdr, together with the Belford 6-pdr, were chosen to arm the fledgling horse artillery in 1782 (this arm received its patent as the Royal Horse Artillery only in 1792). The Desaguliers Long 6-pdr was used in the Peninsula in 1808; it also armed Captain Mercer's RHA troop in 1815. Some were still in use as fortress pieces as late as 1825, but their length and weight made them impractical. Desaguliers' lasting legacy was his carriage designs.

Sir Thomas Blomefield (1744–1822) was appointed ADC to General Conway, Master-General of the Ordnance, and in 1771, in the rank of lieutenant RA, he was ADC to Lord Townshend. After serving in Canada in 1776–77 under Brigadier Phillips RA, in 1780 he was appointed Inspector-General of Ordnance. The problem of bursting guns was widespread, and after failing nearly 500 barrels in proof during his first year he applied himself to better ways of measuring strength and accuracy. He reorganised both the Royal Brass Foundry and the Powder Department from 1783, and with Samuel Walker (see above) he devised a new 'System of Ordnance'. His weapons were introduced for the Royal Artillery from 1784 and Royal Navy from 1788, and his system was officially adopted by both services in 1790. The production of Blomefield's gun tubes commenced in 1787, but due to initial problems with the system, official approval did not come until 1789 or 1790. The Board of Ordnance ordered a new Gun Establishment in late 1790/91. The Blomefield 'System' was only fully implemented *c.*1810/11.

Blomefield based his work on that of Leonhard Euler and the contemporary French designs of Jakob Manson. Blomefield attempted to make artillery more accurate and lighter in weight; he standardised the gun tube lengths to 17 calibres for the 'heavy' pieces – as used by the Austrian Liechtenstein system – and 13 calibres for the 'light' 12-pdr field gun and the 18-pdr and 24-pdr siege guns. Blomefield tubes remained in service with few changes until the 1850s, though their use was far from universal. (Interestingly, a surviving M1760 Light Common 3-pdr was cast by Francis Kinman of London in 1796, and was probably an attempt to reintroduce that calibre.)

The 6-pdr gun was the mainstay of British Napoleonic artillery; it used a 24oz (680g) charge, and had a calibre of 3.668in (93.2mm). The horse artillery used the 5ft-long M1780 Belford 6-pdr on the block-trail carriage, later supplemented by the Blomefield Light 6-pdr. The foot artillery used the heavier 7ft-long M1778 Desaguliers Long 6-pdr and the Blomefield Light 6-pdr on the bracket carriage. Both saw service in Flanders, the Peninsula and at Waterloo, and were still in service in 1827. The Blomefield Long 6-pdr was not in general use; the Blomefield Light 6-pdr was preferred for its superior mobility.

During the 1790s a new Blomefield 9-pdr gun, with a bore length of 17 calibres and weighing 627kg, was tested at Woolwich. It was in production by 1805, but was not in general service. The introduction of the 9-pdr was in the main a matter of economy; in March 1797 the Admiralty ordered the replacing of the iron 9-pdr long guns on the quarterdeck guns of ships of the line with Carronades (normally with 32-pdrs) except for those guns that would fire through the shrouds. In June 1799, this principal was extended to frigates (*see* Lavery, 1987 and Caruana, 1993). This left the Board of Ordnance with a surplus of several million rounds of ammunition. The bronze 9-pdr was disliked: it was heavier than the 6-pdr, needed more horses and a larger crew, and carried less ammunition. It was in fact heavier than the 'Light' Blomefield 12-pdr, and had a shorter range and less hitting-power. Gradually the trend in the British artillery turned towards heavier calibre guns, however, and despite its unpopularity the Blomefield 9-pdr became the 'standard' British field gun by 1815.

Blomefield designed three types of 12-pdr, each being specialised towards a particular function. The Heavy 12-pdr was used in garrison and siege work; the Medium was used in the field, and the Light for the horse artillery. Cockburn (1827) indicates that the Medium 12-pdr (18cwt) was introduced as early as 1788, and the Light 12-pdr in 1798–99 by the Royal Horse Artillery.[124] In 1792 trials were made at Goodwood of the Heavy and Medium Blomefield 12-pdrs against the older weapons of their class. A letter dated 14 February 1794, states that the Medium 12-pdr (18cwt) was to be adopted 'to complete the Park of Artillery'. As the Napoleonic Wars progressed the Medium 12-pdr became the sole weapon of its class; examples exist at the Royal Armouries Museum, Leeds, and one in Montreal has its original block-trail carriage.

Interestingly, the 13-calibre Blomefield Light 12-pdr, 5ft long and weighing 12cwt, was 4cwt (204kg) heavier than its predecessor designed by Armstrong-Frederick. The introduction of the 12-pdr gun to the British army was due to Prussian influence, and to tactical papers by Major William Collier published between 1780 and 1791. The British used both the Light and Medium Blomefield 12-pdrs in field batteries in the Flanders campaign 1794–95 and the Egyptian expedition of 1800, and in the early half of the Peninsular War, between 1808 and 1810.

Howitzers

The M1760 howitzer carriage was 10ft (303cm) long, and William Congreve Snr extended this by 12in in his M1788 Congreve carriage. The howitzer bracket carriage was heavily reinforced with iron strapping. In 1792, Congreve described the Heavy 5½in or 'Royal' howitzer as being the more effective of the two howitzers in use, and argued for the suppression of the 4⅖in (110mm) howitzer due to its inaccuracy at long ranges and lack of hitting-power.

Blomefield designed four models of bronze howitzers to complement his artillery reforms of 1780: 10in, 8in, Heavy 5½in, and Light 5½in calibre with a conical chamber. The 8in and 10in howitzers were considered the mainstay of the siege train.[125] The 8in howitzer was used alongside the 12-pdr gun in foot artillery brigades until 1795.

The Heavy 5½in was over twice the weight of the Light 5½in howitzer (509kg compared to 241kg), but was only 16cm longer. The effective range of both pieces was similar, despite their differences in size: the Heavy 5½in had an effective range of 945m, and the Light of 1015m. Interestingly, both were fired using a 1lb powder charge. They had a maximum elevation of 12 degrees, giving a maximum range of 1,290m for the Light 5½in weapon and 1570m for the Heavy (according to range tables dating from 1820). British howitzers were generally fired at a low trajectory, and shells were bounced or ricocheted on to the target rather like roundshot.

Both models of howitzer initially used the double-bracket carriage and, when limbered, were pulled by four horses. A version of the Desaguliers block-trail carriage was designed for the 5½in howitzer in 1788 and introduced in 1792. Blomefield's new howitzers were considerably smaller and hence more mobile then their predecessors, and were issued to some field batteries. The Light 5½in model was designed for the horse artillery, but proved to be less effective than the Heavy 5½in and was soon phased out. Generally there was one howitzer per battery; the artillery officers of most Continental armies considered that a single howitzer was of very little use, and that two were the absolute minimum number needed.

In 1811, the Foot Artillery transferred their heavy 5½in howitzers to replace their light 5½in howitzers. The Foot Artillery received iron 5½in howitzers on bracket trails. The artillery officer Alexander Dickson thought that the iron howitzer would 'answer very well...[it] is an excellent thing but it wants a better carriage'.[126] However, the existing shells were too large for the iron howitzers so they had to be destroyed.[127]

The ammunition allocation of March 1813 indicates the use of the block-trail and the Desaguliers articulated limber-wagon for the howitzers. In 1813, the howitzer carriage of Ross's Troop RHA 'broke to pieces', and a captured French 24-pdr howitzer carriage was used instead.

Foot Artillery Gun Carriages

From the 17th century the Board of Ordnance employed a master carpenter to oversee the manufacture of carriages in government workshops or by private contractors. In 1728, New Carriage Square was laid out for the construction of gun carriages, probably to designs by Sir John Vanbrugh or Nicholas Hawksmoor. After the burning down of the old carriage buildings in 1802, the Royal Carriage Department's factory would rise over the next three years to become one of the largest engineering workshops in the world, with steam-powered lathes and wood-planing machines installed by Joseph Bramah (1748–1814).[128] In 1805 the Warren at Woolwich was renamed the Royal Arsenal on the suggestion of King George III, and the Grand Stores were built between 1805 and 1814. In 1802–04 convict labour enclosed the site with a high wall, reclaimed additional marshland and built the river wall. In 1809 steam-powered sawmills were built by the Frenchman Marc Isambard Brunel (1769–1849).

In 1803 the Royal Carriage Department was established at Woolwich to standardise design and centralise manufacture under its Inspector, Major-General Edward Fage, who held the post until his death on 3 September 1809. He was succeeded by Colonel (Major-General in 1811) William Cuppage (1756–1832), who died in post; Cuppage designed mountain guns and standardised carriage designs. The post of Second Inspector of the Royal Carriage Department was held several times between 1805 and 1822 by Lieutenant-Colonel Frederick Williams (1768–1846).

The Royal Artillery used two principal types of gun carriage: the Desaguliers block-trail and the (double-) bracket or travelling carriage. As with their ordnance, the Royal Artillery used several generations and types of bracket carriages: the M1760 Muller, M1776 Congreve and M1797 Butler carriages. The principal aim of designs was to make the field artillery lighter and therefore mobile; little work appears to have been done in relation to siege guns and heavy howitzers, which retained Muller carriages until after 1810, when new siege guns were mounted on the block-trail.

M1760 Muller Carriages

Johannes (John) Muller's carriage designs of the Seven Years War were based on his experiences of the War of the Austrian Succession being heavily influenced by the Swedish carriage adopted by the Prussian and the French (qv M1740 Brocard Carriage).[129] He believed that the carriages in use were too heavy and the guns upon them even more so. Conservatism in the Royal Artillery meant that many of his reforms were blocked, until he sought the assistance of the Duke of Cumberland, the victor of Culloden and the brother of King George II;

(Top) Armstrong-Frederick M1760 4⅖in howitzer on a Müller carriage, painted with red lead and with black metalwork. (Bottom) Armstrong-Frederick M1760 8in howitzer on a Müller carriage, painted light grey with black metalwork.

thereafter his proposals were trialled and adopted. He shortened gun carriages, and replaced elevation by means of coins de mire with the elevating screw. By 1780 he was advocating large wheels of at least 5ft diameter, and reformed carriage designs. However, he retained single draft for artillery, and preferred iron to brass gun tubes.[130]

M1776 Congreve Carriages

William Congreve Snr (d.1814) was initially in December 1775, the Inspector of Military Machines and Carriages in America, and two years later appointed Superintendent of Military Machines at Woolwich, through both his own technical innovations under patronage from the Marquis Townshend and other senior officers, including Desaguliers. He was responsible for the design of all artillery vehicles and rolling stock, and it was under his supervision that many of the ideas of Muller, Desaguliers and his own innovations were implemented. Later he became Comptroller of the Royal Laboratory in Woolwich and also headed the artillery school that taught drill and tactics to artillery officers.

In 1775, the Royal Artillery found itself preparing for a possible war in America; despite the reforming zeal of Muller in 1758 urging the construction of light guns and carriages, the army still used large, heavy and relatively immobile guns.[131] The urgency of the situation was clearly realised, since the returns from the Ordnance Department for 1776–77 indicate that the Royal Artillery was re-armed during the two years from 1775.[132]

In 1774 the Pattison 3-pdr with its own specially designed carriage was introduced, followed by the Townshend 3-pdr in 1775; the M1776 Congreve 3-pdr was first ordered in January 1776 'for the American Service'.[133] Howitzers, heavy field guns (Heavy 6-pdr and 12-pdr) and siege guns retained their Muller carriages. The M1776 Congreve carriage was designed to mount the Light Common 6-pdr (4ft 6in) in service from 1760, and the Light Common 3-pdr (3ft 6in) in service from 1766.[134] By mid-August 1776 a total of 73 Congreve M1776 Light 3-pdrs had been produced, as well as 24-pdrs and Desaguliers 6-pdrs.[135] The new 3- and 6-pdr gun tubes were mounted on the M1776 bracket carriage designed by William Congreve Snr were modifications within an existing system of rolling stock and tubes.[136]

In December 1776, Lord Townshend, Master-General of the Ordnance, ordered the Light 6-pdr and Heavy 3-pdr to be mounted on the M1776 Congreve carriage because it had larger wheels than the M1760 Muller, permitted the fitting of quarter-

Blomefield M1798 Heavy 5½in howitzer

This Blomefield M1798 Heavy 5½in howitzer was cast in 1813 by John and Henry King, as engraved on the base ring. It is 96cm long and weighs 500kg . The royal cypher of King George III can be seen on the chase, and the monogram of the Master-General of the Ordnance, the Earl of Mulgrave, between the trunnions. (Courtesy the Trustees of the RAHT; photograph Stephen Summerfield)

sights and use of a more efficient limber.[137] The old side-lockers of the carriage were replaced with removable lockers, and the same wheels were used for the gun carriage and limber.

The basis of the Congreve carriage and limber design was to have to hand all the equipment, ammunition, tools and other material required to maintain and serve the gun. This avoided having a large logistic train, so that each piece was self-sufficient in the field. In Congreve's list of equipment carried with each gun were rope for the gyn, blocks and tackle, sheepskin, hammers and entrenching tools.[138] In 1793, Captain Richard Bogue wrote in his notebook that the side-lockers were to be used for 'common travelling when no enemy is suspected and also when the wagon cannot be sent with it.'[139] This indicates that the side-lockers were removed in action; when the boxes were removed, there was sufficient space for four gunners to ride on the carriage.[140]

The limber and gun carriage wheels were standardised on a universal iron axle, so that if a gun wheel broke it could be replaced with a limber wheel. The wheels, of 4ft 6in (137cm) diameter, were based on the work of Desaguliers; they made the carriage easier to draw and more manoeuvrable over rough or soft ground.[141] Congreve Snr introduced a new elevating system that allowed the piece to fire at 16.5 degrees, twice the elevation of its predecessor.[142] The carriage was lengthened for guns from 94in to 104in (239–264cm) and for howitzers to 132in (11ft, or 335cm).

These revised carriages were an instant success with Royal Artillery officers in the field in North

The Müller carriage of this M1760 Armstrong-Frederick Light Common 3-pdr gun, now in New Orleans, is painted light blue (Prussian Blue and White Lead) with black metalwork. (Anthony Dawson)

America, but not so with the higher ranks of the artillery. In 1777, artillery officers on campaign were calling for the Congreve light gun and carriage applications. Captain Cleveland had already replaced his field guns with the Congreve pattern 6-pdr, despite strong objections from the military establishment. Captain Stephelin was indenting for 'necessary stores for raising Captain Congreve's guns over ditches etc.' Acceptance of Congreve's innovations is evidenced in a report that 'eight of Captain Congreve's Light 3-pdr crossed the Delaware' on 13 March 1778. The Light Carriage was 'an early result of the War of Independence, born of difficulties experienced in moving cumbersome guns over rough roadless terrains and water obstacles.'

Armstrong-Frederick M1760 Light Common 6-pdr on M1776 Congreve carriage painted light grey with black metalwork. (Anthony Dawson)

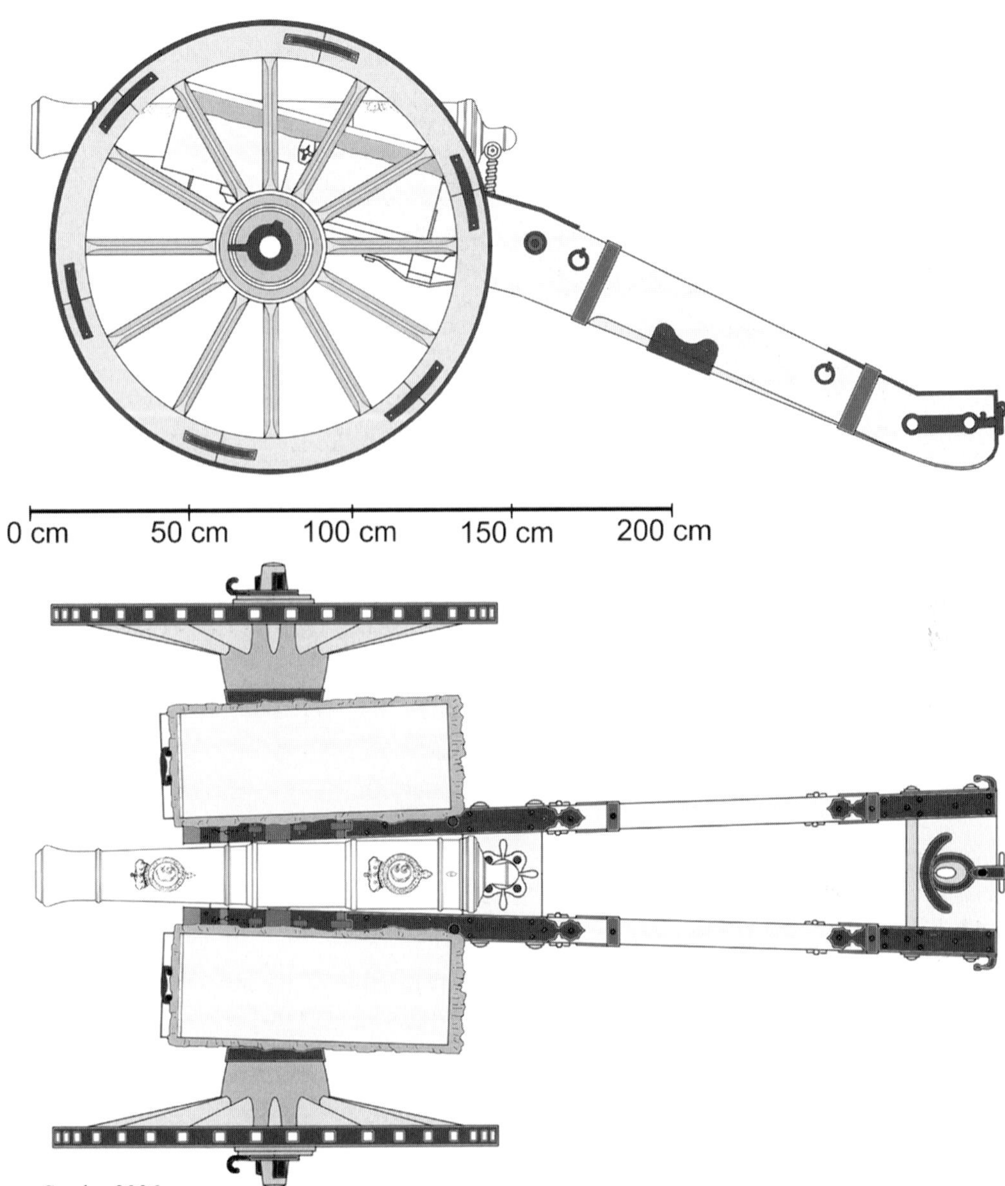

Norman Swales 2006

The British M1776 Congreve bracket carriage. (After Rudyerd, 1793)

The Light Common 6-pdr was superseded in about 1790 by the Belford 6-pdr.[143] Due to human error, the Congreve carriages prepared for the Flanders campaign in 1795 were built with the old pre-1776 elevation system.[144] The gun carriage was also altered to allow for the fitting of quarter-sights.[145]

M1788 Richmond System

In 1788 the Duke of Richmond, Master-General of the Ordnance, ordered that the Congreve system of light carriages be 'extended' to howitzers and heavy field guns, with 5ft carriage and limber wheels – as recommended by Congreve in 1776 – on the

Table 4.2: Guns mounted on the M1776/M1788 Congreve carriage

	Date mounted
M1775 Townshend Light Infantry 3-pdr	1775
M1775 Congreve Light 3-pdr	1775
M1760 Light common 6-pdr	1776
M1778 Long 3-pdr (Desaguliers)	1776
M1778 Long 6-pdr (Desaguliers)	1788
M1760 4⅖in (Coehorn) Howitzer	1788
M1788 5½in (Royal) Howitzer	1788

iron axle in place of the wooden one.[146] The 6-pdr mounted on the Congreve carriage in 1788 was the Desaguliers Long 6-pdr.[147]

The 4⅖in (Coehorn) howitzer and the 5½in (Royal) howitzer – presumably the Blomefield pattern – were mounted on the M1788 Congreve bracket carriage. This was a great improvement over the M1760 Muller; the howitzer carriage could be converted for vertical fire by removing the centre transom.[148] The carriage for the 12-pdr could also be altered using a similar method so that the piece could be fired at elevations up to 30 degrees.[149] Siege guns and heavy howitzers were still mounted on Muller carriages, partially replaced in 1812 by block-trails.

M1797 Butler Carriage

Despite the Congreve carriage serving well in America (1776–83) and Flanders (1795), in 1797 the 6-pdr received the Butler gun carriage.[150] The howitzers and 3-pdr retained the Congreve carriage. Despite being deemed obsolete in Britain, the Congreve carriage and the guns it mounted were still in use as late as 1811 in colonial service.[151] In 1800, battalion – i.e. foot – artillery (6-pdrs) were equipped with light travelling carriages; Adye describes them in 1802, and James in 1805.[152]

During late 1796 the 'Field Officers and Colonels of the Royal Artillery in Committee' studied various proposals for the arming and equipping of the battalion artillery, following the adoption of the

Sadler's 'War Chariot', as depicted by Rowlandson. This was designed to keep up with the cavalry, with two gunners firing its two 3-pdr guns in any direction. (Authors' collection)

Table 4.3: Royal Horse Artillery equipment, 1792

	Horses	Drivers
Two 5½in or Royal Howitzer	12	6
Two Howitzer wagons	12	
Two 3 pdr Desaguliers	12	6
Two wagons	12	6
Two Belford 6-pdr (5 foot) mounted on 3-pdr carriages	12	6
Two wagons	12	6
One forge cart	3	1
One wagon for artificers stores	3	1

Table 4.4: **Arming of the Horse Artillery (1779–1792) and Royal Horse Artillery (1793–1815)**
(The Bedford 6-pdr and Desaguliers Long 3-pdr gradually supplemented by Blomefield 6- and 9-pdrs. [Caruana (1980a), Duncan (1879), Frazer (1859), Leslie (1908) plus Blomefield, Congreve and the Dickson Papers (RAHT)].)

	Light 12-pdr	9-pdr	6-pdr	Long 3-pdr	5½ inch Howitzer
1779–1788	–	–		4	0 or 2
1788–1793	–	–	2	2	2
1794	–	–	4	2	2
1798–1801	2	–	4	–	2
1804	2	–	2	–	2
1805–9	–	–	4	–	2
1810	–	–	5	–	1
1811	–	–	6	–	–
1811	–	4	–	–	–
Oct 1813	–	–	6	–	0
Oct 1813	–	6	–	–	–
1815	–	–	5	–	1
1815	–	5	–	–	1
1815	–	4	–	–	2
1815	–	–	–	–	6
1816 (France)	–	–	4	–	–
(home)	–	–	2	–	–

Desaguliers block-trail for the Royal Horse Artillery. Of the schemes proposed, that of Major James Butler RHA was adopted on 7 March 1797.[153] Butler had worked in 1791–93 on tactics, developing new manoeuvres for the battalion artillery.[154] The Butler carriage utilised many of the standard parts of the Desaguliers block-trail. All gun and howitzer carriage wheels were to be 60in (152cm), and the limber wheels 56in (142cm) in diameter. A universal iron axle was used, and the capsquares were 'on the French principal'.[155] The carriage was parallel; the trail end was rounded off to allow articulation with the limber, and the lunette ring projected beyond the trail end. The 6-pdr carriage was 210cm long, 60cm wide at the trail end, and weighed 595kg.[156] Elevation was as on the Congreve carriage.

The proposed adoption of the Butler carriage resulted in a flurry of indignant correspondence between Congreve, the Board of Ordnance, and the 'Field Officers and Colonels in Committee'.[157] Congreve stated that not enough time had been given to studying the new carriage, and that the decision

Table 4.5: Royal Horse Artillery equipment and horses, 1813 (Nafziger, 1983)
(Note: the 6-pdr troop had 108 draft horses, 6× mules and 71× riding horses; the 9-pdr troop differed in having 120× draft horses.)

	6-pdr Troop	9-pdr Troop
5 gun limbers	30 draft horses	40 draft horses
1 Howitzer limber	6 draft horses	8 draft horses
9× 6-horse ammunition wagons	54 draft horses	54 draft horses
1× 6-horse spare wheel carriage	6 draft horses	6 draft horses
1× 4-horse forge wagon	4 draft horses	4 draft horses
1× 4-horse curricle cart	4 draft horses	4 draft horses
1× 4-horse baggage wagon	4 draft horses	4 draft horses
Officers and surgeon	6 horses	6 horses
Staff sergeants	2 horses	2 horses
Sergeants, corporals, bombardiers	12 horses	12 horses
Mounted gunners	48 horses	48 horses
Farrier and smith	2 horses	2 horses
Collar maker	1 horse	1 horse
Baggage mules	6	6
Total no. of horses and mules	185	197

to adopt it was purely arbitrary.[158] Furthermore, he justifiably claimed that his system had stood the test of actual service, and had won the approbation of two Masters-General and of officers who had used the equipment on campaign, whereas adopting an untested system in wartime was dangerous.

Adye in 1802 noted that the Long 12-pdr, the Light 6-pdr and the Royal (5½in) howitzer were mounted on 'light travelling carriages' i.e. bracket carriages. He further noted that the Butler proposals in regard to wheels, at least, had been adopted: 'All horse artillery carriages, limbers, Long 6-pdr and Long 3-pdr and limbers; carriages of 6-pdr battalion guns and Light 5½in howitzers' used the 5ft diameter wheel. The smaller wheel of 4ft 8in was used for the 'limbers to Light 6-pdr and 5½in howitzers, Medium 12-pdr carriages and limbers.'[159]

On 31 March 1813, it was instructed that new axles and wheels were to be produced, with the tyres bolted and screwed in place instead of nailed, so that the 'felloes would be protected from damage since the nails when driven home had a tendency to split them'.[160] A revised list of wheel types appeared in Adye (1813).[161] New, stronger wheels of Congreve's construction were ordered in 1814, no doubt due to the wheels being 'shook all to pieces' in the Peninsula.[162] Colonel William Robe RA noted in September 1813 a 'very favourable report on the wheels made in the Portuguese manner and they seem to be aware of the advantages gained from that mode'. Scharnhorst confirms the use of the bracket carriage, and also the wheel sizes listed by Adye.[163] Indeed, Scharnhorst in 1806 shows the Butler-pattern carriage being used alongside the M1764 Flanders wagon and the M1797 Congreve limber.

Out of the 52 guns in the Peninsula with the battalion (foot) artillery in 1808, two Light 5½in howitzers and four Light 3-pdrs were of old pattern, which in the words of William Robe made them 'totally inapplicable to the service'. The howitzers were used to form a reserve brigade, and the four 3-pdrs were remounted 'on the present type'; their limbers were converted to double-draft. All the 'old pattern' support rolling stock was considered a

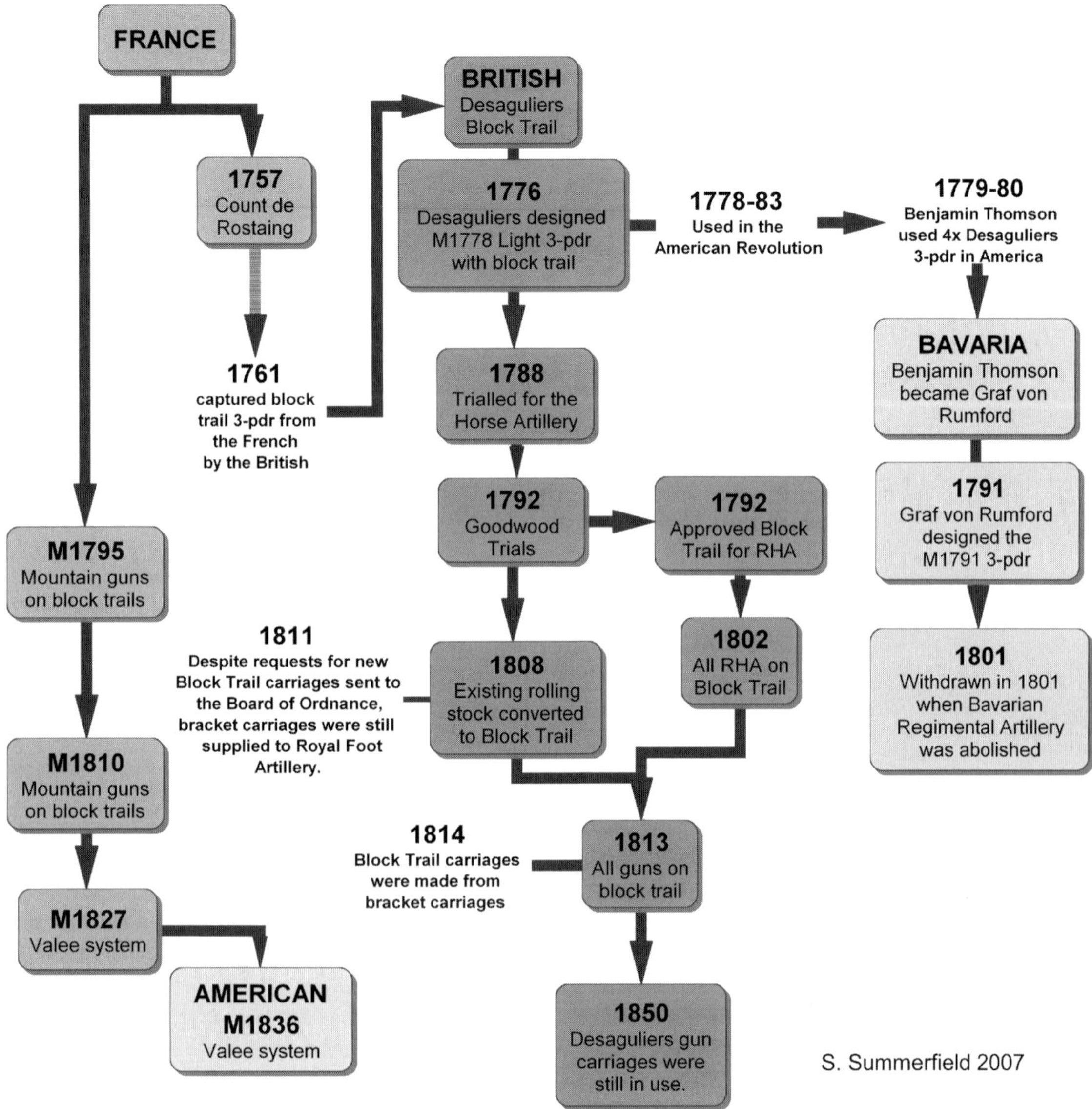

Chart showing evolution of the block trail. Note that British foot artillery were only completely converted to the block trail in 1814, more than twenty years after the Royal Horse Artillery.

'deadweight' and was to be replaced with the new pattern equipment.[164]

By 1814, it is possible that the Desaguliers block-trail for both guns and bronze howitzers was in universal use, with the bracket carriage being retained by the siege guns and the iron 5½in howitzers (introduced in 1813). That the bracket carriage was still manufactured, however, is shown by the returns from Major-General George Glasgow in Canada, who noted in 1811 that despite requesting block-trail carriages, Woolwich was sending him bracket carriages. Of the 33 Light 6-pdrs in service in North America, according to the ordnance returns at least one-quarter were the M1760 Light Common 6-pdrs of 4ft 6in (137cm), mounted on bracketcarriages that had been declared obsolete elsewhere.[165]

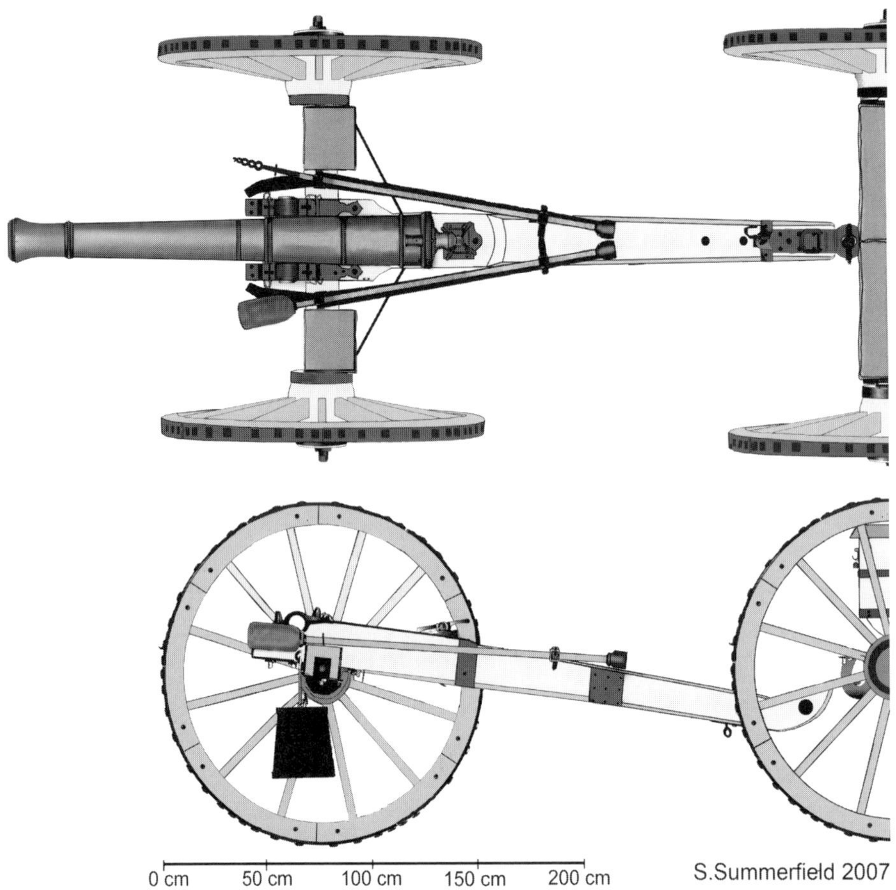

Desaguliers M1778 Long 3-pdr as used by the Royal Horse Artillery. (After a drawing by William Congreve Snr)

Adye's *Pocket Gunner* of 1813 lists all the foot artillery guns as being mounted on 'New Pattern' carriages, although that year the only pieces explicitly listed as being on the block-trail type were the 3-pdr and Light 6-pdr. The phasing-out of the bracket carriage by this date is borne out by the fact that in March 1814 the Ordnance Storekeeper at Quebec was requested to provide six double-bracket carriages for breaking up so as to recycle the iron work, 'to make an equal number of block-trail gun carriages to replace them for the Service of the Field Train Department'.[166]

Royal Horse Artillery Ordnance

William Belford designed the M1780 Belford 6-pdr gun, carrying out experiments during 1778 and trials at Winchester in August–September 1780.[167] An example of the Belford Light 6-pdr gun still survives at Woolwich, cast by Francis Kinman in London in 1793.

Colonel Griffiths Williams, who commanded the Park of the Royal Artillery in 1777–80, was convinced by his service in America of the need for mobile artillery. He had experiment with Horse Artillery in America, and designed the Williams Light 6-pdr gun for use by the horse artillery, and a system of horse artillery utilising his 6-pdr mounted on a 'light Flemish curricle carriage'. These were trialled during 1781–82 against the Desaguliers system of rolling stock for equipping an embryonic horse artillery brigade, but the Desaguliers equipment was judged superior. (During the late 1790s there was a further impractical scheme for horse artillery, sponsored by a unit of artillery volunteers in London who used a 'war chariot' – effectively a four-wheeled coach with a 3-pdr gun mounted on a traversing-platform on its roof!)

In 1788, Congreve suggested that a horse artillery brigade should consist of 4× Long 3-pdr Desaguliers and 2× Royal howitzers; two of the 3-pdrs were subsequently replaced by Belford 6-pdrs.

In August 1792 trials took place at Goodwood to examine options for the re-arming of the horse artillery. Here the Blomefield Medium and Light 12-pdrs, the Desaguliers Long 3-pdr, the Belford 6-pdr and the Light 5½in howitzer were mounted on block-trail carriages. The conclusion was to equip each troop with two Light 5½in howitzers, two Desaguliers Long 3-pdrs and two Belford Light 6-pdrs, on the Desaguliers block-trail. Lieutenant-Colonel Augustus Frazer confirms this establishment.[168] Four gunners travelled on the gun, with the NCO and one supernumerary mounted on horses; the horses were held by a driver when the gun was in action.

The Long 3-pdr gun had a similar range to the Light 6-pdr, and was issued with a modified canister round of 48 balls as opposed to the usual 36. It was also found that the Long 3-pdr could do more execution with case-shot than a Light 6-pdr; indeed, at close range the Long 3-pdr was more effective than the Light 6-pdr with both canister and round-shot, which made it admirably suitable for the horse artillery. Experiments also showed that the Long 3-pdr gun could be loaded and fired eight times in a minute; due to the target being obscured by smoke this rate of fire was highly inaccurate, but still impressive.[169]

Contemporary European thinking, particularly in Prussia, also advocated the use of a Long 3-pdr gun for horse artillery. An anonymous review of contemporary horse artillery published in 1798 noted that 'These guns have, as commonly known, the same range, and a 3-pdr cannonball has the same results against humans and horses as a 6-pdr ball. Not taking in account the advantage there is when transporting the ammunition for the 3-pdr, while at least a third more can be transported at the same weight.' The Long 6-pdr was not more effective than a 12-pdr at close range, but due to its smaller size and lighter ammunition was more mobile and therefore applicable to horse artillery work.

The number of guns per troop was augmented to eight from 1794 until 1804, when it was again reduced to six.[170] On 28 June 1798, the Duke of York – commander-in-chief of the army – ordered that two Light 12-pdr guns be attached to each troop of Royal Horse Artillery. In 1801, General Lawson recommended that the horse artillery receive heavier pieces due to the Long 3-pdr and Light 6-pdr being considerably outclassed by the French horse artillery armed with 8-pdrs and 6.4in howitzers. By 1802 a troop of RHA were armed with two 'Light' 12-pdrs, two 'Light' 6-pdrs and two 5½in howitzers.

In 1808 the troop was equipped with four Light 6-pdrs and two 5½in howitzers, which changed by 1810 to five 6-pdrs and one howitzer.

The two RHA troops (A and I) in the Peninsula mustered only ten guns between them (eight Light 6-pdrs and two Royal howitzers during 1809). By 1811 there were four troops (A, D, E and I) each armed with six Light 6-pdrs. In 1811 the King's German Artillery horse brigades received 9-pdrs as their armament.[171] In September 1813, A (Ross)'s Troop RHA had five Light 6-pdrs and a 5½in howitzer; the troops of F (Smith) and K (Ramsey) had two Long 6-pdrs, three Light 6-pdrs and a heavy 5½in howitzer between them. The 9-pdr was initially introduced to the Foot Artillery, and G (Frazer)'s Troop RHA was issued them in October 1813, mounted on 6-pdr block-trail carriages.[172] For the numbers of vehicles and horses per troop, *see* Table 4.5.[173]

Desaguliers System

General Thomas Desaguliers designed a complete system of artillery of gun tubes, carriages and rolling stock. His tubes were based on those of the French and were tested at Woolwich in 1776, and his 'system' was published in 1778. Desaguliers died two years later; his artillery system of guns and carriages was adopted, but the gun designs were rapidly superseded by the work of Sir Thomas Blomefield in 1790. Desaguliers, like Vallière, attempted to spread the weight of the gun tube and increase the range and accuracy of the weapon by increasing the length of

Blomefield M1794 Light 12-pdr

A Blomefield M1794 Light 12-pdr of 115mm calibre, weighing 616kg and measuring 5ft (1.53m) long. This example, cast by John and Henry King, was proved on 16 March 1798. The block trail is a reproduction made in 1986 based upon the drawings created by the Royal Carriage Department in the 1860s, and so may differ in details from the original carriage. (Courtesy the Board of Trustees of the Royal Armouries; photograph Stephen Summerfield)

the tube. His system was based on a standardised set of four calibres with tubes of 20 calibres in length. Desaguliers lightened the gun tubes and simplified their construction by using thinner tube walls than the previous designs of Armstrong and Armstrong-Frederick and removing extraneous decoration; the dolphins were removed from the smaller calibres.

Desaguliers designed a light block-trail carriage for the Long 3-pdr in *c.*1775, so that it could be used with cavalry in the Prussian manner; these saw service in America from 1776. According to Congreve, Desaguliers' carriage design was based upon a French field gun (probably a M1757 Rostaing 3-pdr) captured on Martinique in 1761 that had a primitive block-trail. The block-trail was introduced for service for the Desaguliers Long 3-pdr and Light 6-pdr in 1776.

William Congreve Snr was ordered by Lord Amherst in 1779 to meet Mr Elliot (the envoy to Prussia) to hear his propositions for forming a corps of artillery for service with cavalry. Congreve stated that he 'waited upon Mr Elliott, and found that Mr Elliot had only an imperfect knowledge of the Prussian artillery attached to the cavalry; upon which Captain Congreve informed Mr Elliott that General Desaguliers had contrived some Long 3-pdr carriages for service of the cavalry, and advised him to wait upon General Desaguliers.'[174]

The Desaguliers 3-pdr carriages were judged 'well adapted for the service proposed', and were adopted. The result of this meeting was that

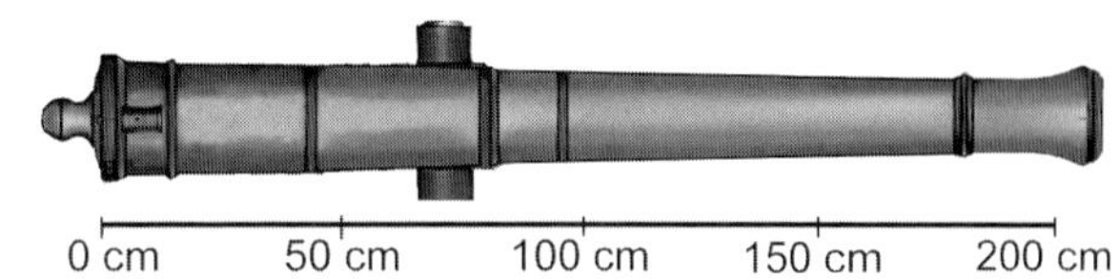

M1778 Desaguliers Long 6-pdr on an M1788 Congreve carriage. (After a drawing by William Congreve Snr)

Desaguliers ordered Congreve to compile a series of manoeuvres for the cavalry artillery, and 'to think whether any addition might be made to their carriages, to enable them to keep up with the cavalry in every situation.'[175] By his own account Congreve was not the designer of the block trail and made only some 'trifling additions' to the design of the block-trail which were 'much approved' by Desaguliers. These consisted of the Desaguliers block-trail 'carrying the same apparatus as the Light 6-pdr, to enable them to follow Troopers when dismounted to dislodge infantry from strong ground'.[176]

The Light 12-pdr, Long 6-pdr and both howitzers were on bracket carriages; the Long 3-pdr and 12-pdr of Desaguliers were on the block-trail and the Light Infantry 3-pdr on the Townshend carriage in 1780 and 1792. The 3-pdr on Desaguliers' block-trail carriage and limber weighed 748kg and the 3-pdr Townshend gun, carriage and limber weighed just 437kg.[177]

Various trials were run by Congreve in August 1779 to 'Ascertain the Degree of Expedition that Light 6-pdr upon New Pattern Carriages, with their full proportion of ammunition and other stores could travel with three horses...' At the end of these trials Congreve concluded that the new pattern gun and carriage, with all its equipment and a three-horse team, could travel at 3.5mph (5.7km/h) for thirty miles.[178]

From December 1781 to January 1782, Captain Congreve and Major Benjamin Stephelin carried out trials on Desaguliers' equipment. Stephelin used six horses to draw the limber with gun attached and two horses drew the spare limber; six artillerymen rode on the vehicles, which carried 100 rounds of ammunition. The trials concluded in March 1782 that the Desaguliers system of field artillery was highly advantageous for battalion or cavalry artillery. Congreve concluded that the Desaguliers block-trail was superior to the double-bracket design due to its being more manoeuvrable and carrying more ammunition and equipment.[179]

The Duke of Richmond, Master-General of the Ordnance, commissioned the Desaguliers system of carriages and rolling stock in 1788.[180] William

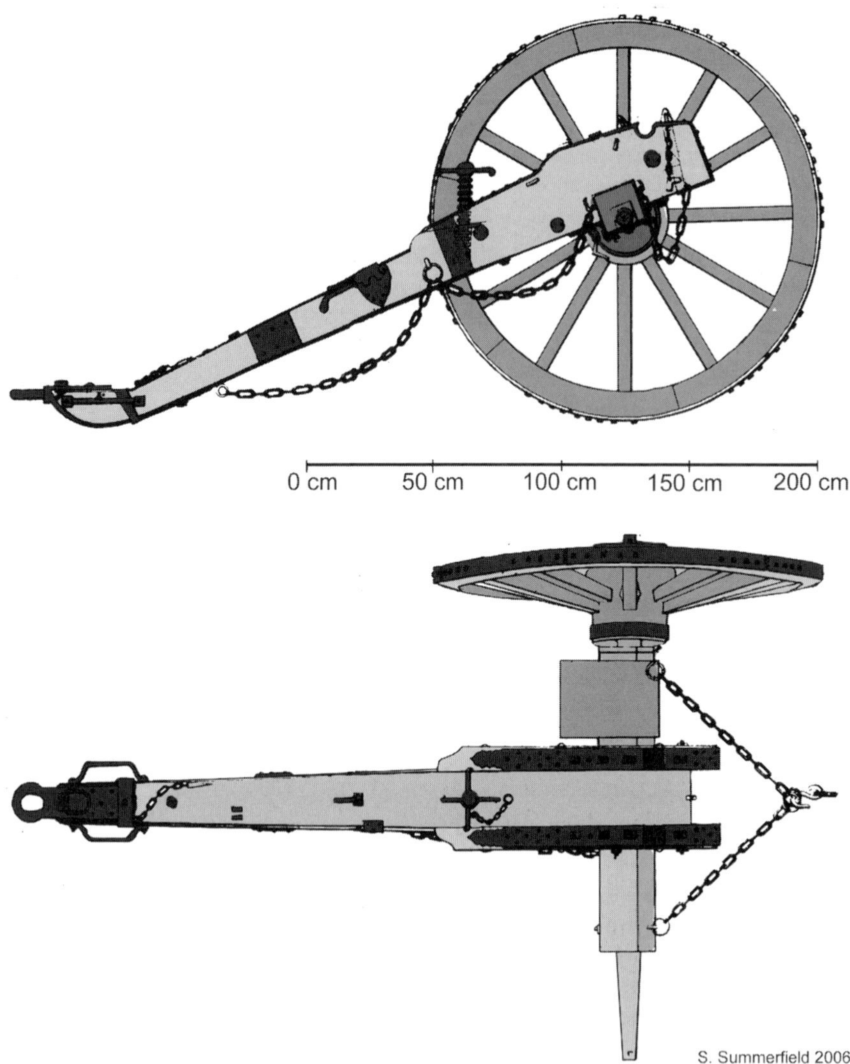

Desaguliers block-trail carriage, after a German drawing by Jacobi (1831) – probably of equipment supplied to the Prussian army. The different elevating system operated under the backplate of the gun tube, permitting tubes other than the 5ft Light 6-pdr Blomefield to be used on this carriage.

Congreve Snr wrote: 'In the year 1788, I had the honour of being employed to construct some wagons and to mount guns and howitzers upon Desaguliers' Principle; also to carry out a comparative view of the expense between General Desaguliers' Principle and Colonel Williams' System of horse artillery.[181] The Willliams system of 'Flemish Curricle Carriage' – probably a galloper gun – was considered inferior, and abandoned.[182]

The Duke of Richmond ordered 'the wheels and axle-trees of the gun carriage and its limber of the same diameter and strength as those of the ammunition wagons, and that the fore wheels and axle-trees of the said carriage should be the same height and strength as the hind ones.'[183] In other words, the wheels were standardised at 5ft (152cm) diameter. In 1773, Desaguliers had made a study of wheels and noted that the optimum wheel size was

Blomefield M1788 Light 6-pdr cast by Francis Kinman in his foundry at Shoe Lane, City of London in 1796 on Victorian block-trail carriage. The foot artillerymen are in the post-1812 uniform. (Courtesy the Trustees of the RAHT; photograph Stephen Summerfield)

approximately 5ft, and that the axle stubs should be inclined downwards so that the wheels splayed outward, and that the spokes should be angled so as to make the wheels concave in profile. He also recommended that the fore and rear wheels of any vehicle be the same size. Congreve says that he was 'from this order...necessarily confined to the figure introduced by General Desaguliers in 1776 from some field carriages which were taken in Martinique in the year 1761, to enable the high wheels to be used with limbers, without hindering them to turn short as common field carriages.'[184]

Congreve strengthened the block, as it was found that the Desaguliers block-trail carriage was not strong enough to prevent it from warping. The wheels and axle for the carriages were based on the scaling for the ammunition wagons. Furthermore, Richmond ordered that iron axles be used, and that a spare arm for the axle and a complete spare wheel was to be carried on the rear of each wagon.[185]

Later commentators have suggested that the block-trail carriage gave a smaller turning-circle for a gun and limber. However, this argument is refuted by Congreve's statement that the block-trail carriage was used in order to make the new carriages turn in the same space as bracket carriages, a conclusion further supported by Valée and Gibbons.[186] All new guns of the Blomefield type were to be mounted on block-trail carriages from 1788. The next major development of the Desaguliers block-trail came in 1792, when the Royal howitzer was mounted on the block-trail, as confirmed by Congreve writing in 1792–93.[187]

On 21 October 1793 the new Horse Artillery received Royal Assent, and the Desaguliers block-trail was officially adopted for this arm.[188] The foot or 'battalion' artillery retained the Congreve light travelling bracket carriages.

The Desaguliers block-trail was not universally liked upon its adoption, mainly due to its weight. Congreve rejected the complaints, claiming that it was as manageable as its predecessor; he suggested that if weight was so much of an issue, then the wooden axle should be reintroduced – which it was not.[189] According to General Lawson, some foot artillery Light 6-pdrs were mounted on block-trails by 1799 and served in Egypt.[190]

The major advantage of the block-trail was that as soon as the gun was unlimbered it could be loaded and fired. It could be manoeuvred more speedily on the battlefield and, due to its large wheels, was able to traverse rough and soft terrain with few problems. The block-trail carriage in horse artillery service required a crew of five men and an NCO, and eight for foot artillery service, whereas earlier bracket carriages and limbers required fifteen men. Furthermore, it could transport upwards of 60 rounds of ammunition as well as its crew.[191]

General Alexander Dickson described the block-trail and its universal limber as superior to the bracket trail, being easier to limber-up and unlimber; furthermore, they stood the test of prolonged firing well and needed few repairs.[192]

HANOVER

Hanover occupied a unique position among the German states by virtue of its monarch (elector) having succeeded as King George I of England in 1714. Hanover became neutral under the Treaty of Basel (1795), and in 1801 was occupied by Prussia. With the Peace of Amiens (1802) the Electorate absorbed the Bishopric of Osnabruck. Hanover was occupied by France in 1803.[193] Prussia exchanged Neuchatel and Ansbach for Hanover in 1805, but Napoleon renounced this agreement, and also annexed Kleve, in February 1806.[194]

M1735 Bruckmann System

General von Bruckmann, who had formed the Hanoverian artillery, designed its ordnance based on the M1732 Vallière system, but used the Prussian system of calibres (*see* Table 4.6). Bruckmann also experimented with a breech-loading gun with a wedge-shaped breech block, but these experiments did not lead to the development of a successful breech-loading design.

The 1762 regulations dictated that the light battalions were armed with two 1-pdr Amusettes and a four-horse cart, carrying 180 roundshot and 20 canister. Each gun carried 35 roundshot and 5 canister. Each of the twenty musketeer battalions and seven grenadier battalions had one 3-pdr gun attached issued with 64 roundshot and 36 canister carried in a four-wheeled cart, and 36 roundshot and 10 canister rounds carried on the gun.

Under these regulations, the 6-pdr guns were grouped into batteries of twelve, each gun being issued 70 roundshot and 30 canister rounds carried in the four-wheeled caisson, as well as 27 roundshot and 13 canister carried on the gun. The 12-pdrs were likewise grouped into batteries of twelve guns, each gun having a caisson containing 100 roundshot and 40 canister, and the gun carrying 27 roundshot and 2 canister. The 30-pdr howitzer had two wagons assigned to it, each carrying 30 bombs, 10 incendiary shells, 10 grenades and 5 canister rounds.

The Hanoverian horse artillery was formed during the Seven Years War (1756–63), and quickly came to be regarded as the best in Europe.

M1780 Trew System

New light guns were introduced between 1780 and 1786 due to experience from the Seven Years War. The new tubes were cast to a ratio of 200:1 of metal to weight of ball; the *Rechtsmaschine* elevating system acted on the back-weight of the gun tube, as in the current Austrian and Prussian systems.

The M1786 equipment was designed for the horse artillery, which was armed with a new 3-pdr and a light 7-pdr howitzer, both drawn by six-horse teams. The regimental artillery was manned by selected men from each battalion rather than by the artillery regiment proper.

The artillery regiment had 24× field guns and 14× howitzers, forming in 1793 two batteries each of 10× 6-pdrs, 4× 7-pdr howitzers and 2× 30-pdr howitzers. The third battery was the flying (horse) artillery, equipped with 4× 3-pdrs and 2× 7-pdr howitzers. Six 12-pdrs formed the heavy reserve battery. This organisation was increased in 1794 to three foot divisions totalling 4× 30-pdr howitzers, 8× 7-pdr howitzers and 20× 6-pdr field guns; the horse artillery had 4× 3-pdrs, 2× 7-pdr howitzers and 3× 6-pdrs. The eighteen infantry battalions were armed with a total of 36× 3-pdrs and 6× 1-pdr Amusettes.

By 1800 the Hanoverian army had adopted the 6-pdr instead of the 3-pdr for their horse artillery. Many officers at the time, including William Congreve Snr, believed that a well-equipped 3-pdr was equal to a 6-pdr in practice. When it was armed with the 3-pdr in the late 1770s, Congreve described the Hanoverian flying artillery as the best in Europe.[195]

M1795 System

Introduced in that year after the experience of the Flanders campaign (1793–95), this had 18-calibre long tubes for all pieces. The system used 3-pdr, 6-pdr and 12-pdr guns, 7-pdr (120mm) and 10-pdr (144mm) howitzers. Based on the surviving

Table 4.6: Hanoverian ordnance M1735, M1780 and M1795 ordnance

	Calibre length	Tube length	Total weight	Tube
Bruckmann M1735				
Long 3-pdr	77mm	208cm	27 calibres	500kg
Short 3-pdr	77mm	185cm	24 calibres	448kg
6-pdr	95mm	257cm	27 calibres	1064kg
12-pdr	120mm	288cm	24 calibres	1904kg
Trew M1780				
Long 3-pdr	77mm	185cm	24 calibres	407kg
Short 3-pdr	77mm	162cm	21 calibres	358kg
6-pdr	95mm	200cm	21 calibres	890kg
12-pdr	120mm	288cm	24 calibres	1530kg
7-pdr Howitzer	120mm	72cm	6 calibres	341kg
30-pdr Howitzer	200mm	110cm	4 calibres	890kg
M1795				
3-pdr	77mm	162cm	21 calibres	358kg
6-pdr	94.5mm	170cm	18 calibres	575kg
12-pdr	120mm	216cm	18 calibres	1000kg
7-pdr Howitzer	120mm	72cm	6 calibres	341kg
10-pdr Howitzer	144mm	86cm	6 calibres	620kg

Hanoverian M1780 6-pdr (left) and 12-pdr (centre) guns, and 30-pdr howitzer (right). These were still heavily influenced by Vallière designs. (Courtesy the Trustees of the RAHT; photograph Steven H. Smith)

gun tubes in the Musée de l'Armée and Kremlin collections, they were cast at Woolwich with Hanoverian calibres. The gun carriages were of the double-bracket type; the horse artillery had a Wurst-style seat that could accommodate four gunners, two further gunners being mounted on the limber. A unique feature of this equipment was the use of flintlock ignition in place of a fuse or loose powder.

Under the 1795 reforms, a battery was to consist of six rather than the eight pieces (four field guns and four howitzers) of the 1780s regulations. The guns had four-horse limbers; the battery had six four-horse caissons, two eight-horse forage wagons, a two-horse field forge, three riding horses and eight spare horses.

In 1803–06 the Hanoverian army came under Prussian and French control. The artillery pieces were used by the French and saw action in the 1805 campaign when they formed the artillery of Marshal Bernadotte's I Corps, since he had to abandon his French guns due to the lack of horses (*see* Chapter 5). Based on returns, these Hanoverian guns were still in use by the French in June 1807. M1795 guns were used by the liberated state of Hanover in 1815, and no English equipment was used until the 1830s.

Hanoverian M1795 6-pdr gun. Notice the parallel cheeks of the bracket trail. It was later used by KGA foot artillery. (Courtesy the Trustees of the RAHT; photograph Steven H. Smith)

King's German Artillery

The King's German Artillery (KGA) was formed in 1803 from personnel of the disbanded Hanoverian army who were withdrawn to Britain. On 1 August 1806 it came under the command of the Board of Ordnance. New gun tubes were issued for their mounted on M1795 bracket carriages, due to the smaller calibre of the British guns: e.g. a Hanoverian 3-pdr had fired 75mm shot (calibre 77mm) and a British 3-pdr fired 70mm shot (calibre 74.4mm). The 1-pdr Amusette and 3-pdr gun were not retained.

The KGA horse artillery retained the M1795 bracket carriage with Wurst seat for the gunners. Unlike their British counterparts, each horse brigade was armed with eight guns. On 1 August 1806 the two horse brigades were each armed with 6× 3-pdr guns and 2× 5½in howitzers. One of the horse artillery brigades served in the disastrous Walcheren campaign of 1809, and had to be completely reconstructed in its aftermath. In 1812, the KGA horse brigades received Blomefield M1805 9-pdr guns.

The foot brigades were equipped with eight pieces. On 1 August 1806 the three field brigades were each armed with 6× Light 6-pdrs and 2× 5½in howitzers; the heavy brigade was armed with 4× 12-pdrs and 2× 8in howitzers. In 1809 in the Peninsula, the King's German Artillery mustered 4x Medium 12-pdrs, 12× Light 6-pdrs, 2× Heavy 5½in howitzers and 2× Light 5½in howitzers. Unlike their British counterparts, all the guns were of the new Röttiger pattern. The 12-pdr brigade had only six pieces (4× 12-pdrs and 2× howitzers).

The KGA in Spain had two eight-gun brigades, and one half-brigade of 12-pdrs that acted as a miniature park. However, due to the lack of horses and other draft animals in the Peninsula, William Robe ordered that they were to be 'manned in a similar way to the English Companies', i.e. reduced to six gun brigades and the spare guns transferred to the Park or garrison duties. In May 1809 the brigades of Captains Gesenius and Teiling had no horses and were unable to move their guns.

The Blomefield M1805 9-pdr gun was adopted for one foot artillery battery and one horse artillery battery in 1812. The gun-teams for the M1795 system guns were:

6 horses (Light 6-pdr, howitzer caisson)
8 horses (Long 6-pdr, 9-pdr, 5½in howitzer)
8 or 10 horses (Medium 12-pdr)

An increase in the number of horses needed to draw a gun probably reflected use of heavier equipment than that used previously. Each brigade, in addition to its six guns, had eight ammunition caissons, two baggage wagons, a field forge, a spare-wheel wagon and a wagon with musket ammunition. Baggage and musket ammunition wagons were drawn by two horses; the field forges had teams of six and the spare-wheel wagon four or six horses.

Captain Von Rettburg's Brigade of Light 6-pdrs at Coimbra on 1 May 1809 had on its establishment the following vehicles, horses and mules:

6 guns	36 horses
6 caissons	4 mules
Cart for small stores	2 mules
Officers	4 horses
NCOs and farriers	3
Spare	7 horses, 5 mules
Total	78 horses, 19 mules

At the same date Captain Heise's Brigade had two field forges, one spare-wheel wagon and two carts for small stores.

Kingdom of Hanover, post-1815

During the march on Paris after the battle of Waterloo, the 4th Foot Battery of the KGA was involved in the storming of Péronne. With the exception of 3rd Company, Foot Artillery, the KGA was disbanded on 24 February 1816, and 3rd Company on 24 May.

In 1816 the 1st Battalion of the Royal Hanoverian Artillery, based in Hanover, was formed from the 1st KGA Horse Battery and the 1st to 5th KGA Foot Batteries. The 2nd KGA Horse Battery formed the nucleus of the 2nd Hanoverian Battalion. The 6th KGA Foot Battery was disbanded and the men distributed among the 1st Hanoverian Battalion. The guns used were those remaining from the M1795 system. The construction of new carriages was superintended by General Augustus Theodor Röttiger (1766–1851).

5 Foreign and Captured Ordnance

INTRODUCTION

Most states had their own unique systems of gun tubes and calibres based on their national unit of measurement (*see* Table 5.1), despite copying the basic technology from each other. The reduction of windage improved the efficiency of the guns, but reduced the ability to use captured or allied ammunition. In Austria in 1753, Liechtenstein initiated the process of reducing the windage of guns that was followed by Gribeauval in France and Dieskau in Prussia. The reduction of windage was the major achievement of the ordnance innovators of the middle decades of the 18th century. Austria and France did this by increasing the diameter of the ammunition and so kept the same bore diameter as before, whereas Prussia reduced the size of the bore in relation to that of the projectiles. Therefore Prussia generally had smaller calibres than most of Europe, with the exception of Britain.

Britain, being isolated from European developments, had its own unique system of guns and calibres; this required the re-arming of the King's German Artillery with new gun tubes in 1803, and the disbanding of the Brunswick Horse Artillery armed with Austrian guns when they entered British service in 1809.

Generally, France used shot of the largest calibre and weight, its greater kinetic energy giving superior penetration of targets. Britain used the smallest shot but with the highest density, because the shot was hammered more; when the lower drag is taken into account, it probably had a similar effect upon the target to the French shot. Austria and Prussia were unable to use French ammunition, but Russia could. The French in an emergency could use captured British 6-pdr ammunition, but there was a large windage. However, the British were unable to use captured French shot unless it was undersized. Just as ammunition that would not fit down the gun tube was useless, ammunition that gave too much windage imposed a severe reduction in both accuracy and range.

Europe did not use anything approaching a system of common weights and measures (*see* the Appendix), so there was great variation in the weight and hence the diameter of 6-pdr cannonballs made in different countries (*see* Table 5.3). This demonstrates the complexity of supply problems for the Coalition allies and the Grande Armée alike. It contributed to the Austro-Bavarian defeat at Hohenlinden (3 December 1800), and later at Hanau (30–31 October 1813). At Hanau the Austro-Bavarian army deployed only 58 out of their 134 guns (68 Austrian and 66 Bavarian) due to lack of ammunition.[196] The Bavarian artillery opposing the 20× 12-pdrs of the Old Guard quickly ceased firing, as only Austrian 12-pdr shot could be provided; the Bavarian artillery train was in Ussenheim, 120km to the south-east.[197] The Austrian 12-pdr ammunition (113.2mm rather than 120mm) left too much windage in the French M1808 ordnance used by the Bavarians, giving poor range and accuracy. By 4pm on 31 October only the Bavarian 11th Battery (3× 12-pdrs), 8th Battery (6× 12-pdrs) and the combined 7th/9th Battery (6× 6-pdrs) had sufficient ammunition to carry on the fight; the Austrians had already exhausted their ammunition.[198] This poor staff work compounded the failure of General Wrede's strategic gamble to delay the retreat of Napoleon's army from Leipzig.

FOREIGN GUNS IN FRENCH SERVICE

Throughout the period, France often relied on captured guns to supplement or replace pieces lost on campaign – especially those from Austria and Prussia, during the Revolutionary Wars.

Table 5.1: Comparison of gun calibres

	3- and 4-pdr	6-pdr	8- and 9-pdr	12-pdr	Medium howitzer	Heavy howitzer
Austria M1753	75.5mm *3-pdr*	95.7mm	none	119.5mm	150mm *7-pdr howitzer*	171mm *10-pdr howitzer*
Baden M1786	77mm *3-pdr*	none	103mm *'6-pdr'*	none	148–153 mm *7-pdr howitzer*	184.5mm *10-pdr*
Baden (1804–14)	84mm *4-pdr M1765*	94.5mm *Bavarian M1800*	none	121mm *French M1808*	148mm *M1800 7-pdr*	151.3mm *M1808 24-pdr*
Bavaria	75mm *3-pdr*	94.5mm	none	117mm	148mm *7-pdr howitzer*	240mm *30-pdr howitzer*
British	73.7mm *3-pdr*	93.2mm	107mm *9-pdr*	117mm	114.8mm *4 2/5in howitzer*	143mm *5 1/2in howitzer*
Danish	75mm *3-pdr*	94mm	none	122mm	130.5mm *10-pdr howitzer*	170mm *20-pdr howitzer*
Dutch	75.2mm *3-pdr*	96mm	105mm *8-pdr*	121mm	151.7mm *24-pdr howitzer*	none
French M1697	84mm *3-pdr*	none	106mm *8-pdr*	121mm	none	none
French M1732	84mm *3-pdr*	none	106mm *8-pdr*	121mm	none	163mm *6.4in M1749 howitzer*
French M1765	86mm *3-pdr*	none	106mm *8-pdr*	121mm	none	163mm *6.4in M1749 howitzer*
French M1803	none	95.8mm	none	121mm	151.5mm *7-pdr howitzer*	170mm *10-pdr M1795 howitzer*
French M1808	none	95.8mm	none	121mm	149mm *24-pdr howitzer*	none
Hanover M1780	77mm *3-pdr*	95mm	none	120mm	120mm *7-pdr howitzer*	200mm *30-pdr howitzer*
Hanover M1795	77mm 3-pdr	94.5mm	none	120mm	120mm *7-pdr howitzer*	144mm *10-pdr howitzer*
Hesse Darmstadt	72mm *3-pdr*	94mm	none	120mm	148mm *7-pdr howitzer*	173mm *10-pdr howitzer*
Piedmont M1786	76.2mm *4-pdr*	none	96.5mm *8-pdr*	122mm *16-pdr*	140mm *7-pdr howitzer*	none
Portuguese	74mm *3-pdr*	95.3mm	109.2mm *9-pdr*	119.4mm	none	none
Prussia M1758	73mm *3-pdr*	95mm	none	122mm	148mm *7-pdr howitzer*	170mm *10-pdr howitzer*
Prussia M1768	73mm *3-pdr*	94mm	none	119mm	148mm *7-pdr howitzer*	170mm *10-pdr howitzer*
Prussia M1809–16	76mm *3-pdr*	91mm	none	119mm	148mm *7-pdr howitzer*	none
Russia M1805	84mm *3-pdr unicorn*	96mm	none	120.9mm	122mm *10-pdr unicorn*	152mm *20-pdr unicorn*
Saxon M1766–72	78.7mm *4-pdr*	none	100.6mm *8-pdr*	115mm	154.8mm *4-pdr Granatstück*	154.8mm *8-pdr howitzer*
Saxon M1810	none	92.6mm	none	115mm	none	154.8mm *8-pdr howitzer*
Spanish Gribeauval	84mm *4-pdr*	none	106.7mm *8-pdr*	121.9mm *Garrison*	none	160mm *6.4in howitzer*
Sweden	76.7mm *3-pdr*	97mm	none	124.1mm	198.5mm *16-pdr howitzer*	207.5mm *20-pdr howitzer*
Württemberg	76mm *3-pdr*	93mm	none	118mm	150mm *7-pdr howitzer*	none

Table 5.2: Comparison of shot diameters

	3- and 4-pdr	6-pdr	8- and 9-pdr	12-pdr	Medium howitzer	Heavy howitzer
Austria	72.8mm *3-pdr*	90.4mm	none	113.2mm	145.7mm *7-pdr howitzer*	163mm *10-pdr howitzer*
Baden M1786	75mm *3-pdr*	none	99mm *'6-pdr'*	none	none	178mm *10-pd howitzer*
Baden (1804–14)	82mm *4-pdr M1765*	91.4mm *Bavarian M1800*	none	118.2mm *French M1808*	146mm *M1800 7-pdr*	146mm *M1808 24-pdr*
Bavaria	72mm *3-pdr*	90mm	none	115mm	146mm *7-pdr howitzer*	236mm *30-pdr howitzer*
British	70.5mm *3-pdr*	88.8mm	101.6mm *9-pdr*	111.8mm	113.1mm *4 2/5in howitzer*	142mm *5 1/2in howitzer*
Danish	73mm *3-pdr*	92.7mm	none	117.1mm	128mm *10-pdr howitzer*	166.5mm *20-pdr howitzer*
Dutch	73mm *3-pdr*	93mm	101mm *8-pdr*	117mm	146mm *24-pdr howitzer*	none
French M1765	82mm *3-pdr*	none	104.1mm *8-pdr*	118.7mm	none	160mm *M1749 6.4in howitzer*
French M1803	none	94mm	none	118.7mm	149mm *7-pdr M1803 howitzer*	164mm *10-pdr M1795 howitzer*
French M1808	none	94mm	none	120mm	146mm *24-pdr M1808 howitzer*	none
Hanover M1780	73mm *3-pdr*	91mm	none	120mm	113mm *7-pdr howitzer*	192mm *30-pdr howitzer*
Hanover M1795	73mm *3-pdr*	91mm	none	113mm	113mm *7-pdr howitzer*	140mm *10-pdr howitzer*
Hesse-Darmstadt	70mm *3-pdr*	90.5mm	none	113.8mm	146mm *7-pdr howitzer*	162mm *10-pdr howitzer*
Piedmont M1786	76.2mm *4-pdr*	none	96.5mm *8-pdr*	122mm *16-pdr*	138mm *7-pdr howitzer*	none
Portuguese	71mm *3-pdr*	91mm	105mm *9-pdr*	114mm	none	none
Prussia	71.8mm *3-pdr*	90.4mm	none	113.9mm	143.8mm *7-pdr howitzer*	166mm *10-pdr howitzer*
Russia M1805	79.2mm *3-pdr unicorn*	91.7mm	none	115.4mm	117mm *10-pdr unicorn*	147mm *20-pdr unicorn*
Saxon M1766–72	75mm *4-pdr*	none	99mm *8-pdr*	114mm	152mm *4-pdr Granatstück*	152mm *8-pdr howitzer*
Saxon M1810	none	91mm	none	114mm	none	152mm *8-pdr howitzer*
Spanish Gribeauval	81.2mm *4-pdr*	none	102mm *8-pdr*	117mm *Garrison*	none	156mm *6.4in howitzer*
Sweden	74.4mm *3-pdr*	92.5mm	none	119.6mm	189.5mm *16-pdr howitzer*	203mm *20-pdr howitzer*
Württemberg	73mm *3-pdr*	90.5mm	none	114.6mm	145mm *7-pdr howitzer*	none

Table 5.3: Comparison of shot weights

	3- and 4-pdr	6-pdr	8- and 9-pdr	12-pdr	Medium howitzer	Heavy howitzer
Austria	1.3kg *3-pdr*	2.7kg	none	5.0kg	7.2kg *7-pdr howitzer*	12.3kg *10-pdr howitzer*
Baden	1.3kg *3-pdr*	2.7kg *Bavarian M1800*	unknown *'6-pdr'*	6.1kg	6.1kg *7-pd howitzer*	6.6kg *10-pdr howitzer*
Bavaria	1.4kg *3-pdr*	3.0kg	none	6.1kg	6.6kg *7-pdr howitzer*	ND *30-pdr howitzer*
British	1.4kg *3-pdr*	2.7kg	4.1kg *9-pdr*	5.4kg	3.5kg *4²/₅in howitzer*	6.8kg *5¹/₂in howitzer*
French M1732	1.8kg *4-pdr*	none	4.0kg *8-pdr*	6.0kg	none	12.4kg *6.4in M1749 howitzer*
French M1765	1.8kg *4-pdr*	none	4.0kg *8-pdr*	6.1kg	none	12.4kg *6.4in M1749 howitzer*
French M1803	none	3.0kg	none	6.1kg	6.6kg *7-pdr M1803 howitzer*	14.6kg *10-pdr M1795 howitzer*
French M1808	none	3.0kg	none	6.1kg	6.1kg *24-pdr M1808 howitzer*	none
Hanover	1.4kg *3-pdr*	3.0kg	none	6.0kg	6.5kg *7-pdr howitzer*	27.7kg *30-pdr howitzer*
Piedmont M1786	1.0g *4-pdr*	none	3.0kg *8-pdr*	6.0kg *16-pdr*	unknown *7-pdr howitzer*	none
Prussia	1.4kg *3-pdr*	3.0kg	none	5.9kg	6.4kg *7-pdr howitzer*	12.3kg *10-pdr howitzer*
Russia	1.0kg *3-pdr unicorn*	2.9 g	none	5.7kg	3.88kg *10-pdr unicorn*	8.1kg *20-pdr unicorn*
Saxon M1766-72	1.0kg *4-pdr*	none	3.74kg *8-pdr*	5.6kg	1.9kg *4-pdr Granatstück*	7.3kg *8-pdr howitzer*
Saxon M1810	none	2.8kg	none	5.6kg	none	7.3kg *8-pdr howitzer*
Württemberg	1.3kg *3-pdr*	3.0kg	none	6.1kg	6.1kg *7-pdr howitzer*	none

(Interestingly, it was only in 1795 that Gaspard Monge issued instructions to cast more French guns.) Austrian and Piedmontese guns were used during the Italian campaign of 1796–97, many of which stayed in service throughout the period, especially the mountain guns.

By the accession of Napoleon as emperor in 1804 the French army therefore had a significant amount of foreign material. Only ordnance captured from Austria, Prussia and Russia with the same calibres as those used by the French were incorporated into the artillery of the Grande Armée. As already mentioned in Chapter 4, during the Austerlitz campaign of 1805, Bernadotte's I Corps left behind some fifteen guns due to lack of horses, and replaced them with thirty-six Hanoverian guns (2× 12-pdrs, 22× 6-pdrs, 6× 3-pdrs and 6× 7-pdr howitzers).

With the creation of the French Empire, Napoleon ordered on 14 April 1806 that the French system of calibres was to be made universal across the Empire (Metropolitan France, Italy, Dalmatia, Westphalia and Holland); he also recommended that the same calibres be used in French protectorates, namely the Confederation of the Rhine and Italy. By this one reform ammunition supply and control would be greatly eased, as three calibres of cannon (3-, 6- and 12-pdr) and two calibres of howitzer (24-pdr and 6.4in) were to be used across Europe. Some states of the Confederation of the Rhine wholly adopted French calibres (Baden, Würzburg and Hesse-Darmstadt), whilst others did so only partially – primarily for the 6-pdr gun (Saxony and Bavaria). Prussia and Austria retained their own systems. Württemberg used Austrian material up to 1809,

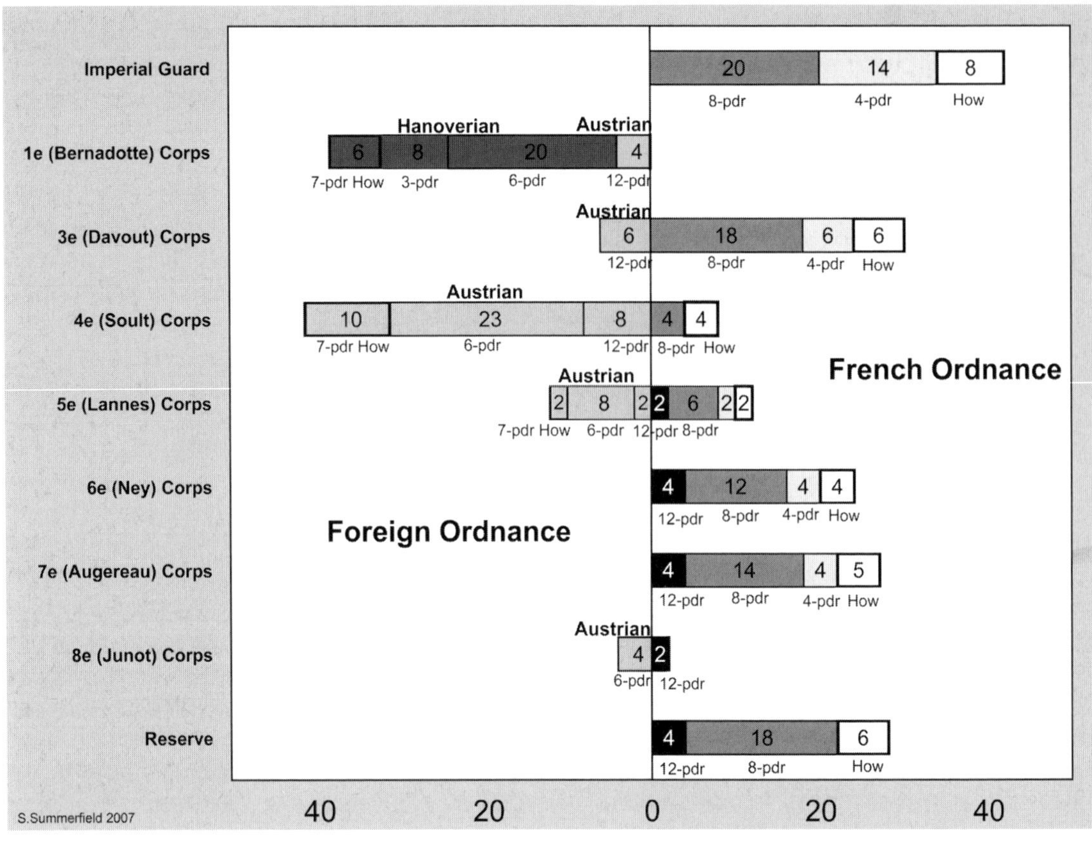

Bar chart showing origins of ordnance used by each corps of the French Grande Armée on 1 November 1806: (left) captured ordnance from Austria and Hanover, (right) French ordnance.

and then alongside their own artillery system based on that of France.

In May 1807, the French field army had 114 Austrian and 34 Hanoverian guns compared to only 128 French guns. In addition there were the Prussian siege guns, manned mainly by allied gunners that Napoleon used to reduce a number of the Prussian fortresses in 1806–07. Many of the Prussian guns were later re-bored to the larger French calibres when they were sold to the Duchy of Warsaw.

After Aspern-Essling in 1809, Napoleon formed regimental artillery using Austrian 3-pdr guns. For Wagram a number of position batteries were formed (consisting of 32× 18-pdrs, 4× 12-pdrs and 2× 6-pdrs), as well as two floating batteries (2× 3-pdrs, 2× 6-pdrs, a howitzer and a 12-pdr) manned by the Sailors of the Imperial Guard. After the heavy losses in Russia in 1812 the use of captured artillery again made up for the lack of French guns.[199]

Baden

When artillery was first raised in 1771, Baden had a single battery of guns commanded by Carl Frederick von Freystedt and Captain Johann Jacob Lux. Baden lacked a gun foundry, and in 1783 that at Mannheim in Bavaria cast 3-pdr guns for Baden. By 1792 the battery had 3× 6-pdrs and 3× 7-pdr howitzers, cast at Mannheim. Interestingly, the calibre of the M1771 6-pdr (103.5mm) was almost the same as a French 8-pdr. A second company was raised in 1803 using the M1783 3-pdr guns. In 1804, French M1765 12-pdrs were introduced. On 1 May 1805, six new Bavarian M1800 6-pdr guns were cast in Mannheim to replace the old M1771 3-pdrs. On

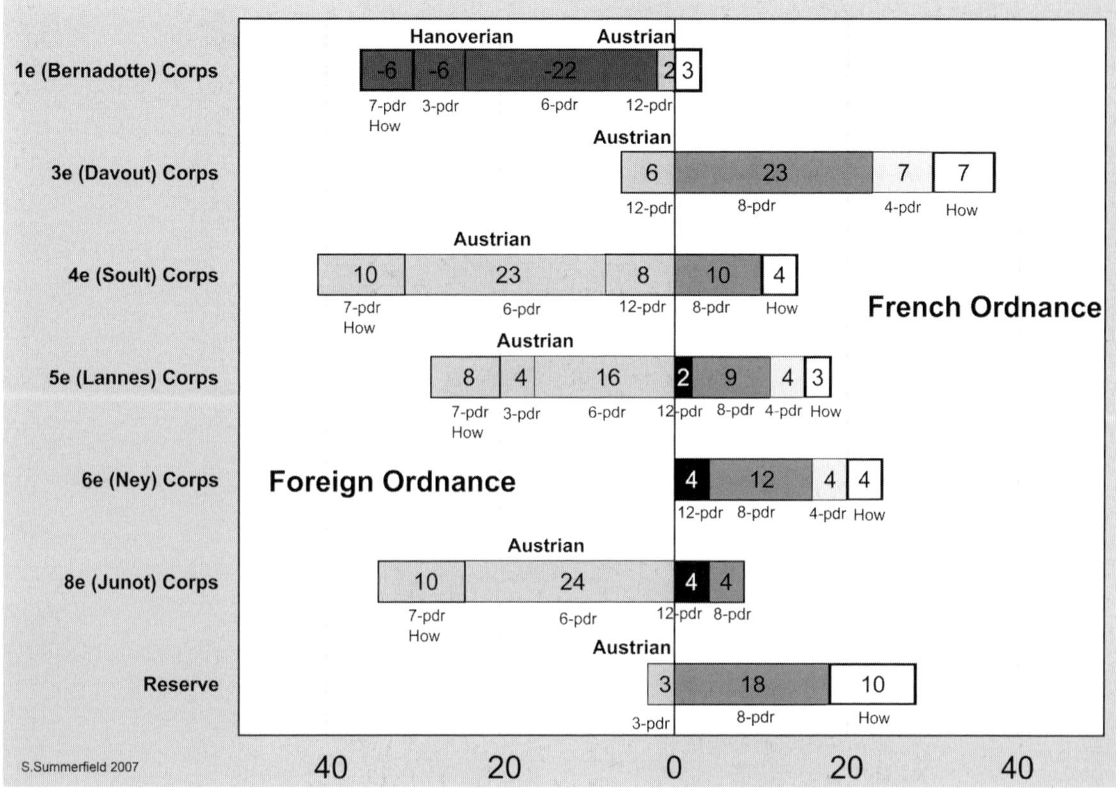

Bar chart showing origins of ordnance used by each corps of the French Grande Armée on 1 May 1807: (left) captured ordnance from Austria and Hanover, (right) French ordnance.

20 January 1806, the Baden artillery had 7× 6-pdrs and 5× 7-pdr howitzers. In January 1806, Baden received 6× 7-pdr howitzers probably of Austrian manufacture.

Upon Baden joining the Confederation of the Rhine, new guns were introduced according to the decree of 14 April 1806 that harmonised the calibre of artillery pieces in Napoleon's Europe. Battery strength varied from six pieces (3× guns and 3× howitzers, or 6× guns) to nine (6× guns and 3× howitzers). On 1 November 1806 a horse artillery company was equipped with 6x French Gribeauval 4-pdr guns; two foot batteries each had 4× 6-pdrs and 2× 7-pdr howitzers, and one foot battery 6× 6-pdrs and 6× 7-pdr howitzers. In 1808 the Baden artillery comprised:

1st (Horse) Battery: 8× Light 6-pdr field guns. Half of the battery was sent to Spain, while the other half-battery (then with 2× 6-pdrs and 2× howitzers) fought in 1809 against Austria.

2nd (Foot) Battery: 6× 6-pdr guns and 2× howitzers. Fought in 1809 against Austria.

3rd (Foot) Battery: 6× 12-pdr guns and 2x howitzers. Sent to Spain in 1808, where they exchanged their guns for 6× Gribeauval 4-pdrs (possibly of Spanish origin), and were brigaded with the 2nd Nassau Infantry in the German Division.

On 15 March 1809, Baden deployed against Austria a total of 8× 6-pdrs, 4× howitzers, 16× 6-pdr caissons (French design), 12× howitzer caissons (French design), 22× infantry ammunition wagons and 14× forage wagons.

On 20 March 1811 eight gun batteries were organised, so bringing the Baden artillery organisation into line with that of France. The decree of 11 February 1811 created a regimental artillery

Table 5.4: Baden artillery

	Calibre	Bore length	Gun tube length	Gun tube weight	Windage	Projectile weight	Charge weight
Baden (pre 1805)							
6-pdr M1771	103.5mm	17 calibres	186cm	ND	ND	ND	ND
3-pdr M1783	77mm	17 calibres	139cm	ND	ND	1300g	409g
10-pdr M1792 Howitzer	184.5mm	4 calibres	96cm	ND	ND	ND	ND
Baden (1804-1813)							
12-pdr (French)	121.3mm	16.8 calibres	210cm	760kg	2mm	6100g	1600g
6-pdr (Bavarian M1800)	94.5mm	17 calibres	170cm	248kg	ND	2740g	800g
4-pdr (Gribeauval)	86mm	16.5 calibres	155cm	295kg	2.1mm	1.8kg	0.8kg
7-pdr Howitzer (Bav. M1800)	148mm	7 calibres	101cm	300kg	2mm	6600g	1000g
7-pdr Austrian Howitzer	153mm	4.1 calibres	94cm	280kg	8.5mm	7500g	572g
Baden (1814)							
6-pdr (French M1808)	95mm	17.2 calibres	180cm	410kg	2.1mm	2600g	1000g
6-pdr Raab M1810 (Saxon)	92.6mm	18 calibres	167cm	392kg	–	2800g	908g
6.4 inch (French) Howitzer	160mm	3 calibres	77cm	327kg	3.9mm	12.4kg	0.8kg
24-pdr (5.9 inch) Howitzer	151.3mm	7 calibres	120cm	327kg	3mm	6100g	1000g

company attached to the infantry for the forthcoming 1812 campaign. Each infantry regiment was issued 2× field guns, 6× caissons, 2× 7-pdr howitzers, 2× howitzer caissons, 4× infantry caissons, and one park wagon. In 1812, Baden gunners also manned one 12-pdr battery (French calibre). In 1811 two guns under Lieutenant Wild accompanied the 2nd Baden Infantry Regiment to Danzig; these were the only Baden guns not lost in the retreat from Russia.

In 1814 the artillery was a mixture of Austrian, French and Saxon pieces (16× Saxon 6-pdrs, 6× Austrian 7-pdr howitzers, 6× French 6.4in howitzers, 6× French 12-pdrs and 6× French 6-pdrs). By 1815 all guns were harmonised to those of the French system, being cast in Bavaria using gunmetal gifted by Napoleon on 30 April 1813.

Denmark

The dual kingdom of Denmark and Norway was primarily involved in naval rather than land warfare. Frederick VI, the regent since 1784, finally succeeded his father on the throne on 13 March 1808.

In 1780, an artillery division had 8× 10-pdr howitzers, 8× 12-pdr guns, 16× 6-pdrs and 8× 3-pdrs, with 8× 1-pdrs issued to the light troops. The five grenadier battalions had 10× Heavy 3-pdrs, and the twenty musketeer battalions 40× Light 3-pdrs.

At the start of the Revolutionary Wars, Denmark used the M1766 artillery system of Prince Karl von Esse. These were well-made pieces with heavy bronze tubes of 1-pdr (Amusette), Light (regimental) 3-pdr, Heavy 3-pdr, 6-pdr and 12-pdr calibres for field artillery, as well as 20-pdr and 36-pdr howitzers. The position guns were 22 calibres long, cast with 200:1 of metal to weight of ball. The Light (regimental) 3-pdr of 16 calibres issued to musketeer battalions was manned by twelve gunners, pulled by two horses, and issued with 100 rounds (80 roundshot and 20 canister) each. The 1-pdr Amusette, pulled by two horses, had 150 ball and 50 canister rounds and a crew of four men.

The efficiency of the Danish 12-pdr was brought into question during the French Revolutionary Wars, so in 1794 a lighter 12-pdr based upon the Austrian M1753 was adopted; the weight of the Danish equipment then in use had hampered the performance of the artillery during the Flanders campaign. The ammunition allocation per piece was:

12-pdr gun – 128 roundshot and 44 canister
6-pdr gun – 166 roundshot, 53 canister
3-pdr gun – 176 roundshot, 58 canister
10-pdr howitzer – 76 shell, 25 canister, 12 firebombs.

Baden artillery officer in front of a M1783 3-pdr regimental gun cast in Mannheim, Bavaria in 1783. Note that the barrel does not have dolphins. (Authors' collection)

Table 5.5: Danish M1766 ordnance

	Calibre	Bore length	Gun tube length	Gun tube weight	Carriage weight	Limber weight
12-pdr	122mm	22 calibres	295cm	1344kg	3136kg	500kg
6-pdr	94mm	22 calibres	208cm	672kg	1960kg	500kg
Heavy 3-pdr	75mm	22 calibres	172cm	336kg	1008kg	ND
Light (regimental) 3-pdr	75mm	16 calibres	130cm	227kg	742kg	ND
1-pdr Amusette	53mm	16 calibres	94cm	184kg	392kg	ND
24-pdr Howitzer	150mm	6 calibres	100cm	300kg	940kg	ND
36-pdr Howitzer	170mm	6 calibres	119cm	354kg	940kg	ND

Danish foot gunners with a Danish 3-pdr

Danish foot gunners leaning against a Danish 3-pdr in 1807, as a ship – probably British – passes their promontory. Note the distinctive black top hat with left brim turned up, secured by a button and loop extending to the crown, topped by a white plume; the uniforms are red coats with blue facings. (By kind permission Landes u. Universitätsbibliothek Darmstadt; photograph Marcus Stein)

Danish M1766 12-pdr

Danish M1766 12-pdr of 122mm calibre, 295cm long and weighing 1,226kg; this piece was cast in 1795 and was used as both a field and a garrison gun. The wreathed monogram of King Christian VII can be seen on the first reinforcement; the base ring is inscribed 17 FRIDRICS WAERCK 95, and the weight is incised on the left trunnion. (Courtesy the Board of Trustees of the Royal Armouries; photograph Stephen Summerfield)

The carriage-mounted chest contained 12 rounds (12-pdr), 24 rounds (3- and 6-pdr), 25 rounds (1-pdr) and 5 shells (10-pdr howitzer).

On 18 December 1800, Denmark signed the armed neutrality pact with Russia and Sweden – joined later by Prussia – to resist British interference with their trade in the Baltic Sea. In 1801, fearing the capture of the Danish fleet by the French, Britain sent a Royal Navy force to Copenhagen, and on 2 April 1801 the Danish fleet and much of the city was destroyed. Denmark remained neutral until 1807, when the British sent a fleet and an army of 18,000 men to forestall Danish entry into the war on the French side. The bombardment of Copenhagen started on 2 September 1807 and ceased on 7 September, when the Danish fleet surrendered.

The Danish army primarily employed 3- and 6-pdr cannon, with some 12-pdrs in the artillery reserve. The Danish 3-pdr and 6-pdr were comparable to the Prussian 6-pdr, but according to Scharnhorst the range was less than that of 6-pdrs produced in France. This difference in efficiency led Napoleon to offer Denmark 8× 6-pdrs and 4× 24-pdr howitzers (French M1808) in order to re-equip the two horse batteries that had 3-pdrs. (In fact, only one was re-equipped by September 1813, with 6× French 6-pdrs, 2× French howitzers, and 2× Danish howitzers.)

In 1809, Denmark provided a foot battery (8× 3-pdrs) and horse battery (2× 3-pdrs) for the protection of the Baltic coast. These were part of the Danish force that stormed Stralsund to put down the von Schill uprising.[200]

In May 1812, Denmark had two 12-pdr batteries, fourteen foot batteries (either 3- or 6-pdr), and five horse batteries, giving her army a ratio of one piece of artillery for every 267 men. Denmark provided four batteries of artillery under Prince Frederick of Hesse to serve in Northern Germany. Artillery units might be either coastal batteries, garrison batteries in fortresses or field batteries. A Danish field battery had 8× guns and 2× howitzers that could be divided into two half-batteries, one with 4× guns and the other with 4× cannon plus 2× howitzers. These were further subdivided into divisions of two pieces.[201] However, in 1813 many batteries had only eight pieces. In that year a Danish division was attached to Marshal Davout's XIII Corps. The advance guard had a 3-pdr foot battery; each of the

Danish M1766 6-pdr of 94mm calibre, 191cm long. Cast in 1783, this piece was captured at Copenhagen on 8 September 1807; the dolphins are in the form of elephant heads. (Courtesy of the Board of Trustees of the Royal Armouries; photograph Stephen Summerfield)

three infantry brigades had a 6-pdr battery, and in reserve was a 3-pdr battery.

On 14 January 1814, Denmark signed the Peace of Kiel with the Coalition allies, losing Norway to Sweden in exchange for Swedish Pomerania and Rugen; Britain restored all captured Danish possessions except Heligoland. In response to the change of sovereignty, Norway mobilised 20,000 men to resist Swedish rule, but Sweden was backed by Britain and Russia. At the Congress of Vienna in June 1815 Denmark lost Swedish Pomerania to Prussia, but received Lauenberg.

Hesse-Darmstadt

In 1752 the Hessian artillery was formed to provide trained gunners for the regimental artillery; only on 7 April 1790 were these formed into the Field Artillery Regiment, under Major Johann Fischer. In 1792–98, Hesse-Darmstadt fought in British and Imperial pay against the French; thereafter she remained neutral until after Austerlitz in 1805. For the captured guns (probably French Vallière and Gribeauval pieces) given to the Landgrave of Hesse-Darmstadt at the beginning of 1793 (*see* Table 5.6).

In 1792, Oberst Georg Gottleib Hahn (1756–1823) succeeded Major Fischer and remained as commander until 1814 – according to some sources, until his death. The regiment was initially of two companies, a third being formed in 1803. In 1793 the regiment had 422 men and 264 horses. A new and lighter 6-pdr was introduced, inspired by the French system, and was cast at Marxburg under the supervision of Oberst Hahn, who oversaw all construction of field guns and attendant rolling stock of Gribeauval style. He also introduced the Prussian M1762 7-pdr and M1763 10-pdr howitzers. The train was militarised in 1796. In August 1796 an equipment return lists 4× 10-pdr howitzers, 8× 7-pdr howitzers, 6× 12-pdr guns, 2× 6-pdrs, 4× 4-pdrs (old) and 11× 24-pdrs.

Table 5.6: Captured ordnance handed over to Hesse-Darmstadt, early 1793

Calibre	Name	Weight (kg)	Cast date
24-pdr	*Le Bien Venu*	2497kg	1772 (Vallière)
16-pdr	*Le Foyable*	1890kg	1774 (Vallière)
12-pdr	*Le Traductour*	825kg	1766
12-pdr	*Le Folatre*	824kg	1787
12-pdr	*Le Brulet*	821kg	1767
4-pdr	*Le Atlas*	289kg	1789
4-pdr	*Le Noulier*	275kg	1767

Table 5.7: Hesse-Darmstadt artillery

	Calibre	Bore length	Tube length	Tube weight
Hesse-Darmstadt (M1752))				
6-pdr M1732	94.5mm	18 calibres	180cm	409kg
3-pdr M1732	72mm	22 calibres	170cm	210kg
Captured French guns (1793–1800)				
12-pdr (Gribeauval)	120mm	18 calibres	21cm	825kg
4-pdr (Gribeauval)	86mm	16.5 calibres	155cm	290kg
Hesse-Darmstadt M1796				
6-pdr M1796 (French inspired)	94mm	16.5 calibres	163cm	377kg
7-pdr M1796 Howitzer (Prussian M1763)	148mm	4.5 calibres	95cm	792kg
10-pdr M1796 Howitzer (Prussian M1762)	173mm	4.4 calibres	94cm	590kg
French M1808 (1810–1813)				
6-pdr	94mm	16.5 calibres	163cm	377kg
24-pdr (5.9 inch) Howitzer	148mm	7 calibres	120cm	327kg

In 1800 the existing 4-pdrs and 12-pdrs were placed in the siege train or garrison. In 1801 the train had 24× 6-pdr ammunition wagons, 12× grenade (shell) wagons, 1× ball wagon, 7× infantry ammunition wagons, 1× field forge, 1× coal wagon, 1× howitzer ammunition wagon, 1× tool cart, 1× augmentation wagon, 2× tent wagons, 1× bread wagon and 4× officers' baggage wagons. On 31 December 1801, the Darmstadt Arsenal had 10× 6-pdrs (old design), 10× M1796 6-pdrs, 7× 1-pdr Amusettes, 6× 7-pdr M1796 howitzers and 1× 24-pdr mortar.

Hesse-Darmstadt was a founder-member of the Confederation of the Rhine. For the 1806 campaign against Prussia she provided a battery of 6× 6-pdrs and 2× 7-pdr howitzers, with 10× 6-pdr caissons, 4× howitzer caissons, 10× infantry caissons, a field forge, an entrenching tool wagon, an iron-and-coal wagon, a tool cart and an officer's baggage wagon.[202] By November 1806 the number of caissons had increased to 18, and spare gun carriages were provided as in the French manner. The battery was present at Jena and at the siege of Graudenz. In 1808 the battery of 8× 6-pdrs and 2× 7-pdr howitzers had 20× caissons, 14× infantry caissons, a field forge, a coal wagon, a tool cart and three baggage wagons. Six 6-pdr guns and one 7-pdr howitzer also saw service in Spain.

The artillery train was formed on 27 November 1810. Ambulances were attached at this time, of the French M1797 light model.

The Hesse-Darmstadt artillery took one battery of 6× 6-pdrs and 2× 24-pdr howitzers to the 1812 campaign in Russia, and the six guns returned to Hesse-Darmstadt in December 1812. The 3× M1796 6-pdrs of 94mm calibre in the Kremlin Museum are 163cm long (muzzle to base ring) and weigh 377kg. They bear the monogram of Ludwig X. Landgraf von Hessen-Darmstadt (1790–1806).

During the battle of Leipzig (16–19 October 1813) the 6× 6-pdrs fired a total of 697 roundshot and 50 canister rounds; the 2× 7-pdr howitzers fired 104 shells and 24 rounds of canister. After Leipzig, Hesse-Darmstadt joined the Coalition allies, and a single eight-gun battery with 152 men was formed.

When the German states prepared to fight Napoleon in 1815 the Hessian artillery provided two batteries, the combined force operating under the Austrian General von Palombini in the corps of Prince von Hessen-Homberg.

Hesse-Darmstadt M1752 6-pdr gun tube at US Military Academy at West Point, NY. (Steven H. Smith)

Hesse-Darmstadt M1796 10-pdr howitzer. (Schloss Friederichstein Museum)

Holland

In 1796 the United Provinces of Holland became the Batavian Republic. It had a foot artillery regiment, a horse artillery battalion and a battalion of train troops. The equipment was a mixture of French Gribeauval and Austrian pieces. In 1799, Holland was invaded by Anglo-Russian forces. In 1805 the contingent from the Batavian Republic formed part of VIII Corps of the Grande Armée.

The Royal Dutch army was formed on 4 July 1806 with the installation of Louis Bonaparte as king. In 1810, Louis abdicated and Holland became part of Metropolitan France. The foot artillery Regiment became the French 9th Artillery Regiment, with Gribeauval and AnXI pieces, and the two horse companies became the cadre for the 7th Horse Artillery Regiment. The latter was headquartered at La Haye; one company was sent on service in Spain and the other was based in Hanover on garrison duties. By a decree of 18 October 1811 the

Dutch foot artillery gunner (left), horse artillery gunner (centre) and trumpeter standing around a limbered 6-pdr gun in c1808. (By kind permission Landes u. Universitätsbibliothek Darmstadt; photograph Marcus Stein)

horse artillery were distributed amongst the other French horse artillery regiments and their Dutch identity was lost. In 1814, the artillery regiment had 23 companies (three more than French artillery regimental establishment) when it was transferred to the new Netherlands army.

Kingdom of Italy

On 17 March 1805, Napoleon unified the remaining northern Italian states to form the Kingdom of Italy (in direct violation of the Treaty of Luneville, 9 February 1801). The kingdom was administered by Napoleon's stepson Eugène de Beauharnais as his viceroy, and was expanded to include Venice (1806), the remaining Italian states up to the border with the Kingdom of Naples (1808), and the southern Tyrol (1810).[203] The Kingdom of Italy was armed with ordnance primarily from Piedmont, mostly M1786, with some from France (*see* Table 5.8). In 1800, General Allix was instructed to form a new artillery train for the French army on campaign in Italy. The Allix M1800 system was cast in Turin by General Allix and based upon Piedmont M1786 designs. (Allix was a competent artilleryman, who later devised his own artillery system in the 1820s.)

On 14 April 1806 artillery schools were established at Alessandrie and Turin, as were two foot artillery regiments. The M1786 guns for the kingdom were ordered to be cast at Pavia because the arsenals at Alessandrie and Turin were being used to produce guns for the French army. All guns for the field army were to be of 3-, 6- and

Table 5.8: Ordnance used by Kingdom of Italy, 1806–1814

Piedmont M1786 guns were cast in Turin and later Pavia. A few Gribeauval, System An XI and M1808 guns cast in France were given to the Kingdom of Italy.

Model	Calibre	Shot diameter	Bore length	Tube length	Weight	Windage	Shot weight	Charge weight
Gribeauval M1765/1777								
12-pdr	120mm	118.7mm	16.5 calibres	216cm	868kg	2.1mm	6000g	1800g
6.4 inch Howitzer	160mm	158.1mm	3 calibres	77cm	327kg	3.9mm	9800g	800g
Piedmontese M1786								
12-pdr	122mm	120mm	16 calibres	224cm	982.8kg	2mm	6000g	1900g
6-pdr	96.5mm	94.5mm	17 calibres	174cm	409.5kg	2mm	3000g	1100g
3-pdr	76mm	74mm	16 calibres	155cm	311.2kg	2.2mm	1000g	800g
7-pdr Howitzer	140mm	138mm	7 calibres	115cm	294.8kg	2mm	ND	ND
AnIX (M1803)								
12-pdr	121.3mm	120mm	16,8 calibres	210cm	760kg	1.3mm	6100g	1958g
6-pdr	95mm	93.9mm	16.6 calibres	170cm	390kg	1.9mm	3000g	1100g
7-pdr Howitzer	151.5mm	149mm	5 calibres	101cm	300kg	2.1mm	6600kg	1000g
M1808 System								
6-pdr	95mm	93.9mm	17.2 calibres	180cm	409.5kg	2.1mm	2600g	1000g
24-pdr Howitzer	148mm	146.1mm	7 calibres	120cm	327kg	2.9mm	6100g	1000g

Table 5.9: Distribution of ordnance and caissons for Kingdom of Italy, 17 July 1806

	Pieces	Caissons	Notes
Palmonava	four 12-pdr, twelve 6-pdr, four Howitzers	60 caissons	Joined II Corps of Grande Armée
Verona	six 12-pdr, four Howitzers, twenty 6-pdr	100 caissons	Retained in arsenal
Pavia	six 12-pdr, six Howitzers, eighteen 6-pdr	–	Sent to Kingdom of Naples
Alessandrie	six 12-pdr, six Howitzers, eighteen 6-pdr some 3-pdr mountain guns	–	Retained in arsenal

12-pdr calibres. On 18 July 1806 the artillery of the Kingdom of Italy had 118 pieces available for its field army; for distribution (*see* Table 5.9).[204] The guns at Palmanava were to be sent to join II Corps of the Grande Armée; those at Pavia were sent to reinforce the army of the Kingdom of Naples. In addition, 52 Dutch guns then in use with the army were withdrawn to the fortresses and arsenals of Osopp, Palmanova, Venice, Legnago, Peschia, Plaisance and Alessandrie; and the old French 4- and 8-pdrs were taken out of service and placed into store. For the number of guns held in reserve by December 1806 (*see* Table 5.10).

Napoleon ordered that the number of guns should be increased to 280 pieces. Stores including gunpowder (as well as Prussian muskets and 186,000 cartridges) were shipped to Italy from the former Prussian fortress of Wesel.

The decree of 8 December 1806 formally organised the artillery of the Kingdom of Italy. Any guns of different calibres from those used in France were to be withdrawn to the arsenals and, where possible, re-bored to French calibres. The decree also handed over to the Kingdom of Italy three parks of French guns; two were kept in reserve at Alessandrie and Genes, and the other was to be used in the field – this consisted of 6× 12-pdrs, 18× 6-pdrs and 6× 24-pdr howitzers. In addition, 30× mountain 3-pdrs were also formed into a reserve brigade. In 1807 the Italian division serving with the Grande Armée in Germany had 2× 12-pdrs, 8× 6-pdrs and 2× 24-pdr howitzers manufactured in France (*see* Table 5.11).

On 7 January 1809 the foot artillery had 72 French guns in service and 12 guns with the horse artillery, supported by 400 vehicles and 2,000 horses. In addition, a further 18 guns of the Italian type were supported by 85 Italian vehicles. In 1811 the reserve guns for the Kingdom of Italy totalled 495 pieces (*see* Table 5.12).

In 1812 the Italian artillery was brigaded with the Imperial Guard, serving 18× 3-pdrs that had been assigned as regimental artillery but instead formed three batteries of conventional foot artillery.

Kleve-Berg

In the summer of 1808, Kleve-Berg formed a single battalion with a foot battery (6× French 8-pdr guns and 2× 6.4in howitzers) and a horse battery (6× 4-pdr guns); an engineer company and a train company were also formed. The foot battery operated as regimental artillery for the 1st to 3rd Berg Infantry Regiments. Berg took part in the Prussian campaign of 1807, sent troops to Spain in 1808–13, and operated against Austria in 1809.

Piedmont M1786 24-pdr field gun. (Steven H. Smith)

On 15 June 1811 a decree directed that the horse artillery battery have 4× 6-pdr cannon and 2× howitzers, with 4× 6-pdr caissons, 2× howitzer caissons, 4× infantry caissons and a park wagon.[205] On 25 June it was decreed that the 1st to 4th Berg Infantry Regiments were each to be equipped with 2× 6-pdr cannon, 3× 6-pdr caissons, 3× infantry caissons, a field forge, a spare gun carriage and a park wagon. According to the returns for 26 September 1811, the 4th Infantry Regiment had had its regimental artillery removed and the vehicles probably issued to the horse artillery battery. On 24 October 1811 the Berg artillery was organised into three artillery companies.

Table 5.10: Ordnance, carriages and vehicles in reserve, Kingdom of Italy, December 1806

	Gun tubes	Carriages	Vehicles
Plaissance	19× 6-pdr,	28× 6-pdr carriages	24 caissons
	2× 12-pdr	6× 12-pdr carriages	6 field forges
		3× 24-pdr Howitzer carriages	3 munitions carts
Alessandrie	6× 12-pdr	4× 12-pdr carriages	28 caissons
		1× 24-pdr Howitzer carriage	12 munitions carts
Turin			71 caissons
Genes			58 caissons

Table 5.11: Equipment of Italian troops with Grande Armée, 1807 (Lechartier, 1907)
(Note: the train had 14× ammunition wagons and 2× field forges.)

	Pieces	Replacement gun carriages	Rounds	Caissons
12-pdr	2	1	630 rounds	6
6-pdr	8	2	2,677 rounds	16
24-pdr Howitzer	2	1	506 rounds	6
Infantry caissons	–	–	137,440 cartridges	12

Table 5.12: Reserve ordnance of Kingdom of Italy established at Alessandrie and supplied by Turin foundry by 1 January 1811

Calibre	At Alessandrie	Moved to Alessandrie	Supplied by 1811	Total guns available
24-pdr Howitzer tubes	143	0	17	
24-pdr Howitzer carriages	71	58	31	160 guns
12-pdr cannon	52	9	68	
12-pdr carriages	49	3	78	130 guns
6-pdr cannon	29	9	101	
6-pdr carriages	29	9	101	130 guns
3-pdr cannon	29	0	46	
3-pdr carriages	29	0	46	75 guns
Total	253 tubes 178 carriages	18 tubes 70 carriages	232 tubes 256 carriages	495 guns

In 1812 the army of Berg served as 1st Brigade, 26th Division, and 30th Light Cavalry Brigade, of IX Corps of the Grande Armée. The contingent fielded 8× French 6-pdr guns and 4× 24-pdr French howitzers. The 1st to 3rd Infantry Regiments each had a regimental artillery section of 2× 6-pdrs.

On 16 January 1813 the foot artillery battery was armed with 4× 6-pdrs with 6× 6-pdr caissons, 4× infantry caissons, a field forge and a powder wagon. The horse artillery battery had been reduced to 2× 6-pdrs and a 24-pdr howitzer, with 3× 6-pdr caissons, a howitzer caisson, an infantry caisson, a field forge and a powder wagon. By July 1813 this battery had been reformed with 4× 6-pdrs and 2× howitzers, and was assigned to the French Imperial Guard.[206]

In November 1813 the Coalition allies invaded Berg, but by this time all Berg units had been disarmed and were treated as prisoners of war by the French. The former Prussian territories reverted to Prussia, and a foot battery and a horse half-battery were organised; the remaining territory was administrated by the Russian governor, General Justus Gruner. From 25 March 1815 the artillery became the Prussian 37th (6-pdr) Battery and the 20th Horse Battery respectively.[207] Later they received Prussian equipment.

Kingdom of Naples

The Kingdom of Naples was formed by the Imperial Decree of 13 April 1806 under Joseph Bonaparte, who was elevated to the throne. He lacked any military interests and did little to build a new army, except for a strong Guard (mostly French). Raising an army in the new kingdom proved to be difficult, due to financial limitations caused in part by the Neapolitan treasury having to pay the French troops assigned to Naples, and the lack of a proper recruiting organisation. The establishment of national conscription on 29 March 1807 eventually addressed this problem.

As a former Bourbon-ruled country, Naples was equipped with Gribeauval ordnance. The field army had some French 8-pdrs, and Neapolitan 6-pdrs that were presumably Austrian or Piedmontese. In July 1806, France sent 6× 12-pdr guns, 6× howitzers and 18× 6-pdr guns to reinforce the artillery.

Poland and the Duchy of Warsaw

Poland was one of France's strongest allies from the time of the Revolutionary Wars. In 1772 she had suffered the First Partition by Austria, Prussia and Russia. In 1792 the Polish Commonwealth started to fight against the dismemberment of the kingdom, and a Second Partition was agreed between Prussia and Russia in St Petersburg on 23 January 1793. In 1795 a new treaty of partition between Austria, Prussia and Russia wiped Poland off the map.

In 1798, two Polish Legions of exiled volunteers were set up by France in the pay of her satellite Cisalpine Republic. These evolved, and from 1808 the successor Vistula Legion was with French forces in Spain. In 1812 it served in Russia as the Division Claparede assigned to the Young Guard.

On 27 November 1806, Murat's cavalry reached Warsaw and liberated part of the Prussian-occupied sector of partitioned Poland. Here Polish military forces began to gather; foot artillery started forming in November 1806, and several companies took part in fighting in Pomerania. General Jan Henryk Dombrowski, in compliance with Napoleon's designs, began forming a 30,000-strong Polish army and planned a widespread uprising; in mid-November he summoned for service former Polish Commonwealth soldiers, and started calling up one conscript from every ten households.

On 15 January 1807, Prince Joseph Poniatowski (1763–1813) was appointed Minister of War in the Polish Directory government. Three days later the 1st to 3rd Artillery Battalions were created, each of three artillery companies, one engineer company and one supply company; these units were attached to the three Legions commanded by Generals Poniatowski, Zajczek and Dombrowski. The 3rd Artillery Battalion of Dombrowski's Legion was the only unit to participate in the campaign of 1807, when it fought in the vicinity of Tczew (Dirschau, eastern Pomerania), participated in the siege of Danzig (Gdansk) that fell on 27 May 1807, and arrived just too late to participate in the victory of Friedland (14 June 1807).

Under the terms of the Treaty of Tilsit (7–9 July 1807), Prussia ceded the land taken from Poland since 1772 to Napoleon. On 12 July 1807, Napoleon created the Duchy of Warsaw, with a constitution that

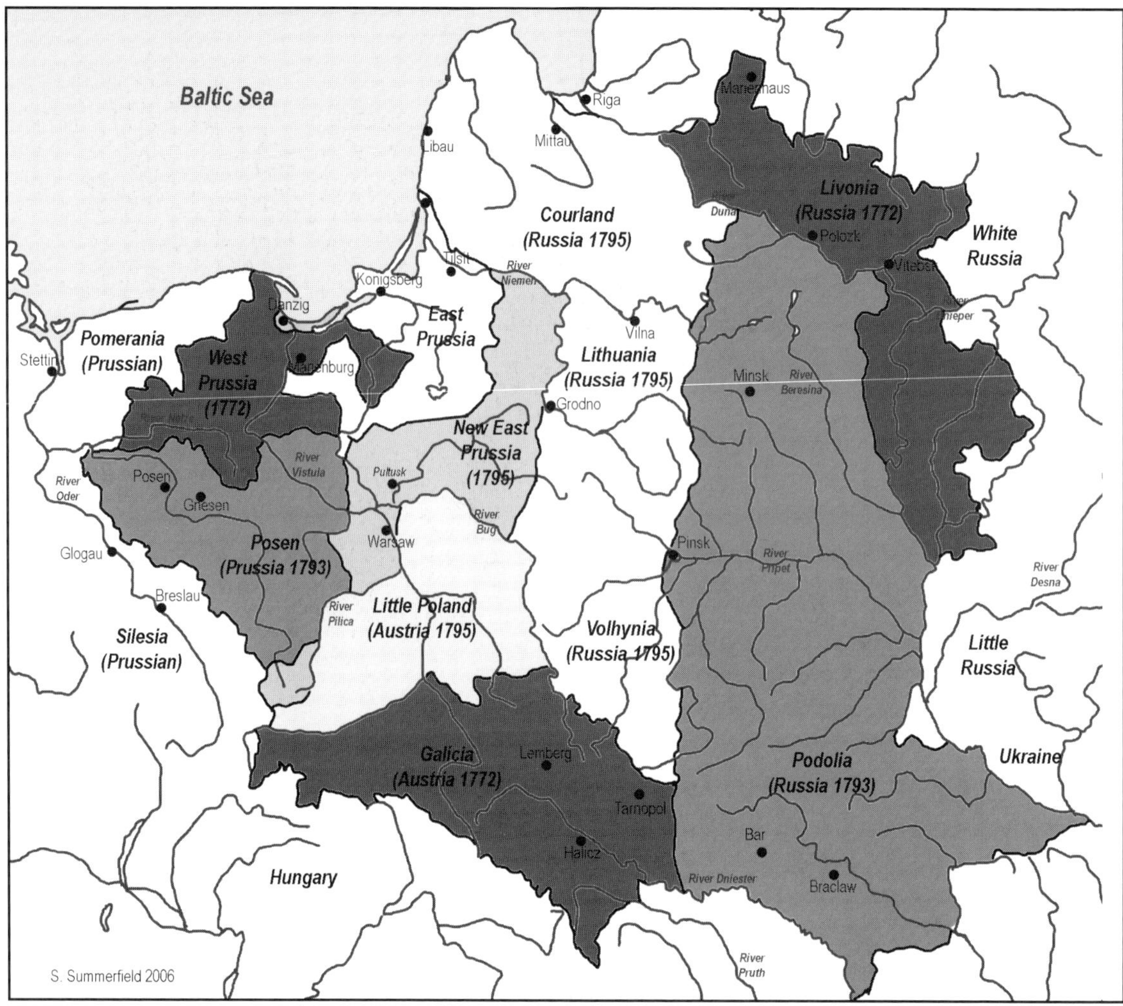

The partitions of Poland in 1772, 1793 and 1795.

eliminated serfdom and created institutions modelled upon those of France.[208] The constitution guaranteed an elected parliament; and Frederick Augustus, King of Saxony, became the Duke of Warsaw, governing from Dresden in Saxony.

This small state, with a population of about 2.5 million people, had an army of 30,000 enlisted men between 20 and 28 years of age. The artillery lacked suitable men and material; veterans from the old Polish Commonwealth army were mostly too old to serve and were unfamiliar with the new guns. The core of the artillery was formed by Polish artillerymen who had served in the Prussian army, returned exiles, and veterans of the artillery of Légion Polonaise d'Italie and Légion du Danube. General Wincenty Aksamitowski became the first temporary commander of the merged technical arms. The highest-ranking positions were occupied by French instructors transferred to the duchy at Poniatowski's request. Polish artillery officers were educated by two Warsaw artillery and engineering schools – the Elementary School, established 1808, and Apprenticeship School, established 1809. The Polish artillery was well trained, although too few in numbers and partially equipped with older guns, mainly from Prussia.

As there was no cannon foundry in the Duchy of Warsaw, there was little standardisation among the

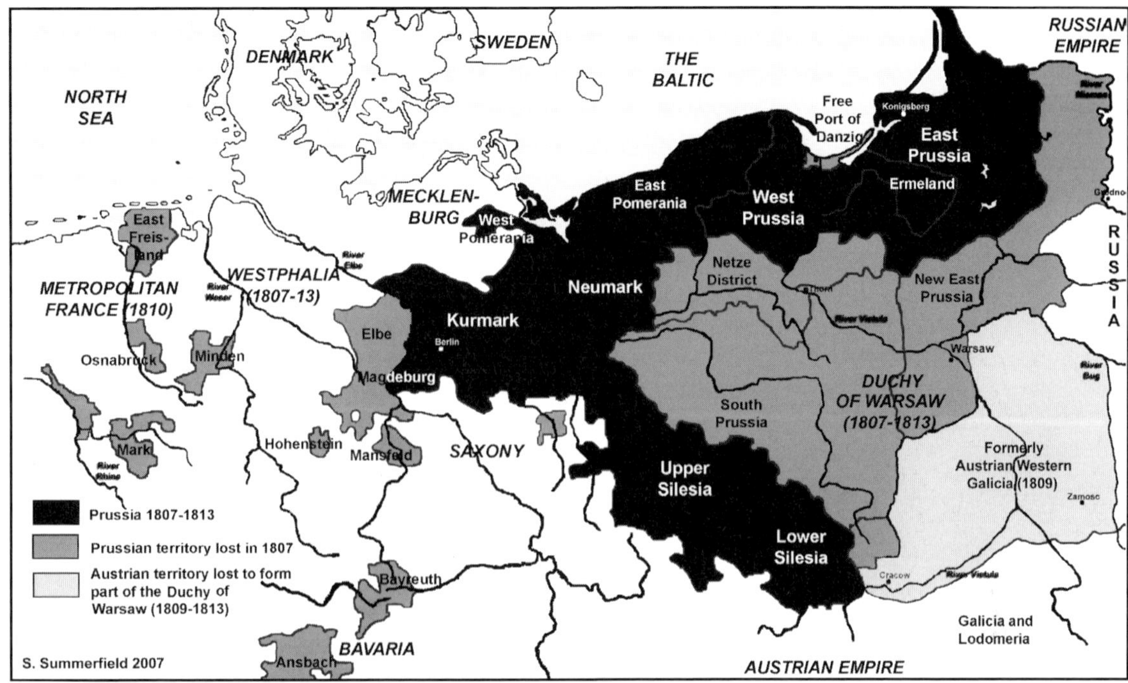

Duchy of Warsaw, 1807–13.

types of ordnance and vehicles, mostly of Austrian and Prussian manufacture. The only French ordnance used before the re-arming of Poniatowski's corps in 1813 was that provided to the Polish Division and the Vistula Legion serving in Spain, and the Danzig Division formed in 1811.

In autumn 1807, Napoleon sold the Poles 204 guns, carriages, ammunition and other equipment captured at Jena-Auerstädt from the Prussians (for 1,997,270 French francs, as agreed by a Franco-Polish commission). With these new guns, the field and garrison artillery of the duchy amounted to some 250 pieces.[209] In November 1807 the organisation of the artillery was as follows:

1st Foot Artillery: 354 men – LtCol Dobrski
2nd Foot Artillery: 597 men – LtCol Górski
3rd Foot Artillery: 389 men – LtCol Hurtig

In 1808 a company of artillery with 4 officers and 145 other ranks was sent to Spain. That same year the Horse Artillery was raised; the first company was organised by Captain W. Potocki, and the second company by Roman Sotyk, who had studied in Paris.[210] In January 1809 the Polish artillery and sappers were organised as follows:[211]

Inspector, Art. and Eng.: Gen J.B. Pelletier (French)
Director of Engineers: Capt J.B. Mallet (French)
Chief-of-Staff of Artillery: Col Górski
Director of Artillery: Col P. Bontemps (French)

1st Foot Arty Bn: 409 men – LtCol Redel
2nd Foot Arty Bn: 137 men – LtCol Górski
3rd Foot Arty Bn: 266 men – LtCol Hurtig
Foot Arty Train Bn: 402 men

1st Horse Bty: 119 men – LtCol W. Potocki
Horse Arty Train Sqn: 119 men

1st Sapper Coy: 79 men
2nd Sapper Coy: 103 men
3rd Sapper Coy: 91 men
Pontoon Coy: 67 men

Just before the 1809 campaign, additional supply columns were attached to the train battalion; these

Duchy of Warsaw Horse Artillery. (Left to right:) officer, 1810; trumpeter, 1807; gunner, 1807; and gunner in stable jacket, 1810. (Pawel Nowaczek)

were disbanded at the end of the hostilities. An artifiser company took care of the repair of equipment and arms. In April 1809, Colonel Pierre Bontemps reported that the duchy had 244 efficient guns, among them 111× field guns and 54× howitzers. Most of the guns were located in fortresses. He considered this number insufficient, noting that only eight mortars could be found within the duchy. Companies were organised in the fortresses of Torun (Thorn), Praga, Serock and Modlin.[212]

On 15 April 1809, Archduke Ferdinand d'Este crossed the border into the duchy with 32,000 Austrian troops and 94 guns. To oppose them Poniatowski, the Minister of War and Commander-in-Chief, had about 18,000 men (including 2,000 Saxons) and 32 field guns. The battle of Raszyn (19 April 1809) was a stalemate; the Austrians failed to crush the fledgling Polish army, whose artillery played a vital role. In May 1809, Poniatowski launched an offensive into Galicia to the rear of Ferdinand's army. Artillery and engineers played a leading part in the capture of Sandomierz (18 May) and Zamosc (20 May), so exposing Archduke Ferdinand's line of communication running south from Warsaw to Krakow.[213] The Poles captured 46 guns. The subsequent defence of Sandomierz (15–18 June) cost the Polish garrison 1,000 dead and wounded plus 42 guns. Archduke Ferdinand evacuated all military stores to Krakow and destroyed the fortifications before he joined Archduke Charles

Spanish crew loading a Gribeauval-type 4-pdr gun in 1813. (Authors' collection)

at Wagram, where Napoleon's victory (5–6 July) decided the outcome of the campaign. At the end of the campaign the army of the duchy thus had a net loss of only four guns, but captured 62 Austrian pieces that were put into immediate service; thus, in effect, the artillery were re-equipped with new Austrian guns from 1809.[214]

As a result of the Treaty of Schönbrunn (14 October 1809), the Duchy of Warsaw was enlarged; it was given four new departments, taking the number to ten, and its population grew to 4.2 million. The army was doubled to 60,000 men (seventeen infantry and sixteen cavalry regiments) divided into four district divisions. The artillery now possessed 306 guns. On 30 March 1810, the Artillery Corps comprised a headquarters; a foot artillery regiment (twelve field companies and four garrison companies); a horse artillery regiment (four batteries each of 4× 6-pdr guns and 2× howitzers); a battalion of sappers, and an artificer company.

In autumn 1810 relations with Russia worsened, and Napoleon provided the Polish fortresses with 50 iron guns, transported at the expense of the King of Saxony from the Western Pomeranian fortress of Stettin (Szczecin). They did not arrive until May 1811, with half going to the fortified town of Torun on the right bank of the Vistula, and the remainder kept on the barges so that they could be sent 145km down-river to Danzig in case of Russian attack. The Poles obtained 34× Prussian 3-pdr guns and carriages from Mainz, to equip regimental artillery formed in October 1810. Six of these guns, intended for the regiments garrisoning Danzig, stayed in the Prussian fortress of Küstrin.[215]

Tsar Alexander's decree of 31 December 1810 to open his ports to British goods, and intelligence of movements by the Russian army towards the duchy at the beginning of 1811, decided Napoleon upon war. As relations with Russia deteriorated further the Duchy of Warsaw spent over 9 million zlotys on fortification.

In early 1812, four foot artillery companies commanded by Colonel Górski went on French pay; the remaining fourteen companies and the two garrison companies were distributed between the several fortresses in the duchy. With the threat of a Russian invasion, the 49 officers and 1,640 foot artillerymen undertook manoeuvres with the infantry and firing exercises, built fortifications and worked with portable cranes. Three companies of the horse artillery regiment commanded by Colonel Hurtig (15 officers and 315 gunners) were quartered in Warsaw and Wocawek on the left bank of the Vistula, and the fourth in Danzig.

In June 1812, V Corps of the Grande Armée, commanded by Poniatowski, comprised the 16th to 18th Infantry Divisions and three light cavalry brigades, totalling more than 36,000 men. General Jean Pelletier commanded the artillery, Colonel Jean Mallet the engineers, Lieutenant-Colonel Artur Potocki the sapper/miner battalion, and Captain Jan Bujalski the company of pontoneers. V Corps took to Russia 48 artillery pieces (6× 12-pdrs, 30× 6-pdrs and 12× Austrian 7-pdr howitzers), plus 20× 3-pdr regimental guns – mostly Prussian. The 16th (Zayonchek), 17th (Dombrowski) and 18th (Kamieniecki) Divisions each had two foot artillery batteries of 4× 6-pdrs and two 7-pdr howitzers, and the reserve had a battery of 6× 12-pdrs and one of 6× 6-pdrs.[216] Two horse batteries, each of 4× 6-pdrs and 2× howitzers, were attached to 4th Light Cavalry Division of Latour Maubourg's 4th Reserve Cavalry Corps.[217] Both the 7th Division (Grandjean) from Macdonald's X Corps, and the 28th Division (Girard) from Victor's IX Corps, had a foot battery of 8× guns and 6× regimental guns.[218]

The Duchy of Warsaw lost only ten guns in Russia. On 10 November 1812, Poniatowski had 45 pieces (excluding the regimental guns, and those guns of 17th Division at Smolensk). The Poles reached Warsaw with 32 guns and all but one of their standards – a remarkable feat of arms. On 25 December 1812, Poniatowski reviewed the remnants of his V Corps at Warsaw. On 5 February 1813 he led the Polish army into Galicia, and in March 1813 he was appointed by Napoleon as commander of VIII Corps.

On 27 June 1813, Napoleon decreed the organisation of VIII Corps with 20 guns brought from Poland and another 24 pieces supplied from French arsenals. He planned to form two Polish infantry divisions with 24 guns, two Polish cavalry divisions with 12 guns, and a reserve with 8× 12-pdr guns. The French guns in fact did not arrive for a long time, so 18× 6-pdr Prussian guns had to be adapted for French ammunition; in mid-June 1813 the first six barrels were sent to a foundry in Saxony to be re-bored.

At the battle of Leipzig (16–19 October 1813) the Polish Corps practically ceased to exist, losing more than 10,000 killed, wounded or taken prisoner.[219] On 19 October many gunners lost their lives and two artillery batteries were abandoned due to the premature demolition of the bridge over the River Elster; the wounded Poniatowski drowned while trying to swim his horse across the river, just four days after being made a Marshal of the Empire. Colonel Bontemps salvaged 38 guns, but had to leave eight of these in Erfurt due to lack of horses, and a further three were abandoned during the retreat to the Rhine. On 1 November 1813 the 27 remaining guns with horses and vehicles reached the fortress of Mainz on the west bank of the Rhine, and these were placed in the arsenal as the Poles retired into France. On 15 December 1813 the artillery numbered only 52 officers and 471 other ranks when they reached Sedan; there Napoleon organised them into four foot artillery companies and a horse artillery company.

For the 1814 campaign in France the Polish artillery was reduced to single foot and horse artillery batteries. The Polish horse battery fought at Brienne (29 January), Montmirail (11 March), Reims (13 March), and Arcis-sur-Aube (20–21 March).[220] The foot artillery prepared cartridges for the infantry until mid-March; on 16 March the battery received six French M1808 6-pdr guns at the Champs de Mars, and arrived on the second day of the battle of Arcis-sur-Aube, where it joined the Artillery of the Guard. On 30 March 1814 the Polish batteries of Walewski, Bujalski and Piêtka defended the St Denis neighbourhood of Paris. When Parisians saw the Polish gunners serving their pieces stripped to the waist and streaming with sweat, they brought them whole casks of wine, saying that if only the

French artillery were fighting like that they would succeed in defending Paris. General Sokolnicki defended the Buttes de Chaumont with three companies of Gardes d'Honneur, young volunteers from the Polytechnic, and Polish gunners who served guns taken from the school. Meanwhile, General Pac was fighting in La Villette.[221] The next day Napoleon abdicated.

On 24 April 1814, Tsar Alexander I accepted the salute of 4,750 Polish soldiers and 50 generals loyal to the defeated Emperor on the fields of St Denis. On 30 May 1814 the remnants of the Polish army, comprising 5,800 officers and men, began their march back to Poland. On 19 August 1814 the artillery reached Poznan. The foot artillery numbered 26 officers and 459 soldiers with 10× guns and 4× 24-pdr howitzers; the horse artillery had 5 officers and 115 gunners, with 6× 6-pdr guns and 141 horses.[222] The guns of French manufacture that had been taken at Leipzig were returned to them. On 30 April 1815, Tsar Alexander I was proclaimed King of Poland.[223] The army of the Polish Kingdom (1815–1830) was re-equipped with Russian guns, the French pieces being relegated to no more than souvenirs of the Napoleonic epoch.

Spain

In 1743, Spain adopted the Vallière system. In the 1770s Jean Maritz II was sent by the King of France to implement the Gribeauval system and to improve the foundries at Seville and Barcelona. In 1783 the Gribeauval system was adopted throughout Spain. According to Adye, the pre-1803 equipment had 12-pdr (123mm), 9-pdr (103mm) and 6-pdr (90mm) guns. In 1803 the head of government, Godoy, attempted to standardise upon French calibres; it appears that the 8-pdr was the heaviest field gun used due to the lack of draft animals. The Vallière guns were assigned to garrison and siege duty, especially the 16-pdrs and 24-pdrs.

A typical foot artillery company in theory had 6× 4-pdrs, 4× 8-pdrs and 2× howitzers. In practice, a foot artillery company might have anything from six to eighteen guns, and the horse artillery six guns. The lack of a train meant that guns were moved by mules or horses hired from contractors. The presence of Gribeauval guns in Spain has caused endless confusion. Interestingly, most if not all the Gribeauval guns used by the French in the Peninsula and by the army of King Joseph had been captured from the Spanish.

It was not until 1816 that any tactical doctrine was written for the artillery, and this was based heavily on French practices.[224]

Westphalia

Westphalia inherited equipment from Brunswick, Hanover and Hesse-Kassel, the latter being 16× 3-pdr regimental guns and 2× 1-pdr amusettes.[225]

The Kingdom of Westphalia was created on 15 November 1807. In December that year the four foot artillery batteries raised were armed with Russian guns that matched French calibres. A year later Napoleon sent some French guns to Westphalia, along with powder and munitions. By 1809 six companies of foot artillery had been raised and one of horse artillery; each of these was armed with 4× 6-pdr guns and 2× 7-pdr howitzers (a total of 28× 6-pdrs and 16× 7-pdr howitzers). By the end of 1811, Westphalia had 1st and 8th Infantry Regiments in Danzig with two guns each; and two horse artillery companies and four foot artillery companies, manning between them 36× guns and 14× howitzers, based in Kassel.

Napoleon wrote to his youngest brother Jerome, King of Westphalia, urging him to establish a 12-pdr battery; this was mentioned in the order of battle for VIII Corps in 1812. The equipment used during the Russian campaign was apparently of French design. The gun tubes were either French- or Prussian-inspired designs mounted on Gribeauval-style carriages:

26× 6-pdr field guns with 4× replacement gun carriages and 41× caissons (1,020 canister rounds, 4,325 roundshot)
8× 24-pdr howitzers with 25× caissons (48 canister rounds, 1,472 shell)
4× 12-pdr field guns with 12× caissons, and 23× infantry caissons.

The train had 9× tool carts, 11× field forges, a coal wagon, an ammunition wagon, 5× pontoon wagons and 11× baggage wagons.

Table 5.13: Ordnance used by Westphalia, 1807–14

	Calibre	Bore length	Tube weight	Carriage weight	Limber weight
Russian					
12-pdr heavy	120mm	16.5 calibres	819kg	672kg	385kg
12-pdr light	120mm	16.5 calibres	475kg	500kg	385kg
6-pdr	95mm	17 calibres	369kg	393kg	385kg
Gribeauval Style					
6-pdr	94.5 cm	18 calibres	380kg	ND	327kg
Prussian M1768					
6-pdr M1768	94.5 cm	18 calibres	380kg	ND	458kg
7-pdr M1763 Howitzer	148mm	4.5 calibres	792kg	ND	458kg
French M1808					
24-pdr Howitzer	148 cm	8 calibres	327kg	ND	327kg
Hanoverian M1795					
6-pdr	94.5mm	18 calibres	672kg	791kg	304kg
12-pdr	120mm	18 calibres	1300kg	1000kg	374kg
7-pdr Howitzer	120mm	6 calibres	341kg	706kg	389kg

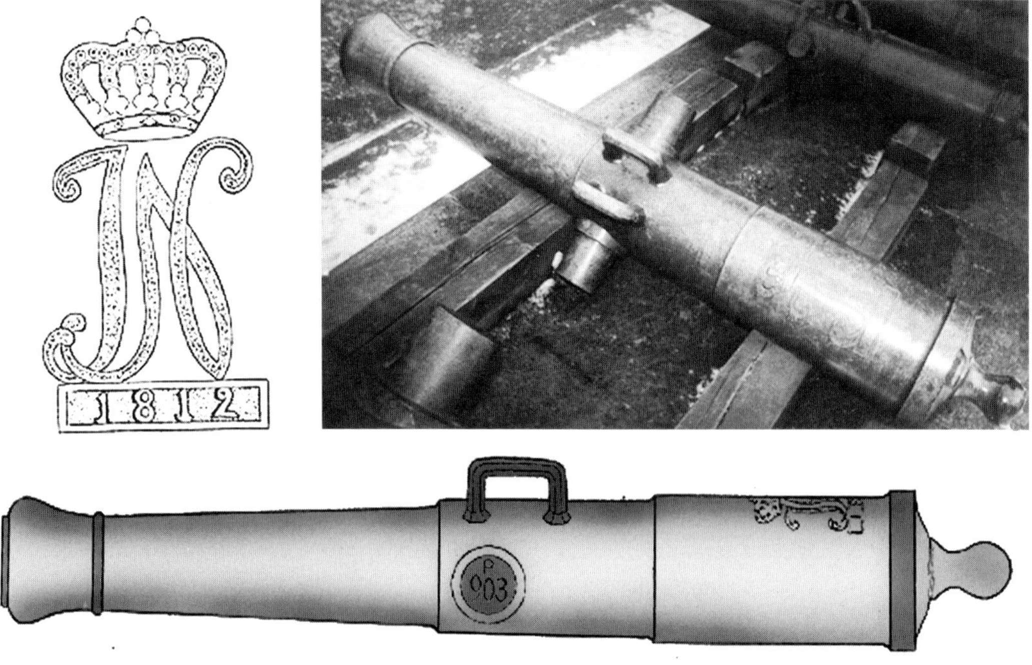

French-type Westphalian 6-pdr gun; (inset) Westphalian royal monogram. (Steven H. Smith)

During 1813 a 5th Artillery Company was formed, just before Westphalia ceased to exist at the end of the year.

FOREIGN GUNS IN COALITION SERVICE

The use of foreign guns in the Coalition was dominated by those supplied by Britain or captured pieces. Interestingly, Russian 10-pud unicorns and iron 18-pdrs, cast in 1785–90 by the Carron company of Scotland, were used in the siege artillery in the Peninsula, and were apparently judged unfit for service.[226]

A letter from Richard Bruckner to Alexander Dickson of 10 July 1813 indicated that the following French guns and equipment were in use by the Royal Artillery:

1st: 6× 12-pdrs, 3× caissons, 1× forge
2nd: 6× 8-pdrs, 3× caissons
3rd: 6× 12-pdrs, 3× caissons
4th: 6× 8-pdrs, 3× caissons, 1× forge
5th: 6× 6.4in howitzers, 12× howitzer caissons.

Brunswick

In 1806 Brunswick was allied to Prussia, and in 1807 Napoleon incorporated Brunswick into the Kingdom of Westphalia. In 1809 the deposed Duke Friedrich Wilhelm enlisted his émigré 'Black Legion' in Austrian service and received Austrian equipment. The artillery was formed as a single battery of horse artillery attached to the duke's hussar regiment. Austria supplied 2× 6-pdr *Kavalerie Artillerie* guns and 2× 7-pdr howitzers, and the 80 gunners, commanded by Lieutenant Genderer, were trained using the Austrian manual.

After the defeat of the Austrians the Duke of Brunswick marched across Germany to join the British fleet at the mouth of the River Weser; his force was shipped to the Isle of Wight, where the artillery was disbanded.

In 1814, Brunswick was once again an independent state. The duke purchased at auction two complete batteries that had been captured the previous year at Leipzig (12× French 6-pdrs, 4× Westphalian 7-pdr howitzers of Prussian design, 32× caissons, 2× field forges and various other equipment).[227]

Kingdom of the Netherlands

On 21 January 1815 the Netherlands had 72× short bronze 12-pdr cannon; 114× 6-pdrs; 83× 3-pdrs; 124× 16-pdr (20cm) stone-firing howitzers; 87× 24-pdr (15cm) iron howitzers; 315× gun-carriages; 238× limbers with ammunition chests; and 144× caissons of mixed origin. There was more than enough ammunition available for all the different ordnance. Many were bronze guns cast in the Hague before 1810, of the modified Dutch M1770 model, while others were French Gribeauval or AnXI (M1803) guns.

The limbers and gun carriages were a mixture of French and Dutch models, so interchangeability was seldom achieved; for example, one artillery battery had seven different kinds of wheels in use. The caissons were badly constructed, heavy and cumbersome. Many of the gun carriages were old and worn out, many of them still with wooden axles; the remainder were new but constructed from unseasoned wood. Horse harness and other artillery equipment were generally lacking. The equipment allocation in 1815 was as follows:

Foot artillery company:
6× short bronze 6-pdr guns, 2× 24-pdr bronze howitzers, 12× 6-pdr caissons, 5× howitzer caissons, 12× caissons loaded with infantry and cavalry cartridges, 3× spare carriages, 2× baggage wagons, 1× field forge

Horse artillery company:
6× short bronze 6-pdr guns, 2× 24-pdr bronze howitzers, 14× 6-pdr caissons, 6× howitzer caissons, 4× caissons with infantry and cavalry cartridges, 3× spare carriages,2× baggage wagons, 1× field forge

12-pdr company:
6× short bronze 12-pdr guns, 2× 24-pdr bronze howitzers, 12× 12-pdr caissons, 5× howitzer caissons, 4× caissons with infantry and cavalry cartridges, 3× spare carriages, 2× baggage wagons, 1× field forge.

Portugal

In the 1790s Portugal had four home-based artillery regiments, each with a regimental establishment of 989 men in one company of bombardiers, one of miners, one of pontoneers and seven of gunners. There were also various independent invalid and fortress companies, and the emphasis was mainly on garrison duties rather than field operations. The regiments were named after their regional headquarters, and were renamed and numbered in 1806: Corte (from 1806, Lisbon, 1st), Algarve (Lagos, 2nd), Alemtejo (Estremoz, 3rd) and Porto (4th). In 1797 two horse artillery companies were raised by the Corte Regiment, but these were disbanded in January 1804.

The Portuguese artillery's cannon were 12-pdrs (119.4mm), 9-pdrs (109.2mm), 6-pdrs (95.3mm) and 3-pdrs (74mm), and howitzers are variously reported as of 5in or 6in calibre. A surviving Portuguese 6-pdr in the Musée de l'Armée has a calibre of 93mm; the tube is 118cm long and weighs 680kg. In 1806 field batteries were each to have 2× 3-pdr guns, 2× 6-pdrs, 1× 9-pdr and 1× howitzer. After the French invasion all regiments were disbanded in December 1807. On 30 September 1808, after the French were defeated by the British expeditionary force, the regiments were ordered re-raised according to the 1806 regulations, but they were short of trained men, guns, and all kinds of equipment.[228]

When Marshal William Beresford (1768–1854) undertook the reorganisation and re-training of the Portuguese army from February 1809 he integrated British officers who, with their well-educated Portuguese counterparts, created efficient field units. Each regiment contributed detachments to form 'brigades' (batteries) for allocation to the divisions of the Anglo-Portuguese field army. British ordnance was also increasingly provided. In August 1809 the following brigades were listed:

Major Alexander Dickson's Division:
- Captain S.J. de Arriaga's (6× 6-pdrs)
- Captain I. José's (4× 6-pdrs)
- Captain J. da Cunha Preto's (6× 6-pdrs)
- *unknown* (6× 3-pdrs)

Major Victor von Arentschild's Division:
- Major von Arentschild's (6× 9-pdrs)
- Captain F.A. Sequeita's (6× 6-pdrs).

In 1810 the Portuguese artillery had eleven formed batteries, though only seven (totalling 42 guns) could be assigned to Wellington's field army due to lack of draft animals; the four remaining batteries were in reserve at Trás os Montes. Brigade/battery organisation was described as similar but not identical to that in British units; manpower was about 300 – e.g. in June 1810, Arentschild's Brigade had 123 gunners from the 1st Regiment and 276 from the second.[229] Mules were used for all draft teams and mounts, and a brigade needed from less than 300 to more than 600 *(see below)*. In July 1811 units in the field with infantry formations were listed as:[230]

Reserve (A. Dickson's) Division:
- S.J. de Arriaga's Bde (6× 6-pdrs) and W. Braun's Bde (6× 9-pdrs) – with Hamilton's Portuguese Infantry
- Lt A. da Costa e Silva's Bde (4× 6-pdrs) – with 6th Division
- J. da Cunha Preto's Bde (6× 6-pdrs) – with 5th Division

Major V. von Arentschild's Division:
- von Arentschild's Bde (6× 9-pdrs) – with 3rd Division
- F.A. Sequeita's Bde (6× 6-pdrs) – with 7th Division.

From May 1812 the 6- and 9-pdr batteries included a single 5½in howitzer in the British manner. In July 1812 an all-howitzer battery was formed; in November 1812 this unit was converted to 9-pdrs and brought up to full strength with men released by the disbanding of a company in Almeida. Equipment allocation to types of brigade in 1813 was as follows:

9-pdr brigade: 5× 9-pdr guns, 1× 5½in howitzer (48× mules); 18× wagons (108× mules), 1× field forge (6× mules), 1× spare-wheel cart (6× mules), 2× stores carts (4× mules), 12× reserve wagons (72× mules); 6× spare draft mules, 14× mules for officers and NCOs, 18× spare riding mules, 84× mules carrying fodder, 12× mules carrying rations

6-pdr brigade: 5× 6-pdr guns, 1× 5½in howitzer (36× mules); 12× wagons (72× mules), 1× field forge (6× mules), 1× spare-wheel cart (6× mules), 2× stores carts (4× mules), 10× reserve wagons (60× mules), 6× spare draft mules; 10× mules for officers and NCOs, 10× spare riding mules, 63× mules carrying fodder, 10× mules carrying rations

Howitzer brigade: 6× 5½in howitzers (48× mules); 26× wagons (208× mules), 1× field forge (6× mules), 1× spare-wheel cart (6× mules), 4× stores carts (8× mules), 18× reserve wagons (144× mules); 14× spare draft mules, 18× mules for officers and NCOs, 28× spare riding mules, 144× mules carrying fodder, 16× mules carrying rations.

Foreign Guns in Prussian Service

The lack of field artillery pieces was made up by gifts of artillery and powder captured by the Russians. Britain supplied gun tubes in 1807 and again in 1813, fitted mainly on British bracket and block-trail carriages or Prussian bracket carriages. Some guns and rolling stock destined originally for the East India Company may also have been used. For example: Captain Vahrenkampff's 24th (6-pdr) Foot Battery had 6× Blomefield Light 6-pdrs on block-trail carriages, 2× Prussian 7-pdr howitzers with wooden axles, and British ammunition wagons; all eight battery NCOs were mounted.

The complex diversity of ordnance used in 1813–15 must have been a logistic nightmare, with different calibres, qualities of gunpowder and spares. The following has been compiled from a number of sources, and gives a flavour of these difficulties.[231] They were not remedied until at least 1820, when all the guns and rolling stock were replaced with the Prussian M1816 system.

6-pdr foot batteries

Three 6-pdr foot batteries were mobilised in 1812 each with 6× Prussian 6-pdrs and 2× 7-pdr howitzers; a further fourteen 6-pdr foot batteries were mobilised in 1813.[232] Two of the latter used French guns.[233] Nine batteries were armed with British 6-pdrs and 5½in howitzers.[234] Five batteries mobilised in 1813, although designated as 6-pdr foot batteries, were armed with heavy (siege) guns.[235] It is unknown whether the 34th (6-pdr) Foot Battery ever received any ordnance.

12-pdr foot batteries

A half-battery was mobilised in 1812 and fully mobilised in 1813.[236] Three batteries had Prussian pieces in 1813.[237] Three batteries mobilised in 1813 were armed with French pieces.[238]

Horse batteries, 1813–15

Three batteries were mobilised with Prussian guns in 1812 and a further seven in 1813.[239] One battery raised in March 1813 from fortress and *Handwerks Artilleristen* (artillery artificers) was armed with Prussian pieces.[240] Five batteries mobilised in 1815 were armed with British guns.[241] Two batteries were armed with Russian guns in 1815 after being transferred from Russian, then British pay.[242] The armament of two further batteries formed in 1813 is unknown.[243]

Foreign Guns in Russian Service

Russia captured huge amounts of equipment during 1812, and most of this was lent or sold to their allies. During their wars against the Turks various Turkish pieces were also pressed into service. For example, the Don Opolchenie Cossack horse artillery half-company formed on 1 August 1812 were armed with Turkish gun barrels taken from the Victory Memorial in Novocherkassk.[244] The Russo-German Legion Foot Battery, commanded by Captain von Maghino and formed in August–October 1813 at Barth/Stralsund from former infantrymen, received eight rather worn British Blomefield 9-pdr cannons.[245]

6 Light and Mountain Ordnance

INTRODUCTION

During the Thirty Years War (1618–48) and English Civil Wars (1642–51) there was a plethora of small-calibre artillery pieces, such as the ¾-pdr robinet, 1¼-pdr falconet and the 2¾-pdr falcon; other small calibre pieces went under such names as the bass, drake and fowl.[246] Interestingly, in the early 18th century the Royal Ordnance still had on its list of brass pieces a 1-pdr and a 1½-pdr cannon, but by 1764 only the Heavy 1½-pdr gun was listed.

Ultra-light, highly portable artillery and mountain guns were designed to traverse awkward country. Their real value was thrown away if they operated in the valleys or low spurs that conventional artillery could occupy. Due to their small wheels, mountain guns could not move as rapidly as field or horse artillery over open ground. They came into their own in terrain where conventional artillery could not go: mountains (such as those of northern Portugal, the Pyrenees, the central spine of Italy and the Alps), or territory where few roads existed (such as North Africa, the Balkans and North America). Their effect upon the morale of the opponent was often out of all proportion to their size.[247]

Mules were the beast of burden for mountain ordnance; hence companies were often nicknamed 'jackass batteries'. If the terrain permitted, the mountain gun and carriage were connected to a *limonière* – a double shaft – and so could be pulled by one of the horses or mules. The mules were graded into three classes: the first class were assigned loads of 150kg, the second class loads of 130kg, and 100kg was the maximum load for the third class. General Gassendi noted that a mule was to carry its load for between six and eight hours.[248]

Ammunition mules were used instead of caissons, each carrying two wooden chests. To load them, four men simultaneously lifted the two chests and hooked them onto special chains attached to the packsaddle.

The ammunition chest was a long, narrow wooden box with an interior measurement of 83cm long, 12cm wide and 24cm deep. French regulations of 1828 called for each mountain howitzer ammunition chest to contain a fixed shell, six special case-shot, and a round of canister. Made of poplar wood, an ammunition chest weighed 9kg empty and 50kg when packed. The carriage of the mountain howitzer was built of oak, except for the axle-tree made of hickory. The wheels were made of oak, and the *limonière* of ash.

When a mountain howitzer was assembled and the shafts detached, the piece was said to be 'in battery'. Six men (one NCO and five gunners) made up the crew for a mountain howitzer, instead of the eight or nine men needed to crew larger pieces. While each man had a specific set of duties to perform in firing the piece, every gunner was trained in every position, so that if one fell another could take over his duties. When the piece was in battery, the ammunition mule stood 15m behind the gun; the other mules were lined up behind. The *limonière* was detached from the carriage and placed alongside the right wheel, pointing to the rear.

AMUSETTES

The Amusette was developed by the French Marshal de Saxe, who intended them to be used with the light infantry; they were introduced into French service in 1748.[249]

In 1776–78 the 1-pdr Amusette was reintroduced to the British artillery by General Thomas Desaguliers, and was nicknamed 'Whiskey'. Generally considered too small for regular service, it appears to have seen considerable use in the American Revolutionary War and in colonial service elsewhere. Amusettes were also used by the British light infantry, to some effect at Tournay (10 May

Table 6.1: Amusettes and ultra-light guns

	Calibre	Bore length	Tube length	Tube weight	Windage	Projectile weight
Austrian						
M1757 1-pdr Amusette	53mm	14.6 calibres	85cm	98kg	3.8mm	450g
M1780 1-pdr Amusette	52.6mm	14.6 calibres	84cm	96kg	3.4mm	450g
British						
M1760 1-pdr	52.4mm	34 calibres	183cm (6')	153kg	ND	454g
M1778 Desaguliers 1-pdr	52.4mm	29 calibres	160cm (5')	127kg	ND	454g
M1793 Blomefield 1-pdr	52.4mm	29 calibres	160cm (5')	128kg	ND	454g
Danish						
1-pdr Amusette	53mm	16 calibres	92cm	184kg	ND	ND
French						
M1743 1-pdr Amusette	53mm	ND	ND	ND	ND	ND
M1757 1-pdr Rostaing	53mm	20.6 calibres	114cm	115kg	ND	ND
Piedmontese						
M1786 1-pdr	53mm	ND	ND	ND	2mm	ND

1794) and Boxtel (14–15 September 1794).[250] Sir Thomas Blomefield tried to improve on the Amusette, and experiments were carried out with the 1-pdr.[251] Blomefield concluded they 'were evidently a failure...[and] no more Amusettes produced'.

In 1801, Adye lists a 5ft and a 7ft brass Amusette still being in service.[252] The Amusette was still in colonial use in India and the West Indies, alongside Light 3-pdrs and Coehorn howitzers, as late as 1853; even more remarkable is that they retained single draft.

The Danish army used the Amusette, and carried out a series of rigorous tests during the autumn of 1796 to compare the 1-pdr with Light 3-pdr and 6-pdr guns. Each piece fired at targets sized like a formed infantry company and a cavalry squadron at 320m range. It was estimated that attacking infantry would take eight minutes to cover that distance, and cavalry four minutes. During the eight-minute test the Amusette fired 48 rounds with 21 hits. The tests concluded that two Amusettes firing at full

M1793 1-pdr Amusette

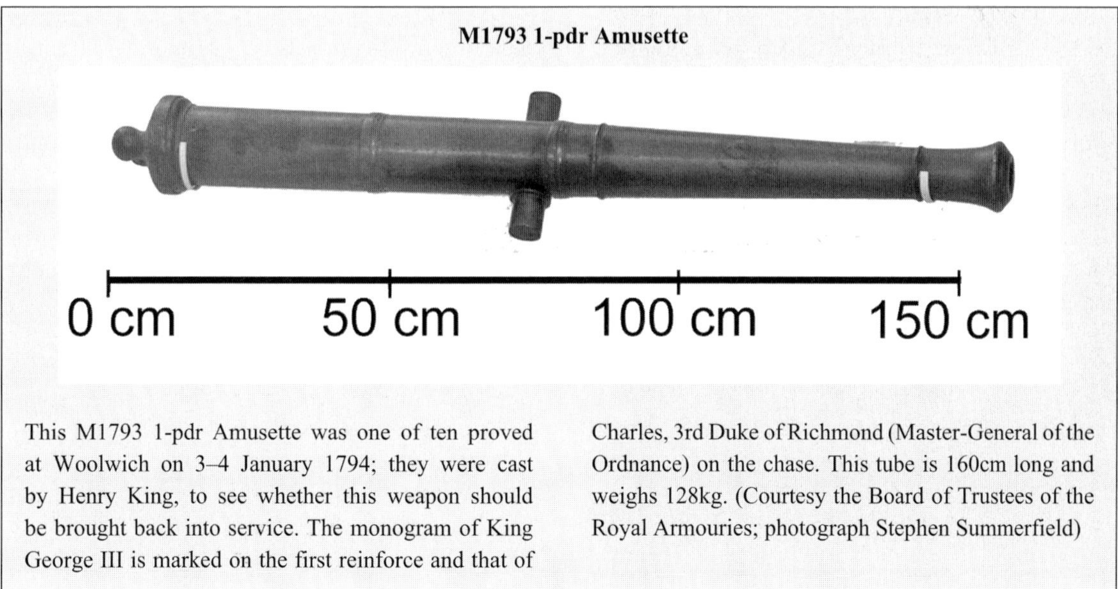

This M1793 1-pdr Amusette was one of ten proved at Woolwich on 3–4 January 1794; they were cast by Henry King, to see whether this weapon should be brought back into service. The monogram of King George III is marked on the first reinforce and that of Charles, 3rd Duke of Richmond (Master-General of the Ordnance) on the chase. This tube is 160cm long and weighs 128kg. (Courtesy the Board of Trustees of the Royal Armouries; photograph Stephen Summerfield)

speed would be at least as effective as a Light 3-pdr or 6-pdr gun. In addition, two Amusettes were cheaper to produce and maintain than the larger pieces.[253]

The small, lightweight Amusette was popular with revolutionary forces. For example, the artillery of the Brabant revolutionaries was composed mainly of 1-pdrs, with a handful of 3-pdrs. These successfully defeated Austrian attempts to regain control of the southern Netherlands. The Brabant Amusettes produced in Liege had an innovative iron ramrod and a mantlet to protect the crew.

The Hanoverian army issued Amusettes to its light troops, crewed by a mixture of experienced artillerymen and Jägers. Light infantry units from Hesse-Kassel used Amusettes during the early years of the French Revolution. They used them at the capture of Frankfurt (2 December 1792) when operating with the Prussian army: 'The light troops divide themselves with their Amusettes to the left and right inside the gardens, and will try to clear the walls with precise shots'.[254]

COALITION ORDNANCE

Austria

The Austrian mountain artillery was established in 1753, when they were armed with a 3-pdr falconette. Prince Eugene, with Oberst Wachterdank, further developed light field guns, mortars and howitzers. During the campaigns of 1757, 1-pdr *Tschaiken* and 2½-pdr howitzers served in the Tyrol and Croatia with the Grenzer frontier troops.[255]

By 1793, Piedmontese materiel had come into service, by which date the Austrian mountain batteries were equipped with 4× 4-pdrs and 2× Coehorn mortars; however, the earlier M1757 1-pdr and M1753 3-pdr pieces remained in service until 1800.[256] Ammunition was carried on five mules, each gun having 168 rounds (124× roundshot and 24× canister). The howitzers were carried on 'Hanoverian beds' on mules. Field guns were drawn by two mules, or disassembled and carried on three mules, with the wheels on the first, carriage on the second and tube on the third.

Britain

In Britain, Colonel James Pattison (1724–1805) was the pioneer of lightweight artillery. The M1773 3-pdr Pattison gun was born out of experience of the French–Indian War (1757–63), which demonstrated the need for highly mobile artillery that could be transported over the most extreme terrain in a country where roads did not exist.

In 1773, Pattison developed 'a very curious and contrived light piece of Artillery, which on emergencies can be carried on men's shoulders'.[257] It was nicknamed the 'Grasshopper', after the unique appearance imparted when it was fitted with its shaft for carrying on the shoulders. It could either be drawn by two horses using a limber; by a single horse in galloper style, when fitted with shafts; or carried by eight men on their shoulders. The Pattison gun could also be transported in wagons, or on three packhorses. In the latter case one carried the gun tube on a wooden packsaddle 'in which it lies firm and secure as when placed on its own carriage'. The second packhorse carried the carriage, and the gun could ready for action within two minutes.[258] Each M1773 3-pdr Pattison gun was issued with 80 rounds of fixed ammunition, transported on a third horse packed in boxes that hooked to each side of the packsaddle. Pattison also developed the 'Hanoverian bed' that enabled a howitzer barrel to be fired like a mortar. In America, Pattison guns were transported in secret in ammunition wagons, 'much to the surprise of the enemy'.

William Congreve Snr developed the Pattison equipment in 1777–78, creating the M1778 Townshend light infantry 3-pdr that was normally referred to as the 'Butterfly'. The carriage was a standard bracket type with 12-round ammunition boxes mounted above both sides of the axle, with a third between the brackets of the trail. 'Butterflies' were still in use in the West Indies in 1811; they saw service in the early stage of the Peninsular War, as their shorter axles were better suited to the narrow or non-existent roads in Spain and Portugal.

'Grasshoppers' were used in Canada as late as 1811–1814, and also saw action during the Peninsular campaigns as mountain artillery; they were certainly in use as early as 1810 in that role, and

Table 6.2: British light and mountain guns

	Calibre	Tube length	Tube length	Bore length	Tube weight	Tube weight
Pattison M1773						
Pattison 3-pdr	74.4mm	3'	91cm	12 calibres	1.7cwt	85kg
Townsend M1778						
Light Infantry 3-pdr	74.4mm	3'	91cm	12 calibres	1.9cwt	96kg
Blomefield						
M1810 Colonial 3-pdr	74.4mm	4'	122cm	16.5 calibres	3cwt	153kg
M1812 Mountain 3-pdr	74.4mm	3'	91cm	12 calibres	2.25cwt	115kg

two, firing hot shot, were described as doing good work against the French at the crossing of the Nive in 1813.

Anglo-Portuguese Mountain Artillery

The concept of ultra-lightweight artillery seems to have lain dormant in Britain until the Peninsular War, despite the experience of the American Revolutionary War. The Portuguese had long experience with mountain artillery; in the rugged, mountainous territory in the north of their country the few roads that existed were often impassable to wheeled vehicles.

Light artillery was manned by both specialist mountain gunners and also by the Royal Navy, who used Light 3-pdrs, 6-pdrs and 12-pdr howitzers when on shore, their equipment being ostensibly similar to that of the mountain artillery.

Lieutenant-Colonel Colquhoun RA, writing in 1842, noted that the equipment used by British mountain artillery was a mixture of improvised 'home-grown' materiel and Portuguese or Spanish. The Light 3-pdr gun of 3ft (91cm) length was used in conjunction with the 4²/₅in or Coehorn howitzer, although the latter had been condemned as next to useless during the American Revolutionary War. The guns were transported on 'pack carriages' or by draft, with a 'shaft carried by the mule attached to the trail of the gun carriage'. In 1811 a new 3-pdr 'for colonial service' was introduced and used in mountain terrain; there were also lightweight versions of 6-pdr guns and 12-pdr howitzers. The gun carriages had narrower axles or span than usual to meet the limitations of the Peninsula roads; the 3-pdr and 6pdr had wheels and axles of 50in (127cm) diameter, and the 12-pdr howitzers 42in (107cm) wheels on axles 44in (112cm) wide. The 12-pdr howitzer might also be mounted on a 'low carriage or bed without wheels' that enabled elevation up to 30 degrees. These could only be carried on packsaddles, and were used by the Royal Artillery in Sicily.

The 12-pdr howitzer tube weighed 127kg and the carriage 57kg; it was considered too short and too heavy, and its pack saddle (weighing 18.6kg) was poorly designed, so that it took three men of 'good stature' to load and unload it. The ammunition mule carried 24 rounds, half of which were spherical case, on an ammunition saddle weighing 20.5kg. The establishment was later changed so that the howitzers operated in pairs, with one mule carrying both beds and the equipment and tools, two further mules the gun tubes, and a final pair the ammunition. The two limber boxes could also be attached to a packsaddle. The maximum weight to be carried by each mountain artillery horse or mule was considered to be 127kg; the animals should ideally be bred in mountainous country, and stand from 14.5 to 15 hands high.

The first regular battery of Portuguese mountain artillery was formed on the orders of Marshal Beresford in May 1809, superintended by Alexander Dickson. This was in response to the damage sustained by the field guns on the 'dreadful mountain roads', which meant that they needed constant repairs or in some cases a complete refit. In addition, Dickson considered light artillery more suitable to the Peninsula: 'I think it ought to be of the lighter kind and requiring fewer mules, than a 6-pdr

A model of the M1773 Pattison light 3-pdr gun. Note the metal frame to support a large ammunition box on the trail, and the elevating screw that supports the gun tube in the manner of a snooker-cue rest. (Courtesy the Board of Trustees of the Royal Armouries; photographs Stephen Summerfield)

brigade, which might prove of more embarrassment than service'.[259]

During June 1809, Lieutenant Colonel Cookson RHA formed a half-brigade of three mountain guns. This unit was initially issued with 2× 3-pdr light guns (probably the M1778 Congreve) and a howitzer (possibly the $4^{2}/_{5}$in) on carriages designed by Colonel William Cuppage, the Inspector of the Royal Carriage Department. These could be carried dismantled on mules, or could be hauled in double draft using the shafts as a trail and an outrigger, with their ammunition carried on pack mules. They were in the field by August 1809.

On 8 November 1809 stores and equipment including 'four cars' were supplied. On 13 December, Dickson and Captain Kelly inspected the stores at Abrantes to ascertain if any mountain equipments were available for the new mountain brigade, but none were in store, so they used what was available: 'English Light 3-pdr carriages of the ordinary construction.' During December three guns and stores were issued from Lisbon 'to complete the Mountain Brigade to six guns'. On 16 December a second lieutenant, a surgeon, four sergeants, five corporals and one drummer were transferred to the mountain brigade. On 21 December the 4th (Mountain) Portuguese Artillery Brigade was inspected by Marshal Beresford, who was 'contented with what he saw'.[260] On 24 December the mountain brigade was at Santarem with Major von Arentschild.

In 1813 the Royal Horse Artillery formed the first regular unit for operation in mountain areas, commanded by Lieutenant Robe RHA (the son of Lieutenant-Colonel William Robe). He established a brigade of mountain guns manned by Portuguese gunners with British drivers and mules – this was because the British were unable to spare any gunners and the Portuguese artillery any mules and drivers. The unit was equipped with three captured French weapons (probably Gribeauval 4-pdrs), and later a further six Portuguese mountain guns from Lisbon were added. The French guns were drawn by horses two abreast, whereas the Portuguese guns were carried on the backs of mules. Dickson thought that to carry guns on packsaddles 'ruined'

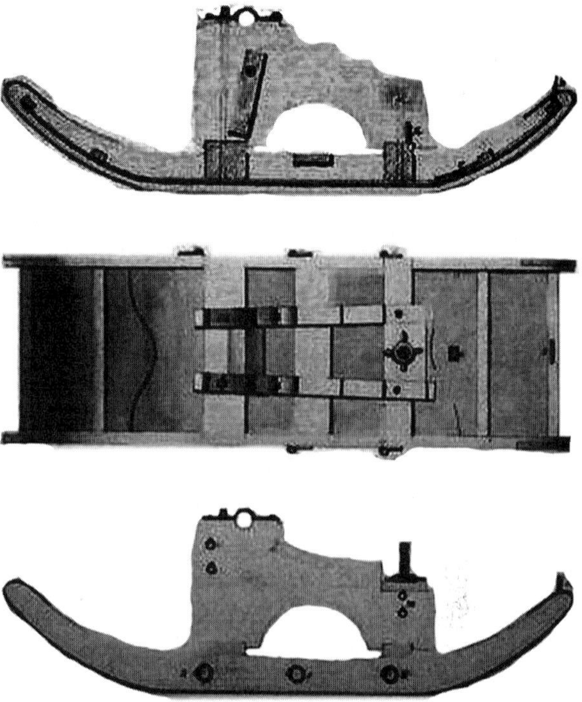

Drawing of a British gun sled for a light 3-pdr gun, designed by R.W. Adye for service in Canada. (Anthony Dawson)

many animals, but that it had the supreme advantage that guns could be conveyed 'by the narrowest foot paths, and up the most difficult steeps'.[261] Dickson's opinion is echoed in an 1853 *Aide Mémoire* which states that a gun on a packsaddle was slow to get in and out of action, the saddle itself too heavy, the gun hard to get into the saddle, and the load too harsh on the draft animal. That the mountain artillery used French equipments is borne out by Colquhoun writing in 1842, who states that the mountain train in 1813 consisted of French 4-pdrs cast in Seville.

British guns were disassembled for packing onto two mules, one carrying the gun tube, *limonière* and gunners' tools, and the other the gun carriage and wheels; the load on each mule was thus greater than in the French practice, and Lord Blayney argued for British artillery to copy the French in this. A British six-gun detachment had 33 mules compared to a French detachment with 39.

On 12 April 1813 the mountain artillery was ordered to hold a position and, according to Dickson, 'they did so to the last extremity, fighting up to the muzzle of the guns, which were captured'.[262] The unit was engaged at the passage of the Bidassoa (7 October 1813) when they were involved in counter-battery fire with their French counterparts. At Vera on 8 October, three French 4-pdr mountain guns were captured and used by the mountain artillery attached to the RHA. They saw action again in the battles of Nivelle (10 November 1813), Arcangues (10 December 1813), Orthes (27 February 1814) and Toulouse (10 April 1814), but the 3-pdr was found too small a calibre to compete with their French counterparts, who were armed with 6-pdr cannon.[263]

The Peninsular campaign provided impetus for greater British interest in mountain artillery, and studies were made of the French, Austrian and Spanish systems. Colquhoun, writing in 1842 and 1849, argued strongly for mountain artillery on the French system, armed solely with howitzers that were transported on pack saddles or using a *limonière* to draw them. The 1853 *Aide Mémoire*, however, utterly rejects pack saddles in favour of light wheeled carriages.

The organisation of the mountain batteries is unknown but may have been similar to that used in

Russian M1805 3-pdr (83mm) field unicorn; tube length 101cm, weight 108.5kg. (Dr S. Efimov)

India in 1803–1816, and by the British in Spain in 1836. During the latter conflict a mountain brigade consisted of 4× 3-pdr guns and 2× 12-pdr howitzers, commanded by three officers with sixty NCOs and other ranks and nine muleteers; there were three riding mules or horses, and thirty-six draft mules. The brigade was divided into front and reserve batteries of three pieces each; there were two ammunition mules per howitzer and one per gun, with 96 rounds carried per gun.

Russia

In 1805, when on campaign two M1805 3-pdr unicorns from heavy position artillery companies were attached to each Jäger regiment, but they were

Russian M1812 ¾-pdr (40mm) light cannon used with light infantry troops; this example was cast in 1812. (Dr S. Efimov)

shown to be ineffective. Some Jäger regiments used other kinds of pieces; Captain Otroshchenko of the 7th Jäger Regiment mentions a 2-pdr gun used by his regiment at the Russian victory over Ney's VI Corps at Guttstadt on 5–6 June 1807. The 3-pdr unicorns were certainly used in the war against Sweden, and possibly against the Turks. They were withdrawn from service by 1810, but a number of these and other light pieces were no doubt pressed into service in the 1812 campaign.

FRANCE

The first step towards mountain artillery equipment in France was made by Marshal de Saxe in 1743, when he introduced the M1743 1-pdr gun and M1743 Light 24-pdr howitzer, to replace a large-calibre M1741 grenade-launcher.[264]

The Count de Rostaing pioneered very light-weight 1-pdr and 4-pdr guns that foreshadowed many of the later developments in mountain and light artillery. In 1757 the 1-pdr gun designed by Rostaing was officially introduced into French service. This had many design features new to artillery that would attract the interest of other ordnance innovators: an iron axle, ammunition boxes mounted on the gun carriage parallel to the tube, crooked handspikes, and the fitting of horse shafts – a *limonière* – to the carriage to enable the gun to be moved by a single horse without a limber. Another innovative aspect of the design was the use of a carriage slightly longer than the total length of the gun tube, and wheels of the same diameter as the tube length; these large wheels made it highly mobile even over rough terrain, and the carriage was sharply curved to accommodate them. Elevation was by a primitive form of *Rechtsmaschine* sliding wedge. The M1757 Rostaing was used during the conquest of Corsica (1768–69), along with a 4-pdr on an *affut-traineau* carriage.[265] Mountain artillery was further developed by du Puget in 1771 and these were incorporated into the Gribeauval system. The old 1-pdr M1757 Rostaing guns were later given to the National Guard artillery units, and finally withdrawn from service in 1797.

M1765 Gribeauval

By 1789 the Gribeauval reforms of 1765–74 had introduced a range of mountain guns mounted on two different types of carriages.

The *affut-porte* corps carriage had two parallel cheeks connected by three horizontal wooden transoms and iron bolts. The trunnion positions were set at the front and at the mid-point of the carriage. At the trail end there was a transom plate and lunette ring that connected to the pintail of the limber. At the head of the carriage were a pair of 66cm spoked wheels; immediately behind was a *chevrette* (iron supporting leg) with 40cm solid timber wheels. These mounted 4-pdr guns, 6-pouce (16.24cm/6.4in) howitzers and 8-pouce (21.66cm/8.5in) mortars.

The *affut-traineau* or gun-sledge carriage lacked the lunette ring; it had 40cm wheels mounted at the trail end, and 16cm *chevrette* wheels. The gun was dragged by a pair of chains connecting to the harness of the mule. These mounted 8-pdr and 12-pdr cannon with an articulating *limonière* limber.

In addition, there were standard Light 4-pdr guns (the old Swedish 4-pdr dating from the 1740s) with a *limonière* rather than a limber, and a 4-pdr with an articulating limber.

The 6-pouce and 8-pouce mortars were mounted on a special form of galloper carriage where the mortar bed slid backwards and forwards on runners to compensate for the recoil when it was fired. The complete vehicle weighed 1800kg and was drawn by four horses hitched in single file. General Gassendi noted in 1809 that 3-pdr and 4-pdr guns were also mounted on galloper carriages for use with light infantry, and these were finally withdrawn by 1825.[266]

Modifications, 1800

The mountain artillery arm was re-established during 1792 for the fighting in northern Italy, and was initially equipped with 1-pdr M1757 Rostaing guns, and 4-pdrs mounted on *affut-traineau* carriages. Soon, captured Piedmont 3-pdr mountain guns were being used alongside the French ordnance; these had unique *chevrette* carriages with folding supports. Piedmont guns formed the basis

French M1757 Rostaing 1-pdr (56mm) gun

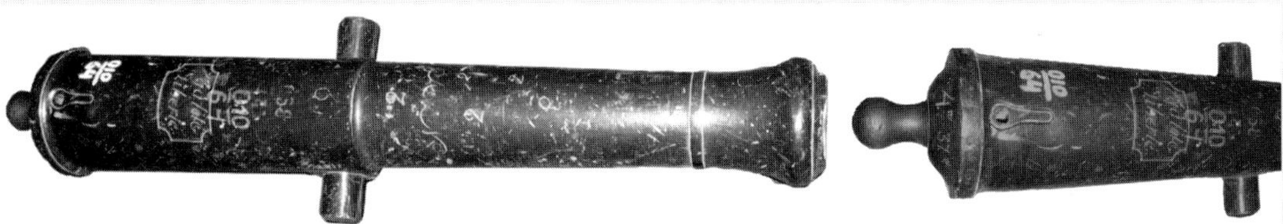

Bronze barrel of a French M1757 Rostaing 1-pdr (56mm) gun, with a length of 91cm and a weight of 77.6kg. The Ottoman Turks captured this piece from the French in Egypt during Napoleon's expedition of 1798–1801. The Russians, in turn, captured it from the Turks in the Russo-Turkish War of 1828–29. (Photograph: Dr S. Efimov)

for the later French mountain batteries. At the capture of Saorgio (24 April 1794) in the French Maritime Alps, General Massena's Army of Italy had nine light mountain guns.[267] By 1795 this figure had doubled.

In 1797 the mountain artillery attached to General Rey's Division consisted of 3× 3-pdrs on Piedmontese *affut-portatif* carriages, 3× 5-pdrs mounted on *affut-traineau* carriages, and a howitzer. The 3-pdrs required fifteen packmules and a field forge with six mules in harness; the 5-pdrs had fourteen packmules and twelve draft mules; and the howitzer had six mules in draft and twenty packmules. The battery had 49 pack and 24 draft mules. The mules carried the guns, ammunition and stores.[268]

By 1800 new caissons, tool carts and field forges were introduced to replace the faulty M1765 system. These were superficially similar to those of the field artillery but with smaller wheels, and used the articulating *limonière* limber with 92cm wheels.

Affut-traineau carriages

Gassendi (1819) confirms the use of 12-, 8-, 6-, 4- and 3-pdr mountain guns as well as 6.4in howitzers on the *affut-traineau* carriage.[269] The iron *chevrettes* were adjustable to three heights, and elevation of the gun tube was by means of quoins.

The M1795 3-pdr mountain gun mounted (81cm long) on the 146cm-long *chevrette* carriage was of Piedmont design, and according to Gassendi (1801) these were first cast in French arsenals in 1795.[270] The M1795 Light 4-pdr mountain gun (81cm long) could be disassembled and manhandled using a carrying pole), or drawn with a limber or a *limonière*. The carriage had parallel sides.

The 8- and 12-pdr *affut-traineau* carriage flared towards the transom; it had two small wheels at the front of the carriage and two larger wheels near the centre of the piece. These large pieces could also be transported in separate parts, with the gun tube on one vehicle and the carriage on the other, linked together and drawn by a *limonière*. The 12-pdr was also mounted on a light carriage and limber.

In Calabria during 1806, Major Grisois of the 1st Horse Artillery Regiment formed a mountain artillery detachment of gunners from the 2nd Company, armed with two each 3-pdrs and mortars, that saw action at Sainte-Euphemie and Maida. They later served under Grisois' command at the siege of Atmantea, with a 12-pdr, 2× howitzers, a mortar and 2× 3-pdr mountain cannon.[271]

M1797 Affut-portatif

These 'portable' M1797 3- and 4-pdr mountain guns were of Piedmont origin and design, and were carried on muleback. The carriage was superficially similar to the French *affut-traineau*, but the wooden transoms were replaced with iron bolts, making them lighter and more mobile. It had two small (41cm) wheels at the trail end of the carriage, made from four pieces of wood bound with iron, and 16cm solid wheels on the *chevrette*. These portable guns were used by the French in Italy from 1797.

Troupes Légère

The *Troupes Légère* used the M1757 1-pdr Rostaing guns, as well as 8-pouce and 6-pouce howitzers,

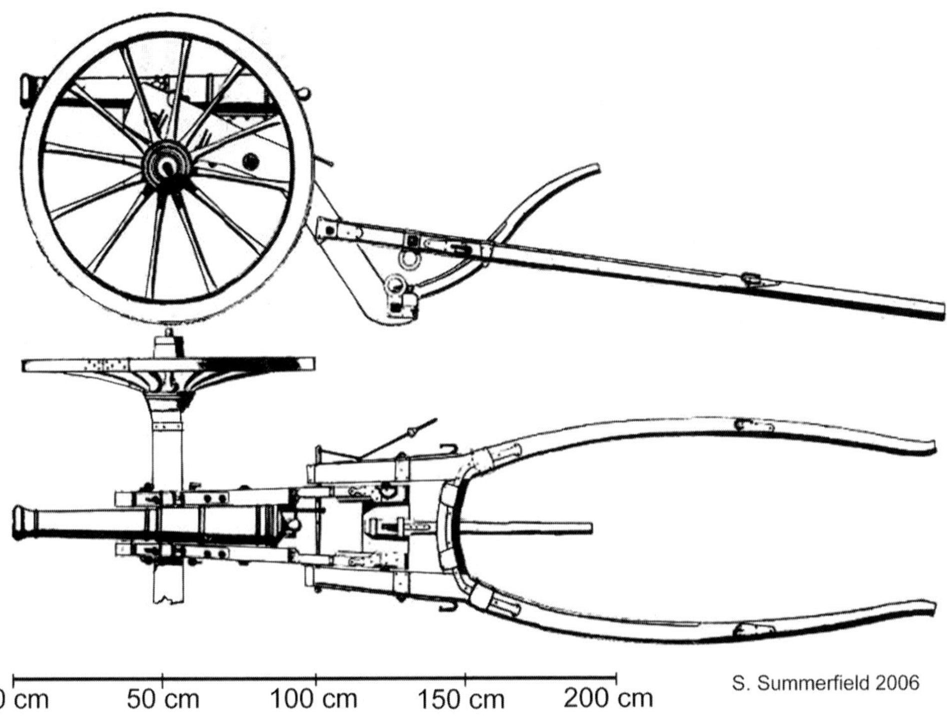

The M1792 1-pdr Rostaing gun with attached limonière existed in a 3-pdr calibre, and an M1765 4-pdr gun tube could also be mounted on the 3-pdr carriage drawn by three horses.

on wheeled 76cm-long lightweight bracket carriages with 124cm wheels, and made to the principles of Rostaing. These were supplemented by the Piedmontese mountain guns on the block trail, which Gassendi notes as being manoeuvrable in the field although heavier than the *troupes légère* carriage then in use.[272] From 1795 the French appear to have constructed their own block-trail carriages for mountain artillery. Some units dispensed with the packmules and drew the gun with two horses attached to the *limonière*.

Used alongside these guns was the Labolle Light 4-pdr designed by Citizen Labolle, an officer in the *Ouvriers*. The carriages were made using standard parts from the arsenals as a matter of economy and expediency. The Labolle carriage could be drawn using a *limonière* or as a sled.

During the 1797 campaign in Italy, 3-pdr, 5-pdr and 7-pdr calibre pieces, along with a howitzer and 11-pdr field guns from Piedmont (Turin) and Lombardy (Milan), were used in place of the larger and more cumbersome French guns (note that these weights are in French *livres de Paris* – *see* the Appendix).[273]

For the planned invasion of England, Napoleon proposed to arm the first wave of troops with Austrian 3-pdr guns or 3-pdr mountain guns on wheeled carriages in preference to the 'useless' Rostaing guns, and a 4 pouce 6 ligne (122mm/4.8in) howitzer.

AnXI/M1803 Reforms

The M1803 equipment had carriages for Gribeauval 4-pdrs, and Piedmont iron 3-pdrs that were fired by means of a flintlock. The two carriages, weighing 150kg, had folding iron *chevrettes* weighing 46kg. At the trail end was a pair of 41cm wooden wheels. The carriage had two trunnion positions, one for firing and the second for travelling. The piece could either be drawn along the ground on its wooden wheels by a human team or four to six

French mountain gun packed onto three mules

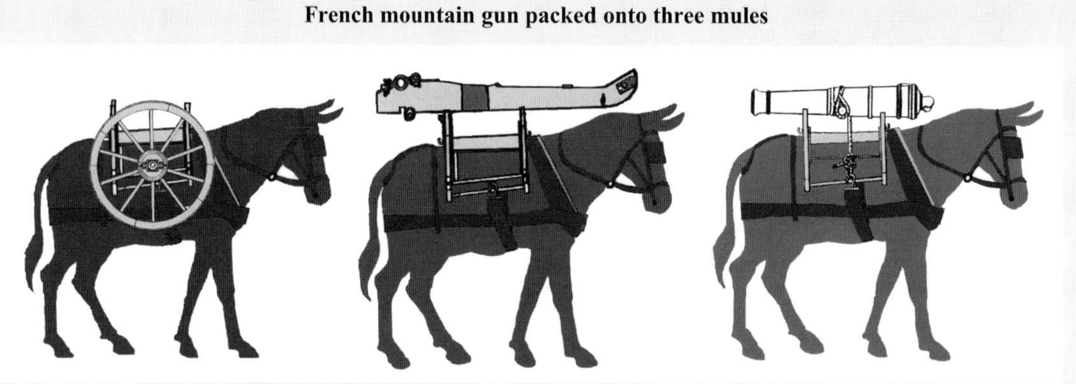

A French mountain gun packed onto three mules. The first carries the gun barrel and the *limonière*; the second, the carriage; and the third, the wheels and the gunner's implements – this gave each mule a load of between 100 and 175kg. Regulations called for the mule carrying the *limonière* to lead, followed at 2m intervals by the other mules, with one driver per mule walking to the left-hand side. To load the lead mule, three men lifted the barrel onto a packsaddle that was fitted with cut-outs to accept the barrel and trunnions. The loads were securely lashed into place.

mules, or manhandled using the *levier brisé*. The M1803 equipment could also be disassembled and carried on four mules (the carriage on one, the gun tube on the second, the ammunition boxes on the third and the gun tools, carrying poles etc on the fourth).

The M1803 6-pdr and 12-pdr mountain gun carriages were fitted with an integral *limonière* for draft by a horse. Elevation was like that on a standard carriage, and the 4-pdr could be elevated up to 21 degrees. The 6-pouce (16.2cm or 6.4in) howitzer was also equipped for mountain service, on the *affut-traineau* carriage; with the *chevrette* removed the piece could be used as a mortar.

Each mountain battery of 47 enlisted men was to have six pieces with 74 mules. A section of 2× mountain guns had 3× gun carriages (one spare), 3× *chevrettes*, 16× ammunition boxes (empty weight 17kg, accommodating 15× roundshot and 5× canister rounds), 2× boxes of pyrotechnic stores (fuses, slowmatch, powder etc), 4× porte-lances, 4× linstocks, 6× sponge-ramrods, 2× water buckets, 2× worms, 6× *coins de mire*, 10× pioneer tools (2× pick-axes, 4× mattocks, 2× earth buckets, 2× rubble buckets), 2× sandbags, 10 *toises* (20m) of rope for *prolonges*, 10× pickets and 4× hammers.[274]

M1810 Peninsula Modifications

During the first years of the French occupation of Spain operations were hampered by the lack of mountain guns. For example, in November 1808 the infantry of I Corps had to leave their 22 guns behind as they were unable to transport them. In order to solve this lack of artillery support Marshal Soult, with Generals Sebastiani and Sénarmont, formed a commission in 1810 to examine the arming and equipping of mountain artillery.

The result of their work was the M1810 mountain artillery that saw the adoption of new light guns and howitzers mounted on the block-trail carriage *(affut à flèche)*, to replace all previous designs.[275] The M1810 equipment was cast in Seville. The block-trail mountain gun used 100cm wheels and a 132cm-long carriage, with the block trail meeting the ground at an angle of 38 degrees. It was fitted with a *limonière* so that it could be drawn by a single animal, or it could be disassembled and carried by pack animals. Equipment lists show that the piece could also be moved by *prolonge* or *bricole*.

The 12-pdr (4.8in) mountain howitzer was specifically designed to be taken apart for pack transport, although it could also be pulled by single draft. Instead of needing a six-horse team like most other guns of the Napoleonic era, a mountain howitzer

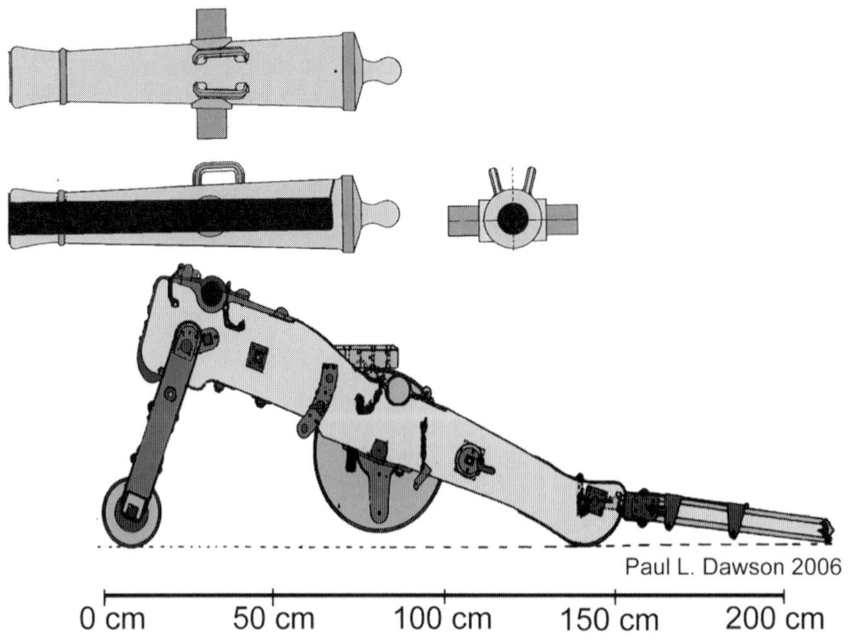

French AnXI (M1803) 6-pdr mountain gun, introduced in 1807.

and two ammunition chests could be carried by three mules through thick forest, across swampy ground or over rough mountain trails where no other gun could go. Although its 120mm bore could handle the same 12-pdr ammunition as a regular 12-pdr gun, a complete mountain howitzer – block-trail carriage, wheels and tube – weighed 215kg, just less than the 4-pdr field gun tube. The howitzer used a smaller carriage than the field gun and 98.5cm wheels; the wooden axle lessened the recoil, and gave an elasticity to the whole carriage. The same kind of packsaddle was used for carrying the tube, carriage, ammunition and field forge. The transom on each side of the saddle had a circular notch cut in it to receive the trunnions of the piece, which was carried with the muzzle to the rear. The first mule carried the barrel and the shafts of the carriage (114kg); the second, the carriage and implements (134kg); and the third, two ammunition chests (108kg).

These new pieces were also issued with a 203cm carrying pole that came apart into two sections, from which the gun barrel was suspended so it could be carried by a group of gunners while the remainder manhandled the carriage. A unique aspect of the design was the pair of ammunition boxes, containing eight shells and powder charges, which strapped to the top of the gun tube.

General Ruty designed the M1811 16.2cm (6.4in) howitzer, the M1811 8-pouce (21.7cm/8.5in) mortar, and M1811 Light 2-pdr, cast in iron and mounted on the block trail. In theory, the M1803 (AnXI) 3-pdr and 6-pdr were also mounted on larger versions of this carriage.

The mountain artillery also boasted its own portable forge designed for country inaccessible to wheeled vehicles, where the small gun carriages could easily suffer damage. The tool boxes were of similar size to the ammunition chests. The first mule carried two boxes totalling 105.5kg including the blacksmith's tools and other necessary materials. The second mule carried two boxes for the carriage-maker's tools, for emergency repairs to gun carriages, and coal (52kg). The hearth was a sheet of iron on an iron frame supported by three legs connected by bolts, so that it could be folded flat. Bellows and a small anvil accompanied the forge.[276]

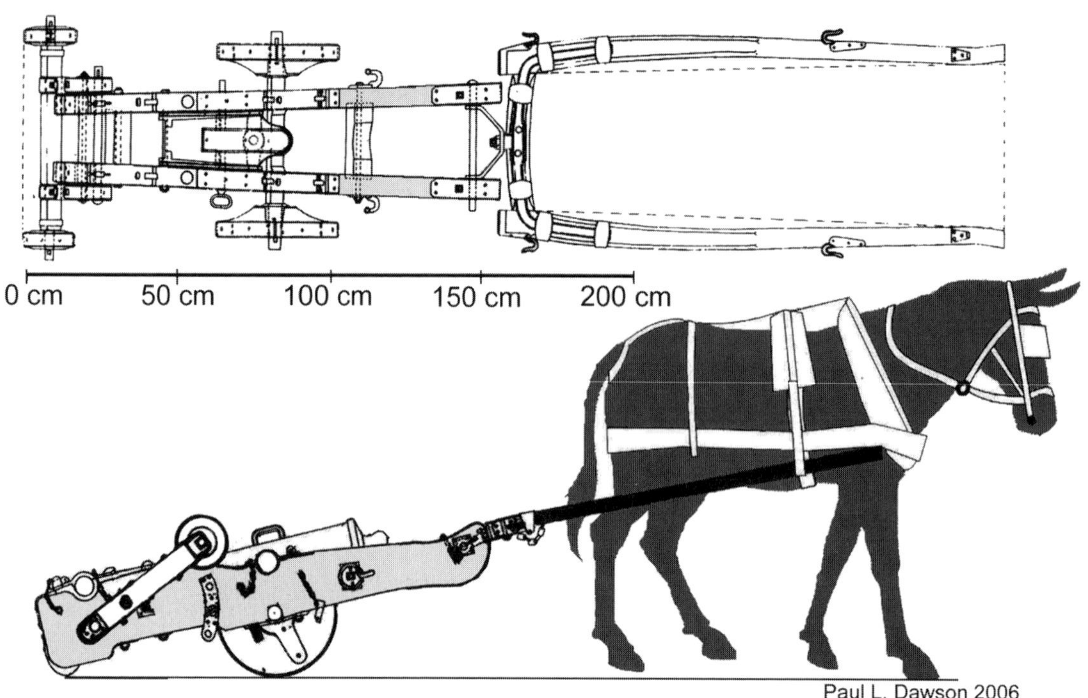

French AnXI (M1803) 6-pdr mountain gun in mule draft.

Official regulations called for mountain howitzers to be organised into six-gun batteries with 39 mules. This was enough pack animals to carry the guns, a spare carriage, tools and gunners' implements, and sufficient ammunition for 48 rounds per gun. In practice, mountain howitzers were deployed in four-gun batteries of two sections, or even in single-gun detachments. Horse artillery units and even a few infantry units also operated mountain howitzers.

In the Peninsula, mountain guns and howitzers were mostly used in small skirmishes, to dislodge guerrillas or small groups of enemy troops from cover, and on scouting missions where the infantry needed artillery support. For instance, Colonel Digeon, the artillery commander of Marshal Ney's VI Corps of the Army of Portugal, ordered that four mountain guns portable on mules should be constructed. However, these pieces also played their part in conventional actions. At Albuera (16 May 1811) the mountain howitzers proved very effective in a normal battlefield artillery role. At the combat at Matara in 1812, General Lamarque noted that two small guns carried into position on muleback fired 50 rounds and forced the Spanish to abandon their positions. The value of such equipment was naturally appreciated when the campaign reached the Pyrenees. In July 1813, at Bentarte and Roncevaux, the French deployed an eight-gun mountain detachment to dislodge the British from their positions. In the combat at Rhune (7 October 1813), General Clauzel deployed eighteen mountain guns; three prepared positions were constructed, of two batteries of four guns each and one of ten guns – this was probably the largest concentration of mountain guns used in the Peninsula. Clauzel successfully defended the bridge at d'Alfara with two mountain guns, and at Nivelle (10 November 1813) he attached great importance to placing the mountain guns in entrenchment.

An irony of this campaign was that the British, who had developed the block trail before the French, used captured French block-trail mountain

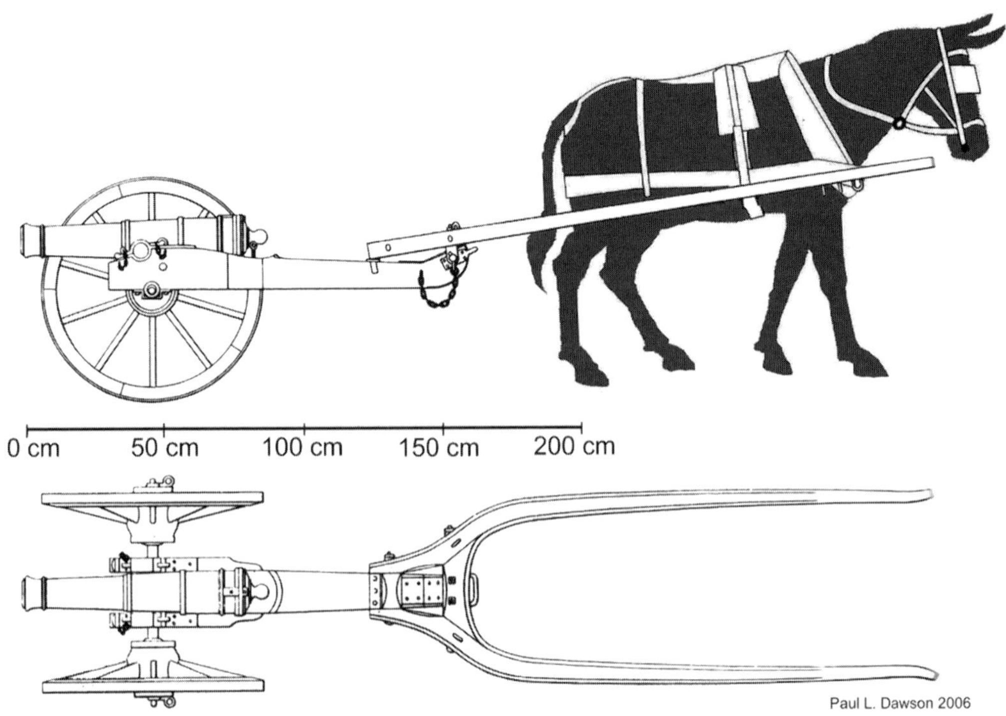

French M1810 6-pdr block-trail mountain gun with limonière *attached for mule draft.*

guns and equipment because they were better than their own. Indeed, Lord Blayney suggested that the British adopt a similar establishment for their own mountain artillery.

The French M1810 equipment saw service in Spain again during 1823, and was adopted by the M1828 Valée artillery system with little or no change; General Faré drew it in 1827.[277]

PIEDMONT

The Piedmontese army was well equipped and experienced for mountain warfare. Their system of mountain guns and carriages was the basis of the mountain guns used by Austria and France during the Revolutionary Wars. They used either the bronze 3-pdr mounted on the *affut-traineau* carriage (the *chevrette* weighing about 60kg), or the block-trail carriage; both types could be packed on muleback. The block-trail carriage was preferred, as the piece stood higher, making it easier to serve for the crew, and less liable to overset when fired.[278] Yet Jean du Teil considered the *affut-traineau* carriage superior, as it could be dragged over any terrain; he noted that ordinary spoked carriage wheels were liable to break when crossing bad roads, whereas solid wooden wheels were more robust.[279]

The bronze 3-pdr gun tube (127cm long and weighing 130kg) was fitted with a flintlock firing mechanism that was deemed more reliable in mountain conditions than match or loose powder. Iron gun tubes were also produced. The elevating system of the block-trail carriage consisted of an iron elevating screw with the upper end formed into a fork; the cascable button fitted into this and was locked in place with a horizontal pin. The *affut-traineau* carriage had an iron elevating plate fixed by a hinge at the head of the carriage, and moved by a short elevating screw. In both methods 3-degree elevation and depression could be obtained.[280]

The *affut à chevrette* was a 113cm wooden carriage with an adjustable 64cm iron support leg (*chevrette*) and a pair of 30cm solid wooden wheels

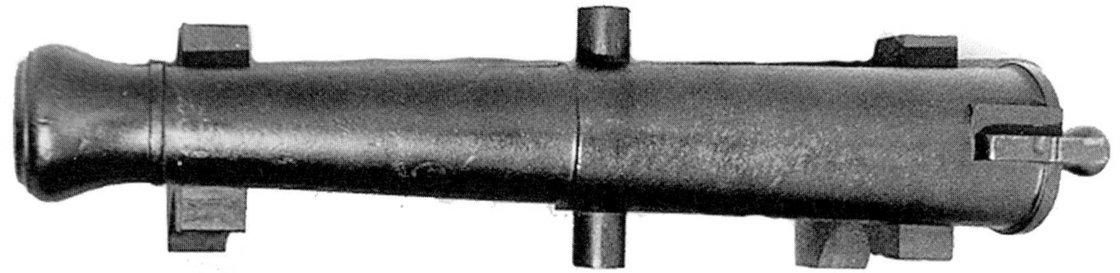

Piedmontese 1-pdr gun, with fittings for a flintlock firing mechanism. (Steven H. Smith)

at the trail end. The elevation system used a vertically mounted bronze screw that connected to the cascable button via a pin, and was reminiscent of that used in Britain. The guns were carried disassembled on the backs of mules.

In addition to the 3-pdr, a light Coehorn howitzer/mortar was also employed. The Coehorn mortar bed was made of a single block of oak or two pieces joined together with bolts. A recess, for the trunnions and part of the breech, was made in the top of the bed, and the trunnions were kept in place by iron plates bolted down over them. Two iron handles were bolted to the bed on each side, so that four men could carry the bed with the mortar in place.[281]

DALMATIA

By the Treaty of Campo Formio (17 October 1797), Austria received Venice with its territories of Istria and Dalmatia. On 26 December 1805, Austria ceded Venice and her territories to the Kingdom of Italy.

In 1806 the Dalmatian artillery was established with 4× 3-pdr guns and 2× 6.4in howitzers cast in Ragusa (Dubrovnik).[282] In the then-Dalmatian capital of Zara (Zadar) the guns were mounted on a form of *affut à chevrette* carriage constructed from modified field gun carriages, with the wheels replaced by a folding iron *chevrette*, and small solid wooden wheels on an iron axle at the trail end. The carriage weighed 115kg and measured 198cm long – somewhat shorter than the regulation 235cm 4-pdr carriage; this suggests that they were modified from Rostaing rather than Gribeauval 4-pdr carriages. The piece was difficult to manoeuvre due to the small wheels, and was top-heavy. In addition, the carriage was too long to fit a mule's back, and it was awkward to raise the *chevrette* leg into position.

In September 1806 a report listed 40× 3-pdr mountain guns in Dalmatia, of French design. In 1807 the 'mountain train' consisted of 44 men and 34 mules serving 2× howitzers and 3× 3-pdr guns, under the command of Chef de Bataillon Mongenet. In July, further pieces were supplied from Ragusa, including 2× 6.4in mortars. The 3-pdr guns were supplied on the ratio of two per infantry division, and each had 54 rounds of ammunition.

In 1808, Marshal Soult became Duke of Dalmatia, and the mountain artillery was transferred to the Kingdom of Italy. By the terms of the Treaty of Schönbrunn (14 October 1809), Dalmatia and the Republic of Ragusa would now form the Illyrian Provinces, part of the French Empire. Under the Congress of Vienna (1815) Austria gained the Illyrian Provinces.

KINGDOM OF ITALY

On 20 September 1806 the Kingdom of Italy had 32× French 3-pdr mountain pieces (probably M1803 (AnXI) rather than Piedmont), and the Kingdom of Naples had 35× 3-pdrs. On 8 December 1806, Napoleon ordered the Kingdom of Italy to form the 1st (Field) Artillery Division and the 2nd (Mountain) Artillery Division with 30× 3-pdr mountain guns of French design and

An impression of Italian mountain artillery. (Authors' collection)

Table 6.3: Dimensions of French mountain guns on *Affut-Traineau* (Gun Sledge) carriage according to Gassendi (1809)

		3 pdr	4 pdr	8 pdr	12 pdr	6.4 inch Howitzer
Gun carriage body	Cheek length	146cm	148cm	191cm	217cm	164cm
	Cheek width	22cm	26cm	41cm	41cm	39cm
Thickness of the cheeks		7cm	8cm	8cm	9cm	9cm
Spacing of the cheeks	At the head	13cm	23cm	27cm	30cm	31cm
	The transom	22cm	23cm	32cm	41cm	31cm
Carriage axle	Length	57cm	72cm	92cm	97cm	81cm
	Square section	4cm	5cm	8cm	8cm	5cm
Gun carriage wheels	Diameter	34cm	41cm	65cm	65cm	37cm
	Thickness	4cm	5cm	7cm	7cm	7cm
Chevrette wheels at the front end	Diameter	16cm	16cm	41cm	41cm	16cm
	Thickness	3cm	5cm	7cm	7cm	5cm
Chevrette iron axle at the front end	Length	101cm	111cm	97cm	97cm	114cm
	Square section	3cm	5cm	7cm	7cm	3cm
Mounting of the chevrette	Height	56cm	77cm			75cm
	Support arms	30cm	41cm			51cm

manufacture. A further 60× 3-pdrs of foreign manufacture (either Austrian or Piedmont origin) were added to this number, suitable for mountain work or use with light troops. Three divisions of 30× guns were formed, with the gunners coming from the foot artillery of the Kingdom of Italy rather than being a specialist unit. The artillery of the Kingdom of Italy was augmented in 1808 by the Dalmatian artillery becoming the 9th and 13th Companies, with 185 men in each company.

SPAIN

The Spanish mountain artillery was based upon that of France, using Light 4-pdr guns mounted on carriages which had a narrower span, i.e. a shorter axle than regular field guns. They were drawn by two mules in tandem, and ammunition was carried on packsaddles. They were withdrawn in 1837 for a system based entirely upon that of France. A uniquely Spanish set-up of mountain artillery, armed with 12-pdr howitzers carried on mules, was authorised in 1844; each gun was served by eight men.

7 Siege, Coastal and Garrison Ordnance

INTRODUCTION

The Revolutionary and Napoleonic Wars were not solely a matter of pitched battles and clashes in the open field. Of all engagements, it has been calculated by one historian that 28% were blockades or sieges of strategic positions; another has suggested that these represented 34% for the whole period 1748–1815.[283] (These figures do not include the numerous engagements between ships and coastal fortifications.)

Fortified towns, cities and ports still dominated the communication routes of Europe, as they had done for centuries, and the free movement of field armies required that they be neutralised or captured. A siege was a costly affair, and a serious commitment in time and resources by the commanding general. In sieges preparatory to assaults the attacker's guns were positioned very close to the defender's position, so elaborate field defences were created to protect the guns from defending fire. The weight and size of the guns meant that once positioned they could only be redeployed with a great deal of effort. This lack of mobility meant that the siege train itself was ponderous, required colossal numbers of draft animals, and moved far slower than the field army. The ammunition would be carried in whatever suitably sturdy vehicles came to hand if those specially designed for that function became damaged.

The siege of Toulon (18 September–18 December 1793) launched the career of Napoleon Bonaparte, but he avoided sieges after his experience of the seven-month siege of Mantua (4 July 1796–2 February 1797). He preferred large-scale engagements which offered opportunities to destroy the enemy's field army. Not surprisingly, he considered that the key to success on the battlefield was weight of fire and mobility, and his most impressive campaigns could be considered as the early 19th-century equivalent of Blitzkrieg warfare. In some theatres, however, and notably in the Peninsula, the terrain and the strategic situation dictated that the holding or capturing of fortified positions was central to the success of campaigns, and here Napoleon's marshals were forced to undertake many such operations.

The heavy cannon (normally 18- or 24-pdrs) were used to breach enemy fortifications at close range. Other batteries were used to silence the defenders' guns, especially if a dominating position could be found. Guns could be fired with a full powder charge to impart the maximum amount of kinetic energy for breaching masonry, or with reduced charges for use with heated shot; the latter was particularly effective against wooden targets (especially ships). Large calibre howitzers and mortars were a vital part of the armoury, due to their ability to throw heavy explosive shells over the walls of the fortress.

ORDNANCE

Heavy Guns

The first European country that attempted to reduce the weight of their siege train and improve the guns' efficiency was Austria. In 1753, Liechtenstein's team of designers developed a series of 12-, 18- and 24-pdr heavy battery guns of 20–22 calibres length; these were about 50% heavier than their field-gun equivalents.[284] The M1764 Medium 12- and 18-pdr were introduced. The greater weight of the gun tubes meant that the carriages needed larger and sturdier wheels than the field guns, and much bulkier axles. The cast-iron M1776 *Verteidigungs* (defence) guns for fortresses and other strongpoints were introduced

Table 7.1: Heavy guns

	Calibre	Bore length	Tube length	Tube weight	Windage	Projectile weight
Austrian bronze siege (Belagerungs) guns						
24-pdr M1756	150mm	22 calibres	353cm	2900kg	ND	10.9kg
18-pdr Long M1780	136mm	24 calibres	336cm	2190kg	5.5mm	8.25kg
18-pdr Short M1753	136mm	18.5 calibres	272cm	2020kg	5.5mm	8.25kg
18-pdr Medium M1764	136mm	20.5 calibres	299cm	2200kg	5.5mm	8.25kg
12-pdr Long M1780	120mm	22 calibres	304cm	1450kg	ND	ND
Austrian iron defence (Verteidigungs) guns						
18-pdr iron M1776	136mm	22 calibres	321cm	ND	5.5mm	8.25kg
12-pdr iron 1776	120mm	22 calibres	304cm	ND	ND	8.25kg
6-pdr iron M1776	96mm	26 calibres	250cm	716kg	ND	ND
British bronze guns						
24-pdr Heavy (bronze) M1788	148mm	16 calibres	290cm (9'6")	2700kg	5.4mm	10.9kg
24-pdr Light Blomefield M1788	148mm	13 calibres	191cm (6'3")	1220kg	5.4mm	10.9kg
24-pdr Medium M1750	148mm	15 calibres	244cm (8')	2087kg	ND	10.9kg
18-pdr Blomefield M1788	134mm	18 calibres	175cm (5'9")	916kg	4.9mm	8.2kg
12-pdr Blomefield M1788	117mm	16 calibres	152cm (5')	612kg	4.4mm	5.5kg
British iron guns						
32-pdr iron M1796	162mm	18 calibres	312cm	2832kg	5.4mm	14.6kg
24-pdr iron M1796	148mm	18 calibres	290cm	2520kg	5.4mm	10.9kg
24-pdr iron M1796	148mm	16 calibres	274cm	2400kg	5.4mm	10.9kg
18-pdr (iron) M1796 Naval	134mm	22 calibres	290cm	2190kg	4.9mm	8.2kg
18-pdr (iron) M1796	134mm	20 calibres	274cm	2030kg	4.0mm	8.2kg
12-pdr iron M1796	117mm	22 calibres	276cm	1680kg	4.0mm	5.5kg
French M1775						
24-pdr M1775	153mm	20 calibres	323cm	2740kg	4.5mm	12kg
16-pdr M1775	134mm	22 calibres	311cm	1990kg	3.9mm	8kg
Long 12-pdr M1775	121mm	23 calibres	293cm	1550kg	3.6mm	6kg
Long 8-pdr M1775	106mm	24 calibres	265cm	1060kg	3.1mm	4kg
Long 4-pdr M1775	84mm	22 calibres	195cm	560kg	2.5mm	2kg
French M1803 (AnXI)						
Short 24-pdr M1803	147mm	16 calibres	279cm	1400kg	2.1mm	12kg
Long 12-pdr M1803	121mm	22 calibres	300cm	700kg	2.1mm	6kg
Piedmontese M1786						
24-pdr M1786	155mm	19 calibres	323cm	2630kg	2mm	12kg
Prussian						
24-pdr pre M1740	149mm	16 calibres	230cm	1150kg	6mm	11.2kg
24-pdr M1744 (Holzendorf)	149mm	16 calibres	230cm	1750kg	6mm	11.2kg
24-pdr M1754 (Dieskau)	149mm	16 calibres	230cm	1764kg	6mm	11.2kg
12-pdr M1731 Brummer	122mm	26 calibres	274cm	1697kg	5mm	5.60kg
12-pdr M1761 Brummer	122mm	22 calibres	262cm	1492kg	5mm	5.93kg

in 6-, 12- and 18-pdr calibres due to improvements in iron-casting and boring technologies. The M1780 Light 12- and 18-pdr siege guns replaced the former long guns, as well as heavy gun tubes of 24 calibres length which had been introduced.

Tests carried out in Vienna in 1777 estimated the lifespan of a gun tube. Three 24-pdrs fired 2,070 roundshot over a 17-day period, and increased the vent only by 2mm. At the same time, 4× 6-pdr gun tubes fired 7,000 roundshot on full charge and

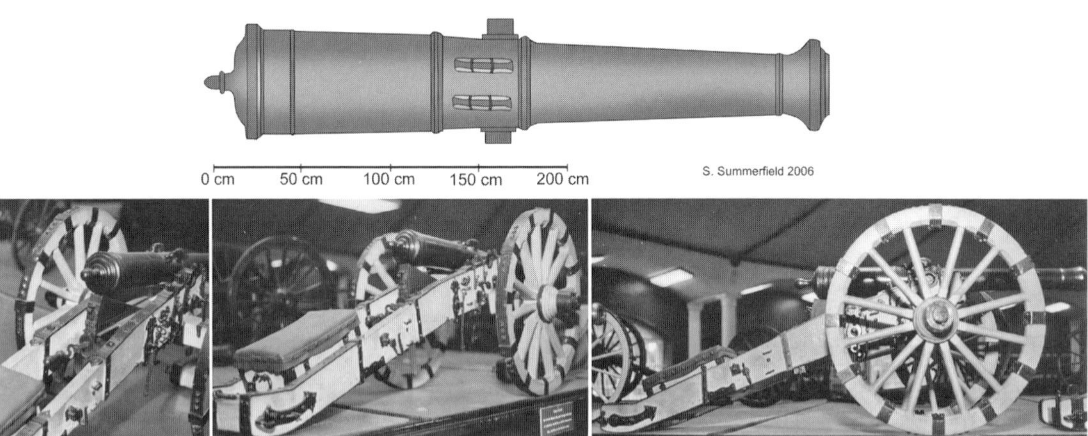

Below a drawing of an Austrian M1756 24-pdr siege gun are three views of a bronze M1753 short 18-pdr siege piece. It has black metalwork, a blackened bronze barrel and an ochre carriage. (Courtesy the Trustees of the RAHT; photographs Norman Swales)

British M1796 Blomefield iron 32-pdr gun

British M1796 Blomefield iron 32-pdr gun for sea or garrison service, made by Walker & Co. The calibre is 162mm, the length 312cm (10ft 3in) and the weight 2838kg (55cwt 3 quarters). Notice the markings on the base ring for the quarter-sights (bottom left), where each mark represented a quarter of a degree of elevation; these were used to align with a mark on the muzzle. The major markings represented 0–3 degrees of elevation. (Courtesy the Board of Trustees of the Royal Armouries; photographs Stephen Summerfield)

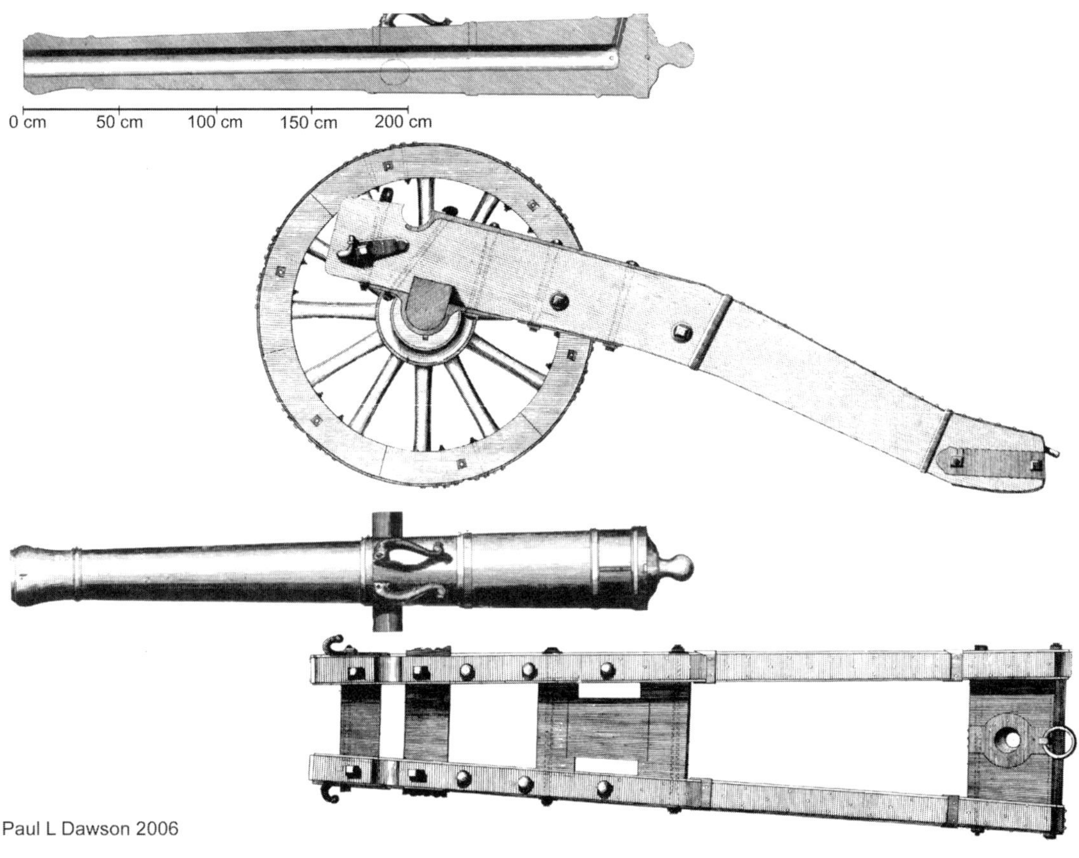

The French M1765 24-pdr siege gun (top) was little altered from the M1732 system and still used elevating quoins. The 16-pdr (bottom) used the same carriage. In 1786 a Rechtsmaschine elevating system was introduced. (After de Scheel)

produced a wear of 2.5–6.5mm. Vent wear beyond 4mm rendered guns unfit for service. Generally gun tubes lasted some 900–1,000 rounds, with the 6.5mm diameter vent expanded by about 2.6mm. As a result of these tests, fewer barrels split in action once the vent had expanded by more than 4mm.[285] For example, during the siege of Kehl (10 November 1796–9 January 1797) five of the 6× 18-pdrs and 19 of the 12-pdr siege guns were failed due to vent expansion beyond the degree permitted.

Britain principally used 24-pdrs for breaching operations. These were mainly cast in bronze until 1811, when the problems experienced at Badajoz rendered them unserviceable due to excessive wear, the vent becoming unbushed and the gun tubes drooping. Sometimes 18-pdrs were used. Dickson states that the calibre of guns employed was often influenced by the ammunition that could be found in sufficient quantity, and was a reason for the variety of different calibres in his siege train.[286] This often meant using ammunition collected from a previous siege, and also firing back the enemy's shot – the solid iron roundshot of that period was almost indestructible unless it hit a very solid obstacle.

The iron guns of 32-, 24-, 18- and 12-pdr calibres used by the siege train came from the Board of Ordnance. The 32-pdr, the heaviest broadside piece employed by the Royal Navy, was not normally used for siege work, although it was often placed in coastal defences. The iron 24-pdrs used at Badajoz (1811) were designed by Thomas Blomefield (M1796) or Armstrong-Frederick (M1760).

In France, Jean-Baptise de Gribeauval's efforts to redesign artillery were concentrated on field and coast defence guns, and the 16- and 24-pdr siege pieces were retained virtually unchanged from

Bavarian Manson 24-pdr siege gun limbered, with the barrel in the travelling position. (Musée de L'Armée)

the Vallière system of 1732. The decoration was removed from the outside of the gun tubes; and the small chambers at the base of the bore were eliminated, as they were difficult to sponge out and made the gun awkward to load. Heavy 12- and 8-pdrs were retained from the M1732 system; these were used to defend gun positions and saps under construction and recently-taken positions, since they could be moved more quickly and easily than the larger calibre guns. The design of their carriages was altered in 1786, when the screw-driven *Rechtsmaschine* was introduced to replace the quoin.

The carriages used for the heavy artillery were virtually unchanged from the M1732 ordnance, and due to the great weight of the gun tubes had only a single trunnion position. Consequently, the gun tube would often be transported separately on a sling cart; only being placed on the carriage with a gyn (field service crane) once the besieged place was reached. The carriages for the 16-pdr and 24-pdr were drawn by four horses, while teams of eight or ten for the 16-pdr and 24-pdr respectively drew the gun tubes on the sling carriages.

In 1792, new gun tubes designed by Jakob Manson were introduced, and carriages with a vertically-mounted screw acting on the bottom of the breech. The next major change came in 1803, when the artillery committee redesigned the siege artillery. The 16-pdr was withdrawn and a Short 24-pdr introduced. The ratio of metal for the gun tube was reduced from 150:1 of shot weight to 120:1. The Long 12- and 6-pdrs were introduced to replace the Long 12- and 8-pdrs of the previous system. The windage of the 24-pdr was reduced, so that the calibre of 5 pouce 6 ligne (5.9in) was the same as that of the 24-pdr howitzer, with commonality of powder charges and shells.

Prussian siege ordnance consisted of 18- and 24-pdr guns, supported by 18-pdr howitzers and a range of mortars. The 24-pdr, with a barrel weight of about 1700kg, was relegated to siege and garrison work from 1759 after it had caused considerable damage at Hohenfriedberg (4 June 1745) and Leuthen (5 December 1757). Many of these guns were used against their previous owners in 1806–07 when Prussian fortresses were besieged by the French and their allies.

This model of a Russian bronze M1757 18-pdr siege gun was presented to the Duke of Wellington in 1815 by the Tsar. (Courtesy the Trustees of the RAHT; photographs Norman Swales)

Model of a Russian bronze M1757 24-pdr siege gun. (Courtesy the Trustes of the RAHT; photographs Norman Swales)

During the 18th century Russia undertook many sieges both in Europe and against the Ottoman Turks. Baron Munnich had formed the Engineer Corps in 1730, and by the time of the Seven Years War this comprised 1,302 officers and men. However, nearly all of them were engaged on civil engineering projects and could not be spared for service with the army, leaving the Russians bereft of specialists. In 1763, the first year of Catherine the Great's reign, Russian siege artillery consisted of 40× 24-pdrs, 20× 18-pdrs, 4× 9-pud mortars, 40× 5-pud mortars, 40× 1-pud unicorns, and the necessary train. The six siege parks were established at St Petersburg, Derpt, Kiev, Belgorod, St Dimitri Fortress and Orenburg.[287]

On 27 February 1797 the artillery was reorganised into three siege (Osadnyi) battalions.[288] On 27 August 1801 the siege artillery consisted of 180 guns – mainly 24-, 18- and 12-pdr cannon with some mortars and unicorns. It was organised into battalions of five companies each.

Heavy Howitzers

Large-calibre howitzers were a vital part of the armoury, due to their ability to throw heavy explosive shells over the walls of fortresses. These required massive firing carriages or mountings to withstand the strain of repeated firing; if they failed, the howitzers were useless.

Austria complemented their heavy guns with 7-, 10- and 12-pdr howitzers. British howitzers of 10in (254mm) and 8in (203mm) calibres were mounted on bracket carriages. Some iron howitzers were developed by 1800.

The French used the M1749 8-pouce howitzer designed in 1749 by Marshal Poitevin, and first cast at Douai. Gribeauval relegated this design to siege and garrison operations. The carriage was drawn by a four-horse team and the howitzer tubes were carried two at a time in a four-horse wagon; once in position the barrel was hoisted into position on the carriage. The carriage design was altered in 1786 when the screw-driven *Rechtsmaschine* replaced

Table 7.2: Heavy howitzers

	Calibre	Tube length	Tube weight	Windage	Projectile weight
Bavarian (Rumford M1791)					
30-pdr M1791 Howitzer	240mm	65cm	508kg	4mm	30kg
British iron Howitzer					
8 inch M1800 iron Howitzer	203mm	122cm (4')	1070kg	3.6mm	22kg
10 inch M1800 iron Howitzer	254mm	152cm (5')	2090kg	4.1mm	41kg
British bronze Howitzer					
8 inch M1760 Müller Howitzer	203mm	91cm (3')	661kg	3.6mm	22kg
10 inch M1760 Müller Howitzer	254mm	120cm (47.5")	1310kg	4.1mm	41kg
10 inch M1791 Howitzer	254mm	140cm (55")	–	4.1mm	41kg
French					
8 pouce M1743 Howitzer	223mm	94cm	540kg	ND	23kg
Prussian					
18-pdr M1744 Linger Howitzer	203mm	130cm	450-480kg	ND	ND
25-pdr M1767/1777 Howitzer	227.5mm	123cm	1106kg	6.7mm	29kg
30-pdr M1762 (Holzendorf) Howitzer	242mm	130cm	1324kg	6.5mm	30kg
Russian					
1 Pud M1757 Unicorn	203mm	305cm	2704kg	ND	16.4kg

the quoin. For the siege of Cadiz (February 1810–August 1812) the topography demanded long-range howitzers. This had been proposed by Colonel Villantroys as part of the M1803 (AnXI) artillery reforms; it was made in 9-pouce, 10-pouce and 11-pouce calibres, and had a range from 5.2 to 5.8km.

In Prussia, the excellent M1744 18-pdr and M1743 10-pdr howitzers designed by Oberst-Leutnant von Holtzmann still seem to have been in use during the Napoleonic Wars, and were turned against the Prussians by the French in their siege operations during the 1806–07 campaign.

The lack of specialists available to the army in Russia led the Inspector-General of Artillery, Peter Shuvalov, to embark on the search for a universal piece of artillery to be used both in the field and for sieges. The result was the gun-howitzer, which became known as the unicorn. After the futile cannonade at Küstrin in 1758, many Russian officers complained that conventional siege artillery would have been better. Shuvalov was adamant about the usefulness of his unicorns, however, claiming that the shell travelled at high velocity on a flat trajectory. According to field tests, the unicorn projectile could penetrate an earthen rampart up to 7ft (2.1m) and the exploding bomb produced a larger crater than a conventional mortar or howitzer shell.

Mortars

Mortars were high-angle weapons that were used exclusively for siege work. Some fired at a fixed elevation of 45 degrees, the range being adjusted by altering the powder charge. Other mortars had trunnions either at the base or the point of balance, clamped by metal caps to sturdy wooden beds; in such cases elevation was adjusted by using quoins. Mortars were normally transported on special four-wheeled carriages.

Siege mortars of calibres up to 450mm (18in) were produced, but most ranged between 8in and 13in. The carriages or beds were bulky, and with the mortar in place weighed from 1.5 to 2.5 tonnes depending on the calibre. Mortars could be carried on a sling cart that allowed the mortar bed to be winched down from the vehicle onto the ground. They fired shells (also known as 'bombs'), and an incendiary round called 'carcass'. The larger shells had two carrying lugs, either side of the fuse housing, to assist in the process of loading by means of hooks. Loading a mortar required the tube to be elevated to the vertical; the powder charge was inserted, either contained within a cartridge or poured loose from a bucket. Up to four gunners

British M1800 iron 10-in howitzer

This model of a British M1800 iron 10-in howitzer was made of brass and ebony, probably by the Royal Carriage Department in the 1820s. This howitzer was drawn by Nelson in 1846, and was still in use during the Crimean War. The 5ft (152cm) gun tube weighed 1070kg and was mounted on an 8ft (244cm) carriage weighing 1863kg. (Courtesy the Board of Trustees of the Royal Armouries; photographs Stephen Summerfield)

then loaded the projectile, whereupon the tube was depressed to 45-degree elevation. The bombardier then calculated the angle of elevation prior to firing. The mortar required a strong platform of timbers, laid at right-angles to the axis of the carriage, over a layer of flat stones.

An anti-personnel mortar termed a Perrier, 6–8 calibres long, fired stones contained within baskets that burst in all directions upon hitting the target.

Coehorn mortars were the smallest, of between 60mm and 120mm calibre; they were named after Baron Menno van Coehorn, a Dutch military engineer and general during the War of the Spanish Succession. These could be carried by two men on poles through the handles fixed to the bed; they fired small shells or hand grenades to ranges of about 140m.

The Austrian M1780 10-, 30- and 60-pdr mortars were 2.8 calibres long. In December 1785 the M1785 6-pdr Coehorn mortar was introduced, and the next year M1786 8- and 16-pdr mortars. In 1794, Oberst-Leutnant Vega, Professor of Mathematics at the

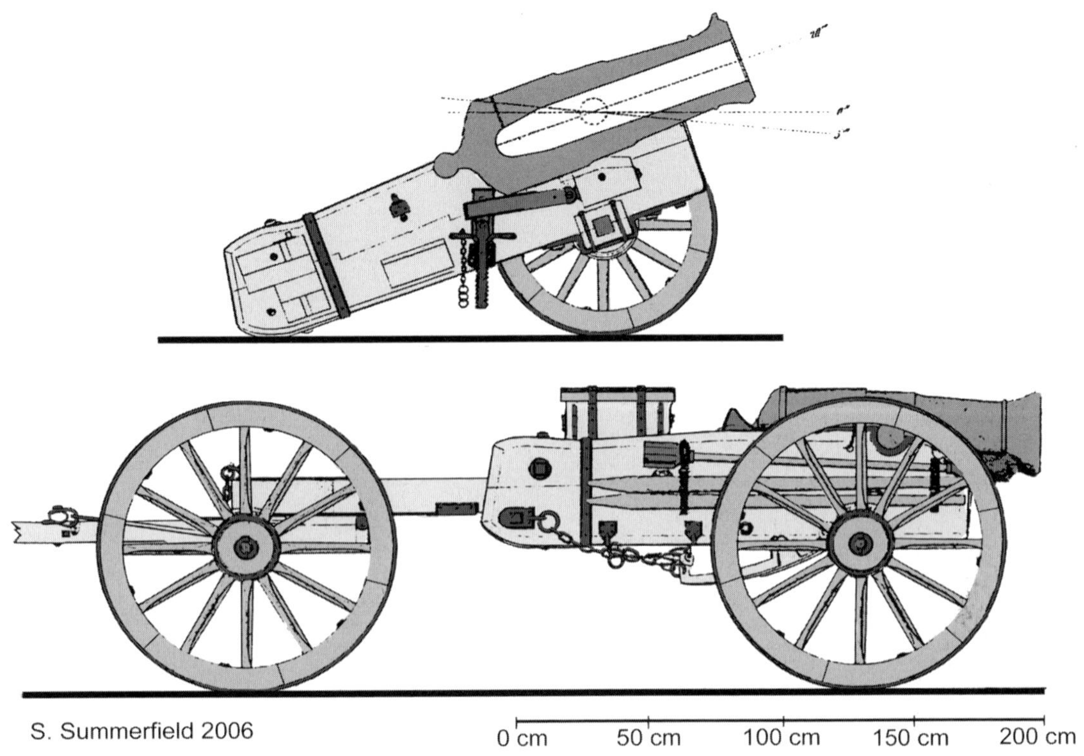

The Prussian M1777 25-pdr howitzer is almost indistinguishable from the British 8in and 10in designs.

Bombardier School in Vienna, reduced Fort Louis – Vauban's masterpiece – within 24 hours, using 16 siege pieces including 3× 10-pdr mortars. As a direct consequence, Vega developed new 30- and 60-pdr long-range mortars. In 1796, using these, the Austrians took Mannheim after a few days' pounding; at an angle of 45 degrees the 30-pdr mortar had a range of 1620m – far greater than the defenders' guns – and the 60-pdr had a range of 1800m.

Britain used bronze or iron mortars, most of the former being cast before 1792. The largest was the 13in (330mm) iron mortar, that could be mounted either on an iron 4.8 tonne garrison bed, a 2.5 tonne land service bed, or a wooden 1.1 tonne bed.[289] At 45-degree elevation the 13in Land Service Mortar had a maximum range of 1940m with a 6lb (2.7kg) charge, and the 10in Land Service 1764m with a 3lb (1.4kg) charge. All British mortars had a tapering chamber based on the designs of Gomer in France.

The French M1732 mortars were replaced in 1769 by the 8-pouce (223mm), the Short 10-pouce (274mm) and the Long 10-pouce (274mm) mortars designed by Gribeauval. The bomb weight was irregularly distributed, which caused damage when fired. A mortar could fire 48 bombs within 24 hours, but this was normally restricted to 30 rounds to avoid excessive wear. J. Berenger – the gun-founder at Douai, and son-in-law of Jean Maritz II – developed the M1775 12-pouce (325mm) mortar, which had a cylindrical rather than a pear-shaped chamber.

In 1785, General de Gomer introduced a chamber shaped like a truncated cone; this ensured that the bomb fitted tightly into the breech of the piece, increased accuracy by equalizing the gas pressure on all sides of the projectile, and avoided the barrel wear of previous mortars. The M1789 8-pouce (223mm), 10-pouce (274mm) and 12-pouce (325mm) Gomer-chambered mortars were adopted; the 8-pouce and 12-pouce remained in use until 1870, and the 10-pouce until 1890.

Model of the Russian bronze M1757 1-pud unicorn. (Courtesy the Trustees of the RAHT; photographs Norman Swales)

Table 7.3: Heavy mortars

	Calibre	Tube length	Tube weight	Windage	Filled shell weight
Austrian mortars					
M1780 10-pdr mortar	171mm	ND	ND	8mm	10.6kg
M1796 30-pdr mortar (Vega)	246mm	ND	ND	11mm	30.5kg
M1796 60-pdr mortar (Vega)	310mm	ND	ND	14mm	61.2kg
M1796 100-pdr mortar	367mm	ND	ND	ND	102kg
British bronze mortars					
8in Land Service mortar (iron)	203mm	100cm	458kg	4.1mm	22kg
10in Land Service mortar (iron)	254mm	80cm	916kg	4.1mm	41kg
13in Land Service mortar (iron)	330mm	64cm	1832kg	3.6mm	93kg
British iron mortars					
4 ⅖in Coehorn mortar	112mm	34cm	38kg	ND	2kg
5½in Royal mortar	143mm	41cm	51kg	ND	6kg
8in Land Service mortar	203mm	86cm	458kg	4.1mm	22kg
10in Land Service mortar	254mm	97cm	916kg	4.1mm	41kg
13in Land Service mortar	330mm	111cm	1272kg	3.6mm	93kg
French mortars					
M1765 8.8in (8 pouce) mortar	223mm	55cm	ND	ND	22kg
M1765 10.8in (10 pouce)	274mm	77cm	1660kg	ND	49kg
M1775 12.8in (12 pouce) mortar (Berenger)	325mm	90cm	2560kg	ND	72kg
M1789 8.8in (8 pouce) Gomer mortar	223mm	ND	ND	ND	22kg
M1789 10.8in (10 pouce) Gomer mortar	274mm	ND	2200kg	ND	49kg
M1789 12.8in (12 pouce) Gomer mortar	325mm	76cm	1040kg	ND	72kg
16in (15 pouce) Perrier	406mm	80cm	ND	ND	50kg
Prussian mortars					
M1775 Coehorn mortar (wrought iron)	105mm	24cm	19kg	2.6mm	2.1kg
7-pdr M1790 Pack mortar (Tempelhoff)	149mm	46cm	87kg	5.2mm	6.1kg
10-pdr M1785 mortar (Tempelhoff	170mm	52cm	182kg	3.7mm	12.6kg
25-pdr M1755 mortar (Linger)	226mm	69cm	397kg	7.1mm	29.0kg
50-pdr M1752 Light Bronze mortar (Breslau)	284mm	72cm	715kg	5.7mm	85.6kg
50-pdr M1769 Bronze mortar (Linger)	284mm	75cm	807kg	5.7mm	85.6kg
50-pdr M1782-96 Bronze mortar (Holtzmann)	284mm	93cm	804kg	5.7mm	85.6kg
140-pdr M1775 Stone mortar	398mm	71cm	874kg	ND	ND
140-pdr M1784/1810 Stone mortar	392mm	88cm	785kg	ND	ND
Russian mortars					
¼ Pud (10-pdr) M1805 mortars	122mm	41cm	73kg	ND	3.9kg
2-Pud M1805 mortar	203mm	ND	ND	ND	32kg
5-Pud M1805 mortar	335mm	111cm	1494kg	ND	82kg

British 4⅖in bronze Coehorn mortar, cast by John and Henry King in 1807 at the Royal Arsenal in Woolwich. Now in the Royal Armouries in Leeds, it has a wooden bed painted light grey. (Courtesy the Board of Trustees of the Royal Armouries)

British iron 8in mortar, on an iron bed painted black. (Courtesy the Board of Trustees of the Royal Armouries; photographs Stephen Summerfield)

New 12-pouce (325mm), 8-pouce (223mm) and 24-pdr (5.9in/152mm) mortars were introduced in 1803. The 24-pdr mortar was later codified into the Valée system, and the design remained in use until as late as 1914. This mortar had only a small iron mounting with the rest of the bed made of timber, and was provided with two lifting eyes on each side so that four men could carry it over rough terrain. At the same time the windage of the 24-pdr was reduced so that the calibre was 5.9in, the same as the 24-pdr howitzer, and thus common powder charges and shells could be employed for both pieces. In 1808, 6-pouce and 8-pouce mortars were introduced.

In Prussia the Linger M1732 10-, 24- and 50-pdr mortars were retained by Frederick the Great. Dieskau introduced the lighter M1755 mortar mounted on a cannon-type carriage, and these replaced the M1732 10-pdr mortars in the siege train. Georg Friedrich von Tempelhoff designed the M1789 10-pdr mortar in 1785, and a mountain mortar (M1790) to supplement the older mortars that were in service.

Russia introduced the 5-, 2- and ¼-pud mortars of the Arakcheev M1805 system, with maximum ranges at a 45-degree angle of 2.6km, 2.4km and 1.8km respectively. The M1805 2-pud mortar could fire one shot every five to seven minutes. During the 1813 campaign mortars were widely used and performed well at, for instance, the siege of Danzig.

DEFENSIVE POSITIONS

Frederick the Great considered heavy artillery to have a key role in assisting the infantry advance,

British iron 13in mortar, on an iron bed painted black. (Courtesy the Board of Trustees of the Royal Armouries; photographs Stephen Summerfield)

Gribeauval M1765 short 10-pouce (10-pdr) mortar of 274mm calibre. (After Manson, 1792)

and that it was important not to let the guns fire too soon. The opening rounds of a battery were the most effective, and the greatest resource at the disposal of the army commander, so timing of the opening salvo was crucial. Austrian doctrine of 1759 argued for the guns to open fire when the target was at musket ranges. Prussian doctrine held that the guns should fire by half-battery in salvos rather than singly.

Batteries were placed in fixed positions, and when used to support an infantry attack they were located, whenever possible, so as to enfilade the enemy mass – to fire into the opposing troops' flank – and the closer the battery could get, the better. However, this tactic required quick reactions to guard against sudden counter-attacks. To some extent this risk could be overcome by leap-frogging batteries forward, or by approaching behind a screen of cavalry or infantry. The latter also increased the surprise factor, and unexpected artillery fire from effective range might rout an inexperienced enemy on its own.

The Austrians used their 18-pdr guns as heavy field artillery, placing them in prepared field fortifications. After 1795 the 18-pdr gun – which required a team of eight heavy draft horses – was less employed, due to a shortage of such animals.[290] Only two such batteries were in the field in 1813.

Prussian M1789 10-pdr (170mm) mortar designed by Templehoff. This example is preserved in the fortress of Torun in Poland. (Pawel Nowaczek)

Russian M1805 ¼-pud mortar on wooden bed; tube length 41cm, weight 73kg. (Dr S. Efimov)

Prussia used 12-pdrs much as the Austrians used their 18-pdrs, as position guns. Until 1760 the position artillery marched in a single column, commanded by the quartermaster of artillery and the wagon-master. Usually several infantry battalions were attached to this column, to provide a pool of labour to extricate the guns from ruts and protect them on the march. While on column of route the heavy artillery pieces were placed at the front of the column with the powder wagons and other carriages to the rear. The artillery was only divided into batteries when it neared the enemy, and would enter the battlefield from either the right or the left.

Duke Ferdinand of Brunswick – commander of the Prussian western theatre in the Seven Years War, and victor at Minden – was forced in 1760 to employ the lighter Austrian 12-pdr as part of the artillery train. This could move as fast as the infantry on the march, and was complemented by lightweight 12-pdrs used by the horse artillery. He also suggested decreasing the number of 12-pdrs in favour of the Heavy 6-pdr, thus reducing the number of horses needed and the length of the train. Ferdinand stated that replacing the cumbersome 12-pdr with the lighter 6-pdr would improve infantry mobility; it would be able to occupy positions more swiftly, and commanders could have confidence that it could be brought into action at a critical point in the battle.[291]

After 1760, Prussian artillery batteries were assigned to the infantry brigades while on column of route, and marched into the battle line along with their infantry. In 1787, six bombardment (position) batteries armed with 6× Heavy 12-pdrs and 2× howitzers were with the field army. For the Jena campaign some twenty years later Prussia had 24 'bombardment pieces', 84× Medium 12-pdrs, 120× Heavy 6-pdrs, 320× Light 6-pdrs, 16× 10-pdr mortars, 76× 10-pdr howitzers and 34× 7-pdr howitzers.

Saxony was one of the few minor German states with a large artillery establishment prior to the French Revolutionary Wars. The Saxons deployed their 8- and 12-pdrs in positional batteries.

Field Fortifications

There were different types of field fortifications. In a defensive action, the position artillery was located behind redoubts (defensive blockhouses or earthen ramparts, usually in the shape of a square but also in polygonal or hexagonal forms); and redans or fleches (small V-shaped earthworks set at a salient angle facing the enemy and usually open in the rear). These were used to cover the front of a deployed field army, advanced posts, bridges, or roads into a town. Often they were hastily erected the night before the battle, and were supported by infantry. A number of field fortifications were constructed so that their fields of fire were mutually supporting in case of enemy attack, but they specialised in counter-battery fire.

Gogel recommended that redoubts should not be placed in isolation in front of the main line of troops, and that the guns should have at least two lines of retreat.[292] The guns used were often of the larger calibres (12-pdr and above), and would be defended by an earthen bank reinforced with gabions (earth-filled baskets). Stacked gabions could also form a parapet to mask the crews while leaving openings for the guns to fire through.

The Austrian artillery manual of 1809 suggested that a timber roof of light construction should be placed over the gun to prevent the gunners from being injured by flying debris. From 1809 the Austrians tended to deploy their positional artillery in prepared field fortifications, in the manner seen at Wagram and Aspern-Essling. The 1807 Austrian *Kavallerie Reglement* advocated that the infantry should advance supported by fire from the heavy position guns, and from a cavalry artillery battery advancing by half-batteries, so the first half was covered by the fire of the second.[293] Austrian doctrine in 1808 allocated all the heavy guns to a permanent battery organisation of 6× 12-pdrs and 2× howitzers that would not deploy by half-batteries. These batteries, once they had achieved their objective, returned to the artillery reserve, leaving the temporary field fortification as an obstacle to troop movement on the battlefield.[294] In exceptional circumstances position batteries were used offensively – as at Lieberwolkwitz (13 October 1813), when two

A sketch of a British defended earthwork emplacement for two Blomefield M1796 iron 12-pdrs on garrison carriages. It has been revetted with timbers, sandbags and gabions as part of the Lines of Torres Vedras in Portugal, 1810–11.

position batteries were advanced by Oberst Stein to deny the French troops a rallying-point.

Where practicable, British heavy guns and howitzers were to be protected by an earthwork 2–3ft (75–100cm) high and fronted with a shallow ditch.[295]

France sometimes assigned the 16-pdrs to the field army, and the Army of Germany used them in considerable numbers in 1794. On 7 June 1794 the Army of the Rhine had 10× 16-pdrs on *affut-fardier* carriages that made them as mobile as field guns, supplementing the 27× 12-pdrs, 19× 8-pdrs, 10× 4-pdrs and 14× howitzers; in addition, 4× Long 12-pdrs and 4× Long 8-pdrs from the siege train were used in the field. In 1800, Auguste des Lespinasse noted that 16-pdr guns were placed in temporary field fortifications in the Austrian manner.

In 1807 Napoleon ordered the construction of redoubts along the Vistula to defend against Russian incursions. In 1809, heavy guns were deployed prior to the battle of Wagram (5–6 July 1809), using mostly captured Austrian ordnance from the Vienna arsenal. In 1813, Napoleon constructed five redoubts around the city of Dresden to defend against the Austrians, Russians and Prussians. The lack of 12-pdrs forced the field army in Spain, and later in Germany after the battle of Katzbach (26 August 1813), to deploy the 16-pdr in the field.

The Prussians also emplaced their 12-pdrs in temporary field fortifications due to their immense weight and lack of mobility.[296]

The Russians were the greatest proponents of position batteries, those established at Borodino being the best examples at this time. On 20 May 1813 the Allies took up positions around Bautzen and the nearby hills with a chain of redoubts and smaller works. The village on the Kreckwitz height was fortified, and abattis of felled trees blocked the roads. The fortifications were so extensive that the French engineers later destroyed no less than 78 Allied redoubts, redans and epaulements.[297]

Fortified Camps

Fortified camps capable of sheltering an entire army played important strategic roles in many of the campaigns, and built upon the success of those of Frederick the Great during the Seven Years War. The most notable in the period were the Lines of Torres Vedras in 1810–12 and the Drissa in 1812.

The Lines of Torres Vedras improved upon the great natural strength of a series of ridges protecting the Portuguese port and capital city, Lisbon, on its peninsula. The Lines dated back to October 1809, when Lieutenant-Colonel Fletcher RE, his Chief of Engineers, was ordered by Wellington to begin construction. In September 1810, Wellington fell back

This French siege gun emplacement depicted in 1824 has changed little from those described by Hulot in 1813 and drawn by Jakobowski in 1786. (Auguste de Moltzheim, L'Armée Français sous la Restauration, 1814–1830, *Editions du Cannonier, Nantes)*

on Lisbon during a carefully paced fighting withdrawal in the face of the advancing French Army of Portugal under Marshal Massena. The Lines were not simply a field entrenchment but a series of solid, all-round defensive positions that could provide mutual support and minimise the concentration of enemy artillery. The first two lines stretched 29 miles (47km) and 22 miles (35km) respectively, from the River Tagus to the Atlantic, supported on both flanks by Royal Navy gunboats, bomb vessels and sloops. The third line protected the evacuation beach on the Tagus, and was considered the strongest. Altogether the system enclosed an area of about 500 square miles (1300km^2), which had been thoroughly provisioned in advance. The Lines were split into five sectors, the redoubts being garrisoned with 1,009 troops from 1st to 3rd Portuguese Artillery Regiments supported by 1,882 volunteers from the Ordenanza (militia):

Alhandra Forts (Maj Joao C. Pinto) – 258 gunners, 182 Ordenanza
Becellas Forts (Col Romao de Arriada, CO 1st Artillery Regt) – 218 gunners, 847 Ordenanza
Monte Agraca Forts (Maj J.J. da Cruz) – 150 gunners, 300 Ordenanza
Torres Vedras Forts (Capt F.J.V. Barreiros) – 150 gunners, 248 Ordenanza
Mafra Forts (Maj Caetano P. Xavier) – 233 gunners, 305 Ordenanza.

FORTRESS AND GARRISON ARTILLERY

Garrison artillery was designed for the defence of permanent fortifications. The carriages for fixed positions were not constrained by weight, and so were designed for efficiency; they often involved traversing-platforms. Where mobility within fortresses was not required, many garrison carriages resembled the naval truck carriage, the stepped wooden cheeks supporting the gun on its trunnions and moving backwards and forwards on four small solid wheels.

Austrian garrison guns were of the same calibre as the siege guns, and were mounted on the same carriage and traversing-platform as introduced into the French service in 1764. On 26 June 1806, the Kingdom of Naples possessed 68× bronze 24-pdrs, 45× bronze 16-pdrs, 19× bronze 12-pdrs, 17× iron 36-pdrs, 40× iron 32-pdrs, 104× iron 24-pdrs, 51× iron 18-pdrs, and 30× iron 12-pdr garrison and coast defence guns, many inherited from Austria. Napoleon's decree of 8 December 1806 on the organisation of the artillery of the Kingdom of Italy noted that Austrian guns were used in Venice, Palmanava and Ossoppo as fortress guns.

Britain used 24-pdr cannon on garrison carriages (weighing 712kg), mortars and carronades.[298] Garrison duty, offering substantial quarters and no cross-country marching, was believed to be within the capabilities of 'invalids' – at that time simply a term for time-expired men, and not implying serious disability. In 1792 the thirty-five Invalid Companies were distributed as follows: in Berwick (3), Chester (2), Dover Castle (1), Guernsey (6), Jersey (6), Kingston-upon-Hull (1), Landgave Fort (1), Scotland (4), Pendennis (1), Plymouth (6), Scilly Isles (1), Sheerness (2) and Tilbury Fort (1). In 1802 these companies were disbanded or formed into Garrison Battalions.[299]

The Royal Garrison Battalion of ten companies was raised on 1 September 1795.[300] On 25 December 1802 the 2nd to 7th Royal Garrison Battalions were formed from the Invalid Companies. On 30 June 1804 they were renamed the Royal Veteran Battalions. The following were formed mostly for home service: 8th (29 December 1804), 9th (21 March 1805), 10th (26 December 1806), 11th (25 April 1807), 12th (25 June 1808), 13th (March 1813 in Lisbon) and the 1st Foreign (1813, from thekgL Garrison Company). By 1816 all had been disbanded.

In October 1804, after the original units had become Royal Veteran Battalions, the 1st–16th Garrison Battalions were formed from the Battalions of Reserve, only to be disbanded in February 1805, and 19,553 men volunteered for the Regular Army. The remaining fit and underage men were formed into the 1st–3rd Garrison Battalions on 25 February 1805 and the 4th–9th Garrison Battalions in December 1806. Most were disbanded in December 1814.

The Battalion of Invalid Artillery was formed for garrison duty within Great Britain. They were stationed at Woolwich (44th, 46th, 48th–50th, 59th–60th Companies), Guernsey (43rd Company), Elizabeth Castle in Jersey (47th Company), Fort George in Scotland (45th Company), Bermuda (64th Company 1794–1807, then to Woolwich), and Ireland (89th Company 1801–07 in Dublin, 1807–19 in Athlone). All were disbanded in February 1819.

Ever since bomb vessels were added to the Royal Navy in the 1680s, their armament of mortars had been operated by the Royal Artillery. The Royal Marine Artillery was formed in 1804 due to the difficulties of the Ordnance Department in manning bomb ketches, and provided shore expeditions with artillery. Three companies were formed at

Portuguese iron 6-pdr cannon cast in 1768; the royal coat of arms can be seen. Interestingly, these are now in Torun fortress in Poland; they are possibly naval guns from a Portuguese ship that was impounded in Danzig. (Pawel Nowaczek)

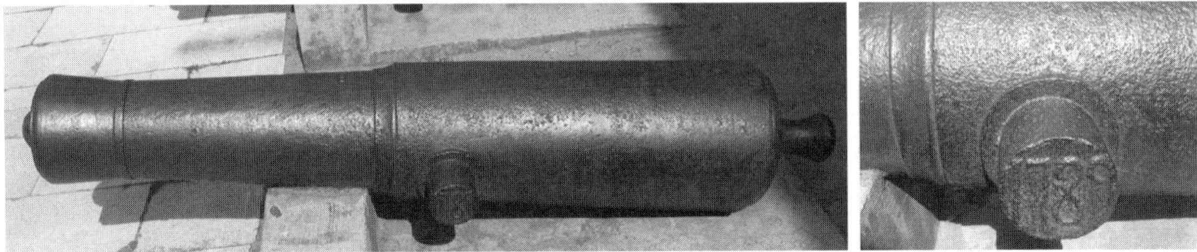

Prussian iron garrison guns cast in 1789, now at Torun in Poland. (Pawel Nowaczek)

Iron 6-pdr with 'PFW' monogram cast in 1768, now on display at Torun, Poland. It may date from the short-lived Polish Confederation. (Pawel Nowaczek)

Portsmouth, Plymouth and Chatham with another later added at Woolwich. By 1805, each artillery company consisted of 1 captain, 3 1st lieutenants, 5 2nd lieutenants, 8 sergeants, 5 corporals, 8 bombardiers, 3 drummers and 62 gunners. For amphibious operations in the Peninsula and America, they were equipped with light howitzers and mountain guns (*see* Chapter 6).

Republican France inherited Vauban fortresses from the 17th century which relied heavily on iron 12- and 16-pdr guns (as these were cheaper to produce). Vauban also argued that the best type of carriage for this application was the naval carriage that he had devised in the early 1690s for the port of Dunkirk, as well as Ypres and Mons. The Vauban fortress carriage dispensed with the rear wheels and had a stubby trail.

When Napoleon came to power in 1799, France had 28 companies of *Cannoniers Sédentaires* dating back to the Ancien Régime, and their number was increased to 30 by 1812. In 1791, the *Cannoniers Sédentaires de Lille* (established 1483) merged with the National Guard. They served with distinction during the sieges of Lille in 1792 by the Austrians

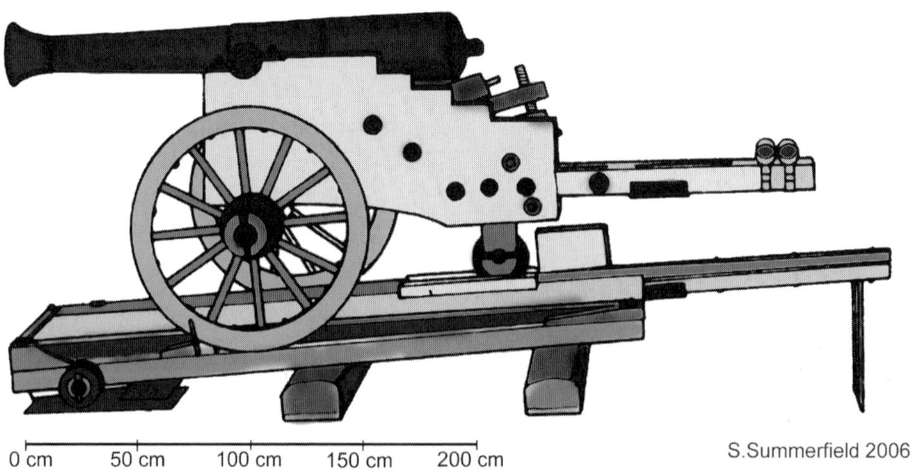

Prussian iron 12-pdr gun on a garrison carriage with traversing-platform.

and 1814 by the Anglo-Prussian forces. This unit was not used exclusively in garrison, and in 1803 formed a two-company battalion; this served in 1809 at Walcheren, where they lost three officers and twenty-four men. The National Guard Artillery was disbanded in 1798, but re-formed in 1812 when two guns were attached to each of the 88 Cohorts of National Guard.

In Holland, French troops captured 250 guns at the Dutch capitulation of Breda (24 February 1793), 150 guns at Geertruidenberg (1–4 March 1793), and 54 guns and 2 mortars at Klundert (1–4 March 1793). A Dutch and Hanoverian garrison at Sluis (17 July–24 August 1794) had 17× 18-pdrs, 15× 24-pdrs, 43× 6-pdrs, 26× 6-pdrs, 5× 16in howitzers and 4× 16in mortars.

Polish fortresses in the Duchy of Warsaw were created to act as obstacles to a Russian invasion. As early as December 1806, Napoleon ordered General Chasseloup-Laubat, Chief Engineer of the Grande Armée, to build a right-bank bridgehead in Praga, and to design a fortress at Modlin at the confluence of the rivers Vistula and Narev, just 28km north-west of Warsaw. Soon the idea of building another fortress at Serock, about 30km from Modlin, was developed.

When war moved into East Prussia in 1807, Torun acted as the supply base for the Grande Armée. Fortification work was halted after the Treaty of Tilsit; the defensive triangle at the confluence of the Vistula and Bugonarwia rivers had served its purpose. The Vistula fortifications played a principal role following the enlargement of the duchy; in 1809 the border with Austria moved further away, and the function of the Modlin–Praga–Serock (and later Zamosc) triangle changed. Napoleon abandoned the project to enhance the fortresses prepared by Pelletier in November 1809 along the Vistula from Krakow to Torun, because he considered them too static, and implying that the Russians would be a future aggressor.

According to Pierre Bontemps, writing on 23 August 1810, the Polish army had 8× bronze 24-pdr guns, 39× 12-pdr fortress guns, 29× 12-pdr field guns, 19× 6-pdr fortress guns, 79× 6-pdr field guns and 29× 3-pdrs. In addition to these bronze guns, they had the following iron pieces: 27× 6-pdrs and 12-pdrs, 29× 10-pdr howitzers, 27× 7-pdr howitzers, 7× captured 8in howitzers (though with no ammunition), and 9× mortars. These iron guns appear to have been of Prussian manufacture; however, most of the howitzers were old and of little use. There were only 78 field guns and 227 garrison guns serviceable. An example of the lack of good artillery was the fortress of Zamosc, the only fortress in the Duchy of Warsaw considered capable of surviving a three-week siege – provided it had 100 guns; but it only had 50 light pieces in its arsenal.

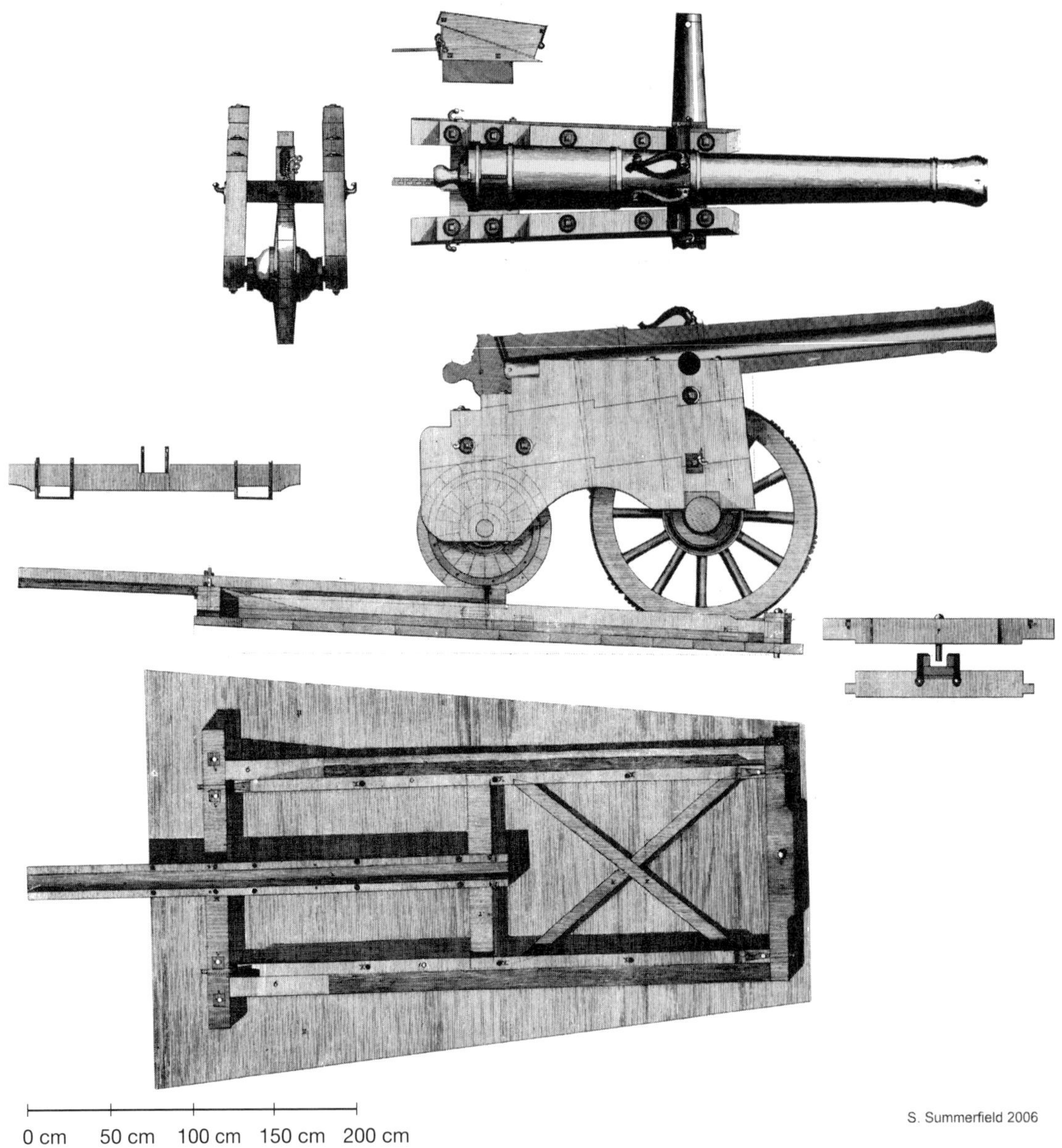

French M1765 Gribeauval 16-pdr garrison carriage. The elevation of the gun tube was by sliding quoins. (After Muy and Gribeauval, 1771)

In the autumn of 1810 relations between the duchy and Russia took a turn for the worse, and Napoleon promised the Polish fortresses 50 iron guns from Stettin; however, due to transport problems during the winter the guns did not arrive until May 1811. Half of them were allocated to Torun, and the rest remained on the barges so they could be sent to Danzig in case of a Russian attack.

Instead of three average-sized fortresses, Napoleon chose to construct one huge fortress halfway down the Vistula: Modlin, at the junction of the Vistula and Narev rivers – which were called

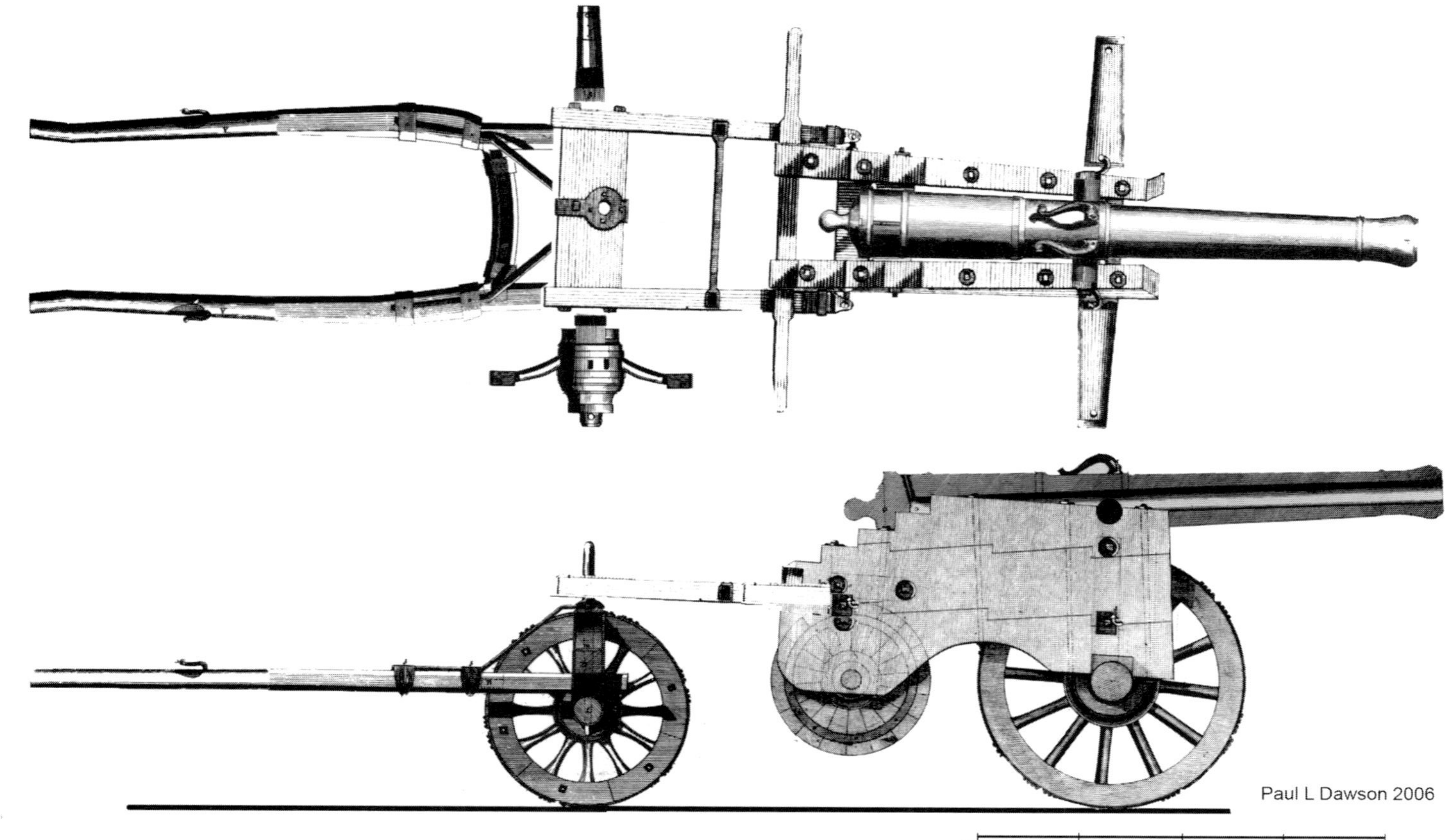

French M1765 Gribeauval garrison carriage for a 16- or 24-pdr gun, attached to a single-draft limber that dated back to the designs of Vallière's M1732 system. (After Muy and Gribeauval, 1771)

French post-1789 garrison and coast defence carriage

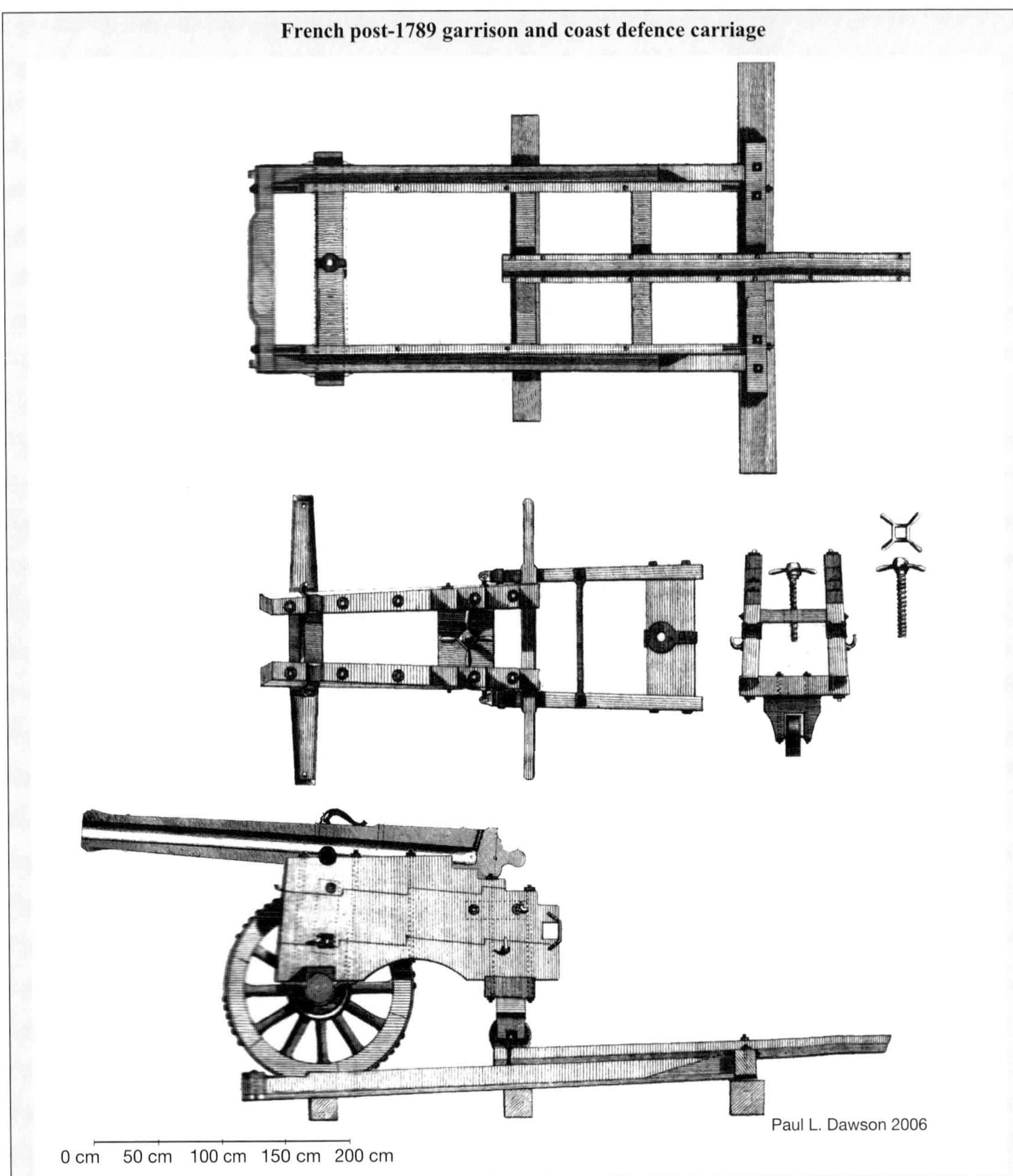

The French post-1789 garrison and coast defence carriage, on a traversing-platform designed by Berthalot. (After Manson, 1792) The elevating screw and small rear wheel were alterations made by Count de Rostaing. In the Gribeauval system, the garrison and coast guns had different wheels from the field artillery; Rostaing made axles and wheels for each calibre of gun interchangeable regardless of carriage, so that a 12-pdr or 8-pdr garrison gun had the same wheels as its counterpart in the siege or field artillery.

French Meunier carriage, with iron gun tube designed by Manson. This was a naval gun carriage mounted on a traversing-platform. (After Manson, 1792)

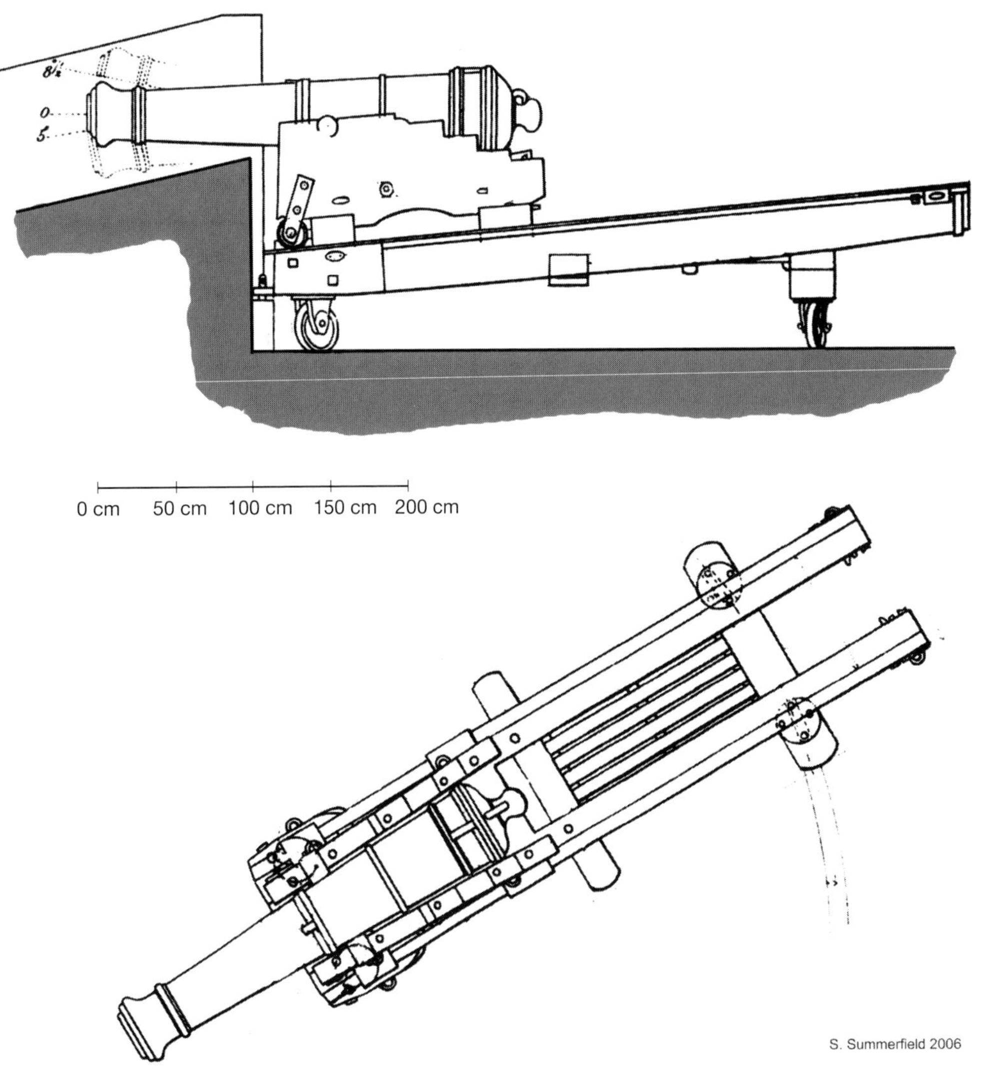

British traversing-platform for a 24-pdr; this had to support the combined weight of 2.3 tonnes (gun tube) and 0.9 tonnes (carriage).

by Napoleon in January 1881 'the Boulevard of the Duchy'. This became central to Warsaw's defence, with a considerable arsenal; in the event of a Russian attack the Polish army would find shelter there to await French aid. The other major fortress was Danzig, called the 'Gibraltar of the Baltic'.

On the eve of war with Russia in 1812 the fortresses of the Duchy of Warsaw had a total of 298 functioning guns, of which 67 were iron.

Prussian Garrison Companies varied in strength, and were composed of men unfit for field service. In 1740, Frederick the Great inherited four of them, at Pillau, Magdeburg, Stettin and Wesel. In 1742 the Silesian Garrison Company was formed at Breslau. In 1748–50 the number of garrison companies was raised to eight by the formation of new companies at Neisse, Glatz and Schweidnitz. Further companies were formed at Cosel (1756), Colberg and Glogau (1770), Königsberg (1777), Silberberg (1782) and

Graudenz (1784). These garrisons were armed with 24-, 12- and 6-pdr guns; after 1780 some of these were of cast iron rather than bronze.

After the huge losses of Dieskau guns at Breslau (1757), M1731 Brummer 12-pdr garrison guns from Glogau were used with devastating effect at Leuthen. These remained a mainstay of Prussian artillery until 1806, despite their unwieldy size and weight. In 1786, Prussia had thirteen garrison artillery companies plus two garrison artillery 'commandos' (detachments), with a total of 63 officers, 142 NCOs, 218 bombadiers, 1,600 gunners and a drummer, manning 6,409 fortress and siege guns. In 1792, sixteen garrison artillery companies of varying strengths were formed.[301] In 1795 the twenty arsenals were commanded by a lieutenant or a captain with a small staff, and came under the Artillery Inspection.[302]

Twenty Prussian 18-, 24- and 36-pdr garrison and coast defence guns from the fortress of Wesel were transported to the Kingdom of Italy in 1807. In addition, large numbers of guns were sold to the Duchy of Warsaw, as noted above.

Russia, with its long borders surrounded by hostile countries including Austria, Poland, Prussia, Sweden and Turkey, maintained a large number of garrisons. The Moscow Garrison Regiment was formed from eight field and three garrison battalions in Moscow on 20 November 1796. The St Petersburg Garrison was reduced to two battalions on forming the Arkharov 1st Musketeer Regiment, and the Schlüsselburg Garrison Battalion was established on 21 November. There were forty-three garrison battalions allotted to divisions, leaving sixty-four unassigned. On 3 December 1796, each battalion had one grenadier and five musketeer companies. On 4 March 1800 most of the garrison battalions were disbanded and the men were used to form line infantry regiments.[303]

The artillery garrisons in fortresses were numbered 1st–69th Companies, and were distributed among ten regions (Okrug) on 8 November 1809. The fortresses won from the Ottomans established new garrison artillery companies in the Dunaiskii (Danube) Okrug in May 1811. The Braila, Giurgiu, and Turnu fortresses were returned to Turkey on 16 May 1812, and consequently their artillery garrisons were relocated. After this the artillery garrison companies in the Danube Region consisted of the 34th at Khotin, 70th at Akkerman and Bendery, 71st–72nd at Izmail, and 72nd at Kiliya.

COAST DEFENCE

Defence of the coastline and ports was essential for any maritime nation. The key problem in the Napoleonic era was the relatively short range of the guns, which naturally dictated their emplacement very close to the shoreline. Coast defence developed from garrison artillery, and only came into its own as a specialism in the middle of the 19th century, with the introduction of accurate long-range rifled guns.

France

The decree of 7 May 1795 re-created the coastal defence artillery to 130 companies, drawn from 14,000 volunteers. However, the infantry had a higher priority, so the bulk of these men were transferred to that arm. On 23 May 1803, 100 new companies of *Cannoniers Garde-Côtes* of about 100 men each were formed, along with 58 garrison companies. By 1805 these were reorganised into 100 mobile companies under the command of the field artillery, and 28 static companies classed as National Guard.

By 1806 the mobile companies of Coast Defence had 160 guns, placed under the command of the local prefect and deployed wherever necessary within his region. By May 1814 some 144 companies had been formed. From their initial formation in 1806 the three Swiss Regiments in the French army (about 3,000 men in total) were destined for the defence of coastal fortresses, harbours and emplacements at Avignon, Rennes and Lille. From 1809, some coastal guard artillery found themselves manning the guns of small frigates called *prames* for protection of anchorages and major harbours, organised into eight flotillas each commanded by a *chef de bataillon*. That year a large number of the 12,000 artillerymen were organised into fourteen companies of artillery, and used to furnish cadre and men to replenish the artillery of the Grande Armée.

An inspection to determine the real situation of coast defences was made in May 1810, and found that 906 places had 3,648 guns manned by 13,000 gunners. The organisation was changed at this time, as Napoleon believed it to be top-heavy and ineffective. On 19 March 1811 two inspectors were appointed – one for the northern coast, one for the southern – with six commissioners classed as artillery engineers, to continue the energetic building of coastal defences and batteries.

In March 1811, mobile columns of 1,000–1,500 men accompanied by 50 cavalry and two field guns were formed, charged with the surveillance of shipping off the Dutch coast, the Spanish frontier and southern Italy. If any enemy shipping was spotted the guns were to be put into action to sink or deter them; it is unknown how effective this was in practice. The bulk of the men for these mobile columns came from the eight naval flotillas disbanded in July 1810. In total, eighteen new battalions were formed.

In June 1812, Napoleon was convinced that it would be far better to replace the infantry and artillery detachments at coastal fortresses and harbours with companies of bombardiers, trained as both infantry and artillery. A total of seventy-two new companies were planned, grouped into four regiments of three battalions each, and reinforced with the artillery drawn from the National Guard cohorts. However, the disastrous losses in Russia that year prevented the issue of the orders for these. In August 1813, the coastal guard artillery and National Guard infantry stationed in the coastal garrisons were incorporated into the Grande Armée, and were replaced by demi-brigades of conscripts of the class of 1814. In May 1814 these were disbanded.

The Maritime Artillery, termed under the Ancien Régime as the *Corps Royal des Canonniers Matelots*, was disbanded in 1792; two garrison regiments were formed the same year, but they too were soon disbanded. On 26 October 1795, seven demi-brigades each of three battalions were formed. The gunners saw service on board ship alongside the gunner-sailors of the fleet; in ports, manning the emplacement guns at the principal forts; and in the construction of equipment and munitions for the coast defence and navy. One company saw service as grenadiers in the Army of Italy in 1800-01, and these personnel often provided the cadre for the companies of military and naval *Ouvriers* (artificers).

On 5 May 1803, the twenty-one battalions were reduced to twelve and formed into four regiments, to which four companies of Ouvriers and four of cadets were added. The first Inspector-General was General Sugny. The artillery park was placed under the command of the artillery director of each principal port. Increasingly these units performed duties as engineers and as staff escorts.

On 24 January 1813 the four regiments (now with some twenty battalions) were transferred from the Naval Ministry to the War Ministry, and formed the backbone of the newly raised army for the German campaign. Ten companies were assigned to the Foot Artillery of the Imperial Guard. About 9,600 naval gunners became grenadiers in Marmont's VI Corps, and served with distinction at Lützen, Bautzen, Leipzig and Hanau; they were disbanded in May 1814. In addition, 17,300 naval gunners were drafted into the army, leaving only 3,700 for service at the ports.

French coastal and garrison ordnance

The same guns were used as by the siege trains, but mounted on garrison, Meunier or depression carriages.

The garrison carriage used in the coast batteries was supposedly designed by Gribeauval in 1748, and was the same as that employed in garrisons. The M1748 garrison carriage was of a naval style, with two limber wheels at the front and a large solid truck wheel, larger than the standard naval type, at the back.[304]

The M1765 traversing-platform, designed to absorb the recoil, was developed by Sieur Berthalot and first built at Auxonne. The Gribeauval garrison gun carriage was set on an elevated platform of three wooden rails rising at a slight angle from a forward pivoting point towards the rear.[305] Under the centre rear of the platform was a small wheel set at right-angles to the timber rails; this ran on a semi-circular iron track, giving 180 degrees of traverse when the platform was moved with handspikes or ropes and pulleys. This allowed the guns of coastal batteries to follow the movement of enemy ships. However, due to the size and cost of this new mounting, many of the 3,000 or so coastal guns remained on naval or garrison carriages, especially the smaller calibres. The 24- and 36-pdr were mounted primarily on the traversing-platform carriage, as they were the least manoeuvrable without it. Berthalot's invention was also applied to fortress guns, not only in France but in most of the major European states including Austria, Britain and Prussia.

The Gribeauval-style garrison carriage became more common after 1780. In 1786, Count de Rostaing greatly improved the M1765 Gribeauval carriages by refitting them with standard field-gun front wheels and replacing the solid timber rear wheel with a small naval truck, to permit the fitting of a vertically-mounted elevating screw.

The M1789 garrison carriage designed by Rostaing lengthened the carriage from 168cm to 196cm, and the front wheels were increased from 132cm to 148cm.[306,307] This increase in wheel diameter permitted increased elevation and depression, from +13 degrees/–15 degrees to +20 degrees/–22 degrees.[308]

Meunier's carriage was similar to the Gribeauval garrison carriage, but ran on either small composite timber wheels or naval trucks. It was in essence a naval carriage mounted on a traversing-platform. Unlike Berthalot's platform, the carriage had two small wheels at the back, and consisted of two rails instead of three. This resulted in the gun firing on a flatter angle than Gribeauval's, and was intended for use inside casemates – unlike Gribeauval's carriage for exposed positions.[309] A version of the Meunier type running on larger wheels also existed, for use on wall tops alongside the Gribeauval type.

The depression carriage enabled the gun to fire downwards at an angle of up to 45 degrees, by means of a pair of blocks-and-tackles set into a rectangular frame mounted on the traversing-platform behind the gun carriage.[310] By means of this lifting system the gun could be depressed and traversed to follow a target below the walls. Once it was elevated, the windlass – which acted on two cables through the blocks-and-tackles – was locked off. This type of gun carriage was used by other countries, primarily the British in Gibraltar.

The M1786 coast defence system was designed in 1785 by General Manson, Inspector-General of the Royal Corps of Colonial Artillery, to replace the guns of the M1778 system that were deemed too long and heavy, and was brought into service on 26 October 1786. Manson's new iron gun tubes were lighter than their predecessors, without mouldings, ornamentation or dolphins. The astragal at the base of the muzzle-swell was removed from the smaller calibre guns, and replaced with a simple ring on the 18-pdr, 24-pdr and 36-pdr. The trunnions on all calibres were reinforced with rimbases. In 1810, flintlocks were introduced. So successful was Manson's M1786 system that it remained in use until 1820.

British coastal ordnance

The defences of Britain were upgraded swiftly under the threat of invasion. The traversing-platform for permanent fortifications permitted the gun crew to train artillery quickly upon moving targets, but it was not fully refined until the early 19th century with its introduction on Martello towers. By 1800 three types of platforms were available, distinguished by the position of the pivot and the racers. Despite manuals of construction laid down by the Board of Ordnance, there was great variation due to local conditions and requirements.

The earliest carriages were constructed of wood, but these soon deteriorated in extreme climates. From the late 18th century carriages and platforms of cast iron were introduced, becoming universal by 1810, despite their brittle nature and tendency to shatter if struck by enemy fire. In response to this the Earl of Chatham, Master-General of the Ordnance, ordered on 9 March 1810 that iron carriages were to be placed in parts of fortifications that were least exposed to enemy fire, and in coast batteries that could not be approached closer than 1,000 yards. Wooden platforms and carriages were kept in store to replace the iron carriages in case of attack.

In early February 1794, HMS *Fortitude* (74 guns) and HMS *Juno* (32 guns) were severely mauled by three guns in a medieval round tower on Mortella Point in the Gulf of San Fiorenzo on the coast of Corsica. In the 150-minute engagement the Royal Navy lost 60 sailors. After a two-day siege mounted by 1,400 soldiers disembarked from the ships, the fort surrendered. The Mortella Point tower was 12m high and 13.7m in diameter with 4.6m-thick walls constructed of stone.[311]

As a result, the standardised design of the 'Martello' (*sic*) Towers built by the British was established as being elliptical in shape and thicker on the seaward side, with a 24-pdr or 36-pdr mounted on a traversing carriage. In 1796 two towers were built at Cape Town and Simon's Town, South Africa. Between 1802 and 1812 a total of 103 Martello Towers of either stone or brick were constructed in eastern and south-eastern England, in response to the threat of French invasion. These were circular or elliptical, with walls between 1.8m and 3.7m thick, and an entrance 3m or more above ground; they resembled an 'upturned flower-pot'.[312]

In the late 1770s, the carronade was invented by Melville, Gascoigne and Miller of the Carron Company; this short, large-bore gun was adopted by the Royal Navy in 1779. The most common were the 32- and 24-pdrs; together with the 68-pdr, these were used for coastal defence, and the latter in the siege train. All carronades of whatever calibre were designed to a standard set of proportions, and were typically a quarter of the weight of a long gun of the same calibre. Unlike other ordnance, Carron supplied both the carronade and the carriage, consisting of a wooden bed with an iron fitting to receive the bolt for the loop of the gun and the slide. The carronade was elevated by means of a screw passing through the cascable.[313]

SIEGES

The techniques pioneered by Marshal Vauban of France (1633–1707) at the siege of the Dutch fortress of Maastricht in 1673 were still followed 150 years later. At Maastricht the trenches of the 'first parallel' were opened on 17–18 June. From these the engineers sapped forward, using zigzag trenches. The 'second parallel' was dug 275m from

Sectioned drawing of a Martello Tower.

During the siege of Gibraltar (1782–85), Lieutenant G.F. Koehler RA designed a depression carriage for downwards fire. This M1782 Koehler depression carriage was similar to a contemporary French design. (Courtesy the Trustees of the RAHT; photographs Stephen Summerfield)

the fortress; and the governor capitulated on 1 July, recognising the inevitable.

Sieges can be divided into four main types. The siege of *containment* involved leaving an observation force of cavalry and light infantry to intercept and frustrate any attempt by the garrison to break-out. Digby Smith (1998) has listed sixty-five fortresses and fortified towns that surrendered upon being formally summoned to do so in the period 1790–1815; nineteen of these were Prussian fortresses that surrendered in 1806.[314]

A brief siege culminating in a place being *taken by storm* often occurred when the attacking commander was short of time and resources. The sixteen examples during the Napoleonic Wars (1805–15), compared to three during the Revolutionary Wars (1793–1801), suggest a change in the nature of campaigns.

The *blockade* was undertaken when the purpose was to deny access to the fortified place, as the preliminary step to the establishment of a siege proper. Digby Smith (1998) lists thirty-eight blockades, of which thirty occurred in 1813–15 upon isolated French garrisons, and were conducted by second-line Coalition forces.

The straightforward *siege* – ranging from the type of unhurried, sequenced operation that punctuated much of the later 17th and 18th centuries, to less formal affairs – occurred during our period on seventy-four occasions.

A siege needed meticulous logistic planning, and had a tendency to use up guns very quickly; the high rate of fire and heavy expenditure of ammunition wore the guns badly, particularly those cast from bronze. The manufacture of new equipment to replace lost or damaged guns and accessories took a long time, and needed to be planned well ahead. (It should be remembered that besieged garrisons might mount sorties not only to 'spike' the vents of the besiegers' guns, but even to destroy or capture such mundane but vital equipment as picks and shovels.) In effect, this meant that production of heavy equipment was undertaken throughout a campaign; for instance, regular shipments from Britain reached Wellington's army in the Peninsula. The French appear to have cast replacement guns in Spain, as being quicker and less risky than bringing new guns from France by road; it certainly put less strain on the always unreliable supply of draft oxen and horses.

One method of supplementing the numbers of guns available to the attacking or defending forces was to assemble guns and ammunition from the stores and fortresses of allies, as well as those captured from the enemy. This often resulted in a hotchpotch of ordnance that was only useful

Table 7.4: British carronades

	Calibre	Bore length	Tube length	Tube weight	Windage	Projectile weight
68-pdr carronade M1790	184mm	7 calibres	201cm	1513kg	2mm	31kg
32-pdr carronade M1794	160mm	6.5 calibres	147cm	920kg	2mm	14.6kg
24-pdr carronade M1808	145mm	7.5 calibres	145cm	670kg	2mm	10.9kg

British 24-pdr carronade

British 24-pdr carronade, weighing 13cwt 2 quarters (687kg). This example is on an iron land carriage; these were normally replaced with wooden carriages when action was expected, because the brittle qualities of cast iron made it shatter dangerously if struck by a ball. (Courtesy the Board of Trustees of the Royal Armouries; photographs Stephen Summerfield)

as long as the calibre of the gun tube matched available ammunition. According to Alexander Dickson, British siege lines often contained French guns firing captured ammunition against French garrisons. The use of old or captured ordnance also meant that extra time had to be spent gauging ammunition to ensure that it fitted, and testing captured stocks of powder and fuses. Another method employed by artillery commanders was to 'borrow' ships' guns (and seamen) whenever possible. For example, 18-pdr guns were taken from a number of Royal Navy frigates for the siege of San Sebastian (7 July–31 August 1813).

A great deal of time was spent in carrying out repairs and testing guns and carriages. The main repair to guns was at the vent, which tended to enlarge by gas wash during prolonged firing. This reduced the power of the gun and greatly increased the chance of its bursting upon discharge. Between sieges, the regimental blacksmiths and other artificers were kept busy. Carriages and their wheels were in constant need of repair, and large parties of wheelwrights were necessary whenever the siege train had to move any distance, with frequent stops to allow the greasing of axles and repair of damaged wheels.

Transporting a siege train was always a major logistical undertaking, and in regions with few and primitive roads waterborne movement was used wherever possible. Heavy ordnance needed massive firing carriages or mountings to withstand the strain of repeated discharges. Wooden-wheeled, unsprung carriages with heavy loads had to move on unsurfaced country roads, not only across the plains but also through the difficult mountain passes of Portugal and Spain. Large numbers of draft animals

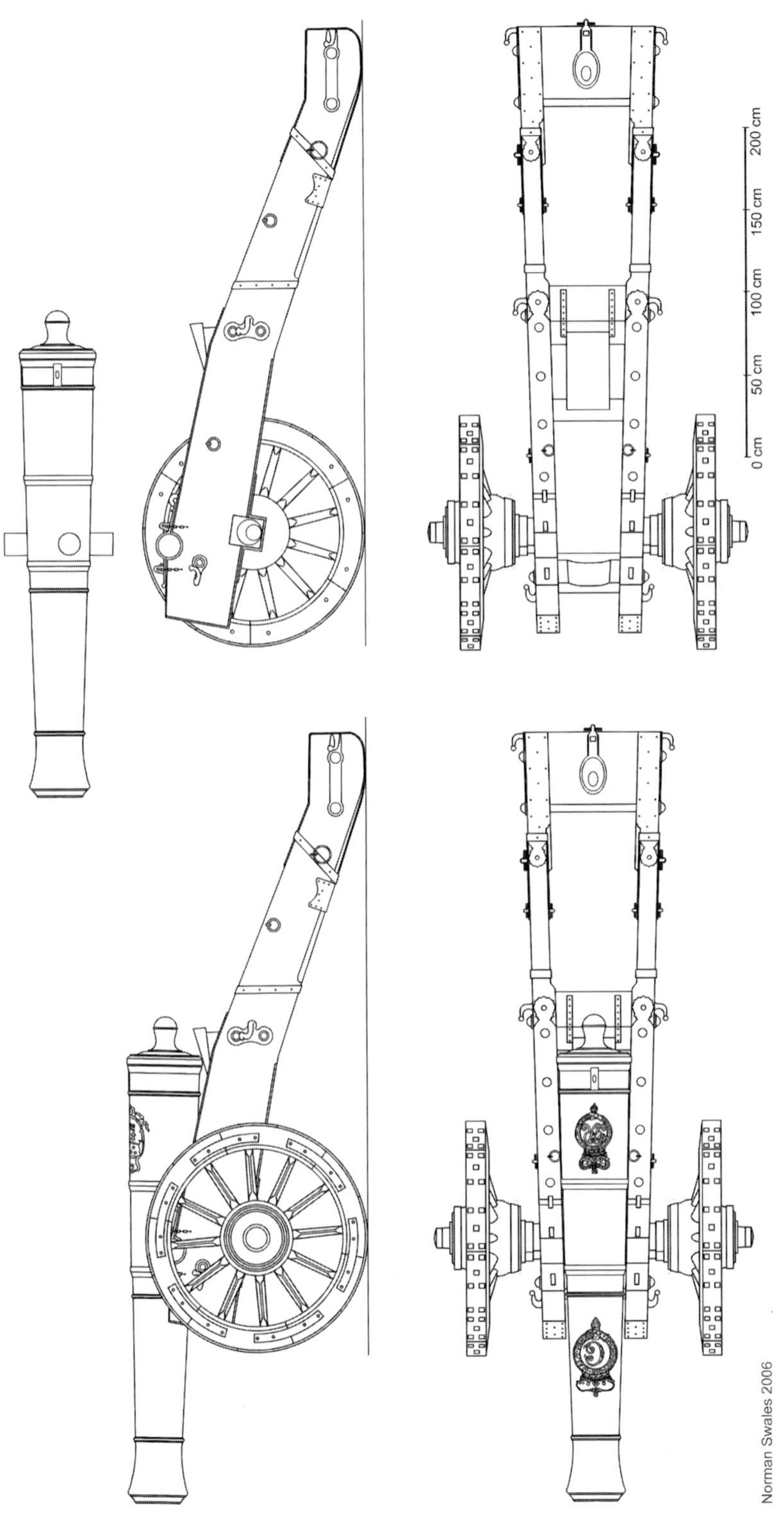

Drawings of a British medium 24-pdr of the 1750s, designed by John Armstrong, that was still in use during the Napoleonic Wars. In 1811 bronze guns of this type were withdrawn due to failure during the siege of Badajoz. The gun weighed 41cwt (2087kg) and was 8ft (244cm) long. (After C.W. Rudyerd, 1793)

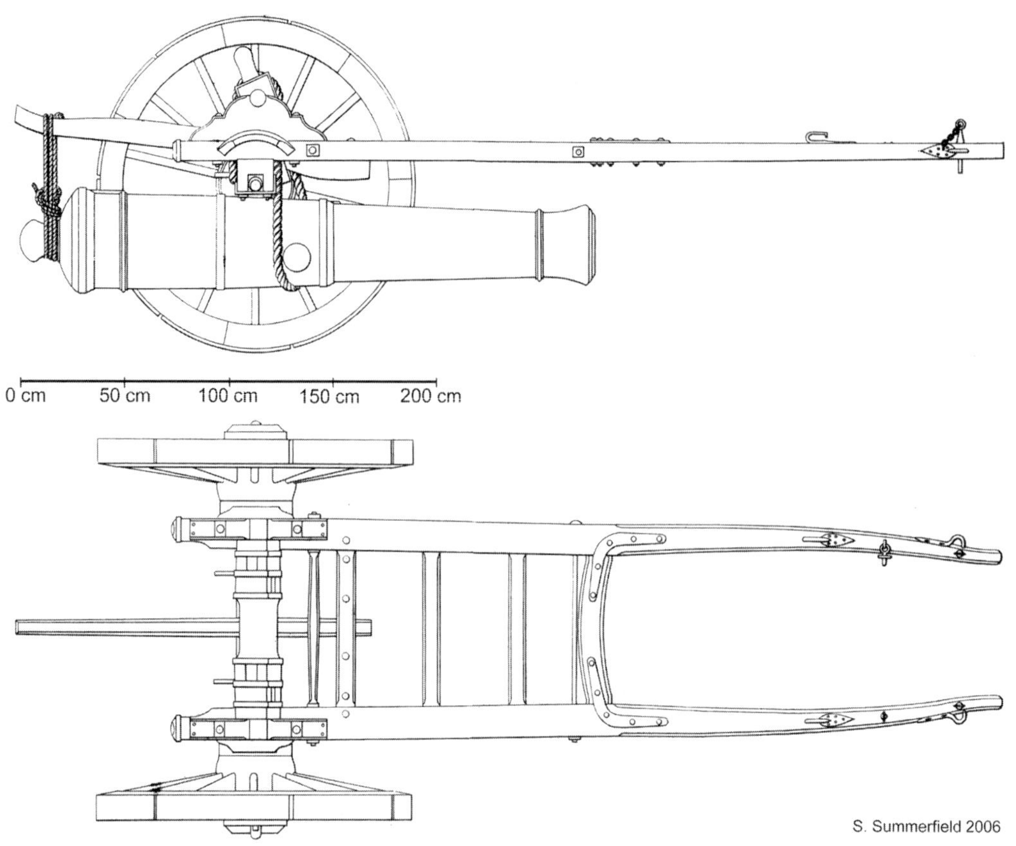

A British sling cart, with a Blomefield iron 24-pdr siege gun slung. The cart was 17ft (5.2m) long, on 5ft (152cm) wheels, and weighed 16.4cwt (835kg). (After Rudyerd, 1793)

were required: for example, a British 24-pdr gun needed at least sixteen oxen. The British siege train for Almeida in 1811 had 1,100 oxen for the guns alone, apart from the very many more needed to transport ammunition, tools and stores. All of these animals had to be fed and watered if they were to be of use to the army, so a great many of the vehicles in the train carried fodder for the oxen and horses. The siege train was a ponderous column which might be 5 miles (8km) long, stretched out on muddy or rutted dirt roads which offered no room to turn around or to overtake; it therefore presented a very vulnerable target. Selecting suitable routes was important, and the train often followed a different road from the rest of the marching army; without that protection, there were many instances of siege trains being captured by the enemy – and their loss might unbalance the strategic plan for an entire season.

When the train did arrive safely, the principal operational aspects of a siege were as follows:

Detailed reconnaissance of the fortress by the besieging force commander, accompanied by the senior engineer officer, would be combined with study of details of any previous siege. From this intelligence the point of attack was selected, to provide the best approach for storming parties to the breaches which the artillery intended to open by bombardment, and for subsequent operations once the stormers got within the fortress. Deception plans would be decided upon, to keep the defenders uncertain as to where and when the main attack would be made, thus delaying the building of additional defences.

The first enfilading batteries were sited about 1km from the fortress walls, in order to silence the defenders' guns while the work of getting other

A French gun crew traversing a bronze M1789 Gomer mortar with handspikes, c.*1828. (Auguste de Moltzheim,* L'Armée Française sous la Restauration, 1814–1830, *Editions du Cannonier, Nantes)*

guns closer in took place. Gun emplacement proceeded under the cover of darkness, to prevent the fortress garrison from interfering with the digging and building work. No attempt would be made at this stage to breach the walls, as the guns were too far away. A large number of different positions had to be taken up in order for this to be achieved, since the defences were designed to make this as difficult as possible. In general, if enfilading batteries could be placed on higher ground they would fire their roundshot by ricochet, to wreck enemy guns and kill men. The practical siting of batteries was, of course, complicated not only by the conformations of terrain but by the nature of the ground itself; for example, at Badajoz in 1811 very thin topsoil over rock greatly increased the difficulties, and the garrison had actually laboured in advance to scrape the earth even thinner.

The breaching batteries, normally of four guns each, would fire at the weakest point of the enemy

Table 7.5: Ammunition provision for a "Standard Package" of British siege guns
(Note: three of these standard 'packages' were supplied for the Siege of San Sebastian, 7 July–31 August 1813.)

Type	No.	Ammunition
24-pdr iron gun	14	1500
8 inch Howitzer	6	600
68-pdr carronade	4	600
10 inch mortar	4	500

defences. The breach was made in a methodical manner: first the guns were fired to batter a horizontal line into the face of the wall about 2m above the ground; vertical lines would then be battered, running from the horizontal up to the base of the parapet walk. These vertical lines would be then used as targets, to be deepened until the wall gave way. This would take an average of four to five days for a battery of 4× 24-pdr guns. During a battering, the heavy roundshot was used to break apart the stone walls, while the 'vertical fire' of the mortars and howitzers used exploding shells to blow away the rubble and expose more of the stonework. Breaching guns needed to be as close as possible, because the velocity of the fired roundshot dropped rapidly as range increased. This made the crews and the labouring infantry vulnerable to enemy fire from the walls.

Breastworks, earthen ramparts, gabions filled with earth and covered approaches (roofed-over trenches) were constructed by working parties provided – unwillingly – by the infantry, in order to protect the batteries. Emplaced batteries would take position on a site floored with timbers and sunken, half-sunken or screened behind a simple earth embankment. A team of twelve infantry workmen would construct an emplacement by half of them digging a ditch with pick and shovel in front of the position to create spoil to fill the gabions, while the other half created an embankment and compacted the spoil, leaving a berm between the two. The gunners would make the gabions and fascines; the latter were lashed bundles of sticks and brush, used to form the lintels over a gabion-built emplacement.

A constant ammunition supply was essential during breaching operations. Ox-drawn ammunition carts transported it to dumps a safe distance from the fortress; mules and men then carried the ammunition to the guns. Parallels and saps (trenches running respectively roughly parallel to, and roughly perpendicular to, the walls) provided additional protection for the labouring attackers as they closed in on the fortress.

Howitzers and mortars would attack the interior of the fortress or strongpoint to help keep defenders away from any breach that was developing. According to Dickson, the British siege artillery used a mixture of exploding shells and spherical case for this task. At night, the attackers would fire special projectiles made of a brightly burning compounds to provide illumination, and incendiary shells ('carcasses') to set fire to buildings near to the breach. Pre-laid canister and roundshot were fired in attempts (often unsuccessful) to prevent the defenders from repairing the damaged defences under cover of darkness.

During sieges, mortars and heavy guns could fire solid shot that had been heated in special ball-ovens. However, the heating of the roundshot caused it to expand and made loading difficult, apart from increasing the possibility of a premature discharge. The Austrians under Field Marshal von Sachsen-Tescen employed this technique at Lille (25 September–8 October 1792), where 20 of 52 guns, howitzers and mortars were worn out or burst. Heated shot was again used during the siege of Valenciennes (25 May–27 July 1793), where the ensuing inferno melted 14,000 French muskets.

A fire-plan for suppressive fire would be needed when the time came to attempt the storming of the breach, in order to help the infantry get as close as possible to the breach before they had to face fire from the defenders. Mortars and howitzers would continue to fire into the fortress to try to prevent the defenders mounting an effective counter-attack force against the stormers.

8 Moving the Guns

The new artillery tactics of Napoleon, Josef Smola and others relied upon the manoeuvrability of the guns and, as importantly, of their supply of ammunition – guns in the front line without sufficient ammunition were obviously useless. All European powers studied the means of ensuring that artillery was mobile and could accompany their troops, especially the cavalry. Mobility of the artillery was improved by the militarisation of the artillery train, the introduction of horse artillery and by improving ammunition provision. Austria, Britain, Russia and Prussia adopted limber ammunition boxes and smaller, lightweight caissons.

Battlefield experience showed that the guns were highly mobile, but they were only one element of a battery. France was the only country that relied upon the ammunition caisson, as their guns carried on average only ten rounds. This hindered the manoeuvrability of the French artillery, since even the horse artillery had to be accompanied by at least one caisson per gun. The ammunition chest mounted on the gun trail was used in emergency, and the guns were fed with ammunition directly from the caisson, thus exposing the caissons to enemy fire in the battery position, where they made a large target.

In other armies, the guns themselves were provided with ammunition on their limbers, and thus could fight as a single unit rather than having a considerable tail of vehicles behind the battery. The battery could deploy quicker, the guns being lighter and – with larger wheels than the caissons – able to move faster and over rougher ground. Not having to deploy caissons meant that fewer men and horses were exposed to enemy fire, and the battery took up less space.

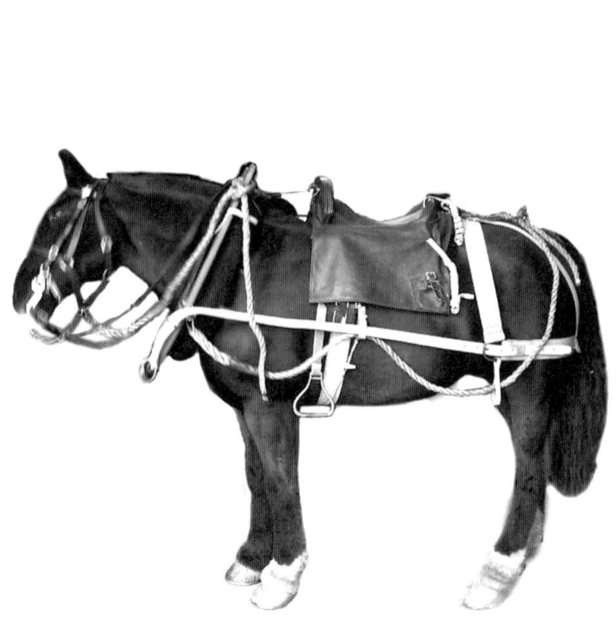

Example of French limber wheel-horse equipment. (Horses Through History)

Reconstruction of a full-weight Gribeauval 12-pdr field gun and limber. (L'Association Britannique de la Garde Impériale, and Horses Through History; photograph Stephen Summerfield)

ARTILLERY DRAFT AND PACK ANIMALS

The main draft animal was the horse, but others were used when these were not available, including mules, oxen and even elephants.

Horses were required to pull the enormous weight of the cannons and ammunition; on average a horse could pull about 320kg. The large number of horses posed a logistical challenge for the artillery, because they had to be fed, maintained, and replaced when worn out or injured.

Artillery horses were generally selected after the cavalry mounts from a pool of high-quality animals. The capacity of a healthy horse to pull a load was affected by the nature of the surface over which the load was being hauled. A single horse can pull 1,360kg a distance of 32–40km per day over a hard-paved road. The weight dropped to 860kg on hard un-metalled ground, and to 500kg on rough ground. These figures were further halved if a rider was carried on the horse's back. As the number of horses in a team increased, the pulling capacity of each extra horse was reduced; e.g. a horse in a team of six had only seven-ninths (78%) the pulling capacity it would have had in a team of two. The goal was that each horse's share of the load should be no more than 320kg.

The daily routine for the artillery would start with the trumpeter sounding the stable call after reveille and roll call, and then water call after breakfast. This same routine for the horses was repeated late in the afternoon. Morning and afternoon drill also meant a workout for the horses, after which they needed to be walked to cool down, combed, and watered again. Obtaining water for the horses was always a problem, especially on the march. If water was some distance from the camp, only half the horses would be sent to water at any one time so that the battery could still be moved in an emergency.

The driver assigned to each pair of horses rode on the left horse; he was responsible for the feeding, watering and grooming of both, and the maintenance of their harness. Skilled riders were required for this service, which demanded the daring of the cavalry trooper with the concentration for precision teamwork. Drivers were issued a leg-guard (an iron plate encased in leather) for their right leg, to prevent injury from the limber pole. During battle, they brought the ordnance into position under the direction of the sergeant. Once the artillery line was established the drivers would dismount, and might lie on the ground with their reins in their hands, depending on the amount of hostile fire being received. The only drivers who were not usually with the battery in battle were those who drove the travelling field forge and battery wagon. This equipment was usually in the rear of the army on the march.

A battery moved at the same speed and over the same distance as the troops to which they were attached. French horse teams could cover 2.6 miles

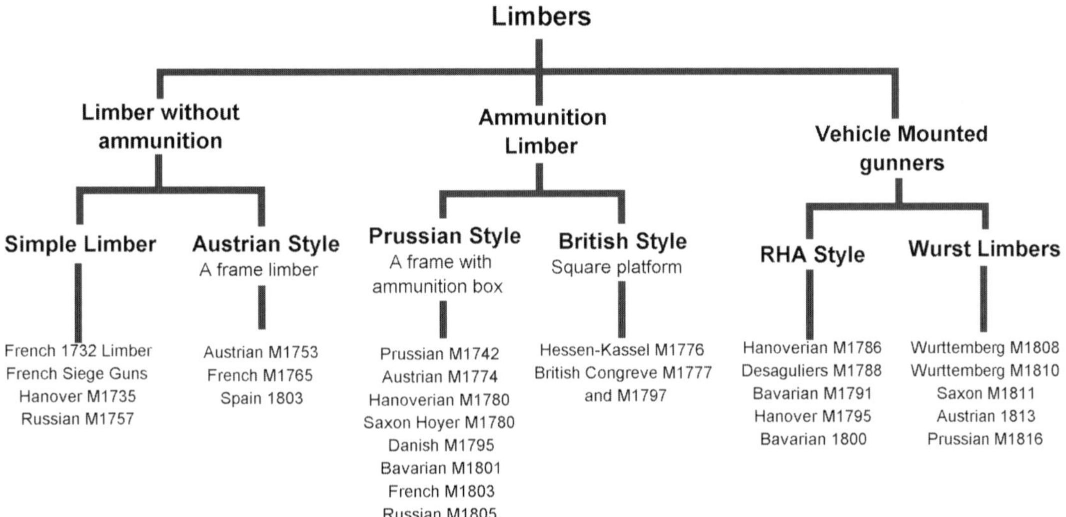

Moving the guns with limbers.

(4.2km) in an hour on a decent road and could travel a maximum of 20 miles (32km) in a day, although a forced march of 50km per day could be performed in emergency.

William Congreve Snr's speed trials with a fully laden gun and Desaguliers M1788 limber concluded that a Light 3-pdr and a 5.5in howitzer drawn by four horses could move at 6–7mph, and with six horses at 10–11mph (16–18km/h). At a 'moderate trot' a fully laden gun 'equipped for horse artillery' could cover 1km in nine minutes, and at the canter could cover 185m in two minutes. This was considerably faster than the pre-Desaguliers equipment that could move no faster than the drivers could walk – i.e. at no more than 4mph (6.4km/h).

An un-laden horse at a brisk trot travels at 5–6mph (8–10km/h), at the canter at 10–11mph (16–18 km/h) and at a flat-out gallop at 20–21 mph (32–34km/h); therefore, Congreve's figures suggest that the fastest gait of the horse teams was no more than the canter, and in general they moved at a moderate walk. In 1793 coach horses were introduced for the Royal Horse Artillery, and were described as being 'able to trot steadily on hard roads at eight miles an hour with a substantial load daily and for long distances without detriment to either bodily condition or soundness'. The artillery horses were expected to trot fast and, according to Captain Whinyates, could gallop on occasion. The fastest a horse artillery team travelled was about 10–15mph (16–24km/h) over short distances. The notion of horse artillery galloping into action is therefore misplaced.

In 1795, Congreve stipulated that a team should rest every 7 miles (11km) for a minimum of half an hour. In other words, the horse teams would move for an hour before resting for half hour. In 1782 he had noted that in bad weather a horse team could expect to rest over two hours after travelling ten miles.

Mules were excellent for pulling heavy loads, but are considered unreliable under fire, when they might buck, kick, and roll on the ground, entangling harnesses and becoming impossible to control. Out of necessity, mules were used in the Peninsula by both sides to haul guns and wagons. An example of this has been given, in Chapter 5, for Portugal.

Mules were very suitable as pack animals for carrying small mountain howitzers and guns that were light enough to be broken down, where their strength and surefootedness was required (*see* Chapter 6). Napoleon favoured the current Austrian practice that had also been followed by a number of German states. Packhorses were also used. 'The most suitable horse for the pack-saddle is the one most nearly approaching the mule in his formation. He should be very strong-backed, and from 14–15 hands high'.[315]

In India, elephants and oxen were often used to pull artillery and wagons or carry supplies. Oxen and bullocks were sometimes used to pull siege artillery in Europe due to lack of suitable horses, especially in the Peninsula, but they were very slow.

LIMBER TYPES

The most common way in which the horse team was attached to the gun was by a limber. A limber is essentially a set of wheels, which fit to the gun carriage to aid its movement over a long distance.

The most common form of limber was that using an 'A'-frame with a single shaft, allowing for tandem harnessing of the horses (e.g. Austrian M1753 and Gribeauval M1765 limbers). The pintail was commonly mounted on the axle; during the 18th century it was moved to the bolster immediately behind the axle, as this made limbering the gun easier and quicker. William Congreve Snr noted in 1776 that this allowed the gun and team to turn shorter, as was frequently necessary to accompany infantry. The mounting of the ammunition box on the limber also acted as a counterweight for the limbered gun carriage, so the limber balanced more evenly and was consequently easier to move by the horse team. In 1741, Ernst von Holtzmann designed the M1742 limber; this was first copied in Austria in 1774, and acted as a point of inspiration for other nations. The French were the only country to retain the limber without the ammunition box, apart from a few years between 1803 and 1808.

The British M1788 design removed the bolsters behind the axle and the pintail was replaced with a bronze hook that connected to a protruding

Modern reconstruction of limbering a Gribeauval 12-pdr gun to a French M1765 limber. (L'Association Britannique de la Garde Impériale, and Horses Through History; photographs: Stephen Summerfield)

lunette ring mounted on the end of the gun trail. The removal of the third bolster reduced the limber body to just longer than the wheel diameter; this improved the turning circle and made the vehicle lighter. France was the only major power to retain long limbers throughout the period; the Austrians altered their limbers in 1813.

The other form of limber relied upon a square platform, with the shafts for the horses or sweep bar attached to the first bolster. When a single sweep bar was used this was often an integral structural element of the platform of the limber. The square-bodied limber was apparently developed in Britain in the 1780s and was restricted to Britain and Bavaria. The 'A'-frame limber was by far the most common type in use, although some had a square platform mounted over the 'A'-frame, as in Hanover, and the French post-1822 Valée limber.

The limber-mounted ammunition box carried more ammunition than the chest carried on the gun carriage itself. The logical conclusion of the carriage-mounted ammunition box was its development into a seat for the gunners to ride on – the so-called 'Wurst' seat used by Austria, Bavaria and Württemberg. Specific types of limber seen during our period were as follows.

Simple Limbers

Developed from the late 17th century onwards, these were simply a pair of wheels on an axle, fitted to the gun carriage via a pintail which passed through the lunette ring on the transom plate of the carriage. The French retained the M1732 Vallière simple limber for the M1748 6.4in howitzers until 1777, and for siege guns throughout the period. General Bruckmann based his Hanoverian M1735 limber design on the current French M1732. It consisted of a single pair of wheels and axle with a small 'A'-frame supporting the central sweep bar. The pintail was replaced with an iron ring, into which passed an iron hook that was located on the trail end of the gun carriage.

The Russian M1757 limbers for 3-, 6-, 8- and 12-pdr guns were supplied by the Master-General of the Artillery Department, and pulled by teams of 2, 7, 9

Drawing of a Vallière limber, exemplifying the simple limbers of the 18th century.

and 15 horses respectively. Each piece was accompanied in the field by two ammunition wagons, carrying 120× roundshot and 30× canister.[316]

Austrian-style or 'A'-frame Limber

This became the most common form, with a single shaft allowing for tandem harnessing of the horses; it was introduced by Austria in 1753 and copied by Gribeauval in France. The Austrian M1753 Liechtenstein limber introduced the central sweep bar or pole, and was a major technological improvement. In the new system, the weight of the limber and gun was taken on the back of two horses rather than one. Four horses rather than one could be hitched to the limber (two to the first bolster acting as wheelers, and two to the swingletree at the end of the sweep-bar). This gave better traction and a better distribution of the weight, so horses could be kept in harness longer, and could move the gun further without getting fatigued as quickly. A common axle was adopted, with just two types of wheels: the 36in (91cm) size served for the limber wheels and the front wheels of the ammunition carts, and the 51in (130cm) for gun carriages and the rear wheels of the carts. The M1753 limber design was copied in Prussia (M1758), France (M1765) and throughout Europe, except Britain, where the two shafts were retained until 1788–97.

The French M1765 Gribeauval limber had team horses harnessed two abreast, and then hitched in tandem. The train drivers rode the left-hand horse of each pair, controlling both. The 12-pdr guns were assigned six horses and the other guns four horses. At least one of the 12-pdr caissons per gun was given a six-horse team while all others were allotted four horses. Unlike the Austrians, followed by the Prussians and Russians, the French horse harness was not standardised, German- and French-style tack being used.

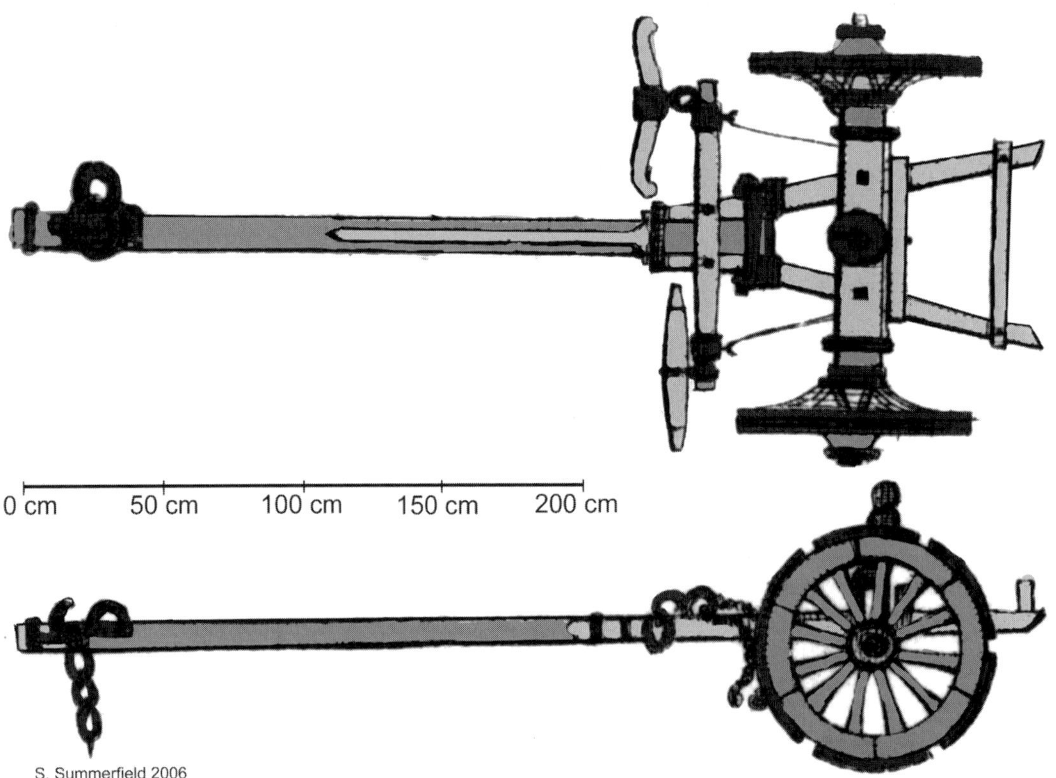

The Austrian M1753 limber could be considered as an 'A'-frame superimposed upon a simple limber, so permitting the limber to be pulled by double draft. Notice the close similarity to the later Gribeauval limber.

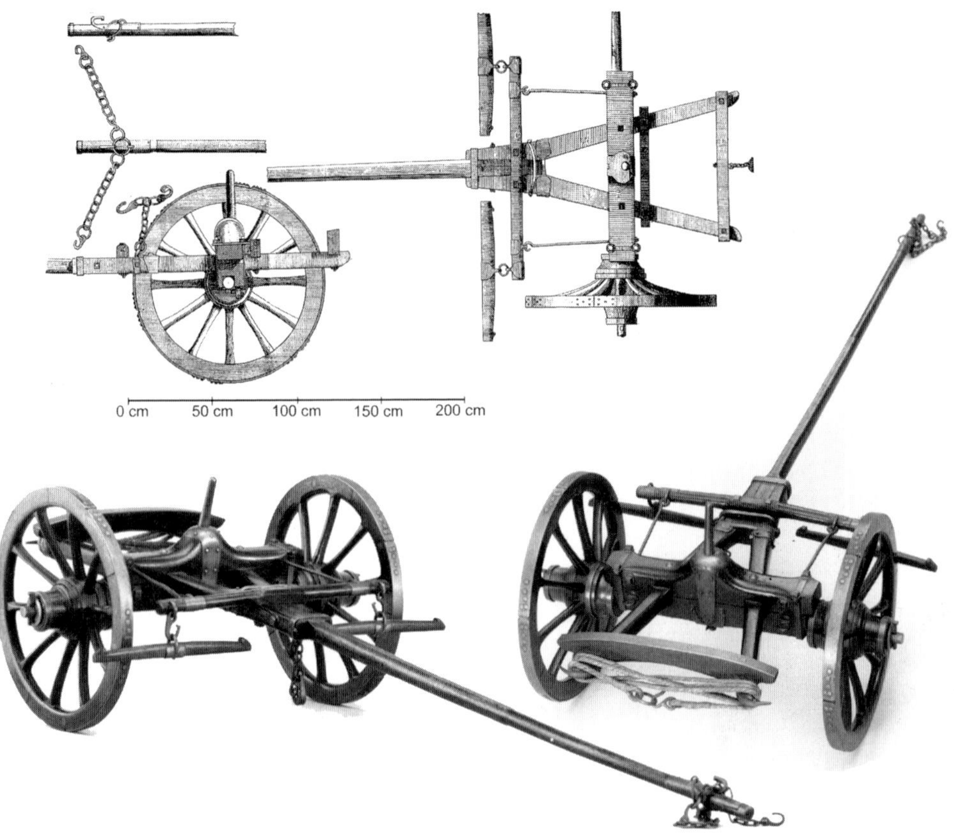

Drawing and model of the Gribeauval limber with 114cm wheels, for the howitzer, 8-pdr and 12-pdr guns. The smaller 4-pdr limber, used with the 6-pdr gun, had 103cm wheels. In 1814 the type illustrated became the universal limber for all French field guns. (Musée de l'Armée)

The lightening of the tubes and the carriages afforded the French artillery a great advantage. According to Otto de Scheel:

The 4-pdr could be drawn by four or even three horses on all types of roads, and eight men, by the means of traces and handspikes placed in the transom plate, were able to advance or retreat in battle even over soft terrain as fast as the infantry could march.

The 8-pdr on good ground was also able to advance in battle with eight men, and on uneven or ploughed ground with eleven, part of whom are to draw the traces, the others to be at handspikes at the aiming curve of the gun and at the transom plate. On the road, the 8-pdr could be pulled freely by four horses.

The 12-pdr could be transported equally well on roads with six horses, and in battle required no more than eleven men to manoeuvre on good ground, but fifteen men or more were required on the most difficult ground, either advancing or retreating.[317]

The Kingdom of Italy, Naples, and (from 1803) Spain used the M1765 Gribeauval limber.

Prussian-style or 'A'-frame Limber with Ammunition Box

This was a great advance on those designed by Liechtenstein, Brocard, Gribeauval and others on several counts. More immediately-available ammunition was carried with the guns, so caissons did not have to follow the battery onto a battlefield, and

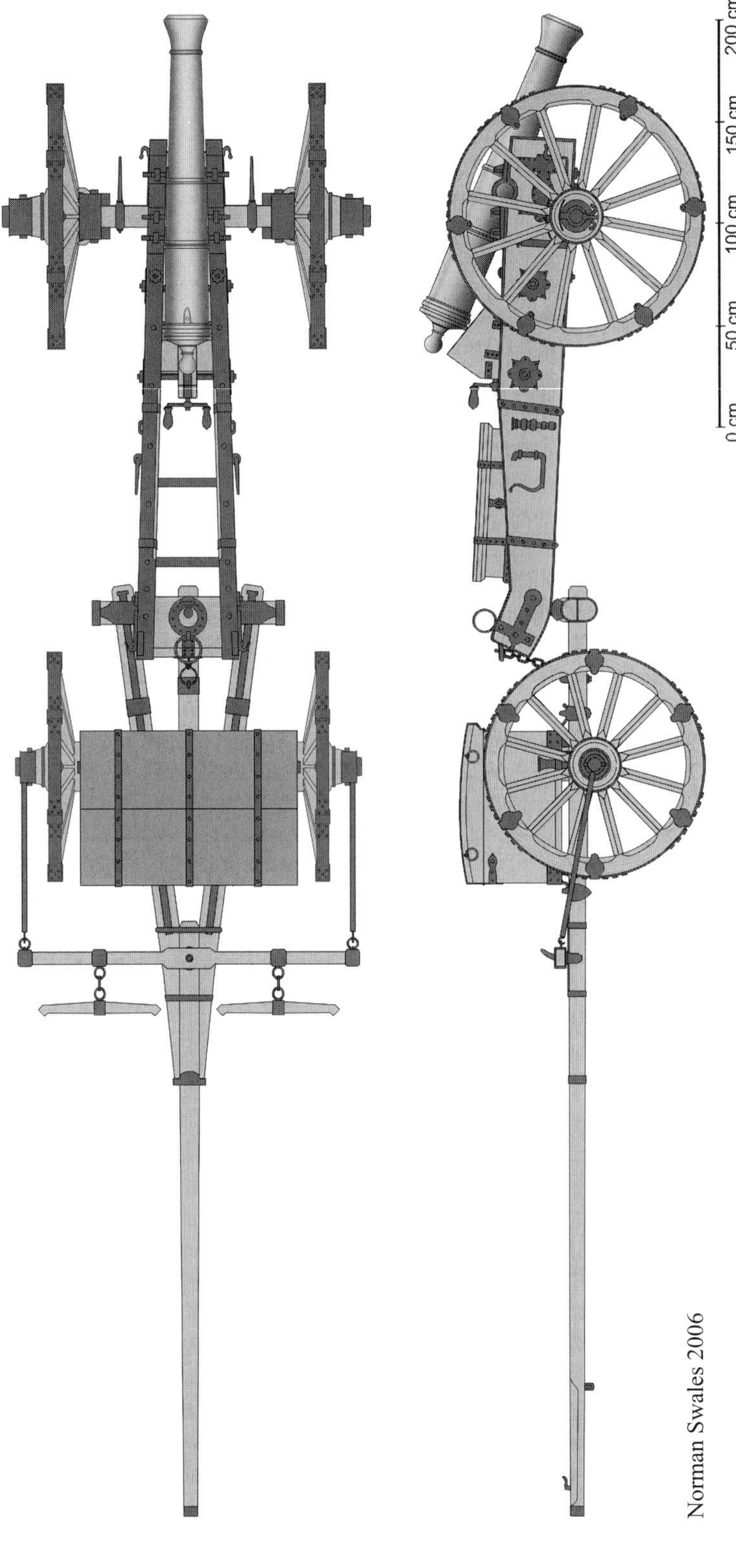

Prussian M1768 limber, of 'A'-frame construction with the pintle moved to the rear, permitting easier limbering.

Austrian M1774 3-pdr limber, now preserved in HMG Vienna. (Dave Hollins)

the guns could fight as a unit without being encumbered by other vehicles. Larger wheels were fitted, raising the height of the shaft, so the team pulled the limber horizontally rather than diagonally, and the limber was less likely to bog down in muddy roads and ploughed fields. The centre of balance of the limber was lowered, making the limbered gun more stable and less liable to overbalance on the move. To counterbalance the weight of the sweep bar, the centre of gravity of the limbered gun via the pintail was placed in the rear of the centre of the axle-tree.

The Prussian M1742 limber was the first with ammunition box mounted; it was designed by Holtzmann, who paid for the production of the first prototype. For movements greater than one mile the limber was used, and each gun had six horses and three drivers. Two ammunition cases were placed on the limber, one with 50× balls, the other

Saxon M1780 'Hoyer' limber. (Joerg Titzer)

with 50× cartridges; later Prussia introduced fixed ammunition. In 1768 an improved M1768 limber was introduced, and this was used by Prussia, with minor improvements, throughout the Napoleonic period.

In 1774, Oberst Maurer moved the ammunition box to the limber to create the Austrian M1774 limber; this meant that the amount of ammunition was no longer restricted to what two men could lift. The weight was now transmitted to the ground and not to the horses' backs as previously, so contributing to the increased traction of the gun on the limber. Under the 1809 regulations, the ammunition box for foot artillery and the Wurst for horse artillery contained ammunition that was available as soon as they unlimbered.

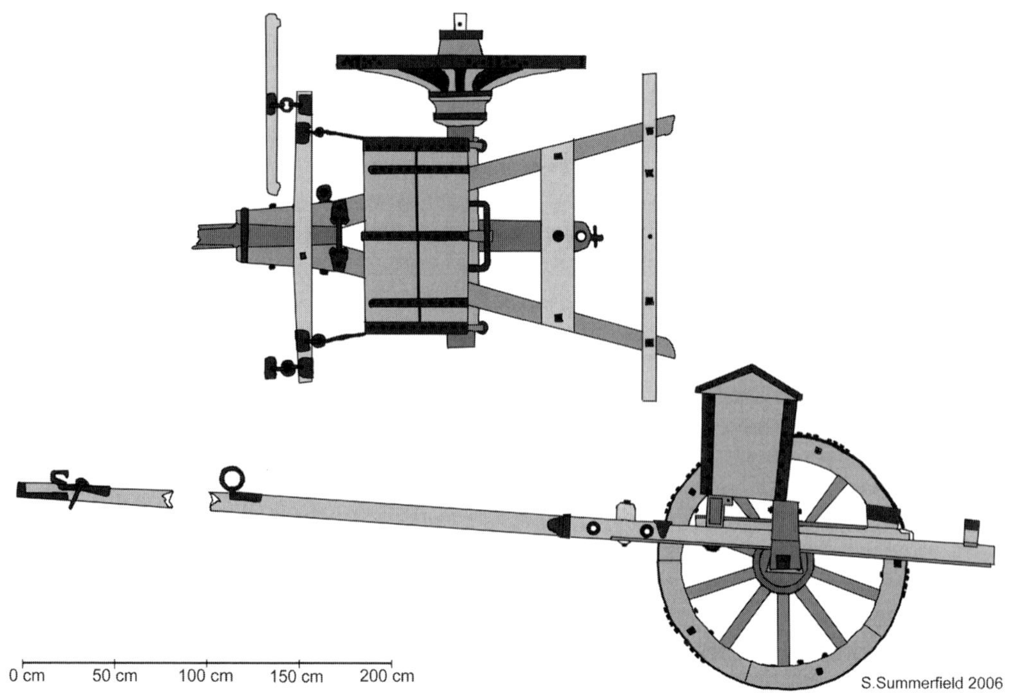

Plan and elevation of French AnXI/M1803 system limber for howitzer, 6-pdr and 12-pdr field guns.

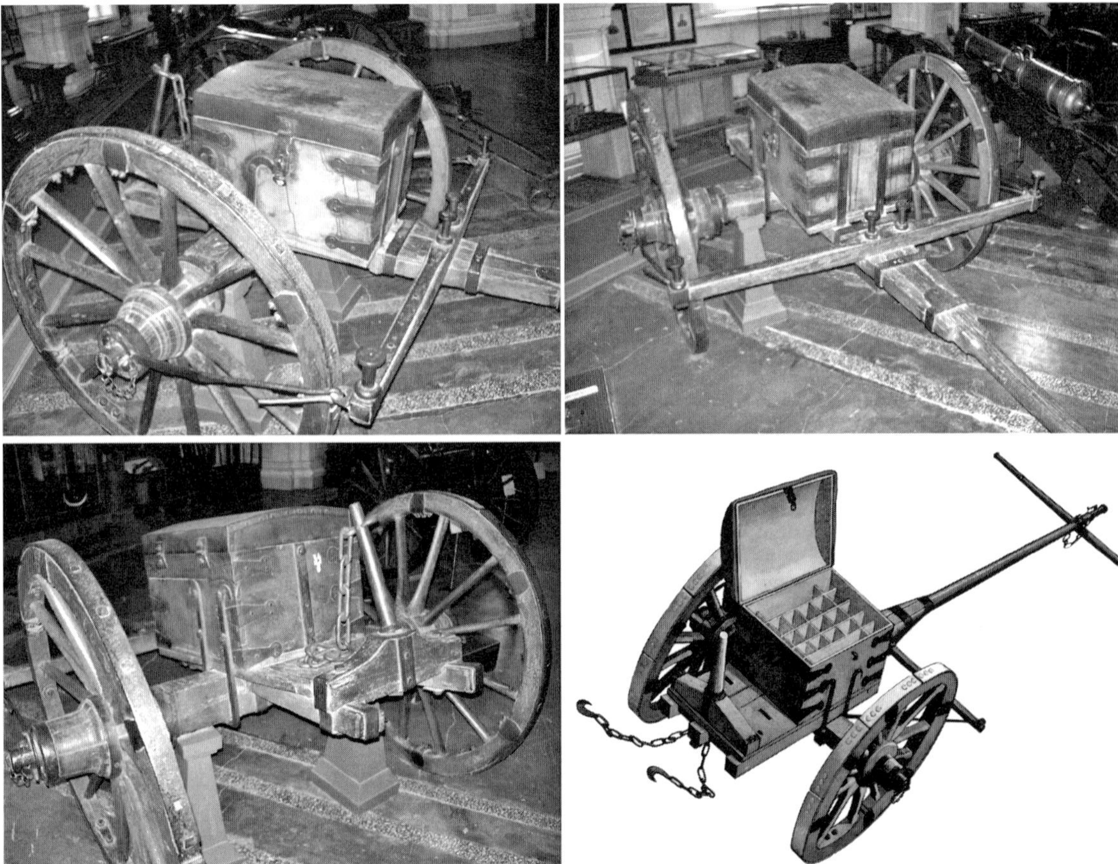

Russian M1805 limber with a closed box, and drawing of limber for 6-pdr gun opened, with 18 'nests' for roundshot. (Dr S.Efimov)

In 1780 a copy of the Prussian M1768 limber was introduced by General Trew into Hanoverian service; in the same year Hoyer introduced it into Saxon service, both being termed M1780 limbers. In 1795, after the dismal performance of her artillery in the Flanders campaign, Denmark introduced a M1795 limber based on the Hanoverian model. In 1801, Jakob Manson introduced the Bavarian M1800 limber based on the Austrian M1774, but the ammunition box was trapezoidal in plan and had a gabled lid.

The French M1803 (AnX1) limber was in turn a copy of the Bavarian M1800 design. According to Valée, the box should have been carried still farther back; the weight on the necks of the wheel-horses was so great when the gun was limbered that without some arrangement for relieving them on the march their necks were soon galled and the horses rendered unfit for service. The new limbers, which supposedly caused more harm to artillery horses than enemy fire, were abandoned, despite being a definite improvement on those used previously; this was probably a reactionary decision by the conservative French artillery establishment. General Gassendi was also critical of the moving of the ammunition chest to the limber; he noted that the box opened away from the gun, so the ammunition servants had to stand behind the horses to access the ammunition, and were likely to come to harm if the horse team moved suddenly.[318] In 1808 the Gribeauval limber was reintroduced; the 12-pdr limber was used for the 12-pdr gun and howitzer, and the 4-pdr limber for the 6-pdr guns.

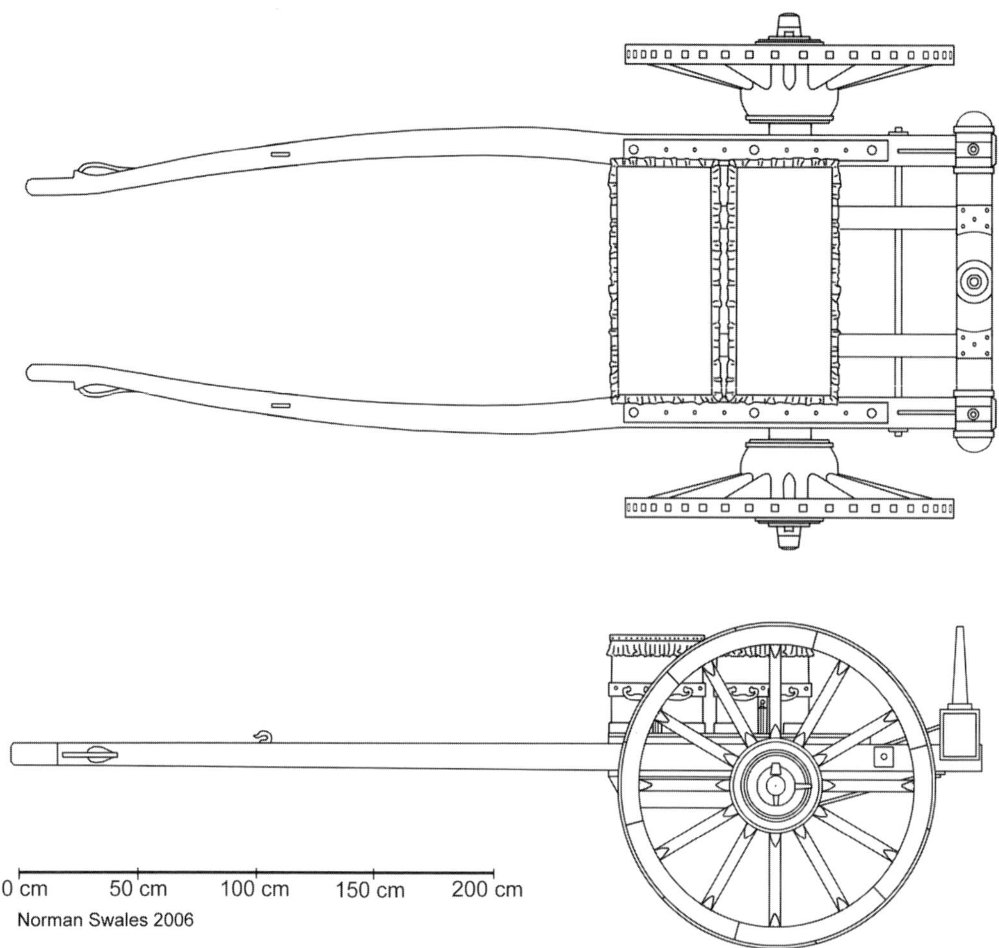

British M1777 Congreve foot artillery limber, with shafts for horses in single draft; this was used by some Royal Artillery foot batteries until 1809. (After Rudyerd, 1793)

The Russian M1805 limber was an 'A'-frame type with a platform, topped by a box covered with sheet iron to protect it from shot. It came in two types, for the heavy and the light artillery. Inside, the box was divided into two parts by a longitudinal partition; one compartment was used for storing tools or two to four charges. The other portion was divided by partitions into cells where part of the ammunition allocation was stored. The 6-pdr cannon, 3-pdr unicorn and ¼-pud (10-pdr) unicorn had 18×, 30× and 12× nests respectively. No ammunition was carried on the ½-pud and 12-pdr limbers. The heavy cannon were drawn by six horses, the light and horse artillery by four horses, and the 3-pdr caissons by two horses. On muddy roads the guns were given double and triple teams of horses, as in Poland 1806–07 and later in France in 1814. A minimum of one horse could pull a 3-pdr unicorn, two horses a light piece and four a heavy piece.

The French M1814 limber was a direct copy of the Manson limbers used in Bavaria from c1805. This was codified in January 1814 for all field guns, and lasted until 1827. It differed from previous designs in that the pintail was moved to the rearmost bolster, and an ammunition box was placed centrally over the axle.

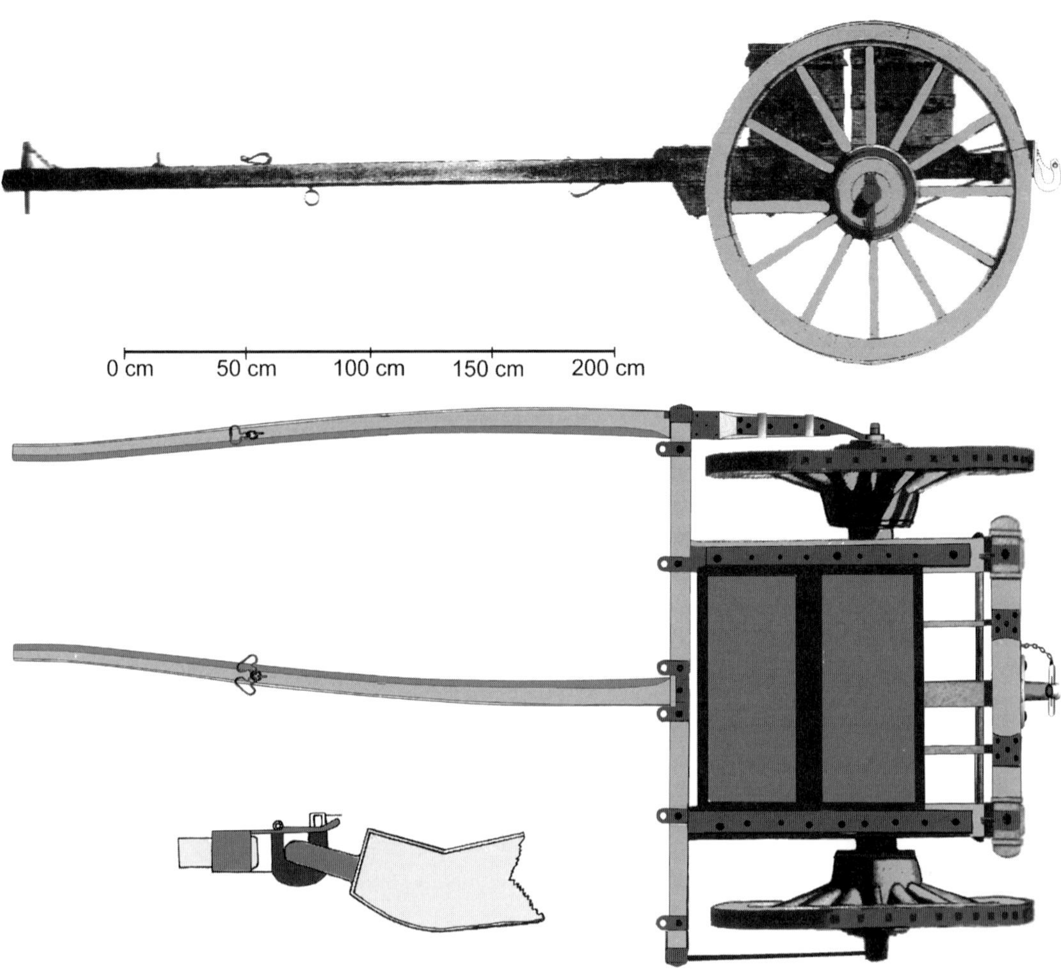

British M1797 Congreve foot artillery limber, a modification of the M1777. (After Scharnhorst (1800) and Rudyerd (1793))

British-style or Square Platform Limber

This differed from the 'A'-frame type in relying on a square platform, with the shafts for the horses or sweep bar attached to the first bolster. When a single sweep bar was used this was often an integral structural element of the platform. The square-bodied limber probably derived from the Hessian limber that Congreve saw in 1776, and was developed by him over the next 20 years; in both cases the pintail was mounted some 45cm behind the axle.[319]

The Congreve M1777 limber had two ammunition boxes on the bed, which were capable of being moved 'regulated upon the principle of the steelyard, so as to form an equilibrium with the trail of the carriage'. The limber was designed to carry 66 rounds of ammunition (44 more than its predecessor) as well as entrenching tools, a gyn, rope, blocks-and-tackles, and other necessary items. Under the limber was a locker in which stores were carried, and various tools were strapped to the axletree. The limber wheels were of the same size (54in, 137cm) and strength as those of the gun carriage, which meant that they could be used to replace a broken gun wheel; furthermore, the limber could

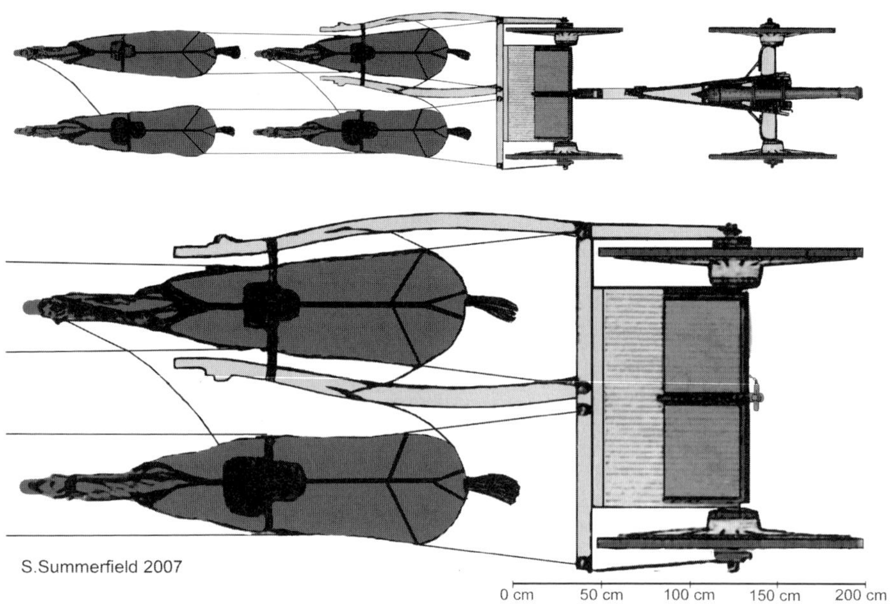

British M1788 Desaguliers limber for the Royal Horse Artillery. (After William Congreve Snr)

transport the gun if the carriage was disabled. The limber had fixed shafts that only allowed single draft, and the strength of horse teams was listed in 1795 as one for the Light 3-pdr, four for the Desaguliers Long 3-pdr, two for the Light 6-pdr, seven for the Desaguliers Long 6-pdr, three for the Light 12-pdr, and ten for the Heavy 12-pdr.

In February 1797, the Congreve M1797 limber was produced by making the shafts of the M1777 adjustable so that the horses could travel two abreast or in line like Desaguliers' designs, at 'only a trifling expense'. It took time for the Congreve limbers to be converted for use with the Butler system. Of 52 guns in the Peninsula in November

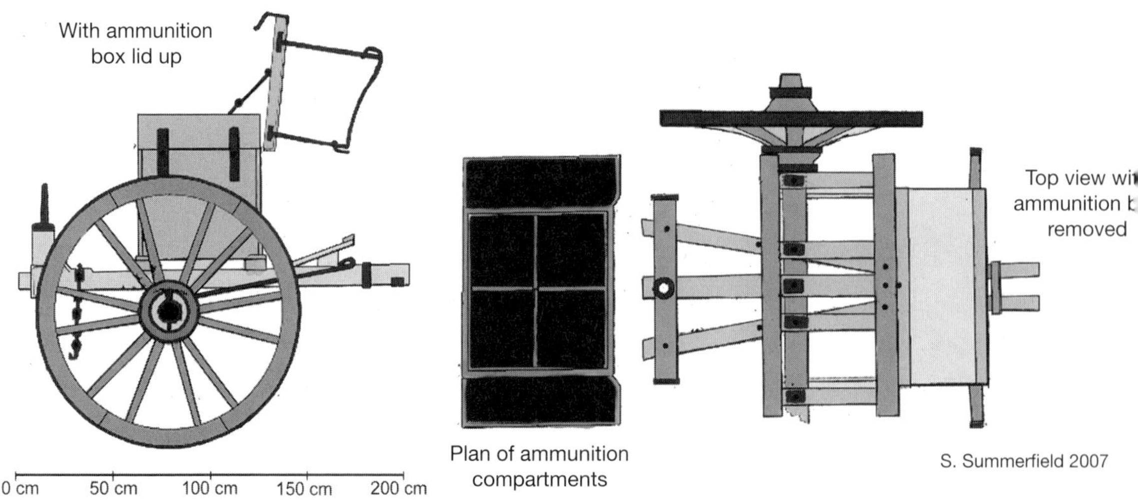

Hanoverian M1795 limber for horse artillery, later used by the King's German Horse Artillery.

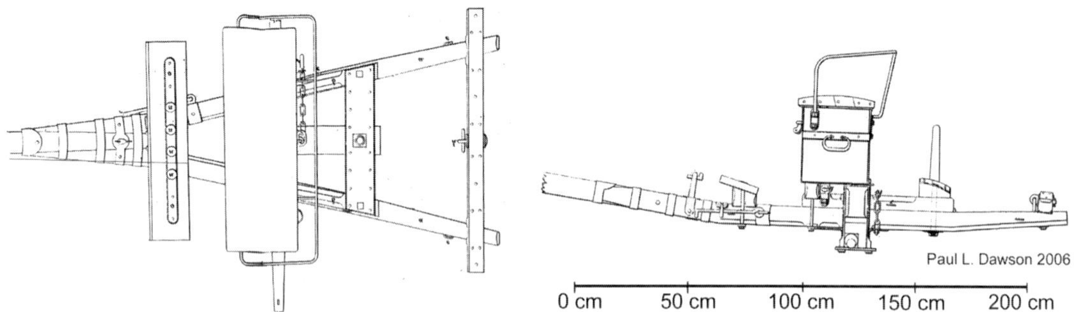

Austrian M1813 Wurst limber, a modified M1774 with a seat for two gunners.

1808, six were 'of the Old Pattern, with single horse draught...totally inapplicable to service'.[320]

Wurst Limbers

The date of transformation of the limber from being a vehicle purely for carrying ammunition to one on which to mount gunners is unknown, but it was a logical progression. (Gunners through the centuries have found many ways to avoid walking.) Perhaps the first country to design a limber especially for the transportation of two gunners was Hanover. The Hanoverian M1786 horse artillery limber had its ammunition box mounted upon a square platform and the pintail replaced with a cast-iron hook mounted on the axle. The box contained either 20× howitzer shells or 76× roundshot. The basics elements of the design were copied by a number of European states.

According to Congreve, the Desaguliers M1788 limber was based on the Hanoverian M1786. The M1788 had a bronze hook connected to a protruding lunette ring mounted on the end of the trail. The limber was built around the universal 5ft 3in (160cm) iron axle (which was embedded in an elm axle-tree box from 1813). On top of the bed there was a pine platform board for the feet of the two seated gunners; behind this was space for the ammunition boxes. These sat slightly to the front of the axle-tree, which transmitted their weight directly onto the horse team. Unlike the Congreve limber, the shafts to which the horses were harnessed were not fixed. Under each limber were four iron sockets into which the shafts were secured, thus enabling the limber to be set up for double- or single-draft. British opinion was that the use of shafts would 'afford greater facilities than the pole for turning', i.e. than the sweep-bar. The splinter-bar also had iron hooks and eyes to which the traces and swing-letrees could be attached 'as required' when double draft was being used.

Like the limber for the M1778 Townshend 3-pdr, the Desaguliers could be used as a mantlet to protect the gun crew from enemy fire. In 1800 the foot and horse artillery used the Desaguliers limber. Each 3-pdr and limber was issued with a team or four horses, with an extra pair available for bad ground or steep gradients. The 6-pdr had a team of six horses and both the 12-pdr and howitzers had eight.[321]

The Bavarian M1791 was a Rumford design that seems to have drawn heavily upon the design of Desaguliers' M1788. The light guns (3- and 6-pdrs) used an ammunition limber that carried four or six gunners instead of the conventional two; each gun had two ammunition limbers, so carried up to twelve gunners. There was also no difference between light artillery and horse artillery.

The Hanoverian M1795 Wurst limber issued to the horse artillery carried 40 rounds of ammunition and two gunners; four more gunners were mounted on the gun carriage. These were later used by the King's German Legion.

The Württemberg M1808 and M1810 Wurst limbers were modified forms of the Austrian M1774, with a padded seat for two gunners.[322] This meant that half the crew for foot artillery could ride upon the vehicles (Wurst limber and Wurst caisson),

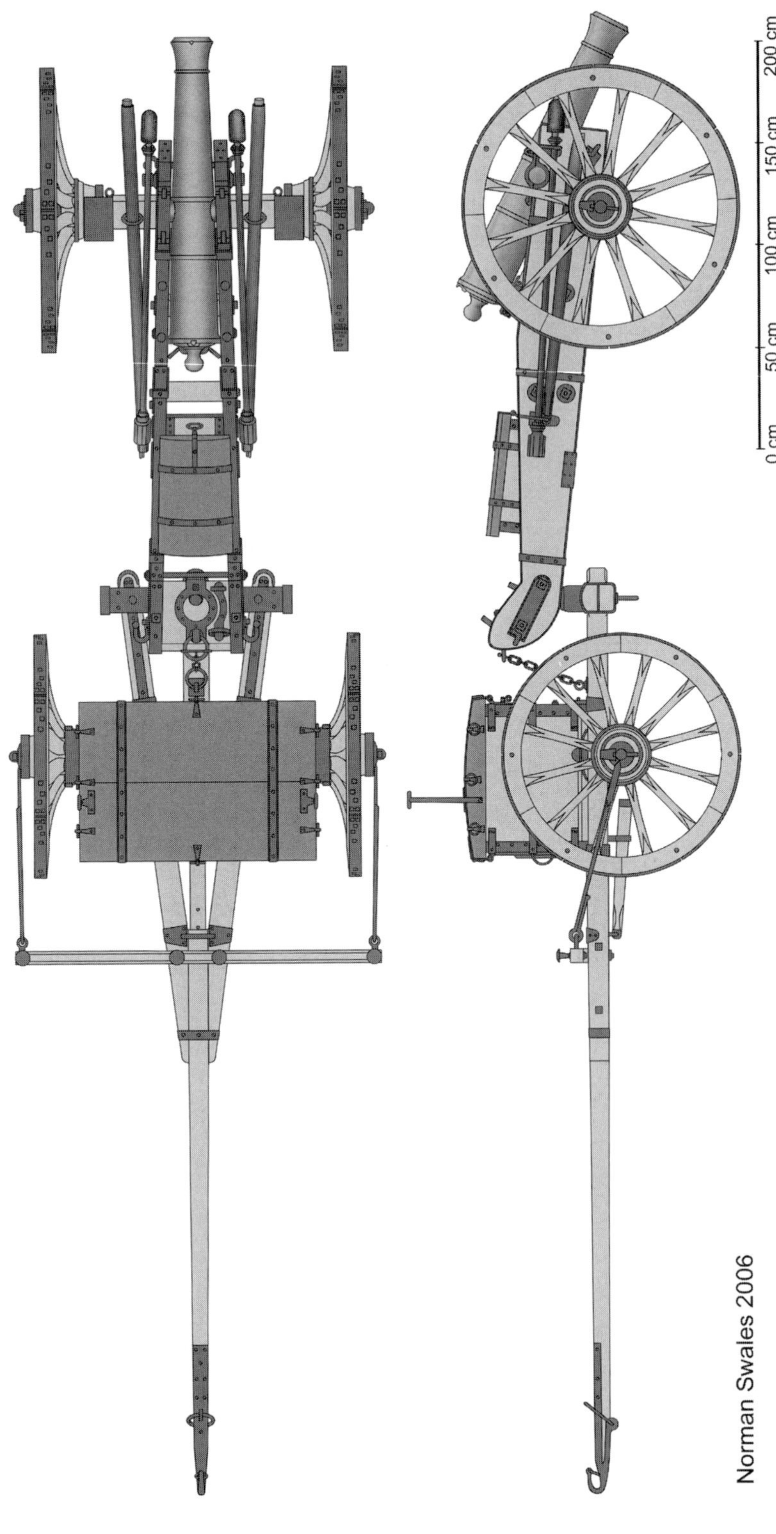

Prussian M1816 Wurst limber for 6-pdr field gun, in fact produced from 1812.

Moving a full-size, full-weight replica of a Gribeauval 12-pdr field gun to its limber using handspikes. (L'Association Britannique de la Garde Impériale, and Horses Through History)

Bricoles attached to a 12-pdr; two gunners wearing bricoles; and six gunners moving the replica 12-pdr – weighing about 1 tonne – across muddy ground. (L'Association Britannique de la Garde Impériale; photographs Jane Dawson)

and all were mounted for light (horse) artillery, with the other half riding upon the Wurst gun carriages. The Saxon M1810 used the smaller 113cm wheels. The Austrian M1813 Wurst limber was the M1774 limber with the ammunition box converted into a seat for the gunners.

The Prussian M1816 Wurst limber, made in small numbers from 1812, had both the ammunition box on the limber and a movable one on the carriage. A 6-pdr gun had an allocation of 45× roundshot, 10× canister and 5× heavy canister, as well as 66× fuses, 568g of gunpowder, 25× portfires and a slowmatch.

ARTILLERY TRAINS

By the beginning of the 19th century most European nations had militarised their artillery trains, so casting off the last of their guild origins. Previously, reliance upon civilian contractors to supply drivers and horse teams to move guns had frequently led to drivers abandoning the guns at the first shot in order to save their lives and horses, leaving the gunners to manhandle their pieces around the battlefield as best they could. For instance, at the battle of Novi (15 August 1799) the French drivers abandoned the guns and caissons in a defile during the retreat and so blocked the line of retreat for the French rearguard.

Austria

Until 1808, Austrian artillery had no permanent transport organisation, so hired civilians and their horses to draw the guns, ammunition carts and baggage wagons. This made sense on purely economic grounds, since a large portion of the *Rosspartei* (train) could be stood down during the winter, and the organisation could be dissolved almost altogether in times of peace. The *Rosspartei* was commanded by a senior wagon-master (*Oberwagenmeister*) and his assistant (*Obergeschirrmeister*), and was divided into sixty troops, each consisting of a wagon-master, two assistants, 80 horses and 160 drivers.[323]

By the War of the Bavarian Succession (1778–79) the artillery train formed part of the larger Army Transport Organisation, but General Johann Theodor Rouvroy noted with distress that the system sank into chaos in the first campaign. In 1783 things improved, when the best horses and drivers from the Army Transport Organisation were drafted to the artillery. In 1798 the Artillery Train was divided into *Fuhrwesen* (with draft horses), *Packwesen* (with packhorses) and *Beschallwesen* (with military remounts, stud, etc). On the battlefield the *Fuhrwesen* drove the supply wagons and carts; however, the other drivers and the ammunition wagon drivers now all wore the white uniforms then in use by the *Rosspartei*.

From 1808 the train was militarised, with the officers enjoying equal status with the rest of the artillery service, operating under a more tolerable military discipline and enjoying better pay. Under the 1809 regulations the drivers all became *Fuhrwesen*, although No.7 (a *Handlanger*) was a horse-holder for the limber team, and brought the horses round for forward movement of the gun.

Britain

Prior to 1715, a train of artillery was created only when the need arose, and the failure to do this in time for the First Jacobite Rebellion forced a major reform. A permanent artillery train was established; although initially only one company in strength, it was enlarged to two companies in May 1716, and reached battalion strength by the time of the Seven Years War. During the 18th century the British army relied solely upon contracting civilian hauliers to move the artillery pieces. In general, the contract went to the lowest bidder, and there were some occasions when they refused to serve on campaign or abroad. At Fontenoy (11 May 1745) the hired drivers from the Low Countries fled during the battle, leaving the guns stranded.[324]

In 1786 the Royal Artillery experimented with militarising its train. In 1792 the Corps of Drivers, Royal Horse Artillery was formed to conduct the guns and vehicles of the new branch of service.[325] Unlike the 'gunner-drivers' of the foot artillery, they were an integral part of each Horse Artillery troop but were technically civilian employees of the Board of Ordnance. In 1804 the RHA drivers were reorganised. The RHA were authorised to have a staff, 58 drivers (increased to 60 on 24 February 1806); and in March 1813 a depot of 40 drivers was formed.[326]

During 1794, the Gunner-Drivers, Corps of Captain Commissaries was established to move the guns and vehicles of the foot artillery.[327] Like the Corps of Drivers, RHA, the Gunner-Drivers were part of the 'Civil List' until 1804.[328] On 1 April 1804 the Brigade of Gunners and Drivers was reformed, with a staff of two adjutants and two veterinary surgeons, and seven Troops each of 689 men; the enlisted men were now part of the Military List of the Board of Ordnance.[329] On 1 January 1806 the Brigade was renamed the Corps of Royal Artillery Drivers, with eleven troops of 554 all ranks. On 1 April 1806 the staff became a major, two adjutants and two veterinary surgeons. In 1808 the Corps had eight Troops, each split into five Sections of 90 all ranks plus specialists. Each troop had 104 officers and specialists and 450 drivers, with 75 riding horses and 945 draft horses. On 13 February 1813 the staff was increased to an adjutant, a veterinary surgeon, and three each quartermasters, sergeant-majors and quartermaster-sergeants. The eleven Troops were each increased by the addition of five carriage and shoeing smiths, five lance-corporals and fifty drivers. Finally, on 21 April 1813, a twelfth Troop was added. The detachment serving 9-pdr field brigades was increased. Even after the creation of these specialist corps, however, civilian drivers and hauliers were still routinely contracted.

The Field Train Department was created to transport the ammunition and equipment for the artillery. The existence of the three wholly separate and fiercely individual organisations caused great difficulties. In practice the Field Train Department were the worst element of the British army. They were described as 'an Augean stable... Many of the officers are negligent and indifferent to their duty...constantly giving their names in sick and in several cases absenting themselves without leave'. Horses were often 'nags' and vehicles poorly maintained. By 1813 the drivers were still considered to be highly undisciplined, unsupervised, with low morale and worn-out uniforms. One report noted that 'They want from the nature of their duty, dispersed in fractional parts, more superintendence than any other corps, and yet...they have not a field officer or superintending power belonging to them'. Captain Swabey RHA called them a 'nest of infamy', and in the Peninsula campaigns listed their chief activities as selling their horses and ammunition to the Portuguese.[330]

France

In 1792–93 four major contractors supplied French artillery horses; by early 1794 it had become a public monopoly, though the horses remained privately owned. This led to such a degeneration of the system that procurement through contractors was re-established in 1795.[331]

On 3 January 1800 the First Consul militarised the artillery train, as an essential prerequisite for his having to implement artillery assaults. By 1805 France had ten *Bataillons du Train d'Artillerie*. Each battalion consisted of five companies, distributed out in wartime to artillery batteries. The élite company, assigned to a horse artillery battery, had the best draft horses and drivers, and the four centre companies were assigned to foot batteries. This gave the foot artillery companies trumpeters, which must have been useful to the battery commanders in coordinating the activities of their men. Originally the train company commanders were sergeants, but this was later changed to a lieutenant's post, and thus one grade lower than the artillery company commander.

In 1805–07 an artillery train company consisted of 2 officers, 7 to 10 NCOs, 2 trumpeters, 2 blacksmiths, 2 harness-makers and 84 privates. In 1808, France had eight artillery train battalions. In 1813, soldiers who had been wounded in the hand and were thus unsuitable for either infantry or cavalry duty were assigned as replacements for the train. In 1815 an artillery train company consisted of a sergeant-major, 4 sergeants, a farrier, 4 corporals, 2 trumpeters, 2 blacksmiths, 2 harness-makers, 24 drivers first class and 60 drivers second class.[332]

A good deal of the effectiveness of the French artillery of the period has to be credited to the efficiency and valour of the artillery train. When a battery moved, the foot gunners marched alongside their gun in two files, and horse artillery rode in two files behind the gun.

Hanover (King's German Artillery)

Unlike the Royal Artillery's Corps of Drivers, the KGA logistics train was an integral part of the

KGA regiment, commanded by Captain Rehwinkel (the Captain Commissary). After the detachment of the men to the tactical units the train remained as a depot for the batteries. The train detachments were commanded by a second-captain, a lieutenant and a driver sergeant, and were carried on the ration strength of each brigade (battery). Each 6-pdr foot and horse brigade had a train detachment of a sergeant, two corporals, a bugler, a blacksmith, two each farriers and collar-makers, a wheelwright and fifty-seven drivers. The 9- and 12-pdr train detachments had two each sergeants and corporals, a bugler, a blacksmith, three farriers, two collar-makers, a wheelwright and ninety-six drivers. Therefore, even though a 9-pdr brigade had 172 gunners, its real strength was 282 all ranks.

Russia

The drivers of the horse teams of the guns and caissons were soldiers throughout this period. In 1803, the drivers of the artillery train wagon teams became soldiers, replacing previously hired civilians.

MANHANDLING GUNS

For short movements on the battlefield, rather than bringing up the horse team and risking exposing it to enemy fire, the gun crew could manhandle the gun into position with drag ropes *(bricoles)*, which were used by Prussia from 1722.[333] They were introduced into Austrian service by Liechtenstein in 1753; and to France by Gribeauval in 1765, after his observation of both services.[334,335] A Prussian manual of the period states:

> In 1722 the *bricole*, that was slung over the shoulder by means of a loop, was hooked on to the hooks on the carriage. In the 1745 campaign, the advancing rope [*Schleppseil*] was used with the 10-pdr [howitzer] and also with the ordinary 6-pdr, but not for the 3-pdr. With the 3-pdr, there was no thick rope, but this was moved by means of the *bricoles* and the traversing spar [a long wooden pole attached to the rear of the carriage].[336]

In the trials of new guns at Strasbourg and Metz in 1764, General Gribeauval championed the use of the *bricole* for short movements on the battlefield.[337] Gribeauval had at his disposal many men who were in favour of the new *bricole*, which he ordered to be used to bring his guns onto the field across flat, hard ground. The gunners proved quite capable of manoeuvring with the body of troops without impeding their movements; there were even times when they out-performed the body of infantry. The military observers were unaccustomed to seeing such speedy movement by artillery manoeuvring without horses. The ease with which the crews could move the new guns was also proved on the sands of Compiègne in northern France.

The *bricole* did not give the French any overall advantage, as it was used by most of the nations of Europe. Ironically enough for Gribeauval, it was an

A firing Russian M1757 20-pdr Unicorn attached to the lead pair of the horses team by the Schleppseil *ready to the advance. (Authors' collection)*

British Light 6-pdr on a M1788 Congreve bracket carriage

These drawings by Pyne, c.1802, show (top) a British Light 6-pdr on a M1788 Congreve bracket carriage being advanced by horse power (*Schleppseil* method) with the Hanoverian truck in place; and (bottom) the gun being bricoled with the 'Hanoverian truck' in place, by men from a light infantry company. Both are guided by an artilleryman with the central handspike. (Courtesy the Trustees of the National Army Museum)

Attaching the prolonge from the replica M1765 limber to the M1765 12-pdr. (L'Association Britannique de la Garde Impériale, and Horses Through History)

important benefit for the 4-pdr 'battalion gun' that he had no desire to add to his system of 8- and 12-pdrs.[338]

In practical tests undertaken by l'Association Britannique de la Garde Impériale, just six men could pull a 12-pdr gun through thick mud with the carriage acting as a sledge, and this is supported by contemporary descriptions. Interestingly, one man can move a Gribeauval 12-pdr field gun like a wheelbarrow for a short distance (10–20m) over hard, level ground by using the handspikes. The trunnions are set just forward of the axle, so making forward movement easier; this would not be possible for guns that had the trunnion on or just behind the line of the axle and using one handspike (hence the Hanoverian truck was used – *see* below). It was found that with two gunners using *bricoles* at the front, far longer distances could easily be covered whether or not the trail was lifted; of course, the more hands are available the easier it is.

MOVING GUNS BY DRAFT WITHOUT LIMBERS

By the mid-18th century most countries had abandoned moving medium and heavy guns without limbers over long distances. The exceptions were the Portuguese prior to 1809, and the Spanish out of necessity. The double-bracket trail served as shafts and double-draft was achieved by means of an outrigger. In the Peninsula mules were used instead of horses to pull the guns, carry the ammunition and even provide the mounts for the officers. This practice persisted throughout the war, even when British-pattern limbers were issued to the Portuguese at the end of 1809. Throughout the 18th century, various designs turned a light gun into, effectively, a two-wheeled cart. These included the French Rostaing M1757 1-pdr, to whose carriage horse shafts were fitted to enable the gun to be moved by a single horse without a limber.

The *Schleppseil*, *prolonge* and 'Hanoverian truck' were developed to move unlimbered guns on the battlefield up to 2km with the assistance of horses. The *prolonge* and *Schleppseil* was a long rope (7-14m long). The difference between them was how they were used.

The *prolonge* connected the gun to the limber so that in emergencies the gun could be retreated rapidly without having to be limbered; this allowed the horse team and limber to be left at a safer distance while being attached to the gun at all times. This method caused many accidents, and tended to

A Hanoverian truck can be seen under the trail transom of the Congreve bracket carriage of this British 12-pdr field gun. (Courtesy the Trustees of the National Army Museum)

damage the gun carriage due to the sudden jerk on a single point of the gun; the gun could overturn, and was difficult to steer. According to General C.S. Valée, writing in 1827, the method was only developed due to the slowness of limbering a Gribeauval gun and moving the ammunition box from the limber to the ground and onto the gun carriage as confirmed by modern field evaluations by the L'Association Britannique de la Garde Impériale. The *prolonge* fell out of favour as it was not as versatile as the *Schleppseil*. The rounded off rear corners of the carriage made it easier to drag. The lightness of the new guns allowed them to be withdrawn in case of a sudden enemy attack without having to be moved to the limber.

The Austrian *Schleppseil* was a 7m long rope with a T-bar fixed to a short chain secured the splinter-bar of the unhitched lead pair of horses. To advance, the *Schleppseil* was attached to the central hook on the gun axle and two gunners lifted the trail end of the gun carriage using the handspike. To retire the gun, the T-bar of the *Schleppseil* was passed through the lunette ring of the transom plate. The Prussians adopted the *Schleppseil* in 1731, the Austrians in 1753, the Saxons in 1772, the British in 1776 and the French finally in 1808.

The Prussians placed a small removable wheel (known in British service as the 'Hanoverian truck') into the pintail hole on the transom plate of the trail, which allowed the gun to be moved on the *Schleppseil* for distances of less than a mile (1.6km) without fatiguing the gun crew. This meant the gun could be moved either by *bricole*, or with the two-horse team attached by a long rope to the centre of the axle-tree, without the need to lift the trail with handspikes. It enabled the gun to be brought quickly into action without the delay of turning the gun and team and unlimbering. When the gun was cleared for firing, the horses were unhooked and led to the rear or to one side, so they could quickly be led back into position to move the gun anew. The team could also be attached to the rear of the gun to facilitate a rapid retreat.

9 The Colours of Artillery Pieces

The colour of artillery carriages and metalwork is a very complex subject of study. Only with further research into interpreting contemporary recipes and re-producing them with natural pigments can a proper idea of the hues and shades be gained. The only synthetic pigment in general use in that period was Prussian Blue. Natural pigments offer great variations.[339] Paints were based on pigments, linseed oil, turpentine and, normally, metallic driers – mainly lead (II) oxide.[340] The pigments were often available in paste form before adding the required amounts of linseed oil, varnish or turpentine according to requirements. The purity, particle size and method of production have a greater influence upon the colour than is the case with dyes.

Bronze gun tubes were normally polished in barracks but often left dull in the field. Iron barrels were painted black or dark brown (a mixture of red lead and black) to help protect them from the weather and prevent rusting. This paint wore off during action, so the gunners spent hours repainting them.

AUSTRIA

From the introduction of Liechtenstein's system in 1753, the gun carriages and wheels were painted with an oil-based dark yellow paint (yellow ochre), and the ironwork with oil-based black paint.[341] The paint gave good protection against damp, giving the wooden parts of the carriage a longer service life and thus reducing the number of new carriages needed after every campaign. The Austrians also blackened their bronze tubes.

BRITAIN

One commonly held misconception about British artillery is that the carriages and limbers were painted dark grey. The prints of Dawes (1792), Pyne (c1800), Atkinson (1807) and Vernet (1813) show variations in colour.[342] William Congreve Snr argued that gun carriages should be left unpainted and the natural wood only waxed.[343] The notebook of Rudyerd (1793) shows brown carriages (but it is unclear whether this is an attempt to show brown paint or natural wood).[344] Some contemporary depictions show gun carriages painted a light blue or buff; and a written description made in January 1812 says that the guns were painted [red] 'lead colour'.[345]

Thus, it seems likely that British gun carriages were either unpainted natural wood or painted light blue, certainly in the early part of the Napoleonic Wars. The adoption of mid- to dark grey only took place in the later Napoleonic period, presumably as the block-trail carriage became more numerous.

The official 'recipe' for the paintwork of the guns thirty-five years later than our period, in c1850, was 1 part Brunswick Black to 24 parts zinc oxide. Brunswick Black when mixed with white had a tendency towards brown. (Zinc oxide was generally not used as a pigment until 1850, being too expensive; it is therefore likely that pipeclay, barytes or lead carbonate was used instead in the earlier period.) The ironwork was painted black, with a mixture of 28 parts of lampblack to 1 part red lead.

The recipe for the black paint used on British naval gun tubes was a mixture of 113g of iron rust (ferric oxides) in 4.54 litres of vinegar (dilute acetic acid). This was left to stand; after a week, 453g of lampblack and 340g of copperas (ferrous sulphate) were stirred in at various intervals over a couple of days. Each gun had five to six coats, applied with a sponge and allowed to dry well between each application; it was finally polished with linseed oil and a soft woollen rag. This resulted in an ebony appearance to the gun tubes.

FRANCE

Up to the 1760s, gun carriages and other items of rolling stock were painted red and the metalwork blackened. By 1775 this had changed to a blue carriage with yellow fleur-de-lise and red wheels. In 1789 the colour was once again changed, to French Artillery Green as the colour for guns, caissons and all rolling stock. However, contemporary prints show many variations:[346]

Berka, published in Prague, shows a wagon of the 8th Artillery Train as painted a light grey-blue (possibly from Prussian paint stocks).

Widow Cherau (1800–05) shows a gun with green wheels and ammunition box, but cheeks painted rust colour (possible red oxide or ferric oxide). Other carriages are shown completely rust coloured with either green or rust-coloured wheels.

Lejeune in his painting of the battle of Marengo shows an 8-pdr with green wheels but a carriage with alternating green and rust coloured zebra stripes.

In an 1806 print of the surrender at Ulm (17 October 1805) a carriage can be seen in yellow ochre and black zebra stripes.

Blue-grey or grey rolling stock was still in use during the Revolutionary Wars.[347]

These variations were no doubt due to the use of older stocks of paint or captured enemy stores, and the inherent variation of using natural pigments. Remember that ochre varies from pale brownish-yellow to orange, and black was likely to have been brownish-black. We must also remember the frailty of the colours used in paintings and watercolours.

In the 1819 *Aide Mémoire à l'Usage de l'Artillerie de France,* General Gassendi recommended the following proportions:[348]

Artillery (olive) green

A mixture of 29.4kg of yellow ochre, 1.5kg of fine black charcoal, and 0.5kg lead (II) oxide in 9.8kg

Contemporary illustrations showing different colours for French artillery equipment; some have the wheels of different colours to the carriage. (Authors' collection)

Table 9.1: Quantity of paint required for a French gun carriage (Gassendi, 1819)[348]
(Note: The new woodwork was primed with red lead, followed by two coats of olive green paint. One coat of red lead and one of black paint were applied to the ironwork.)

	Red lead	Olive paint	Black paint
Field gun-carriage and limber (inc. implements)	6 lb	10 lb	12 oz
Caisson (limber and implements)	8 lb	15 lb	13 oz
Forge with limber	6 lb	10 lb	16 oz
Battery wagon with limber	7 lb	13 lb	14.5 oz
Garrison gun and chassis (inc. implements)	7 lb	14 lb	12 oz
Coastal carriage and chassis (inc. implements)	6 lb	11 lb	16 oz

of linseed oil. The presence of the linseed oil gave a semi-gloss finish to the woodwork. All equipment was given two coats of paint. The 'transparent' first coat had 3.4kg of turpentine added to 6.9kg of Artillery Green paint. For the second coat, 5.9kg of Artillery Green paint was mixed with 1.0kg of cooked oil, 0.5kg of linseed oil and 2.0kg of turpentine. General Gassendi stated that this was sufficient for eighteen caissons.

Olive green paste
A paste was made with 68 parts of pulverised yellow ochre in 37 parts of boiled linseed oil. Then 11 parts of lampblack was mixed with 0.4 parts of turpentine in another container, before combining the two colours. The olive paste was kept in a tin vessel.

Liquid olive green colour
61.5 parts of olive paste and 3.5 parts of lead (II) oxide was stirred into 29.5 parts boiled linseed oil, 5.5 parts turpentine and 2 parts Japan varnish, in a paint-pot.

Black paint for ironwork
Recipe 1: Mix 0.98kg of fine black charcoal and 61g of lead (II) oxide in 0.98kg of linseed oil. The first coat was a mixture of 0.49kg of black paint, 0.49kg of Artillery Green paint and 0.49kg of turpentine. The second coat was 0.12kg of very fine black charcoal in 0.92kg of cooked oil and 0.61kg of turpentine.

Recipe 2: Prepared by grinding 28 parts lampblack in 73 parts of linseed oil, then stirring in 1 part of lead (II) oxide; 1 part of varnish and 1 part of turpentine were added last.

Paint for tarpaulins
1kg of tarpaulin paint was required for each square yard, painted with three coats. Dissolve 6 parts of beeswax in 6 parts of turpentine with gentle heat, then mix warm with 100 parts of liquid olive colour. Add 0.37kg of the beeswax to 7.5 litres of linseed oil, and boil for two hours. Prime the cloth with this mixture, and use the same, in place of boiled oil, for making the paint.

OTHER COUNTRIES

In 1815 the Netherlands artillery, with its mixture of gun and equipment types, varied greatly in colour even within batteries. Mostly they were shades of brown with some in French Artillery Green. It was not until 1826 that the Netherlands army used British material and guns.

In Prussia, gun carriages appear to have been a blue-grey colour with blackened metalwork fittings. Prussian Blue was mixed with either white lead or barytes.[349]

Until 1805, Russian equipment was painted with a red lead that produced a brick red colour, and the metal fittings were painted black. Under the 1805 reforms the colour of Russian guns changed from red

Table 9.2: Artillery colours

Country	Year	Woodwork	Metal fittings
Major states			
Austria	1753–1850	Ochre	Black
Britain	1792–1810?	Unpainted or light blue	Black
	1810–1815	Medium to dark grey	Black
France	upto 1760s	Red (red lead)	Black
	1760s–1789	Blue carriage with red wheels	Black
	1789–1918	Olive green	Black
Prussia	1740–1850	Blue-grey	Black
Russia	Pre 1805	Red	Black
	1805–60	Apple green	Black
Coallition allies			
Brunswick	1809	Ochre (Austrian)	Black
	1813–1815	Olive green	Black
Hanover	1735–1803	Red	Black
	1814–1815	Red with some medium to dark grey	Black
Netherlands	1814–1815	Various shades of brown (red lead and black) with some olive green	Black
Portugal	Pre 1807	Olive green	Black
	1808–1814	Medium blue-grey	Black
KGA	1805–1815	Medium to dark grey, some may have been red	Black
Spain	1807–1815	Dark grey or stained	Black
Sweden	1805–1814	Greenish blue	Black
French allies			
Denmark	1800–1815	Red, blue-grey or grey. Often the sides of caisson were painted black	Bronze or black
Kingdom of Holland	1805–1810	Olive green	Black
Italy	1806–1814	Grey	Black
Naples	1805–1815	Olive green	Black
Duchy of Warsaw	1807–1813	Mainly blue-grey	Black
Switzerland		?	
Confederation of the Rhine			
Baden	1805–1815	Grey to dark grey	Black
Bavaria	1805–1815	Light blue-grey	Black
Berg	1808–1813	Stained wood	Bronze
Hesse-Darmstadt	1805–1815	Mid-blue	Black
Hesse-Kassel	1806–1815	Mid-blue	Black
Saxony	1805–1813	Black to dark brown. Wagons had light blue body, light brown roof and black wheels	Bronze
Westphalia	1806–1813	Olive green but some sources show yellow stripes on wheels	Black
Württemberg	1805–1815	Stained wood	Bronze
Würzburg	1807–1815	Grey	Black

to apple-green with black fittings. This colour seems to have been superficially similar to French Artillery Green, but much darker. It is unclear whether it was made with yellow ochre and lampblack or verdigris.

Saxon gun carriages were stained black with a mix of asphalt, litharge [lead (II) oxide], boiled linseed oil and turpentine. Metal was bronze so was not painted. The handles of gun tools and the bore of the tube were cleaned with vinegar mixed with water. In 1811, Saxon guns apparently changed colour to green, made from 2.5kg of yellow ochre and 25g of black mixed with boiled linseed oil, turpentine and dryings. Saxon artillery also used:

- Black (25kg of lampblack with 1kg of yellow ochre)
- Red (red ochre mixed with lead oxide and boiled linseed oil, turpentine and dryings)
- Brown (red mixed with yellow ochre, lead oxide and lampblack)
- Blue (Prussian Blue and lead (II) oxide)
- Green-grey (unknown composition).

Pigments

The following is an outline of the inexpensive pigments that were available in the 18th and early 19th centuries.[350]

Black

Asphalt is produced by burning high-boiling mineral oils in atmospheric oxygen. Artificial asphalt is obtained by heating coal tar pitch to a high temperature.

Brunswick Black is bitumen or pitch (mineral material containing mainly hydrocarbons), mixed with turpentine and linseed oil, then heated. It is similar to asphalt but somewhat lighter in colour.

Lampblack is brownish-black bituminous soot (80–85% carbon with a small proportion of oily material), obtained from the ignition of tarry beechwood soot that is ground, sieved and extracted with hot water until the water is no longer coloured. Similar products are obtained by extracting lignite (brown coal) tar or humus with ammonia, and precipitating the extract with acetic acid.

White

Barytes is natural barium sulphate [$BaSO_4$], occurring naturally in England (Derbyshire, Cornwall and Devon), Germany (Hessian Odenwald near Neustadt, Waldshut in Baden, near Königsee in Thüringia, etc), Italy and other sites. It was first sorted into pure white, reddish or yellowish, then washed with water and dried, and finally milled three to four times to a very fine powder. It imparts greater covering-power to Chrome Yellow and Prussian Blue.

Pipeclay is aluminium silicate or kaolin [$Al_2O_3.2SiO_2.2H_2O$]

Slate Grey (Stone Grey, Mineral Grey) is hydrated aluminium silicate [$AlHSi_2O_6$] and occurs widely along the Rhine, in Thüringia and elsewhere. The product was crushed and ground, often mixed with other white colours, for grey shades.

White Lead is basic lead carbonate [$(PbCO_3)_2.Pb(OH)_2$] – CI Pigment White 1: Ceruse – and occurs in nature as the mineral hydrocerussite. When used alone it dries to a rather soft surface that weathers to a chalky coat and is readily abraded. It is blackened with hydrogen sulphide to give lead sulphide (PbS).

Zinc White is zinc oxide [ZnO]; it occurs as the mineral zincite, and was probably too expensive to be used as a paint in the period.

Red

Red Lead (lead (II, IV) oxide) [Pb_3O_4] is made by heating litharge [PbO]. The variation in colour depends upon the amount of lead dioxide [PbO_2] they contain (18–34%). Good quality paint contains 25% red lead, and was used to preserve wood and protect ironwork. It had to be mixed with oil and used immediately.

Yellow

Naples Yellow (mainly lead antimonate [$PbO.Sb_2O_5$]) has been used in paints since at least the 13th century. It darkens with time if contaminated with iron, tin or zinc.

Yellow Ochre (Chamois, Imperial Yellow, Ochre, Paris Ochre, etc) is a natural hydrated ferric oxide [$Fe_2O_3.H_2O$] and basic ferric sulphate [iron (III) sulphate] containing alumina (clays), silica (sand), lime, etc. It occurs extensively in England (Cornwall, Derbyshire, Oxfordshire and Surrey), France (Auxerre, Ru, Apt, etc), Germany (Harz Mountains, Thüringia, Bavaria, Westphalia, etc), Spain, Italy (Tuscany), Poland and North America. It ranges from pale yellowish-brown to orange.

Green

Bronze Green is a mixture of charcoal, Prussian Blue and Yellow Ochre.

Brunswick Green was obtained by precipitating copper sulphate, tartaric acid and sodium arsenite with limewater.

Verdigris (Vert de Montpelier) is essentially copper acetates and hydrate copper hydroxides $[Cu(CH_3COO)_2 \cdot \times Cu(OH)_2 \cdot yH_2O]$ in varying proportions. It acts as a wood preserver, and is still used in Russia for painting iron roofs to prevent rust. In varnish, it gives a dark green upon exposure to air.

Blue

Brunswick Blue (Celestine Blue) was an impure Prussian Blue mixed with white pigments such as 50–90% barytes, pipeclay, etc.

Prussian Blue (Berlin Blue, Chinese Blue, Paris Blue, etc) is iron (III) hexacyanoferrate (II). Discovered in 1704 by Diesbach, it is fast to light, acids and alkalis. It has great colour strength: 1 part Prussian Blue will render 640 parts of White Lead perceptibly blue.

Verditer Blue is formed by copper nitrate and gilder's whiting.

Other Components

Driers is a trade term for oxides of lead, manganese and cobalt that are added during the process of boiling linseed oil to accelerate its drying properties; they absorb oxygen from the air and aid the oxidation of the oil. The most common was lead (II) oxide [PbO], also known as litharge or dryings; this exists in two forms, red to reddish-yellow.

Vinegar is dilute acetic acid, probably derived from wine or spirits.

Copperas is ferrous sulphate, iron (II) sulphate.

Linseed oil was obtained from the flax plant from either the Baltic or India. Artist's Linseed Oil is raw linseed oil that has been allowed to stand for a few weeks, then treated with litharge [PbO], and finally bleached by exposure. Boiled Oil is linseed oil that has been boiled with litharge to render the oil more drying and increase its viscosity.

Turpentine was obtained by tapping resinous exudates from pine trees and distilling them. The most important sources were France, Greece, Russia and Spain.

Varnishes are either an oil varnish (resin oil in turpentine) or spirit varnish (natural resin in a volatile solvent). *Japan Varnish* is obtained from blending asphalt varnish with dark-coloured copal or amber varnish to give a dark black-brown varnish.

10 Ammunition: Effectiveness, Characteristics and Supply

INTRODUCTION

One of the primary factors that limited the effectiveness of artillery was poor visibility on the battlefield. Guns often opened fire at distances shorter than the often-quoted theoretical maximum ranges. When the limitations of terrain and the effects of gunpowder smoke on a still day were combined, visibility might be measured in terms of tens of metres only. The first salvo from a battery would be aimed, but any subsequent salvos would have less effect as the target became more obscured by the thick banks of grey-white powdersmoke which hung in the air unless a stiff wind was blowing – and from a convenient direction. Napoleon and Frederick the Great, amongst others, observed that once gunners opened fire they usually continued firing even though their own smoke blocked the view to their front.

The Russian Major-General Kutaisov noted that long-range aimed fire (i.e. beyond 600m), where observation of the enemy was difficult, had to be carried out in a slow and controlled manner, and at such ranges it was only useful for slowing down the deployment of the enemy.[351]

According to eyewitness accounts, some artillery batteries could not tell the difference between friendly and enemy troops as close as 400m, thus negating the theoretical maximum range of 1500m for 12-pdr guns. De Segur wrote that at Borodino in 1812 the smoke was so thick that 'we could only make out the enemy at rare intervals'.[352] Von Brandt wrote of his Vistula Legion infantry on one occasion that the 'gunpowder smoke when fired literally blanketed the battlefield with varying degrees of density. It hung low, needing a stiff breeze to disperse it quickly. Troops were seen fleetingly through gaps in the smoke. Gunners often fired blind into a distant haze. It gave advantage or disadvantage to attacker and defender equally.'

Even without smoke, distinguishing friend from foe was difficult. Only at about 450m can colours be determined; many nations wore uniforms of very similar silhouette, and colours such as the darker blues, greens and browns were always hard to tell apart – especially if troops had been on campaign for weeks or months and their uniforms were dirty and worn. Identification might be possible based on the shape of headdress, but again, many nations followed prevailing fashions and wore black shakos whose differences were only evident at fairly short distances. Wellington complained about the change to the Dragoon and Light Dragoon uniforms in 1812: although the former kept their red jackets they changed their bicorn hats for helmets similar in shape to those of French dragoons; the latter changed their Tarleton helmets for shakos and their dark blue jackets acquired coloured facings similar to those worn by some French units.[353] According to B.P. Hughes, the limits of visibility were as follows (but only if not obscured by smoke or bad weather):[354]

- At 1600m: Infantry on the horizon or field could be seen as a thin black line.
- At 1200m: The formation of the infantry and its strength could be assessed.
- At 800m: Individual movements could be seen.
- At 540m: The spacing of files, numbers and organisation of the body of infantry could be confirmed.
- At 400m: The identity of the unit might just be made out.
- At 320m: Identification of the unit was likely.

The numbers of casualties caused by gunpowder artillery have often been overestimated as much as its psychological effect has been disregarded.

An impression of the amount of smoke produced by a single round fired from a 12-pdr; after a few rounds the gun crew were quite unable to see their target, here a 3-pdr of the Royal Horse Artillery at approximately 350 paces' distance – well within canister range. (Association Britannique de la Garde Impériale)

Of course, the effects of artillery projectiles on the human body could be terrifying, producing 'macerating or avulsing' [i.e. the flesh pulped, or torn off the limbs]...The main cause of death was dismemberment or decapitation. There would be no survival with roundshot, or musket-ball [i.e. canister] at close range.'[355] Cannonballs travelled through the air at subsonic speeds, giving a loud whistling sound as they approached. Even from extreme range, rolling shot would bowl files of men over and cause widespread injury. Shot hitting equipment, wooden vehicles and stony ground would fling the debris in all directions with deadly force, causing even more carnage.

Each gun produced belching white smoke and a flash of flame combined with very loud noise; the latter must have been shocking to a person born in the late 18th century, whose previous experience of noise levels was limited to less than half of that considered normal today, in our age of jet engines and ubiquitous motor vehicles. Artillery frightened and disturbed soldiers, wearing down their resolve and morale. Soldiers of all nations agreed that standing in position under a cannonade, with nothing to do but wait and pray, was the most unpleasant ordeal that they could imagine. With nothing to occupy a soldier's mind, and no way of striking back at the enemy, he had to endure the sight of comrades killed or horribly maimed, perhaps at his side. This was one of the reasons for assigning regimental and battalion guns, whose return fire was probably of more psychological than destructive value.

Mobility upon the battlefield also influenced the effectiveness of the artillery, and severe losses of horses to counter-battery or other fire could be crippling. Mercer stated that his battery lost 140 out of 200 horses at its final deployment area at Waterloo, and that the dead horses had to be freed from the harnesses before the living horses could be regrouped into effective teams. Heavy losses among horses also occurred through natural causes. J.F. Boulart described a scene during the advance into Russia when an overnight storm of near-freezing rain killed nearly 25% of the horses in the artillery train and cavalry, thus seriously hampering the movement of the artillery. Some 40,000 horses may have died in this episode.[356]

FIRE EFFECT

Cannon

Cannons were fired by direct line of sight, so artillerists had to see the target to be effective. Generally the longer the barrel of the cannon the greater was the accuracy at long range but this depends upon the quality of the gunpowder and the windage. Cannons fired roundshot (75% of their ammunition) by either direct or ricochet fire. A cannonball fired by ricochet made about five grazes (if unobstructed), each bounce travelling perhaps half the distance of the previous one, depending upon the state of the ground and other factors. The more grazes it made,

6th Company of the Foot Artillery of the Imperial Guard

This photograph was taken from the position occupied by the 6th Company of the Foot Artillery of the Imperial Guard on the left of the *Grande Batterie* at Waterloo. The farm of La Haye Sainte is seen half a kilometre in front of the battery; the British main line of defence was about the same distance beyond it. (Association Britannique de la Garde Impériale)

the greater the magnitude of the deviations and the corresponding reduction in potential energy. A well-trained gunner would always try to make the first graze just in front of the target, and ricochet the ball through the enemy troop formation at about chest height.

The primary target was massed infantry and cavalry; aiming for dispersed targets was a waste of ammunition due to the inaccuracy of the artillery of this period. The value of oblique (enfilading) fire was stressed by all contemporary manuals; infantry linear formations were particularly vulnerable to flanking fire, although they might not always be easy targets due to their narrow cross-section. Adye also urged gunners to place their guns to create crossfire. He suggested that artillery fire should always take an enemy in the direction of its greatest dimension, so the artillery were placed obliquely or in flank against line, and in front to fire at columns.

Relative Effectiveness at Battle Ranges

Larger-calibre guns (12- and 18-pdrs) had greater penetration and longer range than medium artillery (6- and 8-pdrs) and light artillery (3- and 4-pdrs), due to their greater mass. This was particularly useful for destroying field fortifications, or for denying the enemy a particular area – creating a 'beaten zone' to hinder their troop movements, rather than attempting to hit particular bodies of men.

However, theoretical maximum ranges were usually unimportant. The Prussian General Monhaupt noted that 'a 12-pdr is able to fire its roundshot 460–600m further than a 6-pdr, but this has no influence on the outcome of the battle... A hit at such distance is purely accidental, and a soldier who has campaigned for 20 years or more will not run from the whistle and the strike of such roundshot.'[357]

Many contemporary artillery experts – including Scharnhorst, Monhaupt, and a French observer in 1824 – stated that a 6-pdr was more effective than

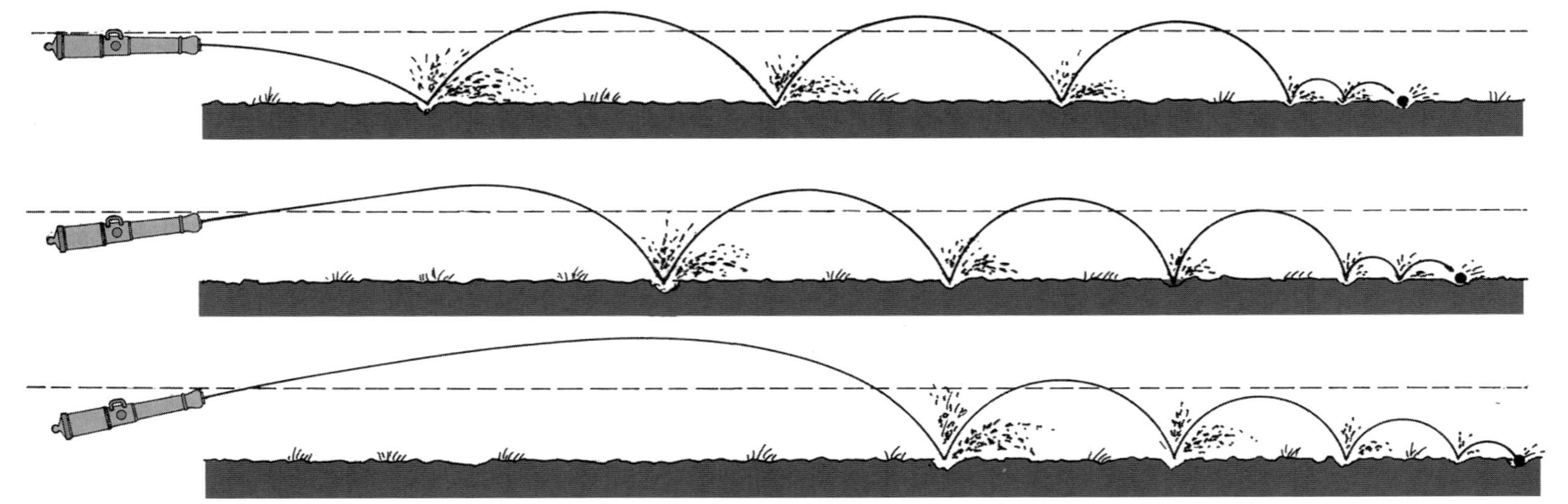

Table 10.1: Hits registered by six-gun batteries of 6-pdr and 12-pdr guns

(Note: The target measured 61.5m by 5.5m. Six guns of each calibre fired roundshot for 30 minutes; each 12-pdr fired an average of 45 rounds and each 6-pdr an average of 60. With canister, each battery fired for one minute.)

	400 m	**500 m**	**600 m**	**700 m**	**800 m**	**900 m**
41 ball Heavy Canister						
12-pdr (9 rounds fired)	No data collected	No data collected	45 (12%) hits	No data collected	36 (10%) hits	
6-pdr (12 rounds fired)	No data collected	No data collected	48 (10%) hits	No data collected	0 (0%) hits	
112 ball Light Canister						
12-pdr (9 rounds fired)	180 (18%) hits	162 (16%) hits	108 (11%) hits	72 (9%) hits	No data collected	
6-pdr (12 rounds fired)	240 (18%) hits	204 (15%) hits	96 (7%) hits	60 (5%)hits	No data collected	
Roundshot						
12-pdr (270 rounds fired)		107 (40%) hits		97 (36%) hits		54 (20%) hits
6-pdr (360 rounds fired)		135 (27.5%) hits		90 (25%) hits		0 (0%) hits

a 12-pdr, both because it could fire quicker and because a 6-pdr roundshot had more effect than a 12-pdr firing canister.[358] The advantages of the 12-pdr were often negated by its slower rate of fire, caused by the weight of the ammunition, the time needed to lay the gun, and its lower battlefield mobility. Indeed, it was estimated in peacetime tests that 5× 6-pdrs had more effect on a target than 4× 8-pdrs.[359] A French officer writing just after the period used Scharnhorst's empirical observations and his own experience to state that two French 8-pdrs had the same effect as three Austrian 12-pdrs; and that 5× 6-pdrs had the same effect as 4× 8-pdrs or 3× 12-pdrs.[360] In addition, a 6-pdr caisson could carry twice as many rounds as a 12-pdr caisson, so fewer caissons were required.

Table 10.1 shows that over a half-hour period at distances of 500m, there were only 107 strikes of the target with 12-pdr shot, compared to 135 strikes by 6-pdr shot. When additional ranks of the enemy were standing behind each other, roundshot would have double or even threefold the effect. At a distance of 400m, at which both calibres fired one round of canister, the 12-pdr had nearly double the effect compared with a 6-pdr; but the smaller piece could be loaded and aimed faster than a 12-pdr. More importantly, the 6-pdr could move 50% faster on firm ground, and this proportion became more favourable on more difficult or sandy ground.

General Allix observed that although the 12-pdr was less mobile than the 6-pdr, it was useful for destroying bridges and field fortifications, and that the consequent delay to an enemy army's progress of one or two days could determine the success or failure of an operation. Conversely, a number of French officers felt that the 12-pdr needlessly encumbered the field army as it struggled to travel over bad roads and undulating terrain. In the middle 1790s Generals Kléber, Desaix and Moreau sought to eliminate the 12-pdr from their respective artillery parks. However, Lespinasse – who replaced Allix – favoured the 12-pdr, and in his *Essai sur l'Organisation de l'Artillerie* he stated that in order for artillery to be effective, it was necessary to amass large batteries and include guns of the heavier calibres. When more power was needed instead of manoeuvrability, or when it was necessary to fire at the enemy effectively at greater ranges (1,500–1,800 paces [1140–1370m]), or to destroy strong artificial obstacles that hamper our attack, the artillery manuals of France, Austria and Prussia all agree that 12-pdr batteries are required. Allix noted that 16-pdrs were instrumental in a number of victories in Spain and, due to the loss of 1,600 guns at Katzbach, Dennewitz and Kulm in 1813; Napoleon took garrison 16-pdrs into the field as an unavoidable expedient.[361]

Table 10.2: Differential solubility at different temperatures
(Anon (2001) Merck Index, 13th Edition, Merck Inc; and Anon (2004) The Combined Chemical Dictionary: Chemical Database, Chapman & Hall)

	0°C	18°C	100°C
Calcium and magnesium ions removed by precipitation			
Calcium carbonate	ND	0.0014g/100ml	ND
Magnesium carbonate	ND	0.011g/100ml	ND
Solubility of chlorides			
Potassium chloride	ND	24g/100ml	57g/100ml
Sodium chloride	35.7g/100ml	38.5g/100ml	39.12g/100ml
Solubility of nitrates			
Calcium nitrate	ND	121.2g/100ml	376g/100ml
Potassium nitrate	13.3g/100ml	35.7g/100ml	247g/100ml
Sodium nitrate	ND	90.9g/100ml	180g/100ml

Table 10.3: Composition of gunpowder from different nations

	Saltpetre	Sulphur	Charcoal (carbon)
Austria (artillery)	70 (66.7%)	15 (14.3%)	20 (19.0%)
Britain (1742)	6 (75%)	1 (12.5%)	1 (12.5%)
Britain (1781)	15 (75%)	2 (10%)	3 (15%)
Chinese (1788)	75.79%	9.05%	15.16%
France (artillery)	6 (75%)	1 (12.5%)	1 (12.5%)
Hanover	5 (71.4%)	1 (14.3%)	1 (14.3%)
Italy	76%	12%	12%
Poland	80%	8%	12%
Portugal	75.7%	10.7%	13.6%
Prussia (1774 coarse)	74.4%	12.3%	13.3%
Prussia (1775 fine)	80%	10%	10%
Prussia (1800)	75%	10%	15%
Prussia (C19th)	75%	11.5%	13.5%
Russia	70%	11.5%	18.5%
Saxony (artillery)	75.8%	8.1%	16.1%
Spain	76.5	10.8	12.7
Swiss (1800/1808)	76%	10%	14%
Sweden (1770)	75%	9%	16%
Sweden (1827)	75%	15%	10%
USA	76%	10%	14%
Württemberg	77.8% (70)	11.1% (10)	11.1% (10)

The Russian Major-General Kutaisov noted that opening fire at 1000m was a waste of ammunition, and that at 600m one could be certain of hitting the target.[362] It was further attested by Scharnhorst and a number of French observers that at 600m a 6-pdr could hit a target with more accuracy and deliver a greater weight of shot onto it than a 12-pdr. They recognised that 600m was perhaps a maximum range for opening an effective cannonade, but that 5× 6-pdrs could fight with more efficiency than 3× 12-pdr and certainly 4× 8-pdrs. Scharnhorst and the French observer in 1824 stated that hitting targets above 600m with roundshot was difficult irrespective of the gun calibre.[363] Napoleon wrote:

> There are a thousand circumstances in war where it is requisite to open fire at a very long range, whether from one bank to the other of a wide river, or to hinder the enemy from encamping and occupying a position which can only be attacked from a distance. Finally, it is a real disadvantage not to reply to an enemy's fire. However, we look to artillery officers not to fire uselessly, for we pretend in no way to attack the fundamental principle that to open fire at a long range under ordinary circumstances is to burn ammunition and to destroy its effect.[364]

Vergnaud stated in 1840 that it was impractical to fire at targets beyond 900m.[365] As the intended target could probably only be confirmed as enemy troops at distances between 800m and 540m, the 12-pdr's theoretical maximum range of 1600m was irrelevant; at 800m or less nearly all of the guns used in the period would have been able to hit the target, and the effective range of 370–320m was within the prescribed ranges even for canister shot. Tests by Muller and others are often cited, but have almost nothing to do with the real effect that artillery had in action; the accuracy of guns in combat was inevitably poorer than during tests conducted in peacetime. Effectiveness in battle depended upon being able to see where you wanted your ball to hit the ground and, as already argued, this was strictly limited by visibility.

In 1824 the French evaluated the most effective ranges of their 12-pdrs and 6-pdrs in a series of tests, and determined that the most effective range on the battlefield was 500–600m. In these tests the 6-pdr was a superior weapon to the 12-pdr at below 700m (*see* Table 10.1).

Howitzers

Before the Seven Years War howitzers had limited deployment with field armies and were almost exclusively found in the siege train. The Austrian von Tielke explored the possibilities of using the howitzer as a battlefield weapon, and noted that a howitzer firing on a high trajectory was extremely useful in hilly and undulating terrain, as it could be fired into hollows or on to the tops of heights to dislodge troops with exploding shell. This realisation led to the change in their deployment from all-howitzer batteries to a mixed battery of guns and howitzers which could perform a more diverse set of functions. This became a self-contained fighting unit able to suit its tactics to the terrain – a flexibility denied to homogenous batteries. In general, howitzers were kept in reserve of the battery and often behind the main gun line.

In 1800, Manson suggested that the firing of shells with a flat trajectory from a longer tube would be more effective than from the short-barrelled de Saxe M1749 howitzer then in use in France as shown by the M1766 *Granatstück* and Russian unicorn gun-howitzer.

One example of the usefulness of howitzers was recorded at the battle of Dennewitz (6 September 1813), where the Prussians were able to take the village of Rohrbeck with howitzer support. The shells and incendiaries set the village on fire, forcing the French to retreat, and allowed the Prussians to take the village with only light casualties.[366]

The cutting of the time-fuse was of crucial importance. Cut it too short, and the shell could explode over the heads of friendly troops; cut it too long, and the shell would land without exploding. In the French service doctrine advocated the busting of shells over the heads of the enemy; in Britain and Russia it was the practice to graze the shell like a roundshot, principally because of the lack of elevation available on the howitzer carriages. The gunners were trained to cut the fuse of the shell so that it exploded soon after the first ricochet, which was to be immediately in front of the enemy troop formations.

In most armies the shells were supplied empty and had to be filled prior to discharge, and the pre-packed fuses cut to length. The fuse had an incremental scale on the side giving a known time, but getting elevation, trajectory and time correct was still a difficult undertaking. It was estimated that a French shell would spread splinters in a 30m sphere. Although effective in siege work, the common shell was not always effective against cavalry and infantry in the open field.

GUNPOWDER

Gunpowder is the physical combination of potassium nitrate, sulphur and charcoal, commonly in the proportions of 75% potassium nitrate, 12.5% sulphur and 12.5% charcoal. Gunpowder is a low explosive rated between 170 and 630m/s depending upon grain size making it in practical terms a good propellant. High-quality, well-preserved gunpowder is slate grey, or shiny black if glazed with graphite; too black a shade indicated either too much charcoal, or the fact that it was wet. Good powder should not cause a stain on the fingers and, when burnt, should not char or leave a residue on a sheet of white paper with black stains indicating too much charcoal, and yellow stains too much sulphur. A brief chronology of the evolutionary development of gunpowder is as follows:

- 220 BC: Chinese alchemists reported an accident while separating gold from silver, and accidentally made gunpowder.[368]
- 950 AD: First use of rockets in China, using 70% potassium nitrate, 20% charcoal, 10% sulphur.
- 1044: Wu ching tsung-yao (*Collection of Essential Military Techniques*) provided accounts of nine gunpowder weapons and three varieties of gunpowder.[369]
- 1267: Roger Bacon (1214–92) was the first person in Europe to mention gunpowder, in his *Opus Majus*.[370]

Barrels containing 100lb of LG blank gunpowder. (Courtesy the Board of Trustees of the Royal Armouries; photographs Stephen Summerfield)

- 1320s: Serpentine gunpowder was produced – a simple mixture of saltpetre, sulphur and charcoal made using a hand pestle and mortar; in storage the mixture settled, leaving the lighter charcoal at the top and the heavier sulphur and saltpetre at the bottom. This method of production gave a finer powder than produced today, but it did not burn efficiently. The problems with fine powder were that it was more hygroscopic than coarse powder; and could be rammed too firmly so the ignition flame passing down the vent would burn the outside of the mass first before igniting it completely.
- 1425: The French perfected 'corned powder': saltpetre, sulphur and charcoal were mechanically mixed with water to form a paste and spread thinly on plates for drying in the sun. When dry this cake was broken up and passed through sieves to produce grains (corns) of the required size – originally three sizes, fine grain for handguns and medium and large grains for cannon. The gunpowder was ballistically stronger and had superior storage properties.[371]
- 1680s: Production of glazed powder. The three ingredients were corned, glazed by introduction of air-dried graphite, dried in a drying house, and finally packed in containers. The more rounded grains had greater moisture resistance, were harder and more uniform.
- 1742: Benjamin Robins devoted the first section of his *New Principles of Gunnery* to the determination of the force of gunpowder.[372]
- 1750s: Britain started to incorporate the three ingredients, then roll them under 10-ton wheels to form 'wheel cake', which was then pressed through wooden rollers to increase specific gravity before it was corned, glazed, dried and packed. This process spread to the rest of Europe by the 1780s and America in 1802.[373]
- 1781: Benjamin Thompson (aka Graf Rumford) published his first challenge to Robins.[374]
- 1783: Gunpowder based on charcoal prepared in cylinders was developed by Robert Watson from an invention by Dr Fordyce; this provided a more powerful and consistent propellant so allowing shorter gun tubes.

- 1785: William Congreve Snr started work at The Warren, Woolwich upon producing cylinder gunpowder.[375]
- 1790: Sir Thomas Blomefield, Inspector-General of Ordnance at The Warren, Woolwich, initiated a series of trials in August that showed that any gun above a 9-pdr could fire double-shotted at 400 yards with a powder charge one-third the shot weight rather than half.
- 1792: The new cylinder powder produced for the Royal Navy and army was marked with red lettering (Red LG) to distinguish it from ordinary powder, marked in blue (Blue LG), or recycled powder, which was marked in white. In the Royal Navy the weaker powder was restricted to close action, salutes or tests, and the cylinder powder was reserved for long-range engagements.[376]
- 1797: Graf von Rumford published *Experiments to determine the force of fired gunpowder* from his experiments made in Bavaria in 1793.[377, 378]
- 1803: The Board of Ordnance realised that the new cylinder gunpowder made replacing the pre-Blomefield iron guns a pressing matter, especially due to a recent spate of bursting guns. The examination, reproofing and, if necessary, withdrawal of older guns was undertaken with 'the utmost dispatch' from March.
- 1810: In February the Ordnance Board finally ordered the return to store of all 'Old Pattern' naval Armstrong and Muller guns.
- 1850s: The steam-drying house was introduced; steam was re-circulated through pipes, making the production of gunpowder safer.

Ingredients

Historically, sulphur mostly originated in Sicily, Iceland and in Ancona, Italy, where it was mined and crudely refined.[379] The presence of rock contaminants required further refining before making the powder.

Although straightforward to produce, charcoal is a complex subject. For gunpowder production soft woods were preferred, including hazel, alder and willow harvested by pollarding in the spring; each branch was cut to length before being stripped of bark. The earliest method of producing charcoal was mound-burning, where the rods were stacked around a central stake and a kiln was formed by sealing the mound with earth. Fire was introduced to the centre after the stake was removed; the charcoal-burner regulated the fire by adding more earth, or making a vent hole opposite the direction of the wind. It required ten to fourteen days and twenty-four-hour supervision to produce suitable charcoal.

In 1783 it was proposed to form charcoal in large iron retorts or ovens called 'cylinders' so permitting better temperature control, a more uniform burn and hence a more efficient gunpowder. The heat from the fire removed the tars and pyroligneous acids that were collected in tubs. After distillation, the charcoal was cooled and crushed. Improvements in gunpowder quality meant that the charge could be reduced; a charge of one-third of the shot weight was standard for the new cylinder powder.

Saltpetre (also known as nitre) was derived naturally or artificially from soil. The inorganic salt of potassium nitrate, with its high oxygen content, aids the combustion of the sulphur and carbon (charcoal). Pure potassium nitrate is not strongly hygroscopic, but when contaminated with other nitrates (especially calcium and magnesium) and sodium chloride (common salt) leads to it dampening quickly.

Potassium nitrate is produced naturally by the decomposition of animal and vegetable detritus in porous, humid soils. Saltpetre imported from India by the East India Company was far superior to supplies of native British saltpetre.[380] In the temperate countries of Europe the concentration in soils of potassium nitrate over the other nitrates of calcium and magnesium is small, due to its high solubility – it is easily washed out by rain. The nitre earth of Bengal in India contained 8.3% potassium nitrate, 3.7% calcium nitrate and the rest calcium carbonate, earth, water, and so forth. British command of the seas, and thus uninterrupted access to nitre earth from the tropics, had the result that British gunpowder was acknowledged as being finer and of higher power than the French.

Synthetic saltpetre is derived from human or animal urine whose main component is urea (H_2NCONH_2), which is metabolised by micro-organisms such as *Micrococcus urea* to ammonium nitrate, which reacts with sodium, potassium, magnesium or calcium salts (predominantly the chloride) to form the nitrate salt. The average yield was 0.75–1kg of saltpetre per 100kg of earth.

The usual method of separating saltpetre was to filter boiling water through a mix of nitrate-bearing earth and wood ash resulting in a liquid containing potassium nitrate with the unwanted inorganic salts and dirt left behind. In this way the highly hygroscopic calcium and magnesium nitrate – the main culprit for spoiling gunpowder – would be removed as their practically insoluble carbonate, as shown in Table 10.2.[381] Potassium nitrate is highly soluble in hot water (247g/100ml at 100°C) while the less soluble salts sediment and the predominantly organic materials were skimmed off the surface. The remaining liquid was cooled causing the potassium nitrate to crystallise because it is far less soluble in cool water with the solubility reduced to 13.3g/100ml at 0°C. The almost unchanged solubility of sodium chloride between 0°C (35.7g/100ml) and 100°C (39.12g/100ml) keeps the undesirable sodium chloride in solution while the nitrates precipitate to the bottom of the vessel. The crude brown saltpetre after the first extraction contained 88% potassium nitrate, and required three more recrystallisations before being pure enough for gunpowder manufacture with less than 0.2% sodium chloride.

From 1665, a private company (Fermes des Poudres) managed gunpowder production in France. In 1775, a new state enterprise *(Regie des Poudres et Saltpetres)* under the direct control of the Ministry of Finance took over gunpowder production. In 1792 France was blockaded, thus cutting the imports of saltpetre, so had to produce it from nitre pits; the quality of French gunpowder was therefore relatively poor, particularly in 1814. In January 1794, France was divided into eight districts for the production of saltpetre. In 1800, Napoleon transferred the supervision of gunpowder production from the Ministry of Finance to the Ministry of War. The Imperial gunpowder organisation spread out from France into the annexed territories including Amsterdam, Rome, the Kingdom of Naples, Westphalia, Spain and the Illyrian Provinces.[382]

The Austrians obtained saltpetre from the soil of part of Lower Hungary. Russia obtained saltpetre from Poland.

The composition of gunpowder from its three ingredients – 75:12:13, corresponding to $2KNO_3$:S:3C – gives the simple equation below:

$$2KNO_3 + S + 3C \rightarrow K_2S + N_2 + 3CO_2$$

When gunpowder is ignited, a huge amount of gas is given off (carbon dioxide and nitrogen) leaving mainly potassium sulphide residue. However, the combustion of gunpowder particularly within a confined space eludes description even by more complex equations with solid residue including potassium carbonate, potassium sulphate, sodium chloride, soot and sulphur.

The method of manufacture rather than the mixture ratio has the greater influence upon the burn rate of gunpowder. Increasing the sulphur content makes the powder keep better. Charcoal is never pure, so includes variable amounts of moisture. The purity of the potassium nitrate is by far the most important factor in effecting the combustion of gunpowder; impurities of sodium chloride and calcium nitrate are very detrimental to its combustion. In addition, the grain size influences the speed of combustion.

In a gun, the pressures generated by the burning gases reach a peak after about 2 calibres (about 10–15m/s) and fall quickly at 4–6 calibres. Artillery-grade powder was coarser than that used for smallarms because cannon required a superior propellant, and a lower initial pressure curve also avoided the threat of rupture. Interestingly, rougher gunpowder burns slower (at 1.0–1.1m/s) than smoother samples (at 0.6–0.8m/s).[383]

Sir William Congreve Snr reported that during the period between 1 January 1789 and 31 August 1810 the British government manufactured and purchased 649,388 barrels of powder, and interestingly 327,750 barrels (50.47%) were returned as unserviceable, to be remade or broken down to recover the potassium nitrate.[384]

IGNITION SYSTEMS

During the Napoleonic period guns were fired by ignition of the main powder charge via priming in the vent, and of the two main methods of priming employed – loose powder, or a priming tube – the latter became almost universal in use. The earliest priming tubes were goose quills either filled with gunpowder, or with a length of quickmatch passed through them. In France, Marshal de Saxe adopted the quill filled with a fine gunpowder mixture in the 1740s. This reached Britain by 1755; and by 1759 tin tubes were in use. The earliest use of ready-made fuses in the Polish service appears to have been by Oberst Geisler during the 1770s; and fuses made from copper tubes were introduced in the Austrian artillery at Oberst Kark Rouvroy's (1750–1816) suggestion in 1780. In Britain, the Royal Navy adopted the flintlock to fire its cannon in the 1780s; Alexander Dickson urged its adoption for field guns, but this was not done until the 1820s.

The composition used in the priming tubes was virtually uniform across Europe. Waxed cartridge-paper, tin or copper sheet measuring 140mm by 50mm was rolled to form a hollow tube. This was filled with fine gunpowder soaked in alcohol (ethanol) and mixed into a fine paste; then a fine bronze wire was passed through the composition, creating an air space down the length of the tube. The end of the tube was filled with the paste and then sealed with a piece of waxed paper tied with string. The French tubes had two 'ears' of quickmatch inserted into the end for better ignition.

The portfire was the main means of lighting the priming tube; this consisted of a much larger waxed paper tube filled with a varying mix of mealed gunpowder, sulphur and saltpetre. They were first introduced to Britain before 1710, to France by 1732, and Liechtenstein introduced them to Austrian service in 1753.

- The British portfire composition in *c.*1750 was: 2.7kg saltpetre, 0.9kg sulphur, and 0.45kg mealed gunpowder combined with linseed oil to make a paste, i.e. 75:24:1 potassium nitrate: sulphur: carbon. The other carbon source was of course the linseed oil. By 1780, the composition was altered to create a faster and cleaner-burning composition: 0.11g saltpetre, 0.45kg sulphur and 0.97kg mealed gunpowder combined with linseed oil, i.e. 56:37:7 potassium nitrate: sulphur: carbon.
- French portfires in *c.*1765 used a similar composition: *(Recipe 1)* 170g saltpetre, 57g sulphur and 85g priming powder, i.e. 75:21.5:3.5 potassium nitrate: sulphur: carbon. *(Recipe 2)* 1.88kg saltpetre, 0.85kg sulphur, 0.34kg priming powder, i.e. 70.4:28.4:1.4 potassium nitrate: sulphur: carbon.

Table 10.4: Ignition systems

Country	Ignition system	Date adopted
Austria	Copper tube filled with fine gunpowder mixture	1780
Britain	Tin or paper tube filled with fine gunpowder mixture	1757
France	Quill or paper tube filled with fine gunpowder mixture	1740s
Italy	Fuses	unknown
Hanover	Flintlocks	1795
Poland	Copper tube filled with fine gunpowder mixture	1770s
Portugal	Tin or paper tube filled with fine gunpowder mixture	1808
Prussia	Paper or copper tube filled with fine gunpowder mixture	1807
Italy	Flintlocks	1808
Russia	Fuses	unknown
Spain	Quill or paper tube filled with fine gunpowder mixture	unknown

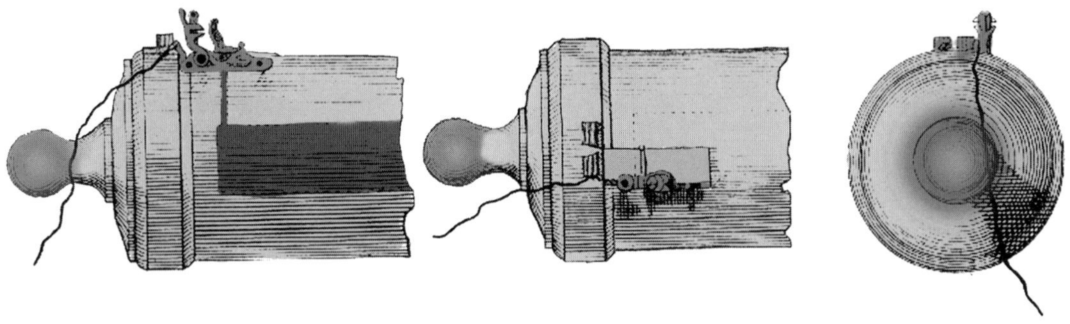

Hanoverian flintlock system. (After Scharnhorst, 1806)

The slowmatch was the old means of firing a gun, and by the 19th century it was relegated to being the source of constant combustion from which the portfires were lit, i.e. with a length smouldering ready to hand on a linstock thrust into the ground near the gun lines. Britain abandoned it as the means of lighting the priming tube in 1788. In Britain, slowmatch was made from hemp cord ('hempen slack') boiled in lees of wine (sediment from fermentation of alcohol). French slowmatch was made from hemp cord that had been soaked in vinegar (acetic acid), saltpetre and brandy, or lees of wine. When dry it was rubbed with mealed powder.

Quickmatch was prepared in a similar way to slowmatch, but instead of hemp the basis was cotton, boiled in a composition of saltpetre, gunpowder and spirits of wine. A British recipe of 1760 contained 0.68kg pulverised saltpetre, 4.54kg mealed powder, 2.27 litres of spirits of wine (ethanol), and 1.70–3.98 litres of water. Quickmatch was also used in French fuses, and in some cases two lengths of quickmatch were passed down a quill tube to make a rudimentary priming tube.

Common Shell Fuses

Fuses for bombs and shells were made of strong, dry wood that was free from knots. According to Gribeauval the best woods for the purpose were linden, lime, ash or very dry alder, though beech could be used if none of these could be obtained. The fuses were turned in a lathe from squared wood, to fit exactly the conical section of the vent left in the case of the bomb. The fuse was filled with a tight-rammed composition of priming powder, saltpetre and sulphur. The top of the fuse was furnished with matches, and each end of the fuse was waterproofed with a mixture of yellow wax and mutton suet.

If the fuse was to be stored away from a magazine or in a caisson, four match threads were neatly arranged on the waterproof cap, and the fuse was then capped with a piece of parchment soaked in brandy, held in placed with lukewarm capping wax. When the wax dried, the portion from the extremity of the fuse to where it touched the body of the bomb was dipped into a molten mixture of black pitch and resin, or black pitch and linseed oil. The outside of the wooden tube was cut with marks at intervals, spaced to indicate half-seconds of burning time, as a guide for the fuse-cutter in the gun crew. The shell was placed in the bore of the howitzer or mortar at an angle to ensure that the fuse was ignited by the propellant charge when the piece was fired.

ARTILLERY AMMUNITION

Cartridges

The majority of field artillery systems of the Napoleonic period used fixed cartridges of propellant, as opposed to loose powder. In Britain the use of cartridges, for the Royal Navy at least, began in the middle of the 17th century, when paper was issued to make cartridges; by 1700 pre-prepared canvas bags were issued to make up into cartridges. Canvas cartridges had a tendency to attract damp but, more importantly, left a great deal of debris in the gun tube. To remedy this, parchment cartridges

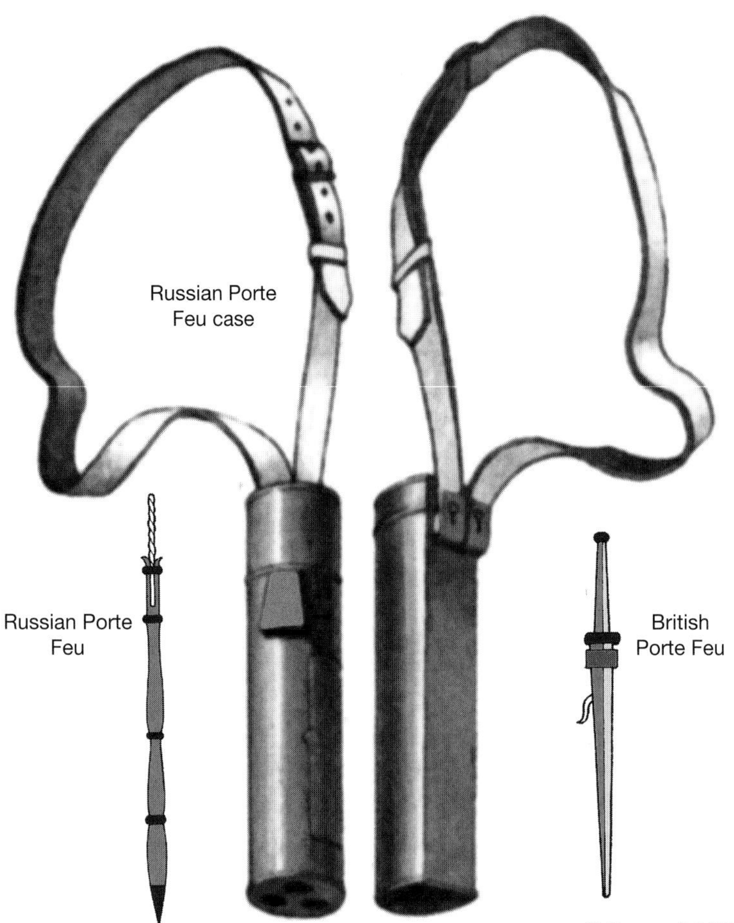

Portfires and their carrying cases; these were made from either leather or copper, to make them both waterproof and flame-retardant.

were adopted in 1720; and from 1755 both the army and navy used flannel, which was essentially self-consuming and left almost no debris or residue in the gun tube after detonation. In 1790, William Congreve Snr argued for the abolition of the fixed charge and also of paper cartridges; he noted that the latter left considerable detritus in the tube after firing, which was 'very dangerous', and also made the sponge stick in the bore.

Flannel cartridges were used by most countries; France using fine serge. Practical tests carried out by L'Association Britannique de la Garde Impériale have shown that with either material some remnants remain in the gun tube; if not removed with the worm or bristle-sponge these will build up over time and cause misfires, by preventing the cartridge from seating at the base of the gun tube.

The cartridge was attached to its projectile – whether roundshot, shell or canister – by tying the bag to an intermediate disc-shaped softwood (pine) sabot or shoe, often grooved for this purpose. Gun captain Johann Haselwander found a usable cartridge grease in 1755, although it was later replaced by an oil covering. Guns were swabbed with water, and at Kolin in 1756 there were problems with the water/grease mix; this formed a gum which built up on the inner surfaces of the gun tube, and reduced the diameter of the bore sufficiently to prevent ammunition being rammed down, thus rendering the piece useless until this encrustation had been scraped out. Some countries, including Russia, retained greased rather than oiled cartridges, and the guns were issued with scrapers specifically designed to scour off this deposit.

(Left to right:) Pass-ball or gauge, callipers, and roundshot attached to their wooden sabots with tin strapping.

Roundshot

The archetypal artillery ammunition, the iron cannonball, was first introduced in the late 16th century. Iron roundshot was cast in clay moulds and then reheated in a kiln to cherry red. It was then placed upon a concave anvil, where it was hammered by water-powered concave hammers. This increased the mass, and ensured that it was spherical and of the correct calibre for the ordnance. France used waterwheel-powered drop-hammers, which were subsequently adopted in America.

Roundshot were checked for shape and size using a pass-ball, couble-square and cylinder, and final checking for size was carried out using callipers. The roundshot were finally polished to make them uniformly smooth, and then painted with red lead to prevent them from rusting. Due to the nature of this process roundshot could not be produced in the field, but in 1781 the Hanoverian artillery officer Schwependick developed a mobile kiln for field manufacture of ammunition; this was further developed by Josef Smola in Austria in 1808.

The first fixed ammunition used by the French consisted of bagged powder with a round fixed to the front, and this was soon copied by the Austrians in 1748. In the Napoleonic period the spherical projectiles were normally attached to the wooden sabot by crossed tin straps.

Canister (Case-shot)

Canister shot had its origins in medieval 'hail-shot'. The canister was made from sheet tin, rolled into a cylinder with the ends crimped over and soldered to secure the top and base plates. In France the canister had wrought-iron top and base plates covered in tin; they were also slightly conical, and had a rope

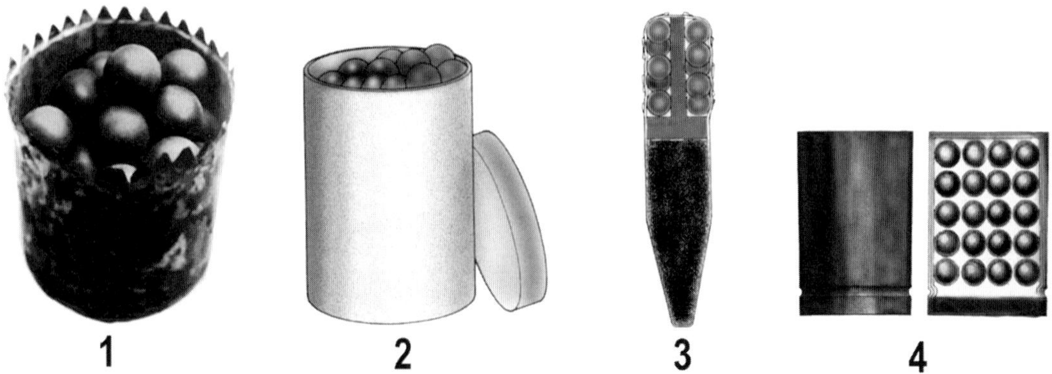

(1) Russian large canister, with lid removed; (2) British light canister; (3) Russian canister for a unicorn gun-howitzer; (4) Austrian canister.

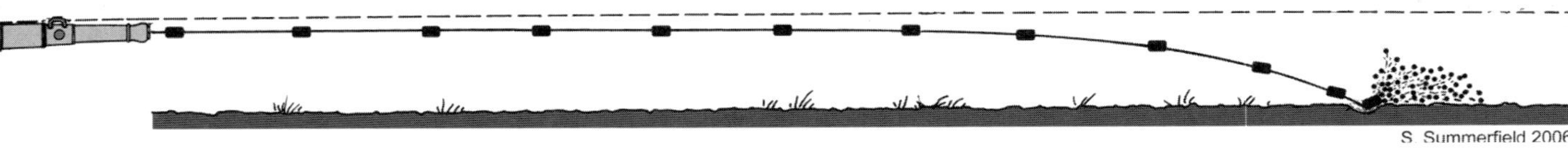

Table 10.5: Table 10.5: Russian tests of light canister
(Note: Rounds were fired at a pinewood panel 1m wide × 2.2m high × 20mm thick.)

	Number of hits on target						
Range	**200 m**	**250 m**	**300 m**	**350 m**	**400 m**	**450 m**	**500 m**
12-pdr Heavy (151 balls)		40 (26%)	22 (15%)	15 (10%)	10 (7%)	6 (4%)	2 (1%)
12-pdr Light (132 balls)	46 (35%)	34 (26%)	19 (14%)	12 (9%)	8 (6%)	4 (3%)	–
6-pdr (99 balls)	32 (32%)	24 (24%)	16 (16%)	8 (8%)	5 (5%)	1 (1%)	–
½ pud Unicorn (151 balls)	53 (35%)	40 (26%)	22 (15%)	15 (10%)	9 (6%)	5 (3%)	2 (1%)
¼ pud Unicorn (151 balls)	44 (29%)	26 (24%	17 (11%)	10 (7%)	7 (5%)	3 (2%)	–
¼ pud Unicorn HA (132 balls)	40 (30%)	22 (17%)	14 (11%)	9 (7%)	7 (5%)	3 (2%)	–
3-pdr Unicorn (38 balls)	10 (26%)	4 (11%)	2 (5%)	–	–	–	–

handle secured to them for ease of handling. The canister was filled with iron balls packed in sawdust; when fired from the gun the canister ruptured upon impact with the ground, and the impact velocity discharged the contents and shards of the casing in all directions – the effect on troops at close range was like that of a giant shotgun. Towards the close of the 18th century a stronger canister round was developed, made from steel in the case of Russia, and France used some iron canisters.

It was imperative that the base of the canister was firmly secured to 'prevent the charge from going through' and the canister rupturing prematurely in the gun tube.[385] French canister shot used by the field armies was constructed from a tin (or in some cases iron) cylinder to the following dimensions:

- 12-pdr: Length 369mm, diameter 116mm, wrought-iron baseplate 7.9mm
- 8-pdr: Length 330mm, diameter 100mm, base 6.8mm
- 4-pdr: Length 264mm, diameter 80mm, base 6.6mm.

These canisters were attached to wooden sabots, which prevented the charge from rupturing the canister in the gun tube. Small-calibre canister could have a fixed charge, e.g. the French 4-pdr had the serge powder cartridge attached. For the larger-calibre field pieces the charge was put in separately. The earlier forms (i.e. pre-Gribeauval) had a tendency to merely crumple or flatten upon impact, therefore being next to useless. Gribeauval stated that 'the shot will infallibly produce twice as much effect as one ball, even on the supposition that the ball should take three men in a line; thanks to this new cartouche, we are able to do three times the execution that was formerly done by our artillery.'

Canister was fired from both guns and howitzers. In Britain, following experience in America since the 1750s, guns were generally double-shotted (i.e. loaded with two canisters) for maximum effect at point-blank range. These were used to great effect against advancing French heavy cavalry at Waterloo; in one case the entire front rank of a cavalry charge was taken down, and none of the following troops could (or would) make their way over the heaving pile of men and horses to their front. Cavalry naturally represented a target twice the size of formed infantry, so the effects were noticeably greater.

Canister had little effect beyond 600m for the 12-pdr, and 500m for the 6-pdr; it had to be used below 400m to be really effective.[386] The Russian Major-General Kutaisov wrote that canister was to be used only between 100 and 320m.[387] In order to discover its effects the Russian artillery carried out a series of tests in 1807. Table 10.5 shows that at 400m the 12-pdr and 6-pdr canister had the same effect, if the latter's faster rate of fire was taken into account. Even at 500m the difference in effect between 12-pdr and 6-pdr canister was negligible; beyond this the effect of canister diminishes greatly. A Prussian manual of 1822 noted that 'Without doubt, the greater part of the military is of the opinion that the effect of canister is far more fearful and murderous than it really is.' Canister was not the most appropriate weapon against narrow formations; it did possess some advantage at close range, where there was no need to aim the piece as accurately as for roundshot, and so it could be fired at a faster rate. The Russian Guard Artillery officer Velyaminov wrote in 1807 that for greater effect the Austrians should have fired roundshot rather than canister at the French crossing the bridge at Lodi in 1796.[388]

Roundshot was at least two to three times more accurate than canister even at less than 500m. The 6-pdr may not have been as accurate as the 12-pdr in terms of roundshot, but its canister was as effective. Canister's lack of accuracy was off-set by being able to hit the target with a greater weight of shot, and thus achieve more hits, if used at the correct ranges. For instance, at the battle of Friedland (14 June 1807) General Sénarmont made an audacious 'artillery charge', advancing his guns and firing roundshot at Russian infantry from as close as 200m, before switching to canister when the range closed still further.

General Allix estimated that three-quarters of all canister balls went uselessly into the ground, and that most of the remainder passed over the target. Roundshot was the most effective ammunition type against dense formations, and possessed sufficient kinetic energy to pass through dozens of men. Canister lacked the penetrative capabilities of roundshot, and rarely inflicted casualties beyond the front

Common shell – (left), section, with fuse in place.

rank. The Russian General Okounef noted that canister had more effect in lowering morale than killing infantry, and had the largest effect when fired against cavalry; notwithstanding the account of Waterloo, quoted above, Okounef claimed that it panicked the horses and disrupted the movements of the cavalry, rather than causing many casualties.[389]

Common Shell

Shell was essentially a hollow cast-iron sphere, filled with a bursting charge. French-made shells had a thicker, slightly flatter base and were thinner at the top; this meant that the shell did not shatter upon being fired, and that it would theoretically land bottom-first.

In Britain, common shell was fired by both howitzers and guns. The 12-pdr field gun fired the same 111.8mm shell as the 12-pdr carronade. In 1802, each horse artillery 12-pdr was issued 14 shells. The shells were fired at a lower trajectory than was the French practice, using ground-grazing ricochets; the shell would have the same effect as a roundshot against massed infantry even if it did not explode, and if it did then it caused even more casualties. In 1792 William Congreve Snr called the common shell a weapon 'powerful enough to dismount any piece of ordnance that an enemy may bring into the field.'[390]

Shells were transported empty and filled either before battle or as needed when being fired. In British service the shell was loaded with its bursting charge immediately before use, by two specialist gunners who also set the fuse. The propellant charge was first loaded into the chamber of the howitzer or mortar and rammed home; the shell

Russian M1805 5-pud mortar; calibre 335mm, length 111cm, weight 1494kg, range 2050 metres. This weapon fired exploding shell (right picture, top centre), case-shot grenades or shrapnel (top right), case-shot in a steel canister (top left) and solid roundshot (bottom centre). (Dr S. Efimov)

Spherical case-shot or shrapnel, devised in Russia in the 1750s and later copied by Prussia, Saxony, France and Britain.

attached to its sabot was then inserted. When fired from a mortar, the large bomb was lowered in using two large hooks connected to rings on the casing. The men serving the howitzers wore special canvas gauntlets akin to flash guards. The British howitzer drill argued for a sheepskin to be shoved down the gun tube after the charge had been loaded and while the shell was being prepared, to prevent any premature discharges.

The Austrian artillery officer von Tielke believed that common shell was more harmful than roundshot; if it could be fired with ricochet, its kinetic energy would force the shell into the middle of a formation of troops prior to bursting.[391] The effectiveness of shell against a body of men was attested by Karl Rohrig, who served at the battle of Leipzig (16–19 October 1813). He noted that his battalion, drawn up in square, sustained more than 100 casualties from a battery of enemy guns and howitzers; one shell which landed in the middle of the square exploded some time later, wounding several men.[392] Russian doctrine was also to set the fuse so that the shell exploded soon after the first graze when it bounced into the enemy formation.

Spherical (Shrapnel's) Case-shot

Canister did not always rupture upon impact; consequently, in the 1750s, Shuvalov of Russia developed a form of exploding canister, which was copied in Prussia and Saxony by 1759, then later by Hanover in the 1770s and France in the 1780s. A combination of a shell and canister was developed, originally called 'case-shot grenades' but

Table 10.6: Russian tests with spherical case, 1807

Distance	Rounds fired	Penetrating hits	Did not penetrate	Total hits on target	Total no. balls per round	Missed the target
230m	10	28	4.7	32.7	50	17.3
300m	15	27	6.8	33.8	50	16.2
400m	17	20	9.3	29.3	50	20.7
470m	11	10.5	7.1	17.6	50	32.4
530m	19	14.3	9	23.3	50	26.7
600m	13	6.1	9	15.1	50	34.9
700m	18	6.2	5,6	11.8	50	38.2

later (and ever since) known as shrapnel after its English progenitor. The round was a shell containing cast-iron or lead projectiles mixed in with the bursting charge. Upon detonation of the charge the small projectiles would shower the enemy, and far more efficiently than conventional canister. Its great disadvantage was that it tended to explode prematurely, a fault not fully rectified until after the Napoleonic wars.[393]

Lieutenant George Henry Shrapnel RA experimented with various means of increasing the range and usefulness of canister-shot. He noted that not all canisters ruptured on impact with the ground, and therefore introduced a bursting charge 'sufficient to rupture the case, which has less thickness of metal than the shell'. This is confirmed by an American artillery manual which states that it 'produces the same effect as the canister, and can be used for much greater distances'.[394] Shrapnel reasoned that if the canister could be made more aerodynamic it would carry further, and that if it had a charge to burst it open the contents would carry on with the 'remaining velocity' of the shell. If the point on the trajectory at which the shell burst was well chosen, the balls would reach the target with lethal velocity.

It is unclear when Shrapnel first arrived at his ideas; but in 1813 he wrote 'Notwithstanding it is nearly 30 years ago since I first exhibited the firing of balls in tin metal cases...', so presumably he first presented his prototypes in the mid-1780s. In 1787, when stationed at Gibraltar, Shrapnel demonstrated to an impressed Major-General O'Hara 'a new method of extending the use of canister shot, to the utmost range of ordnance'. In February 1792 Shrapnel made proposals to the Board of Ordnance for firing canister and grapeshot 'in a more collected manner'. A committee to examine his proposals was convened by the Board, but its findings are unknown; it was not until June 1803 that there was a cautious recommendation to the Board of Ordnance in favour of Shrapnel's case-shot.

An order was placed with the Carron Foundry in August 1803, and rigorous tests were carried out on the new ammunition. The initial design was obviously faulty; there were numerous instances of the shell bursting in the gun tube, and it was found that the cases were too thick. Shrapnel had initially used those cast for common shells, but quickly adopted a very thin casing which was easily ruptured by the small bursting charge.

Shrapnel's case-shot was used by British forces in South America (1806–07), Italy (1806) and Egypt (1807), and against the Danes at Copenhagen (1806). Wellington praised the use of the shot at Rolica and Vimiero (17 and 21 August 1808). However, at Fuentes de Oñoro (3–5 May 1811) it proved to be largely ineffective for both British and Portuguese artillery. On that occasion Wellington was damning, saying that 'they inflict trifling wounds, and kill nobody'. The reason for the round's lack of success in Portuguese hands was probably lack of training.

In 1806 the French captured part of the ammunition train of the British artillery, and Napoleon ordered tests to be carried out on the spherical case-shot recovered. In 1811 a British 5½in howitzer with two ammunition wagons was captured, and General Eble was instructed to study and copy the case-shot among their load (this was despite the Board of Ordnance having decreed that Shrapnel's case-shot should not be used if there was a chance that it could fall into enemy hands). The French report placed great emphasis on the desirability of bursting the shot on the first graze and projecting the contents as far as possible.

During the War of 1812 Shrapnel's case-shot saw considerable use, and in contradiction of the French report British officers serving in Canada estimated that it produced most effect if it burst 40ft (12m) above and in front of the target. These rounds were part of the standard ammunition allocation for horse and foot artillery in 1813, although they were not perfected until after 1815.

In 1807, Russian tests showed their own form of exploding case-shot to be a highly effective weapon; it had increased range and accuracy over standard canister-shot, and the contents spread further.

Incendiary and Illumination Rounds

Howitzers also fired 'carcass-projectiles' to set fire to buildings and other suitable targets. The round was oblong in shape, made from canvas reinforced

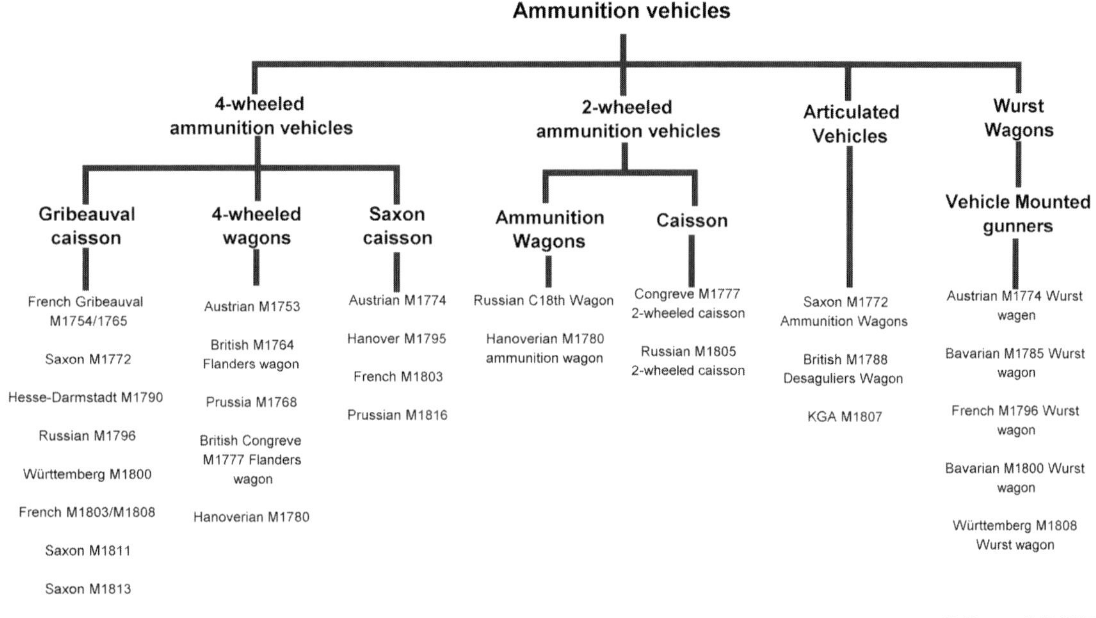

Caissons and ammunition wagons.

with iron hoops and bound with cord. It contained a mixture of turpentine, resin, tallow, sulphur, saltpetre and antimony. The shell could burn for up to 12 minutes, depending on the calibre, and was virtually impossible to extinguish.

The Russian incendiary shell was a hollow-cast cannon ball, with three holes in the casing. It was filled with a mixture of 12 parts gunpowder, 12 parts wood pulp, 7.5 parts resin, 2.5 parts potassium nitrate, 1 part candle fat, 0.5 parts wax, 0.5 parts rosine and 0.06 parts finely chopped flax. The three openings in the shell each contained a fuse; the entire shell was covered with paper, and then with a resin-impregnated linen mat tied with a criss-cross of quickmatch. One of the fuses was passed through the mat and paper so that it would be ignited on discharge.

Russian illumination rounds, like those of the French, were composed of a wooden shell body with a metal baseplate, filled with 1 part antimony, 3 parts portfire mixture, 16 parts sulphur and 20 parts saltpetre. The portfire mixture had 16 parts saltpetre, 4 parts sulphur, 3 parts gunpowder and 0.5 parts carbon.

CAISSONS AND AMMUNITION WAGONS

Of fundamental importance to the way in which a battery could operate was the movement of munitions, using two- or four-wheeled caissons or other vehicles. The four-wheeled caissons can be classified as Gribeauval or Saxon types. These were large, specially designed carts to transport quantities of ammunition with the artillery, and most armies' regulations strictly forbade exposing them to enemy fire. The French caissons carried far more ammunition than those of other nations, and so could not manoeuvre at anything faster than the walk; they tended to bog down in muddy conditions and overturn on uneven ground, and were deemed too cumbersome for use with horse artillery. The horse artillery of other nations were not encumbered by heavy four-horse caissons; Austrian, British and Russian two-wheeled ammunition wagons were of lightweight designs and could manoeuvre at speed.

There were a number of circumstances where the gun-mounted ammunition chests of the French could not be re-supplied with ammunition in time

French M1765 Gribeauval caisson, as used for all calibres of field guns, as well as to convey infantry ammunition. With minor alterations this was still in use until almost 1830. (Musée de l'Armée; photographs Paul Dawson)

(e.g. Dennewitz, Katzbach and Leipzig in 1813), so paralysing or delaying the movement of artillery. At Vauchamp (14 February 1814) the French army surprised the Prussians with a cavalry attack that should have been supported by horse artillery, but the battery could not move the caissons over the rough ground, and so failed to advance for fear that it would soon be out of ammunition. At Waterloo, the battle did not start early in the morning because the mud prevented General Drouot from bringing up the ammunition caissons.

Gribeauval-type Caissons

The M1732 system caissons were based upon the M1697 St Remy designs. With more mobile field pieces it became necessary to increase the mobility of the ammunition caissons destined to supply them. In 1754 new caissons were designed by Gribeauval, and these were later adopted into the Gribeauval system with only slight modifications.

In 1761, Manson modified the Gribeauval caisson to strengthen it by a more logical and convenient distribution of the internal fittings, and by a more secure mode of shutting. The caissons were also lightened: the original design weighed 895kg. The M1765 Gribeauval caisson had a normal load not exceeding 595kg, and the interior set-up was such that they could be altered at will to carry various ammunition types in differing quantities. The large wheels at the rear were the same size as the 8- and 12-pdr gun wheels, so these could be readily exchanged – they ran on the same axle.

The Gribeauval-designed caisson and the accompanying ordnance were used in all Bourbon possessions including France, Spain and Naples. They were also adopted in Saxony in 1769, Hesse-Darmstadt in 1792, Russia in 1796, Württemberg in 1800, and Bavaria in 1801. The caisson design was modified in France in 1808, and the M1808 caisson remained in service until 1827.

Saxon-type Caissons

The Saxon M1810 caisson was very similar to the French M1803. The ammunition boxes were

Watercolour of a Saxon M1769 ammunition wagon, based on the M1765 Gribeauval caisson. (Joerg Titzer)

designed to fit both the limber and caisson, so rather than moving loose munitions as in the French practice, the empty boxes were simply off-loaded from the limber and full boxes loaded on. This made re-arming a battery quicker and safer, and was soon copied by other states, principally by France and Bavaria.

The Saxon M1813 ammunition wagon was a Gribeauval-style caisson and was constructed to replace the losses in Russia. The 12-pdr ammunition wagon carried 65 balls and 10 canister rounds in 15 boxes, and the 6-pdr wagon carried 130 balls and 20 canister rounds also in 15 boxes. In this period it was common for reserve supplies of infantry and cavalry small-arms ammunition to be transported along with the artillery ammunition. Infantry ammunition wagons carried 15,840 cartridges in 22 boxes, with 2,400 musket flints; cavalry wagons carried 18,000 cartridges in 22 boxes with 2,500 flints. The empty wagon weighed 900kg; the empty weights of the boxes were 12-pdr ball (5.6kg), 12-pdr canister (6.5kg), 6-pdr ball (5.4kg), 6-pdr canister (6.1kg), and musket cartridge boxes (4.7kg).

Four-wheeled Ammunition Wagons

The Austrian M1753 ammunition wagon was based on the 174cm universal axle made of elm, with just two types of wheels for all gun carriages and rolling stock. The immediate reserve ammunition was kept some 30m behind the battery when in action. The howitzers and 6-, 12- and 18-pdr guns had larger four-wheeled carts with four-horse teams. Under enemy fire, one ammunition cart per two-gun section was regarded as sufficient. All items of equipment were marked with the gun's number. Every two guns carried a spare drag rope. In action, the immediate reserve ammunition would be replenished by a steady stream of wagons from the park, these vehicles being of the two-wheeled type as they were more mobile.

A single 6-pdr cannon in Austrian foot and horse artillery use had 94 roundshot and 26 canister rounds immediately available in limber boxes and ammunition carts. A 12-pdr cannon had 123 roundshot and 40 canister; a 7-pdr howitzer had 12 canister and 72 shells in ammunition vehicles. The rest of the ammunition was carried in the reserve park. On average, each gun had an allocation of 130–180 rounds.

Saxon M1769 ammunition wagon. (Joerg Titzer)

The British M1764 or 'Flanders pattern' wagon was a four-wheeled vehicle with wickerwork sides, covered with a painted canvas tilt secured over wooden hoops. The vehicle saw active service in America (1775–83), Flanders (1793–95) and Egypt (1801). By 1788 it was considered obsolete, due to the small size of its wheels and the fact that it could only have single draft. In 1801 Major-General Lawson said that 'no carriage appears to want reform more than the common artillery wagon: there is too much of it merely for carrying ammunition, and it is too narrow for baggage or bulky stores'. Lawson noted that if they were to remain the same size then the wasted space should be put to good use by carrying spare parts for guns, tools and other equipment. Due to the way they harnessed to the horses, all the weight bore on the wheel-horse, which caused them to have sore backs or to suffocate. In 1802 Adye said that the park and battalion wagons had not yet been altered from the oldest establishment but that the horse artillery was using the new limber-wagons.

Austrian horse artillery (left) and foot artillery (right) M1774 caissons, c.*1823. (Steven H. Smith)*

The British M1777 Congreve wagon was a modified version of the M1764, notably by having the same size front and rear wheels. Congreve stated that a large four-wheeled wagon was issued to every two guns. Each wagon carried, besides ammunition, a gyn or crane, fork levers, entrenching tools, etc. The Hanoverian M1780 wagon was based on the Flanders wagon used in Britain to support each pair of guns. These were found to be unsuitable and were replaced in 1795 after the Flanders campaign (*see below*).

The Prussian M1768 caissons were larger than the Gribeauval type, and were drawn by four horses. The spare wheels and carriages were carried in so-called 'rack wagons' drawn by four horses. Each battery had only four M1768 caissons and two rack wagons, compared to a French battery with 12–18 caissons. The Prussian caissons were deployed up to 50m behind the limbers. Ammunition supply according to the 1809 regulations was as follows:

6-pdr foot battery: 6× 6-pdr guns and 2× 7-pdr howitzers – 2× cannon caissons, 2× howitzer caissons and 2 × rack wagons.

12-pdr foot battery: 6× 12-pdr guns and 2× 10-pdr howitzers – 6× cannon caissons, 4× howitzer caissons and 2× rack wagons.

6-pdr horse battery: 6× 6-pdr guns and 2× 7-pdr howitzers – 4× cannon caissons, 2× howitzer caissons and 2× rack wagons.

The Prussian M1816 ammunition wagon carried 90 rounds of ball, 17 of light canister, 8 of heavy canister, 2.5lb (1136g) of gunpowder, 127 fuses, 25 portfires and a slowmatch.

The Saxon M1765 infantry ammunition wagon was copied by the Austrians as the M1774 and by the Hanoverians as the M1795 after the poor showing of Hanover's version of the Flanders wagon. The King's German Artillery used the Hanoverian M1795 ammunition wagon until 1807.

Two-wheeled Ammunition Vehicles

The Austrian M1753 two-wheeled ammunition cart was assigned to a 3-pdr, and to every two cavalry artillery guns until 1790 when the latter were replaced by 6× packhorses. The Hanoverian M1780 based on the Flanders wagon was used by the 3-pdr battalion guns.

In 1803, the two-wheeled Russian M1803 ammunition caisson based on the Congreve M1777 wagon was introduced; the four-wheeled caissons of the Gribeauval system had proved too heavy and unmanoeuvrable on rough terrain. An iron-bound wooden box covered with sheet iron was mounted on a two-wheeled limber, with shafts for the horses rather than a sweep bar. The box was divided into cells for the projectiles by a wooden frame: for 12-pdrs it had 40 nests and six compartments for tools, spare fuses, portfires, linstocks, slowmatch, etc. The 6-pdr box had 51 nests, 2 large and 4 small compartments for the

British M1777 Flanders wagon, with standard wheels at front and rear. (Authors' collection)

British ammunition wagon in 1814, showing wheels of different sizes still in use. (Authors' collection)

Saxon M1772 infantry ammunition wagon, copied by Austria as their M1774 and Hanover as the M1795. The Hanoverian version was used by the King's German Artillery until 1807.

Model of the Hanoverian M1780 two-wheeled ammunition cart. (Courtesy the Trustees of the RAHT; photograph Steven H.Smith)

Saxon M1772 caisson for the 4-pdr Granatstück *– an early example of an articulated vehicle. (Joerg Titzer)*

slowmatch, fuses etc. The box for the 20-pdr (½-pud) unicorn had 40 nests; the 10-pdr (¼-pud), 54 nests; and the 3-pdr, 88 nests.

The ½-pud unicorn and 12-pdr cannon required three ammunition caissons pulled by three horses; the ¼-pud unicorn and 6-pdr gun required two three-horse caissons; the 3-pdr unicorn had only one two-horse caisson. On occasion a single horse might be required to move a caisson. In total – including the ammunition on the 6-pdr, ¼-pud unicorn and 3-pdr unicorn – there were 80 ball, 30 canister and 10 incendiary rounds for each 12-pdr; 90 ball and 30 canister for each 6-pdr; and 80 shells, 30 canister and 10 incendiary for each unicorn (the 3-pdr unicorn had 10 ball instead of the incendiary rounds). In battle the caissons were positioned 30 to 40m from the guns. According to the regulations, no more than two gunners were to remain next to a caisson during battle.

Articulated Ammunition Wagons

The Saxon M1772 ammunition wagon for the 4-pdr *Granatstück* (grenade-thrower) carried the ball and charges separately on an articulated vehicle.

British guns carried their ammunition in the side-boxes on the gun itself, in limber boxes and ammunition wagons. The side-boxes were only used when the ammunition wagons could not be sent with the gun. Each gun was provided with two ammunition wagons, plus one spare per half-battery for foot artillery or per division in the horse artillery. The British M1777 limber-caisson designed by William Congreve Snr could carry up to three ammunition boxes. Each gun had two such limber- caissons, with one acting as a limber proper and the other as the caisson.

This simple design was replaced by the M1788 Desaguliers four-wheeled articulated limber-

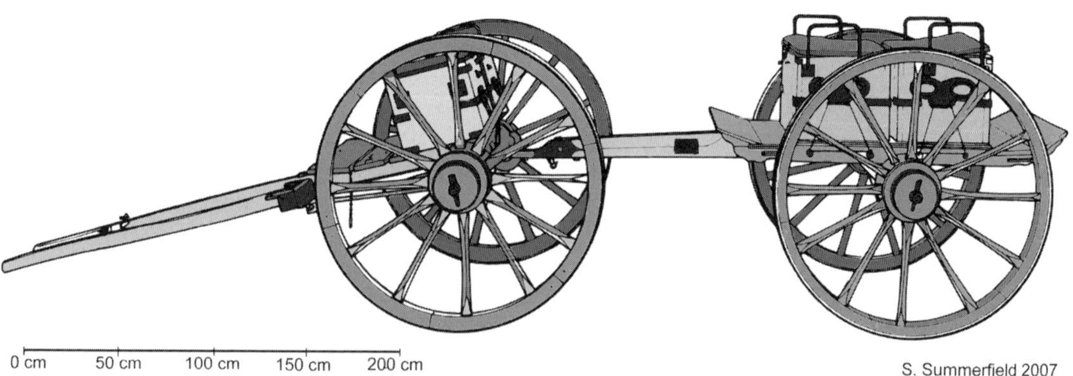

British M1788 Desaguliers articulated limber-wagon.

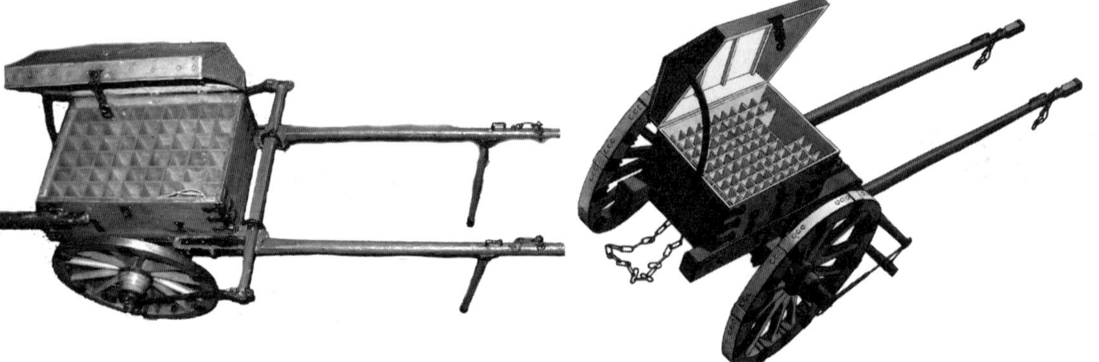

(Left) ⅙th scale model of the Russian M1803 ¼-pud two-wheeled caisson, with 54 nests for ammunition. (St Petersburg Engineers Museum; photograph Dr S. Efimov) (Right) Drawing of a 3-pdr unicorn caisson with 88 nests. (Authors' collection)

wagon, produced by coupling two limbers together. This permitted two gunners to ride on the limber boxes and four on the ammunition boxes at the rear, and was the logical conclusion of what Congreve had attempted to do some years before. The wagon also carried a spare set of shafts for the limber. Due to the universal nature of the Desaguliers wheels and axles it was possible to exchange wheels from various vehicles:

> To this is to be added the great simplicity they afford to the system of field artillery, the limbers being the same as those for the guns, the wheels the same for Light 6-pdr, for all ammunition limber-wagons, and for the forges and store carriages, and they will answer also for 9-pdr on an occasion. Indeed I believe they are quite strong enough for this nature, a 9-pdr with 6-pdr wheels, having for experiment been employed for a 12 month in one of the field batteries under my orders in France, and during that time the gun, three times a week, was marched 12 or 14 miles over the paved roads of that country.[395]

The Desaguliers wagons were far more mobile than the 1764 or Congreve vehicles, due to the large wheels and articulated design: 'The caisson has the same turning capacity and mobility as the gun carriage, so that it can follow the piece in all its manoeuvres if necessary.'[396] The ammunition boxes stowed on the limber-wagon were identical to those used on gun limbers, so re-supply was by simple replacement of empty boxes with full ones.

Model of Württemberg M1810 Wurst ammunition caisson, with a seat for four gunners and another two on the limber. (Rastatt Military Museum)

Wurst Wagons

In order to make moving men across a battlefield faster some countries, especially the lesser German states, developed the Wurst wagon design to carry both men and ammunition. The top of the caisson was covered with a seat of leather padded with horse hair, known as a Wurst seat. In some countries, such as Austria and Württemberg, the Wurst wagon concept was also applied to gun carriages themselves, to carry four or six gunners on the carriage-mounted ammunition boxes. In 1753 the Austrians were the first to experiment with the idea of mounting the gun crew on a vehicle.

The Austrian M1774 Wurst gun carriage of the horse artillery had a large ammunition locker which the gunners rode, by means of a padded leather seat and running boards. This had the advantage that fewer gunners had to ride, fewer horses were required, and the gun could be brought into action quicker.

In 1784, Jakob Manson in Strasbourg took a Gribeauval M1765 caisson and altered it so that six gunners could ride on the ammunition chest. The Bavarian M1785 Wurst wagon was used by the light artillery and was the same as that designed by Manson the previous year for the French army. These were replaced in 1800 by Bavarian M1800 Wurst wagons, also designed by Manson.

The French M1794 Wurst wagon was re-introduced by General Dorsner in 1794 for the Artillerie Légère. According to Adye, the M1794 wagon for the 8-pdr carried 58 roundshot or 30 shells for the 6.4in howitzer.[397] By 1801 most had been withdrawn and converted to carry doctors and medical orderlies. Writing in that year, General Gassendi noted that the Wurst could carry six gunners. Internally, the box had four compartments each subdivided into three; compartments 1 and 4 carried 15 shot and compartments 2 and 3, 18 shot, in total 66 rounds for an 8-pdr. The French Wurst wagon was reintroduced in 1811.

The Württemberg M1808 Wurst ammunition wagon, based on the French caisson, carried 104 rounds, and half the lid had a padded Wurst seat. The front wheels came from a standard 'A'-frame ammunition limber for the light (horse) artillery. In both foot and horse artillery two gunners could ride on the carriage on top of the padded tool box. In theory two more could be mounted on the limber, and in the horse artillery the rest of the gun crew were mounted on the caisson. The remainder of the rolling stock was of Austrian-inspired designs. This Wurst ammunition wagon was copied by Austria,

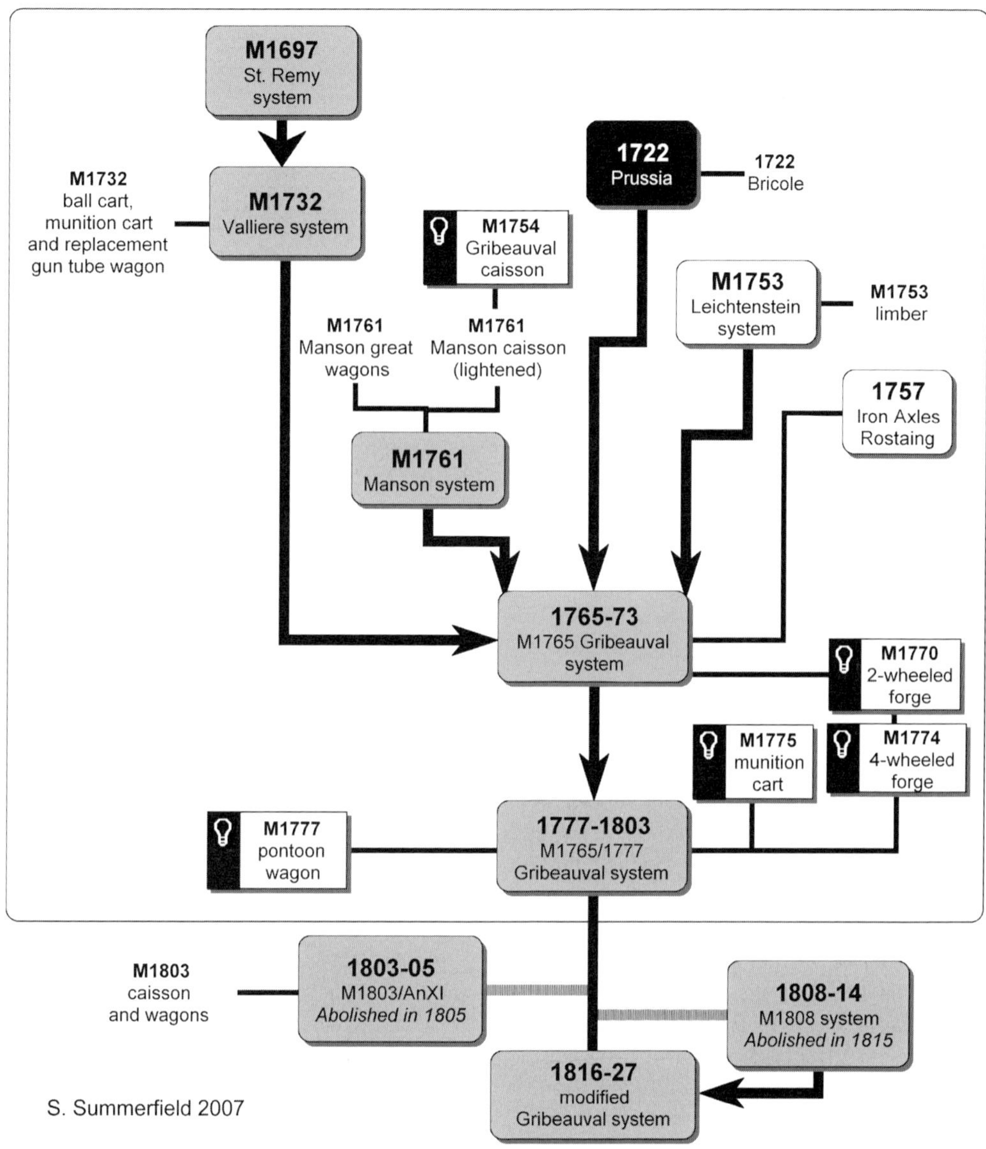

Origins of the Gribeauval rolling stock.

but was not introduced into their service until after the Napoleonic Wars.

The Württemberg M1810 Wurst ammunition wagon, introduced in September 1810, was designed by Karl Fredric Kerner, who had been the Commandant of Light Artillery since 1794. All new items of rolling stock and guns were built to his designs.

OTHER VEHICLES

As well as the caissons, an artillery battery would be accompanied by a bewildering array of other support vehicles, primarily wagons, some of which are described below.

Gribeauval Artillery Vehicles

The Gribeauval system was not an all-encompassing and radical change; it introduced new elements piecemeal, new vehicles being designed when existing material was found to be insufficient for the current needs of the army (*see* accompanying chart). The French M1732 rolling stock including the *charrette à boulets, charrette à munitions* (large and small), *chariot à canon* and the *triqueballe à vis de levage*, and these were all retained. The French M1761 'large wagons' of the artillery park were constructed to the designs of Manson, and were retained after the introduction of the Gribeauval system in 1765/1776.

In 1765, Gribeauval designed a two-wheeled field forge; that was altered to four wheels in 1774. At the same time he added an artificer's wagon that was a modification of his caisson design. In 1770 a mortar carriage that permitted a mortar to be used as a howitzer was adopted; and in 1775 a munitions cart of a more robust design appeared. Each battery also had a tool wagon for general repairs; when in action this was kept in the rear with all the other spares wagons. Smaller tools were kept in a series of wooden boxes inside the caisson along with the other spare items.

In 1803, new wagons and field forges were introduced. It is unknown if any of the attendant rolling stock was ever produced. General Gassendi ordered that all these improvements to the French artillery be abandoned in 1808 – according to General Valée, 'due to overconfidence in the superiority of the Gribeauval system'.[398]

British Artillery Vehicles

During the Napoleonic period the British used at least two generations of support vehicles, that were gradually replaced in piecemeal fashion with those of the Desaguliers pattern by 1813.

Two patterns of forge wagon were in use: the M1760 Muller four-wheeled vehicle and the newer M1788 Desaguliers design based upon the ammunition limber-wagon. In 1808, William Robe wrote that the old pattern forge vehicle was a 'dead weight' and the new vehicle was far superior, not least due to its large wheels. 'The plan of the frame of the limber-wagons is the most proper the folding sides being fixed to it, and the pole lengthened, to admit turning. The limber boxes serving to carry the tools of the wheeler and collar maker.' Robe further stated that it was based upon the limber-wagon design, and

> consists, besides the limber, of a framework of three rails and crossties, on which is fixed the bellows, fireplace, &c. The stock, held up by a prop, serves as a support for a vice. Behind the bellows is placed a coal box, which has to be removed before the bellows can be put in position. In the limber-box are placed the tools for use with the forge, horseshoes, nails, and spare parts (iron) of carriages, harness, &c. One of these forges accompanies each field-battery, and others are provided, equipped for general service with the army.[399]

In 1813, Adye noted that the body of the forge weighed 462kg, the limber 400kg, the bellows 32kg and the anvil 80kg. New bellows weighing only 25kg were proposed in order to lighten the vehicle. The 'stores limber' that accompanied the forge cart was identical to the ammunition wagon, but it carried smiths' tools, iron tools and sundry spares for the guns.

11 Artillery Tactics

INTRODUCTION

Innovative doctrinal changes accompanied the technical improvements to artillery equipment throughout the last decades of the 18th century. The du Teil brothers (Jean and Jean-Pierre) were instrumental in the education of Napoleon in his formative years as a young artilleryman. Notable among the artillerymen of other nations who also changed the way in which artillery was deployed were Josef Freiherr von Smola (1764–1820) of Austria, K.F. Kerner of Württemberg and Ernst Monhaupt (1775–1835) of Prussia.[400]

In France, tactics developed and recommended by Gribeauval and the du Teil brothers were taught in the excellent artillery schools. There were, however, no official regulations governing the tactical employment of the arm, although the French Imperial Guard did publish one for their own use in 1812. Standard operating procedures were developed by both the corps artillery commanders and the corps commanders themselves.

Artillerymen generally attempted to emplace their batteries on slightly elevated ground. Too high an eminence would leave considerable dead ground in front of the position which could not be covered by the guns, so leaving them vulnerable. Generally, firing over the heads of friendly troops was avoided; fuses for shells were apparently unreliable, and the sound of guns behind them and shot passing overhead could unnerve untried conscripts.

The du Teils insisted on both the concentration of guns, and the concentration of their firepower on single targets. This was based upon the thinking of General Count Jacques Antoine Hippolyte de Guibert (1743–90), who had initiated widespread reforms of the French army in 1775, and of Frederick the Great in his instruction to generals printed in 1785; both these commanders recognised the limited accuracy of individual guns. If multiple targets were to be engaged, they should be attacked one at a time or by different batteries. At the battle of Olmutz in 1758, Frederick amassed a battery of 60 guns that battered the flank of the enemy's line with canister; and in 1763 he collected an artillery reserve of 70 pieces.

Under Napoleon, artillery tactics came of age, and could finally claim to be one of the great deciders of battles. The object of the artillery was not to kill men or dismount guns in isolation, but to make gaps appear in the enemy's lines, to stop his attacks, and to support those launched against him. To achieve this, massive concentrations of artillery were required; other nations soon learned the lesson, but they were not as successful in applying it. However, these massed batteries returned battles from the free-flowing actions of the Revolutionary Wars and early Empire to a type of siege-war mentality, leading to battles of attrition as last experienced in the Seven Years War of the mid-18th century.

It was not until Eylau (7–8 February 1807) that Napoleon's view of artillery's potential became fully crystallised. According to General Antoine-Henri Jomini (1779–1869), who wrote *Précis de l'Art de Guerre* (1836), Napoleon determined to increase the artillery of France dramatically; thereafter he massed his guns in unprecedented numbers to prepare the enemy to receive his assaults – a task previously undertaken by swarms of infantry skirmishers.[401] Napoleon recognised that it was the concentration of the 'great battery', rather than simply the numbers of guns employed, that increased its effect; he stated that 'nothing will resist [the great battery], whereas the same number of guns spread out along the line would not give the same result'. Oberst Smola summed up his doctrine of close engagement as follows:

> Advance as close to the enemy line as is possible given the need for the safety of the guns against an unexpected enemy attack. Artillery is rarely decisive

Napoleon supervising a Polish 12-pdr position battery. (Authors' collection)

> at ranges beyond 800 *schritte* [about 500m]; an action at 500 *schritte* [about 300m] will usually last only a few minutes before the outcome is clear. Cavalry guns must make use of their advantage in mobility to undertake skilful attacks, especially in actions against enemy cavalry – a few positions close to the enemy will be more decisive than hour-long cannonades, which will tire the crews and use up ammunition pointlessly. When it is possible to advance against the enemy unnoticed and open fire only at the effective range.

Traditional exponents of artillery such as Frederick the Great, Smola and the du Teil brothers advocated a conservative approach to ammunition, apportioning fire in relation to the importance of the objective so as to save munitions for decisive moments. Napoleon instead increased the ammunition allocation to 300–350 rounds per gun, and advocated continuous fire regardless of the ammunition expenditure. He would later write, 'Never forget that in war all artillery must be with the army and not in the park. Had I possessed 30,000 artillery rounds at Leipzig on the evening of 18 October [1813], today I would be master of the world.'

The decline in quality of the French infantry required an increasing number of guns.[402] Napoleon saw artillery as crucial to stiffen and support infantry, and to minimise casualties by winning battles at the lowest possible cost in lives.[403, 404] He believed that a revolution in tactics, with artillery at its core, had been achieved by advocating massed batteries and near-continuous fire, and that this had fundamentally altered the nature of gunpowder warfare.

During the Napoleonic Wars, therefore, the main difference between the Coalition and the French artillery lay not in the quality of gunners or guns, but in the way in which they were used. Napoleon used artillery offensively, whereas the Coalition allies used theirs to defend their cavalry and infantry.

CLOSE INFANTRY SUPPORT

Battalion Artillery

The attachment of one or two guns to each infantry battalion was an 18th-century practice that lingered into the early 19th century. It was enshrined in Austrian doctrine until 1808, and Prussian doctrine until 1812. Before entering the Confederation of the Rhine most of the German states organised their battalion artillery after the manner of Austria. As the Napoleonic Wars progressed it was found that dispersing the artillery by pairs of guns amongst the infantry made little tactical sense, and the battalion guns were phased out to be replaced by batteries of guns placed between the infantry brigades.

The Prussians placed their battalion guns 50m in front of their infantry to engage the enemy line, and as soon as the advance was ordered the guns in the first line moved into the intervals between the battalions and loaded with roundshot. These pieces were advanced with the infantry by means of *bricoles* until the line had come within 400m of the enemy. At that point they began to fire again, and continued until the battalion to which the guns were attached was engaged with the enemy. Then the guns would also advance upon the enemy, and change to case-shot at 75m; theoretically, after a few such salvos the action would be tipping in their favour. The battalion artillery attached to the second line only started firing if the first line was defeated and retreated through the second line.[405]

Other countries, including Britain and France, placed their battalion guns at the right of the line with the grenadier company – which supposedly had the battalion's biggest men, who were well suited to assist the artillerymen.

Regimental Artillery

This entailed a half- or full battery attached to an infantry regiment of two to four battalions. After the 1805 campaign the use of regimental artillery dragged on in Russia for several years, strongly advocated by Generals Bennigsen, Buxhowden and Miloradovich. Major-General Gogel observed during 1806-07 that infantry regiments competed in keeping their guns in good order, prizing them like their colours, and fought more bravely when supported by artillery. However, Gogel admitted that these pieces hindered the infantry's movements when deployed along their front; that the regimental gunners were less competent than those trained at an artillery school; that infantry officers favoured rapidity of fire over accuracy, and that they often ordered the guns to open fire at too long a range. Gogel argued that it would be better to take all the guns from the infantry and form them into proper batteries.[406] In 1808, Russian regimental artillery was formed on a brigade basis.

In 1809, France introduced regimental artillery using Austrian 3-pdr guns, and in 1811 initiated it among many of its allies.

Post-1800, British doctrine was to deploy their Light 6-pdr guns by half-battery to infantry brigades of two to three battalions, so this could best be described as regimental artillery. In 1813, Adye stated that they were not placed in the intervals between the infantry battalions, and certainly not at the 'front line'; this suggests a change in artillery doctrine as a result of experience during the Napoleonic Wars.[407] He indicated that placing the guns in the line of battle exposed the guns and gunners to enemy fire, and furthermore slowed and hampered the movement of the infantry. Instead, guns were placed so that they were protected by the infantry without hampering them.

British artillery usage in the Peninsula was the exception rather than the norm, due to the poor roads and ultimately a lack of horses or other draft animals to move the guns. In Spain in 1808, a half-brigade (i.e. three guns) was attached to each infantry brigade; this gave a ratio of one gun to every 600 men (compared to the French average of one gun per 250 men). Both half-brigades camped together wherever possible; this allowed all the horses to be grouped together and cared for en masse, thus making best use of the somewhat limited support services.

Divisional Artillery

As First Consul from November 1799, Napoleon organised the army into a modern divisional structure, thus creating semi-autonomous artillery formations under the command of intelligent and aggressive young artillery officers. Napoleon and several of his senior generals were experts at maintaining the offensive tempo on the battlefield, including the efficient co-ordination of artillery fire. The presence of selected officers leading and co-ordinating massed artillery units was one of several important factors in the superior performance of French artillery at this time. The French divisional artillery concept was copied by the larger states of the Confederation of the Rhine, principally Bavaria, Saxony and Württemberg.

When used to support an infantry attack, the battery would once again seek to obtain a position where it could fire into the opposing troops' flank, from the closest practical range. This tactic required quick reactions to guard against sudden counter-attacks, but to some extent this danger could be overcome by leap-frogging batteries forward in alternate sections, or by approaching behind a cavalry or infantry screen. The latter increased the surprise factor,

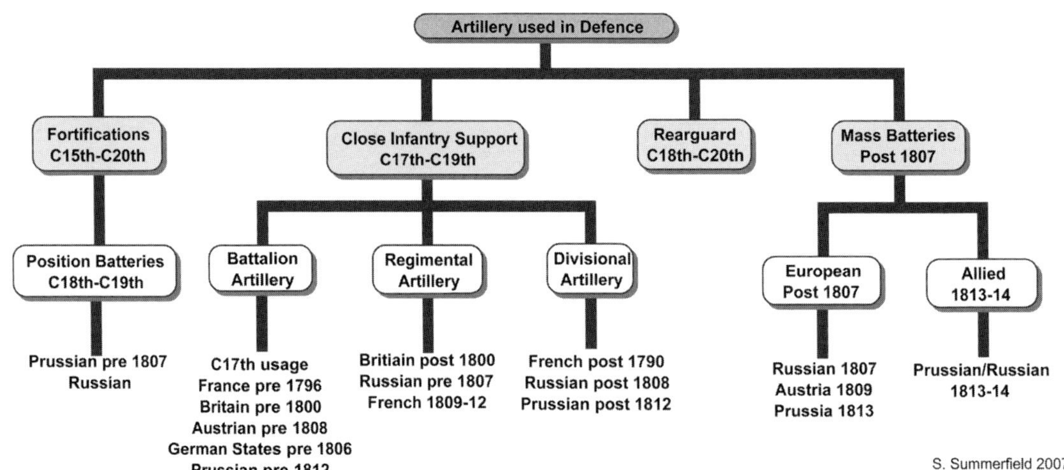

Artillery used in the defence.

often enabling the artillery to rout an inexperienced enemy formation virtually on its own.

Prior to 1810, Russia assigned two position batteries (12-pdrs), three light batteries (6-pdrs) and a horse battery at divisional level. In early 1810 Field Marshal Mikhail Andreas Barclay de Tolly (1761–1818), the Minister of War, wrote the Tsar a report that addressed his philosophy of artillery assignment. He noted that the distribution of guns in the infantry divisions was done on a regular and equal basis, but he said that there were:

> Two considerations on this subject:
>
> (A) It is necessary that the infantry divisions are not encumbered with an excessive quantity of heavy artillery which opposes the rapidity of movements by its transportation difficulties.
>
> (B) The heavy artillery should be judiciously distributed between the infantry divisions, and the excess assigned to the artillery reserve of each army. These reserves should be placed under the immediate authority of the army commander-in-chief, and can be employed with great advantage at the decisive moment of a battle.
>
> In accordance with these considerations, I have the honour to propose that each corps should be assigned reserve artillery batteries composed of heavy and horse artillery.[408]

These words also fairly sum up Napoleon's view of artillery. This shows that Russia was learning to emulate the French; by the beginning of the 1812 campaign when these guidelines were implemented, each infantry division was assigned an artillery brigade that consisted of two light 6-pdr batteries and a position battery of 12-pdr guns. By 1814, Russian foot artillery was considered to be the best among all the Coalition armies. Their service at La Rothière (1 February 1814) was admirable; and at Craonne (7 March 1814) even the French admitted that the Russian gunners served their pieces better than their own artillerymen. However, the Russians still used their artillery defensively.

When the Prussian army was re-organised in 1809 no doctrine on the use of artillery was established, until a series of regulations were issued in 1812 that repeated a set of recommendations on the use of combined arms, and abolished battalion guns. A Prussian brigade (equivalent to a division in other armies) was equipped with one 6-pdr battery and one horse battery. The foot battery operated in two sections posted on the flanks, with the horse battery held in reserve so as to be able to bolster the firepower of whichever flank needed it.

The Prussian regulations of 1812 outlined a standard combined-arms attack. The main body of infantry was formed into two lines covered by a skirmish screen. The cavalry and horse artillery was posted in the rear. The skirmish screen from

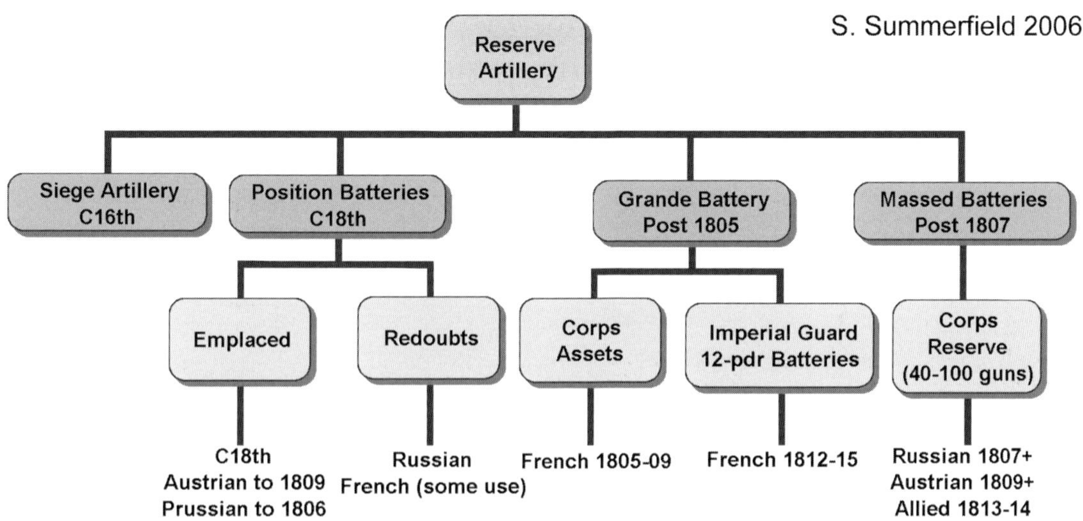

Reserve artillery.

the two fusilier battalions was intended to neutralise the opposing skirmishers and to harass the enemy's formed infantry. The infantry main body was to fix the enemy infantry in place, allowing the artillery to position itself in order to pour in canister and shot at close range. Once sufficient damage had been done, the cavalry would swing out round a flank to sweep the enemy from the field.[409]

RESERVE ARTILLERY

The 18th-century conventions had traditionally placed batteries in a general artillery pool from which they were then parcelled out to temporary corps commanders. Even under this method commanders could mass artillery, as the Austrians did at Marengo (1800) and Aspern-Essling (1809).

Throughout the period the British and Austrian armies continued to use the old pool system, parcelling out individual batteries to brigades or divisions. While the individual batteries were well led, there was little co-ordination between them. The British Reserve Park generally consisted of the 9- and 12-pdr guns, organised by half-brigade to provide heavy support when needed, and were not attached to any infantry units.

In terms of battery position, Adye urged that guns must be placed to create crossfire on the enemy position, and that in some instances it was necessary to concentrate fire upon a particular point by grouping half-brigades together into a single battery. He also suggested the sub-division of brigades, 'thus [the enemy's] fire may be attracted to different objects, whilst your own is directed to one point.' In an attack on the enemy's position or other kind of advance, fire became direct in order not to impede the movement of their own troops. When the advance reached a stage at which guns could no longer fire safely on the objective of the attack, they were directed to switch targets on to the collateral points.

French Corps Artillery and *Grande Batteries*

The development of massed artillery batteries that concentrated fire upon single points represented a tactical change towards relative rigidity. With massed artillery, battery commanders could no longer view their operation at a local level, but were forced to fit into a framework of higher command and control - which, on occasion, did not live up to expectations. The assembly of massed artillery by uniting divisional or corps units into a single Great Battery faced an almost insurmountable obstacle in the jealousy between divisional and corps commanders. Fancy new ideas like corps artillery tactics were all very well in theory; but without its artillery

Artillerie à pied de la Garde Royale

Artillerie à pied de la Garde Royale, c1816, serving a M1765 Gribeauval 12-pdr gun. This uniform was adopted in October 1814 and retained until the regiment was disbanded in 1829. Notice the handspikes used to train the gun, and the *prolonge* rope for attachment to the trail. (August de Moltzheim, *L'Armée Française sous la Restoration,* Editions du Gunsier, Nantes)

a division was vulnerable, and in practice it was only in exceptional cases that very large numbers of guns were concentrated.

Napoleon formed his first *grande batterie* of 30 guns at Lodi (10 May 1796); subsequently, he concentrated 19 at Castiglione (5 August 1796); 18 at Marengo (14 June 1800); two *grande batteries* of 24 and 18 guns at Austerlitz (2 December 1805); and 25 guns at Jena (14 October 1806). From 1807, he employed massed batteries of increasing size.

At Friedland (14 June 1807), General Sénarmont massed 38 guns divided between three provisional batteries. The two main batteries each had 10× 6-pdrs, 2× 4-pdrs and 3× howitzers, and were positioned to produce supporting lines of fire on a single point; they were protected by an infantry battalion and four dragoon regiments. The reserve battery (4× 12-pdrs, 2× 6-pdrs and 2× howitzers) was kept in a covered position. Fire was opened at 400m, and after firing five or six rounds Sénarmont advanced his guns to within 200m of the Russians. After firing a further twenty rounds per gun, the batteries were advanced by *prolonge* until they combined at about 60m from the enemy line; from there, rapid fire with heavy canister broke the Russian infantry to the battery's front, so permitting the French infantry to attack the town of Friedland.

From the beginning, Napoleon had designed the Foot Artillery of the Guard to intervene en masse after the battle had developed, and it was not used in the type of desultory outpost work on which the guns of the Line were often dispersed. At Eylau (7–8 February 1807) the Imperial Guard assembled 40 guns, while St Hilaire's Division mustered only 18, and Sénarmont's just 19 pieces. Eylau appears to have provided Napoleon with confirmation of his artillery doctrine; there and in later battles, the Guard Artillery's 12-pdrs provided the nucleus for ever-larger artillery concentrations.[410] By increasing the strength of the Guard Artillery, Napoleon was able to increase these concentrations of guns, since the Guard was free from the organisational limitations of the Line.

The expansion of the Guard Foot Artillery to over 100 guns was a deliberate act, to allow Napoleon to deploy an artillery corps en masse under his direct command to overcome the failings observed at Wagram (1809). That battle had suffered from a convex rather than a concave battery formation, with consequent dispersion of fire effect; it would have been better to have light guns on the flanks and heavy guns holding the centre, all firing into a fixed point. Wagram also suffered from poor co-operation between Generals Drouot and d'Aboville, and the lack of a co-ordinated infantry attack to follow up the bombardment.

The French were also known for judicious placing of their *grande batteries*; for example, at Borodino (7 September 1812) they placed a massive battery of 80 howitzers in the ravines of the Kolocha river. According to General Yermolov, 'only the heads of the French gunners could be seen, and Russian artillery was unable to silence them.'[411]

In 1813 the Guard Artillery, along with the rest of the Imperial Guard, became a major battle formation rather than a reserve, which led to a particular emphasis on 12-pdrs and 6.54in howitzers. At Lützen (2 May 1813), 60 guns of the Guard artillery appeared from behind a ridge, stopping the enemy in their tracks and preparing the way for Napoleon's infantry counter-attack. However, the infantry quickly overran the beaten zone cleared by the guns, resulting in only a limited French advance. Marmont's central attack at Bautzen (20–21 May 1813) was supported by 76 guns. At Dresden (27 August 1813) the Guard artillery was committed on the second day around Grosse Garten, and cleared the enemy from a wide zone to their front, only to see this advantage squandered. This was repeated at Leipzig (16–19 October 1813), when a mass of 80 Guard guns (including 32× 12-pdrs) blew a convincing hole in the enemy line, but the advantage was not fully exploited. General Drouot earned promotion to *général de division*, and on 24 October 1813 he was made a Count of the Empire.[412]

The Guard was more successfully employed at Hanau (30–31 October 1813), where Drouot deployed 15 guns opposite the enemy main line. First he cleared the woods with two battalions of Guard infantry skirmishers, then defiled through them with 15 guns to such a position as to allow them to take the Bavarian artillery in the flank. Behind the screen of skirmishers he deployed the remainder of the Guard artillery, totalling some 50 guns.

At Ligny (16 June 1815) the Imperial Guard Foot Artillery battered the Prussian centre and contributed to their heavy defeat. The massed artillery at Waterloo (18 June 1815) was hampered, as at Bautzen a couple of years earlier, by the wet ground preventing its early deployment. The effects of the torrential rain of the previous afternoon and night prevented the cannonballs from ricocheting, and made the ground too treacherous for the easy manoeuvre of both guns and infantry.

Russian and Prussian Reserve (Corps) Artillery

The Russians were no strangers to massed artillery, whose use stretched back to Peter the Great at the turn of the 17th–18th centuries.

In December 1806 at Pultusk, a French infantry division under General Gazan advanced against Russian cavalry. These waited until the range had closed, and then wheeled away, exposing 70 guns deployed behind them; Gazan's advance was immediately halted by their murderous fire. At Eylau the following year the Russians employed three powerful batteries of 40, 60 and 70 guns; Marshal Augereau's two French infantry divisions lost 5,200, killed and wounded out of a starting strength of perhaps 7,000 men.[413]

At Borodino (7 September 1812) the Russians amassed a huge artillery reserve, but this failed to be decisive due to the poor co-ordination of Kutusov and the untimely death of the artillery reserve commander, Kutaisov, at the head of a cavalry charge. This failure of a strong artillery reserve does not appear to have been properly analysed by Russian commanders; they continued to favour their assembly, and continued to have real problems in deploying them. For example, at Lützen (2 May 1813) and Bautzen (20–21 May 1813) large reserves of guns were massed, but not employed; it was not until Leipzig (16–19 October 1813) that the Russians managed to get their artillery reserve into action. It was only in 1813 that officers were appointed to command corps-level artillery reserve formations.

When Prussia finally put her army into the field against Napoleon in 1813, it was organised along the lines of the new Russian practice, which saw the beginnings of an increase in the number of independent artillery formations and commanders. The Prussians did not mass their guns in the French manner, but should the necessity arise they had the option of forming 'great batteries' from their corps reserve rather than divisional artillery. However, there are few examples of this being carried out; it was usually prevented by the Prussian troops being distributed throughout multi-national Coalition armies as detached corps, and they did not have the opportunity to form a purely Prussian massed battery until Leipzig in 1813.

The artillery of the brigades and the corps was under the command of the corps artillery commander, who held the rank of Oberst or Oberst-Leutnant. The overall artillery commander was usually a major-general, but he had no reserve under his hand, as in the French manner. In order to exploit an advantage or to commit at the decisive time and place he had to form any concentration by borrowing artillery from the individual corps, thus causing much delay.

HORSE ARTILLERY

The costs of maintaining horse artillery were much higher than foot artillery, and if used in the same way horse batteries would only achieve the same effect; consequently, commanders sought to find more

Russian Guard Artillery battery in 1830. (Authors' collection)

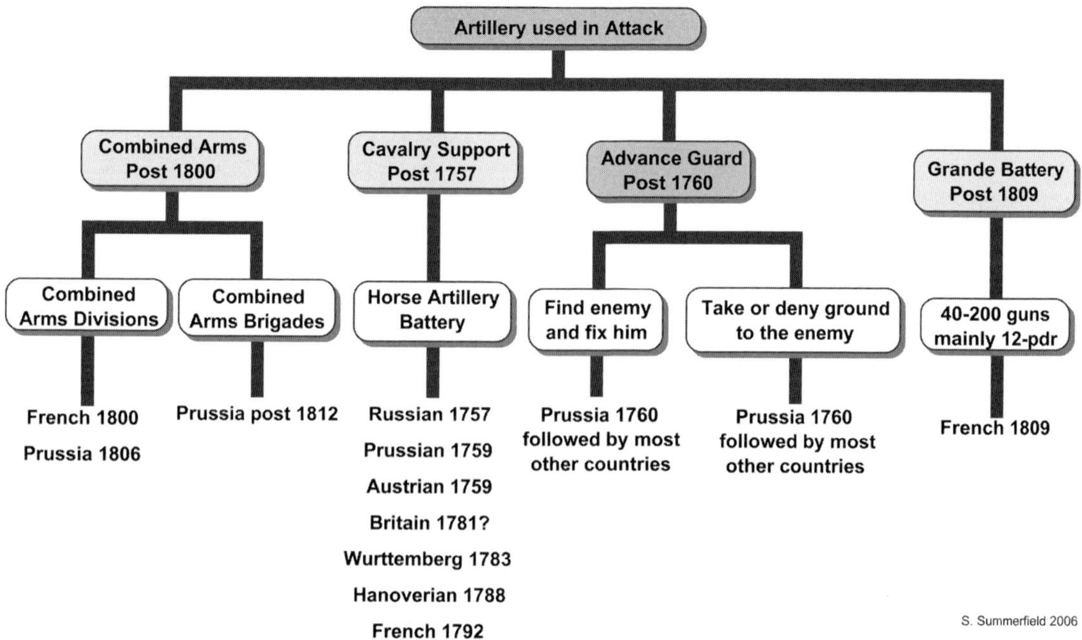

Artillery used in the attack.

effective ways of employing this expensive asset. Although the horse artillery was much quicker to reach a position than foot artillery, it was still hampered by its vehicles and by terrain obstacles. The two main types of horse artillery were used in two distinct ways. Horse-mounted units employed in the Prussian style primarily accompanied cavalry to support their attacks; and *Artillerie Légère* (vehicle- or semi-vehicle mounted) was used to occupy positions quickly to support the infantry and cavalry, rather than to accompany them.

The Prussian General Monhaupt noted in the 1830s that it was a mistake to misuse horse artillery as regimental guns attached to the cavalry, or to reinforce cavalry with horse artillery. This was a failing of the Austrian horse artillery until 1808, and of *Artillerie Légère* in general when deployed as 'cavalry artillery'. During an attack by the cavalry upon enemy cavalry the presence of the horse artillery would hamper the speedy and flexible movement of the former – which was of the utmost importance during such combats.

In France, *Artillerie Légère* was discontinued in 1804 in favour of fully mounted Prussian-style horse artillery. The *Artillerie Légère* was still used by the Austrians, Bavarians, British and Württembergers, and the French re-introduced the arm in 1816. In England, William Congreve Snr noted that upon the formation of the Royal Horse Artillery in 1792 it was recommended that 'this brigade ought never to be stationary, and scarcely ever to act on the defensive'; they were to be a 'flying brigade to support the cavalry attacks and to provide firepower where needed.'[414]

However, in general terms, both types of horse artillery were used in the same ways. It was recommended that when, at a certain point in a battle, the commander-in-chief committed all other troops, the horse artillery should form his last reserve. With its aid he was able to put the crown on his victory, or to limit the price of defeat. With horse artillery alone he might be able to undo the results of mistakes caused by the terrain, by the forces at his disposal, by his subordinates' or by his own doing. He should avoid using horse artillery in a stationary position in the line; treating it like any other artillery denied him the potential of a very useful asset.

With this arm the commander-in-chief was able to occupy speedily any unoccupied and favourable position in front or to the flank of his own lines before the enemy could, by sending in as many cavalry squadrons as the situation dictated, supported by

Gunner of the French 2nd Line Horse Artillery Regiment

Gunner of the French 2nd Line Horse Artillery Regiment, 1816, mounting a horse while carrying a portfire in his left hand. The horse is no more than 14.2 hands high, or he would need a mounting block. The uniform illustrated is essentially that of the Bardin regulations of 1812, though with Royal insignia exchanged for Napoleonic. (August de Moltzheim, *L'Armée Française sous la Restoration,* Editions du Gunsier, Nantes)

horse artillery. In support of light infantry skirmishers or flank guards, horse artillery had a great advantage in speed. Their speed was also advantageous during the retreat, when they could support the withdrawing rearguard to the utmost – a task exemplified by General Marquis of Anglesey's conduct of the mounted rearguard withdrawing from Les Quatre Bras to Mont St Jean on the eve of Waterloo.

12 Artillery Organisation

INTRODUCTION

In parallel with equipment and tactics, the organisation of artillery batteries evolved throughout the period. Most field artillery batteries during the Napoleonic Wars consisted of six guns of the same calibre. Often a howitzer or a section of two were added, based upon battle experience from the Seven Years War that had demonstrated the value of giving a battery the ability to engage an enemy behind cover.

Artillery can be classed as battalion guns (pairs of 3-, 4- or 6-pdrs); regimental (a half- or full battery of 3- or 6-pdrs); brigade artillery (usually a 6-pdr battery); position artillery (12- and 16-pdr batteries); and horse artillery. In general, equipment was only replaced when it was lost or beyond repair; it will come as no surprise to any reader with military experience that obsolescent equipment was kept in piecemeal service for some time after it had been superseded by more modern designs.

FOOT ARTILLERY

Foot artillery batteries were the mainstay of any Napoleonic army; and the mainstay of the foot artillery was the 6-pdr, operated at battalion or regimental/brigade level. Occasionally, they were massed against the enemy line.

Battalion Artillery

As discussed in Chapter 11, as the Napoleonic Wars progressed it was found that dividing the artillery by pairs of guns amongst the infantry units made little tactical sense, and the battalion guns were phased out to be replaced by units assembled higher up the pyramid of organisation. France abolished battalion artillery at the end of the Revolutionary Wars, largely from lack of ordnance, but it persisted in continental Coalition armies until 1808. The allocation of artillery to infantry battalions was abandoned by Britain in about 1800; by Hanover on its occupation in 1803; by Saxony when it joined the Confederation of the Rhine in 1806; by Austria in 1808; and by Prussia, in practice, in 1807, although it was not formally abolished until the Prussian 1812 regulations. Most of the northern German states followed the Prussian practice and the southern states the Austrian practice of battalion guns. When they joined the Confederation of the Rhine the use of battalion guns fell out of favour.

Austria allocated battalion guns to their infantry manned by a combination of gunners and unskilled labour provided by the infantry regiment. The allocation of the guns depended on the terrain and likely opposition: infantry regiments in Italy and the Tyrol, and the Grenzer frontier troops in the Balkans, had 6× 3-pdr guns per regiment. Those operating outside these areas were issued with 6-pdrs instead. In 1808, Austria formed brigade artillery.

From 1799 until 1806, Prussian infantry regiments consisted of two musketeer battalions plus two grenadier companies, and a depot battalion. In wartime the depot formed a third musketeer battalion and the grenadier companies of each pair of regiments formed a grenadier battalion. Two Light 6-pdrs were attached to each of the first two musketeer battalions and to each grenadier battalion; the third musketeer battalion had 3-pdr guns. After the collapse of 1806 each regiment was supposed to consist of two musketeer and one light or fusilier battalion, plus the usual two grenadier companies; the fusilier battalion was theoretically to have two 3-pdr guns. All these guns were officially withdrawn under the 1812 regulations.[415]

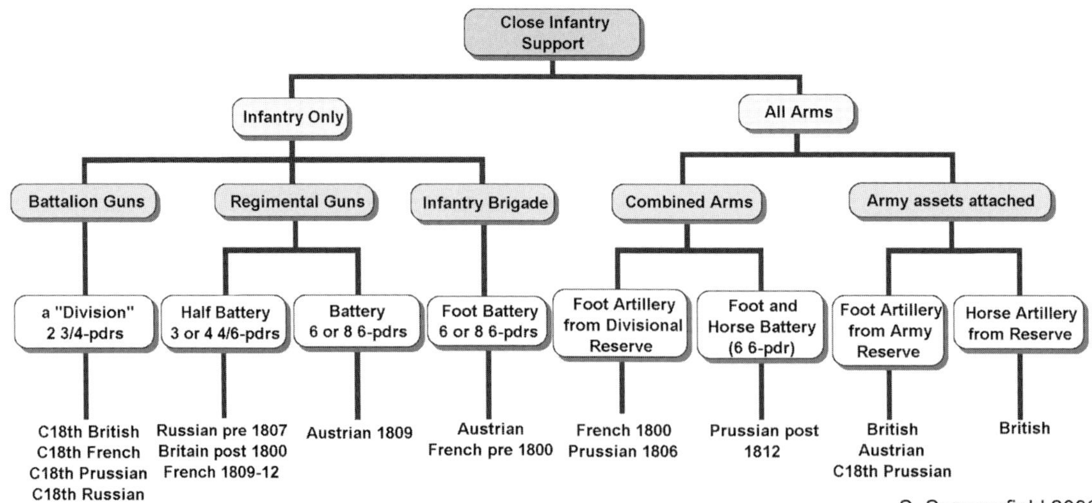

Close infantry support.

Regimental Artillery

Russia attached a half-battery of 4× 6-pdrs and 2× howitzers – with 5 officers, 13 NCOs and 85 gunners – to each infantry regiment of three battalions. In 1803, 3-pdr unicorns were introduced to support Jäger regiments. After 1808, brigade batteries were assigned to infantry support, and the heavy guns to the position batteries. It was only in 1813 that the light artillery became independent.[416]

Napoleon believed that both raw conscripts and seasoned veterans benefited from close support from the artillery.[417] In 1809 the French infantry received regimental artillery; this is often explained as being the direct result of the infantry's decline in tactical quality, but this is too simplistic.[418] In 1812, Davout's I Corps and the Imperial Guard – undeniably the best infantry in the Grande Armée – received the highest allocation of regimental artillery.[419] The intention was rather to give an added punch to the regiments that had expanded, under the 1808 reorganisation, to four–six battalions operating together; the attached guns would give them the ability to perform semi-independent operations. For example, the Young Guard commanded by Dorsenne in Spain could operate independently supported by twelve guns. Generally, the regimental artillery was not a success; after nearly all the regimental guns were lost in Russia, they were not replaced in 1813.

While battalion artillery in Coalition armies served to dissipate the artillery's effects by weakening the army's reserve and field artillery, this was not the case for France in 1809–12 or her allies in 1811–12 (Baden, Berg, Italy, Neufchatel, Switzerland, Saxony and Westphalia).[420] In France, regimental artillery had a separate establishment from field artillery and so did not weaken it. In effect, it freed up field guns from infantry support to be used in larger and higher-level artillery formations, thus enabling the *grande batteries* to be formed without robbing the infantry of dedicated support. In addition, the equipment issued to the French and satellite infantry units was from captured stocks, particularly of Austrian 3-pdr guns.

Brigade Artillery

When Austria and Britain abolished battalion guns, the ordnance was assembled into batteries attached to infantry brigades. On 3 June 1808, Austria designated her artillery batteries as brigade (8× 3-pdr or 6-pdr guns), position (6× 12-pdr and 2× howitzers), or horse (4× 6-pdrs and 2× howitzers). Only the Grenzer battalions retained their 3-pdr battalion guns. With the introduction of permanent batteries,

Russian Foot Artillery Organisation

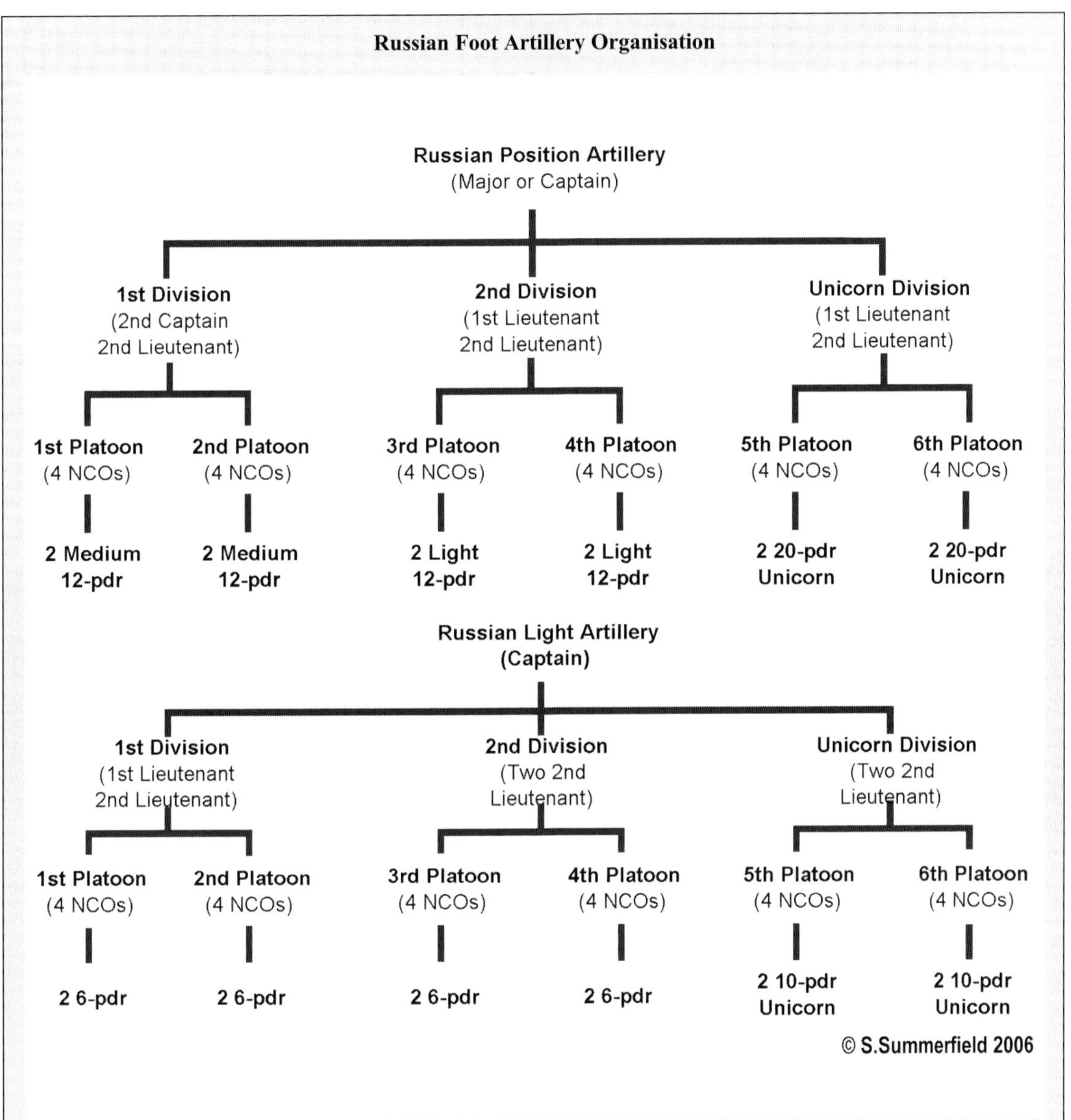

Position battery: 4× medium 12-pdr guns, 4× light 12-pdr guns and 4× ½-pud (20-pdr) unicorns.
1 staff officer, 6 officers, 24 NCOs, 50 bombardiers, 50 gunners, 150 *Handlanger*, 59 non-combatants/specialists; total 340 personnel.

Light artillery company: 8× 6-pdr guns, 4× ¼-pud unicorns.
1 staff officer, 6 officers, 24 NCOs, 35 bombardiers, 35 gunners, 100 *Handlanger*, 42 non-combatants/specialists; total 243 personnel.

Neuchatel Regimental Artillery Company

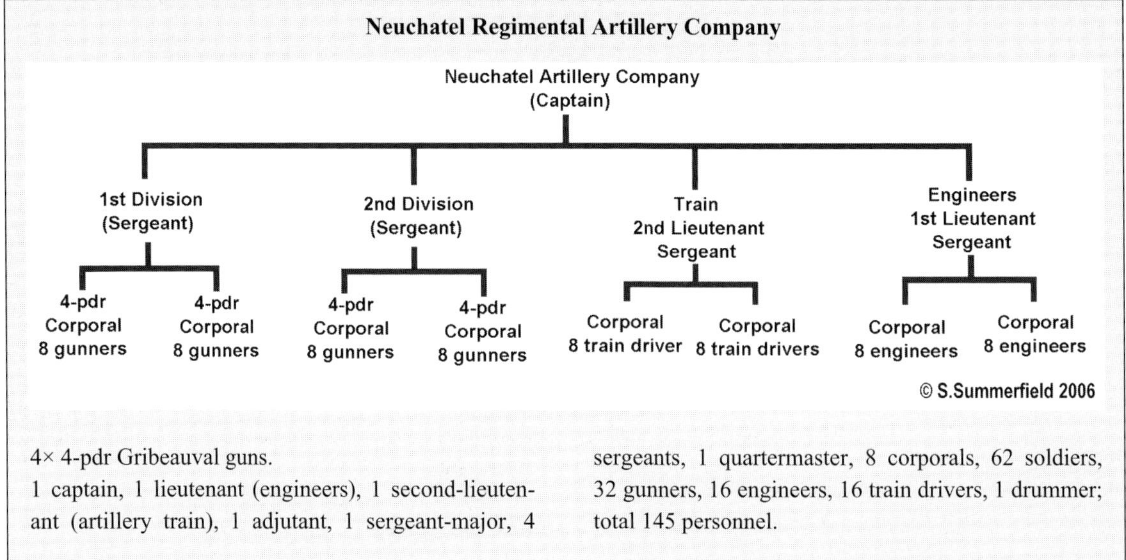

4× 4-pdr Gribeauval guns.
1 captain, 1 lieutenant (engineers), 1 second-lieutenant (artillery train), 1 adjutant, 1 sergeant-major, 4 sergeants, 1 quartermaster, 8 corporals, 62 soldiers, 32 gunners, 16 engineers, 16 train drivers, 1 drummer; total 145 personnel.

the tactical focus turned to deployment in support of the infantry and cavalry brigades and other artillery units.

The British deployed their Light 6-pdr guns by half-batteries (confusingly, termed 'brigades') in support of the infantry brigades of two to three battalions.

Prior to 1806 Prussian guns were distributed between infantry brigades, with apparently little or no regard for what was assigned to any particular brigade; some had horse batteries, others 3-, 6- or 12-pdr foot batteries. (Interestingly, the Reserve Divisions had less artillery.) In 1812 the Prussians conformed to French organisation, with light artillery attached to the brigades. In 1813, a Prussian corps had four brigades (each about the same size as a contemporary French division) each with a foot battery attached, and a corps artillery reserve of 6- and 12-pdr and horse batteries.

Reserve, Divisional and Corps Artillery

Heavy artillery (8-, 9-, 12-pdrs, and sometimes 16- or 18-pdrs) formed in the reserve was used in fixed position batteries, or massed against one sector of the enemy line. Throughout the period the Austrians and British followed the 18th-century practice of an army reserve, where batteries were not assigned to individual brigades, divisions or corps. A British reserve artillery park consisted mainly of 9- and 12-pdr guns organised by half-brigades, to provide heavy support where and when needed.

French divisional artillery comprised 6- or 8-pdr foot batteries and 6-pdr horse batteries. The 12-pdr batteries were assigned at the corps level, with light foot batteries and horse batteries if available. As the period progressed greater use was made of reserve artillery assembled in massed batteries (*see* Chapter 11).

During the Revolutionary Wars the French used whatever artillery they had at their disposal wherever they needed it. Batteries were often distributed amongst the infantry in a support role. Individual batteries might have more than one calibre of gun and one or two howitzers. After 1800 every battery theoretically had six guns of the same calibre, plus two howitzers; however, a glance at the organisation of the artillery for the battle of Friedland (14 June 1807) still shows the use of mixed gun batteries. It also became standard practice to assign at least one foot battery per infantry division, and possibly a horse battery as well.

From 1808, Russians corps level artillery had an artillery brigade comprising a position battery (8× 12-pdrs and 4× 20-pdr unicorns), a horse battery (8× 6-pdrs and 4× 10-pdr unicorns), and one or two

Austrian Artillery Organisation

Austrian 6-pdr Brigade Battery
Captain

- **Half Battery** — Lieutenant
  - **1st Division** — Corporal
    - **6-pdr**: 4 (5) gunners, 6 (8) Handlanger
    - **6-pdr**: 4 (5) gunners, 6 (8) Handlanger
  - **2nd Division** — Corporal
    - **6-pdr**: 4 (5) gunners, 6 (8) Handlanger
    - **6-pdr**: 4 (5) gunners, 6 (8) Handlanger
- **Half Battery** — Lieutenant
  - **3rd Division** — Corporal
    - **6-pdr**: 4 (5) gunners, 6 (8) Handlanger
    - **6-pdr**: 4 (5) gunners, 6 (8) Handlanger
  - **4th Division** — Corporal
    - **6-pdr**: 4 (5) gunners, 6 (8) Handlanger
    - **6-pdr**: 4 (5) gunners, 6 (8) Handlanger
- **Captain**
  - **Train**
  - **Ammunition**

Austrian 6-pdr Battery of 1813
(Captain)

- **Half Battery** — (Lieutenant)
  - **1st Division** — Corporal
    - **6-pdr**: 5 gunners, 8 Handlanger
    - **6-pdr**: 5 gunners, 8 Handlanger
  - **2nd Division** — Corporal
    - **6-pdr**: 5 gunners, 8 Handlanger
    - **6-pdr**: 5 gunners, 8 Handlanger
- **Half Battery** — (Lieutenant)
  - **3rd Division** — Corporal
    - **6-pdr**: 5 gunners, 8 Handlanger
    - **6-pdr**: 5 gunners, 8 Handlanger
  - **Howitzer Division** — Feuerwerker
    - **7-pdr Howitzer**: 6 gunners, 7 Handlanger
    - **7-pdr Howitzer**: 6 gunners, 7 Handlanger
- **Captain**
  - **Train**
  - **Ammunition**

Austrian 12-pdr Position Battery
(Captain)

- **1st Division** — Lieutenant
  - **12-pdr**: Corporal, 4 (5) gunners, 8 (10) Handlanger
  - **12-pdr**: Corporal, 4 (5) gunners, 8 (10) Handlanger
- **2nd Division** — Lieutenant
  - **12-pdr**: Corporal, 4 (5) gunners, 8 (10) Handlanger
  - **12-pdr**: Corporal, 4 (5) gunners, 8 (10) Handlanger
- **Howitzer Division** — Ober-Feuerwerker
  - **7-pdr howitzer**: Feuerwerker, 4 (6) gunners, 7 Handlanger
  - **7-pdr howitzer**: Feuerwerker, 4 (6) gunners, 7 Handlanger
- **Captain**
  - **Train**
  - **Ammunition**

Austrian 6-pdr Horse Battery
(Captain)

- **1st Division** — Lieutenant, Corporal
  - **6-pdr Wurst**: 6 gunners
  - **6-pdr Wurst**: 6 gunners
- **2nd Division** — Lieutenant, Corporal
  - **6-pdr Wurst**: 6 gunners
  - **6-pdr Wurst**: 6 gunners
- **Howitzer Division** — Ober-Feuerwerker
  - **7-pdr howitzer Wurst**: 7 gunners
  - **7-pdr howitzer Wurst**: 7 gunners
- **Captain**
  - **Train**
  - **Ammunition**

6-pdr brigade battery: 8× 6-pdrs; 32 gunners, 48 *Handlanger*
12-pdr position battery: 4× 12-pdrs, 2× 7-pdr howitzers; 20 gunners, 46 *Handlanger*

6-pdr position battery: 4× 6-pdrs, 2× 7-pdr howitzers; 24 gunners (1813, 30), 36 *Handlanger* (1813, 48)
Horse battery: 4× 6-pdr Wurst guns, 2× 7-pdr Wurst howitzers

light batteries (6× 6-pdrs and 6× 10-pdr unicorns). In combat Russian light foot artillery, although a divisional asset, frequently accompanied the battle formations of infantry regiments both in attack and in the defence, being located on their flanks. It could therefore be considered to be deployed as brigade artillery.

From 1812, Prussia organised its artillery along the lines of the new Russian system, which was beginning to increase the number of independent artillery officers to improve co-ordination of fire. The 12-pdr batteries were assigned at corps level and acted as the corps reserve as in the French army. The corps also contained a number of 6-pdr horse and foot batteries depending on availability.

HORSE ARTILLERY

During the 18th century there were a number of proposals and experiments with the goal of bringing field guns quickly to the point of action. Generally, Frederick the Great is considered as the inventor of the horse artillery, after seeing how the Russians operated their light artillery with their cavalry (though some also claim that the Swedes introduced horse

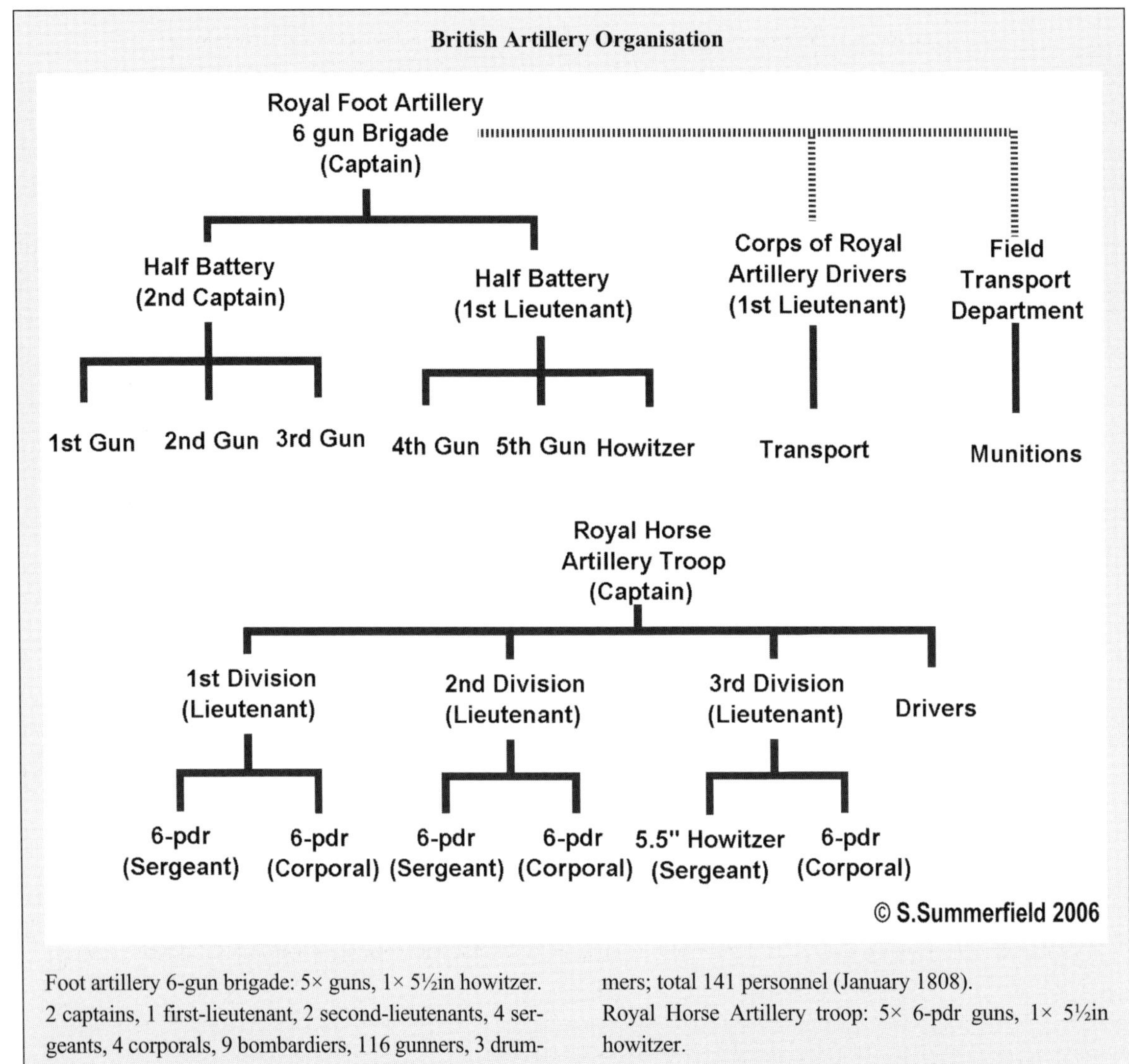

British Artillery Organisation

Foot artillery 6-gun brigade: 5× guns, 1× 5½in howitzer. 2 captains, 1 first-lieutenant, 2 second-lieutenants, 4 sergeants, 4 corporals, 9 bombardiers, 116 gunners, 3 drummers; total 141 personnel (January 1808).
Royal Horse Artillery troop: 5× 6-pdr guns, 1× 5½in howitzer.

Prussian Artillery Organisation 1808–15

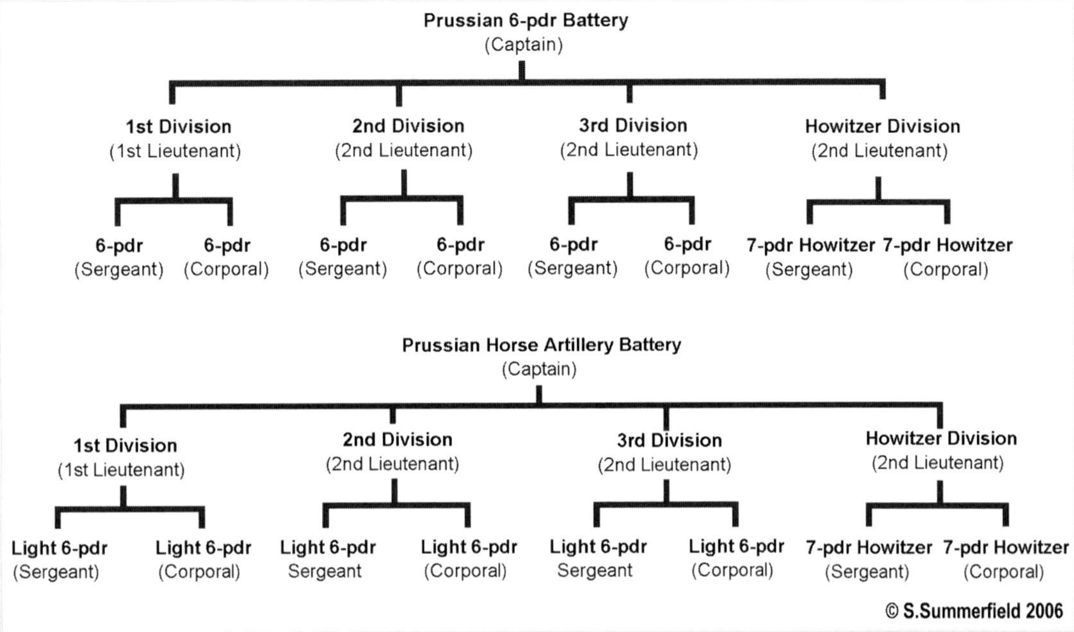

Prussian 6-pdr Battery
(Captain)

1st Division
(1st Lieutenant)
6-pdr (Sergeant)
6-pdr (Corporal)

2nd Division
(2nd Lieutenant)
6-pdr (Sergeant)
6-pdr (Corporal)

3rd Division
(2nd Lieutenant)
6-pdr (Sergeant)
6-pdr (Corporal)

Howitzer Division
(2nd Lieutenant)
7-pdr Howitzer (Sergeant)
7-pdr Howitzer (Corporal)

Prussian Horse Artillery Battery
(Captain)

1st Division
(1st Lieutenant)
Light 6-pdr (Sergeant)
Light 6-pdr (Corporal)

2nd Division
(2nd Lieutenant)
Light 6-pdr Sergeant
Light 6-pdr (Corporal)

3rd Division
(2nd Lieutenant)
Light 6-pdr Sergeant
Light 6-pdr (Corporal)

Howitzer Division
(2nd Lieutenant)
7-pdr Howitzer (Sergeant)
7-pdr Howitzer (Corporal)

6-pdr foot battery: 6× 6-pdr guns, 2× 7-pdr howitzers
Horse battery: 6× light 6-pdr guns, 2× 7-pdr howitzers.

French battery: 6× guns and 2× howitzers

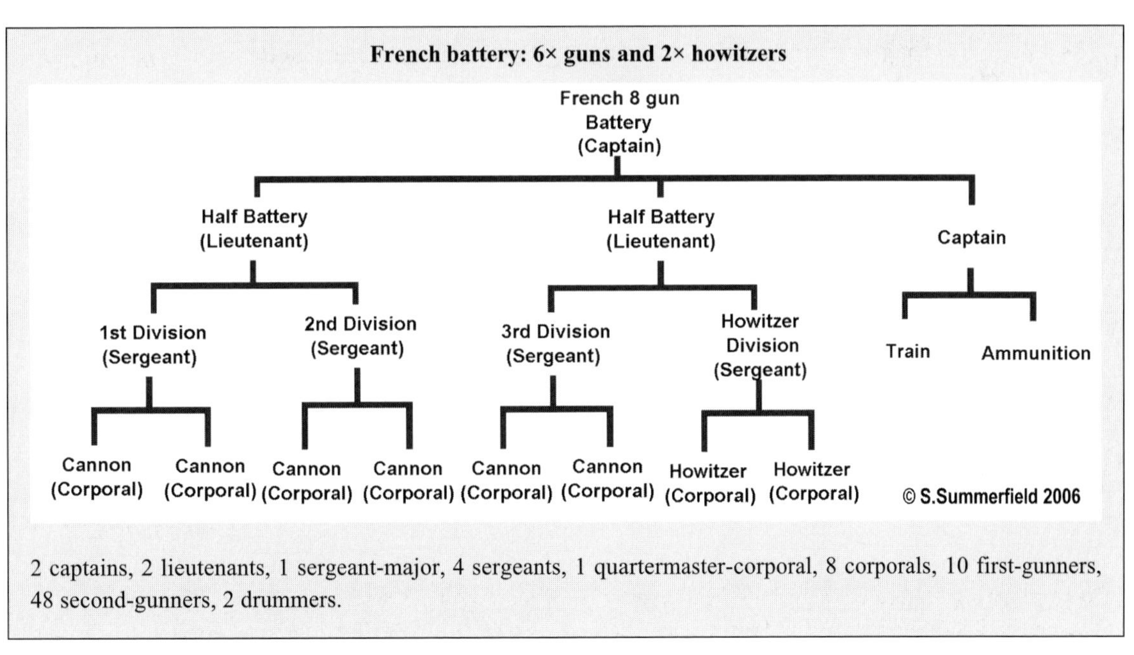

2 captains, 2 lieutenants, 1 sergeant-major, 4 sergeants, 1 quartermaster-corporal, 8 corporals, 10 first-gunners, 48 second-gunners, 2 drummers.

artillery). Frederick adopted it to provide his advance guard with support when it reconnoitred the terrain close to the enemy, and to take the heights in front of enemy positions. To dislodge the enemy from these heights he mounted the crews of an artillery battery, and ordered it to follow the advance guard or another strong cavalry command. These guns were used against the enemy cavalry to great advantage, and particularly when the Prussian cavalry had forced the enemy infantry to form square. Deploying at just beyond musket range (at roughly 200m), these guns could devastate the dense ranks of the squares with canister.

During the period there were three main systems in use, which are categorised by the method used to mount the gun crews:

(1) Prussian system (horse-mounted)
Russia (regimental cavalry guns, 1758)
Prussia (from 1759)
Austria (1759–74)
Württemberg (1783–1801, then 1803–10)
France (from 1792)
Sweden (from 1792)
Bavaria (1799–1804)
Kingdom of Italy (1805–15)
Baden (from 1808)
Kleve-Berg (1808–14)
Westphalia (1808–13)
Britain (from 1816)

(2) Austrian system (vehicle-mounted)
Austria (from 1774)
Britain (1778)
France (1792–1804)
Bavaria (1806–15)
Saxony (1806–15)

(3) Hanoverian system (semi vehicle-mounted)
Hanover (1788–1803, then from 1816)
King's German Artillery (1803–15)
Britain (1804–16)
France (experimental 1784–1800, then from 1811)
Württemberg (1799–1803 and 1810 onwards)

By the 1790s most European armies had introduced horse artillery. In general, horse artillery was designed to get up close to an enemy body of troops, fire as many rounds as possible in support of an attack, and then evacuate the area as quickly as possible. As the horse artillery normally worked at much closer ranges than the foot artillery, it was deemed expedient to use small calibre guns (3-pdrs), since they were light and mobile, and at the ranges involved had a similar effect to a heavier-calibre gun firing canister.

By 1800 most horse artilleries were armed with 6-pdrs, as they could fire larger loads of canister. The French took this idea to its logical conclusion and used 8- and 12-pdr guns in their horse artillery. A decree of 29 August 1805, authorizing the organisation of the Imperial Guard Horse Artillery, stipulated that each of the six companies was to be armed with 4× 8-pdrs, 2× 4-pdrs and 2× howitzers.[421] In 1807 the regiment was armed with a total of 6× 12-pdrs, 12× 8-pdrs, 10× 4-pdrs, and 8× 6.4in howitzers.[422]

Prussian System (Horse-mounted)

In the Prussian system, all the members of the battery were mounted. The teams of horses used to pull the guns had an additional pair, to increase the ability of the battery to accompany the movements of the cavalry. The intention was to give the cavalry firepower, and to enable the horse artillery to seize and defend high ground, giving the impression that infantry held it; this ruse succeeded at the battle of Reichenbach (1762).[423] Johann Friedrich Hoyer, a Saxon artillery officer, noted that the Prussians chose the Light 6-pdr with a tube weight of 409kg, and mounted the whole crew – an NCO and nine gunners – who dismounted to serve the guns. The horses were held further back behind the guns, and when redeploying the guns to another position the need to collect them together always caused trouble and delay. The gun horse team consisted of six horses.

The Austrians, who experienced the effectiveness of the horse artillery at first hand, were the first to imitate the Prussians after their defeat at

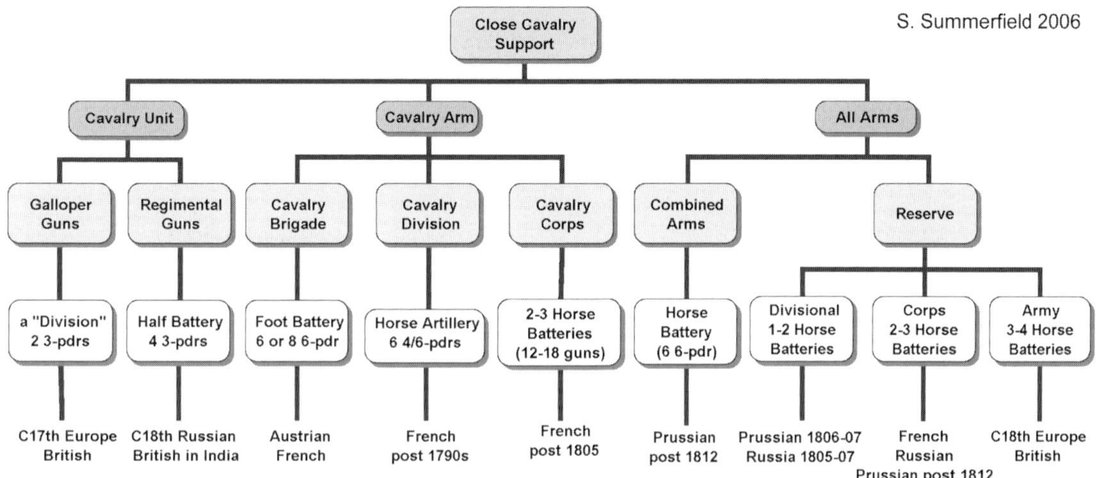

Close cavalry support.

Maxen (21 November 1759). The 12× 3-pdrs were drawn by two teams of four horses, and the unit had a total of 120 horses. The unit was ready for service in June 1760, seeing action later in the year at Prague. In the following year captured Russian horses and equipment formed a second battery of 4× 6-pdrs for use in Silesia. Horse artillery was still somewhat experimental, and in Austria it did not exist as a discrete branch of the artillery until the 1770s – and then in a very different form.

In 1785, the Marquis de Lafayette (1757–1834) saw the Prussian 'flying artillery' in camp in Silesia, and initiated a protracted debate upon the virtues and limitations of horse artillery. Formation was proposed in 1784, but the idea was abandoned, due to its significant cost in money and horses, until 1792.

The Hessian army were the next to adopt an exact copy of the Prussian horse artillery. According to J.F. Hoyer, the Prussians were mistaken in using 6-pdr guns of 18 calibres and weighing 409kg instead of the superior 3-pdr guns. The less cumbersome 3-pdr could be moved faster, and with more than one-third more ammunition carried in the same space. According to Hoyer, in the 1780s

> [Württemberg horse artillery] use 3-pdr and 6-pdr guns, each with two horses, a 'Fuhrmann' [senior driver] with the four horses and two 'Fuhrleuten' [junior drivers]. The latter are in fact artillerymen, armed with a sabre the same as the others. The gun crew is mounted, and consists for the 3-pdr of an NCO and five gunners, for the 6-pdr of an NCO and eight gunners. The horse-holder is seated on the limber. When the gun has to deploy, the horse-holder jumps off the limber to hold the horses of the crew. Limbering is executed as usual, the horse-holder climbing on the limber again. The Duke of Württemberg has a company of this horse artillery with his *Garde*.

Paradoxically, although the fully mounted artillery was quicker to reach its position, it was slower to get into action. The horse-mounted crew members had to find a safe spot to dismount before arriving at their position, but could not leave their horses until the guns were in the correct position and the horse-holder had jumped down from the limber to take over their reins. When limbering up again, the guns had to wait until the crew had mounted again and the horse-holder was once again seated on the limber. Particularly in the case of night surprises, fully mounted horse artillery was notoriously slow to move.[424] Other disadvantages were that Prussian-style horse artillery stripped the best men from the foot artillery, and was costly in horses. A horse battery fired a smaller weight of shot than a foot battery (although the French used 8-pdr horse artillery for a time); and it presented a magnificent target for enemy fire and cavalry attack, with its massed lines of horse-holders, horses and caissons.[425] It also

Prussian horse artillery, 1760, showing M1758 limber and 6-pdr gun.

Russian Horse Artillery Organisation

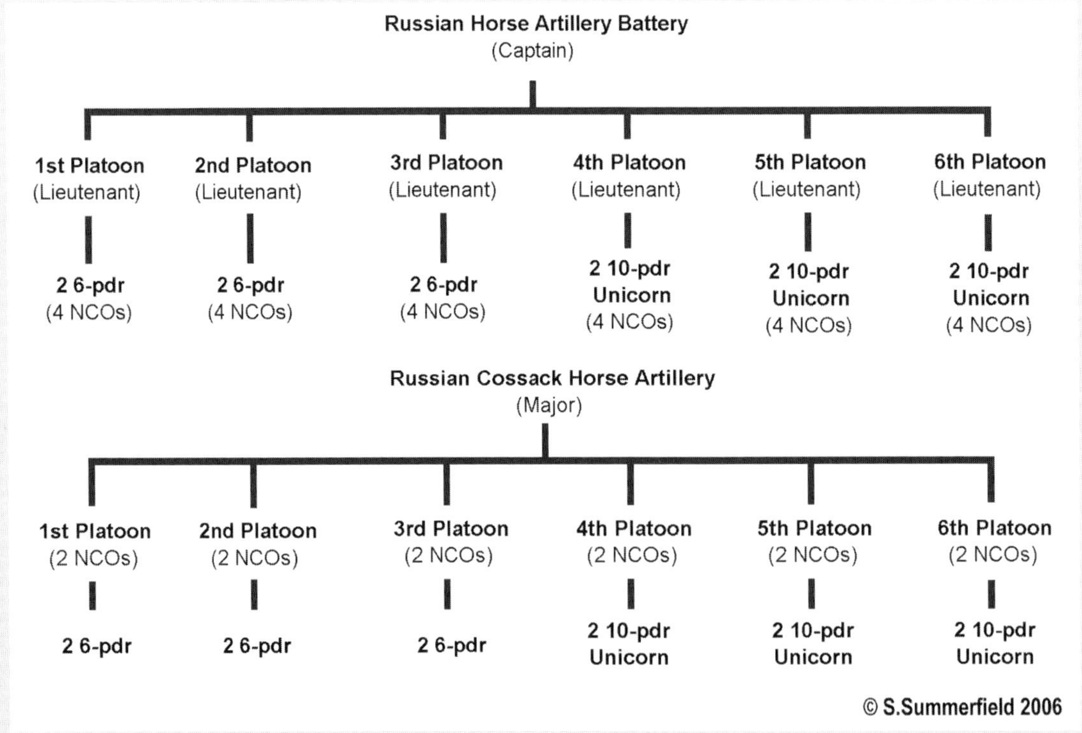

Russian Horse Artillery Battery
(Captain)

1st Platoon (Lieutenant)	**2nd Platoon** (Lieutenant)	**3rd Platoon** (Lieutenant)	**4th Platoon** (Lieutenant)	**5th Platoon** (Lieutenant)	**6th Platoon** (Lieutenant)
2 6-pdr (4 NCOs)	**2 6-pdr** (4 NCOs)	**2 6-pdr** (4 NCOs)	**2 10-pdr Unicorn** (4 NCOs)	**2 10-pdr Unicorn** (4 NCOs)	**2 10-pdr Unicorn** (4 NCOs)

Russian Cossack Horse Artillery
(Major)

1st Platoon (2 NCOs)	**2nd Platoon** (2 NCOs)	**3rd Platoon** (2 NCOs)	**4th Platoon** (2 NCOs)	**5th Platoon** (2 NCOs)	**6th Platoon** (2 NCOs)
2 6-pdr	**2 6-pdr**	**2 6-pdr**	**2 10-pdr Unicorn**	**2 10-pdr Unicorn**	**2 10-pdr Unicorn**

Horse artillery company: 6× 6-pdr guns, 6× ¼-pud (10-pdr) unicorns.
1 staff officer, 6 officers, 24 NCOs ('fireworkers'), 72 bombardiers, 134 gunners, 44 non-combatants/specialists; total 291 personnel.
Cossack horse battery: 6× 6-pdr guns, 6× ¼-pud (10-pdr) unicorns.
1 major, 12 NCOs, 144 artillerymen, 6 craftsmen.

Austrian horse artillery Wurst 6-pdr with crew riding astride the ammunition chest. The off-side horse in the team is ridden by a Handlanger, *who assisted in the manhandling of the piece and was responsible for unloading ammunition from the pack mules. (By kind permission Steven H. Smith)*

took up more space than a foot battery, because of the extended lines.[426]

French cavalry divisions, unlike those of the infantry, did not have permanently attached artillery; when required, horse artillery was attached from the artillery reserve. Sometimes horse artillery batteries were assigned to cavalry divisions or even regiments that acted as rearguards, advance guards or on other duties. Being the most mobile kind of artillery, horse artillery permitted rapid concentration in areas where significant firepower was required, and was an essential part of the artillery reserve.

Austrian System (Vehicle-mounted)

It was in the 1770s that the Austrians considered, and confirmed by experiment, the increased effectiveness of mounting the whole crew on the guns, in order to reach a position and deploy more quickly than Prussian-style horse artillery.[427] The 6-pdr Wurst gun was given a much more elongated carriage than the normal piece, which enabled five men seated one behind the other to ride astride the long ammunition chest mounted on the trail. The gun was pulled by a four-horse team, and was able to advance at the same speed as the cavalry. This concept was unchanged until the 1820s. Each gun had extra ammunition on the limber and on two horses with pack-saddles. When the gun was in position these horses were used to ferry ammunition from the caissons, and formed a reserve for the team in case of need. The sixth crew member, an NCO, was mounted on a separate horse.[428]

The difference between the two concepts was striking. The Austrians were probably slower in their movement from position to position compared to the Prussians, but once there they deployed much more quickly. The only target for the enemy was the gun itself with its crew – much harder to hit than all the extra vehicles and riding horses of the Prussian system.[429] Smola noted in 1827 that the cavalry artillery guns were quicker to unlimber, and that the crew could be at their places in just 10 seconds if running the piece on the *Schleppseil* rope, and remounted on the carriage in just 5 seconds when the piece was to be withdrawn. Although packmules or horses were used to carry ammunition instead of caissons, the train of animals needed was not as long as in the Prussian army. Smola also pointed out that the gun could still operate even after casualties had been taken among the horses, while in the Prussian system the gunners needed individual mounts.[430]

French Artillerie Légère *during the Revolutionary Wars; a Wurst can be seen in the left background. (By kind permission Landes u. Universitätsbibliothek Darmstadt; photograph Marcus Stein)*

Vehicle-mounted artillerymen were also favoured in France from as early as 1784. Upon the first formation of horse artillery in 1791, on 5 June that year the Minister Duportail wrote to Sénarmont, commander of the Metz Division, recommending that the Wurst wagons designed by Manson in 1784 be used in forming the horse artillery. He stated that these 'had great advantages', in that the gunners did not have to be taught to ride and that fewer horses were needed – this saving of expense was not unimportant in time of war.

In 1793, General Eble wrote to the Central Committee of Artillery recommending that the horse artillery use 4-pdr guns and 16-pdr howitzers with the gunners conveyed on Wursts, a system that he considered superior to both foot and horse artillery. He recommended that the Wurst be pulled by six horses with three drivers, and carry seven to eight men. (The use of the 4-pdr was also recommended by Louis Toussard in America.) A report of 1794 concerning the 2nd Company of the 1st Horse Artillery Regiment described the gunners as 'mediocre' in both the artillery and cavalry roles. The same report also stated that of the nine regiments then forming, three were fully mounted and the remaining six were being Wurst-mounted due to the lack of horses. These *Wursts* were used to great effect in the Army of Germany (1794–96) and the Army of Naples (1797–98). The *Artillerie Légère* was used to occupy positions at speed, while the fully-mounted *Artillerie Volante* ('flying artillery') accompanied the cavalry.

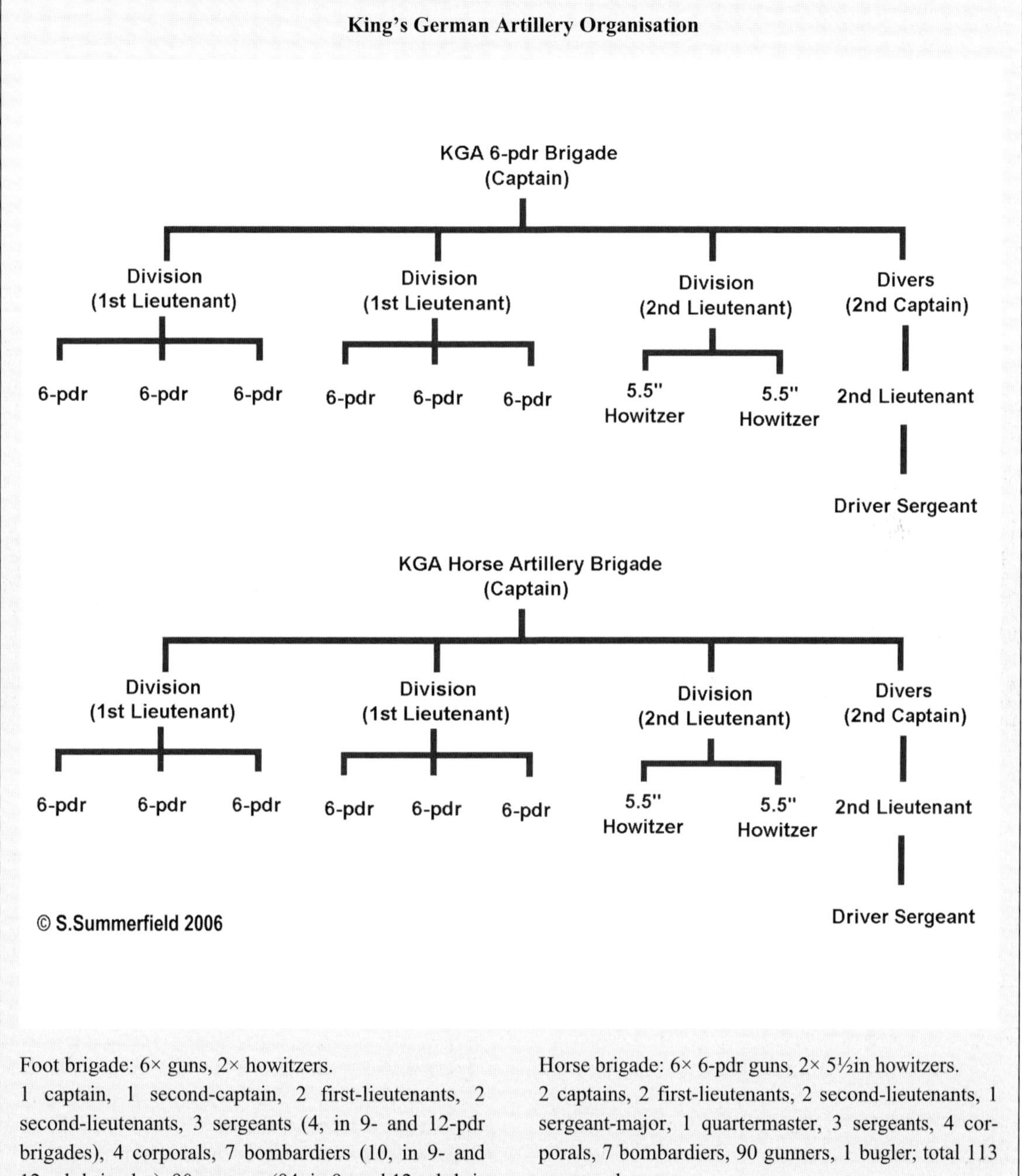

Foot brigade: 6× guns, 2× howitzers.
1 captain, 1 second-captain, 2 first-lieutenants, 2 second-lieutenants, 3 sergeants (4, in 9- and 12-pdr brigades), 4 corporals, 7 bombardiers (10, in 9- and 12-pdr brigades), 90 gunners (94, in 9- and 12-pdr brigades), 1 drummer; total 110–118 personnel.

Horse brigade: 6× 6-pdr guns, 2× 5½in howitzers.
2 captains, 2 first-lieutenants, 2 second-lieutenants, 1 sergeant-major, 1 quartermaster, 3 sergeants, 4 corporals, 7 bombardiers, 90 gunners, 1 bugler; total 113 personnel.

Eble made further comments to the committee in July 1799 advocating the use of vehicle-mounted crews, based on his further experience of operating with them. He argued that mounting every gunner was wasteful in horses, robbing the cavalry of much-needed mounts; and that the service of the cavalryman was not compatible with that of the gunner. By this time the 8-pdr field gun had been taken into service by the horse artillery, as it had more hitting-power than the 4-pdr and could deliver larger loads of canister. The 8-pdr would remain the principal gun for the horse artillery until 1811, when it was replaced by the 6-pdr.

Hanoverian System (Semi Vehicle-mounted)

Shortly before the French Revolutionary Wars the Hanoverians combined the advantages of the Prussian and Austrian systems. The *Geschwinde Artillerie* (fast or flying artillery) used 3-pdrs weighing 273kg, with a large ammunition chest carried on the limber in the Prussian manner. The limber wheels were the same size as the gun carriage wheels, and the pintail used to hitch carriage to limber was replaced with a large hook, mounted directly on the wooden axle block.[431] This had the clear advantage of making both gun and limber the same level, and made the gun carriage quicker to unlimber.

The crew consisted of an NCO and eight gunners. The NCO and four gunners were mounted, while the remaining four gunners rode on the vehicles (two on the gun carriage and two on the limber chest). Six horses drew the gun and limber, and the four riding horses for the mounted gunners could be used to augment the team when crossing soft ground or on bad roads. When a gun was deployed the crew dismounted behind it; one gunner remained with the horses, and the gun was unlimbered by the gunners who had been seated on the carriage.

The Hanoverian horse artillery was considered the finest and fastest in Europe during the Revolutionary Wars. Since half the gunners were vehicle-mounted there were fewer horses involved, and the gun could be brought into action rapidly.[432] This semi vehicle-mounted artillery was copied in Württemberg, and was experimented with for a time in France. It was employed by the King's German Artillery from 1803 until 1815, when they formed the cadre for the new Hanoverian army, and by the Royal Horse Artillery from 1804 to 1816.[433] It is beyond question that this concept of semi vehicle-mounted crews was one of the best for horse artillery: it was proved in battle that the guns were able to follow the cavalry easily even with four gunners riding, and once halted could swiftly be brought into action.

Appendix: Weights and Measures

The conversions to metric equivalents have been corrected to four significant figures. British (Imperial) conversions are given where appropriate.

METRIC SYSTEM

The metric system was adopted by France in 1795 until 1814, and again from 1840 to the present. By 1872, most of Europe had adopted the metric system:

1 kilometre (km) [0.621 miles] = 1,000 metres (m) [1,094 yards]
1 metre (m) [3.281 feet] = 100cm [3.937in] = 1000 millimetres (mm) [0.0397in]
1 tonne [2,205lb] = 1,000 kilograms (kg)
1 kilogram [2.2046lb] = 1000g [0.0353 ounces (oz)]

British (Imperial)

From 1296, London merchants adopted a system of weights known as the 'avoirdupois' from the Old French *aver de peis* ('goods of weight'). The term Imperial dates from the Weights and Measures Act 1824:

1 league (statute) [4.828km] = 3 statute miles
1 statute mile [1.609km] = 1,760 yards = 5,280 feet
1 yard [91.44cm] = 3 feet = 36 inches
1 pace [76.20cm] = 30 inches
1 foot [30.48cm] = 12 inches [25.40mm] = 144 line [2.12mm]
1 long ton [1016kg] = 20 hundredweight (cwt) = 2,240 pounds (lb) [453.6g]
1 hundredweight (cwt) [50.8kg] = 4 quarters (qr) [12.7kg] = 112 pounds (lb) [453.6g]
1 pound (lb) [453.6g] = 16 ounces (oz) [28.35g]

United States of America

The conversions to US weights and measures have been included for American readers. American weights and measures are based upon those used in Britain before 1824.

1 short ton [907.2kg] = 20 short hundredweight (sh cwt) [45.36kg] = 2,000 pounds (lb)
1 pound (lb) [453.6g] = 16 ounces (oz) [28.35g]

Austrian

1 meile [7585m = 4.7141 miles] = 4 klafter [1.896m] = 24,000 fuss [0.3161m]
1 klafter [189.6cm] = 3 schritt (pace) [63.20cm] = 6 fuss (foot) [31.61cm] = 72 zoll (inch) [2.634cm] = 864 linie [0.2195mm]
1 centner (Austrian hundredweight) [56.0kg] = 100 Pfund [0.560kg]
1 pfund (Viennese pound) [560.0g = 1.234677lb] = 16 unze [35g] = 32 loth [17.54g] = 16 pfennig [1.094g]

Dutch (Amsterdam)

The metric system became compulsory in 1820.

1 mile (Dutch) = 5854m
1 elle [68.78cm] = 2.5 voeten [28.31cm]
1 voeten [283.1mm] = 12 diume [23.59mm] = 144 lyne (Dutch line) [2.144mm]
1 pond (Amsterdam pound) [494.1g] = 16 unze (ounce) [30.88g]

French (pre-metric, and 1814-40)

Until 7 April 1795, Revolutionary France continued to use the same measures as the *Ancien Régime*, derived from the Charlemagne system and suffering from a great range of regional variations. These were reintroduced in 1814, but replaced once more with the metric system by the Law of 4 July 1837 which came into force from January 1840.

1 lieue de Paris (league) [4444m = 2.7617 miles] = 2280 toise de Paris
1 lieue de poste (league) [3898m = 2.422 miles] = 2000 toise de Paris
1 toise de Paris [1.949m = 2.1314 yards] = 6 pied de Paris [0.3248m]
1 pied de Paris [32.48cm = 0.3552 yards = 1.0655 feet] = 12 pouce de Paris [2.707cm = 1.0658in] = 144 ligne de Paris [0.2256cm = 0.0888in] = 1728 point de Paris [0.1880mm]
1 millier [489.5kg = 1079.219lb] = 1000 livre (pound) [0.4895kg = 1.0702lb]

1 livre de marc (pound) [489.5g = 1.0792lb] = 16 once poid de marc (ounce) [30.59g = 1.0792 oz]

On 1 February 1812, Napoleon introduced the pseudo-metric form, used until abolished in 1814:

1 lieue (metric league) [4000m = 2.486 miles] = 2000 toise (metric) [2.000m = 2.18727 yards] = 6060 pied (metric) [0.333m]
1 pied (metric) [33.3cm = 0.3645 yard = 13.12in] = 12 pouce (metric) [2.75cm = 1.0936in] = 144 ligne (metric) [0.233cm]
1 double livre [1000g] = 2 livre (metric) [500g = 1.1024lb] = 4 demi-livre [250g] = 8 quarteron [125g] = 1000 grammes

German
Germany, with over 300 states, suffered from a myriad of measurement systems; it was not until 1872 that the metric system came into use throughout Imperial Germany.

Baden
The old measures were based upon those of Fribourg:
1 fuss (Old Baden) [29.1cm = 0.32072 yards] = 12 zoll [24.25mm = 0.9622in]
1 pfund [528.8g = 1.165887lb] = 32 loth [16.52g] = 128 quentchen [4.13g]

In 1810, Baden instigated new weights and measures based upon the metric system:

1 meil [8888m = 5.5234 miles] = 2 stunden [4444m]
1 ruthe [300.0cm] = 10 fuss [30.0cm = 0.3281cm] = 1000 linie [0.30cm]
1 pfund [500.0g = 1.1024lb] = 10 zehning [50.0g] = 100 centass [5.0g] = 1000 pfennig [0.50g]

Bavaria
Bavaria embodied a number of states, with varied weights and measures, until 1810.

1 meil (Anspach) [8633m = 5.3652 miles] = 2880 ruthe [3.00m] = 28800 fuss [0.300m]
1 meil (Munich) [7424m = 4.6143 miles] = 2400 ruthe [3.094m] = 24000 fuss [0.3094m]
1 pfund (Anspach) [509.9g]
1 pfund (Munich) [561.2g = 1.2372lb] = 16 unze [35.08g] = 32 loth [17.54g] = 128 quentchen [4.38g]

On 28 February 1809, King Maximilian Joseph decreed a standardised measurement system throughout his kingdom, to come into force on 1 January 1810.

1 ruthen [291.9m] = 100 zoll
1 fuss [29.19cm] = 12 zoll (inch) [24.33mm] = 144 linie [2.03g]
1 pfund [560.0g = 1.234655lb] = 16 unze [35g] = 32 loth [17.5g] = 128 quentchen [4.375g]

Brunswick
1 miel [10864m = 6.7520 miles] = 34424 Rhenish fuss [1.0297 feet]
1 elle [57.3cm = 0.621 yards] = 2 schuh [28.7cm] = 24 zoll [2.4mm]
1 schiffpfund [130.9kg] = 20 liespund [6.545g] = 280 pfund [0.4675kg]
1 pfund [467.5g = 1.0306lb] = 32 loth [14.51g] = 128 quentchen [3.65g]

Hanover
1 meil [10252m = 6.3779 miles]
1 elle [58.40cm = 0.6386 yards] = 2 fuss [29.20cm] = 24 zoll [2.43cm] = 288 linie [0.203cm]
1 pfund [489.6g = 1.0794lb] = 16 unze [30.6g] = 32 loth [15.3g] = 128 quentchen [3.83g]

Hesse-Kassel
For retail purposes the Berlin *pfund* was used.

1 fuss [28.76cm = 0.3145 yards] = 12 zoll [2.40cm] = 144 linie [0.20cm]
1 pfund [484.2g = 1.0675lb] = 16 unze [30.26g] = 32 loth [15.13g] = 128 quentchen [3.78g]

Hesse-Darmstadt (Frankfort)
Hesse-Darmstadt used Frankfort weights and measures until 1821.

1 fuss [28.5cm = 0.3112 yards] = 12 zoll [23.7mm = 0.9338in] = 144 linie [1.98mm]
1 pfund (Frankfort) [505.3g = 1.1141lb] = 16 unze [31.58g] = 32 loth [15.79g] = 128 quentchen [3.95g]

Prussia (Berlin)
The Prussian system was the most commonly used in northern Germany.

1 miel [7412m = 4.6068 miles] = 2000 ruthe [3.706m] = 24000 rheinfuss [30.9cm]
1 rheinfuss [31.39cm] = 12 zoll [2.615cm] = 144 linie [2.180mm]
1 pfund (pre-1816) [468.5g = 1.032895lb] = 32 loth [14.64g] = 512 pfennig [0.9150g]

Saxony (Leipzig)
1 miel [6793m = 4.2220 miles]
1 elle [56.53cm = 0.6182 yards] = 2 fuss [28.27cm] = 24 zoll [2.35cm] = 240 linie [0.235cm]
1 pfund [467.5g = 1.0306lb] = 16 unze [29.2g] = 32 loth [14.6g] = 128 quentlein [3.65g]

Württemberg
Weights similar to those of Prussia were used. In 1806, the zoll was set at 127 *lignes de Paris*.

1 miel [7406m = 4.6028 miles]
1 fuss [0.3133 yards = 28.7cm] = 10 zoll [1.1280in=2.87cm] = 100 linie [2.87mm]
1 pfund (Leipzig) [467.7g = 1.0311lb] = 32 loth [14.62g]

Other German pound weights:
1 pfund (Cologne) = 440.0g
1 pfund (Middleburg) = 444.5g
1 pfund (Rhineland, Westphalia) = 435.5g

Iberian Peninsula

Portugal
1 legoa (league) [6157m = 3.8265 miles] = 3 milha (mile) [2052m] = 24 estadio [256.5m] = 5616 vara [1.096m]
1 vara (yard) [109.6m] = 5 palmo (short) [21.93cm] = 40 pollegada [2.74cm = 1.0827in]
1 covado [67.72cm] = 3 palmo [22.57cm]
1 pe (foot) [32.85cm] = 12 pollegada (inch) [2.74cm] = linha (line) [0.2281cm]
1 arratel (pound) [459.0g] = 16 onca (ounce) [28.69g] = 128 outava [3.59g]

Spain
The variations in weights and measures between provinces were minor, so the Madrid system is given. The *legua* for Spanish maps and to mark the Great Roads was calculated as equal to 2/35ths of a degree, in 1718–67 as 3.9461 miles, and from 1768 as 4.1508 miles. However, the 'common' league of 3.4234 miles was frequently used. The metric system was compulsory from 1860.

1 legua (1718–68) [6349m = 3.9461 miles] = 7605 vara [83.59cm] = 22815 pie [27.86cm]
1 legua (1768–1860) [6679m = 4.1508 miles] = 4800 paso [1.393m] = 8000 vara [0.8359m] = 24000 pie [0.2786m]
1 common legua [5508m = 3.4234 miles] = 800 cuerda [6.885m] = 6600 vara [0.8359m] = 19800 pie [0.2786m]
1 vara (yard) [83.59cm] = 3 pie or tervia (foot) [27.86cm] = 36 pulgada (inch) [2.322cm] = 432 linea [0.1451cm]
1 tonelada [920.2kg] = 2,000 libra
1 libra (pound) [460.0g] = 16 onza (ounce) [28.76g] = 128 ochava

Italian
There was a great deal of variation before 1861, when the metric system became compulsory.

Genoa (Duchy of Genoa)
1 pie [51.37cm = 0.5618 yards] = 12 once [4.28cm]
1 libbra [348.8g = 0.7690lb] = 12 oncia [29.06g = 0.0641lb]

Milan (Lombardy)
Lombardy used the Milan weights and measures until 1803, when Milan adopted the metric system. This became compulsory in the rest of Italy in 1861. The 'Italian pound' was 1kg.

1 miglio [1856m = 1.1536 miles]
1 braccio (Milan) [59.5cm = 0.6414 yards] = pie [0.4759 yards] = 12 once (inch) [4.958cm = 1.9242in]
1 libbra peso sottile [327.0g = 0.7209lb] = 4 quarto [81.75g] = 28 oncia [11.68g]
1 libbra peso grosso [763.0g = 1.6821lb] = 12 oncia [63.58g] = 288 denaro [2.65g]

Naples (Kingdom of the Two Sicilies)
Units varied between Messina, Palermo and Syracuse.

1 miglio [1845.9m = 1.1593 miles] = 7000 palmo [0.2637m]
1 canna [210.96cm = 2.3068 yards] = 8 palmo [26.37cm = 10.3810in] = 96 oncia [2.20cm = 0.8651in]
1 libbra [320.8g = 0.7072lb] = 12 oncia [26.73g] = 360 trapeso [0.891g]

Papal States (Rome)
1 miglio [1488m = 0.9252 miles]
1 canna [199.2cm = 2.1785 yards] = 2 braccio [99.60cm] = 6 pie [33.17cm = 0.3258 yards] = 8 palmo [24.88cm = 9.8034in] = 24 linea [8.3cm]
1 libbra [346.3g = 0.7476lb] = 12 oncia [28.86g] = 288 denaro [1.20g]

Piedmont (Turin)
1 miglio [2226m = 1.383 miles] = 7600 pie [0.293m]
1 raso [58.6cm] = 2 pie [29.3cm = 0.3746 yards] = 16 oncia [4.281cm]
1 piede liprando [51.38cm = 0.5619 yards] = 12 oncia (inch) [4.281cm = 1.6855in] = 144 punto (point) [0.3568cm]
1 libbra [369.1g = 0.8133lb] = 12 oncia [30.75g] = 96 ottavo [3.84g] = 288 denaro [1.28g]

Venice (Republic of Venice)
1 miglio [1834m = 1.1397 miles] = 1000 passo [1.834m] = 5000 pie [0.3668m]
1 braccio (Venice) [68.3cm] = 2 pie [34.8cm = 13.6775in] =12 palmo [2.9cm = 1.14in]
1 libbra peso grosso [478.5g = 1.0527lb] = 12 oncia [39.88g] = 72 saggio [6.65cm]

Russian
The old system of units lasted until 1831:

1 archine [71.15cm = 0.7780 yards] = 2 stopa [35.57cm] = 24 verschok [2.964cm] = 32 paletz [2.22cm]
1 pud [16.38kg = 36.0676lb] = 40 funt (pound) [0.4095kg = 0.9012lb]
1 funt (pound) [409.5g] = 16 lana (ounce) [25.59g] = 32 loth [12.80g] = 96 zolotnic [4.27g]

From the time of Tsar Peter the Great the artillery *pud* was defined as the weight of a cast-iron ball of 2 British inches (5.08cm) diameter, and a weight of 115 zolotnics:

1 Russian artillery pud = 490.6g

Scandinavian
Denmark and Norway
These differed little one from another.

1 mil (Danish) [7546m] = 2400 rode = 12000 aln [0.6296m] = 24000 fod [0.3148m]
1 aln [62.96cm] = 2 fod [31.48cm = 0.3442 yards] = 24 tomme [1.312cm] = 288 linie [0.109cm]
1 pund (Danish) [499.4g = 1.1009lb] = 16 unze [31.2g] = 32 lod [15.6g] = 128 quintin [3.90g]

Sweden
1 mil (mile) [5344m] = 9,000 aln (ell) [0.5938m] = 18,000 fot (foot) [0.2969m]
1 aln [59.37cm = 0.64763 yards] = 2 fot (foot) [29.69cm] = 24 turn (inch) [2.474cm]
1 turn (inch) [24.74mm] = 12 linie (Swedish inch) [2.062mm]
1 skälpund (pound, food weight) [425.1g] = 16 untz [26.57g] = 32 lod [0.8203g]
1 Swedish pound (iron weight) [340.2g]

Bibliography for the Appendix

Alexander, J.H. (1857), *Universal Dictionary of Weights and Measures, Ancient and Modern*, W.M. Winifie, Baltimore

Allen, R. C. and T. E. Murphy (2005), *Just before the metre, the gram, the litre: Building a Rosetta Stone of Weights and Measures in the Early Modern World*, Tables I (Length) and IV (Weight), Version 05.08, www.nuffield.ox.ac.uk/users/murphy/measures/before_metre.htm

Cararelli, F. (1999), *Scientific Unit Conversion*, 2nd edn, Springer-Verlag, London

Doursther, H. (1840), *Dictionnaire Universel des Poids et Mesures Anciens et Modernes, contenant des Tables de Monnaies de Tous les Pays*, Amsterdam

Kula, W. (1986), *Measures and Men*, Princeton University Press

Ricard, S. (1781), *Traité général du commerce - Édition entiérement refaite d'après un plan nouveau, rédigée & considérablement augmentée*, Vol II, E. van Harrevelt et A. Soetens, Amsterdam

Glossary

ORDNANCE

Affut à chevrette (French) Carriage with *chevrette*.

Affut à flèche (French) Block-trail.

Affut-portatif (French) A Piedmont designed gun-sledge carriage similar to the *affut-traineau*, but with iron bolts instead of wooden transoms making the equipment lighter.

Affut-porte corps (French) A mountain artillery carriage with two parallel cheeks connected by three horizontal wooden transoms and iron bolts. The trunnion positions were set at the front and at the mid-point of the carriage.

Affut-traineau (French) Gun-sledge carriage.

Astragal Small convex molding used in the ornamental work of the cannon tube. It was usually connected with a fillet or flat molding.

Axle (-tree) The rod connecting opposite wheels of a carriage, upon which they rotate.

Base ring The first metal band at the base of the breech of a piece of ordnance, often marked with the name of the caster.

Battery wagon A two-wheeled cart used to carry the tools and supplies necessary to keep the leather, cloth and wooden equipment of the battery in good condition. It was linked to a limber to form a four-wheeled vehicle.

Bed The support or base of a mortar, made of wood or cast iron.

Block-trail (stock-trail) Type of two-wheeled gun carriage with short cheeks supporting the tube, attached each side of a single central beam forming the trail.

Bolster The transverse wooden spar behind the axle and before the sweepbar.

Bore Includes all the drilled out portion of the tube including the chamber (if there is one), the cylinder, and the conical or spherical surface connecting them with the drilled out section.

Bore diameter The internal width of a gun at its muzzle.

Bore length The entire length measurement inside the tube including the chamber, if one was present.

Bracket carriage (travelling carriage) Two-wheeled gun carriage formed from two full-length cheeks, separated by horizontal transoms.

Brass Alloy composed of copper and zinc.

Breech The closed rear part of a gun tube.

Bricole (French) **(men's harnisse or drag rope)** A rope used by a man to drag a gun.

Bronze (gunmetal) Copper and tin alloy, normally containing small quantities of zinc and lead.

Bush A drilled plug inserted into the touch-hole of a gun.

Caisson Specially designed wagon employed for the transportation of ammunition.

Calibre The diameter of the bore of a gun; often quoted by contemporaries in multiples, to define the length of pieces of ordnance.

Capsquare Iron plates that pass over the trunnions of a gun to secure them to the carriage.

Carriage The wheeled support on which a gun is mounted or transported.

Carronade A short-barrelled piece of ordnance made by the Carron iron company in Scotland.

Cascable (cascabel, back-weight) The external extension at the extremity of the breech, of the same diameter as the gun's bore. This facilitated the handling of the piece when mounting and dismounting it.

Cast iron A hard, brittle, impure form of iron obtained by remelting pig iron with limestone.

Chamber The rearmost part of the breech holding the propellant charge for the projectile. The *cylindrical chamber* common in howitzers had a smaller diameter than the main bore, with either a rounded or squared end. The *conical chamber* (or 'Gomer' chamber, after its inventor) was shaped like the frustum of a cone, and was used in mortars and howitzers. The *spherical chamber* was used in early mortars, the sphere being joined to the bore by a small-diameter cylinder.

Chase The part of the gun in front of the trunnions.

Cheek The side-piece of the gun carriage that supported the trunnion.

Chevrette (French) Iron supporting leg used in mountain artillery carriage.

Dolphins (handles) Two handles placed over the centre of gravity of the piece in order to assist in mounting or dismounting; normally found only on bronze pieces. Originally these handles were ornamental and cast to represent dolphins.

Elevating screw Vertical adjustment screw running through the transom of a gun, enabling the rapid elevation of the barrel.

Felloes (fellows, fellies) Curved sections of wood joined to form the circumference of a wheel.

Handspike (trailspike, traversing lever) Wooden lever about 2m long, either straight or with a curved end, used to manoeuvre a gun into place.

***Hausse* sight** (German) A free-swinging sighting piece attached to a seat on the barrel near the breech. The sight consisted of an upright piece of sheet brass with a movable slider. The slider traveled along a graduated scale. At the lower end of the sight was a lead-filled bulb that allowed the scale to remain in a vertical position regardless of the rough ground or the trunnions. This allowed the *hausse* sight to be used when the breech sight and tangent scale were affected by a faulty position of the trunnions.

Howitzer A short-barrelled piece firing explosive shell or canister.

Limber A two-wheeled vehicle used to pull an artillery piece, often fitted with ammunition boxes.

Limonière (French) A double shaft attachment for a horse or mule used to move a mountain gun in draft.

Linchpin Iron pin-and-ring set inserted into the wheel hub of the carriage to prevent the wheel from sliding off the axle.

Lunette (French) An iron ring located on the trail of a gun carriage, used to attach the carriage to the limber.

Mantlet A bullet-proof shield made of wood, rope matting or metal, used to protect gun crews at embrasures.

Mortar A short piece of ordnance for throwing shells at high angles.

Muzzle The mouth of a gun tube.

Muzzle-loader A weapon which had the projectile and charge loaded through the mouth of the bore. The term applies to all types of ordnance in this period.

Nave The central hub of a wheel, uniting the axle and spokes.

Ordnance A term used to describe all kinds of artillery.

Perrier A small type of gun or a mortar used to throw bagged or netted stones as anti-personnel projectiles.

Pintle (pin-tail) An iron upright spike on the limber to connect to the lunette ring on the gun.

Prolonge (French) A 14m-long hempen rope with a hook at one end and a toggle at the other, used to attach the gun to the limber when retiring the gun to a new position.

Quoin (coyne, coin) A wooden wedge used under the breech for raising and depressing a barrel on its carriage.

Rechtsmaschine (*Richtsmachine*: modern German) Screw-driven elevating wedge.

Reinforce The breech half of the barrel, from the breech ring to the ring before the trunnions, made stronger to withstand the detonation of the powder charge.

Rimbase The short cylinder that united the trunnion with the body of the weapon so providing extra strength at the trunnion junction and to limit any sideways movement in the trunnion beds.

Schleppseil (German) A 7m-long drag rope, first used by the Prussians to connect the horse to the gun directly.

Splinter-bar Part of a limber that transfers the traction to the body of the limber. This can be fixed (e.g. French M1765) or pivoting (e.g. Austrian M1753).

Strake Iron strengthening plate fitted to the rim of a wheel.

Sweep-bar Rearmost transverse part of the limber.

Swingletree A pivoted cross bar to which the trains of a horse are fastened so equilibriating the forward and backward motions of the horse's shoulders.

Trail The part of the gun carriage behind the cheeks (on stock-trail pieces), or the rear part of the cheeks (on bracket carriages), that rests on the ground when the gun is unlimbered.

Transom Pieces of wood that join the cheeks of the gun carriage horizontally.

Trucks Small solid wood or iron wheels used on some gun carriages, particularly naval.

Trunnions The two short cylinders projecting from either side of a gun barrel at the point of balance, which rest on the cheeks of the carriage to support and secure the barrel.

Tube The correct term for a gun's barrel.

Tube length The entire length measurement inside the tube including the chamber.

Unicorn (licorne) A Russian gun-howitzer with a conical chamber designed to shoot both roundshot and shell. Its name stems from the early examples having dolphins fashioned in the form of unicorns.

Vent (touch hole) The small hole bored through the breech end of the gun's tube, through which the charge is ignited by means of a fuse or priming powder.

Vent field (vent patch) The area of the breech where the vent is drilled.

Windage The space between the surfaces of the loaded projectile and the inside of the tube; the difference between the bore diameter and the diameter of the projectile.

AMMUNITION AND FIRING

Ammunition The common name for all the types of projectiles fired from the gun tube.

Apron A piece of sheet lead or leather used to protect the vent against the elements when not in action.

Canister (-shot) A metal cylinder containing iron or lead balls packed in sawdust, fired at close range as an anti-personnel projectile.

Carcass A projectile containing an incendiary composition for setting fire to inflammable targets.

Cartridge bag (*cartouche* (French), **powder bag)** Bag filled with measured charge of gunpowder and seated behind the projectile, to be pierced and then ignited via the touch hole.

Charge (powder, service, propellant charge) The amount of gunpowder needed to fire a specified projectile the desired distance.

Field ammunition Projectiles designated for use in field artillery pieces, i.e. solid shot, shell, canister- and case-shot.

Fixed ammunition A pre-assembled projectile complete with sabot and powder bag, that eased handling and permitted an increased rate of fire.

Fuse The means of igniting the propellant charge in a gun, or the bursting charge in a shell; either a length of match, or a tube filled with a highly flammable composition.

Gimlet A heavy metal wire with a wooden handle on one end and a screw at the other, used to remove broken fuses or other obstructions from the vent of a tube.

Grape (grapeshot) Projectile in form of multiple iron balls enclosed in a canvas bag or formed around a stand.

Graze The point where a projectile touches the ground without coming to rest.

Gunner's pouch A leather pouch which fastened to the waist belt, holding the gunner's level, gimlet, vent-spike and chalk.

Gyn A field service crane consisting of a wooden 'A'-frame fitted with a windlass and a series of blocks-and-tackles.

Incendiary shell A hollow projectile with a front compartment for a bursting charge and a rear compartment for a flammable mixture.

Linstock A wooden rod about 75cm long, used to hold a length of smouldering slowmatch for igniting the priming powder in the vent of a gun, or later as a reserve source of ignition from which to light the more portable and efficient portfire. The staff was often tipped with sprung jaws to secure the match, and at the other end an iron ferrule so that it could be thrust into the ground.

Portfire Device for igniting the fuse or priming a gun; a paper tube filled with a flammable mixture that would burn (from full length) for about ten minutes, and could not be extinguished by water. The enclosed *portfire case* of leather or copper held ten or twelve portfires. The *porte-lance* or *portfire stock* was used to hold the portfire. The *portfire cutter* was a strong pair of scissors used to cut the portfire to different lengths.

Powder measure Cylindrical copper utensil with a cutaway flanged end, used to measure and handle loose powder for projectiles and weapons.

Priming Small amount of powder placed in and around the vent of a piece; when ignited, this fired the main charge.

Quadrant A metal or wooden instrument that measured the required degree of elevation of the piece.

Quickmatch Cord made of cotton soaked in spirits and coated with a paste of mealed powder; a metre of quickmatch takes 12–13 seconds to burn.

Rammer Shaped wooden block fitting the bore of a gun, attached to a wooden staff often of elm, poplar or maple, and used to drive the powder cartridge and projectile to the base of the bore in preparation for firing. A combination rammer-and-sponge or rammer-and-brush tool was used with most artillery pieces; these had an absorbent sheepswool sponge or a bristle scouring-brush attached to the opposite end.

Sabot Shallow softwood disc fitting the bore of a gun, attached behind a projectile and sometimes with the cartridge bag attached behind it, to form fixed ammunition. It served as a driving band for the projectile, and helped protect the base of canister-shot.

Saltpetre (nitre) Potassium nitrate (KNO_3)

Shell (common shell) A hollow cast-iron projectile containing a bursting charge, ignited by means of a timed fuse.

Shot (roundshot, solid shot, cannonball) A solid cast-iron spherical projectile

Shrapnel (spherical case-shot) A shell with thinner walls, ignited by means of a timed fuse, and filled with lead or iron balls in a sulphur or pitch matrix around a bursting charge in a thin tin or iron container.

Slowmatch Hemp or flax cord soaked in strong lye; this burns at a rate of 10–13cm per hour.

Sponge Made of sheepskin or coarse, well-twisted woollen yarn, fashioned into a cylindrical bag shape and fastened to a wooden staff, for swabbing the bore of a gun after firing to extinguish any remaining sparks and cool the metal.

Sponge bucket Hooked to the gun carriage on the march, this held water for dipping the sponge-head when washing out the tube.

Thumb stall Made of buckskin with horsehair, etc., stuffed under the pad, this protected against heat when the gunner 'stopped the vent' (placed his finger over the touch hole) during the sponging procedure.

Tompion (tampion) An iron, brass or wooden stopper used to plug the muzzle of artillery pieces to protect the bore when not in action. Many tompions had cork attached for a more secure fit.

Vent punch A tool for clearing the vent of any obstructions. It had an octagonal head with a hole in the centre, and a flat-ended wire brazed to it.

Ventspike (priming wire, priming iron) Wire tool, often of non-ferrous metal to avoid sparks, pointed at one end with a loop grip at the other. It was inserted through the vent to pierce the cartridge bag seated in the bore, thus allowing the flame from the fuse or priming to reach the propellant charge.

Worm (wadhook) An iron tool resembling a large double corkscrew attached to a long wooden staff, to remove debris from the bore of a gun after firing, or to draw a misfired charge.

ORGANISATION

Armoury A manufacturing or storage facility for arms and ordnance.

Arsenal A storage facility for ordnance and ordnance stores. Some arsenals were also used for the construction and repair of ordnance equipment.

Artificer (artisan) Skilled workman responsible for the repair and maintenance of gun carriages and other items of rolling stock.

Artillery park An artillery grouping made up of the spare carriages, reserved supply of ammunition, and the tools and materials for extensive repairs and for making up ammunition for the service of the army in the field. Reserve batteries were usually attached to the field park.

Artillery reserve Designated batteries that were to remain limbered and hitched, ready to move quickly into position during battle. Their purpose was to replace disabled batteries or to move rapidly to where the enemy was massing for an attack.

Battalion/regimental guns Light field pieces attached to infantry units

Battery (1) A number of pieces of ordnance and their equipment; (2) the company of troops charged with serving a certain number of pieces of ordnance; (3) an artillery emplacement

Bombardier An artilleryman versed in the handling of bombs and shells, mortars and howitzers, grenades and fuses.

Brigade (Bde) (1) A British artillery company; (2) a formation of two or more regiments of infantry or cavalry under a single commander.

Company (Co. or Coy) A military unit of about 100–200 men

Corps (army corps) A formation of two or more divisions of infantry, with attached cavalry and artillery, under a single commander. In looser contemporary terms, used generically to refer to any particular military unit.

Division (Div) (1) Two field pieces with attendant vehicles; (2) a formation of two or more brigades of infantry or cavalry under a single commander.

Geschwinde Artillerie (German) Horse Artillery. Literally fast or flying artillery.

Gun captain (gun commander) The most senior rank in a gun's crew, typically an NCO, who was responsible for 'laying' or aiming the piece, and for giving the orders for loading, firing and cleaning the weapon.

Gun crew (detachment) Small number of military personnel responsible for the maintenance, transportation and operation of a single piece of ordnance and its necessary equipment and horses. Support personnel within a battery, company or brigade also included drivers, horse-holders, and specialists such as blacksmiths.

Gunner A member of an artillery crew; or specifically that senior member, usually a junior NCO, who was responsible for actually firing the weapon.

Handlanger (German) An artillery labourer.

Horse artillery (flying artillery) A highly manoeuvrable artillery unit in which all the gunners were mounted or rode on vehicles.

Oberst (German) Colonel.

Oberst-leutnant (German) Lieutenant-Colonel.

Ouvrier (French) *See* Artificer.

Piece The generic term used to denote any artillery weapon.

Sub-division A Royal Horse Artillery unit of one gun, limber, caisson and detachment.

Train (artillery train) The troops responsible for driving the artillery transport and support vehicles.

Notes

1 Napoleon (18 August 1809), 'To General Clarke, Minister of War,' *Correspondence No.15678, 19:361*
2 Napoleon (29 May 1809) 'To General Clarke, Minister of War,' *Correspondence No.15726, 19:58*
3 Napoleon (21 October 1805), 'Proclamation,' *Correspondence No.9405, 11:343*; also (14 February 1807) 'To Empress Josephine,' *Correspondence No.11813, 14:304*; (9 February 1807) 'To Cambacères, Prince Arch-Chancellor,' *Correspondence No.11788*; (11 February 1807) 'To Duroc, Grand Marshal of the Palace,' *Correspondence No.11789, 14:290–291*; (11 February 1807) 'To Empress Josephine,' *No.11798, 14:297*; (25 February 1807) 'To Prince Jerome,' *Correspondence No.11876, 14:332–33*
4 Cook, C. and J. Stevenson (1998), *The Longman Handbook of Modern European History, 1763–1997,* 3rd edn, Longman, London, pp 275–282
5 Seignobos, C. (1904), *A Political History of Contemporary Europe since 1814*, William Heinemann, London, pp 374–375 (trans from 1901 French edn)
6 Scott, H.M. (1990), *Enlightened Absolutism: Reform and the Reformers in Later Eighteenth Century Europe*, London
7 Gill, J.H. (1992), *With Eagles to Glory: Napoleon and his German Allies in the 1809 Campaign*, Greenhill Books, London
8 Hofschröer, P. (1995), *1815, The Waterloo Campaign – Wellington, his German Allies and the Battles of Ligny and Quatre Bras*, Greenhill Books, London
9 Cook and Stevenson (1998), *op cit* p 73
10 Rowe, M. (2001), 'Napoleon and State Formation in Central Europe', in P.G. Dwyer, *Napoleon and Europe*, Longman, London, p 223
11 Lendy, Captain A.F. (1862), *Treatise on Fortification*, W. Mitchell, London, pp 10–23
12 Coignet, J-R. (1928), *The Note-Books of Captain Coignet*, 5th Notebook, Peter Davis Ltd, London
13 Bronze gunmetal has a specific gravity of 8.8 gcm^{-3} compared to 7.207 gcm^{-3} for cast iron. (Captain A. Modecal (1850), *The Ordnance Manual for the Use of the Officers of the United States Army*, 2nd edn, Gideon and Company, Washington, p 409)
14 Roberts, Captain J. (1863), *The Handbook of Artillery for the Service of the United States (Army and Militia)*, D. Van Nostrand, New York, p 10
15 Landmann I. (1801), *The Principles of Artillery reduced into Questions and Answers for use of the Royal Military Academy at Woolwich*, W. Glendinning, London, pp 14–18
16 French bronze (90% copper and 10% tin) has specific gravity of 8.8 gcm^{-3}, and 450 MNm^{-2} (Tottle, C.R., 1984, *An Encyclopaedia of Metallurgy and Materials*, MacDonald and Evans, Plymouth, England, p xvi)
17 Landmann, I. (1801), *op cit*
18 Admiralty gunmetal (British Standard G1) contains 88% copper, 10% tin and 2% zinc; it has a specific gravity of 8.8 gcm^{-3}, and melts at 1010°C. (Tottle, C.R., 1984, *op cit* p xxx)
19 Gunmetal (British Standard LG4) of 88% copper, 7% tin, 2% and 3% lead, has a Brinell Hardness of 70–85. (Tottle, C.R., 1984, *op cit* p xxx)
20 Leslie, Major J.H., ed (1905, r/p 1991), *The Dickson Manuscript,* Ken Trotman, Cambridge
21 Osborne, A.K. (1967), *An Encyclopaedia of the Iron and Steel Industry*, 2nd edn, The Technical Press Ltd, London, pp 62–63
22 Landmann, I. (1801), *op cit* pp 14–18
23 Osborne, A.K. (1967), *op cit* pp 465
24 Douglas, General Sir H. (1860), *A Treatise on Naval Gunnery*, 5th edn, John Murray, London, pp 96–108
25 Lavery, B. (1987), *The Arming and Fitting of English Ships of War*, Conway Maritime Press, London, pp 263–265: Proofing of iron guns
26 Lendy, Captain A.F. (1862), *op cit* pp 6–7
27 Roberts, Captain J. (1863), *op cit* p 124
28 Hurford, R. (2006), personal communication, from internationally renowned wheelwright
29 Lendy, Captain A.F. (1862), *op cit* pp 7–8; Nelson R.J. (1846 r/p 1972), *Gun Carriages, An Aide Memoire to the Military Sciences*, Royal Engineers,

(r/p Museum Restoration Service, Canada) pp 57–64
30 Lendy Captain A.F. (1862), *op cit,* pp 8–20
31 Caruana, A.B. (1997), *The History of English Sea Ordnance (II) The Age of the System 1715–1815*, Jean Boudriot Publications, East Sussex, pp 357–404: See also Lavery, B. (1987), *op cit,* pp 126–134
32 Campana, J. (1901), *L'Artillerie en Campagne 1792–1901*, Berger-Levrault, Paris
33 Susane (1874), *Histoire de l'Artillerie Française*, Hetzel, Paris
34 Rostaing, Comte de (1786), *Aide Mémoire à l'Usage des Bouches de Feu,* Chez Magimal, Paris
35 Dolleczek (1872), *Geschichte der Österreichischen Artillerie*, Vienna
36 Gassendi, J.B. (1809), *Manual d'Artillerie*, Paris
37 Scharnhorst, D.G. von (1812), *Exerzir-Reglement für die Artillerie der Königlich Preussischen Armee*, Berlin
38 *ibid*
39 Trefil, James (2002), *Cassell's Laws of Nature*, Cassell, London
40 Gullberg, Jan (1997), *Mathematics from the Birth of Numbers*, W.W. Norton and Company, London
41 Duffy, Christopher (1981), *Russia's Military Way to the West: Origins and Nature of Russian Military Power 1700–1800*, Routledge, London, p 8
42 Belidor, Bernard Forest de (1731), *Le Bombardier Français, ou, Nouvelle Méthode pour Jeter des Bombes avec Précision. Tables*, Paris
43 Steele, Brett D. (2006), 'Rational Mechanics as Enlightened Engineering: Leonhard Euler and Interior Ballistics', in Buchanan B.J., *Gunpowder, Explosives and the State: A Technological History*, Ashgate Publishing, Aldershot, pp 281–302
44 Dolleczek (1872), *op cit*
45 Schöning, K.W. von, (1844), *Historische-Biographische Nachrichten zur Geschichte der Brandenburgisch Preussischen Artillerie,* Vol 1, Berlin. Schoening notes that the M1731 12-pdr Brummer required 26 horses to draw it; the M1758 Light 12-pdr, 12 horses; the Austrian 12-pdr, 20 horses; the Heavy 6-pdr, 20 horses; the Light 6-pdr, 10 horses; the 10-pdr howitzer, 20 horses; and the 7-pdr howitzer, 10 horses.
46 Anon (1767), *Die Artillerie Lehre zum Gebrauche des kk Feld-Artillerie corps*, Vienna
47 Prokhorov, A.M. (1982), *Great Soviet Encyclopedia*, Collier MacMillan, London Vol 2, p 229
48 Killy, W. and R.Vierhaus (2002), *Dictionary of German Biography*,kg Saur, Munich
49 Dolleczek (1872), *op cit*: Kennard A.N. (1986), *Gunfounding and Gunfounders: A Directory of Cannon Founders from Earliest Times to 1850,* Arms and Armour Press, London, pp 108.
50 Dolleczek (1872), *op cit*
51 Duffy, C. (2000), *The Army of Frederick the Great*, 2nd edn, Emperor's Press, Chicago: see also Guddat, M. (1992), *Kanoniere, Bombardierer, Pontoniere: Die Artillerie Freidrichs des Grossen,* Verlag E.S. Mittler & Sohn GmbH, Herford und Bonn
52 *ibid*
53 *ibid*
54 Scharnhorst, D.G. von (1812), *op cit*
55 Decker, Carl von (1828), *Traité d'Artillerie*, Paris
56 Prokhorov, A.M. (1982), *op cit*, Vol 19
57 Dolleczek (1872), *op cit*
58 *ibid*
59 *ibid*
60 Markevich, A.I. (1820-24), *A Manual to the Art of Artillery*, St Petersburg
61 Zhmodikov, A. and Y. (2003), *Tactics of the Russian Army in the Napoleonic Wars, Vol 1*, The Nafziger Collection, p 63
62 Dolleczek (1872), *op cit*
63 *ibid*
64 *ibid*
65 Jackson, M.V. and C. de Beer (1973), *Eighteenth Century Gun Founding*, Smithsonian Institute Press, Washington, pp 16–20: Ffoulkes, C. (1937), *The Gun-Founders of England with a List of English and Continental Gun-Founders from the XIV to XIX Centuries,* Cambridge University Press, pp 8–20: Kennard, A.N. (1986), *op cit,* pp 19–22
66 Valliere (5 June 1732), 'Letter to the General of Artillery of the Republic of Geneva,' *SHAT, Casting Artillery 4w43*; see also Director of Lyon foundry (20 October 1732), 'Report,' *SHAT, Casting Artillery 5w16*
67 Belidor (1731) *op cit* recommended charges were 4.1kg for the 24-pdr gun; 2.7kg for the 16-pdr; 2.3kg for the 12-pdr; 1.4kg for the 8-pdr; and 0.9kg for the 4-pdr.
68 Persy, N. (1832), *Elementary Treatise on the Forms of Guns & Various Systems of Artillery*, Museum Restoration Service, Canada
69 Ordinance of the King (11 March 1744) 'Payment for the testing of the parts of the gun intended for service with the field artillery,' Versailles, *SHAT, Casting Artillery 4w1*

70 Jean Maritz (1 January 1754), 'Letter,' *SHAT Casting Artillery 9A4*: see also Kennard, A.N. (1986), *op cit,* pp 108–109

71 Ordinance (21 December 1761), *SHAT Private Papers, 1K311 Box 12*; see also, Maritz, J. (1763) 'Notebooks,' *SHAT, Casting Artillery 3w134*

72 Müy and Gribeauval (1771), *Collection Complète de la Nouvelle Artillerie Construite dans les Arceneaux Metz et Strasbourg,* Paris. [Erroneously referred to as the 1765 Gribeauval Treatise.]

73 d'Urtubie, T.B.S.D. (1787), *Manual de l'Artilleur, Contenant tous les Objects dont la Connaissance est nécessaire aux Officiers et Sous Officiers d'Artillerie*, 2nd Edition, Chez Magimal, Paris: See also the editor's introduction Graves, D., ed. (1984), *Otto de Scheel's Treatise on Artillery*, Museum Restoration Service, Canada

74 Gillespie, C.C. (Oct 1998), 'Engineering the Revolution', in *Technology and Culture*, 39(4), pp 733–754. See also Monge, G. (1794), *Description de l'Art de Fabriquer les Canons*, Paris

75 Lombard, Professor Jean Louis (1781–83), *Traité du mouvement des projectiles appliqué aux bouches à feu*, Paris

76 According to Otto de Scheel (1795), the Hausse sight was invented by Gribeauval, and this error has been perpetuated by other authors.

77 Haythornthwaite, P.J. (1998), *Who was Who in the Napoleonic Wars*, Arms & Armour Press, London, p 211

78 Nafziger, G.F. (1993a), *The Armies of the Kingdom of Bavaria and the Grande Duchy of Wurzburg 1792–1815*, The Nafziger Collection

79 Xylander, R. Ritter von (1905), *Geschichte des 1. Feld-Artillerie-Regiments Prinz-Regent Luitpold*, Vol I, E.S. Mittler, Berlin

80 The French throughout most of the period used the *pouce de Paris*, and is often mistakenly considered to be the same as the Imperial inch. In fact, 1 *pouce de Paris* = 2.707cm (1.0658in).

81 Maritz J. (1763) 'Notebooks,' *SHAT, Casting Artillery 3w134*; see also Ordinance (21 December 1761), *SHAT, Private Papers 1k311, Box 12*,

82 Maritz J. (1 October 1754), 'Letter from Rochefort,' *SHAT, Casting Artillery 9A4*

83 Manson, J. (1792), *Tables de Construction de Principal attirails de l'Artillerie proposé au approvées depuis 1764 jusque en 1789 par M. de Gribeauval*, Paris: [When compared to the plates of Müy and Gribeauval (1771) *op cit*, the M1765 system had evolved markedly.]: See also Decker, M. (1989), *Les Canons de Valmy; Catalogue de l'Exposition Tenue au Musée de l'Armée*, Paris

84 Nardin, P. (2002), 'Le Comité de l'Artillerie et ses Réalisations des Origines à 1870', in *RIHM*, No. 82, Commission Française d'Histoire Militaire

85 *ibid*

86 *ibid*

87 *ibid*

88 Susane (1874), *op cit*; Gassendi, J.B. (1819), *Aide Mémoire à l'Usage d'Artillerie de France*, Chez Magimal, Paris; Fave, I. (1845), *Histoire et Tactique de Trois Armes et Particulièrement de l'Artillerie*, Paris; Fave (1871), *Études sur le Passé et l'Avenir de l'Artillerie*, Vol 5, Librairie Militaire, Paris

89 Gassendi, J.B. (1819), *Aide Mémoire...*, Vol I, p 111. Gassendi reproduces the AnXI report on pp 118–200 of Vol I.

90 Susane (1874), *op cit*

91 Gassendi, J.B. (1819), *op cit*, Vol I, pp 115–116

92 Gassendi, J.B. (1819), *op cit*, Vol I, p 118

93 Dahlgren, A. (1856), *Shells and Shell Guns*, King & Baird, Philadelphia, pp 7–14

94 Gassendi, J.B. (1819), *op cit*, Vol I, p 239

95 Ballada, A., *Dessins des bouches à feu et des constructions de l'artillerie après l'arrêt du 11 Floréal AnXI*, SHAT; also Challeat, J. (1933), *Histoire Technique de l'Artillerie de Terre en France pendant un Siècle 1816–1919*, Imprimerie National, Paris; Fave, I. (1871), *op cit*; Susane (1874), *op cit*

96 Nardin, *op cit*; also Gassendi (1819), *op cit*; Susane (1874), *op cit*; and Fave (1845), *op cit*

97 Menkov, A. (2005), personal communication. French guns captured in Russia are as follows. Casting dates of French tubes bearing the imperial crown:

- 58× 12-pdrs: 1× AnXII, 1× AnXII, 1× M1809, 3× 1810, 9× 1811
- 184× 6-pdrs: 5× AnXII, 6× AnXIV, 46× 1807, 99× 1808, 13× M1809, 1× 1810, 1× 1811
- 60× 5.9in (24-pdr) howitzers: 9× AnXII, 36× AnXIII, 12× AnXIV, 1× 1806

There were also 25× 6.4in howitzers (Gribeauval) all predating the imperial coronation, supporting the edict that none were to be produced post-1805.

At Dresden in 1813, 260 tubes were captured and placed in the Kremlin:

- French: 1× 4-pdr, 43× 6-pdrs, 10× 12-pdrs, 24× howitzers
- Austrian: 5× 3-pdrs, 15× 6-pdrs, 1× 12-pdr

- Prussian: 2× 3-pdrs, 18× 6-pdrs
- Holland: 5× 6-pdrs
- Bavarian: 4× 6-pdrs
- Westphalian: 4× 6-pdrs, 1× howitzer
- Italian (Kingdom of Italy): 7× 3-pdrs
- Saxon: 10× 12-pdrs, 10× 8-pdrs, 4× 6-pdrs, 28× 4-pdrs, 15× howitzers, 8× mortars.
- Origins unknown: 16× 12-pdrs, 16× 6-pdrs, 1× mortar
- Russian: 8 pieces – no description.

This clearly shows the use of captured guns by the French in 1813. The Prussian and Austrian guns could conceivably be those used by the Polish.

98 Nardin, *op cit;* also Gassendi (1810 and 1819), *op cit*

99 Gassendi, J.B. (1819), *op cit*, Vol I, pp 21–24

100 Nardin, *op cit*; also Challeat (1933), *op cit*

101 Mathew and Harrison (2004), *op cit*, Vol 54, pp 403–406

102 *SHAT, Box C2-538*

103 Palmer, A. (1984), *An Encyclopaedia of Napoleon's Europe*, St Martin's Press, New York, pp 83, 194, 245–246

104 Hoyer, J.F. (1798), 'Uber die reitende Artillerie', in *Neues Militairisches Magazin – Historischen und Scientifischen Inhalts*, Vol 1, Part 2, pp 3–14, Leipzig: (1802), 'Uber den Gebrauch der reitenden Artillerie', in *Neues Militairisches Magazin – Historischen und Scientifischen Inhalts*, Vol 2, Part 4, pp 10–14, Leipzig

105 Kerner, K.F. (1803), *Betrachtungen über der Reitende Artillerie: Organisation, Gebrauch und Tactic*, Friederich Nast, Ludwigsburg, pp 12–14

106 Jackson and de Beer (1973), *op cit* p 145: see also Kennard, A.N. (1986), *op cit,* pp 136

107 Hunt, R. (1853), *A Treatise on the Improvement and Present State of the Manufactures in Metal, Vol 1: Iron and Steel*, London, pp 75–76; also Jones, C. (17/10/2006), personal communication

108 Hunt, R. (1853), *op cit* p 76

109 Jackson and de Beer (1973), *op cit* pp 17–20. See also Kennard, A.N. (1986), *op cit,* pp 148–9 and 158 (spelt Johann Jakob Ziegler)

110 Jackson and de Beer (1973), *op cit,* pp 21–30 and 146. See also Ffoulkes, C. (1937), p 65.

111 Jackson and de Beer (1973), *op cit,* pp 28–29, 146

112 *ibid* pp 38–39

113 *ibid* pp 35–37, 146

114 *ibid* pp 49–52, Caruana (1997) *op cit*, pp9–11

115 Jackson and de Beer (1973), *op cit,* pp 53–66, 146

116 *ibid* pp 64–65, 146

117 Caruana, A.B. (1983). "Sir Thomas Blomefield and the Blomefield System of Ordnance," 21(3), *Canadian Journal of Arms Collecting*, 21(3), pp 95–100: Lavery, B. (1989) 'Carronades and Blomefield Guns,' in Smith, R.D. ed., *British Naval Armaments,* Royal Armouries Conference Proceedings 1, pp 15–28: Caruana, A.B. (1997), *op cit,* pp 257–266

118 John, A.H. (1951), *The Walker Family: Iron Founders and Lead Manufacturers*, Council for the Preservation of Business Archives pp 1–19; also Baker, H.G. (1945), *Samuel Walker and his Partners*, Society for the Preservation of Old Tools, Sheffield

119 Hunt, R. (1853), *op cit* p 77

120 John, A.H. (1951), *op cit* p 34

121 Mathew and Harrison (2004), *op cit*, Vol 15, pp 893–894: also Valentine, A. (1970), *The British Establishment 1760–1784*, University of Oklahoma Press, pp 86–87

122 Cockburn, John (1827) shows the use of the Long 6-pdr; he describes it as being of 'great precision. Inconvenient in travelling and in serving' [Cockburn, John (1827), *Notes on Artillery,* Cadet NoteBooks*,* RAHT, Woolwich]

123 Mathew and Harrison (2004), *op cit*, Vol 6, pp 253-255; also Valentine, A. (1970), *op cit* pp 86–87

124 Cockburn, John (1827), *Notes on Artillery,* Cadet Notebooks*,* RAHT, Woolwich

125 The 10in howitzer was a very hefty lump of metal, weighing 25cwt and measuring 107cm long, which required the barrel to be removed and transported on its own travelling carriage. The 10in howitzer was 118cm long; the 8in, 94cm; the 'Heavy' 5.5in, 66cm; and the 'Light' 5.5in howitzer, 56cm.

126 Leslie, Major J.H., ed (1905, r/p 1991), *op cit* p 462

127 *ibid* p 730

128 Smiles, S. (1863), *Iron Workers and Tool Makers*, London

129 Rogers, Colonel H.C.B. (1971), *Artillery through the Ages*, Military Book Society, pp 59–60. See also (1992) *The Concise Dictionary of National Biography*, Vol 2, p 2120

130 Rogers (1971), *op cit* pp 59–61

131 *ibid*

132 In 1775 (6× 12-pdrs, 2× 6-pdrs and 6× 3-pdrs); 1776 (12× 12-pdrs and 84× 3-pdr); and 1777 (only a single 3-pdr). [Jackson and de Beer, *op cit*]

133 Caruana, A.B. (1979b), *Grasshoppers and Butterflies,* Museum Restoration Service, Canada,

p3ff, pp 69–70; [Jackson and de Beer, *op cit* pp 53–59]

134 Caruana, A.B. (1977), *The Light 6-pdr Battalion Gun of 1776*, Museum Restoration Service, Bloomfield, pp 5–11; Landmann (1764), *A Table of the Length Weight, Calibres and Diameters of shot of brass guns of each nature according to the Present Establishment...*, RAHT; *see also* Caruana (1979b), *op cit*

135 Jackson and de Beer (1973), *op cit* p 58; see also Caruana (1979b), *op cit* p 7

136 Caruana, A.B. (1977), *op cit* pp 5–8

137 *ibid*

138 Caruana, A.B. (1977), *op cit* p 13

139 Bogue, R. (1793), *Cadet Notebook*, RAHT, Woolwich; see also Congreve Snr quoted in Caruana (1977), *op cit* p 19

140 Lawson, Major General (1801), 'Memorandum of Artillery Arrangements and Alterations made in Carriages, Harness and Ammunitions', in (1884) *Proceedings of the Royal Artillery Institution*, XII (4), pp 207–220

141 Congreve Snr quoted in Caruana (1977), *op cit* pp 13–17

142 Congreve Snr quoted in Caruana (1977), *op cit* p 19

143 Caruana, A.B. (1977), *op cit* p 5

144 Congreve Snr, W. (1800), *An Account of some of the cases in the Practice of Artillery which might be taught by the Officers of the Royal Military Respository,* RAHT, Woolwich

145 Congreve Snr quoted in Caruana (1977), *op cit* pp 11, 19; see also Congreve Snr (1800), *op cit*

146 Congreve Snr, W. (11 7 12 February 1797), letters, RAHT

147 Congreve Snr, W. (1797), *op cit*; see also Congreve Snr (1778), *A Table of the Length, and Weight of Brass Guns*, RAHT, Woolwich. In February 1797 Congreve Snr stated that in 1786 Long 6-pdrs up to 12cwt and howitzers were mounted on his carriage; from the table of lengths and weights by Congreve Snr (1778) the only gun fitting that description is that of Desaguliers.

148 James, C. (1805), *A New and Enlarged Military Dictionary: or an Alphabetical Explanation of Technical Terms*, London

149 Anon (1795), *Questions upon Artillery*, RAI, Woolwich

150 Congreve Snr, W. (1797), *op cit;* also Farrington, A. (7 February 1797), 'Letter,' *RAHT,* Woolwich

151 Major-General George Glasgow (1811), Letter, *RAHT,* Woolwich: "He requested from Canada, block-trail carriages for his Light common 6-pdrs in 1811; the carriages sent by Woolwich were Congreve Snr's pattern, as they were in stock and 'more suitable' for the guns Glasgow listed"

152 Congreve Snr, W. (1800), *op cit;* also Adye, Captain R.W. (1802), *The Little Gunner and Pocket Bombardier*, 3rd Edn, London; James, C. (1805), *op cit*

153 Farrington, Anthony (7 March 1797), 'Letter,' *RAHT,* Woolwich

154 Smith, S. (2006), personal communication

155 Farrington, Anthony (7 March 1797), *op cit*

156 Scharnhorst, D.G. von (1806), *Handbuch für die Artillerie*, Berlin

157 Congreve Snr, W. (1797), *op cit*

158 Congreve Snr, W. (12 February 1797), 'Letter,' *RAHT,* Woolwich

159 Adye, Captain R.W. (1802), *op cit*

160 Franklin, C.E. (2000), *British Rockets of the Napoleonic and Colonial Wars*, Spellmount, Staplehurst, Kent, p 35

161 Adye, Captain R.W. (1813), *Bombardier and Pocket Gunner*, 7th Edn, London

162 Anon (7 April 1814), 'Letter,' *RAHT,* Woolwich

163 Scharnhorst, D.G. von (1806), *op cit*

164 Return by Lieutenant-Colonel William Robe, 1 November 1808, PRO W055/1194, p 52

165 Graves, D. (2005), personal communication

166 *ibid*

167 Mathew and Harrison (2004), *op cit*, Vol 4, pp 888–889

168 Lieutenant-Colonel Augustus Frazer confirms that the horse artillery were initially equipped with 3-pdrs, Light 6-pdrs and 5.5in howitzers, mounted on the Desaguliers carriage [Frazer, Col. Sir Augustus (1859, r/p 2001), *Letters of Colonel Sir Augustus Simon Frazer...,* (r/p Naval and Military Press, East Sussex.)]. See also Duncan, Major F. (1879), *History of the Royal Regiment of Artillery,* Vol II, John Murray, London p 34

169 Duncan Drummond, William Congreve Snr and Thomas Blomefield (19 August 1792 and 20 December 1792) 'Letters to the Duke of Richmond,' *RAHT,* Woolwich

170 Duncan *ibid* pp 35–36

171 PRO WO 55/1194, Letters from Officers – Foreign

172 Leslie, Major J.H., ed (1905, r/p 1991), *op cit* p 1076

173 Park, S.J. and G.F. Nafziger (1983), *The British Military: Its System and Organisation 1803–1815*, RAFM Co, Ontario
174 Congreve Snr, W. (c1780), *An Account of the Proposals for the Management of the Heavy Three Pounder contrived by General Thomas Desaguliers for the service of Cavalry, made by Captain William Congreve in 1779*, Woolwich
175 *ibid*
176 Congreve Snr, W. (nd), *An Account of Carriages*, *RAHT*, Woolwich
177 Caruana, A.B. (1977), *op cit*, p 16ff
178 Caruana, A.B. (1977), *op cit* p 24
179 Congreve Snr, W. (1782), *op cit*
180 Congreve Snr, W. (nd), *Paragraphs on the Several Ideas which Captain Congreve Proposed to General Desaguliers for the Management of his Heavy 3-pdr when Attached to Cavalry*, RAHT; also Congreve Snr (nd), *An Account of the Field Pieces ordered to be Constructed by His Grace the Duke of Richmond in the Year 1788*, RAHT; Congreve Snr (1788), letter concerning Duke of Richmond's orders, RAHT
181 *ibid*
182 Congreve Snr, W. (1788), letter concerning the Desaguliers and Griffiths systems, Royal Artillery Insitution, Woolwich
183 Congreve Snr, W. (nd), *An Account of the Field Pieces ordered to be constructed...*, RAHT
184 *ibid*
185 *ibid*
186 *ibid*; see also Congreve Snr (nd), *Paragraphs on the Several Ideas...*
187 Congreve Snr, W. (nd), letters concerning the Goodwood trials, RAHT. Congreve Snr notes that 'In August 1792 the Duke of Richmond ordered General Drummond, Colonel Blomefield and myself to meet and to give... a plan for pieces of Ordnance of General Desagulier's Construction'.
188 Caruana (1977), *op cit* p 16
189 Congreve Snr, W. (nd), *An Account of Carriages*, RAHT
190 Lawson, Major General (1801), *Memorandum of Alterations...*
191 Congreve Snr, W. (nd), *An Account of Carriages*, RAHT
192 Leslie, Major J.H., ed (1905, r/p 1991), *op cit*
193 Hofschröer, P. (1989), *The Hanoverian Army of the Napoleonic Wars*, Osprey Publishing, London
194 Connelly, O. (1965), *Napoleon's Satellite Kingdoms*, Free Press Paperback, Ontario, p 13
195 Congreve Snr, W. (1785)
196 Smith, D. (1998), *The Greenhill Napoleonic Wars Data Book*, Greenhill Books, London, pp 473–475
197 Nafziger, G.F. (1996), *Napoleon at Leipzig: The Battle of Nations 1813*, p 271
198 *ibid* pp 275–278
199 At the outset of the autumn campaign of 1813 the French artillery was made up of French and foreign material, *SHAT, C2-536*
200 Snorrason, T. (1970), 'The Assault on Stralsund 1809', in *Tradition*, London, No.52 (Part I), No.53 (Part II)
201 Cassin-Scott, J. (1976), *Scandinavian Armies in the Napoleonic Wars*, Osprey Publishing, London
202 The 6-pdr caisson had 660× 6-pdr roundshot, 240× 6-pdr canister rounds; the howitzer caisson, 216× 7-pdr howitzer shells, 32× 7-pdr canister, 184× 1lb howitzer powder charges, 64× ¼lb charges; the infantry caisson held 46,800 musket cartridges, 11,520 rifle cartridges, 1,800 pistol cartridges, 900 carbine cartridges and 12,000 flints.
203 Palmer, A. (1984), *op cit* pp 157–158
204 General Sorbier (18 July 1806), 'Report to Napoleon'
205 Nafziger, G.F. (1993b), *The Armies of Westphalia and Cleve-Berg 1806–1815*, Nafziger Publication, p 64
206 Nafziger, G.F. (1993b), *op cit* pp 65–66
207 Summerfield, S. (2006) *Prussian Artillery*, NARG Publications
208 The Duchy of Warsaw is the correct title for this state, although it is commonly referred to today as the Grand Duchy of Warsaw. Article 5 of the Treaty of Tilsit, which created the duchy; the Convention that transferred it to Saxony; and Article 1 of the Act of the Congress of Vienna, which effectively abolished it, all refer to it in French as the *Duché de Varsovie*. Similarly, the duchy's constitution refers to it in German as *Herzogtum Warschau*; and its coins bore the Latin inscription FRID.AVG. REX SAX.DVX VARSOV (Fridericus Augustus, Rex Saxonia, Dux Varsovia – 'Frederick Augustus, King of Saxony, Duke of Warsaw').
209 Gembarzewski, Bronislaw (1904), *Wojsko Polskie*, Warsaw
210 Morawski, R. and A. Nieuwazny (2004), *Army of Duchy of Warsaw: Artillery, Engineers and Sappers*, Warsaw (trans Pawel Nowaczek)
211 *ibid*
212 Praga fortress is now situated in a suburb of Warsaw on the right bank of the Vistula; Serock fortress is

30km north of Warsaw. Modlin fortress (in Polish, Twierdza Modlin) was one of the largest 19th-century fortresses in Poland. It is located at the confluence of the Rivers Narew and Vistula near the town of Modlin on the Narew, some 28km north-west of Warsaw.

213 Zamosc is a town in south-eastern Poland, 88km south-east of Lublin and 60km south of Chelm.

214 Gembarzewski, B. (1904), *op cit*

215 *ibid*

216 Smith, D. (2002), *Armies of 1812: The Grande Armée and the Armies of Austria, Prussia, Russia and Turkey*, Spellmount, Staplehurst, Kent, pp 127–130

217 Smith, D. (2002), *op cit* pp 154–155

218 *ibid* pp 142–144, 191–192

219 Nafziger, G.F. (1996), *op cit*

220 Smith, D. (2001), *Leipzig*; Petre, L.F. (1912, r/p 1974) *Napoleon's Last Campaign in Germany*, Arms & Armour Press, London

221 Kukiel, Dr M. (1912), *Dzieje Oreza Polskiego w Epoce Napoleonskiej 1795–1815*, Zdzisław Rzepecki i Ski, Poznań, Poland.

222 Gembarzewski, B. (1904), *op cit*

223 Dallas, G. (1997), *The Final Act: The Roads to Waterloo*, Henry Holt, New York, pp 249, 356

224 See Morla, T. de (1816), *Tratado de Artillerie Para el Uso de la Academia de Caballeros Cedetes del Real Cuerpo de Artilleria, Dividido en Tres Tomos y Otro de Laminas, Que tartan de las Principales Functiones de los Oficiales de este Cuerpo en pas y en Guerra*, Segovia. Part of this work is translated in Nafziger, G.F. (1996), *Imperial Bayonets*, Greenhill Books, London.

225 For general information about the Westphalian army see Lunsmann, F.O. (1934), *Die Westfalische Armee*, Hanover

226 Dickson (22 February 1812), in Leslie, Major J.H., ed (1905, r/p 1991), *op cit*

227 Hofschröer, P. (1998), *1815: The Waterloo Campaign – Wellington, his German Allies and the Battles of Ligny and Quatre Bras*, Greenhill Books, pp 77–80

228 Chartrand, R. (2001), *The Portuguese Army of the Napoleonic Wars (3)*, Osprey Publishing, Oxford, pp 3–4

229 *ibid* p 5

230 Howard, R.A. (1979), *The Portuguese Regular Army 1806-14*, Napoleonic Association

231 Compiled from various sources, including: Decker, H. von (1866), *Geschichte Rückblicke auf die Formation der Preussischen Artillerie*, Berlin; Pietsch, P. von (1963), *Die Formations und Uniformierungs-Geschichte des Preussischen Heeres 1808–1914*, Vols 1 and 2, Hamburg; Hofschröer, P. (1984), *Prussian Landwehr and Landsturm 1813–15*, RAFM, Ontario; Jany, C. (1910), *Urklungliche Beiträge und Forschungen zur Geschichte des Preussischen Heeres*, Vols III and IV, Berlin; Nafziger, G.F. (1996), *The Prussian Army 1792–1815, Vol III: Cavalry and Artillery*, The Nafziger Collection; Digby Smith (1998), *op cit*

232 The 1st–3rd 6-pdr Foot Batteries were mobilised in 1812 with six Prussian 6-pdrs and two 7-pdr howitzers.

233 6-pdr foot batteries mobilised in 1813 used French guns: *4th Guard* (Guard uniforms); *5th–9th & 12th–16th*, and *17th & 18th* (British uniforms). The *10th 6-pdr Ft Bty* had 6× French 6-pdrs and 2× Prussian 7-pdr howitzers. The *19th 6-pdr Ft Bty* was mobilised 5 May 1813 with 4× French 6-pdrs that had been captured at Vehlitz on 5 April and Halle on 2 May; during the armistice it was increased to 7× French 6-pdrs and 1× Prussian 7-pdr howitzer.

234 The following 6-pdr foot batteries were armed with British 6-pdrs and 5½in howitzers: *20th 6-pdr Ft Bty* – 4× 6-pdrs with British iron barrels, 2× 5½in howitzers (British RA uniforms); *24th 6-pdr Ft Bty* – 6× British 6-pdrs, 2× British 5½in howitzers, 5× British caissons (British RA uniforms; *25th 6-pdr Ft Bty* – 12× British 6-pdrs, no howitzers, 5× British caissons (British RA uniforms); *26th 6-pdr Ft Bty* – 6× British 6-pdrs, 2× British 5½in howitzers, 5× British munition wagons); *27th 6-pdr Ft Bty* – 6× British 6-pdrs, 2× British 5½in howitzers (British uniforms); *30th 6-pdr Ft Bty* – 3× British 6-pdrs, 1× 5½in howitzer (formed in Colberg); *31st 6-pdr Ft Bty* – British 6-pdrs; *32nd 6-pdr Ft Bty* – British 6-pdrs (British uniforms); *33rd 6-pdr Ft Bty* – formed late 1813, probably with British 6-pdrs (became *13th Horse Arty Bty* in March 1815).

235 6-pdr foot batteries armed with siege guns: *21st 6-pdr Ft Bty* – 6× heavy guns (Reserve uniforms); *21st 6-pdr Foot Battery* – 6× heavy guns (Reserve uniforms); *22nd 6-pdr Ft Bty* – heavy guns (British uniforms); *23rd 6-pdr Ft Bty* – heavy guns (Reserve uniforms); *28th & 29th 6-pdr Ft Btys* – British siege guns (British uniforms).

236 12-pdr batteries armed with Prussian equipment (1812): *3rd 12-pdr Bty* – 3× Prussian 12-pdrs, 2×

10-pdr howitzers on mobilisation; in 1813 this was increased to 6× Prussian 12-pdrs, 2× 10-pdr howitzers.

237 12-pdr batteries armed with Prussian equipment (1813): *1st 12-pdr Bty* – 8× Prussian 12-pdrs, 2× 10-pdr howitzers (in Jan 1813); 4× Prussian 12-pdrs, 2× 10-pdr howitzers (in Apr 1813); 8× Prussian 12-pdrs, 2× 10-pdr howitzers (in Aug 1813). *2nd 12-pdr Bty* – 8× Prussian 12-pdrs, no howitzers; *6th 12-pdr Bty* – 6× 12-pdrs, 2× 10-pdr howitzers.

238 12-pdr batteries armed with French equipment (1813): *4th 12-pdr Bty* – 6× French 12-pdrs (captured at Halberstadt), 2× 10-pdr howitzers, 4× British caissons (British uniforms); *5th 12-pdr Bty* – 6× French 12-pdrs, 2× 24-pdr howitzers (British uniforms); *7th 12-pdr Bty* – 3× French 12-pdrs, 1× French 24-pdr howitzer.

239 The *1st–3rd Horse Artillery Batteries* were mobilised in 1812, each with 6× Prussian 6-pdrs, 2× 7-pdr howitzers. The following horse batteries mobilised in 1813 were armed with Prussian equipment: *4th (Guard) and 5th–9th Horse Arty Btys* – each 6× Prussian 6-pdrs, 2× 7-pdr howitzers; *10th Horse Arty Bty* – same equipment (British uniforms); *12th Horse Arty Bty* – same equipment (Reserve uniforms).

240 In 1813 the Fritz Horse Arty Bty was armed with 3× Prussian 3-pdrs, 1× 7-pdr howitzer, with 2× caissons.

241 Horse artillery batteries armed with British 6-pdrs and 5.5½in howitzers in 1813–15: *11th Horse Arty Bty* – 8× British 6-pdrs, no howitzers (British uniforms); *14th Horse Arty Bty* (formed from Fritz Horse Arty Bty in March 1815) – 6× 6-pdrs; *15th Horse Arty Bty* – probably British 6-pdrs; *16th Horse Arty Bty* (formed from 27th 6-pdr Ft Bty) – 6× 6-pdrs, 2× 5½in howitzers; *17th Horse Arty Bty* (formed from 32nd 6-pdr Ft Bty) – British 6-pdrs.

242 The 18th and 19th Horse Arty Btys formed in 1813 from the 1st and 2nd Russo-German Horse Btys respectively were armed with Russian 6-pdr guns and 10-pdr (¼-pud) unicorns.

243 The 13th and 20th Horse Arty Btys were formed in late 1813 with unknown equipment.

244 Conrad, M. (1996), 'Some notes on the Don Cossack Artillery 1812,' *Mark Conrad Homepage*, http://home.comcast.net/~markconrad/MYDON.html (accessed 9 April 2006)

245 Summerfield, S. (2005), *Cossack Hurrah: Russian Irregular Cavalry Organisation and Uniforms during the Napoleonic Wars*, Partizan Press

246 Norton (1626), *The Gunners Glasse* and Eldred (1646), *Ordinance at Dover Castle*, list all these pieces. However, the anonymous 1639 and 1643 *Tables of the Trayne of Ordinance* list only the robinet, falconet and falcon, with the other small guns presumably fallen into disuse by that date.

247 Callwell, Colonel C.E. (1906, r/p 1990), *Small Wars: A Tactical Textbook for Imperial Soldiers*, Greenhill Books, London, pp 307–308

248 Gassendi, J.B. (1819), *op cit*

249 Chandler, D. (1976), *The Art of Warfare in the Age of Marlborough*, B.T. Batsford, London, p 191

250 Uythoven, G. van (2005), 'The Amusette and its use during the Revolutionary Wars,' *Van Uythoven Revolutionary and Napoleonic Wars Website*, http://home.wanadoo.nl/g.vanuythoven/Amusette.htm (accessed 20 August 2006)

251 The Blomefield 1-pdr amusette that survives in the Tower of London weighs 2cwt 2qrs 3lbs (128kg) and 5ft long (152cm); it was cast in 1793 by John and Henry King, Woolwich. [Blackmore, H.L. (1976), *The Armouries of the Tower of London (I) Ordnance,* HMSO, London, pp 63–64]

252 Adye, Captain R.W. (1802), *op cit,* 3rd edn

253 Uythoven, G. van (2005), *op cit*

254 Hoyer, J.F. (1799), *Neues Militairisches Magazin*, Vol 1, Part 5, p 34

255 Duffy, C. (2000), *Instruments of War: the Austrian Army in the Seven Years' War*, The Emperor's Press, Chicago, p 284

256 Dolleczek (1872) *op cit* pp 331–332

257 Caruana, A.B. (1979b), *op cit*

258 *ibid*

259 Leslie, Major J.H., ed (1905, r/p 1991), *op cit*

260 *ibid*

261 *ibid*

262 *ibid* pp 870–871

263 Oman, Sir C. (1930, r/p 1997), *A History of the Peninsular War*, Vol VII, Greenhill Books, London, pp 174–200, 239–43, 356–70, 465–75

264 Rouquerol, G. (1895), *Artillerie au début de les Guerres de Révolution*, Berger-Levrault, Paris

265 du Teil (1778 r/p 1925), *De l'Usage de l'Artillerie Nouvelle dans la Guerre de Campagne,* Paris

266 Rouquerol, G. (1895), *op cit*

267 A village just 40km north-east of Nice. Smith, Digby (1998), *op cit*, p 74

268 Napoleon (24 January 1797), 'To General Auguste de Lespinasse discussing mountain artillery;' from (March 1837) 'Note sur quelques modifications à

faire aux bats de l'Artillerie de Montagne,' *Journal des Sciences Militaires*

269 Cotty, H. (1830), *Supplément au Dictionnaire d'Artillerie*, Paris, p 182
270 Gassendi, J.B. (1801), *op cit*
271 Grisois, L. (1909), *Mémoires 1792–1822*, Vol 1, Plon-Nourit, Paris
272 Gassendi, J.B. (1819), *op cit*
273 Napoleon (24 January 1797), 'To General de Lespinasse' – *see* note 268 above
274 Gassendi, J.B. (1819), *op cit* Vol 2
275 Gibbons, J. (1861), *The Artillerist's Manual*, D. Van Nostrand, New York
276 Gibbon, J. (1861), *op cit*
277 Captain Caffort stated that the M1810 3-pdr and M1810 12cm howitzer were used extensively in 1814; that the same equipment was used in 1823; and that it was identical to that of Valée.
278 Toussard, L. (1809), *The American Artillerist's Companion*, New York, pp 169–176
279 du Teil (1778), *op cit*
280 Toussard, L. (1809), *op cit* pp 169–176
281 Gibbons, J. (1861), *op cit*
282 Morillon, M. (March 2006), 'L'Artillerie de Montagne sous le Premier Empire', in *Soldats Napoléoniens* No.9, Paris
283 Calculated from Smith, D. (1998), *op cit:* D. Chandler counted 289 major sieges among 568 engagements (1749–1815), compared to 167 sieges and 144 engagements (1680–1748); Chandler, D. (1998), 'Siege warfare in the Peninsula, 1808–14', in I. Fletcher (1998), *The Peninsular War: Aspects of the Struggle for the Iberian Peninsular*, Spellmount Ltd, p 47.
284 Dolleczek (1872), *op cit*
285 Hollins, D. (2003), *Austrian Napoleonic Artillery 1792–1815*, Osprey Publishing, Oxford, p 33
286 Leslie, Major J.H., ed (1905, r/p 1991), *op cit*
287 Nafziger, G.F., and W.Warren (1996), *The Imperial Russian Army 1763–1815*, Vol 2, The Nafziger Collection
288 Viskovatov A.V. (1841), *Historical Description of the Clothing and Arms of the Russian Army, Vol 7a: Organisation 1796–1801*, St Petersburg (trans M. Conrad, 2006)
289 Landmann, I. (1801), *op cit*, pp 22–23
290 *ibid*
291 Collier, W. (1785), *An Inquiry into the use and advantages that may probably be derived from the introduction of a light nature of artillery for all field services*; see also Congreve Snr, W. (1780), *A description of the sorts of Artillery used by the Prussian artillery*. Both RAHT.
292 Zhmodikov, A. and Y. (2003), *op cit* Vol II
293 Hollins, D. (2005), personal communication
294 *ibid*
295 Adye, Captain R.W. (1802), *op cit,* 3rd edn
296 Duffy, C. (2000), *op cit*
297 Nafziger, G.F. (1993), *Lützen and Bautzen*, Emperor's Press, Chicago
298 Landmann, I. (1801), *op cit* p 20
299 McKenna, M.C. (2004), *The British Army and its Regiments and Battalions 1793–1815*, The Nafziger Collection
300 In 1795 a Garrison Battalion had a lieutenant-colonel, major, adjutant, quartermaster, surgeon (with two assistants in 1797) and a chaplain. The ten companies each had a captain, lieutenant and ensign.
301 Brieg, Breslau, Colberg, Danzig, Glatz, Glogau, Graudenz. Königsberg, Cosel, Magdeburg, Neisse, Plassenburg, Schweidnitz, Silberberg, Stettin and Wesel each had a garrison company; Küstrin and Pillau had smaller detachments.
302 The arsenals in Berlin, Breslau, Brieg, Colberg, Cosel, Küstrin, Danzig, Glatz, Glogau, Graudenz, Königsberg, Magdeburg, Niesse, Pillau, Schweidnitz, Silberberg, Spandau, Stettin, Wesel and Wulzberg.
303 Viskovatov, A.V. (1841), *op cit* Vol 7a
304 d'Urtubie, T. (1786), *op cit* p 58
305 d'Urtubie, T. (1786), *op cit* pp 50–51
306 Gassendi, J.B. (1819), *op cit*, Vol 1, p 132
307 *ibid* p 105
308 *ibid* p 29
309 *ibid* pp 32–33
310 *ibid* p 33
311 Floyd, D.E. (1991), 'United States Martello Towers' in *Fortress*, No.9, pp 47–56
312 Sutcliffe, S. (1973), *Martello Towers*, Cranbury, New Jersey
313 Lavery, B. (1989), *Nelson's Navy: The Ships, Men and Organisation 1793–1815*, revised edn, Conway Maritime Press, pp 82–87
314 Although not complete, this is certainly a wonderful survey of the engagements in the period; see Smith, D. (1998), *op cit.*
315 Gibbons, J. (1861), *op cit* p 363
316 Nilius (1904), *History of Artillery Equipment*, Moscow
317 de Scheel, Otto (1795), *Mémoires d'Artillerie*, Chez Magimal, Paris

318 Gassendi, J.B. (1819), *op cit*
319 Congreve Snr, W., (1770s), Notebooks, RAHT
320 Leslie, Major J.H., ed (1905, r/p 1991), *op cit*
321 Letter from William Congreve Snr to Duke of Richmond, September 1792; see also letter to Duke of Richmond from Duncan Drummond, William Congreve Snr and Thomas Blomefield, 19 August 1792.
322 Weissenbach, Strack von (1882), *Geschichte der Königlich Württembergischen Artillerie*, Stuttgart
323 Duffy, C. (2000), *Instruments of War...*, pp 279–280
324 Haythornthwaite, P.J. (1988), *Wellington's Specialist Troops,* Osprey Publishing, London
325 PRO, WO 47/2555, Proceedings of the Board of Ordnance
326 PRO, WO 24/608 to /621; also MacArthur, R. (06/04/2004) personal communication
327 PRO, WO 47/2557, Proceedings of the Board of Ordnance
328 Park, S.J. and G.F. Nafziger (1983), *The British Military...* See also PRO WO 24/608 to /621
329 A captain, 5× first-lieutenants, a second-lieutenant, 5× farriers and smiths, 15× shoeing smiths, 10× collar-makers, 10× wheelers, 5× staff-sergeants, 15× sergeants, 15× corporals, 20× lance-corporals, 5× trumpeters, 500× drivers and 2× rough-riders. [Park and Nafziger (1983), *op cit*; see also PRO WO 24/608 to /621]
330 Haythornthwaite, P.J. (1988), *op cit*; see also Haythornthwaite, P.J. (1994), *The Armies of Wellington*, Arms & Armour Press, London
331 Laurema, M. (1956), *L'Artillerie de Campagne Française pendant les Guerres de Révolution: Évolution de l'Organisation et de Tactique*, Helsinki
332 *ibid*
333 Decker (1828), *op cit*
334 Dolleczek (1872), *op cit*
335 du Teil (1778 r/p 1925), *De l'Usage de l'Artillerie Nouvelle dans la Guerre de Campagne 1778*, Paris
336 Decker (1828), *op cit*. See also Malinovsky L. and R. Bonnin (1982), *Geschichte der Brandenburgische-Preussichen Artillerie*, Wiesbaden
337 Graves, D. (1984), *Otto de Scheel's Treatise on Artillery*, Museum Restoration Service, Canada
338 *ibid*
339 Summerfield, S. (unpublished), *Monograph on Dyes,* Oil and Colour Chemist Association
340 Buxbaum, G. (1998), *Industrial Inorganic Pigments*, 2nd edn, Wiley-VCH, Weinheim, Germany
341 Hollins, D. (2003), *op cit*
342 Henry, C. (2004), *British Napoleonic Artillery 1793–1815 (1)*, Osprey Publishing, Oxford
343 Congreve Snr, W. (1792), 'Letter,' *RAHT,* Woolwich
344 Rudyerd, C.W. (1793 r/p 1970), *Course of Artillery at the Royal Military Academy...,* RAI (r/p Museum Restoration Service, Canada)
345 Adye, (1813), *op cit*, 7th edn
346 Chartrand, R. (2003), *Napoleon's Guns 1792–1815 (1)*, Osprey Publishing, Oxford
347 Weiss, Hans-Karl (2006), personal communication
348 Gassendi, J.B. (1819), *op cit*
349 Anon (1924), *Colour Index*, Society of Dyers and Colourists, Bradford
350 *ibid*
351 Zhmodikov, A. and Y. (2003), *Tactics of the Russian Army in the Napoleonic Wars*, Vol II, The Nafziger Collection
352 de Segur, P. (1825), *History of the Expedition to Russia Undertaken by the Emperor Napoleon in the Year 1812*, London
353 Nofi, A.A. (1993), *The Waterloo Campaign June 1815*, Greenhill Books
354 Hughes, B.P. (1974), *Firepower: Weapon Effectiveness on the Battlefield, 1630–1850*, Purnell Book Services, London
355 As stated by Mick Crumplin – a retired surgeon, who had conducted over 30 years of research into Napoleonic medical history – in Wilson, D. (2003), *Battlefield Detectives*, Granada Media, London
356 Captain Mercer's account of the Waterloo campaign is an exceptionally clear account of artillery in action in this period, although he was writing so long after the event that a number of his dates and facts are in error. Equally good memoirs from the French side are those of Pion des Loches and J.F. Boulart, written closer to the times they describe.
357 Monhaupt (1836), *Uber den Gebrauch Reitendern Artillerie,* Berlin
358 Scharnhorst, D.G. von (1806), *op cit*; Monhaupt (1836), *op cit*; Anon (1824), *Observations sur les Changements qu'il Paraitrait Utile d'Apporter au Matériel et au Personnel de l'Artillerie*, Paris
359 Anon (1824), *Observations...*
360 Caramna (1830), 'Du service de l'artillerie en campagne', in *Spectateur Militaire*, Vol 6, pp 409–462
361 D.M. (1827), 'System d'artillerie de campagne du General Allix', in *Spectateur Militaire*, Vol 2; see also Okounef, N.A. (1832), *Examen Raisonné*

de Proprietés de Trois Arms de Leur Emploi dans le Batailles et de Leur Rapport Entre Elles, Paris

362 Zhmodikov, A. and Y. (2003), *op cit*, Vol II

363 Anon (1824), *Observations...*

364 Napoleon, cited in Dawson, P.L.(2005), 'System AnXI,' *The Napoleon Series* www.napoleon-series.org/ (accessed 21/4/2006)

365 Vergnaud, A.D. (1840), *Nouveau Manuel Complet d'Art Militaire*, Paris

366 Okounef, N.A. (1832), *op cit*

367 Howard, R.A. (1996), 'The evolution of the process of powder making from an American perspective', in Buchanan, B.J., *Gunpowder: the History of an International Technology*, Bath University Press, p 3

368 Akhavan, J. (1996), *The Chemistry of Explosives*, Royal Society of Chemistry, London, pp 3–24

369 Pan, J. (1996), 'The origin of rockets in China', in Buchanan, *op cit* pp 25–32

370 Hellemans, A. and B. Bunch (1988), *The Timetables of Science*, Simon and Schuster, London

371 Hall, B.S. (1996), 'The corning of gunpowder and development of firearms in the Renaissance', in Buchanan, *op cit* pp 87–120

372 Robins, B. (1742, r/p 1972) *New Principles of Gunnery*, Richmond Publishing, Surrey, pp 1–15

373 Crocker, G. (1986), *The Gunpowder Industry*, Shire Publications, Aylesbury

374 Rumford (1781), 'An account of some experiments upon gunpowder', in Brown, S.B., ed (1968–70), *The Collected Works of Count Rumford*, Harvard University Press, Vol IV, pp 386

375 West, J. (1991), *Gunpowder, Government and War in the Mid-Eighteenth Century*, Woodbridge, Suffolk, and Rochester, New York, pp 183–184

376 Lavery, B. (1987), *op cit*

377 Rumford (1797), 'Experiments to determine the force of fired gunpowder', in Brown (1968–70), *op cit*, Vol IV, pp 395–471

378 Mauskopf, S.H. (1996), 'From Rumford to Rodman: the scientific study of the physical characterisation of gunpowder in the first part of the 19th century', in Buchanan, *op cit* pp 277–295

379 Buchanan, B.J. (1996), 'Meeting standards: Bristol Powder Makers in the Eighteenth Century', in Buchanan, *op cit* pp 237–252

380 *ibid*

381 Curtis, W.S. (1996), 'The deterioration of Gunpowder and some of the methods used to combat it', in Buchanan, *op cit* pp 253–259

382 Bret, P. (1996), 'The organisation of gunpowder production in France, 1775–1830', in Buchanan, *op cit* pp 261–274

383 Hall, B.S. (1996), *op cit* pp 87–120

384 Walker, J. (1814), *Remarks on the Safe Conveyance and Preservation of Gunpowder*, London

385 de Scheel, Otto (1795), *op cit*

386 Nafziger, G.F. (1996), *Imperial Bayonets*, Greenhill Books

387 Zhmodikov, A. and Y. (2003), *op cit*, Vol II

388 *ibid*

389 Okounef, N.A. (1832), *op cit*

390 Congreve Snr, W. (1792), 'Letter,' *RAHT*, Woolwich

391 Tielke, J.G. (1787), *An Account of some of the most remarkable events of the war and Treatise on several branches of the military art* (trans Craufurd, C. and R.), London

392 Rohrig cited in Brett-James (1970), *Europe Against Napoleon: The Leipzig Campaign, 1813, from Eyewitness Accounts*, London

393 Henry, C. (2004), *British Napoleonic Artillery 1793–1815 (1)*, Osprey Publishing, Oxford

394 Tousard, L. (1809), *American Artillerist's Companion*, Washington

395 Congreve Snr, W. (1792), 'Letter,' RAHT

396 *ibid*

397 Adye, Captain R.W. (1813), *op cit*, 7th edn

398 Valée (1827)

399 Robe, William (1808), Collected Letters, RAI

400 Kerner, K.F. (1803), *op cit*

401 Jomini, A.H. (1855), *Précis de l'Art de la Guerre*, Paris

402 Napoleon (18 August 1809), 'To General Clarke, Minister of War, *Correspondence No.15678, 19:361*

403 Napoleon (29 May 1809), 'To General Clarke, Minister of War,' *Correspondence No.15726, 19:58*

404 Napoleon, correspondence (21 October 1805) 'Proclamation,' *Correspondence No.9405, 11:343*; also (14 February 1807) 'To Empress Josephine,' *Correspondence No.11813, 14:304*; (9 February 1807) 'To Cambacères, Prince Arch Chancellor,' *Correspondence No.11788*; (11 February 1807) 'To Duroc, Grand Marshal of the Palace,' *Correspondence No.11789, 14: 290–291*; (11 February 1807) 'To Empress Josephine,' *Correspondence No.11798, 14:297*; (25 February 1807), 'To Prince Jerome,' *Correspondence No.11876, 14:332–33*

405 Nosworthy, B. (1990), *The Anatomy of Victory: Battle Tactics 1689 to 1763*, Hippocrene Books, New York
406 *ibid*
407 Adye, Captain R.W. (1813), *op cit*, 7th edn
408 Zhmodikov, A. and Y. (2003), *op cit* Vol II
409 Nafziger G.F. (1996), *Imperial Bayonets*
410 McConachy, B. (2001), 'The Roots of Artillery Doctrine: Napoleonic Artillery Tactics Reconsidered', *Journal of Military History*, 65 (3), pp 617–640
411 Zhmodikov, A. and Y. (2003), *op cit* Vol II
412 Tabeur, J. (2004), *Le Général Drouot*, Editions Historique Teissedre
413 Marshal Augereau
414 Congreve, W. (1792), 'Letter,' *RAHT*, Woolwich
415 Scharnhorst, D.G. von (1812), *op cit*
416 Zhmodikov, A. and Y. (2003), *op cit* Vol II
417 Napoleon, (29 May 1809) 'To General Clarke, Minister of War,' *Correspondence No.15723, 31:328–329*
418 McConachy, B. (2001), *op cit*
419 Pivka, O. von (1977), *The Armies of 1812*, Patrick Stephens, Cambridge
420 Zhmodikov, A. and Y. (2003), *op cit* Vol II
421 Batteries, *SHAT, Xab 57–59*
422 Anon (1807), 'Situation du Matériel à 1er Mai 1807', cited in Lechartier (1907), *Les Services de l'Arrière à la Grande Armée*, pp 578–579
423 McConachy, B. (2001), *op cit*
424 Griffith, P. (1976), *French Artillery*, Almark, Surrey
425 Hoyer, J.F. (1798), *op cit*, Vol 1, Part 2, pp 3–14; and (1802), *op cit*, Vol 2, Part 4, pp 10–14
426 Anon (1824), *Observations...*
427 Hollins, D. (2005), personal communication
428 Hoyer (1798) *op cit*, also (1802) *op cit*
429 *ibid*
430 Smola, Josef Freiherr von (1827), *Das Österreichische Kavallerie Geschütz in Vergleiche mit den Reitenden Artillerie Anderen Staaten*, Vienna
431 J.Saint-Ledger (1795) 'Letter to William. Congreve Snr,' *RAHT*, Woolwich
432 *ibid*
433 Weissenbach, Strack von (1882), *op cit*; also Smith, Digby (2006), personal communication

Bibliography

The following are the most useful references for further reading on the various subjects covered in this book. It is not an exhaustive list of the letters, documents, books, memoirs and journals that have been consulted.

Abbreviations: HMSO = Her Majesty's Stationery Office, London: PRO = Public Record Office: RAHT = Royal Artillery Historical Trust, Woolwich: RAI = Royal Artillery Institute (now RAHT): r/p = reprint: SHAT = Service Historique de L'Armee de Terre (French Army Historical Service): trans = translated

Contemporary Sources on Artillery

Adye, Captain R.W. (1800–27), *Bombardier and Pocket Gunner*, eight editions, London [British artillery dictionary]

Anon (1767), *Die Artillerie Lehre zum Gebrauche des kk Feld-Artillerie corps*, Vienna [Austrian artillery manual]

Anon (1803), *Essai Général de la Tactique,* Paris [French tactical treatise]

Anon (1820), 'Über Zwölfpfündige und Haubitz-Batterien', in *Militair-Wochenblatt Vol 5*, Berlin

Anon (1824), *Observations sur les Changements Qu'il Paraitrait Utile d'Apporter au Matériel et au Personnel de l'Artillerie,* Paris [French treatise comparing their artillery to Britain, Prussia and Russia]

Belidor, Bernard Forest de (1731), *Le Bombardier Français, ou, Nouvelle Méthode pour Jeter des Bombes avec Précision. Tables*, Paris [Mathematical treatise]

Brunet, M.A. (1842), *Histoire Générale de l'Artillerie*, Anselin, Paris

Cotty, H. (1830), *Supplément au Dictionnaire d'Artillerie*, Paris

'D.M.' (1827), 'Système d'artillerie de campagne du General Allix', in *Spectateur Militaire* Vol 2, Paris

Dahlgren, A. (1856), *Shells and Shell Guns*, King & Baird, Philadelphia

Decker, Carl von (1828), *Traité d'Artillerie*, Paris [Treatise on how to use guns by a Prussian Major General of Artillery]

Douglas, General Sir H. (1860), *A Treatise on Naval Gunnery*, 5th edn, John Murray, London

Fave, I. (1854), *Emperor Napoleon's New System of Artillery,* London

Gassendi, J.B. (1801, 1809, 1819), *Aide Mémoire a l'Usage d'Artillerie de France*, Chez Magimal, Paris [The most comprehensive firearms treatise of the period at over a thousand pages]

Gibbons, John (1861), *The Artillerist's Manual*, D. Van Nostrand, New York [Comprehensive tactical and constructional treatise on artillery with a useful history of what went on before]

James, C. (1805), *A New and Enlarged Military Dictionary: or an Alphabetical Explanation of Technical Terms*, London

Jomini, A.H. de (1838) *Précis de l'Art de la Guerre*, Paris (r/p 1993), *The Art of War*, (r/p Greenhill Books, London)

Kerner, K.F. (1803), *Betrachtungen über der Reitende Artillerie: Organisation, Gebrauch und Tactic*, Friederich Nast, Ludwigsburg

Landmann, I. (1801), *The Principles of Artillery Reduced into Questions and Answers for Use of the Royal Military Academy at Woolwich*, W. Glendinning, London

Le Bourg, (1845), *l'Artillerie de Campagne Française Pendant les Guerres de Revolution*, Paris

Le Gupil, (1812), *Administration des Masses*, Paris

Lendy, Captain A.F. (1862), *Treatise on Fortification*, W. Mitchell, London

Lespinasse, A. (1800), *Essai sur l'Organisation de l'Armée de l'Artillerie,* Paris [Important essay on the reorganisation of the French Artillery]

Lombard, Professor Jean Louis (1781–83), *Traité du movement des projectiles appliqué aux bouches à feu*, Paris

Manson, Marshal du Camp J. (1792), *Tables de Construction de Principal attirails de l'Artillerie proposé au approvées depuis 1764 jusque en 1789 par M. de Gribeauval*, Paris [Translates as "The principal tables of construction showing changes proposed and approved between 1764 and 1789 by Mr Gribeauval." This was Manson 1792 modifications of the Gribeauval system]

Markevich, A.I. (1820–24), *A Manual to the Art of Artillery*, St Petersburg [Russian artillery manual]

Modecal, Captain A. (1850), *The Ordnance Manual for the Use of the Officers of the United States Army*, 2nd edn, Gideon and Company, Washington

Monge, G. (1794), *Description de l'Art de Fabriquer les Canons*, Paris

Monhaupt, General (1836), *Uber den Gebrauch Reitendern Artillerie,* Berlin [Prussian horse artillery manual]

Muller, John (1780 r/p 1977), *A Treatise on Artillery*, 3rd edition, John Millan, Whithall (r/p Museum Park Service, Canada) [First published in 1757 and had only minor correction by the publisher so is only valid for pre-1760s British artillery]

Müller, H. (1873), *Die Entwicklung der Feld-Artillerie in Bezug auf Material, Organization und Taktik von 1815 bis 1870*, Berlin [History of Prussian Artillery and tactics influenced by von Scharnhorst]

Müy and Gribeauval (1771), *Collection Complète de la Nouvelle Artillerie Construite dans les Arceneaux Metz et Strasbourg,* Paris [Erroneously referred to as the 1765 Gribeauval Treatise]

Persy, N. (1832 r/p 1979), *ElementaryTreatise on the Forms of Cannon & various Systems of Artillery,* Museum Restoration Service, Canada [Translated for the use of the Cadets of the US Military Academy from the lectures of Professor N. Persy of Metz, France]

Nelson, R.J. (1846 r/p 1972), Gun Carriages, An Aide Memoire to the Military Sciences, Royal Engineers, (r/p Museum Restoration Service, Canada) [Scale drawings from the 1846 publication.]

Roberts, J. (1863), *The Handbook of Artillery for the Service of the United Sates (Army and Militia) with the Manual of Heavy Artillery, including that of the New Iron Carriage*, New York [A useful US artillery manual that looks at the previous systems]

Robins, B. (1742, r/p 1972) *New Principles of Gunnery*, Richmond Publishing, Surrey

Rostaing, Comte de (1786), *Aide Mémoire à l'Usage des Bouches de Feu,* Chez Magimal, Paris [The 1792 edition entitled *Manuel du Canonier* had all the references to the king removed]

Scharnhorst, D.G. von (1806), *Handbuch für die Artillerie*, Vol 1–3, Berlin [Scharnhorst's comprehensive survey of European artillery systems]

Scharnhorst, D.G. von (1812), *Exerzir-Reglement für die Artillery der Königlich-Preussischen Armee*, Berlin [The 1812 Prussian artillery manual]

Scheel, Otto de (1795), *Mémoires d'Artillerie; contenant L'Artillerie Nouvelle ou les Changements Faits Dans L'Artillerie Francaise en 1765,* 2nd edn, Chez Magimal, Paris [This presented the M1765 Gribeauval system without the subsequent modifications by Manson and others by 1792]

Graves, D. ed. (1800 r/p 1984), *Otto de Scheel's Treatise on Artillery*, Museum Restoration Service, Canada [reprint of the Jonathan Williams 1800 translation of Otto De Scheel (1795) *Mémoires d'Artillerie,* 2nd Edition on the unmodified M1765 Gribeauval system]

Schels, J.B. von (1813), *Leichte Truppen; kleiner Krieg. Ein praktisches Handbuch für Offiziere aller Waffengattungen*, Vol 1, Section 2, Vienna [Austrian light and horse artillery manual]

Smola, Josef Freiherr von (1827), *Das Österreichische Kavallerie Geschütz in Vergleiche mit den Reitenden Artillerie Anderen Staaten*, Vienna

Smola, Josef Freiherr von (1839), *Handbuch für Kaiserlich-Königliche Österreichische Artillerie-Offiziere,* Vienna [Austrian artillery manual]

du Teil, J.P.B. (1778, r/p 1925), *De l'Usage de l'Artillerie Nouvelle dans la Guerre de Campagne*, Paris: (r/p 2003), *The New Use of Artillery in Field Wars, Necessary Knowledge*, The Nafziger Collection [A Victorian translation of du Teil (1778)]

Tielke, J.G. (1787), *An Account of some of the most Remarkable Events of the War and Treatise on several Branches of the Military Art* (trans Craufurd, C. and R.), London [An Austrian review of the Seven Years War and War of Bavarian Succession]

Tousard, L. (1809), *American Artillerist's Companion*, Washington [American interpretation of French Artillery Tactics]

d'Urtubie, T.B.S.D. (1787), *Manual de l'Artilleur, Contenant tous les Objets dont la Connaissance est nécessaire aux Officiers et Sous Officiers d'Artillerie*, 2nd Edition, Chez Magimal, Paris [French artillery manual]

Vergnaud, A.D. (1840), *Nouveau Manuel Complet d'Art Militaire,* Paris [Compares the Valée system to what went before]

Memoirs and Comtemporary Papers

Bogue, R. (1793), *Cadet Notebook*, RAHT, Woolwich

Caramna (1830), 'Du Service de l'Artillerie en Campagne', in *Spectateur Militaire*, Vol 6, pp 409–62, Paris

Cockburn, John (1827), *Notes on Artillery,* Cadet Notebooks, RAHT, Woolwich

Congreve (1770–1814) *Collected Papers,* RAHT [Unpublished manuscripts]

Frazer, Col. Sir Augustus (1859, r/p 2001), *Letters of Colonel Sir Augustus Simon Frazer, KCB, commanding the Royal Horse Artillery in the Army under the Duke of Wellington written during the Peninsular and Waterloo campaigns* (r/p Naval and Military Press, East Sussex)

Grisois, L. (1909), *Mémoires 1792–1822*, Plon-Nourit, Paris [Memoirs of General Grisois who commanded the Imperial Guard Artillery in 1812 campaign]

Hoyer, J.F. (1798), 'Uber die reitende Artillerie', in *Neues Militairisches Magazin – Historischen und Scientifischen Inhalts*, Vol 1, Part 2, pp 3–14, Leipzig: (1802), 'Uber den Gebrauch der reitenden Artillerie', in *Neues Militairisches Magazin – Historischen und Scientifischen Inhalts*, Vol 2, Part 4, pp 10–14, Leipzig [History and usage of horse artillery]

Lawson, Major General (1801), 'Memorandum of Artillery Arrangements and Alterations made in Carriages, Harness and Ammunitions', in (1884) *Proceedings of the Royal Artillery Institution*, XII (4), pp 207–220

Leslie, Major J.H., ed (1905, r/p 1991), *The Dickson Manuscript,* RAI (r/p Ken Trotman, Cambridge)

Marmont, A. (1859), *De l'Esprit des Institutions Militaires*, Paris [Marshal Marmont]

Mercer, A.C. (1870), *Journal of the Waterloo Campaign,* London [Royal Horse Artillery]

Morla, T. de (1816), *Tratado de Artillerie Para el Uso de la Academia de Caballeros Cedetes del Real Cuerpo de Artilleria, Dividido en Tres Tomos y Otro de Laminas, Que tartan de las Principales Functiones de los Oficiales de este Cuerpo en pas y en Guerra*, Segovia. (Part of this work is translated in Nafziger, G.F. (1996), *Imperial Bayonets*, Greenhill Books, London)

Napoleon (1795–1821), *Correspondance de Napoléon Ier,* www.histoire-empire.org/correspondance_de_napoleon/correspondance_de_napoleon.htm, Bibliothèque Nationale, Paris. [Correspondence of Napoleon]

Bonaparte, Napoleon (1821), 'Notes on Artillery' cited in *The Artillery Revue* (1897), Vol XXIV

Porbeck, von (1802), 'Feldzug der Verbündeten in Braband und Flandern 1793' in *Neues Militairische Magazin,* Vol 2, Part 5, Leipzig [to Holland]

Rudyerd, C.W. (1793 r/p 1970), *Course of Artillery at the Royal Military Academy,* RAI (r/p Museum Restoration Service, Canada)

Segur, P. de (1825), *History of the Expedition to Russia Undertaken by the Emperor Napoleon in the Year 1812*, London

Artillery

Bailey, Maj. Gen. J.B.A. (2004), *Field Artillery and Firepower,* Naval Institute Press, Maryland

Blackmore, H.L. (1976), *The Armouries of the Tower of London (I) Ordnance,* HMSO, London

Ffoulkes, C. (1937), *The Gun-Founders of England with a List of English and Continental Gun-Founders from the XIV to XIX Centuries,* Cambridge University Press

Haythornthwaite, P.J. (1979), *Weapons and Equipment of the Napoleonic Wars,* Blandford Press, Poole

Hughes, B.P. (1974), *Firepower: Weapon Effectiveness on the Battlefield, 1630–1850,* Purnell Book Services, London

Kaestlin, J.P. (1963), *Catalogue of the Museum of Artillery in the Rotunda at Woolwich,* Part I: *Ordnance* and Part II: *Personal Arms*, HMSO, London

Kemp, A. (1980), *Weapons and Equipment of the Marlborough Wars,* Blandford Press, Poole

Kennard, A.N. (1986), *Gunfounding and Gunfounders: A Directory of Cannon Founders from Earliest Times to 1850,* Arms and Armour Press, London

Kiley, Kevin F. (2004), *Artillery of the Napoleonic Wars 1792–1815,* Greenhill Books, London

Nilius (1904), *History of Artillery Equipment,* Moscow [History of Russian artillery and comparing it to European artillery]

Peterson, H.L. (1969), *Roundshot and Rammers: an Introduction to Muzzle-loading Land Artillery in the United States,* South Bend Replicas Inc., Indiana

Rogers, H.C.B. (1971), *Artillery through the Ages,* Military Book Society, London

Tarassuk, L. and Blair, C. (1979), *The Complete Encyclopaedia of Arms and Weapons,* Simon and Schuster, New York

Wise, T. (1979), *Artillery Equipment of the Napoleonic Wars*; Osprey Publishing, London

Biography, History and Organisation

Anon (1810), *War Office Army Lists for 1808 & 1809*, C. Roworth, London

Chandler, D.G. (1966), *The Campaigns of Napoleon,* London

Chandler, D.G. (1979 r/p 1993), *Dictionary of the Napoleonic Wars,* Greenhill Books, London

Emsley, C. (1993), *The Longman Companion to Napoleonic Europe,* Longman, London

Haythornthwaite, P.J. (1998), *Who Was Who in the Napoleonic Wars,* Arms & Armour Press, London

Johnson, R. (1984), *Napoleonic Armies: A Wargamer's Campaign Directory 1805–15,* Arms & Armour Press, London

Killy, W. and R.Vierhaus (2002), *Dictionary of German Biography*,kg Saur, Munich

Mathew, H.C.G. and B.Harrison (2004), *Oxford Dictionary of National Biography*, Oxford University Press

Mullie, M.C. (1851), *Biographie des Célébrités Militaires des Armées de Terre et de Mer,* Vols I and II, Paris

Nafziger, G.F. (1988), *Napoleon's Invasion of Russia*, Presidio Press, Novato CA

Nafziger, G.F. (1993), *Lützen and Bautzen;* (1994) *Napoleon at Dresden;* (1996), *Napoleon at Leipzig*, Emperor's Press, Chicago

Oman, Sir C., (1903–30, r/p 1995–2000), *A History of the Peninsular War*, Vols I–X, Greenhill Books, London

Palmer, Alan (1984), *An Encyclopaedia of Napoleon's Europe*, St Martin's Press, New York

Prokhorov, A.M. (1982), *Great Soviet Encyclopedia*, 30 Volumes, Collier MacMillan, London

Quintin, D. and B., eds (1996), *Dictionnaire des Colonels de Napoléon,* Paris

Six, G. (1934), *Dictionnaire Biographique des Généraux et Amiraux Français de la Révolution et de l'Empire 1792–1814*, Vols I and II, Paris

Smith, Digby (1998), *The Greenhill Napoleonic Wars Data Book,* Greenhill Books, London

Valentine, A. (1970), *The British Establishment 1760-1784*, University of Oklahoma Press

Gunpowder and Ammunition

Brown, S.B., ed (1968–70), *The Collected Works of Count Rumford*, Vols I–V, Harvard University Press

Buchanan, B.J., *Gunpowder: the History of an International Technology*, Bath University Press

Crocker, G. (1986), *The Gunpowder Industry*, Shire Publications, Aylesbury

Caruana, A.B. (1979a), *British Artillery Ammunition 1780,* Museum Restoration Service, Canada

Gillispie, C.C. (1998), 'Engineering the Revolution', in *Technology and Culture*, 39(4), pp 733–754

Hellemans, A. and B.Bunch (1988), *The Timetables of Science*, Simon and Schuster, London

Kelly J. (2004), *Gunpowder, A History of the Explosive that Changed the World,* Atlantic Books, London

Walker, J. (1814), *Remarks on the Safe Conveyance and Preservation of Gunpowder*, London

West, J. (1991), *Gunpowder, Government and War in the Mid-Eighteenth Century*, Woodbridge, Suffolk and Rochester, New York

Tactics

Chandler, D. (1976), *The Art of Warfare in the Age of Marlborough*, B.T. Batsford

Griffith, P. (1998), *The Art of War of Revolutionary France 1789–1802*, Greenhill Books, London

Hamley, Sir E.B. (1900), *Operations of War,* 5th edn, William Blackwood and Sons, London

Nafziger, G.F. (1996), *Imperial Bayonets*, Greenhill Books, London

Nosworthy, B. (1990), *The Anatomy of Victory: Battle Tactics 1689 to 1763,* (1996), *With Musket, Guns and Sword: Battle Tactics of Napoleon and His Enemies,* Hippocrene Books, New York

Austria

Dolleczek, A. (1872), *Geschichte der Österreichischen Artillerie,* Vienna [History of Austrian Artillery to 1870]

Duffy, C. (2000), *Instruments of War: The Austrian Army in the Seven Years' War*, Emperor's Press, Chicago

Hollins, D. (2003), *Austrian Napoleonic Artillery 1792–1815*, Osprey Publishing, Oxford

Rothenburg, G. (1982), *Napoleon's Great Adversaries: the Archduke Charles and the Austrian Army 1792–1814*, B.T. Batsford, London

Britain

Baker, H.G. (1945), *Samuel Walker and his Partners*, Society for the Preservation of Old Tools, Sheffield

Caruana, A.B. (1977) *The Light 6-pdr Battalion Gun of 1776*: (1979b) *Grasshoppers and Butterflies, The Light 3-pounders of Pattison and Townshend*, Museum Restoration Service, Canada

Caruana, A.B. (1980a), 'The Introduction of the Block-Trail Carriage', *Canadian Journal of Arms Collecting*, 18 (1), pp 3–16

Caruana, A. B. (1980b), 'The Light 3 Pounder of William Congreve'. 18(2) pp 66–70

Caruana, A.B. (1983), 'Sir Thomas Blomefield and the Blomefield System of Ordnance,' 21(3), *Canadian Journal of Arms Collecting*, 21(3), pp 95–100

Caruana, A.B. (1994 and 1997), *The History of English Sea Ordnance,* Volume I and II, Jean Boudriot Publications, East Sussex

Dawson, A.L. (2006), 'Some notes on the Royal Artillery in the Peninsula 1808,' *NARG Publications* and *The Napoleon Series*, www.napoleon-series.org/ (accessed 20 February 2006)

Duncan, Major F. (1879), *History of the Royal Regiment of Artillery,* Vol II, John Murray, London

Haythornthwaite, P.J. (1988), *Wellington's Specialist Troops,* Osprey Publishing, London

Haythornthwaite, P.J. (1994), *The Armies of Wellington*, Arms & Armour Press, London

Henry, C. (2004), *British Napoleonic Artillery 1793-1815 (1) and (2)*, Osprey Publishing, Oxford

Hughes, B.P. (1969), *British Smooth-Bore Artillery: The Muzzle Loading Artillery of the 18th and 19th Century*, Stackpole Books, USA

Jackson, M.V. and C. de Beer (1973), *Eighteenth Century Gun Founding*, Smithsonian Institute Press, Washington

John, A.H. (1951), *The Walker Family: Iron Founders and Lead Manufacturers*, Council for the Preservation of Business Archives

Lavery, B. (1987), *The Arming and Fitting of English Ships of War 1600–1815*: (1989) *Nelson's Navy: The Ships, Men and Organisation 1793–1815*, Conway Maritime Press, London

Law, LtCol M.E.S. (1952), *Battery Records of the Royal Artillery Woolwich,* RAI

Leslie, Major J.H. (1908), *The Services of the Royal Regiment of Artillery in the Peninsular War 1808–1814*, Hugh Rees Ltd, London

McConnell, David (1988), *British Smooth-bore Artillery: A Technological Study to Support the Identification, Acquisition, Restoration, Reproduction and Interpretation of Artillery at National Historic Parks in Canada,* National Historic Parks and Sites, Canada

Oman, Sir C. (r/p 1986), *Wellington's Army 1808–1814,* Greenhill Books, London

Park, S.J. and G. Nafziger (1983), *The British Military: Its System and Organisation 1803–1815*, RAFM Co, Ontario

Smith, R.D. ed. (1989), *British Naval Armaments,* Royal Armouries Conference Proceedings 1

Wilkinson-Latham, R. (1973), *British Artillery on Land and Sea 1790–1820,* David and Charles, Newton Abbot

British Allies

Beamish, L.N. (1832, 1837), *History of the King's German Legion,* Vols I and II, London

Cassin-Scott, J. (1976), *Scandanavian Armies in the Napoleonic Wars*, Osprey Publishing, London

Centeno, J. (2004), 'Portuguese Artillery of the Napoleonic Wars', *The Napoleon Series*, www.napoleon-series.org/ (accessed 1 June 2006)

Esdaile, C.J. (1988), *The Spanish Army in the Peninsula*, Manchester

Grehan, J. (1998), 'Wellington's Fighting Cocks: The Portuguese Army in the Peninsular,' in Ian Fletcher, *The Peninsular War: Aspects of the Struggle for the Iberian Peninsula*, Spellmount Ltd, Staplehurst, Kent, pp 173–183

Hartmann, Sir G.J. von (1901), *Der Königlich Hannoversche,* 2nd edn, Berlin [Hanoverian Army]

Hofschröer, P. (1989), *The Hanoverian Army of the Napoleonic Wars*, Osprey Publishing, London

Hofschröer, P. (1998), *1815 The Waterloo Campaign: Wellington, his German Allies and the Battles of Ligny and Quatre Bras,* Greenhill Books, London

Howard, R.A. (1979), *The Portuguese Regular Army 1806–14*, Napoleonic Association

Nafziger, G.F. (1990), *Napoleon's German Enemies: The Armies of Hanover, Brunswick, Hesse-Cassel and the Hanseatic Cities (1792–1815)*

Pivka, O. von (1975), *Spanish Armies of the Napoleonic Wars*: (1985), *Brunswick Troops 1809–15*, Osprey Publishing, London

Reitzenstein, J.F. von (1896, 1897, 1900), *Das Geschützwesen und die Artillerie in den Landen Braunschweig und Hannover von der ersten Anwendung eines Pulvergeschützes 1365 bis auf die Gegenwart,* Vols I–III, Leipzig [Brunswick and Hanoverian Artillery]

Schwertfeger, B. (1907), *Geschichte der Königlich Deutschen Legion 1803–1816,* Vols I and II, Hanover and Leipzig [King's German Legion]

Sichart, V. (1866–98), *Geschichte der Königlich Hannoverschen Armee*, Vols I–V, Hanover and Leipzig [Hanoverian Army]

Confederation of the Rhine

Anon (1984), *Unter dem Greifen. Altbadisches Militär von der Vereinigung der Markgrafschaften bis zur Reichsgründung 1771–1881,* Friends of Rastatt Castle Museum, Germany

Gärtner M., P. Bunde and E. Wagner (2003), 'Le Régiment d'Infanterie du Grande Duché de Hesse "Prince Heritier" pendant la Campagne d'Espagne 1808–1812', in *Soldats Napoléoniens: Les Troupes Françaises, Alliées et Coalisées,* Hors Serie 1, pp 36–45

Gill, J.H. (1992), *With Eagles to Glory: Napoleon and his German Allies in the 1809 Campaign,* Greenhill Books, London

Greessler and Tognarelli (1892), *Geschichte des 2. Württembergischen Feldartillerie Regiments Nr 29 Prinzeregent Luitpold Von Bayern*, Stuttgart

Haillot, C.-A. and H. de Giustiniani (1851), *Statistique Militaire et Recherches sur l'Organisation et les Institutions Militaires des Armées Étrangères*, Bourgogne et Martinet, Paris

Lunsmann, F.O. (1934), *Die Westfalische Armee*, Hanover

Nafziger, G.F. (1993a), *Armies of the Confederation of the Rhine 1806–15,* Vol 1 and 2: (1993b), *The Armies of the Kingdom of Bavaria and the Grand Duchy of Würzburg 1792–1815*: (1993c), *The Armies of Westphalia and Cleve-Berg 1806–1815,* The Nafziger Collection, USA

Nafziger, G.F., M.T. Wesolowski and T.Devoe (1991), *The Poles and Saxons of the Napoleonic Wars,* Emperor's Press, Chicago

Pigeard, A. (1990), 'L'Artillerie à Pied Saxonne 1806–1813', in *Tradition Magazine*, Paris, No.16

Shafer, K. and E. Wagner (1996), 'Des Landgraflich Hessiche Artilleriekorps: Uniformierung der Hessen-Darmstaditschen Artillerie 1790–1803', in *Depesche Magazine,* No.28

Weissenbach, Strack von (1882), *Geschichte der Königlich Württembergischen Artillerie,* Stuttgart

Xylander, R. Ritter von (1905), *Geschichte des 1. Feld-Artillerie-Regiments Prinz-Regent Luitpold,* E.S. Mittler, Berlin

France

Anon (1900), *Historique des Corps de Troupes de l'Armée Française,* Paris

Anon (1977), 'Artilleurs Français 1720–1830', in *Carnet de La Sabretache*, Numéro Spécial

Ballada, A. (1987), *Dessins des bouches de feu et construction de l'artillerie d'après l'arrêt du 11 Floréal AnXI,* SHAT

Buat, E. (1911) *L'Artillerie de Campagne - son Histoire, son Évolution, son État Actuel*, Alcan, Paris

Campana, J. (1901), *L'Artillerie en Campagne 1792–1901*, Berger-Levrault, Paris

Challeat, J. (1933), *Histoire Technique de l'Artillerie de Terre en France pendant un Siècle (1816–1919),* Imprimerie Nationale, Paris

Chartrand, R. (2003), *Napoleon's Guns*, Vols 1 and 2, Osprey Publishing, Oxford

Dawson, P.L. (2003), 'Napoleon's Foot Gunners: The Guard Foot Artillery': (2004), 'French Artillery in 1807': (2004), 'The Artillery of System AnXI,' *NARG Publications*, Wakefield and *The Napoleon Series*, www.napoleon-series.org/ (accessed September 2005)

Dawson, P.L. (2005), 'System AnXI,' *NARG Publications*, Wakefield

Decker, M. (1989), *Les Canons de Valmy; Catalogue de l'Exposition tenue au Musée de l'Armée*, Paris

Decker, M. (1990), 'L'Artillerie Impériale Mai 1804–Avril 1814', in *Souvenir Napoléon*, pp 2–24

Elting, J.R. (1988), *Swords around a Throne: Napoleon's Grande Armée*, Macmillan, New York

Fallou, L. (1901), *Le Garde Impériale (1804–1815),* Paris

Fave, I. (1845), *Histoire et Tactique de Trois Armes et Plus Particulièrement de l'artillerie de Compagne*, Paris

Fave, I. (1862), *Études sur le Passé et l'Avenir d'Artillerie*, J.Dumaine, Paris

Fave, I. (1871), *Études sur le Passé et l'Avenir de l'Artillerie,* Vol I–V, Paris [Five volume series]

Fieffe, E. (1854), *Histoire des Troupes Étrangers au service de France,* Vols I and II, Paris

Fieffe, E. (1859), *Napoléon 1er et la Garde Impériale,* Paris

Griffith, P. (1976), *French Artillery,* Almark, London

Haythornthwaite, P.J. (1988), *Napoleon's Specialist Troops*, Osprey Publishing, London

Head, M. (1970), *French Napoleonic Artillery*, Almark, London

Hennebert, E. (1887), *L'artillerie,* Paris

Laurema, M. (1956), *L'Artillerie de Campagne Française Pendant les Guerres de Révolution: Évolution de l'Organisation et de Tactique,* Helsinki

Lechartier, (1907), *Les Services de l'Arrière à la Grande Armée*, Paris

Martin, Y. (2004), 'French Artillery: 1789-1800' in *The Napoleon Series*, www.napoleon-series.org/ (accessed 10 August 2005)

Martinien, A. (1899), *Tableaux par Corps et par Batailles des Officiers tués et blessés pendant les Guerres de l'Empire 1805–1815,* Paris

Nardin, P. (2002), 'Le Comité de l'artillerie et ses réalisations des origins à 1870', in *Revue International d'Histoire Militaire,* No.82

Okounef, N.A. (1832), *Examen Raisonné de Proprietés de Trois Arms de Leur Emploi dans le Batailles et de Leur Rapport Entre Elles*, Paris

Picard, E. and L. Jouan (1906), *L'artillerie Française au XVIIIe siècle*, Paris

Pigeard, A. (2003), *L'Artillerie Napoléonienne et le Génie,* Hors Serie 23, *Tradition Magazine*, Paris

Rouquerol, G. (1895), *Artillerie au début de les Guerres de Révolution*, Berger-Levrault, Paris

Royal Engineers (1846–52), *Aide-Memoire to the Military Sciences*, John Weale, London [The 2nd expanded edition was published in 1857–60]

Susane (1874), *Histoire de l'Artillerie Française*, Hetzel, Paris

Tabeur, J. (2004), *Le Général Drouot*, Editions Historique Teissedre

Wilkinson-Latham, R. (1975), *Napoleon's Artillery*, Osprey Publishing, London

French Allies

Berjaud, Frédéric (2003), 'L'Infanterie du Bataillon de Neuchatel 1807–1814', in *Soldats Napoléoniens: Les Troupes Françaises, Alliées et Coalisées,* Hors Serie 1, pp 21–28

Chelminski, J. and H. Malibran (1913), *L'Armée du Duché de Varsovie 1807–1815,* Paris

Connelly, O. (1965), *Napoleon's Satellite Kingdoms*, Free Press Paperback, Ontario

Crociani, P. and M. Brandani (1969), 'Napoleon's Italian Army', in *Tradition*, London, No.43 (Part I), No.44 (Part II), No.46 (Part III), No.47 (Part IV), No.48 (Part V)

Dempsey, G.C. (2002), *Napoleon's Mercenaries: Foreign Units in the French Army under the Consulate and Empire,* Greenhill Books, London

Gembarzewski, Bronislaw (1904), *Wojsko Polskie*, Warsaw

Guye, A. (1964), *Le Bataillon de Neuchatel dit les Canaris au service de Napoléon 1807–1814*, La Baconniere, Neuchatel

Morawski, R. and A. Nieuwazny (2004), *Wojsko Ksietwa Warszawskiego Pelta,* Warsaw (trans Pawel Nowaczek)

Pivka, O. von (1979), *Napoleon's Italian and Neapolitan Troops*, Osprey Publishing, London

Netherlands

d'Auzon de Boisminart, W.P (1840, 1848), *Gedenkschriften van den Majoor W.P. d'Auzon de Boisminart - Tijdvak van De Veldtocht in Rusland*, Gravenhage, Amsterdam

Es, N.J.A.P.H. van (1898), *Het Historisch Museum van het Korps Rijdende Artillerie*, Vol I, Arnhem

Haythornthwaite, P.J. (1995), *Netherlands Troops of the Napoleonic Wars*, Pireme Publishing

Sypesteijn, Jhr J.W. van (1852), *Geschiedenis van het Regiment Nederlandse Rijdende Artillerie*, Zaltbommel, Holland

Uythoven, G. van (1999), *Voorwaarts Bataven!*, Zaltbommel, Holland

Prussia

Decker, H. von (1866), *Geschichte Rückblicke auf die Formation der Preussischen Artillerie*, Berlin

Duffy, C. (2000), *The Army of Frederick the Great*, 2nd edn, Emperor's Press, Chicago

Guddat, M. (1992), *Kanoniere, Bombardierer, Pontoniere: Die Artillerie Freidrichs des Grossen,* Verlag E.S. Mittler & Sohn GmbH, Herford und Bonn

Haythornthwaite, P.J. (1992), *Frederick the Great's Army (3): Specialist Troops,* Osprey Publishing, London

Hofschröer, P. (1984), *Prussian Landwehr and Landsturm 1813–15*, RAFM Co, Ontario

Hofschröer, P. (2003), *Prussian Staff and Specialist Troops 1791–1815*, Osprey Publishing, Oxford

Jany, C. (1910), *Urklungliche Beiträge und Forschungen zur Geschichte des Preussischen Heeres,* Vols III and IV, Berlin

Luvass, J. (1966), *Frederick the Great on the Art of War*, New York Free Press

Malinovsky, L. and R. Bonnin (1982), *Geschichte der Brandenburgische-Preussichen Artillerie,* Weisbaden

Nafziger, G.F. (1996), *The Prussian Army 1792–1815, Vol III: Cavalry and Artillery*: (2001), *The Prussian Army of Friedrich der Grosse (1740–1787), Vol 2: Saxon, Cavalry and Technical Troops*, Nafziger Collection

Pietsch, P. von (1963), *Die Formations und Uniformierungs-Geschichte des Preussischen Heeres 1808–1914*, Vols 1 and 2, Hamburg

von Schöning, K.W. von, (1844–45), *Historische-Biographische Nachrichten zur Geschichte der Brandenburgisch Preussischen Artillerie,* 3 vols, Berlin

Summerfield, S. (2006), *Prussian Artillery,* NARG Publications, Wakefield

Russia

Anon (1962), *A History of Artillery of Our Country*, Vol 1, Moscow

Duffy, Christopher (1981), *Russia's Military Way to the West: Origins and Nature of Russian Military Power 1700–1800*, Routledge, London

Nafziger, G.F. (1983), *The Russian Army 1800–1815*, RAFM Co, Ontario

Smirnov, A.A. (1998), 'Arakcheev's' Artillery. Russian field artillery of the system of 1805', *Reference* Informational *Publication,* Moscow (trans 2001)

Summerfield, S. (2005), *Cossack Hurrah: Russian Irregular Cavalry Organisation and Uniforms during the Napoleonic Wars*, Partizan Press

Summerfield, S. (2007), *Brazen Cross of Courage*, Partizan Press

Viskovatov, A.V. (1841), *Historical Description of the Clothing and Arms of the Russian Army,* Vol 7a: *Organisation 1796–1801,* St Petersburg (trans Mark Conrad, 2006)

Viskovatov, A.V. (1851), *Historical Description of the Clothing and Arms of the Russian Army,* Vol 10a: *Organisation 1801–1825*, St Petersburg (trans Mark Conrad, 1993 – On Military Matters, NJ)

Viskovatov, A.V. (1857), *Historical Description of the Clothing and Arms of the Russian Army,* Vol 12: *Army and Garrison Artillery, Army Sappers and Pioneers, Field and Garrison Engineers, 1801–1825*, St Petersburg (trans Mark Conrad, 2005)

Zhmodikov, A. and Y. (2003), *Tactics of the Russian Army in the Napoleonic Wars,* Vols I and II, The Nafziger Collection

Index

Page numbers in *italic* refer to illustrations.